Glencoe Spanish 2

¡Buen viaje!

Protase E. Woodford

Conrad J. Schmitt

Teacher's Manual

Glencoe McGraw-Hill

New York, New York   Columbus, Ohio   Woodland Hills, California   Peoria, Illinois

Glencoe/McGraw-Hill

A Division of The **McGraw·Hill** *Companies*

Send all inquiries to:
Glencoe/McGraw-Hill
21600 Oxnard Street, Suite 500
Woodland Hills, CA 91367

ISBN: 0-02-641518-6 (Teacher's Wraparound Edition)

Printed in the United States of America.

2 3 4 5 6 7 8 9 071 08 07 06 05 04 03 02 01 00 99

National Standards Glencoe Correlation
¡Buen viaje! Spanish 2

NATIONAL STANDARDS FOR FOREIGN LANGUAGE LEARNING

OBJECTIVES	STUDENT EDITION PAGE REFERENCES
COMMUNICATION	
Communicate in Languages Other Than English	
Standard 1.1: Students engage in conversations, provide and obtain information, express feelings and emotions, and exchange opinions.	0, 28, 54, 84, 122, 150, 178, 216, 244, 272, 300, 336, 366, 396
Standard 1.2: Students understand and interpret written and spoken language on a variety of topics.	0, 28, 54, 84, 122, 150,, 178, 216, 244, 272, 300, 336, 366, 396
Standard 1.3: Students present information, concepts, and ideas to an audience of listeners or readers on a variety of topics.	80, 81, 111, 112, 147, 148, 175, 176, 204, 205, 241, 242, 269, 270, 297, 298, 325, 326, 363, 364, 393, 394, 419, 420
CULTURES	
Gain Knowledge and Understanding of Other Cultures	
Standard 2.1: Students demonstrate an understanding of the relationship between the practices and perspectives of the culture studied.	18, 74, 76, 77, 106, 140, 143, 170, 198, 200, 234, 236, 237, 262, 264, 320, 321, 356, 359, 414
Standard 2.2: Students demonstrate an understanding of the relationship between the products and perspectives of the culture studied.	20, 44, 46, 47, 104, 168, 171, 201, 265, 290, 292, 293, 318, 358, 388
CONNECTIONS	
Connect with Other Disciplines and Acquire Information	
Standard 3.1: Students reinforce and further their knowledge of other disciplines through the foreign language.	22, 48, 78, 108, 144, 172, 202, 238, 266, 294, 322, 360, 390, 416
Standard 3.2: Students acquire information and recognize the distinctive viewpoints that are only available through the foreign language and its cultures.	

NATIONAL STANDARDS FOR FOREIGN LANGUAGE LEARNING

ACTFL Proficiency Guidelines

The ***Glencoe Spanish*** series, Levels 1, 2, and 3, follow a logical progression through the ACTFL Proficiency Levels from Novice through Advanced. The initial chapters of ***¡Buen viaje!*** Level 1, for example, present and practice the formulaic language typical of the Novice level: greetings, expressions of courtesy, numbers, days, and dates. Later chapters of ***¡Buen viaje!*** Level 1 have students describing in some detail, expressing likes and dislikes, narrating in present and past, which are language behaviors representative of the Intermediate-Mid and -High levels.

It should be noted that it would be extremely rare for a student to perform at the same ACTFL level across all four language skills. What is usually to be expected is that the student will demonstrate a higher level of performance in receptive skills than in production skills. An Intermediate level speaker may be a fairly competent Advanced level listener. An Advanced level reader might be an intermediate level writer.

It is also the case that in the ***¡Buen viaje!*** materials, as in real life, the language level varies within any given situation. Superior level writers may leave notes written at an Advanced or even at an Intermediate level. Advanced level speakers may respond to a question with a single word, a response usually associated with the Novice level. Nevertheless, the steady, overall progression of complexity from Novice to Advanced holds true throughout the series.

Generic Descriptions

GENERIC DESCRIPTIONS—SPEAKING

Novice	The Novice level is characterized by the ability to communicate minimally with learned material.
Novice-Low	Oral production consists of isolated words and perhaps a few high-frequency phrases. Essentially no functional communicative ability.
Novice-Mid	Oral production continues to consist of isolated words and learned phrases within very predictable areas of need, although quality is increased. Vocabulary is sufficient only for handling simple, elementary needs and expressing basic courtesies. Utterances rarely consist of more than two or three words and show frequent long pauses and repetitions of interlocutor's words. Speaker may have some difficulty producing even the simplest utterances. Some Novice-Mid speakers will be understood only with great difficulty.
Intermediate	The Intermediate level is characterized by the speaker's ability to: ♦ create with the language by combining and recombining learned elements, though primarily in a reactive mode; ♦ initiate, minimally sustain, and close in a simple way basic communicative tasks; and ♦ ask and answer questions.
Intermediate-Low	Able to handle successfully a limited number of interactive task-oriented and social situations. Can ask and answer questions, initiate and respond to simple statements and maintain face-to-face conversation, although in a highly restricted manner and with much linguistic inaccuracy. Within these

limitations, can perform such tasks as introducing self, ordering a meal, asking questions, and making purchases. Vocabulary is adequate to express only the most elementary needs. Strong interference from native language may occur. Misunderstandings frequently arise, but with repetition, the Intermediate-Low speaker can generally be understood by sympathetic interlocutors.

Intermediate-Mid Able to handle successfully a variety of uncomplicated, basic and communicative tasks and social situations. Can talk simply about self and family members. Can ask and answer questions and participate in simple conversations on topics beyond the most immediate needs, e.g., personal history and leisure time activities. Utterance length increases slightly, but speech may continue to be characterized by frequent long pauses, since the smooth incorporation of even basic conversational strategies is often hindered as the speaker struggles to create appropriate language forms. Pronunciation may continue to be strongly influenced by first language and fluency may still be strained. Although misunderstandings still arise, the Intermediate-Mid speaker can generally be understood by sympathetic interlocutors.

Intermediate-High Able to handle successfully most uncomplicated communicative tasks and social situations. Can initiate, sustain, and close a general conversation with a number of strategies appropriate to a range of circumstances and topics, but errors are evident. Limited vocabulary still necessitates hesitation and may bring about slightly unexpected circumlocution. There is emerging evidence of connected discourse, particularly for simple narration and description. The Intermediate-High speaker can generally be understood even by interlocutors not accustomed to dealing with speakers at this level but repetition may still be required.

Advanced The Advanced level is characterized by the speaker's ability to:
- converse in a clearly participatory fashion;
- initiate, sustain, and bring to closure a wide variety of communicative tasks, including those that require an increased ability to convey meaning with diverse language strategies due to a complication or an unforeseen turn of events;
- satisfy the requirements of school and work situations; and
- narrate and describe with paragraph-length connected discourse.

Advanced Plus Able to satisfy the requirements of a broad variety of everyday, school, and work situations. Can discuss concrete topics relating to particular interests and special fields of competence. There is emerging evidence of ability to support opinions, explain in detail, and hypothesize. The Advanced-Plus speaker often shows a well-developed ability to compensate for an imperfect grasp of some forms with confident use of communicative strategies, such as paraphrasing and circumlocution. Differentiated vocabulary and intonation are effectively used to communicate fine shades of meaning. The Advanced-Plus speaker often shows remarkable fluency and ease of speech but under the demands of Superior-level, complex tasks, language may break down or prove inadequate.

Superior The Superior level is characterized by the speaker's ability to:
- participate effectively in most formal and informal conversations on practical, social, professional and abstract topics; and
- support opinions and hypothesize using native-like discourse strategies.

Able to speak the language with sufficient accuracy to participate effectively in most formal and informal conversations on practical, social, professional, and abstract topics. Can discuss special fields of competence and interest with ease. Can support opinions and hypothesize, but may not be able to tailor language to audience or discuss in depth highly abstract or unfamiliar topics. Usually the Superior level speaker is only partially familiar with regional or other dialectical variants. The Superior level speaker commands a wide variety of interactive strategies and shows good awareness of discourse strategies. The latter involves the ability to distinguish main ideas from supporting information through syntactic, lexical and suprasegmental features (pitch, stress, and intonation). Sporadic errors may occur, particularly in low-frequency structures and some complex high-frequency structures more common to formal writing, but no patterns of error are evident. Errors do not disturb the native speaker or interfere with communication.

GENERIC DESCRIPTIONS—LISTENING

These guidelines assume that all listening tasks take place in an authentic environment at a normal rate of speech using standard or near-standard norms.

Novice-Low
: Understanding is limited to occasional isolated words, such as cognates, borrowed words, and high-frequency social conventions. Essentially no ability to comprehend even short utterances.

Novice-Mid
: Able to understand some short, learned utterances, particularly where context strongly supports understanding and speech is clearly audible. Comprehends some words and phrases from simple questions, statements, high-frequency commands and courtesy formulae about topics that refer to basic personal information or the immediate physical setting. The listener requires long pauses for assimilation and periodically requests repetition and/or a slower rate of speech.

Novice-High
: Able to understand short, learned utterances and some sentence-length utterances, particularly where context strongly supports understanding and speech is clearly audible. Comprehends words and phrases from simple questions, statements, high-frequency commands and courtesy formulae. May require repetition, rephrasing and/or slowed rate of speech for comprehension.

Intermediate-Low
: Able to understand sentence-length utterances that consist of recombinations of learned elements in a limited number of content areas, particularly if strongly supported by the situational context. Content refers to basic personal background and needs, social conventions and routine tasks, such as getting meals and receiving simple instructions and directions. Listening tasks pertain primarily to spontaneous face-to-face conversations. Understanding is often uneven; repetition and rewording may be necessary. Misunderstandings in both main ideas and details arise frequently.

Intermediate-Mid
: Able to understand sentence-length utterances that consist of recombinations of learned utterances on a variety of topics. Context continues to refer primarily to basic personal background and needs, social conventions and somewhat more complex tasks, such as lodging, transportation, and shopping. Additional content areas include some personal interests and activities, and a greater diversity of instructions and directions. Listening tasks not only pertain to spontaneous face-to-face conversations but also to short routine telephone conversations and some deliberate speech, such as simple announcements and reports over the media. Understanding continues to be uneven.

Intermediate-High
: Able to sustain understanding over longer stretches of connected discourse on a number of topics pertaining to different times and places; however, understanding is consistent due to failure to grasp main ideas and/or details. Thus, while topics do not differ significantly from those of an Advanced level listener, comprehension is less in quality and poorer in quality.

Advanced
: Able to understand the main ideas and most details of connected discourse on a variety of topics beyond the immediacy of situation. Comprehension may be uneven due to a variety of linguistic and extralinguistic factors, among which topic familiarity is very prominent. These texts frequently involve description and narration in different time frames or aspects, such as present, nonpast, habitual, or imperfective. Texts may include interviews, short lectures on familiar topics, and news items and reports primarily dealing with factual information. Listener is aware of cohesive devices but may not be able to use them to follow the sequence of thought in an oral text.

Advanced Plus	Able to understand the main ideas of most speech in a standard dialect; however, the listener may not be able to sustain comprehension in extended discourse which is propositionally and linguistically complex. Listener shows an emerging awareness of culturally implied meanings beyond the surface meanings of the text but may fail to grasp sociocultural nuances of the message.
Superior	Able to understand the main ideas of all speech in a standard dialect, including technical discussion in a field of specialization. Can follow the essentials of extended discourse that is propositionally and linguistically complex, as in academic/professional settings, in lectures, speeches, and reports. Listener shows some appreciation of aesthetic norms of target language, of idioms, colloquialisms, and register shifting. Able to make inferences within the cultural framework of the target language. Understanding is aided by an awareness of the underlying organizational structure of the oral text and includes sensitivity for its social and cultural references and its affective overtones. Rarely misunderstands but may not understand excessively, rapid, highly colloquial speech or speech that has strong cultural references.

GENERIC DESCRIPTIONS—READING

These guidelines assume all reading texts to be authentic and legible.

Novice-Low	Able occasionally to identify isolated words and/or major phrases when strongly supported by context.
Novice-Mid	Able to recognize the symbols of an alphabetic and/or syllabic writing system and/or a limited number of characters in a system that uses characters. The reader can identify an increasing number of highly contextualized words and/or phrases including cognates and borrowed words, where appropriate. Material understood rarely exceeds a single phrase at a time, and rereading may be required.
Novice-High	Has sufficient control of the writing system to interpret written language in areas of practical need. Where vocabulary has been learned, can read for instructional and directional purpose standardized messages, phrases or expressions, such as some items on menus, schedules, timetables, maps, and signs. At times, but not on a consistent basis, the Novice-High level reader may be able to derive meaning from material at a slightly higher level where context and/or extralinguistic background knowledge are supportive.
Intermediate-Low	Able to understand main ideas and/or some facts from the simplest connected texts dealing with basic personal and social need. Such texts are linguistically noncomplex and have a clear underlying internal structure, for example chronological sequencing. They impart basic information about which the reader has to make only minimal suppositions or to which the reader brings personal interest and/or knowledge. Examples include messages with social purposes or information for the widest possible audience, such as public announcements and short, straightforward instructions dealing with public life. Some misunderstanding will occur.
Intermediate-Mid	Able to read consistently with increased understanding simple connected texts dealing with a variety of basic and social needs. Such texts are still linguistically noncomplex and have a clear underlying internal structure. They impart basic information about which the reader has to make minimal suppositions and to which the reader brings personal interest and/or knowledge. Examples may include short, straightforward descriptions of persons, places, and things written for a wide audience.
Intermediate-High	Able to read consistently with full understanding simple connected texts dealing with basic personal and social needs about which the reader has personal interest and/or knowledge. Can get some main ideas and information from texts at the next higher level featuring description and narration. Structural complexity may interfere with comprehension; for example, basic grammatical relations may be misinterpreted and temporal references may rely primarily on lexical items. Has some difficulty with

the cohesive factors in discourse, such as matching pronouns with referents. While texts do not differ significantly from those at the Advanced level, comprehension is less consistent. May have to read material several times for understanding.

Advanced	Able to read somewhat longer prose of several paragraphs in length, particularly if presented with a clear underlying structure. The prose is predominantly in familiar sentence patterns. Reader gets the main ideas and facts and misses some details. Comprehension derives not only from situational and subject matter knowledge but also from increasing control of the language. Texts at this level include descriptions and narration such as simple short stories, news items, bibliographical information, social notices, personal correspondence, routinized business letters and simple technical material written for the general reader.
Advanced Plus	Able to follow essential points of written discourse at the Superior level in areas of special interest or knowledge. Able to understand parts of texts that are conceptually abstract and linguistically complex, and/or texts that treat unfamiliar topics and situations, as well as some texts that involve aspects of target-language culture. Able to comprehend the facts to make appropriate inferences. An emerging awareness of the aesthetic properties of language and of its literary styles permits comprehension of a wider variety of texts, including literary. Misunderstandings may occur.
Superior	Able to read with almost complete comprehension and at a normal speed expository prose on unfamiliar subjects and a variety of literary texts. Reading ability is not dependent on subject matter knowledge, although the reader is not expected to comprehend thoroughly texts which are highly dependent on knowledge of the target culture. Reads easily for pleasure. Superior-level texts feature hypotheses, argumentation and supported opinions and include grammatical patterns and vocabulary ordinarily encountered in academic/professional reading. At this level, due to the control of general vocabulary and structure, the reader is almost always able to match the meanings derived from extra-linguistic knowledge with meanings derived from knowledge of the language, allowing for smooth and efficient reading of diverse texts. Occasional misunderstandings may still occur; for example, the reader may experience some difficulty with unusually complex structures and low-frequency idioms. At the Superior level the reader can match strategies, top-down or bottom-up, which are most appropriate to the text. (Top-down strategies rely on real-world knowledge and prediction based on genre and organizational scheme of the text. Bottom-up strategies rely on actual linguistic knowledge.) Material at this level will include a variety of literary texts, editorials, correspondence, general reports and technical material in professional fields. Rereading is rarely necessary, and misreading is rare.

GENERIC DESCRIPTIONS—WRITING

Novice-Low	Able to form some letters in alphabetic system. In languages whose writing systems use syllabaries or characters, writer is able to both copy and produce the basic strokes. Can produce romanization of isolated characters, where applicable
Novice-Mid	Able to copy or transcribe familiar words or phrases and reproduce some from memory. No practical communicative writing skills.
Novice-High	Able to write simple fixed expressions and limited memorized material and some recombinations thereof. Can supply information on simple forms and documents. Can write names, numbers, dates, own nationality, and other simple autobiographical information as well as some short phrases and simple lists. Can write all the symbols in an alphabetic or syllabic system or 50–100 characters or compounds in a character writing system. Spelling and representation of symbols (letters, syllables, and characters) may be partially correct.

Intermediate-Low — Able to meet limited practical writing needs. Can write short messages, postcards, and take down simple notes, such as telephone messages. Can create statements or questions within the scope of limited language experience. Material produced consists of recombination of learned vocabulary and structures into simple sentences on very familiar topics. Language is inadequate to express in writing anything but elementary needs. Frequent errors in grammar, vocabulary, punctuation, spelling and information of nonalphabetic symbols, but writing can be understood by natives used to the writing of nonnatives.

Intermediate-Mid — Able to meet a number of practical writing needs. Can write short, simple letters. Content involves personal preferences, daily routine, everyday events, and other topics grounded in personal experience. Can express present time and at least one other time frame or aspect consistently, e.g., nonpast, habitual, imperfective. Evidence of control of the syntax of noncomplex sentences and basic inflectional morphology, such as declensions and conjugation. Writing tends to be loose collection of sentences or sentence fragments on a given topic and provides little evidence of conscious organization. Can be understood by natives used to the writing of nonnatives.

Intermediate-High — Able to meet most practical writing needs and limited social demands. Can take notes in some detail on familiar topics and respond in writing to personal questions. Can write simple letters, brief synopses and paraphrases, summaries of biographical data, work and school experiences. In those languages relying primarily on content words and time expressions to express time, tense, or aspect, some precision is displayed; where tense and/or aspect is expressed through verbal inflection, forms are produced rather consistently, but not always accurately. An ability to describe and narrate in paragraphs is emerging. Rarely uses basic cohesive elements, such as pronominal substitutions or synonyms in written discourse. Writing, though faulty, is generally comprehensible to natives used to the writing of nonnatives.

Advanced — Able to write social correspondence and join sentences in simple discourse of at least several paragraphs in length on familiar topics. Can write simple social correspondence, take notes, write cohesive summaries and resumes, as well as narratives and descriptions of a factual nature. Has sufficient writing vocabulary to express self simply with some circumlocution. May still make errors in punctuation, spelling, or the formation of nonalphabetic symbols. Good control of the morphology and the most frequently used syntactic structures, e.g., common word order patterns, coordination, subordination, but makes frequent errors in producing complex sentences. Uses a limited number of cohesive devices, such as pronouns, accurately. Writing may resemble literal translations from the native language, but a sense of organization (Rhetorical structure) is emerging. Writing is understandable to natives not used to the writing of nonnatives.

Advanced Plus — Able to write about a variety of topics with significant precision and in detail. Can write most types of social and informal business correspondence. Can describe and narrate experiences fully but has difficulty supporting points of view in written discourse. Can write about the concrete aspects of topics relating to particular interests and special fields of competence. Often shows remarkable fluency and ease of expression, but under time constraints and pressure writing may be inaccurate. Generally strong in either grammar or vocabulary, but not in both. Weakness and unevenness in one of the foregoing or in spelling or character writing formation may result in occasional miscommunication. Some misuse of vocabulary may still be evident. Style may still be obviously foreign.

About the Authors

CONRAD J. SCHMITT

Conrad J. Schmitt received his B.A. degree magna cum laude from Montclair State College, Upper Montclair, NJ. He received his M.A. from Middlebury College, Middlebury, VT. He did additional graduate work at Seton Hall University and New York University. Mr. Schmitt has taught Spanish and French at the elementary, junior, and senior high school levels. He was Coordinator of Foreign Languages for Hackensack, New Jersey, Public Schools. He also taught Spanish at Upsala College, East Orange, NJ; Spanish at Montclair State College; and Methods of Teaching a Foreign Language at the Graduate School of Education, Rutgers University, New Brunswick, NJ. He was editor-in-chief of Foreign Languages and Bilingual Education for McGraw-Hill Book Company and Director of English language Materials for McGraw-Hill International Book Company. Mr. Schmitt has authored or co-authored more than eighty books, all published by Glencoe, or other divisions of the McGraw-Hill Companies. He has addressed teacher groups and given workshops in all states of the U.S. and has lectured and presented seminars throughout the Far East, Europe, Latin America, and Canada. In addition, Mr. Schmitt has travelled extensively throughout Spain, Central and South America, and the Caribbean.

PROTASE E. WOODFORD

Protase "Woody" Woodford has taught Spanish at all levels from elementary through graduate school. At the Educational Testing Service in Princeton, NJ, he was Director of Test Development, Director of Language Programs, Director of International Testing Programs and Director of the Puerto Rico Office. He was appointed "Distinguished Linguist" at the U.S. Naval Academy in 1988. He is the author of over two dozen Spanish and English language textbooks for schools and colleges. He has served as a consultant to the American Council on the Teaching of Foreign Languages (ACTFL), the National Assessment of Educational Progress, the College Board, the United Nations Secretariat, UNESCO, the Organization of American States, the U.S. Office of Education, the United States Agency for International Development (AID), the World Bank, the Japanese Ministry of International Trade and Industry, and many ministries of education in Asia, Latin America, and the Middle East. In 1994 he was invited to chair the National Advisory Council on Standards in Foreign Language Education. Mr. Woodford served on the Board of Directors of the Northeast Conference during the period 1982–85. He received the 1993 NYSFLT National Distinguished Leadership Award, and the 1994 Central States Paul Simon Award for Support of Language and International Studies. From 1996–2000 he served as Chairman of the Board of Trustees, Center for Applied Linguistics.

Contents

Introduction

Welcome to *Glencoe Spanish*: Levels 1, 2, and 3, the junior high and high school Spanish series from Glencoe/McGraw-Hill, a Division of the McGraw-Hill Companies. Every element in this series has been designed to help you create an atmosphere of challenge, variety, cooperation and enjoyment for your students. From the moment you begin to use *Glencoe Spanish,* you will notice that not only is it packed with exciting, practical materials and features designed to stimulate young people to work together towards language proficiency, but that it goes beyond by urging students to use their new skills in other areas of the curriculum.

Glencoe Spanish uses an integrated approach to language learning. The introduction and presentation of new material, reinforcement of previously learned material, evaluation, reviews and activities in *Glencoe Spanish* are designed to span all four language skills.

Another characteristic of this series is that students use and reinforce these new skills while developing a realistic, up-to-date awareness of the Hispanic culture.

The Teacher's Edition you are reading has been developed based on the advice of experienced foreign language educators throughout the United States in order to meet your needs as a teacher both in and out of the foreign language classroom. Here are some of the features and benefits which make *Glencoe Spanish* a powerful set of teaching tools:

- flexible format
- student-centered instruction
- balance among all four language skills
- contextualized vocabulary
- thorough, contextual presentation of grammar
- an integrated approach to culture

Features and Benefits

FLEXIBLE FORMAT While we have taken every opportunity to use the latest in pedagogical developments in order to create a learning atmosphere of variety, vitality, communication and challenge, we have also made every effort to make the *Glencoe Spanish* series "teacher-friendly."

Although the Student Textbook and the Teacher's Edition provide an instructional method, every minute of every class period is not laid out. Plenty of room for flexibility has been built in to allow you to draw on your own education, experience and personality in order to tailor a language program that is suitable and rewarding for each individual class.

A closer look at the most basic component, the Student Textbook, serves as an example of this flexibility. Each chapter opens with two sections of vocabulary (**Vocabulario: Palabras 1** and **Palabras 2**) each with its own set of activities. **Vocabulario** is followed by **Estructura,** consisting of a series of grammar points, each with accompanying activities. But there is nothing which says that the material must be presented in this order. The items of vocabulary and grammar are so well integrated that you will find it easy, and perhaps preferable, to move back and forth between them. You may also wish to select from the third and fourth sections of each chapter (the **Conversación** and **Lecturas culturales** sections) at an earlier point than that in which they are presented, as a means of challenging students to identify or use the chapter vocabulary and grammar to which they have already been introduced.

These options are left to you. The only requirement for moving successfully through the Student Textbook is that the vocabulary and grammar of each chapter be presented in their entirety, since each succeeding chapter builds on what has come before.

In the Student Textbook, there is a marked difference between learning activities (**Práctica**) and communication-based activities (**Actividades comunicativas),** both of which are provided in each chapter. The former serve as their name implies, as activities for the acquisition and practice of new vocabulary and structures; while the latter are designed to get students communicating in open-ended contexts using the Spanish they have learned. You can be selective among these, depending on the needs of your students. The abundance of suggestions for techniques, strategies, additional practice, chapter projects, independent (homework) assignments, informal assessment, and more, which are provided in this Teacher's Edition—as well as the veritable banquet of resources available in the wide array of ancillary materials provided in the series—are what make *Glencoe Spanish* truly flexible and "teacher-friendly." They provide ideas and teaching tools from which to pick and choose in order to create an outstanding course.

STUDENT-CENTERED INSTRUCTION Today's classroom is comprised of students who have different learning styles, special needs, and represent different cultural backgrounds. The emphasis on student-centered instruction provided by *Glencoe Spanish* allows the teacher to capitalize on and deal positively with such diversity and encourages students to become involved in their own learning.

Glencoe Spanish anticipates the requirements of today's classroom by offering ideas for setting up a cooperative learning environment for students. Useful suggestions to this end accompany each chapter, under the heading COOPERATIVE LEARNING, in this Teacher's Edition. Additional paired and group activities occur in the Student Textbook (**Actividades comunicativas),** and in other headings such as Additional Practice in the Teacher's Edition. Besides cooperative learning strategies, *Glencoe Spanish* contains many other student-centered elements that allow students to expand their learning experiences.

Here are some examples: suggestions are offered in the Teacher's Edition for out-of-class chapter projects on topics related to the chapter theme and "For the Younger Student," activities aimed primarily at the middle school/junior-high student.

In the Student Textbook, new grammatical material is divided into "bite-sized" lessons, so as not to be intimidating. The Writing Activities Workbook provides a self-test after every unit of chapters, so that students can prepare alone or in study groups for teacher-administered quizzes and tests. The Audio Program allows students to work at their own pace, stopping the cassette (or compact disc) whenever necessary to make directed changes in the language, or to refer to their activity sheets in the Student Tape Manual. The Computer Testmaker component consists of pre-made tests, along with the option of tailoring these ready-made tests, or creating all-new tests.

These and other features discussed elsewhere in this Teacher's Manual have been designed with the student in mind. They assure that each individual, regardless of learning style, special need, background, or age, will have the necessary resources for becoming proficient in Spanish.

Balance Among All Four Language Skills

Glencoe Spanish provides a balanced focus on the listening, speaking, reading, and writing skills throughout all phases of instruction. It gives you leeway if you wish to adjust the integration of these skills to the needs of a particular individual, group or class. Several features of the series lend themselves to this: the overall flexibility of format, the abundance of suggested optional and additional activities and the design of the individual activities themselves. Let's look at some sections of a typical chapter as examples of the other two characteristics mentioned.

If the suggested presentation is followed, students are introduced to new words and phrases in **Vocabulario** by the teacher, and/or by the audiocassette or compact disc presentation. The focus is on listening and speaking through modeling and repetition. The **Práctica** which accompany the **Vocabulario** section can be done with books either closed (accentuating

listening and speaking) or open (accentuating reading, listening and speaking). However, these **Práctica** can just as well be assigned or reassigned as written work if the teacher wishes to have the whole class or individuals begin to concentrate on reading and writing. Throughout the **Vocabulario** section, optional and additional reinforcement activities are suggested in the Teacher's Edition. These suggestions address all four language skills. Later in each chapter, students are asked to combine the material learned in **Vocabulario** with material from the grammar section (**Estructura**) using a combination of listening, reading, writing and speaking skills in the process.

Reading and writing activities are brought into play early in the *Glencoe Spanish* series. The authors realize that communication in Spanish includes the use of reading and writing skills and that these skills are indispensable for the assimilation and retention of new language and the organization of thought.

Let's take a closer look at how each of the four skills is woven into the Student Textbook, the Teacher's Edition and the ancillary materials.

LISTENING   You the teacher are the primary source for listening, as you model new vocabulary, dialogs, structure and pronunciation, share your knowledge of Spanish culture, history and geography, talk to students about their lives and your own, or engage in culturally oriented activities and projects. As always, it is your ability to use Spanish as much as possible with your students, both in and outside of the classroom, which determines how relevant and dynamic their learning experience will be.

Glencoe Spanish offers numerous ways in which to develop the listening skill. There are teacher-focused activities, which provide the consistent modeling that students need. Teachers who use the Audio Program will find that these recordings help students become accustomed to a variety of voices, as well as rates of speed. Activities in which students interact with each other develop listening spontaneity and acuity.

In the Student Textbook, new vocabulary will be modeled by the teacher. Students' attention to the sounds of the new words can be maximized by presenting this material with books closed and using the Vocabulary Transparencies to convey meaning. Following each **Palabras** segment are several **Práctica** activities for rehearsing the new vocabulary. These can also be done with books closed. With each vocabulary presentation there are **Actividades comunicativas,** in which students may work in pairs or groups and must listen to each other in order to find information, take notes or report to others on what was said in their group. In **Estructura,** students listen as the teacher models new grammatical material and then are given a chance to practice each structure in several **Práctica** and **Actividades comunicativas** situations. Once again, closing the book will provide increased focus on the listening skill. The next section of each chapter is **Conversación,** in which a real-life dialog is modeled either by the teacher or by playing the recorded version from the Audio Program. The last section of each chapter, **Culminación,** offers more listening-intensive activities **(Actividades orales)** where students must be able to understand what their partners say in order to play out their role.

In addition to the Student Textbook, the Teacher's Edition offers several other listening-based activities correlated to the chapters. Some of these listening activities are "Total Physical Response" (Level 1) and "Pantomime" (Level 2). Here students must perform an action after listening to a spoken command. There are other listening-based activities suggested under the heading "Cooperative Learning" and often under "Additional Practice," both of which appear in the Teacher's Edition.

The Audio Program has two main listening components. The first is practice-oriented, wherein students further reinforce vocabulary and grammar, following directions and making changes in speech. They can self-check their work by listening to the correctly modeled utterances, which are supplied after a pause.

The second part of the program places more attention on the receptive listening skills. Students listen to language in the form of dialogs, announcements, or advertisements—language delivered at a faster pace and in greater volume—and then are asked to demonstrate their understanding of the main ideas and important details in what they have heard. The

Student Tape Manual contains activity sheets for doing this work. The Teacher's Edition contains the complete transcript of all audio materials to assist you in preparing listening tasks for your class.

More listening practice is offered through the Video Program. This material corresponds to and enriches that in the Student Textbook, and gives students a chance to hear variations of the language elements they have been practicing, as spoken by a variety of native speakers. Students' listening comprehension can be checked and augmented by using the corresponding print activities in the Video Activities Booklet.

SPEAKING Most of the areas of the Student Textbook and the Teacher's Edition mentioned above simultaneously develop the speaking skill. After hearing a model in the **Vocabulario** or **Estructura** sections, students will repeat it, either as a whole class, in small groups, or individually. From these models, they will progress to visual ones, supplied by the Vocabulary Transparencies or the photos and graphics in the textbook. The real thrust in the **Práctica** accompanying these two sections is to get students to produce this new material actively. In the **Actividades comunicativas,** students have the opportunity to apply what they have learned by asking for and giving information to their classmates on a given topic. Here, and in the **Conversación** sections, students are engaged in meaningful, interesting sessions of sharing information, all designed to make them want to speak and experiment with the language. The suggestions in the "About the Language" section in the Teacher's Edition enrich speaking skills by offering variants of expressions and speech mannerisms currently popular in Hispanic culture, especially among teenagers, so that from the start your students will be accustomed to speaking in a way that is accurate and reflective of contemporary Spanish. In the Student Textbook, previously presented material is constantly recycled in the communication based activities, so that students' speaking vocabularies and knowledge of structure are always increasing. The length of utterances is increased over time, so that when students complete *Glencoe Spanish* Level 1 they will have acquired an appreciation of the intonation and inflection of longer streams of language. To assist you in fine-tuning your students' speech patterns, the **Pronunciación** section is presented in each chapter of Level 1.

The speaking skill is stressed in the first part of each recorded chapter of the Audio Program, where pauses are provided for the student to produce directed, spoken changes in the language. This is an excellent opportunity for those students who are self-conscious about speaking out in class to practice speaking. The Audio Program gives these students a chance to work in isolation. The format of making a change in the language, uttering the change and then listening for the correct model improves the speaking skill. The Audio Program can serve as a confidence-builder for self-conscious students, allowing them to work their way gradually into more spontaneous speech with their classmates.

The packet of Situation Cards provides students with yet another opportunity to produce spoken Spanish. They place the student into a contextualized, real-world situation. Students must ask and/or answer questions in order to perform successfully.

READING Each chapter of the Student Textbook has readings based on the chapter theme under the heading **Lecturas culturales.** Each of these readings is accompanied by a series of comprehension activities called **Después de leer,** which focus on useful strategies for vocabulary-building and recognizing word relationships, which students can carry over into other readings. The optional readings in each chapter **(Lecturas opcionales),** are shorter, and are intended to be read with less attention to detail. In the next section of each chapter, **Conexiones,** students again use their reading skills albeit to a lesser degree. Here students have a chance to stretch their reading abilities in Spanish by reading basic information they may have already learned in other academic subjects. The material has been carefully written to include themes (as well as words and structures) which students have learned in previous chapters. The **Conexiones** sections are optional. You can choose to use them for independent reading, as a home-work assignment with in-class followup, or as an intensive in-class activity.

After every unit of chapters of the Student Textbook, *Glencoe Spanish* provides a unique section called **Vistas.** This presentation was prepared by the National Geographic Society. Each **Vista** focuses on one Spanish-speaking country via a dazzling display of photos representative of both that country's past as well as its present. Students have the opportunity to read the photo captions accompanying these **Vista** pages.

The Writing Activities Workbook offers additional readings under the heading **Un poco más.** These selections and the accompanying activities focus on reading strategies such as cognate recognition, related word forms and the use of context clues. In addition to the reading development above, students are constantly presented with authentic Spanish texts such as announcements from periodicals, telephone listings, transportation schedules, labeled diagrams, floor plans, travel brochures, school progress reports and many others, as sources of information. Sometimes these documents serve as the bases for language activities, and other times they appear in order to round out a cultural presentation, but, in varying degrees, they all require students to apply their reading skills.

WRITING Written work is interwoven throughout the language learning process in *Glencoe Spanish.* The activities, which occur throughout the **Vocabulario** and **Estructura** sections of each chapter in the Student Textbook, are designed in such a way that they can be completed in written form as well as orally. Frequently, you may wish to reassign activities which you have gone through orally in class as written homework. The Teacher's Edition makes special note of this under the topic "Independent Practice." At the end of each chapter of the Student Textbook, direct focus is placed on writing in the **Culminación** section, under the heading **Actividades escritas.** Here there are one or more activities that encourage students to use the new vocabulary and structure they have learned in the chapter to create their own writing samples. These are short and may be descriptive, narrative, argumentative, analytical or in the form of dialogs or interviews. Often a context is set up and then students are asked to develop an appropriate written response.

The Writing Activities Workbook is the component in which writing skills receive the most overt attention. All of the activities in it require writing. They vary in length from one word answers to short compositions.

They are designed to focus on the same vocabulary and grammar presented in the corresponding chapter of the Student Textbook, but they are all new and all contextualized around fresh visual material or situational vignettes. Since they often have students making lists, adding to charts and labeling, they provide an excellent means for students to organize the chapter material in their minds and make associations which will help them retain it. As students' knowledge of Spanish increases, longer written pieces are required of them. One workbook section entitled **Mi autobiografía** has students write installments of their own autobiographies. This is an effective way of stretching student writing skills. It also challenges students to personalize the Spanish they have been studying.

Students are also asked to make implicit use of writing almost everywhere in the series. They are constantly taking notes, listing, categorizing, labeling, summarizing, comparing or contrasting on paper. Even the Audio Program and the Video Program involve students in writing through the use of activity sheets. By choosing among these options, you can be sure that your students will receive the practice they need to develop their writing skills successfully.

Contextualized Vocabulary

From the moment students see new words at the beginning of each chapter in **Glencoe Spanish,** they see them within an identifiable context. From the start, students learn to group words by association, thereby enhancing their ability to assimilate and store vocabulary for long-term retention. This contextualization remains consistent throughout the practice, testing and recycling phases of learning.

In the **Vocabulario** section, each of the **Palabras** segments contains a short exchange or a few lead-in sentences or phrases which, together with colorful visuals, establish the context of the topic. Other vocabulary items which occur naturally within this topic are laid out among additional visuals, often as labels. The result is that students see at a glance the new language set into a real-life situation which provides "something to talk about"—a reason for using the language. The accom-

panying activities enrich the context of the language. The items to each **Historieta** activity are related so that when taken together they form a meaningful vignette or story. In other sections of the chapter, these words and phrases are reintroduced frequently.

Moreover, future chapters build on vocabulary and grammar from previous ones. Chapter themes introduced in Level 1 are reintroduced in Level 2 along with additional related vocabulary. Special attention has been given to vocabulary in the reading sections of the series as well. For example, in the **Lecturas culturales,** students are encouraged to stretch their vocabularies in order to get as much meaning as possible from the selections. In addition to glossed words and frequent use of cognate recognition, the corresponding **Después de leer** activities are there to help them with this.

Thorough, Contextual Presentation of Grammar

A quick look through the chapters of **Glencoe Spanish** Levels 1 and 2 will show the role grammar plays in the overall approach of the series. Although grammar is by no means the driving force behind the series, it is indeed an important aspect. Grammar is presented as one of seven sections in each chapter. What makes this series particularly effective is that, as well as being thorough, the presentation of grammar runs concurrent with, and is embedded in, the chapter-long situational themes. Students are presented with Spanish structure both directly, as grammar, and also as a set of useful functions. These will aid in communicating, expanding and improving their Spanish across the four skills, and learning about Hispanic culture as well as other areas of the school curriculum. Another important series characteristic is that the presentation of grammar has been divided into short, coherent "doses," which prevent grammar from becoming overwhelming to the student.

Throughout this series you will see that as you teach the various grammar topics, student interest remains high because each activity relates to a communicative topic and the format always varies. As is the case with many of the vocabulary activities, the individual practice items in the grammar activities are often related to each other contextually, in order to heighten student interest. All such activities are labeled **Historieta.**

You will find that it is easy to move in and out of the teaching of grammar, dipping into the other sections of a chapter or other components as you see fit. The grammar segments are short and intelligently divided. Each one provides a good sense of closure; they are taught in one section, are included as much as possible in the others; and have a coherent contextual theme.

Aside from the Student Textbook and Teacher's Edition, with their focus on grammar in the **Estructura** section of each chapter and in the **Repasos** after every unit, *Glencoe Spanish* offers students opportunities to practice grammar in other components as well. Chapter by chapter, the Writing Activities Workbook provides ample tasks in which students must put to writing the new structures on which they have been working in class. The Audio Program includes recorded sections in every chapter of the Student Tape Manual which correspond directly to **Estructura** in the Student Textbook. Students' knowledge of grammar is evaluated in the Chapter Quizzes and in the Testing Program. Each grammatical structure is practiced in other components, such as the Expansion Activities, Situation Cards, and Video Program.

An Integrated Approach to Culture

True competence in a foreign language cannot be attained without simultaneous development of an awareness of the culture in which the language is spoken. That is why *Glencoe Spanish* places such great importance on culture. Accurate, up-to-date information on Hispanic culture is presented either implicitly or explicitly throughout every phase of language learning and in every component of the series.

The presentation of Spanish in each chapter of the Student Textbook is embedded in running contextual themes. These themes richly reflect the varied cultures of Latin America, Spain and Hispanic communities in the U.S. Even in chapter sections which focus primarily on vocabulary or grammar, the presence of culture comes through in the language used as examples or items in activities, as well as in the content of the accompanying illustrations, photographs, charts, diagrams, maps or other reproductions of authentic documents in Spanish. This constant, implicit inclusion of cultural information creates a format which not only aids in the learning of new words and structures, but piques student interest, invites questions and stimulates discussion of the people behind the language.

Many culturally oriented questions raised by students may be answered in the sections devoted to culture: **Lecturas culturales,** and **Conexiones.** Through readings, captioned visuals and guided activities, these sections provide fundamental knowledge about such topics as family life, school, restaurants, markets, sports, transportation, food, hotels, offices and hospitals, among many others. This information is presented with the idea that culture is a product of people-their attitudes, desires, preferences, differences, similarities, strengths and weaknesses-and that it is ever changing. Students are always encouraged to compare or contrast what they learn about Hispanic culture with their own, thereby learning to think critically and progress towards a more mature vision of the world. For more information on this unique feature, read the section immediately following, and also the section entitled **ORGANIZATION OF THE STUDENT TEXTBOOK.**

All of the cultural material described in the Student Textbook can be augmented by following a variety of suggestions in the Teacher's Edition. There are guidelines for culturally rich instruction and activities, as well as useful, interesting facts for the teacher, under headings such as Chapter Projects, Geography Connection, History Connection, Critical Thinking Activity, Did You Know?, and others.

Throughout the Teacher's Edition, there are sections entitled About the Language. In each of these sections, teachers are given regional differences for lexical items such as **el carril, la pista, la vía, la banda, el canal**— all of which can refer to the lane of a highway, or **el autobús, la guagua, el camión, el micro**—all of which can refer to a bus. In addition to lexical regionalisms, explanations are given for structural variations: **contestar** versus **contestar a; jugar** versus **jugar a.**

Series Components

In order to take full advantage of the student-centered, "teacher-friendly" curriculum offered by *Glencoe Spanish*, you may want to refer to this section to familiarize yourself with the various resources the series has to offer. Both Levels 1 and 2 of *Glencoe Spanish* contain the following components:

- Student Edition
- Teacher's Edition
- Writing Activities Workbook
- Writing Activities Workbook, Teacher's Edition
- Audio Program (Cassette or Compact Disc)
- Student Tape Manual
- Student Tape Manual, Teacher's Edition (tapescript)
- Transparency Binder
- Video Program (Videocassette or Videodisc)
- Video Activities Booklet
- Computer Testmaker Software (Windows/Macintosh)
- Expansion Activities
- Situation Cards
- Lesson Plans
- Block Scheduling Lesson Plans
- Electronic Teacher's Classroom Resources
- Online Internet Activities
- Mindjogger Videoquiz (Videocassette or Videodisc)
- Chapter Quizzes with Answer Key
- Testing Program with Answer Key
- Performance Assessment
- CD-ROM Interactive Textbook
- Spanish for Spanish Speakers: *Nosotros y nuestro mundo*

Organization of the Student Textbook

REPASO The Level 2 textbook begins with seven review sections, A through G, which together make up the initial **Repaso.** These sections review all of the salient grammatical points and vocabulary topics presented in Level 1. Review sections A through D reintroduce content that was presented in Level 1, Chapters 1–7. Review sections E through G review material that was presented in Level 1, Chapters 8–14. The "Overview" topic on the corresponding Teacher's Edition page points out more specifically which grammar topics and vocabulary are being reviewed in each of these sections. For example, **Repaso** section A reviews vocabulary needed to describe school, school supplies, and clothing (Level 1, Chapters 1 through 4). From a grammatical perspective, this section reviews the present tense of **-ar** verbs, and the verbs **ir, dar,** and **estar.** (Level 1, Chapters 1 through 4). Each initial **Repaso** section includes practice activities to help students further internalize these review topics.

Following the initial **Repaso,** each chapter of Level 2 is divided into the following sections:

◆ **Vocabulario (Palabras 1 & Palabras 2)**

◆ **Estructura**

◆ **Conversación**

◆ **Lecturas culturales**

◆ **Conexiones**

◆ **Culminación**

VOCABULARIO The new vocabulary is laid out in two segments, **Palabras 1** and **Palabras 2.** Each of these presents new words in a cultural context in keeping with the theme of the chapter. Ample use is made of labeled illustrations to convey meaning and to provide an interesting introduction to the new vocabulary. The contextual vignettes into which the vocabulary items are embedded make use of the same grammatical structures which will be formally addressed in the chapter, and recycle words and structures from previous chapters. Accompanying each **Palabras** segment is a series of **Práctica** and **Actividades comunicativas** that require students to use the new words in context. These practice activities employ techniques such as short answer, matching, multiple choice and labeling. Many of the **Práctica** activities are contextual, forming coherent vignettes. For this reason they bear the additonal label **Historieta.** Each time **Historieta** appears as part of the activity title, it means that the answers form a short story.

The **Práctica** lend themselves well to any variations you might wish to apply to their delivery (books open, books closed, done as a class, in groups or pairs, written for homework). The activities labeled **Actividades comunicativas** are communicative-based. These are more open-ended activities, requiring students to personalize the new language by performing such tasks as gathering information from classmates, interviewing, taking notes, making charts or reporting to the class.

ESTRUCTURA This is the grammar section of each chapter. It is conveniently and logically divided into two to four segments to aid in student assimilation of the material. Each segment provides a step-by-step description in English of how the new grammatical structure is used in Spanish, accompanied by examples, tables and other visuals. Each segment's presentation is followed by a series of flexible **Práctica** and **Actividades comunicativas,** designed along the same lines as those which accompany the **Vocabulario** section, and focusing on the grammar point. As in **Vocabulario,** the presentation of the new structures and the subsequent activities are contextualized. The **Práctica** activities labeled **Historieta** always fit together in vignettes to enhance meaning. These vignettes are directly related to the overall chapter theme or a theme from a previous chapter. The **Estructura** section makes regular use of the new vocabulary from **Palabras 1** and **Palabras 2,** allowing for free interplay between these two sections of the chapter. This thorough yet manageable layout allows you to adapt the teaching of grammar to your students' needs and to your own teaching style.

CONVERSACIÓN Now that students have had a chance to see and practice the new items of vocabulary and grammar for the chapter, this section provides a recombined version of the new language in the form of an authentic, culturally rich dialog. This can be handled in a variety of ways, depending on the teacher and the class and as suggested by accompanying notes in the Teacher's Edition. Teacher modeling, modeling from the recorded version, class or individual repetitions, reading aloud by students, role-playing or adaptation through substitution are some of the strategies suggested. The dialog is accompanied by one or more **Después de conversar** activities which check comprehension and allow for some personalization of the material. Then students are invited once again to recombine and use all the new language in a variety of group and paired activities in the **Actividades comunicativas** that follow. New vocabulary and expressions are sometimes offered here, but only for the sake of richness and variation, and not for testing purposes

LECTURAS CULTURALES These readings are about people and places from Latin America and Spain, offering further cultural input to the theme of the chapter and providing yet another recombination of the chapter vocabulary and grammar. As is always the case with *Glencoe Spanish*, material from previous chapters is recycled. Following the **Lecturas culturales** reading are **Después de leer** comprehension activities based on the reading, along with activities that give students a chance to experiment with and expand their Spanish vocabularies by using strategies such as searching for synonyms, identifying cognates, completing cloze activities, matching and others. Note that the second and third reading selections among the

Lecturas culturales are optional, and they are clearly labeled as such.

CONEXIONES This section offers yet another type of reading by presenting topics from other areas of the curriculum, allowing students to reinforce and further their knowledge of these disciplines through the study of Spanish. The focus is on the interdisciplinary content rather than the language itself. By engaging your students in some or all of these readings, you will encourage them to stretch their Spanish reading skills in order to obtain useful, interesting information which will be of great service to them in their other academic courses. You will be giving students the opportunity to judge for themselves the added insight that the study of Spanish offers to their overall education. The **Conexiones** section in each chapter is optional.

CULMINACIÓN This wrap-up section requires students to consolidate material from the present as well as previous chapters in order to complete the tasks successfully. **Culminación** provides an opportunity for students to assess themselves on their own and to spend time on areas in which they are weak. You the teacher can pick and choose from these activities as you see fit. The first segment of **Culminación** consists of **Actividades orales,** where students must use the Spanish they have learned to talk about various aspects of themselves: likes, dislikes, favorite activities, hobbies or areas of expertise, among others. This is followed by **Actividades escritas** which encourages students to apply their knowledge of Spanish in written form. The **Vocabulario** page reviews the words and expressions that were taught in the current chapter, listing them by functional category. The **Vocabulario** serves as a handy reference resource for both the student and the teacher. Finally, the **Tecnotur** page previews three key multimedia components of the *Glencoe Spanish* series, the Video Program, the CD-ROM Interactive Textbook (an electronic version of the Student Textbook), and the Online Internet Activities.

After each unit of chapters, the following special sections appear in *Glencoe Spanish*:

◆ **Repasos**

◆ **Vistas**

REPASOS This review section, designed to coincide with the more comprehensive Unit Tests in the Testing Program, occurs after chapters 4, 7, 11, and 14 in the Student Textbook. In each **Repaso,** the main vocabulary and grammar points from the previous chapters are recycled through a variety of new activities and dialogs. While in the individual chapters new grammar was divided into smaller, "bite-sized" portions to aid in the planning of daily lessons and help students assimilate it, now it is reviewed in a more consolidated format. This allows students to see different grammatical points side by side for the first time, to make new connections between the different points, and to progress toward a generative, "whole grammar." For example, in the **Repaso** following Chapter 4 of Level 2, students review the conjugations of irregular verbs in the preterite. They also review the imperfect tense. They practice these structures as they talk about train travel, eating in a restaurant, and a trip to Chichicastenango. This material was previously spread out among the first four chapters of Level 2.

Every possible combination of vocabulary and grammar does not reappear in the **Repaso,** but by carefully going through these activities and referring to the preceding chapters, students will be encouraged to make necessary connections and extrapolations themselves and therefore develop a true, working knowledge of the Spanish they have studied. The **Repaso** is designed to be used by students studying alone, in study groups or as a whole class with teacher guidance.

VISTAS The **Vista**s were prepared by National Geographic Society. Their purpose is to give students greater insight, through colorful and inviting images, into the cultures and people of four different Spanish-speaking countries. In Level 2, these countries are Chile, Costa Rica, Peru, and Guatemala. The first two pages of each **Vista** focus on the traditional aspects of the country, while the final two pages portray the contemporary look and feel of that particular country. Students are encouraged to look at the photographs on the **Vista** pages for enjoyment. If they would like to talk about the photographs, let them say anything they can, using the vocabulary they have learned to this point.

LITERATURA At the back of the Level 2 Student Textbook, there is a special section entitled **Literatura** consisting of four brief literary selections:

Platero y yo by Juan Ramón Jiménez
La Muralla by Nicolás Guillén
El Cohítre, Una leyenda puertorriqueña by
    Ester M. Feliciano Mendoza
Tierra by Gregorio López y Fuentes

The literary selections provide an additional opportunity to develop students' reading skills in an enjoyable and rewarding context. Each literary selection can be read following the completion of the corresponding unit of chapters. For example, after completing Chapter 4, students will be prepared to read ***Platero y yo*** by Juan Ramón Jiménez with relative ease. The exposure to literature early in one's study of a foreign language should be a pleasant experience. As students read these selections it is not necessary that they understand every word. Explain to them that they should try to enjoy the experience of reading literature in a new language. As they read they should look for the following:

- Who are the main characters
- What are they like
- What are they doing—what's the plot
- What happens to them—what's the outcome

These literary readings are totally optional. The point in time you choose to introduce your students to them is your decision.

Suggestions for Teaching the Student Textbook

Teaching the Initial Review Chapter in Level 2

The first day of class, teachers may wish to reiterate the importance of the Spanish language, and reasons for continuing the learning process in the second year. Some suggestions are:

◆ Show students a map (the maps located in the back of the Student Textbook can be used) to remind them of the extent of the Spanish-speaking world.

◆ Have students discuss the areas within North America in which there are a high percentage of Spanish speakers. Ask them to name local Spanish-speaking sources including any individuals or groups they may know in their community.

◆ Make a list of place names such as San Francisco, Los Angeles, El Paso, Las Vegas, or names in your locality that are of Spanish origin.

◆ Explain to students the possibility of using Spanish in numerous careers such as: government, teaching, business, (banking, import/export), tourism, translating.

◆ The first day teachers will also want to find out whether their students used a Hispanic name in last year's Spanish class. If not, this is a good time to give students a Hispanic first name, or to let them take a new one, if they wish.

The **Repaso** sections A through G in Level 2 are designed to give students a concise review of all the essential material taught in level 1 in a *systematic* fashion. Each section is designed to take two or three days of instruction. **Repaso** sections A, B, C, and D review material from Level 1, Chapters 1 through 7; sections E through G review the content of Chapters 8 through 14. Depending upon the amount of material covered in first year Spanish, student aptitude, and your own teaching preference, you may decide to review some or all of the **Repaso** sections at the beginning of the school year. Many teachers will use the **Repaso** sparingly, delving into these sections as required in order to ensure a smooth transition into new material beginning with Chapter 1 of Level 2. Above all, we would urge you not to spend more than a few weeks on the **Repaso** before moving along to Chapter 1. It is always possible to return to these review sections later if necessary.

Teaching Various Sections of the Chapter

One of the major objectives of the *Glencoe Spanish* series is to enable teachers to adapt the material to their own philosophy, teaching style, and students' needs. As a result, a variety of suggestions are offered here for teaching each section of the chapter.

Vocabulario

The **Vocabulario** section always contains some words in isolation, accompanied by an illustration that depicts the meaning of the new word. In addition, new words are used in contextualized sentences. These contextualized sentences appear in the following formats: 1) one to three sentences accompanying an illustration, 2) a short conversation, 3) a short narrative or paragraph. In addition to teaching the new vocabulary, these contextualized sentences introduce, but do not teach, the new structure point of the chapter. A vocabulary list summarizing all of the words and expressions taught in the **Vocabulario** section appears at the end of each chapter in the Student Textbook.

General Techniques

◆ The Vocabulary Transparencies contain all illustrations necessary to teach the new words and phrases. With an overhead projector, they can easily be projected as large visuals in the classroom for those teachers who prefer to introduce the vocabulary with books closed. The Vocabulary Transparencies contain no printed words.

◆ All the vocabulary in each chapter (**Palabras 1** and **Palabras 2**) is recorded on the Audio Program. Students are asked to repeat the isolated words after the model.

Specific Techniques

OPTION 1 Option 1 for the presentation of vocabulary best meets the needs of those teachers who consider the development of oral skills a prime objective.

◆ While students have their books closed, project the Vocabulary Transparencies. Point to the item being taught and have students repeat the word after you or the audiocassette (or compact disc) several times. After you have presented several words in this manner, project the transparencies again and ask questions such as:
¿Es la computadora?
¿Qué es?
¿Es el teclado?
¿Es el ratón o el disco compacto? (Level 2, Chapter 3)

◆ To teach the contextualized segments on the **Palabras** pages, project the Vocabulary Transparency in the same way. Point to the part of the illustration that depicts the meaning of any new word in the sentence, be it an isolated sentence or a sentence from a conversation or narrative. Immediately ask questions about the

sentence. For example, the following sentence appears in Level 2, Chapter 4: **José fue a una tienda de ropa.**
Questions to ask are:
¿José fue a una tienda de ropa o a una papelería?
¿Quién fue a una tienda de ropa?
¿Adónde fue José?

◆ Dramatizations by the teacher, in addition to the illustrations, can also help convey the meaning of many words such as **cantar, bailar,** etc.

◆ After this basic presentation of the **Palabras** vocabulary, have students open their books and read the **Palabras** section for additional reinforcement.

◆ Go over the activities in the **Palabras** section orally.

◆ Assign the activities in the **Palabras** section for homework. Also assign the corresponding vocabulary activities in the Writing Activities Workbook. If the **Palabras** section should take more than one day, assign only those activities that correspond to the material you have presented.

◆ The following day, go over the activities that were assigned for homework.

OPTION 2 Option 2 will meet the needs of those teachers who wish to teach the oral skills but consider reading and writing equally important.

◆ Project the Vocabulary Transparencies and have students repeat each word once or twice after you or the audiocassette (compact disc).

◆ Have students repeat the contextualized sentences after you or the audiocassette as they look at the illustration.

◆ Ask students to open their books. Have them read the **Palabras** section. Correct pronunciation errors as they are made.

◆ Go over the activities in each **Palabras** section.

◆ Assign the activities in the **Palabras** section for homework. Also assign the vocabulary activities in the Writing Activities Workbook.

◆ The following day, go over the activities that were assigned for homework.

OPTION 3 Option 3 will meet the needs of those teachers who consider the reading and writing skills of utmost importance.

- Have students open their books and read the **Palabras** items as they look at the illustrations.
- Give students several minutes to look at the **Palabras** words and vocabulary activities. Then go over the activities.
- Go over the activities the following day.

Additional Activities

Teachers may use any of the following activities occasionally. These can be done in conjunction with the options previously outlined.

- After the vocabulary has been presented, project the Vocabulary Transparencies or have students open their books and make up as many original sentences as they can, using the new words. This can be done orally or in writing.
- Have students work in pairs or small groups. As they look at the illustrations in the textbook, have them make up as many questions as they can. They can direct their questions to their peers. It is often fun to make this a competitive activity. Individuals or teams can compete to make up the most questions in three minutes. This activity provides the students with an excellent opportunity to use interrogative words.
- Call on one student to read to the class one of the vocabulary activities that tells a story. Then call on a more able student to retell the story in his or her own words.
- With less able groups you can have one student go to the front of the room. Have him or her think of one of the new words. Let classmates give the student the new words from the **Palabras** until they guess the word the student in the front of the room has in mind. This is a very easy way to have the students recall the words they have just learned.

Estructura

The **Estructura** section of the chapter opens with a grammatical explanation in English. Each grammatical explanation is accompanied by many examples. Verbs are given with complete paradigms. In the case of other grammar concepts such as the imperfect versus the preterite, many examples are given in order to contrast these two tenses. Irregular patterns are grouped together to make them appear more regular. Whenever the contrast between English and Spanish poses problems for students in the learning process, a contrasting analysis between the two languages is made. Two examples of this are the reflexive construction in Level 1 and the subjunctive in Level 2. Certain structure points are taught more effectively in their entirety and others are more easily acquired if they are taught in segments. An example of the latter is the presentation of the preterite of irregular verbs in Chapters 1 and 2 in Level 2. In Level 1, Chapter 8, the object pronouns **me, te, nos** are presented immediately followed by **lo, la, los, las** in Chapter 9, and **le, les** in Chapter 10. Both direct and indirect objects are then consolidated in Level 2 in the **Repaso** section, and are later recycled in Chapter 10.

Learning Activities

The activities that follow the grammatical explanation are presented from simple to more complex. In the case of verbs with an irregular form, for example, emphasis is placed on the irregular form, since it is the one students will most often confuse or forget. In all cases, students are given one or more activities that force them to use all forms at random. The first few activities that follow the grammatical explanation are considered learning activities because they assist the students in grasping and internalizing the new grammar concept. These learning activities are immediately followed by test activities—activities that make students use all aspects of the grammatical point they have just learned. This format greatly assists teachers in meeting the needs of the various ability levels of students in their classes. Every effort has been made to make the grammatical explanations as succinct and as complete as possible. We have purposely avoided extremely technical grammatical or linguistic terminology that most students would not understand. Nevertheless, it is necessary to use certain basic grammatical terms.

Certain grammar activities from the Student Textbook are recorded on the Audio Program. Whenever an activity is recorded, it is noted with an appropriate icon in the Teacher's Edition.

The activities in the Writing Activities Workbook also parallel the order of presentation in the Student Textbook. The Resource boxes and the Independent Practice topics in the Teacher's Edition indicate when certain activities from the Writing Activities Workbook can be assigned.

Specific Techniques for Presenting Grammar

OPTION 1 Some teachers prefer the deductive approach to the teaching of grammar. When this is the preferred method, teachers can begin the **Estructura** section of the chapter by presenting the grammatical rule to students or by having them read the rule in their textbooks. After they have gone over the rule, have them read the examples in their textbooks or write the examples on the chalkboard. Then proceed with the activities that follow the grammatical explanation.

OPTION 2 Other teachers prefer the inductive approach to the teaching of grammar. If this is the case, begin the **Estructura** section by writing the examples that accompany the rule on the chalkboard or by having students read them in their textbooks. Let us take, for example, the positioning of direct object and indirect object pronouns when they are used together in a sentence. The examples the students have in their textbooks (Level 2, page 163) are:

Ella nos sirvió el helado.	**Ella nos lo sirvió.**
El mozo me dio la llave.	**El mozo me la dio.**
Él me vendió los libros.	**Él me los vendió.**
Papá te hizo las reservaciones.	**Papá te las hizo.**

In order to teach this concept inductively, teachers can ask students to do or answer the following:

- Have students identify the subjects of all the sentences.
- Have students find a pronoun which refers to a person in all the sentences.
- Ask: What do we call these pronouns which refer to people, but which are not the subjects of the sentences?
- Have students identify the direct objects in the sentences in the left column.
- Have students identify the direct objects in the sentences in the right column.
- Ask: What do we call these pronouns which have replaced the direct objects?
- Ask: How many object pronouns are there in ech of the sentences in the right column?
- Ask: When a sentence has two object pronouns, which comes first, the direct object pronoun or the indirect object pronoun?
- Ask: Where do both of these pronouns occur in relation to the verb?

By answering these questions, students have induced, on their own, the rule from the examples. To further reinforce the rule, have students read the grammatical explanation and then continue with the grammar activities that follow. Further suggestions for the inductive presentation of the grammar topics are given on the relevant page of this Teacher's Edition, at the point of use.

Specific Techniques for Teaching Structure Activities

In the development of the *Glencoe Spanish* series, we have purposely provided a wide variety of activities in the **Estructura** section so that students can proceed from one activity to another without becoming bored. The types of activities they will encounter are: short conversations, answering questions, conducting or taking part in an interview, making up questions, describing an illustration, filling in the blanks, multiple choice, completing a conversation, completing a narrative, etc. In going over the activities with students, teachers may want to conduct the activities themselves or they may want students to work in pairs. The **Estructura** activities can be done in class before they are assigned for homework or they may be assigned before they are done. Many teachers may want to vary their approach.

All the **Práctica** and **Actividades comunicativas** in the Student Textbook can be done with books open. Many of the activities such as question-answer, interview, and transformation can also be done with books closed.

Types of Activities

HISTORIETA ACTIVITIES The answers to many question activities build to tell a complete story. For this reason, these activities are labeled **Historieta.** Once you have gone over the activity by calling on several students (Student 1 answers items numbered 1, 2, 3; Student 2 answers items numbered 4, 5, 6 etc.), you can call on one student to give the answers to the entire activity. Now the entire class has heard an uninterrupted story. Students can ask one another questions about the story, give an oral synopsis of the story in their own words, or write a short paragraph about the story.

ACTIVIDADES COMUNICATIVAS These activities assist students in working with the language on their own. All **Actividades comunicativas** are optional. In some cases, teachers may want the whole class to do the activities. In other cases, teachers can decide which activities the whole class will do. Another possibility is to break the class into groups and have each group work on a different activity.

PERSONAL QUESTIONS OR INTERVIEW ACTIVITIES Students can easily work in pairs or teachers can call a student moderator to the front of the room to ask questions of various class members. Two students can come to the front of the room and the activity can be performed as follows—one student takes the role of the interviewer and the other takes the role of the interviewee.

COMPLETION OF A CONVERSATION See Chapter 6, **Práctica D,** page 162 as an example. After students complete the activity, they can be given time either in class or as an outside assignment to prepare a skit for the class based on the conversation.

Conversación

SPECIFIC TECHNIQUES Teachers may wish to vary the presentation of the **Conversación** section from one chapter to another. In some chapters, the dialog can be presented thoroughly and in others it may be presented quickly as a reading activity. Some possible options are:

◆ Have the class repeat the dialog after you twice. Then have students work in pairs and present the dialog to the class. The dialog does not have to be memorized. If students change it a bit, all the better.

◆ Have students read the dialog several times on their own. Then have them work in pairs and read the dialog as a skit. Try to encourage them to be animated and to use proper intonation. This is a very important aspect of the **Conversación** section of the chapter.

◆ Rather than read the dialog, students can work in pairs, having one make up as many questions as possible related to the topic of the dialog. The other students can answer his/her questions.

◆ Once students can complete the **Después de conversar** activities that accompany the dialog with relative ease, they know the dialog sufficiently well without having to memorize it.

◆ Students can tell or write a synopsis of the dialog.

Lecturas culturales

SPECIFIC TECHNIQUES:

OPTION 1 Just as the presentation of the dialog can vary from one chapter to the next, the same is true of the **Lecturas culturales** readings. In some chapters, teachers may want students to go over the reading selection very thoroughly. In this case all or any combination of the following techniques can be used.

- Give students a brief synopsis of the reading selection in Spanish.
- Ask questions about the brief synopsis.
- Have students open their books and repeat several sentences after you or call on individuals to read.
- Ask questions about what was just read.
- Have students read the story at home and write the answers to the activities that accompany the reading selection.
- Go over the **Después de leer** in class the next day.
- Call on a student to give a review of the reading in his/her own words. Guide students to make up an oral review. Ask five or six questions to review the salient points of the reading selection.
- After the oral review, the more able students can write a synopsis of the reading selection in their own words.

It should take one to two class periods to present a given **Lecturas culturales** reading, depending upon how thoroughly you want your students to know the material.

OPTION 2 When teachers wish to present a reading selection less thoroughly, the following techniques may be used:

- Call on an individual to read a paragraph.
- Ask questions about the paragraph read.
- Assign the reading selection to be read at home. Have students write the answers to the **Después de leer** activities that accompany the reading.
- Go over the **Después de leer** activities the following day.

OPTION 3 With some reading selections, teachers may wish merely to assign them to be read at home and then go over the activities the following day. This is possible since the only new material in the readings consists of a few new vocabulary items that are always footnoted.

Lecturas opcionales

The reading selections that are labeled **Lectura opcional** provide additional reading topics that are based on the general cultural theme of the chapter. You can omit any or all of these selections, or you may choose certain selections that you would like the whole class to read. The same suggestions given earlier can be followed. Teachers may also assign the optional reading selections to different groups. Students can read the selection outside of class and prepare a report for those students who did not read that particular selection. This activity is very beneficial for slower students. Although they may not read the selection, they learn the material by listening to what their peers say about it. The **Lecturas opcionales** can also be done by students on a voluntary basis for extra credit.

Conexiones

The purpose of the **Conexiones** is to offer readings from other areas of the school curriculum. These readings are optional. You may choose any of the following approaches:

OPTION 1: INDEPENDENT READING Have students read the selection and do the post-reading activities as homework, which you collect. This option is least intrusive on class time and requires a minimum of teacher involvement.

OPTION 2: HOMEWORK WITH IN-CLASS FOLLOWUP Assign the reading and post-reading activities as homework. Review and discuss the material in class the next day.

OPTION 3: INTENSIVE IN-CLASS ACTIVITY This option includes a pre-reading vocabulary presentation, in-class reading and discussion, assignment of the activities for homework, and a discussion of the assignment in class the following day.

Organization of the Teacher's Edition

One important component which adds to the series' flexible, "teacher-friendly" nature, is the Teacher's (Wraparound) Edition, of which this Teacher's Manual is a part. A complete method for the presentation of all the material in the Student Textbook is provided—basically, a complete set of lesson plans—as well as techniques for background-building, additional reinforcement of new language skills, creative and communicative recycling of material from previous chapters and a host of other alternatives from which to choose. This banquet of ideas has been developed and conveniently laid out in order to save valuable teacher preparation time and to aid you in designing the richest, most varied language experience possible for you and your students. A closer look at the kinds of support in the Teacher's Edition will help you decide which ones are right for your pace and style of teaching and for each of your classes.

The topics in the Teacher's Edition can be divided into two general categories:

1. **Core topics,** appearing in the left- and right-hand margins, are those which most directly correspond to the material in the accompanying two-page spread of the Student Textbook. Core topics consist of suggestions for presenting the corresponding material on the student page, as well as general notes (**¡OJO!**) to the teacher about the material being presented on the student page. In addition to core topics, enrichment topics are included in the side margins when space permits.

2. **Answers and enrichment topics** are found in the bottom margin of the Teacher's Edition. The enrichment topics offer a wide range of options aimed at getting students to practice and use the Spanish they are learning in diverse ways, individually and with their classmates, in the classroom and for homework. The enrichment

topics also include tips to the teacher on clarifying and interconnecting elements in the Spanish language, Hispanic culture, geography and history—ideas that have proved useful to other teachers and which are offered for your consideration.

Description of Major Topics in the Teacher's Edition

CHAPTER OVERVIEW At the beginning of each chapter a brief description is given of the language functions which students will be able to perform by chapter's end. Mention is made of any closely associated functions presented in other chapters. This allows for effective articulation between chapters and serves as a guide for more successful teaching.

NATIONAL STANDARDS Due to the importance of standards in second language learning, we have signaled student pages where the National Standards apply most obviously. Of the five National Standards, the Communication standard is consistently identified early in each chapter, since communication in Spanish is the most fundamental objective throughout the *Glencoe Spanish* series. Examples of the other four National Standards—Cultures, Connections, Comparisons, and Communities—are cited as they are manifested on specific pages in the Student Textbook.

TEACHING VOCABULARY (STRUCTURE, CONVERSATION, PRONUNCIATION, READING)
Step-by-step suggestions for the presentation of the material in all of the major sections in each chapter—**Vocabulario, Estructura, Conversación, Lecturas culturales**—are presented in the left- and right-hand margins. These are suggestions on what to say, whether to have books open or closed, whether to perform tasks

individually, in pairs or in small groups, expand the material, reteach, and assign homework. These are indeed suggestions. You may wish to follow them as written or choose a more eclectic approach to suit time constraints, personal teaching style and class "chemistry." Please note, however, that the central vocabulary and grammar included in each chapter's **Vocabulario** and **Estructura** sections are intended to be taught in their entirety, since this material will appear in succeeding chapters.

Answers for all the **Práctica** and **Actividades comunicativas** in each chapter section are consistently located at the bottom of the page. Because individual student answers to the **Actividades comunicativas** will vary, they are usually not provided. However, whenever practical, model answers to the **Actividades comunicativas** are given, along with key words, expressions and structures that will likely be used in the answers.

BELL RINGER REVIEWS

These short activities recycle vocabulary and structures from previous chapters and sections. They serve as effective warm-ups, urging students to begin thinking in Spanish, and helping them make the transition from their previous class to Spanish. Minimal direction is required to get the Bell Ringer Review activity started, so students can begin meaningful, independent work in Spanish as soon as the class hour begins, rather than wait for the teacher to finish administrative tasks, such as attendance, etc. Bell Ringer Reviews occur consistently throughout each chapter of Levels 1 and 2.

ABOUT THE SPANISH LANGUAGE

Since Spanish is such a growing, living language, spoken in so many different places of the world by people of different cultures and classes, the usage and connotation of words can vary greatly. Under this topic, information is offered on the many differences that exist. The most important aspect of this topic is the presentation of regionalisms. In the student text itself, we present those words that are most universally understood. The many regional variants are then given under the "About the Spanish Language" topic.

VOCABULARY EXPANSION

These notes provide the teacher handy access to vocabulary items which are thematically related to those presented in the Student Textbook. They are offered to enrich classroom conversations, allowing students more varied and meaningful responses when talking about themselves, their classmates or the topic in question. Note that none of these items, or for that matter any information in the Teacher's Edition, is included in the Chapter Quizzes, or in the Testing Program accompanying *Glencoe Spanish*.

COGNATE RECOGNITION

Since the lexical relationship between Spanish and English is so rich, these notes have been provided to help you take full advantage of the vocabulary building strategy of isolating them. The suggestions occur in the **Vocabulario** section of each chapter and are particularly frequent in Level I in order to train students from the very beginning in the valuable strategy of recognizing cognates. Various methods of pointing out cognates are used, involving all four language skills, and the activities frequently encourage students to personalize the new words by using them to talk about things and people they know. Pronunciation differences are stressed between the two languages. The teacher notes also call attention to false cognates when they occur in other chapter sections.

INFORMAL ASSESSMENT

Ideas are offered for making quick checks on how well students are assimilating new material. These checks are done in a variety of ways and provide a means whereby both teacher and students can monitor daily progress. By using the "Informal Assessment" topic, you will be able to ascertain as you go along the areas in which students are having trouble, and adjust your pace accordingly or provide extra help for individuals, either by making use of other activities offered in the Teacher's Edition or devising your own. The assessment strategies are simple and designed to help you elicit from students the vocabulary word, grammatical structure, or other information you wish to check. Because they occur on the same page as the material to which they correspond you may want to come back to them again when it is time to prepare students for tests or quizzes.

RETEACHING These suggestions provide yet another approach to teaching a specific topic in the chapter. In the event some students were not successful in the initial presentation of the material, a reteaching activity offers an alternate strategy. At the same time, it provides successful students another chance to further consolidate their learning.

HISTORY CONNECTION Following these suggestions can be seen as a very effective springboard from the Spanish classroom into the history and social studies areas of the curriculum. Students are asked to focus their attention on the current world map, or historical ones, then they are invited to discuss the cultural, economic and political forces which shape the world with an eye on Hispanic influence. The notes will assist you in providing this type of information yourself or in creating projects in which students do their own research, perhaps with the aid of a history teacher. By making the history connection, students are encouraged to either import or export learning between the Spanish classroom and the history or social studies realms.

GEOGRAPHY CONNECTION These suggestions encourage students to use the maps provided in the Student Textbook as well as refer them to outside sources in order to familiarize them with the geography of Hispanic America and Spain. These optional activities are another way in which *Glencoe Spanish* crosses boundaries into other areas of the curriculum. Their use will instill in students the awareness that Spanish class is not just a study of language but an investigation into a powerful culture that has directly or indirectly affected the lives of millions of people all over the globe. By studying geography, students will be urged to trace the presence of Hispanic culture throughout Europe and the Americas. The notes also supply you the teacher with diverse bits of geographical and historical information which you may decide to pass on to your students.

Additional Topics in the Teacher's Edition

CHAPTER PROJECTS Specific suggestions are given at the start of each chapter for launching individual students or groups into a research project related to the chapter theme. Students are encouraged to gather information by using resources in school and public libraries, visiting local Hispanic institutions or interviewing Spanish-speaking people or other persons knowledgeable in the area of Hispanic culture whom they may know. In Chapter 3, for example, they are asked to compare their own educational system with one from a Spanish-speaking country. These projects may serve as another excellent means for students to make connections between their learning in the Spanish classroom and other areas of the curriculum.

LEARNING FROM PHOTOS AND REALIA Each chapter of *Glencoe Spanish* contains many colorful photographs and reproductions of authentic Spanish documents, filled with valuable cultural information. In order to help you take advantage of this rich source of learning, notes have been provided in the way of additional, interesting information to assist you in highlighting the special features of these up-to-date photos and realia. The questions that appear under this topic have been designed to enhance learners' reading and critical thinking skills.

TOTAL PHYSICAL RESPONSE (LEVEL 1) At least one Total Physical Response (TPR) activity is provided with each **Palabras** segment that makes up the **Vocabulario** section of the chapter. Students must focus their attention on commands spoken by the teacher (or classmates) and demonstrate their comprehension by performing the task as requested. This strategy has proven highly successful for concentrating on the listening skill and assimilating new vocabulary. Students are relieved momentarily of the need to speak—by which some may be intimidated— and yet challenged to show that they understand spoken Spanish. The physical nature of these activities is another of their benefits, providing a favorable change of pace for students, who must move about the room and perhaps handle some props in order to perform the tasks. In addition, Total Physical Response is in keeping with cooperative learning principles, since many of the commands require students to interact and assist each other in accomplishing them.

COOPERATIVE LEARNING Several cooperative learning activities are included in each chapter. These activities include guidelines both on the size of groups to be organized and on the tasks the groups will perform. They reflect two basic principles of cooperative learning: (a) that students work together, being responsible for their own learning, and (b) that they do so in an atmosphere of mutual respect and support, where the contributions of each peer are valued. For more information on this topic, please see the section in this Teacher's Manual entitled COOPERATIVE LEARNING.

ADDITIONAL PRACTICE There are a variety of additional practice activities to complement and follow up the presentation of material in the Student Textbook. Frequently the additional practice focuses on personalization of the new material and employs more than one language skill. Examples of Additional Practice activities include having students give oral or written descriptions of themselves or their classmates; asking students to conduct interviews around a topic and then report their findings to the class. The additional practice will equip you with an ample, organized repertoire from which to pick and choose should you need extra practice beyond that in the Student Textbook.

INDEPENDENT PRACTICE Many of the activities in each chapter lend themselves well to assignment or reassignment as homework. In addition to providing extra practice, reassigning on paper activities that were performed orally in class makes use of additional language skills and aids in informal assessment. The suggestions under the Independent Practice heading in the bottom margin of the Teacher's Edition will call your attention to activities that are particularly suited to this. In addition to reassigning activities in the Student Textbook as independent practice, additional

sources are suggested from the various ancillary components, especially the Writing Activities Workbook.

CRITICAL THINKING ACTIVITY To broaden the scope of the foreign language classroom, suggestions are given that will encourage students to make inferences and organize their learning into a coherent "big picture" of today's world. These and other topics offered in the enrichment notes provide dynamic content areas to language skills and their growing knowledge of Hispanic culture. The guided discussions suggested, derived from the chapter themes, invite students to make connections between what they learn in the Spanish class and other areas of the curriculum.

DID YOU KNOW? This is a teacher resource topic where you will find additional details relevant to the chapter theme. You might wish to add the information given under this topic to your own knowledge and share it with your students to spur their interest in research projects, enliven class discussions and round out their awareness of Hispanic culture, history or geography.

FOR THE YOUNGER STUDENT This topic pays special attention to the needs of younger students. Each chapter contains suggestions for meaningful language activities and tips to the teacher that cater to the physical and emotional needs of these youngsters. There are ideas for hands-on student projects, such as creating booklets or bringing and using their own props, as well as suggestions for devising games based on speed, using pantomime, show and tell, performing skits and more.

FOR THE NATIVE SPEAKER This feature has been provided with the realization that the modern Spanish-as-a-second-language class in the U.S. often includes students whose first language is Spanish. These students can provide the class, including the teacher, with valuable information about Hispanic culture as well as the living Spanish language they use in their everyday lives. "For the Native Speaker" invites them to share this information in an atmosphere of respect and trust. There are often lexical and structural variations in the parlance of native speakers from different areas of the Spanish-speaking world. "For the Native Speaker" points out, or asks the native speakers to point out, many of these variations. When such variations are caused by the interference of English—for example, the inclusion of the indefinite article with professions and nationalities (**Juan es un médico**)—the interference is pointed out, and native speakers are guided in practicing the corrected structure. Such correction is handled with sensitivity. The idea is more to inform native speakers that borrowed words and structures are not used in all situations, rather than to make value judgments as to which usage is right and which is wrong.

Additional Ancillary Components

All ancillary components are supplementary to the Student Textbook. Any or all parts of the following ancillaries can be used at the discretion of the teacher.

Writing Activities Workbook

The workbook offers additional writing practice to reinforce the vocabulary and grammatical structures in each chapter of the Student Textbook. The workbook activities are presented in the same order as the material in the Student Textbook. The activities are contextualized, often centering around line art illustrations. Workbook activities employ a variety of elicitation techniques, ranging from short answers, matching and answering personalized questions, to writing paragraphs and brief compositions. To encourage personalized writing, there is a special section in each chapter entitled **Mi autobiografía.** The workbook provides further reading skills development with the **Un poco más** section, where students are introduced to a number of authentic readings for the purpose of improving their reading comprehension and expanding their vocabulary. The **Un poco más** section also extends the cultural themes presented in the corresponding Student Textbook chapter. The Writing Activities Workbook includes a Self-Test after Chapters 4, 7, 11 and 14. The Writing Activities Workbook, Teacher's Edition provides the teacher with all the material in the student edition of the Writing Activities Workbook, plus the answers—whenever possible—to the activities.

The Audio Program (Cassette or Compact Disc)

The recorded material for each chapter of *Glencoe Spanish*, Levels 1 and 2, is divided into two parts— **Primera parte** and **Segunda parte.** The **Primera parte** consists of listening and speaking practice for the **Vocabulario (Palabras 1** and **Palabras 2)** and the **Estructura** sections of each chapter. There is also a dramatization of the **Conversación** dialog from the Student Textbook, and a pronunciation section. The **Segunda parte** contains a series of activities designed to further stretch students' receptive listening skills in more open-ended, real-life situations. Students indicate their understanding of brief conversations, advertisements, announcements, etc., by making the appropriate response on their activity sheets located in the Student Tape Manual.

Student Tape Manual

The Student Tape Manual contains the activity sheets which students will use when listening to the audio recordings. The Teacher's Edition of the Student Tape Manual contains the answers to the recorded activities, plus the complete tapescript of all recorded material.

Transparency Binder

There are five categories of overhead transparencies in the Transparency Binder accompanying *Glencoe Spanish*, Level 2. Each category of transparencies has its special purpose. Following is a description:

◆ VOCABULARY TRANSPARENCIES These are full-color transparencies reproduced from each of the **Palabras** presentations in the Student Textbook. In converting the **Palabras** vocabulary pages to transparency format, all accompanying words and phrases on the **Palabras** pages have been deleted to allow for greater flexibility in their use. The Vocabulary Transparencies can be used for the initial presentation of new words and phrases in each chapter. They can also be used to review or reteach vocabulary during the course of teaching the chapter, or as a tool for giving quick vocabulary quizzes. With more able groups, teachers can show the Vocabulary Transparencies from previous chapters and have students make up original sentences using a particular word. These sentences can be given orally or in writing.

◆ **BELL RINGER REVIEW TRANSPARENCIES** These are identical to the Bell Ringer Reviews found in each chapter of the Teacher's Edition. For the teacher's convenience, they have been converted to transparency format.

◆ **COMMUNICATION TRANSPARENCIES** For each chapter in Levels 1 and 2 of the series there is one original composite illustration which visually summarizes and reviews the vocabulary and grammar presented in that chapter. These transparencies may be used as cues for additional communicative practice in both oral and written formats. There are 14 Communication Transparencies for Level 1, and 14 for Level 2.

◆ **MAP TRANSPARENCIES** The full-color maps located at the back of the Student Textbook have been converted to transparency format for the teacher's convenience. These transparencies can be used when there is a reference to them in the Student Textbook, or when there is a history or geography map reference in the Teacher's Edition. The Map Transparencies can also be used for quiz purposes, or they may be photocopied in order to provide individual students with a black and white version for use with special projects.

◆ **FINE ART TRANSPARENCIES** These are full-color reproductions of works by well known Spanish-speaking artists including Velázquez, Goya, and others. Teachers may use these transparencies to reinforce specific culture topics in both the **Lecturas culturales** sections, as well as the **Conexiones** sections of the Student Textbook.

The Video Program (Videocassette or Videodisc)

The Video Program for Level 2 consists of two 45-minute videos and an accompanying Video Activities Booklet. Together, they are designed to reinforce the vocabulary, structures, and cultural themes presented in the corresponding chapter of the Student Textbook. The **Glencoe Spanish** Video Program encourages students to be active listeners and viewers by asking them to respond to each video episode through a variety of previewing, viewing and post-viewing activities. Students are asked to view the video episode multiple times as they are led, via the activities in their Video Activities Booklet, to look and listen for more detailed information in the video episode they are viewing.

Video Activities Booklet

The Video Activities Booklet is the companion piece to the video episodes. For each chapter there are a series of pre-viewing, viewing, and post-viewing activities on Blackline Masters. These activities include specific instructions to students on what to watch and listen for as they view a given video episode. The Video Activities Booklet also contains Teacher Guidelines for using the video medium, culture notes, a chapter-by-chapter synopsis of each video episode, and a complete video script.

Expansion Activities

For each chapter of the Student Textbook, there are several activities on Blackline Masters which provide further opportunities for students to practice their communication skills in motivating, game-like formats. Some activities are designed for paired work, while others are whole class activities, and still others, such as the crossword puzzles, can be done individually. Any or all of these activities can be used in block scheduling configurations, or as independent practice.

Situation Cards

This is another component of *Glencoe Spanish* aimed at developing listening and speaking skills through guided conversation. For each chapter of the Student Textbook, there is a corresponding set of guided conversational situations printed on hand-held cards. Working in pairs, students use appropriate vocabulary and grammar from the chapter to converse on the suggested topics. Although they are designed primarily for use in paired activities, the Situation Cards may also be used in preparation for "the speaking portion of the Testing Program or for informal assessment." Additional uses for the Situation Cards are described in the Situation Cards package, along with specific instructions and tips for their duplication and incorporation into your teaching plans. The cards are in Blackline Master form for easy duplication.

Lesson Plans

Flexible lesson plans have been developed to meet a variety of class schedules. The various support materials are incorporated into these lesson plans at their most logical point of use, depending on the nature of the presentation material on a given day. For example, the Vocabulary Transparencies and the Audio (Cassette or Compact Disc) Program can be used most effectively when presenting the chapter vocabulary. On the other hand, the Chapter Quizzes are recommended for use one or two days after the initial presentation of vocabulary, or following the presentation of a specific grammar topic. Because student needs and teacher preferences vary, space has been provided on each lesson plan page for the teacher to write additional notes and comments in order to adjust the day's activities as required.

Block Scheduling Lesson Plans

The Block Scheduling Lesson Plans have been developed to show how the material may be distributed over the Level 2 Spanish course in a typical 90-day block scheduling framework. The plans may be used as presented or, they are flexible enough to allow for the teacher's own creative adaptation. There are no specific time limits placed on any teaching activity. Space has been provided on each day's lesson plan for the teacher to write additional and/or alternate teaching activities to those suggested. The plans include use of the numerous support materials comprising the Level 2 teaching package.

Internet Activities

The On-line Internet Activities serve as a dynamic, real-world connection between cultural themes introduced in *Glencoe Spanish,* and related topics available via the Internet. In addition to serving as an innovative avenue for cultural reinforcement, the activities encourage both students and teachers to view the Internet as an engaging and valuable tool for learning the Spanish language. Through this medium, students are able to further their knowledge of the Spanish language, as well as increase their opportunities for participating in Spanish-speaking communities around the world.

The Internet Activities include directions for the activities and instructions for downloading and printing the student response sheets and accompanying background teacher information, all on a chapter-by-chapter basis. Students will find the information required to complete each Internet activity by going to one or more of the Web sites whose addresses are provided on the Glencoe Foreign Language Home Page.

Assessment

CHAPTER QUIZZES WITH ANSWER KEY This component consists of short (5 to 10 minute) quizzes, designed to help both students and teachers evaluate quickly how well a specific vocabulary section or grammar topic has been mastered. For both Levels 1 and 2, there is a quiz for each **Palabras** section (vocabulary) and one quiz for each grammar topic in the **Estructura** section. The quizzes are on Blackline Masters. All answers are provided in an Answer Key at the end of the Chapter Quizzes booklet.

Maratón Mental
Mindjogger Videoquiz

This multimedia program, available on either videocassette or videodisc, offers hours of informal assessment opportunities within a game show format. The videoquizzes combine oral questioning, written questions that appear on the screen, and engaging visuals. By incorporating these modes of communication, the shows are geared to both auditory and visual learners. This multi-facted approach is helpful in facilitating group learning.

For each chapter of *Glencoe Spanish,* Levels 1 and 2, there is a videoquiz. There are three rounds to each videoquiz, with each round slightly more difficult than the previous one. Students can be organized into cooperative groups or teams. Each team should be supplied with a set of answer cards provided in the Mindjogger package. During each round, questions are asked by the game show hostess, and a time limit in which to answer each question is announced.

Testing Program
with Answer Key

The Testing Program booklet consists of two types of Chapter Tests, both on Blackline Masters.

The first Chapter Test is discrete-point in nature, and uses evaluation techniques such as fill-in-the-blank, completion, short answers, true/false, matching, and multiple choice. Illustrations are frequently used as visual cues. The tests measure vocabulary, grammar and culture concepts via listening, speaking, reading, and writing formats. (As an option to the teacher, the Listening section of each Chapter Test has been recorded by native Spanish speakers.) For the teacher's convenience, the Chapter Tests have been designed so that different sections of the test can be measured on different days. For example, the Listening Test can be administered separately from the Reading, Writing and Speaking Tests. Likewise, the Speaking Test can be administered on a different day than the Reading and Writing Test, etc. All Chapter Tests can be administered upon the completion of each chapter of the Student

Textbook. The Unit Tests can be administered upon the completion of each **Repaso** section of the Student Textbook, following Chapters 4, 7, 11, and 14.

The Blackline Master Testing Program booklet also contains Chapter Proficiency Tests. These measure students' mastery of each chapter's vocabulary and grammar on a more global, whole-language level.

Computer Testmaker Software

The Computer Testmaker Software, available for Windows PC and Macintosh platforms, offers teachers the option of simply printing out ready-made chapter tests, or customizing a ready-made test by selecting certain items, and/or adding original test items. For more information, see the User's Guide accompanying the Testmaker Software.

Performance Assessment

In addition to the tests described earlier, the Performance Assessment tasks provide an alternate approach to measuring student learning, compared to the more traditional paper and pencil tests. The performance assessment tasks include teacher-student interviews, individual and small-group research tasks with follow-up presentations, and skits that students perform for the class. The Performance Assessment tasks can be administered after every unit of chapters in the textbook. They appear in conjunction with the **Repaso** following Chapters 4, 7, 11, and 14.

Spanish for Spanish Speakers:
Nosotros y nuestro mundo

Each of the fourteen chapters takes into account the diversified background of these students—many of whom have a very strong command of the Spanish language and others who have a somewhat limited knowledge of the Spanish language. The textbook also attempts to take into account the specific problems facing the teacher of classes with native Spanish speakers. In some cases, the native-speaking students are placed in separate courses an in other cases, they are in classes with English-speaking students learning Spanish as a foreign language. For these reasons *Nosotros y nuestro mundo* can be used as a basal textbook in courses for native speakers, or it can be used as an adjunct to the *Glencoe Spanish* series in classes that have both native speakers of Spanish and English. In the latter case, it is presumed that the teacher will have less time with their students and a fair amount of the material will need to be acquired by students through independent study or cooperative group work.

Organization of *Nosotros y nuestro mundo*

Each chapter of the Spanish for Spanish speakers textbook is divided into the following sections:

Nuestro conocimiento académico
Nuestro idioma
Nuestra cultura
Nuestra literatura
Nuestra creatividad
Nuestras diversiones

Cooperative Learning

Cooperative learning provides a structured, natural environment for student communication that is both motivating and meaningful. When students develop friendly relationships in their cooperative groups and become accustomed to the multiple opportunities to hear and rehearse new communicative tasks, the filter that prevents many students from daring to risk a wrong answer when called upon to speak in front of a whole class can be minimzed. The goal of cooperative learning is to provide opportunities for learning in an environment where students contribute freely and responsibly to the success of the group. The key is to strike a balance between group goals and individual accountability. Group (team) members plan how to divide the activity among themselves, then each member of the group carries out his or her part of the assignment. Cooperative learning provides each student with a "safe," low-risk environment rather than a whole-class atmosphere. As you implement cooperative learning in your classroom, we urge you to take time to explain to students what will be expected of every group member—listening, participating, and respecting other opinions.

In the Teacher's Edition, cooperative learning activities have been written to accompany each chapter of the Student Textbook. These activities have been created to assist both the teacher who wants to include cooperative learning for the first time, and the experienced practitioner of cooperative learning.

Classroom Management: Implementing Cooperative Learning Activities

Many of the suggested cooperative learning activities are based on a four-member team structure in the classroom. Teams of four are recommended because there is a wide variety of possible interactions. At the same time the group is small enough that students can take turns quickly within the group. Pairs of students as teams may be too limited in terms of possible interactions, and trios frequently work out to be a pair with the third student left out. Teams of five may be unwieldy in that students begin to feel that no one will notice if they don't really participate.

If students sit in rows on a daily basis, desks can be pushed together to form teams of four. Teams of students who work together need to be balanced according to as many variables as possible: academic achievement in the course, personality, ethnicity, gender, attitude, etc. Teams that are as heterogeneous as possible will ensure that the class progresses quickly through the curriculum.

Following are descriptions of some of the most important cooperative learning structures, adapted from Spencer Kagan's Structural Approach to Cooperative Learning, as they apply to the content of **Glencoe Spanish.**

ROUND-ROBIN Each member of the team answers in turn a question, or shares an idea with teammates. Responses should be brief so that students do not have to wait long for their turn.

Example from Level 1, Preliminary Lesson D, Days of the week:

> Teams recite the days of the week in a round-robin fashion. Different students begin additional rounds so that everyone ends up needing to know the names of all the days. Variations include starting the list with a different day or using a race format, i.e., teams recite the list three times in a row and raise their hands when they have finished.

ROUNDTABLE Each student in turn writes his or her contribution to the group activity on a piece of paper that is passed around the team. If the individual student responses are longer than one or two words, there can be four pieces of paper with each student contributing to each paper as it is passed around the team.

A TO Z ROUNDTABLE Using vocabulary from Level 1, Chapters 11 and 13, students take turns adding one word at a time to a list of words associated with plane or train travel in A to Z order. Students may help each other with what to write, and correct spelling. Encourage creativity when it comes to the few letters of the alphabet that don't begin a specific travel word from their chapter lists. Teams can compete in several ways: first to finish all 28 letters; longest word; shortest word; most creative response.

NUMBERED HEADS TOGETHER Numbered Heads Together is a structure for review and practice of high consensus information. There are four steps:

Step 1: Students number off in their teams from 1 to 4.

Step 2: The teacher asks a question and gives the teams some time to make sure that everyone on the team knows the answer.

Step 3: The teacher calls a number.

Step 4: The appropriate student from each team is responsible to report the group response.

Answers can be reported simultaneously, i.e., all students with the approrpiate number either stand by their seats and recite the answer together, or they go to the chalkboard and write the answer at the same time. Answers can also be reported sequentially. Call on the first student to raise his or her hand or have all the students with the appropriate number stand. Select one student to give the answer. If the other students agree, they sit down, if not they remain standing and offer a different response.

Example from Level 1, Chapter 2, Telling Time:

Step 1: Using a blank clockface on the overhead transparency, or the chalkboard, the teacher adjusts the hand on the clock.

Step 2: Students put their heads together and answer the question: **¿Qué hora es?**

Step 3: The teacher calls a number.

Step 4: The appropriate student from each team is responsible to report the group response.

Pantomimes

Give each team one card. Have each team decide together how to pantomime for the class the action identified on the card. Each team presents the pantomime for ten seconds while the rest of the teams watch without talking. Then each of the other teams tries to guess the phrase and writes down their choice on a piece of paper. (This is a good way to accommodate kinesthetic learning styles as well as vary classroom activities.)

Example from Level 1, Chapter 4 vocabulary. The teacher writes the following sentences on slips of paper and places them in an envelope:

1. **Hablan.**
2. **Hablan por teléfono.**
3. **Estudian en la biblioteca.**
4. **Escuchan discos.**
5. **Miran la televisión.**
6. **Preparan una merienda.**
7. **Toman un refresco.**
8. **Bailan.**
9. **Cantan.**
10. **Llegan a una fiesta.**

Each team will draw one slip of paper from the envelope and decide together how to pantomime the action for the class. As one team pantomimes their action for 30 seconds, the other teams are silent. Then the students within each team discuss among themselves what sentence was acted out for them. When they have decided on the sentence, each team sends one person to write it on the chalkboard.

INSIDE/OUTSIDE CIRCLE Students form two concentric circles of equal number by counting off 1-2, 1-2 in their teams. The ones form a circle shoulder to shoulder and facing out. The twos form a circle outside the ones to make pairs. With an odd number of students, there can be one threesome. Students take turns sharing information, quizzing each other, or taking parts of a dialog. After students finish with their first partners, rotate the inside circle to the left so that the students repeat the process with new partners. For following rounds alternate rotating inside and outside circles so that students get to repeat the identified tasks, but with new partners. This is an excellent way to structure 100% student participation combined with extensive practice of communication tasks.

Other suggested activities are similarly easy to follow and to implement in the classroom. Student enthusiasm for cooperative learning activities will reward the enterprising teacher. Teachers who are new to these concepts may want to refer to Dr. Spencer Kagan's book Cooperative Learning, published by Resources for Teachers, Inc., Paseo Espada, Suite 622, San Juan Capistrano, CA 92675

Student Portfolios

The use of student portfolios to represent long-term individual accomplishments in learning Spanish offers several benefits. With portfolios, students can keep written records of their best work and thereby document their own progress as learners. For teachers, portfolios enable us to include our students in our evaluation and measurement process. For example, the content of any student's portfolio may offer an alternative to the standardized test as a way of measuring student writing achievement. Assessing the contents of a student's portfolio can be an option to testing the writing skill via the traditional writing section on the chapter or unit test.

There are as many kinds of portfolios as there are teachers working with them. Perhaps the most convenient as well as permanent portfolio consists of a three-ring binder which each student will add to over the school year and in which the student will place his or her best written work. In the *Glencoe Spanish* series, selections for the portfolio may come from the Writing Activities Workbook; the more open-ended activities in the Student Tape Manual and the Video Activities Booklet, as well as from written assignments in the Student Textbook, including the **Actividades escritas** section. The teacher is encouraged to refer actively to student's portfolios so that they are regarded as more than just a storage device. For example, over the course of the school year, the student may be asked to go back to earlier entries in his or her portfolio in order to revise certain assignments, or to develop an assignment further by writing in a new tense, e.g., the preterit. In this way the student can appreciate the amount of learning that has occurred over several months time.

Portfolios offer students a multidimensional look at themselves. A "best" paper might be the one with the least errors or one in which the student reached and synthesized a new idea, or went beyond the teacher's assignment. The Student Portfolio topic is included in each chapter of the Teacher's Edition as a reminder that this is yet another approach the teacher may wish to use in the Spanish classroom.

Glencoe Spanish 2 CD-ROM Interactive Textbook

The **Glencoe Spanish 2** CD-ROM Interactive Textbook is a complete curriculum and instructional system for Spanish students. The four-disc CD-ROM program contains all elements of the Student Textbook with enhancements that include video, animation, audio, interactive activities, and games. Although especially suited for individual or small-group use, the Interactive Textbook can be connected to a large monitor or LCD panel for whole class instruction. With this flexible, interactive system, you can introduce, reinforce, or remediate any part of the **Glencoe Spanish** Level 2 curriculum at any time.

The CD-ROM program has four major components—Contents, Games, References and Portfolio.

The Contents Menu

The following selections can be found in the Contents menu.

VOCABULARIO Vocabulary is introduced in thematic contexts. New words are introduced and communication activities based on real-life situations are presented.

ESTRUCTURA Students are given explanations of Spanish structures. They then practice through contextualized activities.

CONVERSACIÓN Interactive video enhances this feature comprised of real-life dialogs. Students may listen to and watch a conversation and then choose to participate as a character as they record their part of the dialog.

LECTURAS CULTURALES These readings give students the opportunity to gain insight into Hispanic culture. They are also able to hear the readings in Spanish. The similarities and differences between Hispanic and U.S. cultures are emphasized.

CONEXIONES These readings address other areas of the school curriculum, thereby reinforcing knowledge from other disciplines through the study of Spanish.

CULMINACIÓN End-of-chapter activities require students to integrate the concepts they have learned. Special **Actividades interactivas,** located here as well as in earlier sections of the chapter, allow students to practice listening and speaking skills in simulated conversations. An on-screen character asks a series of questions and the user responds by recording his or her answers.

The **Culminación** section includes a **Vocabulario** review that is linked to the glossary (Reference Menu). By clicking on the **Expansión cultural** photo, students can listen to an expanded version of the photo caption. The **Culminación** section also provides a link to the Glencoe Foreign Language Web site.

REPASO In this section, students participate in a variety of review activities.

LITERATURA These short selections from Spanish literature provide rewarding reading opportunities.

VISTAS The photos featured in this section were prepared by the National Geographic Society. The Vistas in Level 1 focus on Mexico, Spain, Puerto Rico, and Ecuador. Those in Level 2 showcase Peru, Chile, Costa Rica, and Guatemala.

The Games Menu: *Juegos de repaso*

There are two game formats: *¿Cuánto sabes?* and *¡El tucán pregunta!* The games are designed as Self-Tests. The content lets the user review vocabulary and structure concepts for a particular chapter in a motivating and enjoyable format.

The References Menu

The References menu contains the following selections:

MAPS Students can access the maps of the Spanish-speaking world: Spain, Mexico and Central America, and South America.

VERBS The verb charts reproduce all of the verbs highlighted at the back of the Student Textbook.

GLOSSARY Students can search this interactive Spanish/English glossary and hear the words pronunced in Spanish.

The Portfolio Menu

The Portfolio menu reinforces the writing skill. There are a variety of writing templates from which to choose, in order to create dialogs, write postcards and letters, and short essays. The writing samples can be saved to the hard drive. These writings tasks can also be recorded and played back.

For more information, see the User's Guide accompanying the *Glencoe Spanish 2* CD-ROM Interactive Textbook.

Suggestions for Correcting Homework

Correcting homework, or any tasks students have done on an independent basis, should be a positive learning experience rather than mechanical busywork. Following are some suggestions for correcting homework. These ideas may be adapted as the teacher sees fit.

1. Put the answers on an overhead transparency. Have students correct their own answers.

2. Ask one or more of your better students to write their homework answers on the chalkboard at the beginning of the class hour. While the answers are being put on the chalkboard, the teacher involves the rest of the class in a non-related activity. At some point in the class hour, take a few minutes to go over the homework answers that have been written on the board, asking student to check their own work. You may then wish to have students hand in their homework so that they know this independent work is important.

3. Go over the homework assignment quickly in class. Write the key word(s) for each answer on the chalkboard so students can see the correct answer.

4. When there is no correct answer, i.e., "Answers will vary," give one or two of the most likely answers. Don't allow students to inquire about all other possibilities however.

5. Have all students hand in their homework. After class, correct every other (every third, fourth, fifth, etc.) homework paper. Over several days, you will have checked every student's homework at least once.

6. Compile a list of the most common student errors. Then create a worksheet that explains the underlying problem areas, providing additional practice in those areas.

Pacing

¡BUEN VIAJE! **Level 2** has been developed so that it may be completed in one school year. However, it is up to the individual teacher to decide how many chapters will be covered. Although completion of the textbook by the end of the year is recommended, it is not necessary. The important structures of Levels 1 and 2 are reviewed in new contexts in *¡Buen viaje!* **Level 3** under the chapter heading **Repaso de estructura.**

The establishment of lesson plans helps the teacher visualize how a chapter can be presented. By emphasizing certain aspects of the program and de-emphasizing others, the teacher can change the focus and the approach of a chapter to meet students' needs and to suit his or her own teaching style and techniques. They include some of the suggestions and techniques that have been described earlier in this Teacher's Manual. For detailed, day by day lesson plans, see either the Lesson Plans booklet, or the Block Scheduling Lesson Plans booklet.

Glencoe Spanish 2

¡Buen viaje!

Glencoe Spanish 2

¡Buen viaje!

ABOUT THE FRONT COVER
Puerto Vallarta, México   The Church of Guadalupe is one of the most prominent landmarks in the resort town of Puerto Vallarta, located on the Pacific coast. The area in front of the church is the Plaza de Armas. Puerto Vallarta is the second largest resort town in Mexico.

ABOUT THE BACK COVER
(top) El Parque del Retiro, Madrid; *(middle)* Machu Picchu, Perú;
(bottom) Mijas (Andalucía), España

NATIONAL GEOGRAPHIC SOCIETY

The colorful and inviting **Vistas** featured in this textbook were designed and developed by the National Geographic Society's Educational Division. Their purpose is to give greater insight into the people and places found in the Spanish-speaking countries listed below.

VISTAS DE CHILE
pages 118–121

VISTAS DE COSTA RICA
pages 212–215

VISTAS DEL PERÚ
pages 332–335

VISTAS DE GUATEMALA   pages 426–429

Glencoe Spanish 2

¡Buen viaje!

PROTASE E. WOODFORD

CONRAD J. SCHMITT

**Glencoe
McGraw-Hill**

New York, New York   Columbus, Ohio   Woodland Hills, California   Peoria, Illinois

National Geographic Society

The **National Geographic Society**, founded in 1888 for the increase and diffusion of geographic knowledge, is the world's largest nonprofit scientific and educational organization. Since its earliest days, the Society has used sophisticated communication technologies and rich historical and archival resources to convey knowledge to a worldwide membership. The Education Division supports the Society's mission by developing innovative educational programs—ranging from traditional print materials to multimedia programs including CD-ROMs, videodiscs, and software.

Meet our Authors

Conrad J. Schmitt

Conrad J. Schmitt received his B.A. degree magna cum laude from Montclair State College, Upper Montclair, NJ. He received his M.A. from Middlebury College, Middlebury VT. He did additional graduate work at Seton Hall University and New York University. Mr. Schmitt has taught Spanish and French at the elementary, junior, and senior high school levels. In addition, he has travelled extensively throughout Spain, Central and South America, and the Caribbean.

Protase E Woodford

Protase "Woody" Woodford has taught Spanish at all levels from elementary through graduate school. At Educational Testing Service in Princeton, NJ, he was Director of Test Development, Director of Language Programs, Director of International Testing Programs and Director of the Puerto Rico Office. He has served as a consultant to the United Nations Secretariat, UNESCO, the Organization of American States, the U.S. Office of Education, and many ministries of education in Asia, Latin America, and the Middle East.

Glencoe/McGraw-Hill

A Division of The McGraw·Hill Companies

Send all inquiries to:
Glencoe/McGraw-Hill
21600 Oxnard Street, Suite 500
Woodland Hills, CA 91367

ISBN: 0-02-641517-8 (Student Edition)
ISBN: 0-02-641518-6 (Teacher's Wraparound Edition)

Printed in the United States of America.

2 3 4 5 6 7 8 9 10   003   08 07 06 05 04 03 02 01 00 99

Contenido

Repaso

CAPÍTULO *1*
Un viaje en tren

CONTENIDO

CAPÍTULO 4
De tiendas

CAPÍTULO 8
Emergencias médicas

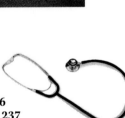

CAPÍTULO *11*
El coche y la carretera

CAPÍTULO *14*
Profesiones y oficios

Literatura

Apéndices

REPASO A

OVERVIEW

There are seven **Repasos (A–G)** at the beginning of **¡Buen Viaje! Level 2.** In **Repaso A** students review vocabulary dealing with school, getting to school, and buying school supplies and clothing. In the **Estructura** section, students review the present tense of **-ar** verbs and the verbs **ir, dar,** and **estar.**

Students practice this vocabulary and these structures as they talk about school, after-school activities, and shopping for clothes.

Las compras para la escuela

R 1

La calle Serrano You may wish to ask the following questions about the photo of calle Serrano, a shopping and residential street in the upscale area of Salamanca in Madrid:

¿Es de noche o es de día?

¿Es una calle bonita?

¿Hay muchas tiendas en la calle?

¿Hay mucho tráfico?

RESOURCES

📁 Workbook, pages R 1–R-6

🔔 Bell Ringer Review
Transparencies R-1–R-2

🔔 Bell Ringer Review

Use BRR Transparency R-1, or write the following on the board:
Write as many words as you can think of associated with school.

TEACHING VOCABULARY

 Before you begin your presentation, you may wish to ask students to say anything they can about the illustrations. If you find that they have a good command of the vocabulary, you can skip this review material and do the **Práctica** activities immediately.

A. Have students open their books. Point to individual items in the illustrations and have the class repeat **el bus escolar**, for example. Then build to the complete sentences.

B. As you present the sentences, ask comprehension questions such as: **¿Llegan los alumnos a la escuela? ¿Quiénes llegan? ¿Adónde llegan? ¿Llegan a eso de las ocho menos cuarto? ¿A qué hora llegan?**

C. After reviewing the vocabulary orally, have students read the material for additional reinforcement.

Vocabulario

Los alumnos llegan a la escuela a las
ocho menos cuarto.
Algunos toman el bus escolar.
Otros van a la escuela a pie.

Los alumnos estudian mucho.
Toman apuntes.
Escuchan a la profesora cuando habla.
La profesora enseña.

José está en la papelería.
Necesita materiales escolares.
Compra un cuaderno, un lápiz y
un bolígrafo.

Teresa está en la tienda de ropa.
Compra una blusa para llevar a la escuela.
Mira la blusa.
Paga en la caja.

Práctica

A HISTORIETA En la escuela

Contesten.

1. ¿Cómo llegan los alumnos a la escuela? ¿Toman el bus, van en carro o van a pie?
2. ¿A qué hora llegan a la escuela?
3. ¿Con quién hablan los alumnos cuando entran en la sala de clase?
4. ¿Quiénes toman exámenes y quién da los exámenes?
5. ¿Sacan los alumnos notas altas?
6. ¿Prestan ellos atención cuando la profesora habla?

B HISTORIETA A la papelería

Escojan.

1. Alicia necesita materiales escolares. ¿Adónde va ella?
   a. a la cafetería   **b.** a la tienda de ropa   **c.** a la papelería
2. ¿Con quién habla Alicia en la papelería?
   a. con el empleado   **b.** con el profesor   **c.** con el mesero
3. ¿Qué compra Alicia en la papelería?
   a. un refresco   **b.** un pantalón corto   **c.** un cuaderno
4. ¿Dónde paga Alicia?
   a. cien pesos   **b.** en la caja   **c.** en el parque
5. ¿En qué lleva ella los materiales escolares?
   a. en una mochila   **b.** en un cuaderno
   c. en una asignatura

C HISTORIETA En la tienda de ropa

Contesten según se indica.

1. ¿Adónde va Roberto? (a la tienda de ropa)
2. ¿Qué necesita? (una camisa de mangas cortas)
3. ¿Busca una camisa verde? (no, roja y azul)
4. ¿Qué talla usa? (38)
5. ¿Compra Roberto una camisa? (sí)
6. ¿Cuánto cuesta? (125 pesos)
7. ¿Dónde paga Roberto? (en la caja)

Calle Florida, Buenos Aires, Argentina

REPASO A

≈ R 3

REPASO A
Vocabulario

Práctica

A **Práctica A** can be done orally with books closed.

EXPANSION After going over **Práctica A**, call on a student to retell the story in his or her own words.

B Have students read **Práctica B** aloud.

C **Práctica C** can be done orally with books closed.

¡OJO! After going over the **Práctica** activities in class, you may have students write them for homework for additional reinforcement. Since this is review work, however, you may find that it is not necessary to have students do this. Try to get through these review lessons as quickly as possible.

Learning From Photos

Calle Florida, Buenos Aires, Argentina Remind students that Calle Florida is a lovely shopping street in the heart of Buenos Aires.

You may wish to ask the following questions about the photo:
¿Dónde está el muchacho?
¿Qué mira?
¿Qué opinas? ¿Es cara o barata la camisa? ¿Cuesta mucho o poco?

ANSWERS

Práctica

A 1. Los alumnos toman el bus (van en carro, van a pie) a la escuela.
2. Llegan a la escuela a las ocho menos cuarto.
3. Los alumnos hablan con ___ cuando entran en la sala de clase.
4. Los alumnos toman exámenes y los profesores dan exámenes.
5. Sí (No), los alumnos (no) sacan notas altas.

6. Sí (No), ellos (no) prestan atención cuando la profesora habla.

B 1. c   **4.** b
2. a   **5.** a
3. c

C 1. Roberto va a la tienda de ropa.
2. Necesita una camisa de mangas cortas.
3. No, busca una camisa roja y azul.
4. Usa la talla 38.
5. Sí, Roberto compra una camisa.
6. Cuesta 125 pesos.
7. Roberto paga en la caja.

R 3

TEACHING THE CONVERSATION

A. Call on two students to read the **Conversación** aloud using as much expression as possible.

B. After the conversation has been read, go over the **Después de leer** activity.

Learning From Realia

Papelería Monog You may wish to ask the following questions:

¿Es Monog el nombre de una papelería o de una tienda de ropa?

¿Qué venden en la tienda Monog?

¿Dónde está?

¿Quién es la propietaria?

Conversación

La apertura de clases

PACO: Elena, ¿cómo estás?
ELENA: Muy bien, Paco. ¿Y tú?
PACO: Bien. ¿Adónde vas?
ELENA: Voy a la papelería. Necesito comprar algunas cosas para la apertura de clases.
PACO: Verdad. Septiembre una vez más. ¡Es increíble!

EDICIÓN EN CD-ROM

MARÍA MOLINER

DICCIONARIO DE USO DEL ESPAÑOL

PRIMERA EDICIÓN

Después de conversar

 A Contesten.

1. ¿Con quién habla Elena?
2. ¿Cómo está Paco?
3. ¿Son amigos Elena y Paco?
4. ¿Adónde va Elena?
5. ¿Qué necesita ella?
6. ¿De qué hablan los dos amigos?

PAPELERIA
MONOG

TODO PARA EL ESTUDIANTE
TODO PARA LA OFICINA
Y MIL COSAS MAS.

Rosa María de Valdéz
PROPIETARIA

Av. Obregon 721
Tel. y Fax 2-54-55

Nogales, Sonora, Mex.

ANSWERS

Después de conversar

A 1. Elena habla con Paco.
2. Paco está bien.
3. Sí, Elena y Paco son amigos.
4. Elena va a la papelería.
5. Ella necesita comprar algunas cosas para la apertura de clases.
6. Los dos amigos hablan de la apertura de clases.

Estructura

Presente de los verbos en -ar

1. Review the forms of the present tense of regular **-ar** verbs.

MIRAR	miro	miras	mira	miramos	*miráis*	miran
TOMAR	tomo	tomas	toma	tomamos	*tomáis*	toman

2. Remember, to make a sentence negative you put **no** before the verb.

No hablamos francés. Hablamos español.

3. Remember to use **tú** when talking to a friend, family member, or person your own age. Use **Ud.** when speaking to an adult, a person you do not know well, or someone to whom you wish to show respect.

¿Tú estudias español, Roberto?
¿Y Ud., señora? ¿Ud. también estudia español?

Práctica

A **Entrevista**   Contesten personalmente.

1. ¿En qué escuela estudias?
2. ¿Cómo llegas a la escuela por la mañana?
3. ¿Cuántos cursos tomas?
4. ¿En qué llevas los materiales escolares?
5. ¿Estudian mucho los alumnos de tu escuela?
6. ¿Sacan Uds. buenas notas?
7. ¿Toman Uds. muchos exámenes?
8. ¿Escuchan Uds. cuando la profesora habla?

Universidad Iberoamericana,
Ciudad de México

Bell Ringer Review

Use BRR Transparency R-2, or write the following on the board:
Use the following expressions in a sentence.
estudiar mucho
tomar apuntes
prestar atención
sacar notas

TEACHING STRUCTURE

Presente de los verbos en -ar

A. Have students read the forms of the **-ar** verbs aloud.
B. Write the two verbs on the board and underline the endings.
C. Read the information in Step 3 to the class. Review this point as quickly as possible.

Práctica

A **Práctica A** can be done as an interview. Have one student ask the question and another respond.

ANSWERS

Práctica

A 1. Estudio en la Escuela ___.
2. Llego a pie (en carro, en bus).
3. Tomo ___ cursos.
4. Llevo los materiales escolares en una mochila.
5. Sí (No), los alumnos de mi escuela (no) estudian mucho.
6. Sí, (No, no) sacamos buenas notas.
7. Sí, (No, no) tomamos muchos exámenes.
8. Sí, (No, no) escuchamos cuando...

Estructura

⊹Práctica⊹

B Have students do **Práctica B** with books open.

Learning From Photos

Una fiesta en la Ciudad de Guatemala Ask the following questions about the photo:

¿Están en una fiesta los jóvenes?

¿Cuántos muchachos hay? ¿Y cuántas muchachas hay?

¿Qué llevan?

¿Qué toman?

¿Dónde está la casa?

¿Dónde está Guatemala?

TEACHING STRUCTURE

Los verbos ir, dar, estar

A. Have students look at the verbs on page R 6. Point out to them that the endings are the same as regular **-ar** verbs except for the **yo** form.

B. Have students repeat **estoy, doy, voy.** Then have them repeat all the forms.

C. Read the explanation about **al** in Step 2 aloud.

R 6

B HISTORIETA En la fiesta

Completen.

1. Durante la fiesta todos nosotros _____. (bailar)
2. Felipe _____ el piano. (tocar)
3. Mientras él _____ el piano, Elena y Carlos _____. (tocar, cantar)
4. ¿ _____ Uds. refrescos durante la fiesta? (preparar)
5. ¿ _____ Uds. fotos durante la fiesta? (tomar)
6. Sí, y todos nosotros _____ las fotografías. (mirar)

Una fiesta en la Ciudad de Guatemala

Los verbos ir, dar, estar

1. Note that the verbs **ir, dar,** and **estar** are the same as regular **-ar** verbs in all forms except **yo.**

ESTAR	estoy	estás	está	estamos	*estáis*	están
DAR	doy	das	da	damos	*dais*	dan
IR	voy	vas	va	vamos	*vais*	van

2. The preposition **a** often follows the verb **ir.** Remember that **a** contracts with **el** to form one word—**al.**

   Voy al café. No voy a la tienda.

ANSWERS

Práctica

B 1. bailamos
   2. toca
   3. toca, cantan
   4. Preparan
   5. Toman
   6. miramos

 **Práctica**

A **HISTORIETA** Voy a la escuela.

Contesten.

1. ¿Vas a la escuela?
2. ¿A qué hora vas a la escuela?
3. ¿Con quién vas a la escuela?
4. ¿Están Uds. en la escuela ahora?
5. ¿Cómo van Uds. a la escuela?

B **HISTORIETA** A la tienda de ropa

Completen.

Yo _____ (ir) a la tienda de ropa.
1

Emilio _____ (ir) también. Él y yo
2

(nosotros) _____ (estar) en la tienda.
3

Yo _____ (comprar) una camiseta
4

y él _____ (comprar) un blue jean.
5

Nosotros no _____ (necesitar)
6

mucha ropa porque _____ (llevar)
7

uniforme a la escuela.

Elena y Tomás _____ (llevar)
8

uniforme a la escuela también. Ellos _____ (ir) a una escuela en las
9

afueras de Lima, en Miraflores.

Estepona, España

Actividades comunicativas

A ¿Cuándo? ¿En clase, después de las clases o en la fiesta?
Work with a classmate. He or she will suggest an activity. You will tell
where you and your friends typically take part in the activity.

B En la tienda de ropa You are at a clothing store. You need to buy
some things. Your partner will be the sales clerk. Have a conversation
with each other. Then reverse roles.

JUEGO ¿Quién es? Work in small groups. One person tells what
someone in the class is wearing. The others have to guess who it is. If
several people are wearing the same thing, the person giving the clues
will have to give more details.

 Práctica

A **Práctica A** can be done orally
with books closed.

B Go over **Práctica B** with books
open.

Writing Development

Have students rewrite the information from **Práctica B** in
paragraph form.

Actividades comunicativas

¡OJO! **Práctica** versus
**Actividades comunica-
tivas** All activities which provide
guided practice are labeled
Práctica. The more open-ended
communicative activities are labeled
Actividades comunicativas.

Learning From Photos

Estepona, España You may
wish to ask the following ques-
tions about the photo:
¿Dónde está el muchacho?
¿Qué hay en la tienda?
¿Qué mira el muchacho?
¿De qué color es?

ANSWERS

Práctica

A 1. Sí, voy a la escuela.
2. Voy a la escuela a las ___.
3. Voy a la escuela con ___.
4. Sí, (No, no) estamos en la escuela
ahora.
5. Vamos a la escuela a pie (en carro,
en bus).

B 1. voy
2. va
3. estamos

4. compro
5. compra
6. necesitamos
7. llevamos
8. llevan
9. van

Actividades comunicativas
A and **B** Answers will vary.

OVERVIEW

In **Repaso B** students review the vocabulary they need to describe people and things and to identify nationalities.

In the **Estructura** section, they review the verb **ser** and agreement of nouns and adjectives.

Students practice this vocabulary and these structures as they talk about their friends, classes, and teachers.

Amigos y alumnos

R 9

La Plaza Mayor You may wish to ask the following questions about the photo of the students seated at a café on the Plaza Mayor in Madrid:

¿Están los jóvenes en un café?

¿Está en la Plaza Mayor el café?

¿Está en Madrid la Plaza Mayor?

¿Qué toman los jóvenes?

¿Qué hay en la mesa?

¿Qué llevan los jóvenes?

RESOURCES

📁 Workbook, pages R 7–R 10
📖 Bell Ringer Review
   Transparencies R-3–R-5

Bell Ringer Review

Use BRR Transparency R-3, or write the following on the board: Write any words you can use to describe a person.

TEACHING VOCABULARY

A. Students should be quite familiar with this vocabulary. It should be possible to review it very quickly.

B. Call on a student to read the sentences below each illustration.

C. Ask questions about the sentences. Then have students say anything they can about the illustrations.

⬥Práctica⬥

A and **B** **Práctica A** and **B** can be done orally with books closed.

Vocabulario

Es María Gorostiza.
Ella es mexicana.
Es rubia y bastante alta.
María es de Guadalajara.
Ella es alumna en el Colegio Hidalgo.

Felipe y Teresa son amigos.
Ellos son alumnos en la misma escuela.
Son alumnos buenos. Son inteligentes.
Y ellos son bastante cómicos.

⬥Práctica⬥

A **HISTORIETA** María Gorostiza

Contesten.

1. ¿De qué nacionalidad es María Gorostiza?
2. ¿De dónde es?
3. ¿Cómo es ella?
4. ¿Es ella alumna?
5. ¿Dónde es alumna María?

B **HISTORIETA** Felipe y Teresa

Corrijan las oraciones falsas.

1. Felipe y Teresa son hermanos.
2. Ellos son alumnos en escuelas diferentes.
3. Ellos son alumnos muy malos.
4. No son inteligentes.
5. Son muy serios y tímidos.

ANSWERS

Práctica

A 1. María Gorostiza es mexicana.
2. Es de Guadalajara.
3. Es rubia y bastante alta.
4. Sí, ella es alumna.
5. Es alumna en el Colegio Hidalgo.

B 1. Felipe y Teresa son amigos.
2. Ellos son alumnos en la misma escuela.
3. Ellos son alumnos buenos.
4. Son inteligentes.
5. Son bastante cómicos.

Conversación

¿De dónde son?

JULIO: ¡Hola!
ROSA: ¡Hola! ¿Qué tal?
JULIO: Bien, ¿y tú?
ROSA: Bien. Oye, ¿eres un amigo de Teresa Irizarry, ¿no?
JULIO: Sí, soy Julio Arenal.
ROSA: ¿De dónde eres, Julio?
JULIO: ¿Yo? Soy de San Juan. Y tú eres de Ponce como Teresa, ¿no?
ROSA: Sí, soy ponceña.

Después de conversar

 Contesten.
1. ¿Son puertorriqueños los dos muchachos?
2. ¿De dónde es Julio?
3. ¿Es Julio un amigo de Teresa Irizarry?
4. ¿De dónde son Teresa y Rosa?

Ponce, Puerto Rico

TEACHING THE CONVERSATION

A. Call on two students to come to the front of the class. Have them read the **Conversación** with as much expression as possible.
B. Have students make up their own conversations with similar information. Ask for volunteers to present their conversations to the class.
C. Now quickly do the **Después de conversar** activity.

Learning From Photos

Ponce, Puerto Rico Ponce is the second largest city in Puerto Rico. It is on the Caribbean coast in the southern part of the island.

ANSWERS

Después de conversar
A 1. Sí, los dos muchachos son puertorriqueños.
2. Julio es de San Juan.
3. Sí, Julio es un amigo de Teresa Irizarry.
4. Teresa y Rosa son de Ponce.

Estructura

Presente del verbo ser

Review the forms of the irregular verb **ser.**

| SER | soy | eres | es | somos | *sois* | son |

Práctica

 A Entrevista Contesten personalmente.
1. ¿Quién eres?
2. ¿De qué nacionalidad eres?
3. ¿Dónde eres alumno o alumna?
4. ¿Cómo es tu escuela?

B HISTORIETA El amigo de Andrés
Completen con **ser.**

Yo ____₁ un amigo de Andrés. Andrés ____₂ muy simpático. Y él ____₃ gracioso. Andrés y yo ____₄ dominicanos. ____₅ de la República Dominicana.

La capital de la República Dominicana ____₆ Santo Domingo. Nosotros ____₇ alumnos en un colegio en Santo Domingo. Nosotros ____₈ alumnos de inglés. La profesora de inglés ____₉ la señorita White. Ella ____₁₀ americana.

Fortaleza de Orzama, Santo Domingo

Acrílico sobre tela de Tony Capellán. Arma de doble filo

Arte dominicano en Puerto Rico

 Bell Ringer Review

Use BRR Transparency R-4, or write the following on the board:
Answer.
1. ¿Quién eres?
2. ¿De dónde eres?
3. ¿De qué nacionalidad eres?

TEACHING STRUCTURE

Presente del verbo ser

Quickly go over the forms of **ser** and have students do the **Práctica** activities.

Práctica

A Have students work in pairs and ask each other the questions in **Práctica A.**

Writing Development

After going over **Práctica B** have students rewrite the story in their own words.

Learning From Realia

Fortaleza de Orzama, Santo Domingo Santo Domingo is the capital of the Dominican Republic. The Dominican Republic and Haiti form the island of Hispaniola. Hispaniola was discovered during Columbus' first voyage in 1492.

ANSWERS

Práctica
A 1. Soy ___.
2. Soy americano(a), etc.
3. Soy alumno(a) en la Escuela ___.
4. Mi escuela es ___.

B 1. soy   6. es
2. es   7. somos
3. es   8. somos
4. somos   9. es
5. Somos   10. es

R 12

Sustantivos, artículos y adjetivos

1. Spanish nouns are either masculine or feminine. Most nouns ending in **o** are masculine and most nouns ending in **a** are feminine. The definite articles **el** and **los** accompany masculine nouns; **la** and **las** accompany feminine nouns.

el alumno	los alumnos	la amiga	las amigas
el curso	los cursos	la escuela	las escuelas

2. An adjective must agree with the noun it describes or modifies. Adjectives that end in **o** have four forms.

el amigo sincero	los amigos sinceros
la amiga sincera	las amigas sinceras

3. Adjectives that end in **e** or a consonant have only two forms.

el curso interesante	los cursos interesantes
la asignatura interesante	las asignaturas interesantes
el curso difícil	los cursos difíciles
la asignatura difícil	las asignaturas difíciles

Unas amigas argentinas, Buenos Aires

 Bell Ringer Review

Use BRR Transparency R-5, or write the following on the board: Write the following in the plural.
1. Él es americano.
2. La muchacha es bonita.
3. El colegio es moderno.
4. El curso es fácil.

TEACHING STRUCTURE

Sustantivos, artículos y adjetivos

As you go over the explanation, have students repeat the words and phrases in Steps 1–3 after you. Point to a specific person or object as you use the definite article.

Learning From Photos

Unas amigas argentinas, Buenos Aires You may wish to ask the following questions about the photo of the girls in the Parque Florida in Buenos Aires:
¿Cuántas muchachas hay en la fotografía?
¿De dónde son ellas?
¿Están en un parque?
¿Tienen bicicletas?
¿Hay edificios altos cerca del parque?

Estructura

Práctica

A Have students say as much about the girl as they can in their own words.

Writing Development

After going over **Práctica B** orally in class, have students write about what they see in the photo.

C **RECYCLING** You may also review time by asking students questions about the school schedule.

Learning From Photos

En la colonia de San Ángel, Ciudad de México San Ángel is a lovely, rather quiet colonial section in the southern part of Mexico City. Every Saturday there is a popular market in San Ángel. It is called **El bazar sábado**.

Práctica

A **Julia** Describan a la muchacha.

Una muchacha de San Juan, Puerto Rico

B **Los amigos** Describan al grupo de amigos.

En la colonia de San Ángel, Ciudad de México

C **Mi clase favorita** Describan su clase favorita.

ANSWERS

Práctica
A, B, and C Answers will vary.

Actividades comunicativas

A **¡Qué clase tan difícil!** Work in groups of three or four. In each group, rate your courses as **fácil, difícil, regular, aburrido, fantástico.** Tally the results and report the information to the class.

B **En Venezuela** You are spending the summer with a family in Venezuela. Tell your Venezuelan "brother" or "sister" (your partner) all you can about your Spanish class and your Spanish teacher. Answer any questions he or she may have. Then reverse roles.

Salto Ángel, Venezuela

C **Cursos** You are speaking with an exchange student from Peru (your partner). He or she wants to know about your school, your schedule, and your classes. Tell as much as you can about your school and then ask him or her about school life in Peru.

Una alumna de Lima, Perú

Actividades comunicativas

¡OJO! The **Actividades comunicativas** allow students to use the vocabulary and structures of the chapter in open-ended, real-life situations. They also give students another opportunity to use words and structures from previous chapters.

Have students work on as many activities as you wish. You may also allow them to select those activities they want to do. Different groups can work on different activities.

Learning From Photos

Una alumna de Lima, Perú
Have students look at the photo and say as much as they can about it.

ANSWERS

Actividades comunicativas
A, B, and **C** Answers will vary.

OVERVIEW

In **Repaso C** students review family and house vocabulary and discuss some of their daily activities.

In the **Estructura** section, they review the present of -**er** and -**ir** verbs, the verb **tener,** and possessive adjectives.

Students practice this vocabulary and these structures as they talk about their families, homes, and neighbors.

La familia

La familia y las palomas This family feeding the pigeons is in the Plaza de Mayo in Buenos Aires, Argentina.

Point to the pigeons and give students the word **las palomas.** Explain to students: **La familia da de comer a las palomas.**

You may wish to have students describe each member of the family and tell what the weather is like in the photo.

R 17

🔔 Bell Ringer Review

Use BRR Transparency R-6, or write the following on the board: Complete.
1. **El hermano de mi padre es mi ___.**
2. **La hija de mis tíos es mi ___.**
3. **Yo soy ___ ___ de los padres de mis padres.**
4. **Los padres de mis padres son mis ___.**

TEACHING VOCABULARY

A. Have students open their books to page R 18. As you review the vocabulary, have students repeat the words and sentences after you.

B. Ask questions such as: **¿Es la familia Ramos? ¿Cuántas personas hay en la familia Ramos? ¿Dónde tienen ellos una casa? ¿En qué país viven ellos? ¿Son hondureños?**

C. Once you have asked your questions about all the illustrations, have students say anything they can about them.

Vocabulario

Es la familia Ramos.
En la familia Ramos hay cinco personas.
Ellos tienen una casa en San Pedro Sula.
Ellos viven en Honduras.

Su casa tiene siete cuartos.

La familia está en la sala.
La señora Ramos lee un libro.
Su esposo lee el periódico.
José ve la televisión.
Una hermana de José escribe una carta.

En el mercado venden frutas y vegetales.
Venden carne también.
La señora compra un kilo de tomates.
Los tomates están a 50 pesos el kilo.

❧Práctica❧

A | HISTORIETA La familia Ramos

Contesten.

1. ¿Cuántas personas hay en la familia Ramos?
2. ¿Tienen ellos una casa o un apartamento?
3. ¿Dónde viven ellos?
4. ¿Cuántos cuartos tiene su casa?
5. ¿Cuáles son los cuartos de la casa?

San Miguel de Allende,
México

B | **Expresiones** Pareen.

1. leer	**a.** mucho en la escuela
2. escribir	**b.** al quinto piso
3. vivir	**c.** una novela
4. aprender	**d.** un alumno bueno y serio
5. vender	**e.** una carta con bolígrafo
6. comer	**f.** una limonada
7. ver	**g.** en una casa particular
8. ser	**h.** una emisión deportiva
9. subir	**i.** discos en una tienda
10. beber	**j.** carne, ensalada y papas

JUEGO **¿Cuáles son?** Contesten.

1. ¿Cuáles son algunas cosas que comemos?
2. ¿Cuáles son algunas cosas que bebemos?
3. ¿Cuáles son algunas cosas que leemos?
4. ¿Cuáles son algunas cosas que escribimos?

❧Práctica❧

¡OJO! Go over the **Práctica** activities as quickly as possible. If students appear to have a good command of the vocabulary, it is not necessary that they write the activities.

If, however, you feel students need additional reinforcement of the vocabulary, have them write the activities after you go over them orally in class.

JUEGO You may wish to have students work in small groups to play this game. See which group can come up with the longest list for each category.

Learning From Photos

San Miguel de Allende, México Students learned something about San Miguel de Allende in **¡Buen viaje! Level 1.** Ask them if they remember anything about San Miguel.

You may also wish to have them say as much as they can about the house in the photo.

ANSWERS

Práctica

A 1. Hay cinco personas en la familia Ramos.
2. Tienen una casa.
3. Ellos viven en Honduras.
4. Su casa tiene siete cuartos.
5. Son la sala, el comedor, la cocina, el cuarto de baño y tres cuartos (recámaras).

B	
1. c	6. j
2. e	7. h
3. g	8. d
4. a	9. b
5. i	10. f

TEACHING THE CONVERSATION

A. Call on two students to read the **Conversación** aloud.

B. Then go over the **Después de conversar** activity.

GEOGRAPHY CONNECTION

Málaga, España Have students locate Málaga on the map of Spain on page 451. Málaga is a port on the Mediterranean. It is considered the gateway to the famous resorts of the Costa del Sol.

Conversación

¿Dónde viven?

TOMÁS: Elena, ¿tienes una familia grande?

ELENA: Sí, bastante grande. Somos seis.

TOMÁS: ¿Viven Uds. aquí en la capital?

ELENA: Sí, vivimos en la calle Mayor. Nuestro apartamento está en el edificio Bolívar.

 Después de conversar

A Contesten.

1. ¿Con quién habla Tomás?
2. ¿Tiene Elena una familia bastante grande?
3. ¿Cuántas personas hay en su familia?
4. ¿Viven ellos en la capital?
5. ¿En qué calle viven?
6. ¿Dónde tienen un apartamento?

Málaga, España

ANSWERS

Después de conversar

A 1. Tomás habla con Elena.
2. Sí, Elena tiene una familia bastante grande.
3. Hay seis personas en su familia.
4. Sí, ellos viven en la capital.
5. Viven en la calle Mayor.
6. Tienen un apartamento en el edificio Bolívar.

Estructura

Presente de los verbos en -er e -ir

1. Review the following forms of regular **-er** and **-ir** verbs.

COMER	como	comes	come	comemos	*coméis*	comen
BEBER	bebo	bebes	bebe	bebemos	*bebéis*	beben
VIVIR	vivo	vives	vive	vivimos	*vivís*	viven
SUBIR	subo	subes	sube	subimos	*subís*	suben

2. Note that the **-er** and **-ir** verbs have the same endings in all forms except **nosotros** (and **vosotros**).

comemos   vivimos
coméis   vivís

Las Ramblas, Barcelona, España

Bell Ringer Review

Use BRR Transparency R-7, or write the following on the board:
Do the following.
1. Write five things you can eat.
2. Write three things you can drink.
3. Write the names of the three meals.

TEACHING STRUCTURE

Presente de los verbos en -er e -ir

A. Have students repeat all of the verb forms after you.

B. Write two of the verbs on the board and have students repeat all forms after you.

C. Read Step 2 aloud and underline the endings to emphasize that **-er** and **-ir** verbs have the same endings in all forms except **nosotros** (and **vosotros**).

Learning From Photos

Las Ramblas, Barcelona, España Las Ramblas is a wide thoroughfare in downtown Barcelona. It is a beautiful street with many flower shops and cafés. It is in the old section of town called the **barrio gótico** and it is a favorite spot for strolling.

Bell Ringer Review

Use BRR Transparency R-8, or write the following on the board: Write an original sentence with each of the following verbs.

vivir
leer
escribir
aprender

 **Práctica**

¡**OJO!** Go over the **Práctica** activities orally in class. If you feel students need additional review, have them write them for homework.

GEOGRAPHY CONNECTION

Barcelona, España Have students locate Barcelona on the map of Spain on page 451, or use the Map Transparency.

Barcelona has long rivaled Madrid as an industrial and commercial center. Barcelona is a beautiful city rich in history that enjoys an active cultural life. It is also a thriving Mediterranean port.

Práctica

A Tú y tus amigos Contesten.

1. ¿Qué comes cuando vas a un café?
2. ¿Qué bebes cuando estás en un café?
3. ¿Qué aprenden tú y tus amigos en la escuela?
4. ¿Qué leen Uds. en la clase de inglés?
5. ¿Qué escriben Uds.?
6. ¿Comprenden los alumnos cuando la profesora de español habla?
7. ¿Reciben Uds. notas buenas en todas sus asignaturas?

B HISTORIETA En un café

Completen.

En el café los clientes _____ (ver) al mesero.
1
Ellos _____ (hablar) con el mesero. Los clientes
2
_____ (leer) el menú y _____ (decidir) lo que van
3   4
a tomar. Los meseros _____ (tomar) la orden
5
y _____ (escribir) la orden en un cuaderno
6
pequeño o un bloc. Los meseros no _____ (leer)
7
el menú. Y los clientes no _____ (escribir)
8
la orden.

Barcelona, España

ANSWERS

Práctica

A 1. Cuando voy a un café como ___.
2. Cuando estoy en un café bebo ___.
3. Mis amigos y yo aprendemos ___ en la escuela.
4. Nosotros leemos ___ en la clase de inglés.
5. Nosotros escribimos ___.
6. Sí (No), los alumnos (no) comprenden cuando la profesora de español habla.

7. Sí (No), nosotros (no) recibimos notas buenas en todas nuestras asignaturas.

B 1. ven
2. hablan
3. leen
4. deciden
5. toman
6. escriben
7. leen
8. escriben

El verbo tener

1. Review the forms of the irregular verb **tener.**

TENER   **tengo**   **tienes**   **tiene**   **tenemos**   *tenéis*   **tienen**

2. Note that the expression **tener que** followed by an infinitive means "to have to."

Tenemos que estudiar y aprender mucho.

A   HISTORIETA   Mi familia

Contesten.

1. ¿Tienes una familia grande o pequeña?
2. ¿Cuántos hermanos tienes?
3. ¿Cuántos años tienen ellos?
4. ¿Y cuántos años tienes tú?
5. ¿Tienen Uds. un perro o un gato?
6. ¿Tiene tu padre o tu madre un carro?
7. En la escuela, ¿tienes que estudiar mucho?
8. ¿Y tienen que trabajar mucho tus padres?

Barcelona, España

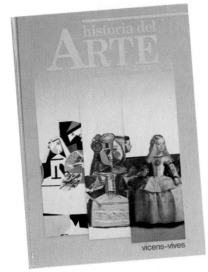

B   HISTORIETA   La familia Bravo

Completen con **tener.**

La familia Bravo ____ un piso o
apartamento en Madrid. Su piso ____ seis
cuartos. Está en Salamanca, una zona muy
bonita de la ciudad. Muchas calles en la zona
Salamanca ____ los nombres de artistas
famosos—la calle Goya, la calle Velázquez.

Hay cuatro personas en la familia Bravo.
Teresa ____ diecisiete años y su hermano
____ quince años. Ellos ____ un perro
adorable.

TEACHING STRUCTURE

El verbo tener

A. Have students repeat the forms of the verb **tener.**

B. Read the information about **tener que** to the class.

C. Have students make up additional sentences using **tener que.**

Práctica

A **Práctica A** can be done in pairs as an interview.

Writing Development

After going over **Práctica B** orally, have students rewrite the information in their own words in paragraph form.

ANSWERS

Práctica

A 1. Tengo una familia grande (pequeña).

2. Tengo ___ hermanos(as). (No tengo hermanos[as]).

3. Ellos tienen ___ años.

4. Yo tengo ___ años.

5. Sí, nosotros tenemos un perro (un gato). (No, no tenemos un perro [un gato]).

6. Sí, mi padre (mi madre) tiene un carro.

7. Sí, (No, no) tengo que estudiar mucho en la escuela.

8. Sí (No), mis padres (no) tienen que trabajar mucho.

B 1. tiene

2. tiene

3. tienen

4. tiene

5. tiene

6. tienen

Estructura

1. Review the forms of the possessive adjectives **mi**, **tu**, and **su**. These adjectives have only two forms.

> **¿Dan una fiesta tu hermana y tus primos?**
> **Sí, mi hermana y mis primos dan una fiesta.**
> **Todos sus amigos van a recibir una invitación a su fiesta.**

2. The possessive adjective **nuestro** has four forms.

> **Nuestro primo, nuestra tía y nuestros abuelos viven todos en Madrid.**

Práctica

Bell Ringer Review

Use BRR Transparency R-9, or write the following on the board:
Answer.
1. **¿Dónde vives?**
2. **¿Tienes una familia grande o pequeña?**
3. **¿Cuántos años tienes?**
4. **Y tu hermano(a), ¿cuántos años tiene?**
5. **¿Tienen Uds. un perro o gato?**

TEACHING STRUCTURE

Adjetivos posesivos

A. Have students open their books to page R24. Go over Steps 1 and 2 with them. Have them read the model sentences aloud.

A. After you have gone over the explanation with them, ask students to make up some original sentences using the possessive adjectives.

Práctica

¡OJO! Go over the **Práctica** activities orally in class. Assign them for written homework if you feel additional review and reinforcement are necessary.

A  **HISTORIETA** *Mi familia y mi casa*

Contesten.
1. ¿Dónde está tu casa o tu apartamento?
2. ¿Cuántos cuartos tiene tu casa o tu apartamento?
3. ¿Cuántas personas hay en tu familia?
4. ¿Dónde viven tus abuelos?
5. Y tus primos, ¿dónde viven?

B **HISTORIETA** *Nuestra casa*

Completen.

Nosotros vivimos en _____ *(name of city or town).* ___1___ casa está en la calle _____ *(name of street).* ___2___ padres tienen un carro. ___3___ carro es bastante nuevo. Yo tengo una bicicleta. ___4___ bicicleta está en el garaje con el carro de ___5___ padres. Nosotros tenemos un perro. ___6___ perro es adorable. ___7___ perro está en el jardín. Mi hermano y ___8___ amigos siempre juegan en el jardín alrededor de ___9___ casa.

Learning From Realia

You may wish to ask the following question about the realia:
¿Es *Hogares* una revista o un periódico?

ANSWERS

Práctica

A 1. Mi casa (Mi apartamento) está en ___.
2. Mi casa (Mi apartamento) tiene ___ cuartos.
3. Hay ___ personas en mi familia.
4. Mis abuelos viven en ___.
5. Mis primos viven en ___.

B 1. Nuestra
2. Nuestros
3. Nuestro
4. Mi
5. mis
6. Nuestro
7. Nuestro
8. sus
9. nuestra

Actividades comunicativas

A **Apartamentos** With a classmate, look at this plan of the fourth floor of an apartment building. A different family lives in each of the two apartments. Give each family a name. Then say as much as you can about each family and their activities. Don't forget to describe their apartment. Be as original as possible.

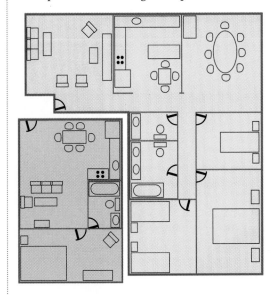

B **En el café** Work in groups of three or four. You're all friends from Chile. After school you go to a café where you talk about lots of things—school, teachers, friends, home, family, etc. One of you will be the waiter or waitress. You have to interrupt the conversation once in a while to take the orders and serve. Take turns.

Viña del Mar, Chile

Actividades comunicativas

¡OJO! Have students work on as many activities as you wish. You may also allow them to select those activities they want to do. Different groups can work on different activities.

A Encourage students to be as creative as possible when doing this activity. They can make up a lot of funny things.

B Have students present their conversations to the entire class.

GEOGRAPHY CONNECTION

Viña del Mar, Chile This is a beautiful summer resort on the Pacific Ocean just west of Santiago, the capital of Chile. Have students locate Santiago on the map of South America on page 452, or use the Map Transparency.

ANSWERS

Actividades comunicativas
A and **B** Answers will vary.

REPASO D

OVERVIEW

In **Repaso D** students review vocabulary associated with team sports.

In the **Estructura** section they review the present tense of stem-changing verbs and expressions with **aburrir, interesar,** and **gustar**.

Students practice this vocabulary and these structures as they talk about the sports and teams that they like.

Los deportes

R 27

El Estadio Azteca You may wish to ask the following questions about the photo of this famous stadium in Mexico City:

¿Hay muchos espectadores en el estadio?

En tu opinión, ¿cuántos espectadores hay?

¿Dónde están los jugadores?

¿Se divierten los espectadores?

RESOURCES

📁 Workbook, pages R 19–R 24
🔔 Bell Ringer Review
Transparencies R-10–R-12

🔔 Bell Ringer Review

Use BRR Transparency R-10, or write the following on the board:
Do the following.
1. Write six words associated with soccer.
2. Write five words associated with baseball.
3. Write four words associated with tennis.

TEACHING VOCABULARY

A. Have students open their books to page R 28. Ask them questions such as: **¿Cuántos equipos hay? ¿Qué juegan? ¿Qué empieza? ¿Adónde vuelven los jugadores? ¿Qué quieren hacer los dos equipos?**
B. Have students repeat the mini-conversation with as much expression as possible.
C. After going over the specific vocabulary on this page, have students say all the words they remember that are associated with team sports.

Vocabulario

Los dos equipos juegan (al) fútbol.
Empieza el segundo tiempo.
Los jugadores vuelven al campo de fútbol.
Los dos equipos quieren ganar.

Elena, ¿te gusta el béisbol?

Sí, me gusta. Pero me gusta más el fútbol.

Sí, me gusta mucho. ¿Y a ti?

A mí, no. Me aburre.

Es un partido de béisbol.
El jugador batea la pelota.
Luego corre de una base a otra.

Práctica

A **HISTORIETA** El juego de fútbol

Contesten según se indica.

1. ¿Cuántos tiempos hay en un juego de fútbol? (dos)
2. ¿Cuántos jugadores hay en un equipo de fútbol? (once)
3. ¿Dónde juegan fútbol? (en el campo de fútbol)
4. ¿Quién guarda la portería? (el portero)
5. ¿Qué bloquea? (el balón)
6. ¿Quieren perder los dos equipos? (no, ganar)
7. ¿Pierde un equipo si el tanto queda empatado? (no)

B ¿Qué deporte es? Escojan.

1. El jugador lanza el balón con el pie.
2. Hay cinco jugadores en el equipo.
3. Hay nueve partidas en el partido.
4. El jugador corre de una base a otra.
5. El portero para o bloquea el balón.
6. El jugador tira el balón y encesta.

C Gustos Contesten.

1. ¿Cuáles son los deportes que a ti te gustan?
2. ¿Cuáles son los comestibles que te gustan?
3. ¿Cuáles son los cursos que te interesan?
4. ¿Cuáles son algunas cosas que no te gustan, que te aburren?

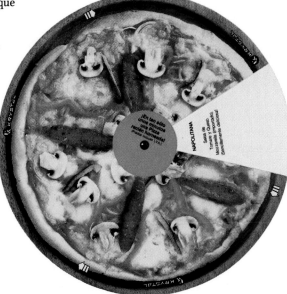

REPASO D
Vocabulario

Práctica

A Go over **Práctica A** orally with books closed.

EXPANSION After going over **Práctica A** have one or more students describe a soccer game in their own words. They can use **Práctica A** as a guide.

B **Práctica B** can be done as a game.

C **Práctica C** gives students the opportunity to recycle a great deal of general vocabulary from **¡Buen viaje! Level 1.**

ANSWERS

Práctica

A 1. **En un juego de fútbol hay dos tiempos.**
2. **En un equipo de fútbol hay once jugadores.**
3. **Juegan fútbol en el campo de fútbol.**
4. **El portero guarda la portería.**
5. **Bloquea el balón.**
6. **No, los dos equipos quieren ganar.**
7. **No, un equipo no pierde si el tanto queda empatado.**

B 1. **fútbol**
2. **baloncesto**
3. **béisbol**
4. **béisbol**
5. **fútbol**
6. **baloncesto**

C Answers will vary.

R 29

TEACHING THE CONVERSATION

A. Call on two students to read the **Conversación** aloud with as much expression as possible.

B. After students have read the conversation, do the **Después de conversar** activity.

Conversación

Un partido importante

TADEO: Isabel, ¿quieres ir al café Solís con nosotros?

ISABEL: Gracias, Tadeo, pero no puedo. Quiero ver el partido.

TADEO: ¿De qué partido hablas?

ISABEL: El Real juega contra el Valencia.

TADEO: ¿Cuál es tu equipo favorito? ¿Cuál te gusta más?

ISABEL: El Real.

Después de conversar

 Contesten.

1. ¿Adónde van los amigos de Tadeo?
2. ¿Quiere ir con ellos Isabel?
3. ¿Por qué no puede ir?
4. ¿Qué quiere ver?
5. ¿Qué equipos juegan?
6. ¿Cuál es el equipo favorito de Isabel?

ANSWERS

Después de conversar

A 1. **Los amigos de Tadeo van al café Solís.**
2. **No, Isabel no quiere ir con ellos.**
3. **No puede ir porque quiere ver el partido.**
4. **Quiere ver el partido.**
5. **El Real juega contra el Valencia.**
6. **El Real es el equipo favorito de Isabel.**

Estructura

Verbos de cambio radical

1. Review the following forms of stem-changing verbs. Remember that the **e** changes to **ie** in all forms except **nosotros** (and **vosotros**).

| EMPEZAR | empiezo | empiezas | empieza | empezamos | *empezáis* | empiezan |
| PERDER | pierdo | pierdes | pierde | perdemos | *perdéis* | pierden |

2. The following verbs change the **o** to **ue** in all forms except **nosotros** (and **vosotros**).

| VOLVER | vuelvo | vuelves | vuelve | volvemos | *volvéis* | vuelven |
| PODER | puedo | puedes | puede | podemos | *podéis* | pueden |

3. The verb **jugar** also has a stem change.

| JUGAR | juego | juegas | juega | jugamos | *jugáis* | juegan |

 **Práctica**

A **HISTORIETA** Un juego de béisbol

Completen.

El juego de béisbol ____₁ (empezar) a las tres y media. Habla Teresa:

—Hoy yo ____₂ (querer) ser la pícher.

La verdad es que Teresa ____₃ (ser) una pícher muy buena. Ella ____₄ (jugar) muy bien. Nosotros ____₅ (tener) un equipo bueno. Todos nosotros ____₆ (jugar) bien. Nuestro equipo no ____₇ (perder) mucho.

Caracas, Venezuela

🖐 Bell Ringer Review

Use BRR Transparency R-11, or write the following on the board:
Complete.

1. Nosotros ___ en ___. (vivir)
2. Mi primo ___ francés y yo ___ español. (estudiar)
3. Nosotros no ___ en la misma clase. (estar)
4. Yo ___ alumno(a) en la Escuela ___. (ser)

TEACHING STRUCTURE

Verbos de cambio radical

A. Have students repeat all the verb forms after you.

B. Then have students repeat all the **nosotros** forms.

C. Now have them repeat all the **yo** forms to contrast the stem change.

 **Práctica**

✏ Writing Development

After going over **Práctica A** orally, have students rewrite the information in their own words in paragraph form.

Learning From Photos

Caracas, Venezuela Have students say anything they can about the photo.

R 31

ANSWERS

A 1. empieza
2. quiero
3. es
4. juega
5. tenemos
6. jugamos
7. pierde

Estructura

Práctica

B Students can ask each other these questions.

 Encourage students to give as many answers as they can. Elicit multiple responses so students can review the use of the infinitive after an auxiliary verb.

TEACHING STRUCTURE

Verbos como aburrir, interesar y gustar

As you go over the explanation and the **Práctica** activities, have students point to themselves as they say **me** and have them look at a friend as they say **te**.

B **HISTORIETA** Una fiesta

Contesten.

1. ¿Quieres ir a la fiesta?
2. ¿Quieren Uds. bailar durante la fiesta?
3. ¿A qué hora empieza la fiesta?
4. ¿Puedes llegar a tiempo?
5. ¿Pueden Uds. tomar el bus a la fiesta?
6. ¿A qué hora vuelven Uds. a casa?

JUEGO Puedo, quiero, prefiero

1. **Puedo...** Tell all that you can do.
2. **Quiero...** Tell all that you want to do.
3. **Quiero pero no puedo...** Tell all that you want to do but for some reason you cannot do.
4. **No quiero porque prefiero...** Tell something you don't want to do because you prefer to do something else.

Verbos como **aburrir, interesar** y **gustar**

1. The verbs **interesar** and **aburrir** function the same in Spanish and English.

> **¿Te aburre el arte?**
>   *Does art bore you?*
> **¿Te aburren los deportes?**
>   *Do sports bore you?*
> **No, los deportes me interesan.**
>   *No, sports interest me.*

2. The verb **gustar** functions the same as **interesar** and **aburrir. Gustar** conveys the meaning "to like," but it actually means "to be pleasing to."

> **¿Te gusta el béisbol?**
>   **Sí, me gusta mucho.**
> **¿Te gustan los deportes?**
>   **Sí, me gustan.**

GUIA BREVE DE LA MEZQUITA CATEDRAL Y MUSEO DIOCESANO DE BELLAS ARTES DE CORDOBA

ANSWERS

Práctica

B 1. Sí, (No, no) quiero ir a la fiesta.
2. Sí, (No, no) queremos bailar durante la fiesta.
3. La fiesta empieza a las ___.
4. Sí, (No, no) puedo llegar a tiempo.
5. Sí (No), nosotros (no) podemos tomar el bus a la fiesta.
6. Nosotros volvemos a casa a las ___.

Práctica

A **Gustos** Sigan el modelo.

> **¿A mí? ¿Los tomates?**
> **Me gustan mucho los tomates.**

1. ¿A mí? ¿El pescado?
2. ¿A mí? ¿Los vegetales?
3. ¿A mí? ¿La carne?
4. ¿A mí? ¿El jamón?
5. ¿A mí? ¿Los mariscos?

B **¿Sí o no?** Contesten.

1. ¿Te interesan o te aburren las matemáticas? ¿Te gustan o no?
2. ¿Te interesa o te aburre la historia? ¿Te gusta o no?
3. ¿Te interesan o te aburren las ciencias? ¿Te gustan o no?
4. ¿Te interesa o te aburre la literatura? ¿Te gusta o no?
5. ¿Te interesa o te aburre la geografía? ¿Te gusta o no?

C **¿Qué te gusta hacer?** Contesten según los dibujos.

1.
2.
3.
4.

Actividades comunicativas

A **No soy muy aficionado(a).** Work with a classmate. Tell him or her what sport you don't want to play because you don't like it. Tell him or her what you prefer to play. Then ask your classmate questions to find out what sports he or she likes.

B **Mi equipo favorito** Work with a classmate. Tell him or her about your favorite team. Tell all about the sport and tell why you really like this team in particular. Then ask your classmate about his or her favorite team. Do you by chance have the same favorite team?

JUEGO **¿Qué deporte es?** Work with a classmate. Give him or her some information about a sport. He or she has to guess what sport you're talking about. Take turns.

Práctica

A and **B** Have students do **Práctica A** and **Práctica B** orally using as much expression as possible.

C Have students refer to the illustrations as they do **Práctica C.**

Actividades comunicativas

Let students choose the activity or activities they wish to take part in.

ANSWERS

Práctica

A 1. Me gusta mucho el pescado.
2. Me gustan mucho los vegetales.
3. Me gusta mucho la carne.
4. Me gusta mucho el jamón.
5. Me gustan mucho los mariscos.

B 1. Me interesan (Me aburren) las matemáticas. Sí, (No, no) me gustan.
2. Me interesa (Me aburre) la historia. Sí, (No, no) me gusta.
3. Me interesan (Me aburren) las ciencias. Sí, (No, no) me gustan.
4. Me interesa (Me aburre) la literatura. Sí, (No, no) me gusta.
5. Me interesa (Me aburre) la geografía. Sí, (No, no) me gusta.

C 1. Me gusta cantar.
2. Me gusta comer.
3. Me gusta leer.
4. Me gusta escuchar música.

Actividades comunicativas
A and **B** Answers will vary.

R 33

REPASO E

OVERVIEW

In **Repaso E** students review vocabulary dealing with airline travel and airports. In the **Estructura** section, students review the present tense of verbs with an irregular **yo** form, the difference between **saber** and **conocer,** and the present progressive.

Students practice this vocabulary and these structures as they plan a trip to a Spanish-speaking country and role-play making airline reservations.

Un viaje en avión

BIENVENIDOS
A
GUATEMALA

VOLAMOS PARA MANTENER LA PAZ

R 35

Learning From Photos

Aeropuerto Internacional, Ciudad de Guatemala You may wish to ask the following questions about this photo of the Guatemala City airport:

En tu opinión, ¿es grande o pequeño el aeropuerto?

¿Está cerca de la ciudad?

¿Son modernos los edificios que están cerca del aeropuerto?

¿Crees que mucha gente vive cerca del aeropuerto?

Bell Ringer Review

Use BRR Transparency R-13, or write the following on the board: Write original sentences using the following verbs.

mirar

tomar

leer

escribir

vivir

TEACHING VOCABULARY

¡OJO! Before you begin your presentation, you may wish to ask students to say anything they can about the illustrations. If you find that they have a good command of the vocabulary, you can skip this review material and do the **Práctica** activities immediately.

A. Have students open their books to page R 36. As you present the sentences, ask comprehension questions such as: **¿La agente revisa los boletos o revisa las maletas? ¿La agente tiene que revisar los pasaportes también? ¿El vuelo 102 sale con destino a México o con destino a Chile? ¿Sale a tiempo o sale con una demora?**

B. After reviewing the vocabulary orally, have students read the material for additional reinforcement.

Vocabulario

Los pasajeros están en el aeropuerto.
La agente de la línea aérea revisa los boletos (billetes).
Tiene que mirar los pasaportes también.

Los pasajeros hacen un viaje en avión.
El vuelo 102 con destino a México sale de la puerta diez.
El vuelo está saliendo a tiempo.
No sale con una demora.

Los pasajeros traen bastante equipaje de mano.
Ponen su equipaje de mano debajo del asiento.

✦Práctica✦

A HISTORIETA En el aeropuerto

Contesten.

1. ¿Están en el aeropuerto los pasajeros?
2. ¿Hacen un viaje en avión?
3. ¿Hablan con la agente de la línea aérea?
4. ¿Qué tiene que revisar la agente?
5. ¿Para dónde sale el vuelo?
6. ¿Está saliendo a tiempo o con una demora?
7. ¿Qué traen los pasajeros?
8. ¿Dónde ponen su equipaje de mano?

B ¿Sí o no? Digan que sí o que no.

1. El avión aterriza cuando sale.
2. El avión despega cuando llega a su destino.
3. Un vuelo internacional es un vuelo que va a un país extranjero.
4. Los agentes de la línea aérea que trabajan en el mostrador en el aeropuerto son los asistentes de vuelo.
5. La tripulación consiste en los empleados que trabajan a bordo del avión.

Aerolínea Mexicana

MEXICANA®
Aterrice con nosotros.

 Bell Ringer Review

Use BRR Transparency R-14, or write the following on the board: Write five words associated with an airport.

✦Práctica✦

A **Práctica A** can be done orally with books closed.

EXPANSION After going over **Práctica A**, call on a student to retell the story in his or her own words.

B Have students correct the false statements in **Práctica B**.

 After going over the **Práctica** activities in class, you may have students write them for homework for additional reinforcement. Since this is review work, however, you may find that it is not necessary to have students do this. Try to get through these review lessons as quickly as possible.

Learning From Photos

En el aeropuerto You may wish to ask the following questions about the top photo on page R 37:
¿Están haciendo cola los pasajeros delante del mostrador de la línea aérea?
¿Es larga la cola?
¿Cuántas personas hay en la cola?
¿Tienen mucho equipaje los pasajeros?
¿Tienen que facturar su equipaje?

ANSWERS

Práctica

A 1. Sí, los pasajeros están en el aeropuerto.
2. Sí, hacen un viaje en avión.
3. Sí, hablan con la agente de la línea aérea.
4. La agente tiene que revisar los boletos.
5. El vuelo sale para ___.
6. Está saliendo a tiempo (con una demora).

7. Los pasajeros traen equipaje de mano.
8. Ponen su equipaje de mano debajo del asiento.

B 1. No.
2. No.
3. Sí.
4. No.
5. Sí.

R 37

Bell Ringer Review

Use BRR Transparency R-15, or write the following on the board:
Complete the following.
1. Yo ___ un viaje. (hacer)
2. Yo ___ el viaje en avión. (hacer)
3. Yo ___ para el aeropuerto. (salir)
4. Yo ___ en taxi. (salir)
5. Yo ___ la maleta en la maletera del taxi. (poner)
6. Yo___ adonde yo ___. (saber, ir)

TEACHING THE CONVERSATION

A. Have the entire class repeat the **Conversación** once after you.
B. Call on two students to read the conversation using as much expression as possible.
C. Go over the **Después de conversar** activity.

EXPANSION

Have one or more students retell the information from the conversation in narrative form.

R 38

Conversación

En el aeropuerto

FELIPE: Están anunciando la salida de nuestro vuelo, ¿no?
ALEJANDRA: Sí, sí. Es nuestro vuelo.
FELIPE: ¿De qué puerta sale?
ALEJANDRA: Sale de la puerta once.
FELIPE: ¿Tenemos que pasar por el control de seguridad?
ALEJANDRA: Sí, tienen que tomar unos rayos equis de nuestro equipaje de mano.

Después de conversar

 Corrijan las oraciones.
1. Están anunciando la llegada del vuelo de Felipe y Alejandra.
2. Su vuelo va a salir de la puerta dos.
3. Ellos tienen que pasar por migración.
4. Tienen que tomar unos rayos equis de sus boletos y pasaportes.

R 38

REPASO E

Estructura

Presente de algunos verbos irregulares

1. Many verbs that are irregular in the present tense are irregular only in the **yo** form. All other forms are regular. Study the following verbs that have a **g** in the **yo** form.

hacer	hago
poner	pongo
traer	traigo
salir	salgo

2. The verbs **saber** and **conocer** also have an irregular **yo** form.

saber	sé
conocer	conozco

Saber is used to express knowledge of simple facts. **Conocer** means "to know" in the sense of to be acquainted with someone or something.

> **Yo sé que Madrid está en España. Yo conozco Madrid.**
> **Yo conozco a Eduardo también. Yo sé que él es de Madrid.**

Madrid, España

⟿ Práctica ⟿

A HISTORIETA **Un viaje imaginario**

Contesten.

1. ¿Haces un viaje a España?
2. ¿Haces el viaje en avión?
3. Antes, ¿haces las maletas?
4. ¿Qué pones en las maletas?
5. ¿Cuándo sales?
6. ¿Sales para el aeropuerto en taxi?
7. ¿A qué hora sale tu vuelo?
8. A bordo del avión, ¿dónde ponen los pasajeros su equipaje de mano?
9. ¿Conoces la ciudad de Madrid?
10. ¿Sabes hablar español?

IBERIA   TARJETA DE EMBARQUE

		INFORMACION AL PASAJERO			
Vuelo	Destin	Hora Limite / Puerta		Clase	Su asiento
IB3127	MAD	12.45	15	C	8C

LUNA/GABRIEL

LIS/22APR   C 048

Conserve esta tarjeta hasta su destino

ANSWERS

Práctica

A 1. Sí, (No, no) hago un viaje a España.
2. Sí, (No, no) hago el viaje en avión.
3. Sí (No), antes, (no) hago las maletas.
4. Pongo ___ en las maletas.
5. Salgo a las ___.
6. Sí, (No, no) salgo para el aeropuerto en taxi.
7. Mi vuelo sale a las ___.
8. A bordo del avión, los pasajeros ponen su equipaje de mano debajo del asiento.
9. Sí, (No, no) conozco la ciudad de Madrid.
10. Sí, (No, no) sé hablar español.

REPASO E
Estructura

TEACHING STRUCTURE

Presente de algunos verbos irregulares

A. Have students repeat the **yo** form of these verbs several times.

B. Write all the forms of two or three of the verbs on the board to show students that all forms other than **yo** conform to the regular pattern.

C. Have students repeat all forms.

D. Read the explanation in Step 2 about the use of **saber** and **conocer** to the class. Have students repeat the model sentences aloud.

⟿ Práctica ⟿

A Go over **Práctica A** orally with books closed.

EXPANSION Have a student retell all of the information in **Práctica A** in his or her own words.

Learning From Realia

Have students find the following information:

1. **nombre del pasajero**
2. **número del vuelo**
3. **destino**
4. **fecha del vuelo**
5. **hora de salida**
6. **puerta**
7. **número del asiento**

Explain: **El pasajero está viajando en Clase C. C es el código para** *Business Class.*

Estructura

B Have students prepare **Práctica B** before you go over it in class.

TEACHING STRUCTURE

El presente progresivo

A. Read Steps 1 and 2 aloud to the class.

B. Have students repeat the model sentences.

B **La maleta** Completen con **hacer, poner** o **salir.**

1. Juan _____ su maleta. Él _____ una camisa en la maleta. Él _____ para Málaga.
2. Nosotros _____ nuestra maleta. Nosotros _____ blue jeans en la maleta porque _____ para Cancún en México.
3. ¿Tú _____ tu maleta? ¿Qué _____ en la maleta? ¿Para dónde _____?
4. Mis padres _____ su maleta. Ellos _____ muchas cosas en la maleta. Ellos _____ su maleta porque _____ para Miami.

Málaga, España

El presente progresivo

1. The present progressive tense is used to express an action or activity that is presently going on.

2. To form the present progressive, you use the present tense of the verb **estar** and the present participle. Review the forms of the present participle.

hablar	**hablando**
comer	**comiendo**
salir	**saliendo**

¿Qué está haciendo Teresa?
Teresa está esperando el avión porque está saliendo para México.

ANSWERS

Práctica

B 1. **hace, pone, sale**
   2. **hacemos, ponemos, salimos**
   3. **haces, pones, sales**
   4. **hacen, ponen, hacen, salen**

 **Práctica**

A HISTORIETA En el aeropuerto

Contesten según se indica.

1. ¿Adónde están llegando los pasajeros? (al aeropuerto)
2. ¿Cómo están llegando? (en taxi)
3. ¿Adónde están viajando? (a Colombia)
4. ¿Cómo están haciendo el viaje? (en avión)
5. ¿Dónde están facturando su equipaje? (en el mostrador de la línea aérea)
6. ¿Qué está mirando la agente? (los boletos y los pasaportes)

Providencia, Colombia

Actividades comunicativas

A **Un boleto para Monterrey** Work with a classmate. You want to fly from your hometown to Monterrey, México. Call the airline to get a reservation. Your partner will be the reservations agent. Before you call, think about all the information you will need to give or get from the agent: date of departure, time, arrival time in Monterrey, flight number, price, etc. Take turns.

B **Un viaje** You know quite a bit about several Spanish-speaking countries. Work with a classmate. Choose a country you would both like to visit. Discuss how you plan to get there and what you are going to do and see there.

Monterrey, México

C **El aeropuerto** Work with a classmate. Look at the illustration of the many activities taking place at an airport. Tell all about the illustration in your own words.

Estructura

 **Práctica**

A Go over **Práctica A** orally with books open.

Actividades comunicativas

¡OJO! The **Actividades comunicativas** allow students to use the vocabulary and structures in open-ended, real-life situations. They also give students another opportunity to use words and structures learned previously.

Have students work on as many activities as you wish. You may also allow them to select those activities they want to do. Different groups can work on different activities.

Learning From Photos

Providencia, Colombia Providencia is a mountainous rural island off the northern coast of Colombia. It has very few tourist accommodations but it has good swimming and is a scuba diver's and snorkeler's paradise. The fish and plant life off its shores are fascinating.

Monterrey, México Monterrey, capital of the state of Nuevo Laredo, is the third largest city in Mexico with a population of around three million people. It is a very important industrial center.

ANSWERS

Práctica

A **1.** Los pasajeros están llegando al aeropuerto.
2. Están llegando en taxi.
3. Están viajando a Colombia.
4. Están haciendo el viaje en avión.
5. Están facturando su equipaje en el mostrador de la línea aérea.
6. La agente está mirando los boletos y los pasaportes.

Actividades comunicativas

A, B, and **C** Answers will vary.

R 41

OVERVIEW

In **Repaso F** students review the vocabulary they need to discuss their daily routines and some good health or hygiene practices.

In the **Estructura** section, they review the uses of **ser** and **estar** and reflexive verbs.

Students practice this vocabulary and these structures as they talk about a typical day and a visit to the doctor.

La rutina y la salud

R 43

Una familia guatemalteca
Have students say whatever they can about the photo of the family from Guatemala City. You may wish to ask them the following questions to get them started:
¿Qué hay en la mesa?
¿Qué está comiendo la familia?
¿Qué ropa llevan?

RESOURCES

 Workbook, pages R 31–R 36

Bell Ringer Review
Transparencies R-16–R-18

Bell Ringer Review

Use BRR Transparency R-16, or write the following on the board:
Match the following words:

1. **cepillar**	a. **la cena**
2. **peinar**	b. **el almuerzo**
3. **desayunar**	c. **el desayuno**
4. **almorzar**	d. **el cepillo**
5. **cenar**	e. **el peine**

TEACHING VOCABULARY

A. Have students open their books to page R 44 and look at the photos.

B. Have them repeat the sentences two or three times after you.

Vocabulario

Estefanía está bien. Ella se levanta cada mañana a las seis y media.

Ella se lava la cara.

Se peina.
Estefanía se mira en el espejo cuando se peina.

Juan no está bien hoy.
Está enfermo.
Tiene fiebre.
Tiene (una) tos.
Está en cama.

Juan va al consultorio de la médica.
Está en el consultorio.
La médica examina a Juan.

Práctica

A HISTORIETA La rutina diaria

Contesten.

1. ¿A qué hora se levanta Claudia cada mañana?
2. ¿Ella se desayuna en casa?
3. Después de desayunarse, ¿se cepilla los dientes?
4. ¿Se lava la cara?
5. ¿A qué hora se acuesta ella cada noche?

B La salud   Digan que sí o que no.

1. Cuando estamos cansados, queremos dormir.
2. Cuando estamos enfermos, vamos a ver al médico.
3. Tenemos que ir al hospital cuando tenemos un catarro.
4. Tenemos fiebre cuando tenemos la gripe.
5. Estamos contentos y nos sentimos bien cuando tenemos la temperatura elevada.
6. Tenemos que guardar cama cuando tenemos dolor de cabeza.

JUEGO   El cuerpo   ¿Cuáles son los nombres de todas las partes del cuerpo que sabes en español?

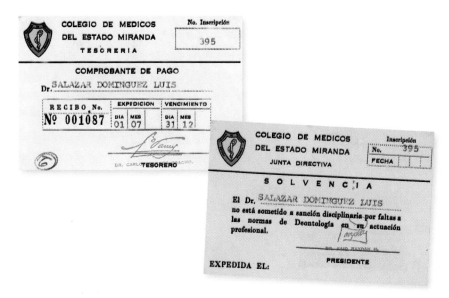

Práctica

A   Go over **Práctica A** orally with books closed.

B   Have students correct the false statements in **Práctica B.**

 You may wish to have each student do this individually and see who can prepare the longest list.

ANSWERS

Práctica

A 1. Claudia se levanta cada mañana a las ___.
2. Sí (No), ella (no) se desayuna en casa.
3. Sí (No), después de desayunarse, (no) se cepilla los dientes.
4. Sí, (No, no) se lava la cara.
5. Ella se acuesta a las ___ cada noche.

B 1. Sí.
2. Sí.
3. No.
4. Sí.
5. No.
6. No.

TEACHING THE CONVERSATION

A. Call on two students to read this short conversation to the class.

B. Go over the **Después de conversar** activity.

Learning From Realia

El dolor de cabeza Have students read the ad. You may wish to explain to them that **¿Es muy perro?** means *Is it awful, really bad?* Have them tell you in their own words what the ad means.

Conversación

¿Cómo estás?

SANDRA: ¿Cómo estás, Pepe?
PEPE: La verdad es que no me siento muy bien.
SANDRA: ¿Estás enfermo? ¿Qué tienes?
PEPE: Tengo dolor de garganta y estoy cansado.
SANDRA: Pues, sabes donde está la consulta del médico, ¿no?

Después de conversar

A Contesten.
1. ¿Cómo está Pepe?
2. ¿Cómo se siente él?
3. ¿Qué tiene?
4. ¿Tiene mucha energía?
5. ¿Está cansado?
6. ¿Adónde debe ir?

El dolor de cabeza
¿es muy perro?

DISPRINA va a la cabeza en alivio pronto y efectivo.
Y no irrita el estómago.

sanofi

DISPRINA se deshace por ti.

ANSWERS

Después de conversar

A 1. No está bien.
   2. Él no se siente bien.
   3. Tiene dolor de garganta.
   4. No, no tiene mucha energía.
   5. Sí, está cansado.
   6. Debe ir a la consulta del médico.

Estructura

Ser y estar

1. The verbs **ser** and **estar** both mean "to be." **Ser** is used to tell where someone or something is from. It is also used to describe an inherent trait or characteristic.

   > **Roberto es de Miami.**
   > **Él es inteligente y guapo.**

2. **Estar** is used to tell where someone or something is located. It is also used to describe a temporary state or condition.

   > **Roberto es de Miami pero ahora está en Madrid.**
   > **Madrid está en España.**
   > **Roberto está muy contento en Madrid.**

 Práctica

A HISTORIETA ¿En qué clase estás?

Contesten.

1. ¿Estás en la escuela ahora?
2. ¿Dónde está la escuela?
3. ¿En qué clase estás?
4. ¿Está la profesora en la clase también?
5. ¿Cómo es la profesora?
6. Y, ¿cómo es la clase de español?
7. ¿De dónde es la profesora?
8. ¿Y tú, ¿de dónde eres?
9. ¿Cómo estás hoy?
10. Y la profesora, ¿cómo está?

Alumnos mexicanos, Ciudad de México

Bell Ringer Review

Use BRR Transparency R-17, or write the following on the board: List all of your family members and tell where each of them is right now.

TEACHING STRUCTURE

Ser y estar

A. Have students open their books to page R 47. Now read the explanation to the class.
B. Have students give additional examples for each use of **ser** and **estar**.
C. Write some of their examples on the board and have the class read them aloud.

Práctica

A **Práctica A** can be done orally with books closed.

ANSWERS

Práctica

A 1. Sí, (No, no) estoy en la escuela ahora.
2. La escuela está en ___.
3. Estoy en la clase de español.
4. Sí, la profesora está en la clase también.
5. La profesora es ___.
6. La clase de español es ___.
7. La profesora es de ___.
8. Yo soy de ___.
9. Hoy (no) estoy bien.
10. La profesora (no) está bien.

R 47

❖Práctica❖

Writing Development

After going over **Práctica B,** have students write about Ángel in their own words.

🔔 Bell Ringer Review

Use BRR Transparency R-18, or write the following on the board: Make a list of all of your daily morning activities.

TEACHING STRUCTURE

Verbos reflexivos

A. Write one of the verb paradigms from page R 48 on the board or on a transparency.

B. Circle the reflexive pronoun in each sentence, underline the subject pronoun and draw a line from the reflexive pronoun to the subject pronoun to stress that they refer to the same person.

C. Explain to students that in a negative sentence **no** comes right before the reflexive pronoun.

B **HISTORIETA** Ángel

Completen con ser o estar.

Ángel ____₁ de Caracas. Él ____₂ muy simpático. ____₃ gracioso también. Ahora Ángel ____₄ en Nueva York. ____₅ estudiante en la universidad. Ángel ____₆ muy contento en Nueva York.

Nueva York ____₇ en el nordeste de los Estados Unidos. La Ciudad de Nueva York ____₈ muy grande y ____₉ muy interesante. A Ángel le gusta mucho Nueva York.

Caracas, Venezuela

Verbos reflexivos

The subject of a reflexive verb both performs and receives the action of the verb. Each subject has its corresponding reflexive pronoun. Review the following forms.

INFINITIVE	LEVANTARSE	ACOSTARSE
yo	me levanto	me acuesto
tú	te levantas	te acuestas
él, ella, Ud.	se levanta	se acuesta
nosotros(as)	nos levantamos	nos acostamos
vosotros(as)	*os levantáis*	*os acostáis*
ellos, ellas, Uds.	se levantan	se acuestan

ANSWERS

Práctica

B 1. es
2. es
3. Es
4. está
5. Es
6. está
7. está
8. es
9. es

Práctica

A ¿Y tú?   Contesten personalmente.

1. ¿A qué hora te acuestas?
2. ¿Te duermes enseguida?
3. Y, ¿a qué hora te despiertas?
4. Cuando te despiertas, ¿te levantas enseguida?
5. ¿Te lavas en el cuarto de baño?
6. ¿Te desayunas en casa?
7. Después, ¿te cepillas los dientes?

B Su rutina   Describan cada dibujo.

1. Ellos
   Nosotros
   Uds.

2. Yo
   Ella
   Tú

Actividades comunicativas

A Un día típico   Work with a classmate. Compare a typical day in your life with a typical day in your partner's life. Then tell what activities you have in common.

B En la consulta del médico   This is really a busy doctor's office. There is a lot going on at the same time. With a classmate, describe all that you see in the illustration.

Práctica

A **Práctica A** can be done orally as an interview. It can also be done as a paired activity.

B Have students refer to the photos when doing **Práctica B**.

Actividades comunicativas

 Allow students to choose the activities they wish to participate in or choose those you consider most appropriate.

ANSWERS

Práctica

A Answers will vary but may include:
1. Me acuesto a (eso de) las ___.
2. Sí, (No, no) me duermo enseguida.
3. Me despierto a (eso de) las ___.
4. Sí (No), cuando me despierto, (no) me levanto enseguida.
5. Sí, (No, no) me lavo en el cuarto de baño.
6. Sí, (No, no) me desayuno en casa.
7. Sí (No), después, (no) me cepillo los dientes.

B 1. Ellos se peinan.
   Nosotros nos peinamos.
   Uds. se peinan.
2. Yo me lavo la cara.
   Ella se lava la cara.
   Tú te lavas la cara.

Actividades comunicativas
A and **B** Answers will vary.

R 49

OVERVIEW

In **Repaso G** students review the vocabulary they need to talk about activities people do on summer and winter vacations.

In the **Estructura** section, they review the preterite of regular verbs and object pronouns.

Students practice this vocabulary and these structures as they talk about what season they prefer and where they would like to vacation.

El verano y el invierno

Learning From Photos

En la playa en México After reviewing the vocabulary, have students look at this photo of the Fiesta Americana Hotel in Quintana Roo and say anything they can about it.

R 51

Bell Ringer Review

Use BRR Transparency R-19, or write the following on the board: Write at least five things you do when you are on vacation.

TEACHING VOCABULARY

A. Have students open their books to page R 52. Review the vocabulary using suggestions given for previous review lessons.

B. After reviewing the specific vocabulary on this page, have students give additional vocabulary they remember that deals with summer and winter activities.

Vocabulario

Raúl pasó el verano en la playa.
Nadó en el mar.

Tomó el sol.
Volvió a casa muy bronceado.

Susana pasó una semana en una estación de
    esquí.
Tomó el telesilla para subir la montaña.
Subió en el telesilla.

Ella bajó la pista para expertos.
No bajó la pista para principiantes.

❖Práctica❖

A HISTORIETA En la playa

Contesten.

1. ¿Fue José a la playa?
2. ¿Nadó en el mar?
3. ¿Esquió en el agua?
4. ¿Se sentó en la arena?
5. ¿Tomó el sol?
6. ¿Volvió a casa muy bronceado?

Acapulco, México

Los Andes, Chile

B HISTORIETA En la estación de esquí

Contesten.

1. ¿Fueron a una estación de esquí los amigos?
2. ¿Salieron ellos muy temprano por la mañana?
3. ¿Pasaron el día entero en las pistas?
4. ¿Subieron la montaña en el telesilla?
5. ¿Bajaron la pista para expertos o para principiantes?
6. ¿Volvieron a casa el mismo día?

❖Práctica❖

A and **B** **Práctica A** and **B** can be done orally with books closed.

EXPANSION After going over **Práctica A** and **B**, call on one or more students to retell all the information from the activities in their own words.

Learning From Photos

Acapulco, México and Los Andes, Chile Have students describe the weather in each of the photos. Then ask them to name articles of clothing they would need in each place.

ANSWERS

Práctica

A 1. Sí (No), José (no) fue a la playa.
2. Sí, (No, no) nadó en el mar.
3. Sí, (No, no) esquió en el agua.
4. Sí, (No, no) se sentó en la arena.
5. Sí, (No, no) tomó el sol.
6. Sí, (No, no) volvió a casa muy bronceado.

B 1. Sí (No), los amigos (no) fueron a una estación de esquí.

2. Sí (No), ellos (no) salieron muy temprano por la mañana.
3. Sí, (No, no) pasaron el día entero en las pistas.
4. Sí, (No, no) subieron la montaña en el telesilla.
5. Sí, (No, no) bajaron la pista para principiantes (expertos).
6. Sí, (No, no) volvieron a casa el mismo día.

TEACHING THE CONVERSATION

A. Have two students read the **Conversación** to the class, using as much expression as possible.

B. Go over the **Después de conversar** activity.

RECYCLING

Have students identify all the items pictured on the page. Now ask them to make up original sentences using these words.

Conversación

¿Qué hicieron los amigos?

JOSÉ:	¿Adónde fuiste ayer, Adriana?
ADRIANA:	Fui a casa de Elena.
JOSÉ:	¿Y… ?
ADRIANA:	Jugamos tenis.
JOSÉ:	¿Tiene Elena una cancha de tenis?
ADRIANA:	No, hay canchas en un parque cerca de su casa. Pero Elena tiene una piscina.
JOSÉ:	¿Sí? ¿Nadaron Uds.?
ADRIANA:	Sí, nadamos después de jugar tenis.

Málaga, España

Después de conversar

A Digan que sí o que no.

1. José fue con Adriana a casa de Elena.
2. La casa de Elena tiene una cancha de tenis.
3. Adriana y Elena jugaron tenis.
4. Jugaron en una cancha en un parque.
5. Nadaron también.
6. Nadaron en una piscina en el parque.

ANSWERS

Después de conversar

A 1. No.
2. No.
3. Sí.
4. Sí.
5. Sí.
6. No.

Estructura

El pretérito

1. Review the forms of the preterite of regular verbs.

INFINITIVE	NADAR	COMER	SUBIR
yo	nadé	comí	subí
tú	nadaste	comiste	subiste
él, ella, Ud.	nadó	comió	subió
nosotros(as)	nadamos	comimos	subimos
vosotros(as)	*nadasteis*	*comisteis*	*subisteis*
ellos, ellas, Uds.	nadaron	comieron	subieron

2. The forms of the verbs **ir** and **ser** are the same in the preterite. The meaning is made clear by the context of the sentence.

fui   fuiste   fue   fuimos   *fuisteis*   fueron

3. The preterite is used to express an event or action that began and ended at a definite time in the past.

Ellos pasaron el año pasado en México.
Fueron a Acapulco.

Práctica

A **HISTORIETA** En la escuela

Contesten.

1. ¿Fuiste a la escuela ayer?
2. ¿A qué hora llegaste a la escuela?
3. ¿Hablaste con el/la profesor(a) de español?
4. ¿Tomaste un examen?
5. ¿En qué curso tomaste el examen?
6. ¿Saliste bien en el examen?
7. ¿Comiste en la cafetería de la escuela?
8. ¿A qué hora volviste a casa?

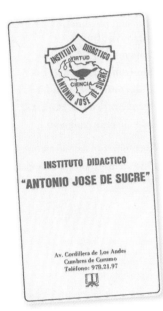

INSTITUTO DIDACTICO
"ANTONIO JOSE DE SUCRE"

Av. Cordillera de Los Andes
Cumbres de Curumo
Teléfono: 978.21.97

Bell Ringer Review

Use BRR Transparency R-20, or write the following on the board: Write down six things you did this past weekend.

TEACHING STRUCTURE

El pretérito

A. Have students repeat the verbs in Steps 1 and 2 after you.
B. Write one form of a verb on the board and challenge volunteers to fill in the rest of the paradigm.
C. Read Steps 2 and 3 to the class aloud.
D. Have students make up additional sentences, using the past tense.

Práctica

A **Práctica A** can be done orally with books closed.

ANSWERS

Práctica

A 1. Sí, (No, no) fui a la escuela ayer.
2. Llegué a la escuela a (eso de) las ___.
3. Sí, (No, no) hablé con el/la profesor(a) de español.
4. Sí, (No, no) tomé un examen.
5. Tomé el examen en (mi curso de) ___. (No tomé un examen.)
6. Sí, (No, no) salí bien en el examen.
7. Sí, (No, no) comí en la cafetería de la escuela.
8. Volví a casa a (eso de) las ___.

Práctica

B **Práctica B** can be done orally with books closed. Have students write **Práctica B** as a homework assigment.

TEACHING STRUCTURE

Los pronombres de complemento

A. Have students open their books to page R 56. Now read the explanation to the class.

B. Write some examples from Step 2 on the board. As you write them, draw a line from **el boleto** to **lo**, etc., so students can visualize what word the pronoun replaces. **Note** This point is rather difficult for students and it will be reviewed again.

B **Muchas actividades** Contesten.

1. ¿Fuiste al cine ayer?
   ¿Viste una película?
   ¿Tomaste un refresco en el cine?

2. ¿Salieron Uds. anoche?
   ¿Fueron a una fiesta?
   ¿Bailaron y cantaron durante la fiesta?

3. ¿Esquió Sandra?
   ¿Subió la montaña en el telesilla?
   ¿Bajó la pista para expertos?

4. ¿Pasaron los amigos el fin de semana en la playa?
   ¿Te escribieron una tarjeta postal?
   ¿Nadaron y esquiaron en el agua?

CANAL SUR	
8.00	TELETRASTO (Infantil) «LA FAMILIA BIONICA», «EL INSPECTOR GADGET», «TRAS-TO»
9.00	HOSPITAL
10.00	ANDALUCIA NUESTRA
10.30	VECINOS
11.00	LAS MAÑANAS DE CANAL SUR
12.00	CINE MATINAL «LAS PROTEGIDAS»
13.30	SIEMPRE HAY UNA SUEGRA
14.30	EL DIARIO 1
15.00	EL TIEMPO
15.05	PIGMALION
15.30	IMAGINA

Los pronombres de complemento

1. The object pronouns **me, te,** and **nos** can be either a direct or an indirect object. Note that the object pronoun precedes the conjugated verb.

Él me miró.   **Él me habló por teléfono.**
¿Te invitó Carlos?   **¿Te dio una invitación?**

2. Lo, los, la, and **las** function as direct objects only. They can replace either persons or things.

Pablo compró el boleto .   **Pablo lo compró.**
Pablo compró los boletos .   **Pablo los compró.**
Teresa compró la raqueta .   **Teresa la compró.**
Teresa compró las raquetas .   **Teresa las compró.**
Yo vi a los muchachos .   **Yo los vi.**

3. Le and **les** function as indirect objects only.

Yo le escribí una carta (a él, a ella, a Ud.).
Yo les escribí una carta (a ellos, a ellas, a Uds.).

ANSWERS

Práctica

B 1. Sí, (No, no) fui al cine ayer.
Sí, (No, no) ví una película.
Sí, (No, no) tomé un refresco en el cine.

2. Sí, salimos anoche.
Sí, fuimos a una fiesta.
Sí, bailamos y cantamos durante la fiesta.

3. Sí (No), Sandra (no) esquió.
Sí, (No, no) subió la montaña en el telesilla.
Sí, (No, no) bajó la pista para expertos.

4. Sí (No), los amigos (no) pasaron el fin de semana en la playa.
Sí, me escribieron una tarjeta postal.
Sí, nadaron y esquiaron en el agua.

 **Práctica**

A HISTORIETA A la consulta del médico

Contesten.

1. ¿Fuiste a la consulta del médico?
2. ¿Te habló el médico?
3. ¿Te examinó?
4. ¿Te dio una diagnosis?
5. ¿Te recetó unos antibióticos?

B Aquí lo tienes. Sigan el modelo.

la toalla
Aquí la tienes.

1. la toalla playera
2. la crema bronceadora
3. el bañador
4. el traje de baño
5. los anteojos para el sol
6. los boletos para el telesilla
7. los esquís
8. las raquetas

C HISTORIETA En el aeropuerto

Completen con **le** o **les**.

La señora Iturria fue al mostrador de la línea aérea. Ella _____ habló
al agente. _____ habló en español; no _____ habló en inglés. Ella _____
dio su boleto y él lo miró. Ella _____ dio su pasaporte también.

A bordo del avión los asistentes de vuelo _____ hablaron a los
pasajeros. _____ dieron la bienvenida a bordo y _____ explicaron las
reglas de seguridad.

Actividades comunicativas

A Las estaciones
Work with a classmate. Tell whether
you prefer summer or winter. Explain why you prefer one
over the other. Tell what you do during that season.
Take turns.

B ¡A viajar!
Look at these postcards.
Work with a classmate. Tell where you
would prefer to go and why. Take turns.

Práctica

¡OJO! Go over all the **Práctica**
orally in class. Have stu-
dents write each of the **Práctica** for
homework. Go over it again the next
day in class.

Actividades comunicativas

Have students choose the activities
they wish to participate in.

ANSWERS

Práctica

A 1. Sí, (No, no) fui a la consulta del
médico.
2. Sí (No), el médico (no) me habló.
3. Sí, (No, no) me examinó.
4. Sí, (No, no) me dio una diagnosis.
5. Sí, (No, no) me recetó unos
antibióticos.

B 1. Aquí la tienes.
2. Aquí la tienes.
3. Aquí lo tienes.
4. Aquí lo tienes.
5. Aquí los tienes.
6. Aquí los tienes.
7. Aquí los tienes.
8. Aquí las tienes.

C 1. le   5. le
2. Le   6. les
3. le   7. Les
4. le   8. les

Actividades comunicativas
A and B   Answers will vary.

Chapter 1 Overview ◆◆◆◆◆◆◆◆◆◆◆◆◆◆◆◆◆◆◆◆◆◆

SCOPE AND SEQUENCE pages 0–27

TOPICS	FUNCTIONS	STRUCTURE	CULTURE
◆ Train travel ◆ Travel-related activities	◆ How to use words and expressions related to train travel ◆ How to describe various types of trains and train services ◆ How to tell what people say ◆ How to talk about events or activities that took place at a definite time in the past	◆ **Hacer, querer,** and **venir** in the preterite ◆ Irregular verbs in the preterite ◆ **Decir** in the present	◆ José Luis and Maripaz take the AVE train to Seville ◆ Taking the train from Cuzco to Machu Picchu ◆ La Plaza de Armas, Cuzco ◆ Machu Picchu ◆ The 24-hour clock and the metric system

CHAPTER 1 RESOURCES

PRINT	MULTIMEDIA

Planning Resources

Lesson Plans
Block Scheduling Lesson Plans

Interactive Lesson Planner

Reinforcement Resources

Writing Activities Workbook
Student Tape Manual
Video Activities Booklet
Web Site User's Guide

Transparencies Binder
Audiocassette/Compact Disc Program
Videocassette/Videodisc Program
Online Internet Activities
Electronic Teacher's Classroom Resources

Assessment Resources

Situation Cards
Chapter Quizzes
Testing Program
Performance Assessment

Maratón mental Mindjogger Videoquiz
Testmaker Computer Software (Macintosh/Windows)
Listening Comprehension Audiocassette/Compact Disc
Communication Transparency: C-1

Motivational Resources

Expansion Activities

Café Glencoe: www.cafe.glencoe.com
Keypal Internet Activities

Enrichment

Spanish for Spanish Speakers

Fine Art Transparency: F-1

Chapter 1 Planning Guide

SECTION	PAGES	SECTION RESOURCES
Vocabulario Palabras 1 **En la estación de ferrocarril**	2–5	Vocabulary Transparencies 1.1 Audiocassette 2A/Compact Disc 2 Student Tape Manual, TE, pages 1–4 Workbook, pages 1–2 Chapter Quizzes, page 1 CD-ROM, Disc 1, pages 2–5
Vocabulario Palabras 2 **En el tren**	6–9	Vocabulary Transparencies 1.2 Audiocassette 2A/Compact Disc 2 Student Tape Manual, TE, pages 5–6 Workbook, pages 3–4 Chapter Quizzes, page 2 CD-ROM, Disc 1, pages 6–9
Estructura **Hacer, querer y venir en el pretérito** **Verbos irregulares en el pretérito** **Decir en el presente**	10–15	Workbook, pages 5–8 Audiocassette 2A/Compact Disc 2 Student Tape Manual, TE, pages 7–9 Chapter Quizzes, pages 3–5 Computer Testmaker CD-ROM, Disc 1, pages 10–15
Conversación **En la ventanilla** **Pronunciación: Las consonantes ñ, ch**	16–17	Audiocassette 2A/Compact Disc 2 Student Tape Manual, TE, pages 9–10 CD-ROM, Disc 1, pages 16–17
Lecturas culturales **En el AVE** **De Cuzco a Machu Picchu** *(opcional)*	18–21	Testing Program, pages 17–18 CD-ROM, Disc 1, pages 18–21
Conexiones **Conversiones aritméticas** *(opcional)*	22–23	Testing Program, page 18 CD-ROM, Disc 1, pages 22–23
Culminación **Actividades orales** **Actividades escritas** **Vocabulario** **Tecnotur**	24–27	¡Buen viaje! Video, Episode 1 Video Activities, pages 61–65 Internet Activities www.glencoe.com/sec/fl Testing Program, pages 15–17; 124; 168; 189–190 CD-ROM, Disc 1, pages 24–27

OVERVIEW

In this chapter students will learn to talk about a train trip. In order to do this they will learn vocabulary related to the train station and train travel. They will also continue to learn how to talk about past events by learning the preterite forms of some irregular verbs. The cultural focus of the chapter is on train travel in Spain and Latin America.

National Standards

✿ *Communication*

In Chapter 1 students will communicate in spoken and written Spanish on the following topics:
- purchasing a train ticket and consulting a timetable
- getting through a train station
- traveling on board a train

Students will obtain and provide information about these topics and learn to engage in conversations with a ticket agent, train conductor, and fellow passengers as they fulfill the chapter objectives listed on this page.

Pacing

Chapter 1 will require approximately six to eight days. Pacing will vary according to the length of the class, the age of your students, and student aptitude.

Block Scheduling

See the Block Scheduling Lesson Plans Booklet for suggestions on how to present the chapter material within a block scheduling framework.

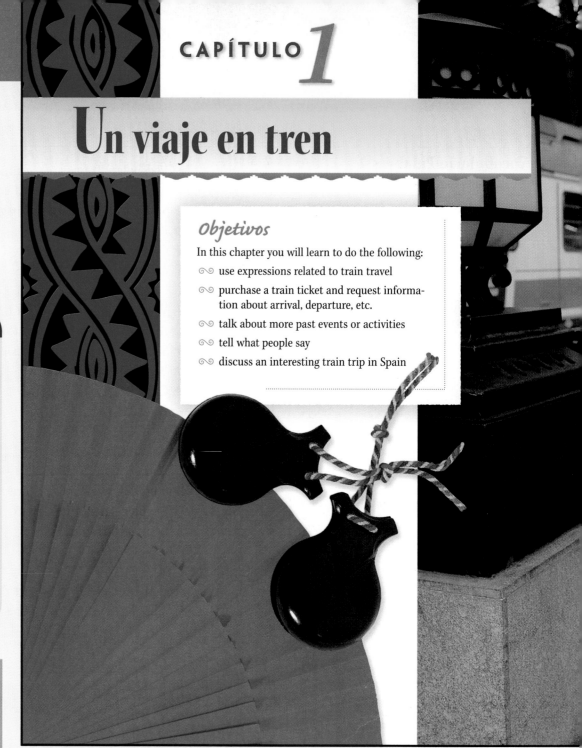

Un viaje en tren

Objetivos

In this chapter you will learn to do the following:
- ෨ use expressions related to train travel
- ෨ purchase a train ticket and request information about arrival, departure, etc.
- ෨ talk about more past events or activities
- ෨ tell what people say
- ෨ discuss an interesting train trip in Spain

inter**NET**
CONNECTION

The **Glencoe Foreign Language Web site** (http://www.glencoe.com/sec/fl) offers three options that enable you and your students to experience the Spanish-speaking world via the Internet:
- The online **Actividades** are correlated to the chapters and utilize Hispanic Web sites around the world. For the Chapter 1 activity, see student page 27.

- The **Correspondencia electrónica** section provides information on how to set up a keypal (pen pal) exchange between your class and a class in the Spanish-speaking world.
- At **Café Glencoe,** the interactive "after-school" section of the site, you and your students can access a variety of additional online resources, including interactive games. The Chapter 1 crossword puzzle practices the chapter vocabulary and structures.

uno 1

Spotlight On Culture

Artefacto The decorative photo shows **castañuelas,** which are typically played during the dancing of flamenco. The fan, called **un abanico,** is also used in certain flamenco dances.
Fotografía This photo was taken at the **Estació de Sants** in Barcelona. Note that the name of the station is in **Catalán.** There are two other train stations in Barcelona.

Learning From Photos

La Estació de Sants You may wish to ask the following questions about the photo after presenting the new vocabulary on pages 2–3:
¿Dónde están los jóvenes?
¿Qué está mirando la muchacha?
¿El muchacho tiene un plano de qué ciudad?
¿Cómo se llama el periódico que tiene el muchacho?
¿Cuántos trenes ves en la foto?

Teacher Notes

Chapter Projects

Un viaje en tren Have groups plan a rail trip through Spain using a guide such as the one from Eurail (available at many travel agencies). Give them a time limit and have them include at least one overnight stay. They should plan arrival and departure times and the length of each stop on the itinerary. Groups can describe their trip to the class.

TECHNOLOGY OPTION In the Chapter 1 Internet activity students visit the RENFE Web site to plan a train trip in Spain. You may wish to have students do this activity as a project. (For more information, see the Internet Connection, page 27.)
Una ciudad Have the groups select one city from their itinerary and find out some information about it. They can do a brief report for a presentation to the class.

📖 Bell Ringer Review

Use BRR Transparency 1-1, or write the following on the board: Complete the following sentences.
1. Los pasajeros hacen ___ en el mostrador de la línea aérea.
2. Los pasajeros ___ su equipaje.
3. Los pasajeros en un aeropuerto tienen que pasar por ___.
4. Los pasajeros tienen que mostrar su ___.

TEACHING VOCABULARY

A. Have students close their books. Present the vocabulary using Vocabulary Transparencies 1.1 (A & B).
B. Now have students open their books and repeat the new words and sentences after you or the recording on Cassette 2A/Compact Disc 1.
C. Have students act out the short dialogue on page 2.

Vocabulario

PALABRAS 1

En la estación de ferrocarril

el tablero de llegadas

el tablero de salidas

el quiosco

el horario

MADRID ALMERIA GRANADA

la sala de espera

Un billete para Madrid, por favor.

¿En primera o en segunda?

En segunda—de ida y vuelta.

el billete de ida y vuelta

el billete sencillo

la ventanilla

2 ∾ *dos*

CAPÍTULO 1

Pantomime

Pantomime 1
Getting ready
A piece of paper with the word **maleta** written on it can represent a suitcase.
Begin
___, levántate y ven acá, por favor.
Vas a hacer algunos gestos. Aquí tienes una maleta.
Toma la maleta. Mira la maleta.
Abre la maleta. Pon la ropa en la maleta.
Cierra la maleta.
Ve al teléfono. Llama un taxi.

Toma la maleta y ve a la calle.
Espera el taxi.
El taxi llega. Pon la maleta en la maletera del taxi. Abre la puerta del taxi.
Sube al taxi. Siéntate.
Gracias, ___. Y ahora puedes volver a tu asiento.

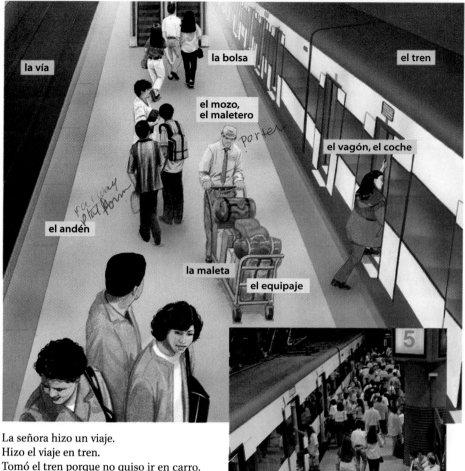

la vía

la bolsa

el tren

el mozo, el maletero

porter

el vagón, el coche

el andén

railway platform

la maleta

el equipaje

La señora hizo un viaje.
Hizo el viaje en tren.
Tomó el tren porque no quiso ir en carro.
Subió al tren.

El mozo vino con el equipaje.
El mozo puso el equipaje en el tren.
Los mozos ayudaron a los pasajeros con su equipaje.

El tren salió del andén número cinco.
Algunos amigos estuvieron en el andén.

VOCABULARIO

tres ∽ **3**

D. As you present the new vocabulary, intersperse it with questions such as the following:

¿La muchacha compra un billete en primera o segunda clase?
¿Compra un billete sencillo o de ida y vuelta?
¿Subió al tren o bajó del tren la señora?
¿Tiene el mozo bolsas y maletas?
¿Qué tiene el mozo?
¿Dónde puso el equipaje?

Have students answer with complete sentences or sometimes just have them use the specific word or phrase that responds to the question word.

INFORMAL ASSESSMENT

ABOUT THE SPANISH LANGUAGE

◆ The word **el billete** is used in Spain. **El boleto** is used in Latin America. The expression *to buy a ticket* is **sacar un billete** in Spain and **comprar un boleto** in Latin America.

◆ **El tablero** is the word used for arrival or departure board. In some stations there is a modern type of TV screen that is called either **la pantalla** or **el monitor**.

1. After presenting all the vocabulary from **Palabras 1,** show the Vocabulary Transparencies again and let students identify items at random.

2. Now have students make up questions about what they see on the transparencies. You may answer the questions or have them call on other students to answer.

Pantomime

Pantomime 2
Getting ready
Have your desk be **la ventanilla**. One student can be **el agente** and another student can be **el pasajero.** Numbers on the board can represent **los andenes.** A piece of paper with the word **boleto** or **billete** can be the ticket.
Begin
___, **levántate y ven acá.**
Ésta es la estación de ferrocarril.

Estamos en la sala de espera. Dame la maleta. Ve a la ventanilla. Compra un boleto.
Págale al agente.
Toma tu boleto. Mira el boleto.
Pon el boleto en tu bolsillo.
Ven acá. Toma la maleta.
Busca el andén número dos.
Ve al andén. Espera el tren.
Aquí viene el tren. Sube al tren.
Gracias, ___. Regresa a tu asiento.

3

Práctica

¡OJO! **Práctica** When students are doing the **Práctica** activities, accept any answer that makes sense. The purpose of these activities is to have students use the new vocabulary. They are not factual recall activities. Thus, do not expect students to remember specific information from the vocabulary presentation when answering. If you wish, have students use the photos on this page as a stimulus, when possible.

Historieta Each time **Historieta** appears, it means that the answers to the activity form a short story. Encourage students to look at the title of the **Historieta** since it can sometimes help them do the activity. It is recommended that you go over all the **Práctica** in class before assigning them for homework.

A Have students retell the story from **Práctica A** in their own words.

B After completing **Práctica B,** have students ask questions about the incorrect choices from this activity.

Writing Development
Have students write the answers to **Práctica A** in a paragraph to illustrate how all of the items tell a story.

Práctica

A HISTORIETA En la estación de ferrocarril

Contesten según se indica.

1. ¿Cómo vino la señora a la estación? (en taxi)
2. ¿Dónde puso sus maletas? (en la maletera del taxi)
3. En la estación, ¿adónde fue? (a la ventanilla)
4. ¿Qué compró? (un billete)
5. ¿Qué tipo de billete compró? (de ida y vuelta)
6. ¿En qué clase? (segunda)
7. ¿Dónde puso su billete? (en su bolsa)
8. ¿Qué consultó? (el horario)
9. ¿Adónde fue? (al andén)
10. ¿De qué andén salió el tren? (del número dos)
11. ¿Por qué hizo la señora el viaje en tren? (no quiso ir en coche)

Atocha, una estación de ferrocarril en Madrid

En la estación de Atocha

B HISTORIETA Antes de abordar el tren

Escojan.

1. ¿Dónde espera la gente el tren?
   a. en la ventanilla   b. en la sala de espera
   c. en el quiosco
2. ¿Dónde venden o despachan los billetes?
   a. en la ventanilla   b. en el equipaje
   c. en el quiosco
3. ¿Qué venden en el quiosco?
   a. boletos   b. maletas
   c. periódicos y revistas
4. ¿Qué consulta el pasajero para verificar la hora de salida del tren?
   a. la llegada   b. la vía   c. el horario
5. ¿Quién ayuda a los pasajeros con el equipaje?
   a. el mozo   b. el tablero   c. el andén
6. ¿De dónde sale el tren?
   a. de la ventanilla   b. del andén
   c. del tablero

ANSWERS

Práctica

A 1. La señora vino a la estación en taxi.
2. Puso sus maletas en la maletera del taxi.
3. En la estación fue a la ventanilla.
4. Compró un billete.
5. Compró un billete de ida y vuelta.
6. Compró un billete en segunda.
7. Puso su billete en su bolsa.
8. Consultó el horario.
9. Fue al andén.

10. El tren salió del andén número dos.
11. La señora hizo el viaje en tren porque no quiso ir en coche.

B 1. b
2. a
3. c
4. c
5. a
6. b

C HISTORIETA El billete del tren

Contesten.

1. ¿De qué estación sale el tren?
2. ¿Adónde va el tren?
3. ¿Cuál es la fecha del billete?
4. ¿A qué hora sale el tren?
5. ¿Está el asiento en la sección de fumar o de no fumar?
6. ¿Qué clase de billete es?
7. ¿Con qué pagó el/la pasajero(a)?

Actividad comunicativa

A **RENFE (Red Nacional de Ferrocarriles Españoles)**
You're in Spain and you want to
visit one of the cities on the map.
A classmate will be the ticket
agent. Get yourself a ticket and
ask the agent any questions you
have about your train trip.

Learning From Realia

Billete y Reserva Have students
look at the train ticket on this
page. Ask them to guess what
the word **metálico** means under
Forma de pago. What do we say
in English instead of **metálico?**
(cash)

Actividad comunicativa

¡OJO! **Práctica versus
Actividades comunica-
tivas** All activities which provide
guided practice are labeled
Práctica. The more open-ended
communicative activities are labeled
Actividades comunicativas.

A You may wish to have some students present their skits to the class.
TECHNOLOGY OPTION In the
Chapter 1 Internet activity students
visit the RENFE Web site to plan a
train trip in Spain. You may wish to
have students do the Internet activity first and then have them do
Actividad A, using the real information from the site. (See the Internet
Connection, page 27.)

Learning From Photos

**Atocha, una estación de ferro-
carril en Madrid** (page 5) Until
recently Atocha was falling into
disuse and serving very few destinations. There was even talk of
closing the station. Instead the
station was completely reno-
vated for the inauguration of the
high speed AVE train in 1992.
Today it serves points south and
east of Madrid. Chamartín station serves trains heading north
and to Barcelona. The Norte station is primarily for local trains
serving the western suburbs.

ANSWERS

Práctica
C 1. El tren sale de la estación de Atocha.
2. El tren va a Ciudad Real.
3. La fecha del billete es 06/07.
4. El tren sale a las 15:30.
5. El asiento está en la sección de no
fumar.
6. Es un billete de segunda clase.
7. El/La pasajero(a) pagó en metálico.

Actividad comunicativa
A Answers will vary.

5

🔔 Bell Ringer Review

Use BRR Transparency 1-2, or write the following on the board:
Complete the following.
La compañía de aviación anuncia la ___ de su ___ 102 con ___ a Madrid. Pasajeros deben abordar por la ___ número tres. Embarque inmediato.

TEACHING VOCABULARY

A. Have students close their books. Present the vocabulary, using Vocabulary Transparencies 1.2 (A & B). Have students repeat each word or expression two or three times after you or Cassette 2A/Compact Disc 1.

B. Ask the following questions as you present the vocabulary: **¿Los jóvenes están en el tren o están en la ventanilla? ¿Qué tiene que ver el revisor? ¿Hay muchos o pocos asientos libres en el coche? ¿Los pasajeros toman asiento o se sientan en el pasillo? ¿Qué hacen los pasajeros en el coche-cama? ¿En el coche-comedor? ¿El tren sale a tiempo o sale tarde? ¿Sale con retraso? ¿Dónde bajan los pasajeros?**

En el tren

el revisor

Reservodo
ocupado
libre
el asiento, la plaza
el pasillo

la litera
el coche-cama

6 ∿ *seis*

CAPÍTULO 1

Pantomime

Getting ready
Set up an area in front of the classroom as **el tren** and place three chairs together. Tell students that those chairs are the seats in the train. Then call on one student to act as **el/la pasajero(a).**

Begin
___, levántate y ven acá, por favor.
Sube al tren. Busca tu asiento.
Pon tu maleta en el asiento. Abre la maleta.

Saca un libro de la maleta.
Cierra la maleta.
Pon la maleta en el compartimiento.
Siéntate. Toma tu asiento.
Abre tu libro. Lee el libro.
Gracias, ___. Y ahora puedes volver a tu asiento.

el coche-comedor,
el coche-cafetería

El tren salió a tiempo.
No salió tarde.
No salió con retraso (con una demora).

ABOUT THE SPANISH LANGUAGE

Note that we have used the expression **bajar del tren**, which is grammatically correct. In many areas of Latin America one will hear **bajarse del tren**. In contemporary novels, you sometimes see both **bajar** and **bajarse** in the same work.

bajar(se) del tren

transbordar

Los pasajeros van a bajar en la próxima parada (estación).
Van a transbordar en la próxima parada.

VOCABULARIO

siete 〰 **7**

7

✦Práctica✦

A B and **C** After going over **Práctica A, B,** and **C** students can summarize all the information in their own words.

Did You Know?

En tren Students have already learned about the importance of air travel in South America in **¡Buen viaje! Level 1,** Chapter 11.

Train travel in South America can be very interesting but in many areas it is not convenient (and in some cases it is nonexistent). In addition to long distances, there are often mechanical delays, flooding during the rainy season, and rugged terrain, all of which can make travel slow and tedious. The railway service is fairly good in Argentina and Chile. Most of Chile's 5,200 miles of track run north to south.

✦Práctica✦

Santiago de Chile

A HISTORIETA En el tren

Contesten.

1. Cuando llegó el tren a la estación, ¿subieron los pasajeros a bordo?
2. ¿El tren salió tarde?
3. ¿Con cuántos minutos de demora salió?
4. ¿Vino el revisor?
5. ¿Revisó él los boletos?

Madrid, España

B HISTORIETA El tren

Contesten según la foto.

1. ¿Tiene el tren compartimientos?
2. ¿Tiene el coche o vagón un pasillo central o lateral?
3. ¿Cuántos asientos hay a cada lado del pasillo?
4. ¿Hay asientos libres o están todos ocupados?
5. ¿Está completo el tren?
6. ¿Hay pasajeros de pie en el pasillo?

C HISTORIETA Un viaje en tren

Completen.

1. Entre Granada y Málaga el tren local hace muchas ____.
2. No hay un tren directo a Benidorm. Es necesario cambiar de tren. Los pasajeros tienen que ____.
3. Los pasajeros que van a Benidorm tienen que ____ en la próxima ____ o ____.
4. ¿Cómo lo sabes? El ____ nos informó que nuestro tren no es directo.

ANSWERS

Práctica

A 1. Sí, cuando el tren llegó a la estación, los pasajeros subieron a bordo.
2. Sí (No), el tren (no) salió tarde.
3. Salió con una demora de ___ minutos.
4. Sí, el revisor vino.
5. Sí, él revisó los boletos.

B 1. No, el tren no tiene compartimientos.
2. El coche (vagón) tiene un pasillo central.
3. Hay dos asientos a cada lado del pasillo.
4. Hay asientos libres.
5. No, el tren no está completo.
6. No, no hay pasajeros de pie en el pasillo.

C 1. paradas
2. transbordar
3. transbordar, parada, estación
4. revisor

8

Actividades comunicativas

A **¿Qué tienes que hacer?** Work with a classmate. You are spending a month in Madrid and your Spanish hosts are taking you to San Sebastián. You're trying to pack your bags and their child (your partner) has a lot of questions. Answer his or her questions and try to be patient. The child has never taken a train trip before.

¿Dónde nos sentamos en el tren?

Nos sentamos en un compartimiento.

Madrid

San Sebastián

B **De Santiago a Puerto Montt** You're planning a trip from Santiago de Chile to Puerto Montt. A classmate will be your travel agent. Get as much information as you can about the trip from Santiago to Puerto Montt. It gets rather cold and windy there and it rains a lot. You may want to find out if there are frequent delays. The following are some words and expressions you may want to use with the travel agent.

reservar

el número de paradas

el horario

la tarifa

el boleto de ida y vuelta

la demora

primera (segunda) clase

VOCABULARIO

nueve 9

Actividades comunicativas

¡OJO! These activities encourage students to use the chapter vocabulary and structures in open-ended situations. It is not necessary to have them do all the activities. Choose the ones you consider most appropriate.

A Before students begin this activity, have them make a list of questions they will ask. You may wish to have students present their conversations to the class.

B Have students working on **Actividad B** locate **Puerto Montt** on the map of South America on page 452.

GEOGRAPHY CONNECTION

Puerto Montt You may either have students look up some information on Puerto Montt on the Internet or give them the following information.

Puerto Montt is a city of some 120,000 inhabitants, many of German descent. A large number of its small houses are unpainted and one can see the Germanic influence in the architecture. In bakery shop windows there are still signs in Spanish and German—**Pasteles** and **Kuchen.**

Puerto Montt is the northernmost town in Chilean Patagonia. The weather can be very harsh with strong winds and a great deal of rain. The train trip to Puerto Montt from Santiago takes 20 hours.

Learning From Photos

Madrid This view of Madrid is looking up the Gran Vía from Cibeles. The Gran Vía is a very busy street with hotels, night clubs, clothing stores, jewelery stores, bookstores, and **cafeterías**.

San Sebastián, España This sophisticated city arcs around the lovely beach called La Concha seen in the photo on this page. Because the Isla de Santa Clara protects the city from the storms that come from the Bay of Biscay, this beach is one of the calmest beaches on the northern coast of Spain.

ANSWERS

Actividades comunicativas

A Answers will vary. Students should use the vocabulary from **Palabras 1** and **2.**

B Answers will vary. Students should use as many words as possible from the colored boxes.

Estructura

Bell Ringer Review

Use BRR Transparency 1-3, or write the following on the board: Write original sentences using each of the following expressions in the present tense.

> **hacer un viaje**
> **poner la ropa en la maleta**
> **salir para la estación de ferrocarril**
> **venir en tren**

TEACHING STRUCTURE

Relating more past actions

A. Have students open their books to page 10. Read Steps 1 and 2 to the class.

B. Have the class repeat the verb forms aloud.

C. Call on an individual to read the model sentences.

D. Point out to students that all these irregular verbs have the ending **e** in the **yo** form.

Note Many of the verbs students will be learning in this chapter are not used very frequently in the preterite. For this reason, it is recommended that you do not spend a great deal of time on this topic. The most important verbs are **venir, hacer,** and **poner.**

Relating more past actions
Hacer, querer y venir en el pretérito

1. The verbs **hacer, querer,** and **venir** are irregular in the preterite. Note that they all have an **i** in the stem and the endings for the **yo, él, ella,** and **Ud.** forms are different from the endings of regular verbs.

INFINITIVE	hacer	querer	venir
yo	hice	quise	vine
tú	hiciste	quisiste	viniste
él, ella, Ud.	hizo	quiso	vino
nosotros(as)	hicimos	quisimos	vinimos
vosotros(as)	*hicisteis*	*quisisteis*	*vinisteis*
ellos, ellas, Uds.	hicieron	quisieron	vinieron

2. The verb **querer** has several special meanings in the preterite.

| **Quise ayudar.** | *I tried to help.* |
| **No quise ir en carro.** | *I refused to go by car.* |

A HISTORIETA ¿Cómo viniste?

Contesten.

1. ¿Viniste a la estación en taxi?
2. ¿Viniste en un taxi público o privado?
3. ¿Hiciste el viaje en tren?
4. ¿Hiciste el viaje en el tren local?
5. ¿Lo hiciste en tren porque no quisiste ir en coche?

Lima, Perú

ANSWERS

Práctica

A 1. Sí, vine a la estación en taxi.
2. Vine en un taxi público.
3. Sí, hice el viaje en tren.
4. Sí, (No, no) hice el viaje en el tren local.
5. Sí, lo hice en tren porque no quise ir en coche. (No, no lo hice en tren porque quise ir en coche.)

Learning From Photos

Lima, Perú You may wish to ask the following questions about the photo:

¿Cómo se llama la estación de ferrocarril en Lima?

¿Está hablando el joven con el taxista?

¿Cuántas maletas tiene el joven?

10

B · No quisieron. Completen.

1. —Ellos no ___(1)___ (querer) hacer el viaje.

   —¿No lo ___(2)___ (querer) hacer?

   —No, de ninguna manera.

   —Pues, ¿qué pasó entonces? ¿Lo ___(3)___ (hacer) o no lo

   ___(4)___ (hacer)?

   —No lo ___(5)___ (hacer).

2. —¿Por qué no ___(6)___ (venir) Uds. esta mañana?

   —Nosotros no ___(7)___ (venir) porque no ___(8)___ (hacer) las
   reservaciones.

3. —Carlos no ___(9)___ (querer) hacer la cama.

   —Entonces, ¿quién la ___(10)___ (hacer)?

   —Pues, la ___(11)___ (hacer) yo.

   —¡Qué absurdo! ¿Tú la ___(12)___ (hacer) porque él no la ___(13)___ (querer)
   hacer?

Actividades comunicativas

A **¡Rebelde!** A friend of yours (your classmate) is in trouble with his
or her parents because he or she didn't do as told. Find out what your
friend didn't do and why. Use the model as a guide.

¿Hiciste la cama?

No.

¿Por qué no hiciste la cama?

No hice la cama porque no quise.

*hacer la maleta
reservar un taxi
comprar los billetes
llamar a los parientes
hacer las reservaciones
leer el horario*

B **¿Qué hiciste durante el fin de semana?**
With a classmate, take turns asking each other what you and other
friends did over the weekend.

Práctica

A **Práctica A** on page 10 practices the **tú** and **yo** forms.

B Have students present **Práctica B** as a series of mini-conversations.

Actividades comunicativas

¡OJO! These activities encourage students to use the chapter vocabulary and structures in open-ended situations. It is not necessary to have them do all the activities. Choose the ones you consider most appropriate.

A Ask for volunteers to role-play the model dialogue. Have them do one or two examples from the handwritten list on the right before students work on their own in pairs.
EXPANSION Encourage students to come up with their own list of things they were supposed to do.

B This is a good warm-up activity to begin the class period. Students might begin by saying: **¿Qué hiciste durante el fin de semana?** or **¿Qué hicieron Uds. durante el fin de semana?**

ANSWERS

Práctica

B
1. quisieron	8. hicimos
2. quisieron	9. quiso
3. hicieron	10. hizo
4. hicieron	11. hice
5. hicieron	12. hiciste
6. vinieron	13. quiso
7. vinimos	

Actividades comunicativas

A Answers will vary but should follow the model.

B Answers will vary.

TEACHING STRUCTURE

Describing more past actions

A. Have students open their books to page 12. Read Steps 1 and 2 to the class.
B. Have the class repeat the verb forms from the chart.
C. Call on an individual to read the model sentences in Step 2.

FINE ART CONNECTION

«Vista de Toledo» de El Greco

Show Fine Art Transparency F-1 of this painting by El Greco from the Transparency Binder. You may wish to have students read the background information accompanying this transparency, and have them do the related activities.

EXPANSION Have students look at a photo of Toledo today. Ask them if they see a resemblance between today's photo and El Greco's painting done about four centuries ago.

Describing more past actions
Verbos irregulares en el pretérito

1. The verbs **estar**, **andar**, and **tener** are irregular in the preterite. They all have a **u** in the stem. Study the following forms.

INFINITIVE	estar	andar	tener
yo	estuve	anduve	tuve
tú	estuviste	anduviste	tuviste
él, ella Ud.	estuvo	anduvo	tuvo
nosotros(as)	estuvimos	anduvimos	tuvimos
vosotros(as)	*estuvisteis*	*anduvisteis*	*tuvisteis*
ellos, ellas, Uds.	estuvieron	anduvieron	tuvieron

2. The verb **andar** means "to go," but not to a specific place. The verb **ir** is used with a specific place.

> **Fueron a Toledo.**
> *They went to Toledo.*

> **Anduvieron por las plazas pintorescas de Toledo.**
> *They wandered through (walked around) the picturesque squares of Toledo.*

«Vista de Toledo» de El Greco

ABOUT THE SPANISH LANGUAGE

In Spain the verb **andar** means *to walk.* **Caminar** is used in Latin America. **Ir a pie** means *to go on foot* and **dar un paseo** or **pasear(se)** means *to take a walk.*

3. The verbs **poder, poner,** and **saber** are also irregular in the preterite. Like the verbs **estar, andar,** and **tener,** they all have a **u** in the stem. Study the following forms.

INFINITIVE	poder	poner	saber
yo	pude	puse	supe
tú	pudiste	pusiste	supiste
él, ella, Ud.	pudo	puso	supo
nosotros(as)	pudimos	pusimos	supimos
vosotros(as)	pudisteis	pusisteis	supisteis
ellos, ellas, Uds.	pudieron	pusieron	supieron

4. Like **querer,** the verbs **poder** and **saber** have special meanings in the preterite.

Pude parar.	*(After trying hard) I managed to stop.*
No pude parar.	*(I tried but) I couldn't stop.*
Yo lo supe ayer.	*I found it out (learned it) yesterday.*

✦Práctica✦

A **HISTORIETA** ¿Dónde está mi tarjeta de identidad estudiantil?

Contesten según se indica.

1. ¿Estuviste ayer en la estación de ferrocarril? (sí)
2. ¿Tuviste que tomar el tren a Toledo? (sí)
3. ¿Pudiste comprar un billete de precio reducido? (no)
4. ¿Tuviste que presentar tu tarjeta de identidad estudiantil? (sí)
5. ¿Dónde la pusiste? (no sé)
6. ¿La perdiste? (sí, creo)
7. ¿Cuándo supiste que la perdiste? (cuando llegué a la estación)

Toledo, España

ESTRUCTURA

trece ∾ **13**

D. Have the class repeat the verb forms from the chart in Step 3.
E. Point out to students that all these irregular verbs have a **u** in the stem.
F. Call on an individual to read the model sentences from Step 4.

✦Práctica✦

A Allow students to refer to the verb charts on these two pages as they do the activity.

Writing Development
Have students write a note telling someone what happened in **Práctica A.**

HISTORY CONNECTION

Toledo, España Toledo is one of the most magnificent cities in Spain. The rock on which it stands was inhabited in prehistoric times. The Romans came in 192 B.C. and built a large fort where the Alcázar now stands. Toledo was inhabited by the Iberians, Romans, Visigoths, and the Moors who arrived early in the 8th century.

Alfonso VI, aided by El Cid, took Toledo from the Moors in 1085. During the Renaissance Toledo was a center of humanism. It began, however, to decline in the 16th century. The expulsion of the Jews in 1492 had severe economic consequences, and the decision in 1561 to make Madrid the center of the court led to its political decline. The years El Greco spent in Toledo (1572 to his death in 1614) were the years of Toledo's decline.

ANSWERS

Práctica

A 1. **Sí, ayer estuve en la estación de ferrocarril.**
2. **Sí, tuve que tomar el tren a Toledo.**
3. **No, no pude comprar un billete de precio reducido.**
4. **Sí, tuve que presentar mi tarjeta de identidad estudiantil.**
5. **No sé dónde la puse.**
6. **Sí, creo que la perdí.**
7. **Supe que la perdí cuando llegué a la estación.**

B For additional practice, have students retell the story in their own words.

TEACHING STRUCTURE

◆ Telling what people say

A. Have students open their books to page 14 and repeat the forms of the verb **decir** after you.

B. Write the forms of the verb on the board. Underline the stem for each form.

C. Now do the **Práctica** on page 15.

Learning From Realia

Banco de Guatemala The **quetzal** is the monetary unit of Guatemala. The **quetzal** is a multicolored bird and it is the national symbol of Guatemala.

Ask students: **¿Cuántos quetzales hay en la página 14?**

B **HISTORIETA** En el mercado

Completen.

El otro día yo ____ (estar) en
1
el mercado de Chichicastenango,
en Guatemala. Ramón ____ (estar)
2
allí también. Nosotros ____ (andar)
3
por el mercado pero no ____ (poder)
4
comprar nada. No es que no ____
5
(querer) comprar nada, es que no
____ (poder) porque ____ (ir) al
6   7
mercado sin un quetzal.

Chichicastenango, Guatemala

◆ **T**elling what people say
Decir en el presente

The verb **decir** *(to say)* is irregular in the present tense. Study the following forms.

INFINITIVE	decir
yo	digo
tú	dices
él, ella, Ud.	dice
nosotros(as)	decimos
vosotros(as)	*decís*
ellos, ellas, Uds.	dicen

Práctica

A **¿Qué dices?** Sigan el modelo.

> ¿Qué dices de la clase de español?

> Pues, yo digo que es fantástica. Estoy aprendiendo mucho.

1. ¿Qué dices de la clase de matemáticas?
2. ¿Qué dices de la clase de inglés?
3. ¿Qué dices de la clase de biología?
4. ¿Qué dices de la clase de educación física?
5. ¿Qué dices de la clase de historia?

B **¿Qué dicen todos?** Completen con la forma apropiada del presente de **decir.**

Yo ____ que quiero ir en tren pero Elena me ____ que prefiere
tomar el avión. Ella y Tomás también ____ que no hay mucha
diferencia entre la tarifa del avión y la tarifa del tren.

—¿Qué ____ tú?

—Yo ____ que es mejor ir en tren.

—Bien. Tú y yo ____ la misma cosa. Estamos de acuerdo.

Nº 10320
ENTRADA *gratuita*
MUSEO NACIONAL DEL
FERROCARRIL

Práctica

A Have students do **Práctica A** as a mini-conversation, working in pairs.

EXPANSION Have students think of additional topics to talk about, such as their school teams and clubs. For example:

—**¿Qué dices del equipo de fútbol?**
—**Pues, yo digo que es fantástico porque está ganando.**

B This activity uses all forms of **decir.**

 There is no more new material to present in this chapter. The sections that follow recombine and reinforce the vocabulary and structures that have already been introduced.

Learning From Realia

Museo nacional del ferrocarril This museum is in Madrid. Ask students: **¿Tienes que pagar por la entrada?**

ANSWERS

Práctica

A All answers follow the model.

B 1. digo
2. dice
3. dicen
4. dices
5. digo
6. decimos

15

Conversación

RESOURCES

🎧 Audiocassette 2A/CD1
💿 CD-ROM, Disc 1, page 16

🔔 Bell Ringer Review

Use BRR Transparency 1-5, or write the following on the board: Write four things passengers must do when they check in at an airport.

TEACHING THE CONVERSATION

A. 🎧 Have students close their books. Read the conversation to them or play Cassette 2A/Compact Disc 1.
B. Have the class repeat each line after you once.
C. Call on two students to read the conversation with as much expression as possible.
D. After completing the conversation, have students summarize it in their own words.
E. After presenting the conversation, go over the **Después de conversar** activity. If students can answer the questions with relative ease, move on. Students should not be expected to memorize the conversation.

TECHNOLOGY OPTION

💿 On the CD-ROM (Disc 1, page 16), students can watch a dramatization of this conversation. They can then play the role of either one of the characters and record themselves in the conversation.

Learning From Photos

En la ventanilla The photo on this page was taken at the Toledo train station, which has beautiful mosaics and tilework.

16

En la ventanilla

PASAJERA: Un billete para Madrid, por favor.
AGENTE: ¿Sencillo o de ida y vuelta?
PASAJERA: Sencillo, por favor.
AGENTE: ¿Para cuándo, señorita?
PASAJERA: Para hoy.
AGENTE: ¿En qué clase, primera o segunda?
PASAJERA: En segunda. ¿Tiene Ud. una tarifa reducida para estudiantes?
AGENTE: Sí. ¿Tiene Ud. su tarjeta de identidad estudiantil?
PASAJERA: Sí, aquí la tiene Ud.
AGENTE: Con el descuento son tres mil pesetas.
PASAJERA: ¿A qué hora sale el próximo tren?
AGENTE: Sale a las veinte y diez del andén número ocho.
PASAJERA: Gracias.

Después de conversar

Contesten.

1. ¿Dónde está la señorita?
2. ¿Adónde va?
3. ¿Qué tipo de billete quiere?
4. ¿Para cuándo lo quiere?
5. ¿En qué clase quiere viajar?
6. ¿Es alumna la señorita?
7. ¿Hay una tarifa reducida para estudiantes?
8. ¿Qué tiene la señorita?
9. ¿Cuánto cuesta el billete con el descuento estudiantil?
10. ¿A qué hora sale el tren?
11. ¿De qué andén sale?

16 ∽ *dieciséis*

CAPÍTULO 1

ANSWERS

Después de conversar

1. La señorita está en la ventanilla.
2. Va a Madrid.
3. Quiere un billete sencillo.
4. Lo quiere para hoy.
5. Quiere viajar en segunda (clase).
6. Sí, la señorita es alumna.
7. Sí, hay una tarifa reducida para estudiantes.
8. La señorita tiene su tarjeta de identidad estudiantil.
9. Con el descuento estudiantil el billete cuesta tres mil pesetas.
10. El tren sale a las veinte y diez.
11. Sale del andén número ocho.

Actividades comunicativas

A **El horario** Look at the train schedule. With a classmate, ask and answer as many questions as you can about it.

B **Vamos a Barcelona.** You and a classmate are spending a semester in Spain. You will be going to Barcelona for a couple of days. One of you is going to fly and the other is going to take the train. Compare your trips: time, cost, and what you have to do the day of departure.

Madrid Toledo

Válido desde el 29 de mayo a 24 de septiembre d

TIPO DE TREN	REGIONAL	REGIONAL	REGIONAL	REGIONAL	REGIONAL
PRESTACIONES	2.ª	2.ª	2.ª	2.ª	2.ª
ORIGEN				MADRID CH. 9.25	
MADRID-ATOCHA					
VILLAVERDE BAJO		7.20	8.25		10.55
LOS ANGELES		7.26	8.33	9.39	11.03
SAN CRISTOBAL DE LOS ANGELES		7.30	8.36		11.05
GETAFE-INDUSTRIAL		7.33	8.38		11.08
PINTO		7.36	8.41		11.11
VALDEMORO		7.41	8.46		11.16
CIEMPOZUELOS		7.47	8.52		11.19
ARANJUEZ		7.52	8.57		11.27
CASTILLEJO-AÑOVER	6.20	8.03	9.08		11.36
VILLAMEJOR		8.13	9.18	10.11	11.53
ALGODOR					
TOLEDO-INDUSTRIAL	6.37				12.03
TOLEDO	6.50	8.22	9.44	10.40	12.09
DESTINO		8.29			12.16
OBSERVACIONES	L M X J V S – (1)	Diario (2)	L M X J V – – (4)	· · · · · S D (3)	Diario

OBSERVACIONES:
(1) No circula 25-VII y 15-VIII.
(2) Efectua parada en Santa Catalina (7.26).
(3) Circula 25-VII y 15-VIII.
(4) No circula 25-VII y 15-VIII. Diario hasta Aranjuez.
(5) Efectua parada en Santa Catalina (14.31).

(L) Lunes (V) Viernes
(M) Martes (S) Sábado
(X) Miércoles (D) Domingo
(J) Jueves

PRONUNCIACIÓN

Las consonantes ñ, ch

The **ñ** is a separate letter of the Spanish alphabet. The mark over it is called a **tilde.** Note that it is pronounced similarly to the *ny* in the English word *canyon.* Repeat the following.

señor	**otoño**	**España**
señora	**pequeño**	**cumpleaños**
año		

Ch is pronounced much like the **ch** in the English word *church.* Repeat the following.

coche	**chaqueta**
chocolate	**muchacho**

Repeat the following sentences.

> **El señor español compra un coche cada año en el otoño.**
> **El muchacho chileno duerme en una cama pequeña en el coche-cama.**
> **El muchacho pequeño lleva una chaqueta color chocolate.**

A Give students a few minutes to study the train schedule before they begin the activity.

B Students should write down their answers and then compare notes with their partners.

TECHNOLOGY OPTION Students may use the Portfolio feature on the CD-ROM to record their conversations.

TEACHING PRONUNCIATION

A. Most students have no particular problem with these sounds. Have them pronounce each word carefully after you or the recording on Cassette 2A/ Compact Disc 1.

B. Have students open their books to page 17. Call on individuals to read the words and sentences.

C. All model sentences on page 17 can be used for dictation.

TECHNOLOGY OPTION

In the CD-ROM version of the Pronunciation section (Disc 1, page 17), students will see an animation of the cartoon on this page. They can also listen to, record, and play back the words and sentences presented here.

ANSWERS

Actividades comunicativas

A Answers will vary.

B Answers should include the time of departure, the cost of the trip, and a brief description of what they have to do the day they leave.

National Standards

✿ *Cultures*
The reading about the AVE train in Spain and the related activities on page 19 allow students to demonstrate an understanding of the importance of train travel in Spain.

TEACHING THE READING

Pre-reading

A. Have students open their books to page 18 and read the information in the Reading Strategy.

B. Tell them that the illustration at the bottom of the page is of **un ave**.

C. Then have them scan the **Lectura** and the photos to look for the connection between the bird and the train.

D. Have students locate Madrid and Sevilla on the map of Spain on page 451.

Reading

A. Call on a student to read three or four sentences aloud.

B. Intersperse the oral reading with comprehension questions from **Después de leer Activity A,** page 19.

Post-reading

A. Assign the reading and the **Después de leer** activities on page 19 for homework.

B. Have a student summarize the reading selection in his or her own words.

TECHNOLOGY OPTION

💿 Students may listen to a recorded version of the **Lectura** on the CD-ROM, Disc 1, pages 18–19.

Lecturas CULTURALES

Reading Strategy

Interpretation of images

Reading passages sometimes use images as a symbol to create an impression. Many times these images are animals. If you are able to identify an image, it is helpful to stop for a moment and think about the qualities and characteristics of the particular symbol the author is using in his or her imagery. Then when you have finished reading, go back and think about how the two images being compared are alike.

EN EL AVE

José Luis y su hermana, Maripaz, pasan dos días en Sevilla. Vinieron a visitar a sus abuelos. El viaje que hicieron de Madrid, donde viven, fue fantástico. Tomaron el tren y llegaron a Sevilla en sólo dos horas y quince minutos. Salieron de Atocha en Madrid a las 17:00 y bajaron del tren en Sevilla a las 19:15. ¿Es posible recorrer el trayecto[1] Madrid–Sevilla en dos horas quince minutos? Es una distancia de 538 kilómetros. ¡Es increíble!

[1]recorrer el trayecto *cover the route*

A bordo del AVE

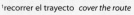

18 ⌒ *dieciocho*

CAPÍTULO 1

Independent Practice

Assign any of the following:
1. **Después de leer** activities, page 19
2. Workbook, pages 9–11
3. CD-ROM, Disc 1, pages 18–19

Sí, es increíble, pero es verdad. El nuevo tren español de alta velocidad es uno de los trenes más rápidos del mundo. Viaja a 250 kilómetros por hora. El tren se llama el AVE. ¿Por qué el AVE? Porque el tren vuela como un ave o pájaro.

José Luis y Maripaz tomaron el AVE. Según ellos, el viaje fue fantástico. ¿Por qué? Primero la velocidad. Pero el tren es también muy cómodo². Lleva ocho coches en tres clases. Los pasajeros pueden escuchar música estereofónica o mirar tres canales de video. El tren también dispone de³ teléfono por si acaso⁴ un pasajero quiere o necesita hacer una llamada telefónica.

²cómodo *comfortable*
³dispone de *has available*
⁴por si acaso *in case*

Plaza de España, Sevilla

Torre del Oro, Sevilla

Plaza de España, Sevilla

Después de leer

A Una visita a los abuelos
Contesten.

1. ¿Quiénes hicieron un viaje de Madrid a Sevilla?
2. ¿Quiénes vinieron a Sevilla, José Luis y su hermana o sus abuelos?
3. ¿Cómo hicieron el viaje?
4. ¿Qué tal fue el viaje?
5. ¿Cuánto tiempo tardó el viaje?
6. ¿A qué hora salieron de Madrid?
7. ¿A qué hora llegaron a Sevilla?

B Información Busquen la información.

1. uno de los trenes más rápidos del mundo
2. el nombre del tren
3. el número de coches que lleva el tren
4. el número de clases que tiene
5. algunas comodidades que el tren ofrece a los pasajeros

LECTURAS CULTURALES *diecinueve* 19

HISTORY CONNECTION

Plaza de España, Sevilla The grandiose structure on the Plaza de España was designed by the architect Aníbal González. It was Spain's pavillion at the 1929 Hispanic-American Exhibition Fair. There are four bridges over the ornamental lake. One of the bridges is seen here. Each bridge represents one of the medieval kingdoms of the Iberian peninsula.

La Torre del Oro, Sevilla, España This famous monument is on the banks of the Guadalquivir in Seville. A twelve-sided tower, it was built by the Moors in 1220. In times of attack they closed off the harbor by attaching a chain from this tower to another tower (no longer in existence) on the opposite bank of the river. In 1248, however, an admiral named Ramón de Bonifaz was able to break through the barrier, allowing Fernando III to capture the city. The Torre del Oro today houses a naval museum.

There is controversy as to how the tower got its name. Some say it got its name from the golden color of its tiles, **azulejos.** Other claim that is was once a warehouse for gold from the New World.

ANSWERS

Después de leer

A
1. **José Luis y su hermana, Maripaz, hicieron un viaje de Madrid a Sevilla.**
2. **José Luis y su hermana vinieron a Sevilla.**
3. **Hicieron el viaje en el tren.**
4. **El viaje fue fantástico.**
5. **El viaje tardó dos horas quince minutos.**
6. **Salieron de Madrid a las 17:00.**
7. **Llegaron a Sevilla a las 19:15.**

B
1. **el tren español de alta velocidad**
2. **el AVE**
3. **ocho**
4. **tres**
5. **música estereofónica, tres canales de video, teléfono**

Después de leer

A Allow students to refer to the reading to look up the answers, or you may use this activity as a testing device for factual recall.

B Have individual students read the appropriate phrase or sentence aloud. Make sure all students find the information in the **Lectura.**

LECTURA OPCIONAL

TEACHING TIPS

 This reading is optional. You may skip it completely, have the entire class read it, have only several students read it, or assign it for extra credit.

A. Have students locate Cuzco on the map of South America on page 452, or use the Map Transparency.

B. Have students read the passage quickly as they look at the photos that accompany it. The photos will increase their comprehension because students will be able to visualize what they are reading about.

C. Have students discuss the information that they find interesting.

VIDEO CONNECTION

Machu Picchu The **¡Buen viaje! Level 3 Video Program** has a segment on Machu Picchu. You may want to show this video in connection with this reading.

LECTURA OPCIONAL

DE CUZCO A MACHU PICCHU

Un viaje muy interesante en tren es el viaje de Cuzco a Machu Picchu en el Perú. Cada día a las siete de la mañana, un tren de vía estrecha[1] sale de la estación de San Pedro en Cuzco y llega a Machu Picchu a las diez y media. Cuzco está a unos 3.500 metros sobre el nivel del mar. El tren tiene que bajar a 2.300 metros para llegar a Machu Picchu. Tiene que bajar 1.200 metros y en el viaje de regreso tiene que subir 1.200 metros.

Pero, ¿quiénes toman el tren para ir a Machu Picchu? Es un tren que lleva a muchos turistas que quieren ir a ver las famosas ruinas de los incas. Machu Picchu es una ciudad entera, totalmente aislada[2] en un pico andino al borde de[3] un cañón. Un dato histórico increíble es que los españoles no descubrieron a Machu Picchu durante su conquista

[1] de vía estrecha *narrow gauge*
[2] aislada *isolated*
[3] al borde de *on the edge of*

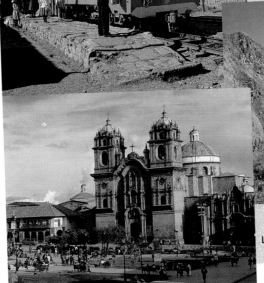

El valle del Urubamba, Perú

La Plaza de Armas, Cuzco

del Perú. Los historiadores creen que Machu Picchu fue el último refugio de los nobles incas al escaparse[4] de los españoles.

Machu Picchu fue descubierto por Hiram Bingham, el explorador y senador de los Estados Unidos, en 1911. ¿Cómo llegó Bingham a Machu Picchu en 1911? ¡A pie! Y aún hoy hay sólo dos maneras de ir a Machu Picchu—a pie o en el tren que sale a las siete y media de Cuzco.

[4]al escaparse *upon escaping*

Machu Picchu

Después de leer

A ¿Sí o no? Digan que sí o que no.

1. Machu Picchu está a una altura más elevada que Cuzco.
2. El tren que va de Machu Picchu a Cuzco tiene que subir 1.200 metros.
3. El viaje de Cuzco a Machu Picchu toma tres horas y media.
4. Hay muy pocos turistas en el tren a Machu Picchu.
5. En Machu Picchu hay ruinas famosas de los incas.
6. Machu Picchu fue una ciudad de los incas.
7. Los españoles descubrieron la ciudad de Machu Picchu durante su conquista del Perú.
8. Hiram Bingham fue un senador de los Estados Unidos.
9. Él también fue a Machu Picchu en tren.

LECTURAS OPCIONALES   *veintiuno* **21**

INFORMAL ASSESSMENT

You may use the **Después de leer** activity as a testing device to see how well students understood the reading selection.

Learning From Photos

Machu Picchu, Perú The top photo on page 20, taken through a stone portal or doorway, gives us a beautiful view of one of the many terraces at Machu Picchu. Many of the original stone buildings have been reconstructed. However, since the original roofs were made of thatch, they have not been rebuilt.

El tren a Machu Picchu (page 20) This is the train that takes tourists from Cuzco to Machu Picchu.

El valle del Urubamba, Perú (page 20) This valley is referred to as the "Sacred Valley of the Incas." The name "Inca" originally applied to the royal family only. Today it is used to describe the people as a whole.

La Plaza de Armas, Cuzco (page 20) Cuzco is a city of 200,000 people. Its population is a blend of Indian, **mestizo,** and Spanish cultures. In the days of the Incas, the Plaza de Armas was called Huacaypata. This square was lined with the sumptuous palaces of the dead and mummified Incas, and with the imperial residences of the living Incas. Today, the palaces have been replaced by Spanish mansions. The first floors of these mansions are occupied by small stores and restaurants.

Conexiones

LAS MATEMÁTICAS

CONVERSIONES ARITMÉTICAS

When traveling through many of the Spanish-speaking countries, you will need to make some mathematical conversions. For example, train as well as plane schedules and hours for formal events, radio, and television are given using the twenty-four-hour clock. The metric system rather than the English system is used for weights and measures. Let's take a look at some of the conversions that must be made.

La hora

Cuando lees el horario para el tren o un anuncio para un programa cultural, dan la hora usando las 24 horas. La una (1:00) es la una de la mañana y las doce (12:00) es el mediodía. Las trece (13:00), una hora después del mediodía, es la una de la tarde y las veinticuatro horas (00:00) es la medianoche.

Nuestros amigos José Luis y Maripaz salieron de Madrid a las 17:00 y llegaron a Sevilla a las 19:15. Es decir que salieron de Madrid a las 5:00 de la tarde y llegaron a las 7:15 de la tarde.

El sistema métrico—pesos y medidas[1]

Pesos
Las medidas tradicionales para peso en los Estados Unidos son la onza, la libra y la tonelada. En el sistema métrico decimal, las medidas para peso están basadas en el kilogramo, o kilo.

[1] pesos y medidas *weights and measures*

ABOUT THE SPANISH LANGUAGE
Terms from the English system—**el pie, la yarda, el galón**—are very seldom heard in Spanish.

Hay mil gramos en un kilo. El kilo es igual a 2,2 libras. Una libra estadounidense es un poco menos de medio kilo.

Líquidos
Las medidas para líquidos en los Estados Unidos son la pinta, el cuarto y el galón. En el sistema métrico es el litro. Un litro contiene un poco más que un cuarto.

Distancia y altura
Para medir la distancia y la altura en los Estados Unidos usamos la pulgada, el pie, la yarda y la milla. El sistema métrico usa el metro.

El metro es un poco más que una yarda. Un kilómetro (mil metros) es 0,621 millas—un poco más que media milla.

✎ Después de leer ✎

A **La hora** Read the schedule on page 400 and give the arrival and departure times of the trains using our system.

B **El sistema métrico** Contesten según las fotografías.

1. ¿Cuánto cuesta un litro de gasolina?
2. ¿Cuál es el límite de velocidad?
3. ¿Cuánto cuesta un litro de leche?
4. ¿Cuánto cuesta un kilo de carne?

L AS MATEMÁTICAS
CONVERSIONES ARITMÉTICAS

¡OJO! The material in this section will probably be of more interest to students who like math and science. It is, however, useful for all because, when travelling through most areas of the Spanish-speaking world, one has to use the metric system.

A. Have students read the introduction in English on page 22.
B. Now have them read the selection quickly. Students should already be familiar with the metric terms used in the reading.
C. Explain to students that here are some basic strategies to use when reading unfamiliar material. They should learn to: (1) recognize cognates and (2) derive meaning from context.
D. Now do the **Después de leer** activities.

ANSWERS

Después de leer
A Answers will vary.

B 1. **Un litro de gasolina super cuesta 118.6 pts.**
2. **El límite de velocidad es de 60 kilómetros por hora.**
3. **Un litro de leche cuesta 99 pts.**
4. **Un kilo de carne cuesta 1395 pts.**

Culminación

RECYCLING

The **Actividades orales** and the **Actividad escrita** allow students to use the vocabulary and structures from this chapter in open-ended, real-life settings.

Actividades orales

¡OJO! Encourage students to say as much as possible when they do these activities. Tell them not to be afraid of making mistakes since the goal of the activities is real-life communication. If someone in the group makes an error, allow the others to politely correct him or her.

Let students choose the activities they would like to do.

A You may wish to assign one type of travel to each group.

B **TECHNOLOGY OPTION**
In the CD-ROM version of this activity (Disc 1, page 24), students can interact with an on-screen native speaker and record their voice.

Student Portfolio

Have students keep a notebook containing their best written work from each chapter. These selected writings can be based on assignments from the Student Textbook, the Writing Activities Workbook, and the Communication Activities Masters. The two activities on page 25 are examples of writing assignments that may be included in each student's portfolio.

In the Workbook, students will develop an organized autobiography **(Mi autobiografía).** These workbook pages may also become a part of their portfolio. See the Teacher's Manual for more information on the Student Portfolio.

Actividades orales

A **El tren, el bus o el avión**　Work in groups of three or four. Discuss the advantages **(las ventajas)** and the disadvantages **(las desventajas)** of bus, train, and air travel. In your discussion, include such things as speed, price, location of stations, and anything else you consider important.

B **¿Qué vamos a hacer?**　You and a classmate are on a bus on the way to the train station in Madrid. There's an awful traffic jam **(un tapón, un atasco).** You know you are going to miss your train. Discuss your predicament with one another and figure out what you can do.

La estación de ferrocarril, Málaga

ANSWERS

Actividades orales
A and **B**　Answers will vary.

Independent Practice

Assign any of the following:
1. Activities, pages 24–25
2. Workbook, **Mi autobiografía,** page 12
3. Situation Cards
4. CD-ROM, Disc 1, Chapter 1, **Juego de repaso**

Actividad escrita

A **En la estación de ferrocarril** Look at the illustrations and write a paragraph about them.

Writing Strategy

Writing a descriptive paragraph

Your overall goal in writing a descriptive paragraph is to enable the reader to visualize your scene. To achieve this you must select and organize details that create an impression. Using a greater number of specific nouns and vivid adjectives will make your writing livelier.

Un viaje excelente

Write about a trip you took to a place you love. The place can be real or imaginary. Describe how and where you went, and when. Then describe what the weather is like in that place and what clothing you need there. Continue by writing about what you saw and how you got to each place you visited. In your description of the place, try to make your readers understand what it is about the place that you think is so great.

Actividad escrita

A You may wish to have students work in pairs to write this paragraph.

Writing Strategy

Writing a descriptive paragraph

A. Have students read the Writing Strategy on page 25.
B. Your students may enjoy writing about a trip to Machu Picchu or one of the other beautiful tourist destinations in the Spanish-speaking world. To help stimulate your students' "creative juices," have them find a photo in the textbook of a place they'd like to visit. Ask them to look at the photo for inspiration as they do the Writing Strategy activity on page 25.

ANSWERS

Actividad escrita
A Answers will vary.

Writing Strategy
Answers will vary.

VOCABULARY REVIEW

The words and phrases in the **Vocabulario** have been taught for productive use in this chapter. They are summarized here as a resource for both students and teacher. This list also serves as a convenient resource for the **Culminación** activities on pages 24 and 25. There are approximately four cognates in this vocabulary list. Have students find them.

Teacher Notes

Vocabulario

GETTING AROUND A TRAIN STATION

la estación de ferrocarril
la ventanilla
el billete, el boleto
  sencillo
  de ida y vuelta
la sala de espera
el mozo, el maletero
el equipaje
la maleta
la bolsa
el tablero de llegadas, de salidas

el horario
el quiosco
el tren
el andén
la vía
en segunda (clase)
en primera (clase)

DESCRIBING ACTIVITIES AT A TRAIN STATION

bajar(se) del tren
subir al tren
transbordar
salir a tiempo
  con retraso, con una demora

ON BOARD THE TRAIN

el coche, el vagón
el pasillo
el compartimiento
el asiento, la plaza
  libre
  ocupado(a)
  reservado(a)
completo(a)
el coche-cama
el coche-comedor, el coche-cafetería
la litera
el revisor
la parada
en la próxima parada

26

TECNOTUR

VIDEO

¡Buen viaje!

EPISODIO 1 ▶ Un viaje en tren

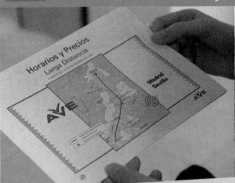

Juan Ramón y Teresa hacen un viaje en tren a Sevilla.

En Sevilla visitan varios lugares interesantes.

CD-ROM

Expansión cultural

Muchos españoles creen que Sevilla es la ciudad más bonita del mundo.

interNET CONNECTION

In this video episode, Juan Ramón and Teresa take the AVE from Madrid to Seville. To plan your own train trip, go to the **Capítulo 1** Internet activity at the Glencoe Foreign Language Web site:

http://www.glencoe.com/sec/fl

TECNOTUR

veintisiete ⁓ **27**

OVERVIEW

This page previews three key multimedia components of the **Glencoe Spanish** series. Each reinforces the material taught in Chapter 1 in a unique manner.

VIDEO

The Video Program allows students to see how the chapter vocabulary and structures are used by native speakers in an engaging story. It is best to show the video episode as a final activity for Chapter 1.
Note You may wish to show the video introduction to your students before playing the Chapter 1 episode. This segment will reacquaint them with the five main characters, or introduce them to your students, as the case may be.

A. Before viewing this episode, have students read the video photo captions. Ask: **¿Cómo se llama el tren? ¿De qué ciudad sale el tren?**
B. Now show the Chapter 1 video episode. See the Video Activities Booklet for detailed suggestions for using this resource.

CD-ROM

A. Have students read the **Expansión cultural** photo caption on page 27.
B. In the CD-ROM version of **Expansión cultural** (Disc 1, page 27), students can listen to additional recorded information about Sevilla.

INTERNET

Teacher Information and Student Worksheets for this activity can be accessed at the Web site.

Video Synopsis

In this episode Juan Ramón and Teresa take the AVE train from the Atocha station in Madrid to Sevilla. They purchase their tickets and get on board. During the trip Juan Ramón tapes the train, the countryside, and Teresa. While on board they discuss whether Sevilla or San Juan, Puerto Rico, is the most beautiful city in the world. When in Sevilla Juan Rámon films various sites for the Web page. On the night train back to Madrid, Juan Rámon shares his impressions with us of the AVE and Sevilla.

Chapter 2 Overview ◆◆◆◆◆◆◆◆◆◆◆◆◆◆◆◆◆◆◆

SCOPE AND SEQUENCE pages 28–53

TOPICS	FUNCTIONS	STRUCTURE	CULTURE
◆ Restaurants ◆ Foods and eating utensils	◆ How to order food or beverage at a restaurant ◆ How to identify eating utensils and dishes ◆ How to make a reservation at a restaurant ◆ How to explain how you like certain foods prepared ◆ How to talk about present and past events and activities	◆ Stem-changing verbs in the present ◆ Stem-changing verbs in the preterite	◆ Typical cuisine from Mexico ◆ Typical cuisine from Spain ◆ Typical foods from the Caribbean ◆ Regional vocabulary in the Spanish-speaking world

CHAPTER 2 RESOURCES

PRINT	MULTIMEDIA

Planning Resources

Lesson Plans Block Scheduling Lesson Plans	Interactive Lesson Planner

Reinforcement Resources

Writing Activities Workbook Student Tape Manual Video Activities Booklet Web Site User's Guide	Transparencies Binder Audiocassette/Compact Disc Program Videocassette/Videodisc Program Online Internet Activities Electronic Teacher's Classroom Resources

Assessment Resources

Situation Cards Chapter Quizzes Testing Program Performance Assessment	**Maratón mental** Mindjogger Videoquiz Testmaker Computer Software (Macintosh/Windows) Listening Comprehension Audiocassette/Compact Disc Communication Transparency: C-2

Motivational Resources

Expansion Activities	Café Glencoe: www.cafe.glencoe.com Keypal Internet Activities

Enrichment

Spanish for Spanish Speakers	Fine Art Transparency: F-2

SECTION	PAGES	SECTION RESOURCES
Vocabulario Palabras 1 **En el restaurante**	30–33	Vocabulary Transparencies 2.1 Audiocassette 2B/Compact Disc 2 Student Tape Manual, TE, pages 13–15 Workbook, pages 13–14 Chapter Quizzes, page 6 CD-ROM, Disc 1, pages 30–33
Vocabulario Palabras 2 **Más alimentos o comestibles**	34–37	Vocabulary Transparencies 2.2 Audiocassette 2B/Compact Disc 2 Student Tape Manual, TE, pages 15–18 Workbook, pages 15-16 Chapter Quizzes, page 7 CD-ROM, Disc 1, pages 34–37
Estructura **Verbos con el cambio e → ie en el presente** **Verbos con el cambio e → ie, o → ue en el pretérito**	38–41	Workbook, pages 17–18 Audiocassette 2B/Compact Disc 2 Student Tape Manual, TE, pages 18–19 Chapter Quizzes, pages 8–10 Computer Testmaker CD-ROM, Disc 1, pages 38–41
Conversación **En el restaurante** **Pronunciación: La consonante x**	42–43	Audiocassette 2B/Compact Disc 2 Student Tape Manual, TE, pages 20–21 CD-ROM, Disc 1, pages 42–43
Lecturas culturales **La comida mexicana** **La comida española** *(opcional)* **La comida del Caribe** *(opcional)*	44–47	Testing Program, pages 21–22 CD-ROM, Disc 1, pages 44–47
Conexiones **El lenguaje** *(opcional)*	48–49	Testing Program, page 22 CD-ROM, Disc 1, pages 48–49
Culminación **Actividades orales** **Actividades escritas** **Vocabulario** **Tecnotur**	50–53	¡**Buen viaje!** Video, Episode 2 Video Activities, pages 66–68 Internet Activities www.glencoe.com/sec/fl Testing Program, pages 19–21; 125; 169; 191 CD-ROM, Disc 1, pages 50–53

CAPÍTULO 2

OVERVIEW

In this chapter students will learn how to order food in a restaurant. To do this they will learn expressions needed to speak with a server, vocabulary associated with utensils, and additional items of food. They will continue to narrate in the present and past by learning the present and preterite of stem-changing verbs they can use at a restaurant—**pedir, servir, repetir.** The cultural focus of the chapter is on some typical cuisines of the Spanish-speaking world.

National Standards

Communication

In Chapter 2 students will learn to communicate in spoken and written Spanish on the following topics:
- ordering a meal
- describing a restaurant experience
- discussing cuisines of the Spanish-speaking world

Students will obtain and provide information about these topics and engage in conversations that would typically take place at a restaurant as they fulfill the chapter objectives listed on this page.

Pacing

Chapter 2 will require approximately six to eight days. Pacing will vary according to the length of the class, the age of your students, and student aptitude.

Block Scheduling

See the Block Scheduling Lesson Plans Booklet for suggestions on how to present the chapter material within a block scheduling framework.

En el restaurante

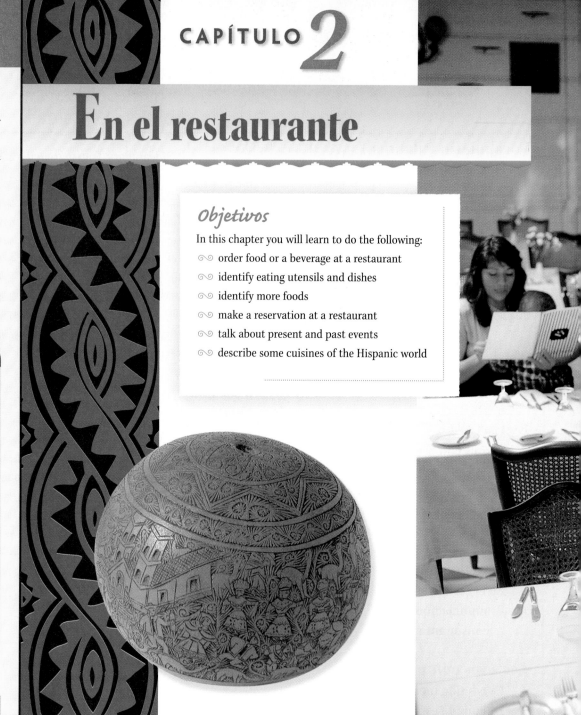

Objetivos

In this chapter you will learn to do the following:
- order food or a beverage at a restaurant
- identify eating utensils and dishes
- identify more foods
- make a reservation at a restaurant
- talk about present and past events
- describe some cuisines of the Hispanic world

interNET CONNECTION

The **Glencoe Foreign Language Web site** (http://www.glencoe.com/sec/fl) offers three options that enable you and your students to experience the Spanish-speaking world via the Internet:
- The online **Actividades** are correlated to the chapters and utilize Hispanic Web sites around the world. For the Chapter 2 activity, see student page 53.

- The **Correspondencia electrónica** section provides information on how to set up a keypal (pen pal) exchange between your class and a class in the Spanish-speaking world.
- At **Café Glencoe,** the interactive "after-school" section of the site, you and your students can access a variety of additional online resources, including interactive games. In Chapter 2, the click-and-drag game practices the table setting.

Spotlight On Culture

Artefacto The Andean area has produced the most superb folk art of the South American continent. The pre-Columbian peoples of the area excelled in weaving, pottery-making, and gold- and silver-smithing. It is said that Peru's artisans may produce the most interesting and varied crafts on the continent, and some of the finest in the world. On page 28 we see a Peruvian carved gourd.

There is a wonderful exhibit of pre-Columbian artifacts at the Museo de Antropología y Arqueología in Lima.

Fotografía The restaurant shown on this page is also in Lima.

Learning From Photos

Al restaurante Ask the following questions about the photo after presenting the new vocabulary in this chapter:

¿Es un restaurante económico o elegante?

¿Lleva un smoking el mesero?

¿Está poniendo la mesa el mesero?

Identifica todo lo que ves en la mesa.

¿Cuántas personas hay en la familia que está en el restaurante?

¿Cómo está vestido el papá? ¿Qué lleva?

¿Qué leen la mamá y el papá?

veintinueve ∽ **29**

Chapter Projects

Visita a un restaurante hispano Plan a class outing to an inexpensive restaurant that serves food from a Spanish-speaking country. If possible, distribute the restaurant's menu in advance so students can think about what they will order. You may also have them use the menus to practice ordering in Spanish.

La cocina hispana Prepare a dish from one of the Spanish-speaking countries, or have students prepare some Hispanic foods and bring them to class. A number of typical dishes are described in this chapter. Students can go to the library to find recipes for these dishes.

TECHNOLOGY OPTION The Chapter 10 Internet activity utilizes Hispanic cuisine Web sites. If you are looking for recipes, you and your students may want to access the links for this activity. See page 28 for the address of the **Glencoe Foreign Language Web site.**

🔔 Bell Ringer Review

Use BRR Transparency 2-1, or write the following on the board: Write a list of the foods you have learned.

TEACHING VOCABULARY

A. Have students close their books. Show Vocabulary Transparencies 2.1 (A & B). Point to individual items and have students repeat each word or expression two or three times after you or Cassette 2B/Compact Disc 2.

B. Intersperse the presentation with simple questions that enable students to use the new words. For example: **¿Tienes hambre? ¿Quieres comer? ¿Tienes sed? ¿Qué pone el mesero? ¿Usas la taza para beber o para cortar la carne?** Have students answer with complete sentences or sometimes have them use just the word or expression that responds to the question.

C. After presenting the vocabulary orally, have students open their books and read the new vocabulary aloud. You can have the class read in chorus or call on individuals to read. Intersperse with questions such as those outlined above.

30

Vocabulario

PALABRAS 1

En el restaurante

El mesero pone la mesa.

el camarero, el mesero

el vaso

Tengo hambre.

Tengo hambre y quiero comer.

Tengo sed.

Tengo sed y quiero beber algo.

la sal

la pimienta

la taza

el platillo

el plato

la cuchara

la cucharita

el tenedor

la servilleta

el cuchillo

el mantel

Pantomime

Getting ready

Teach the following words by using the appropriate gestures as you say each expression: **cubre, dobla, a la derecha, a la izquierda, deja.**

Pantomime 1

Begin

___, ven acá, por favor.
Vas a poner la mesa.
Cubre la mesa con un mantel.
Dobla las servilletas.
Pon un plato en la mesa.

Luego pon la cucharita y el cuchillo a la derecha.
Pon el tenedor a la izquierda. Gracias, ___.

Pantomime 2

Begin

___, ven acá, por favor.
Vas a hacer unos gestos.
Toma el menú. Abre el menú.
Lee el menú. Cierra el menú.
Corta la carne con el cuchillo. Come.
Bebe. Deja una propina para el mesero.
Gracias, ___. Regresa a tu asiento.

La señorita pide el menú.

El cocinero fríe las papas.
Está friendo las papas.

El mesero le sirve la comida.

La señorita pide la cuenta.
El servicio no está incluido.
Ella deja una propina.

✦Práctica✦

¡OJO! **Práctica** When students are doing the **Práctica** activities, accept any answer that makes sense. The purpose of these activities is to have students use the new vocabulary. They are not factual recall activities. Thus, do not expect students to remember specific information from the vocabulary presentation when answering. If you wish, have students use the photos on this page as a stimulus, when possible.

Historieta Each time **Historieta** appears, it means that the answers to the activity form a short story. Encourage students to look at the title of the **Historieta** since it will sometimes help them do the activity.

A Have students work with a partner.

EXPANSION Ask students to volunteer additional items. For example: **Para tomar una limonada, una sopa, etc.**

B After going over **Práctica B,** have students retell the story in their own words.

Writing Development

Have students write the answers to **Práctica B** in a paragraph to illustrate how all of the items tell a story.

Learning From Realia

Alkalde The name of the restaurant on the check is Alkalde. It is a Basque restaurant. The Basques are considered to be the best cooks in Spain.

A **¿Qué necesitas?** Contesten según el modelo.

¿Para tomar leche?
Para tomar leche necesito un vaso.

1. ¿Para tomar agua?
2. ¿Para tomar café?
3. ¿Para comer la ensalada?
4. ¿Para comer el postre?
5. ¿Para cortar la carne?

Madrid, España

B **HISTORIETA** En el restaurante

Contesten.

1. ¿Cuántas personas hay en la mesa?
2. ¿Tiene hambre María?
3. ¿Pide María el menú?
4. ¿Le trae el menú el mesero?
5. ¿Qué pide María?
6. ¿El mesero le sirve?
7. ¿El mesero le sirve bien?
8. Después de la comida, ¿le pide la cuenta al mesero?
9. ¿Le trae la cuenta el mesero?
10. ¿Paga con su tarjeta de crédito María?
11. ¿María le da (deja) una propina al mesero?
12. Después de la comida, ¿tiene hambre María?

ANSWERS

Práctica

A 1. **Para tomar agua necesito un vaso.**
2. **Para tomar café necesito una taza.**
3. **Para comer la ensalada necesito un tenedor.**
4. **Para comer el postre necesito una cucharita (un tenedor).**
5. **Para cortar la carne necesito un cuchillo.**

B 1. **Hay una persona en la mesa.**
2. **Sí, María tiene hambre.**
3. **Sí, María pide el menú.**
4. **Sí, el mesero le trae el menú.**
5. **María pide ___.**
6. **Sí, el mesero le sirve.**
7. **Sí, el mesero le sirve bien.**
8. **Sí, le pide la cuenta al mesero después de la comida.**
9. **Sí, el mesero le trae la cuenta.**
10. **Sí (No), María (no) paga con su tarjeta de crédito.**
11. **Sí, María le da (deja) una propina al mesero.**
12. **No, María no tiene hambre después de la comida.**

C Palabras relacionadas Busquen una palabra relacionada.

1. la mesa   a. el servicio
2. la cocina   b. la bebida
3. servir   c. el cocinero
4. freír   d. la comida
5. comer   e. el mesero
6. beber   f. frito

Alcalá de Henares, España

D HISTORIETA El mesero pone la mesa.

Completen.

1. Para comer, los clientes necesitan
   ____, ____, ____ y ____.
2. Dos condimentos son la ____ y la
   ____.
3. El mesero cubre la mesa con ____.
4. En la mesa el mesero pone una
   ____ para cada cliente.
5. El niño pide un ____ de leche y sus
   padres piden una ____ de café.
6. Ellos tienen ____ y piden una
   botella de agua mineral.

Actividad comunicativa

A En el restaurante Look at the
advertisement for a restaurant in
Santiago de Chile. Tell as much as
you can about the restaurant based on
the information in the advertisement.
A classmate will tell whether he or
she wants to go to the restaurant
and why.

Aquí
está
Coco

El sabor de los mejores
pescados y mariscos del
Pacífico Sur, preparados
como usted quiera, en un
ambiente agradable e
informal.

C This activity helps students
learn to identify word families.

Actividad comunicativa

¡OJO! Práctica versus Actividades comunicativas
All activities which provide guided
practice are labeled **Práctica.** The
more open-ended communicative
activities are labeled **Actividades
comunicativas.**

A Students should base their
descriptions on both the descriptive
paragraph and the two photos in this
ad. Explain to the class that the
phrase **e informal** is not a spelling
error. After they have done **Palabras
2,** pages 34–35, see how many
seafood items they can identify in
this ad.

Learning From Realia

Aquí está Coco There is something in this ad that would tell
you that the restaurant must be
in South America. What is it?
(del Pacífico Sur)

Independent Practice

Assign any of the following:
1. Workbook, pages 13–14
2. Activities, pages 32–33
3. CD-ROM, Disc 1, pages 30–33

ANSWERS

Práctica

C 1. e
2. c
3. a
4. f
5. d
6. b

D 1. **un plato, un tenedor, un cuchillo,
   una cucharita (una cuchara)**
2. **sal, pimienta**

3. **un mantel**
4. **servilleta**
5. **vaso, taza**
6. **sed**

Actividad comunicativa

A Answers will vary; however, students
should mention the type of dishes served
(pescados y mariscos) and whether the
restaurant is formal or informal.

RESOURCES

 Vocabulary Transparencies 2.2 (A & B)

📁 Student Tape Manual, TE, pages 15–18

🎧 Audiocassette 2B/CD2

📁 Workbook, pages 15–16

📁 Quiz 2, pages 7–8

💿 CD-ROM, Disc 1, pages 34–37

🔔 Bell Ringer Review

Use BRR Transparency 2-2, or write the following on the board: Complete with the past tense.

1. **Anoche yo no ___ en casa. (comer)**
2. **Mis amigos y yo ___ en un restaurante. (comer)**
3. **Yo ___ al restaurante en el metro pero mis amigos ___ el autobús. (ir, tomar)**
4. **El mesero nos ___ un servicio muy bueno. (dar)**

TEACHING VOCABULARY

A. Have students close their books. Then model the new vocabulary on pages 34–35 using Vocabulary Transparencies 2.2 (A & B). Have students repeat each word or expression two or three times after you or the recording on Cassette 2B/Compact Disc 2.

B. Clarify any cuts of meat that are not evident. For example, students may not know the following: **carne de res** *(beef)*, **ternera** *(veal)*, **cerdo** *(pork)*, **cordero** *(lamb)*.

C. Have students read the dialogue on page 35 aloud, using as much expression as possible. You may want to have several students perform the telephone conversation for the class.

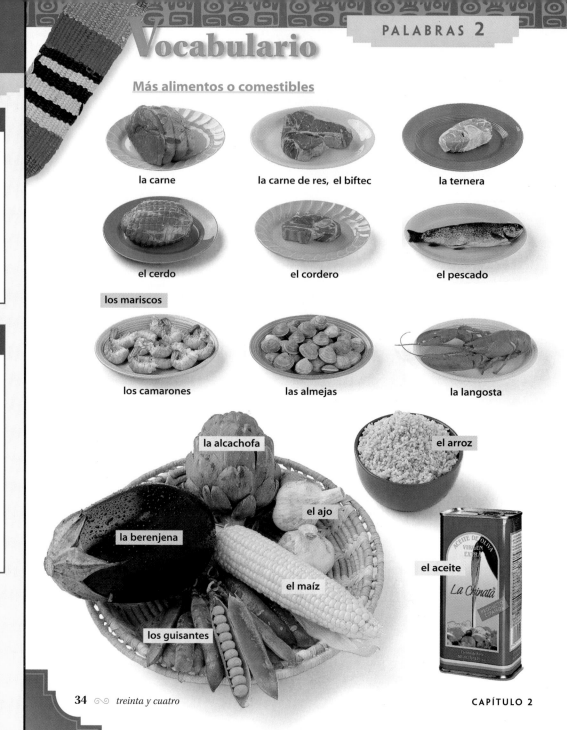

Más alimentos o comestibles

la carne

la carne de res, el biftec

la ternera

el cerdo

el cordero

el pescado

los mariscos

los camarones

las almejas

la langosta

la alcachofa

el arroz

el ajo

la berenjena

el aceite

el maíz

los guisantes

Pantomime

Begin

(Estudiante 1), levántate y ven acá, por favor.
Estamos en el restaurante Mendoza.
Siéntate, (Estudiante 1).
Toma el menú.
Ábrelo.
Lee el menú.
Llama al mesero.
(Estudiante 2), ven acá. Tú vas a ser el mesero.
(Estudiante 1), pídele al mesero lo que

quieres comer.
(Estudiante 2), escribe lo que pide.
Ve a la cocina.
Vuelve con la comida.
Sirve la comida.
Pon los platos en la mesa.
(Estudiante 1), come.

Ah, tenemos un problema. Pediste la carne bien hecha y el mesero te sirvió la carne casi cruda. Llama al mesero.

(continued on page 35)

La joven pidió un biftec.
El mesero sirvió el biftec.
La comida está rica, deliciosa.

¡Diga!

Quisiera reservar una mesa, por favor.

Sí, señor. ¿Para cuándo?

Para esta noche a las nueve y media.

¿Cuántas personas?

Cuatro.

¿A nombre de quién, por favor?

A nombre de Julio Amaral.

Conforme, señor.

Pantomime

(Estudiante 2), ve a la mesa.
(Estudiante 1), dale el plato.
Pide la cuenta.
Mira la cuenta.
Saca el dinero de tu bolsillo o de tu cartera.
Paga.
Levántate.
Sal del restaurante.
Gracias, (Estudiante 1). Ahora puedes volver a tu asiento.
Y tú también, (Estudiante 2). Gracias.

VOCABULARY EXPANSION

You may wish to introduce the following expressions:

bien hecho(a), cocido(a)	*well done*
a término medio	*medium*
casi crudo, no muy cocido(a)	*rare*

A waiter will frequently ask: **¿Qué les apetece?**
(What would you like to order?)

ABOUT THE SPANISH LANGUAGE

◆ Explain to students the difference between **La comida está buena** and **La comida es buena.** (**La comida está buena** significa que la comida está deliciosa, que está muy rica, que tiene buen sabor. **La comida es buena** significa que es buena para la salud. **Contiene vitaminas, etc.**)

◆ **El maíz** is the most universal word for corn. In Mexico, however, you will hear **el elote** and in certain areas of South America **el choclo.**

◆ In addition to **la alcachofa** you will also hear **la cotufa.**

◆ There are several ways to say *shrimp.* There are some differences in type and size but words you will hear in addition to **el camarón** are **la gamba** (usually small shrimp in Spain), **el langostino** (large, but not a lobster) and **la quisquilla.**

◆ There are many ways to say *steak* in Spanish. **Biftec** and **bistec** are commonly used. You will also hear **filete** and **entrecote. Filete**, however, can be a filet of any type of meat or fish. **El entrecote** is meat only. The word **lomo** refers to any cut from the loin area. **Lomo de carne de res** is similar to a sirloin steak. **Solomillo** or **lomo fino** is similar to a tenderloin or filet mignon. In many areas of Latin America **el churrasco** is a grilled steak.

Práctica

¡OJO! It is recommended that you go over all the **Práctica** in class before assigning them for homework.

A After doing **Práctica A**, go back to page 34 and ask students whether or not they like the other food items on that page.

B After doing **Práctica B**, have one or two students retell the story in his or her own words.

Learning From Photos

Caracas, Venezuela Have students describe what they see in these Venezuelan photos in their own words.

A ¿Te gusta(n) o no te gusta(n)? Contesten según las fotos.

1.
2.
3.
4.
5.
6.

B HISTORIETA Cenó en el restaurante.

Contesten.

1. ¿Fue Victoria al restaurante anoche?
2. ¿Quién le sirvió?
3. ¿Pidió Victoria un biftec?
4. ¿Pidió también una ensalada?
5. ¿Le sirvió el mesero una ensalada de lechuga y tomate?
6. ¿Le sirvió una comida deliciosa o una comida mala?

Caracas, Venezuela

ANSWERS

Práctica

A 1. (No) me gusta el biftec.
2. (No) me gusta el pescado.
3. (No) me gustan los camarones (las gambas).
4. (No) me gusta la ensalada.
5. (No) me gusta el maíz.
6. (No) me gustan las almejas.

B 1. Sí, Victoria fue al restaurante anoche.
2. El mesero le sirvió.
3. Sí (No), Victoria (no) pidió un biftec.
4. Sí, (No, no) pidió una ensalada.
5. Sí (No), el mesero (no) le sirvió una ensalada de lechuga y tomate.
6. Le sirvió una comida deliciosa (mala).

C ¿Qué te gusta? Contesten personalmente.

1. ¿Te gusta la ensalada?
2. ¿Te gusta la ensalada con aceite y vinagre?
3. ¿Te gusta el biftec?
4. ¿Te gusta el sándwich de jamón y queso?
   ¿Te gusta más con pan tostado?
5. ¿Te gusta la tortilla de queso?
6. ¿Te gustan los huevos con jamón?

Actividades comunicativas

A **Una reservación** You call a restaurant in Buenos Aires. The head-waiter (a classmate) answers. Make a reservation for yourself and a group of friends.

B **¿Qué recomienda Ud.?**
Here's a menu from a very famous restaurant in Madrid. In fact, it's the oldest restaurant in the city, dating from 1725. There are many items on the menu that you will be able to recognize. A classmate will be the server. Ask what he or she recommends and then order.

C Students can do this activity in pairs.

EXPANSION You can have students expand **Práctica C** into a mini-conversation:
—¿Te gusta la ensalada?
—Sí, mucho. ¿Y a ti te gusta?
—Sí, me gusta. (No, no me gusta.)

Actividades comunicativas

¡OJO! These activities encourage students to use the chapter vocabulary and structures in open-ended situations. It is not necessary to have them do all the activities. Choose the ones you consider most appropriate.

A Students should use the dialogue on page 35 as their model.

B The famous **Casa de Botín** restaurant specializes in **cordero asado** and **cochinillo asado**. **Cochinillo** is called **lechón** in Latin America. You may also wish to point out that the word **carta** is used here, rather than **menú**.

ANSWERS

Práctica

C 1. Sí, (No, no) me gusta la ensalada.
2. Sí, (No, no) me gusta la ensalada con aceite y vinagre.
3. Sí, (No, no) me gusta el biftec.
4. Sí, (No, no) me gusta el sándwich de jamón y queso. Sí, (No, no) me gusta más con pan tostado.
5. Sí, (No, no) me gusta la tortilla de queso.
6. Sí, (No, no) me gustan los huevos con jamón.

Actividades comunicativas

A Answers will vary.

B Answers will vary depending on what students choose from the menu.

Estructura

- Workbook, pages 17–18
- Student Tape Manual, TE, pages 18–19
- Audiocassette 2B/CD2
- Quizzes 3–4, pages 9–10
- Computer Testmaker
- CD-ROM, Disc 1, pages 38–41

Bell Ringer Review

Use BRR Transparency 2-3, or write the following on the board: Answer the following questions.

1. ¿Te gusta la carne?
2. ¿Te gustan los mariscos?
3. ¿Cuáles son algunas legumbres que te gustan?
4. ¿Te gusta el postre?
5. ¿Qué gusta beber?

TEACHING STRUCTURE

Describing more present activities

A. Have students open their books to page 38. Write the verb forms on the board. Underline the stem and have students repeat each form after you.
B. **Note** Oral practice with these verbs is important because, if students pronounce them correctly, they will be inclined to spell them correctly.
C. When going over the verb **seguir**, review with students the following sound-spelling correspondence: **ga, gue, gui, go, gu.**

Práctica

A Students will answer using the **yo** form.

D̲escribing more present activities
Verbos con el cambio e → i en el presente

The verbs **pedir, servir, repetir, freír, seguir** *(to follow)*, and **vestirse** *(to get dressed)* are stem-changing verbs. The **e** of the infinitive stem changes to **i** in all forms of the present tense except the **nosotros** and **vosotros** forms. Study the following forms. Note the spelling of **seguir.**

INFINITIVE	pedir	servir	seguir	vestirse
yo	pido	sirvo	sigo	me visto
tú	pides	sirves	sigues	te vistes
él, ella, Ud.	pide	sirve	sigue	se viste
nosotros(as)	pedimos	servimos	seguimos	nos vestimos
vosotros(as)	*pedís*	*servís*	*seguís*	*os vestís*
ellos, ellas, Uds.	piden	sirven	siguen	se visten

Práctica

A Lo que yo pido   Digan si piden lo siguiente o no.

1.
2.
3.
4.
5.
6.

ANSWERS

Práctica
A All answers begin with **Sí, (No, no) pido...**
1. ... una langosta.
2. ... queso.
3. ... papas.
4. ... un pollo.
5. ... una botella de agua mineral.
6. ... una ensalada.

B Lo que pedimos en el restaurante Sigan el modelo.

A Juan le gusta el pescado.
¿Qué pide él?

Él pide pescado.

1. A Teresa le gustan los mariscos. ¿Qué pide ella?
2. A Carlos le gusta el biftec. ¿Qué pide él?
3. A mis amigos les gustan las legumbres. ¿Qué piden ellos?
4. A mis padres les gusta mucho la ensalada. ¿Qué piden ellos?
5. Nos gusta el postre. ¿Qué pedimos?
6. Nos gustan las tortillas. ¿Qué pedimos?
7. ¿Qué pides cuando tienes sed?
8. ¿Qué pides cuando tienes hambre?

C HISTORIETA Vamos al restaurante.

Completen.

Cuando mi amiga y yo ____ (ir) al restaurante, nosotros ____
₁   ₂
(pedir) casi siempre una hamburguesa. Yo la ____ (pedir) con lechuga
₃
y tomate y ella la ____ (pedir) con queso. A mi amiga le ____ (gustar)
₄   ₅
mucho las papas fritas. Ella ____ (decir) que le ____ (gustar) más
₆   ₇
cuando el cocinero las ____ (freír) en aceite de oliva.
₈

D Entrevista Contesten personalmente.

1. Cuando vas a un restaurante, ¿qué pides?
2. ¿Pides papas? Si no pides papas, ¿pides arroz?
3. ¿Qué más pides con la carne y las papas o el arroz?
4. ¿Quién te sirve en el restaurante?
5. Si te sirve bien, ¿qué le dejas?

Actividad comunicativa

A ¿Por qué no pides… ? You're in a restaurant with a friend (a classmate). You are hungry and thirsty, but you don't know what to order. Your friend will suggest something. Then you decide.

Marbella, España

B **Práctica B** reviews the use of **gustar** as it practices stem-changing verbs.

C After going over **Práctica C,** students can summarize the information in their own words.

D **Práctica D** may be done in pairs.

Actividad comunicativa

A In this activity, the first student can begin by asking: **¿Te gusta(n)… ?** or **¿Por qué no pides… ?**

TECHNOLOGY OPTION Students can use the Portfolio feature on the CD-ROM to record this conversation.

ANSWERS

Práctica
B 1. Ella pide mariscos.
2. Él pide biftec.
3. Ellos piden legumbres
4. Ellos piden ensalada.
5. Pedimos postre.
6. Pedimos tortillas.
7. Cuando tengo sed pido ___.
8. Cuando tengo hambre pido ___.

C 1. vamos
2. pedimos
3. pido
4. pide
5. gustan
6. dice
7. gustan
8. fríe

D 1. Cuando voy a un restaurante, pido ___.

2. Sí, (No, no) pido papas. Sí, si no pido papas, pido arroz. (No, si no pido papas, no pido arroz.)
3. Pido ___.
4. El mesero me sirve en el restaurante.
5. Si me sirve bien le dejo una propina.

Actividad comunicativa
A Answers will vary.

39

TEACHING STRUCTURE

Describing more activities in the past

A. Have students repeat the verb forms shown in the charts on page 40, paying particular attention to the stem changes and correct pronunciation.

A The items in **Práctica A** describe an unfortunate experience in a restaurant.

EXPANSION After going over **Práctica A,** have students make up original stories about a horrible experience in a restaurant. This will be done as a narrative.

Note This is a good preparatory activity for **Actividad comunicativa A,** page 41. In that activity students "converse" with the restaurant manager about a problem with their meal and the service.

Describing more activities in the past
Verbos con el cambio e → i, o → u en el pretérito

1. The verbs **pedir, repetir, freír, servir,** and **vestirse** have a stem change in the preterite. The **e** of the infinitive stem changes to **i** in the **él** and **ellos** forms.

INFINITIVE	pedir	repetir	vestirse
yo	pedí	repetí	me vestí
tú	pediste	repetiste	te vestiste
él, ella, Ud.	pidió	repitió	se vistió
nosotros(as)	pedimos	repetimos	nos vestimos
vosotros(as)	*pedisteis*	*repetisteis*	*os vestisteis*
ellos, ellas, Uds.	pidieron	repitieron	se vistieron

2. The verbs **preferir, divertirse,** and **dormir** also have a stem change in the preterite. The **e** in **preferir** and **divertirse** changes to **i** and the **o** in dormir changes to **u** in the **él** and **ellos** forms.

INFINITIVE	preferir	divertirse	dormir
yo	preferí	me divertí	dormí
tú	preferiste	te divertiste	dormiste
él, ella, Ud.	prefirió	se divirtió	durmió
nosotros(as)	preferimos	nos divertimos	dormimos
vosotros(as)	*preferisteis*	*os divertisteis*	*dormisteis*
ellos, ellas, Uds.	prefirieron	se divirtieron	durmieron

A **HISTORIETA** Servicio bueno o malo

Contesten según se indica.

1. ¿Qué pediste en el restaurante? (una ensalada)
2. ¿Cómo la pediste? (sin aceite y vinagre)
3. ¿Cuántas veces repetiste «sin aceite y vinagre»? (dos veces)
4. Y, ¿cómo sirvió el mesero la ensalada? (con aceite y vinagre)
5. ¿Qué hiciste? (pedí otra ensalada)
6. ¿Qué pidió tu amigo? (puré de papas)
7. ¿Y qué pasó? (el cocinero frió las papas)
8. ¿Qué sirvió el mesero? (papas fritas)
9. ¿Pidieron Uds. una bebida? (sí)
10. ¿Qué pidieron para beber? (una limonada)
11. ¿Qué sirvió el mesero? (un té)
12. ¿Le dieron Uds. una propina al mesero? (no)

ANSWERS

Práctica

A 1. Pedí una ensalada en el restaurante.
2. La pedí sin aceite y vinagre.
3. Repetí «sin aceite y vinagre» dos veces.
4. El mesero sirvió la ensalada con aceite y vinagre.
5. Pedí otra ensalada.
6. Mi amigo pidió puré de papas.
7. El cocinero frió las papas.
8. El mesero sirvió papas fritas.
9. Sí, pedimos una bebida.
10. Pedimos una limonada.
11. El mesero sirvió un té.
12. No, no le dimos una propina al mesero.

B HISTORIETA Preparando la comida

Completen con el pretérito.

Anoche mi hermano y yo ___₁ (preparar) la comida para la familia.
Yo ___₂ (freír) el pescado. Mi hermano ___₃ (freír) las papas.
Mamá ___₄ (poner) la mesa. Y papá ___₅ (servir) la comida. Todos
nosotros ___₆ (comer) muy bien. A todos nos
___₇ (gustar) mucho el pescado. Mi hermano y mi papá ___₈
(repetir) el pescado. Luego
yo ___₉ (servir) el postre,
un sorbete. Después de la comida
mi hermano tomó una siesta.
Él ___₁₀ (dormir) media hora.
Yo no ___₁₁ (dormir). No me
gusta dormir inmediatamente
después de comer.

Valparaíso, Chile

Actividad comunicativa

A **Lo siento mucho.** You're in a restaurant and you're fed up with
the waiter. He hasn't done a thing right. Call over the manager
(a classmate) and tell him or her all that happened. He or she will
apologize and say something to try to make you happy.

B   After doing **Práctica B,** have
several students retell the story in
their own words.

Learning From Photos

Valparaíso, Chile   Have students describe the family members and their activities in the photo on page 41.

Actividad comunicativa

A   Have students examine the illustration accompanying **Actividad A** carefully. There are quite a few things that have gone wrong! Before students begin to work on their conversations, you may wish to ask them to describe the people in the illustration and have them say what's wrong. See who can come up with the longest list.

¡OJO!   There is no more new material to present in this chapter. The sections that follow recombine and reinforce the vocabulary and structures that have already been introduced.

ANSWERS

Práctica

B
1. preparamos
2. freí
3. frió
4. puso
5. sirvió
6. comimos
7. gustó
8. repitieron
9. serví
10. durmió
11. dormí

Actividad comunicativa

A Answers will vary.

🔔 Bell Ringer Review

Use BRR Transparency 2-5, or write the following on the board: Write three things you would possibly say to or ask a waiter at a café.

TEACHING THE CONVERSATION

A. 🎧 Have students close their books. Tell them that they will hear a conversation between Teresa, Paco, and a waiter. Then read the conversation to them or play Cassette 2B/Compact Disc 2.

B. After introducing the conversation, you may wish to set up a café in the classroom and have groups of students perform the conversation for the class.

C. Have students summarize the conversation in their own words.

D. After presenting the conversation, go over the **Después de conversar** activity. If students can answer the questions with relative ease, move on. Students should not be expected to memorize the conversation.

TECHNOLOGY OPTION

💿 On the CD-ROM (Disc 1, page 42), students can watch a dramatization of this conversation. They can then play the role of either of the characters and record themselves in the conversation.

Conversación

En el restaurante

TERESA: ¿Tiene Ud. una mesa para dos personas?
MESERO: Sí, señorita. Por aquí, por favor.
TERESA: ¿Es posible tener un menú en inglés?
MESERO: Sí, ¡cómo no!
PACO: Teresa, no necesito un menú en inglés. Lo puedo leer en español. (El mesero les da un menú en inglés.)
PACO: No sé por qué ella me pidió un menú en inglés.
MESERO: No hay problema. Le traigo uno en español.
PACO: Gracias.
TERESA: Pues, Paco, ¿qué vas a pedir?
PACO: Para mí, la especialidad de la casa.
TERESA: Yo también pido la especialidad de la casa.

Después de conversar

Completen.

1. ¿Para cuántas personas quiere la mesa Teresa?
2. ¿Tiene el mesero una mesa libre?
3. ¿Qué tipo de menú pide Teresa?
4. ¿Necesita un menú en inglés Paco?
5. ¿Sabe él por qué ella le pidió un menú en inglés?
6. ¿Qué va a pedir Paco?
7. Y Teresa, ¿qué pide ella?

42 ∽ *cuarenta y dos*

CAPÍTULO 2

ANSWERS

Después de conversar

1. **Teresa quiere la mesa para dos personas.**
2. **Sí, el mesero tiene una mesa libre.**
3. **Teresa pide un menú en inglés.**
4. **No, Paco no necesita un menú en inglés.**
5. **No, no sabe por qué ella le pidió un menú en inglés.**
6. **Paco va a pedir la especialidad de la casa.**
7. **Ella también pide la especialidad de la casa.**

Actividades comunicativas

A **Fuimos al restaurante.** You and your parents went to a restaurant last night. A classmate will ask you questions about your experience. Answer him or her.

B **Preferencias** Work with a classmate and discuss whether you prefer to eat at home or in a restaurant. Give reasons for your preferences.

PRONUNCIACIÓN

La consonante x

An x between two vowels is pronounced much like the English x but a bit softer. It's like **a gs: examen → eg-samen.**
Repeat the following.

exacto	**examen**
éxito	**próximo**

When x is followed by a consonant, it is often pronounced like an s. Repeat the following.

extremo   explicar   exclamar

Repeat the following sentence.
El extranjero exclama que baja en la próxima parada.

Actividades comunicativas

A Students can base their answers on any outing to a restaurant with their parents. They may wish to use the conversation on page 42 as a model.

B Students should use the verb **preferir** for this exchange.

TECHNOLOGY OPTION In the CD-ROM version of this activity (Disc 1, page 43), students can interact with an on-screen native speaker and record their voices.

TEACHING PRONUNCIATION

¡OJO! Whenever **x** is followed by a consonant in Spanish, it is pronounced as **s.** There are no exceptions to this rule.

There is, however, a variation in the pronunciation of **x** between two vowels. In some areas the **x** in the word **exacto,** for example, is pronounced like **s (esacto),** and in others it is **gs (eg-sacto).**

A. Have students repeat the words after you or the recording on Cassette 2B/Compact Disc 2. Have them imitate very carefully.

B. Have students open their books to page 43. Call on individuals to read the words and sentence carefully.

C. All model sentences on page 43 can be used for dictation.

TECHNOLOGY OPTION

In the CD-ROM version of the Pronunciation section (Disc 1, page 43), students will see an animation of the cartoon on this page. They can also listen to, record, and play back the vowels, words, and sentences presented here.

Learning From Realia

Si tienes hambre, llámanos Have students take a look at the ad to see how much of the vocabulary they already know. Ask if they can guess what **a domicilio** means *(home delivery).* The expression for *take out* is **para llevar.**

ANSWERS

Actividades comunicativas

A Answers will vary.

B Answers will vary; however, students will typically begin the conversation by asking: **¿Prefieres comer en casa o en el restaurante?**

43

National Standards

Cultures The reading about Mexican cuisine on page 44 and the related activity on page 45 familiarize students with typical Mexican food and dishes.

TEACHING THE READING

Pre-reading

A. Have students open their books and do the Reading Strategy activity on page 44. Then ask them what they think the reading is about.

B. Have students tell some things they already know about Mexican food.

Reading

A. Now have students open their books. Call on individuals to read.

B. Intersperse oral reading with some comprehension questions. Then continue reading.

Post-reading

A. Have students tell what they see on the plate at the bottom of the page.

B. Go over the **Después de leer** activity orally on page 45. Then assign it for homework. Go over the activity again the following day.

TECHNOLOGY OPTION

Students may listen to a recorded version of the **Lectura** on the CD-ROM, Disc 1, page 44.

Lecturas CULTURALES

Reading Strategy

Thinking while reading
Good readers always think while reading. They think about what the passage might be about after reading the title and looking at the visuals. They predict, create visual images, compare, and check for understanding, and continually think while the author is explaining.

LA COMIDA MEXICANA

Es muy difícil decir lo que es la comida hispana porque la comida varía mucho de una región hispana a otra.

Aquí en los Estados Unidos la comida mexicana es muy popular. Hay muchos restaurantes mexicanos. Algunos sirven comida típicamente mexicana y otros sirven variaciones que vienen del suroeste de los Estados Unidos donde vive mucha gente de ascendencia mexicana.

La base de muchos platos mexicanos es la tortilla. La tortilla es un tipo de panqueque. Puede ser de harina[1] de maíz o de trigo[2]. Con las tortillas, los mexicanos preparan tostadas, tacos, enchiladas, etc. Rellenan[3] las tortillas de pollo, carne de res o frijoles y queso.

[1]harina *flour*
[2]trigo *wheat*
[3]Rellenan *They fill*

San Miguel de Allende, México

44 ∽ *cuarenta y cuatro*

Learning From Photos

San Miguel de Allende, México Ask the following questions about the photo:

¿Dónde está la señora? ¿Está en la cocina o en el comedor?

¿Qué está haciendo ella? ¿Tortillas o arroz?

¿De qué son las tortillas? ¿De papas o de maíz?

Independent Practice

Assign any of the following:
1. **Después de leer** activity, page 45
2. Workbook, pages 19–21
3. CD-ROM, Disc 1, pages 44–45

Después de leer

A **La comida mexicana** Contesten.

1. ¿Varía mucho la cocina hispana de una región a otra?
2. ¿Dónde es popular la comida mexicana?
3. ¿De dónde vienen muchas variaciones de la cocina mexicana?
4. ¿Qué sirve de base para muchos platos mexicanos?
5. ¿Qué es una tortilla? ¿De qué puede ser?
6. ¿De qué rellenan las tortillas?

SECRETARIA DE EDUCACION, CULTURA
Y RECREACION
MUSEO CASA
"DIEGO RIVERA"
GUANAJUATO, GTO.
COOPERACION N$ 5.00

«El cultivo del maíz» de Diego Rivera

LECTURAS CULTURALES

cuarenta y cinco 〜 **45**

Después de leer

A Allow students to refer to the reading to look up the answers, or you may use this activity as a testing device for factual recall.

FINE ART CONNECTION

«El cultivo del maíz» de Diego Rivera Throughout his life Diego Rivera was vitally interested in the suffering of Mexico's poor. Ask the class why he would do a painting depicting someone cultivating corn. (Corn is extremely important to Mexico because it is the sustenance for Mexico's poor. Corn is for Mexico what potatoes, bread, or rice would be to people in other parts of the world.)

EXPANSION Show Fine Art Transparency F-2 of this painting by Diego Rivera, from the Transparency Binder. You may wish to have students read the background information accompanying this transparency and have them do the related activities.

ANSWERS

Después de leer

A **1.** Sí, la comida hispana varía mucho de una región a otra.
2. La comida mexicana es popular aquí en los Estados Unidos.
3. Vienen del suroeste de los Estados Unidos.
4. La tortilla sirve de base para muchos platos mexicanos.

5. Una tortilla es un tipo de panqueque. Puede ser de harina de maíz o de harina de trigo.
6. Rellenan las tortillas de pollo, carne de res o frijoles y queso.

LECTURA OPCIONAL 1

LECTURA OPCIONAL 1

National Standards

Cultures
This reading about Spanish cuisine and the related activity on this page familiarize students with some typical foods from Spain.

TEACHING TIPS

¡OJO! This reading is optional. You may skip it completely, have the entire class read it, have only several students read it, or assign it for extra credit.

A. Have students read the passage quickly as they look at the photos that accompany it. The photos will increase comprehension because students can visualize what they are reading about.

B. Have students discuss what information they find interesting.

Learning From Photos

Barcelona, España Have students look at the three photos on this page to see how many items they can identify.

Barcelona, España

LA COMIDA ESPAÑOLA

En España, como en México, hay tortillas también. Pero hay una gran diferencia entre una tortilla mexicana y una tortilla española. La tortilla española no es de maíz. El cocinero español prepara la tortilla con huevos. La tortilla española, que es muy típica, lleva patatas (papas) y cebollas[1].

La cocina española es muy buena y muy variada. Como España es un país que tiene mucha costa, muchos platos españoles llevan marisco y pescado. Y los cocineros preparan muchos platos con aceite de oliva.

[1]cebollas *onions*

Después de leer

A **La cocina española** Contesten.

1. ¿Cuál es la diferencia entre una tortilla española y una tortilla mexicana?
2. ¿Qué lleva la típica tortilla a la española?
3. ¿Por qué llevan marisco y pescado muchos platos españoles?
4. ¿Qué usan muchos cocineros españoles para preparar una comida?

ANSWERS

Después de leer

A **1.** La tortilla española no es de maíz. El cocinero español la prepara con huevos.

2. Lleva patatas y cebollas.

3. Muchos platos españoles llevan marisco y pescado porque España es un país que tiene mucha costa.

4. Usan aceite de oliva para preparar una comida.

LA COMIDA DEL CARIBE

En el Caribe, en Puerto Rico, Cuba y en la República Dominicana, la gente come muchos mariscos y pescado. Es natural porque Puerto Rico, Cuba y la República Dominicana son islas. Pero la carne favorita de la región es el puerco o el lechón[1]. No hay nada más delicioso que un buen lechón asado[2]. Sirven el lechón con arroz, frijoles (habichuelas) y tostones. Para hacer tostones el cocinero corta en rebanadas[3] un plátano, una banana grande, verde y dura. Luego fríe las rebanadas en manteca[4].

[1]lechón *suckling pig*
[2]asado *roast*
[3]rebanadas *slices*
[4]manteca *lard*

Humacao, Puerto Rico

Después de leer

A **¿Lo sabes?** Busquen la información.

1. algunos países de la región del Caribe
2. por qué come la gente muchos mariscos y pescado en la región del Caribe
3. una carne favorita de los puertorriqueños, cubanos y dominicanos
4. lo que sirven con el lechón asado
5. lo que son tostones

LECTURAS OPCIONALES

cuarenta y siete **47**

LECTURA OPCIONAL 2

National Standards

Cultures This reading about Caribbean cuisine and the related activity on page 47 familiarize students with some typical foods from the Spanish-speaking countries of the Caribbean.

TEACHING TIPS

¡OJO! This reading is optional. You may skip it completely, have the entire class read it, have only several students read it, or assign it for extra credit.

A. Have students read the selection to themselves.
B. Now have students do the **Después de leer** activity on page 47.

Learning From Photos

Los platos del Caribe Have students look at the top photo on this page. Point out to them that the dish in the foreground contains **arroz, tostones,** and **habichuelas rosadas.** Tell them that red beans are favored in Puerto Rico and black beans are favored in Cuba.

On the plate in the background to the right, there are **tostones, arroz blanco,** and **asopao. Asopao** is a type of stew made with rice. It has more liquid than a **paella.** There are **asopaos de pollo, de camarones,** and **de jueyes** (*land crabs*).

GEOGRAPHY CONNECTION
Humacao, Puerto Rico This town is on the western coast of Puerto Rico. The well-known resort and condominium complex **Palmas del Mar** is in Humacao.

ANSWERS

Después de leer

A **1.** **Puerto Rico, Cuba y la República Dominicana**
2. **porque son islas**
3. **el puerco o el lechón**
4. **arroz, frijoles (habichuelas) y tostones**
5. **rebanadas de plátano fritas en manteca**

Conexiones

National Standards

Connections

This reading about linguistic differences in the Spanish-speaking world establishes a connection with another discipline, allowing students to reinforce and further their knowledge of the humanities through the study of Spanish.

Comparisons

This reading on regional differences in pronunciation and vocabulary in Spanish and the related activities, which illustrate the same concepts in English, give students a better understanding of the nature of language.

¡OJO! The readings in the **Conexiones** section are optional. They focus on some of the major disciplines taught in schools and universities. The vocabulary is useful for discussing such topics as history, literature, art, economics, business, science, etc.

You may choose any of the following ways to do this reading on linguistic differences in the Spanish-speaking world.

Independent reading Have students read the selections and do the post-reading activities as homework, which you collect. This option is least intrusive on class time and requires a minimum of teacher involvement.

Homework with in-class follow-up Assign the readings and post-reading activities as homework. Review and discuss the material in class the next day.

Intensive in-class activity This option includes a pre-reading vocabulary presentation, in-class reading and discussion, assignment of the activities for homework, and a discussion of the assignment in class the following day.

LAS HUMANIDADES

EL LENGUAJE

As we already know, Spanish is a language that is spoken in many areas of the world. In spite of the fact that the Spanish-speaking world covers a large area of the globe, it is possible to understand a speaker of Spanish regardless of where he or she is from. Although there are regional differences, these differences do not cause serious comprehension problems.

However, pronunciation does change from area to area. For example, people from San Juan, Puerto Rico; Buenos Aires, Argentina; and Madrid, Spain have pronunciations that are quite different one from the other. However, the same is true of English. People from New York, Memphis, and London also have a distinct pronunciation but they can all understand one another.

The use of certain words will also change from one area to another. This is particularly true in the case of words for foods. Let's look at some regional differences with regard to vocabulary.

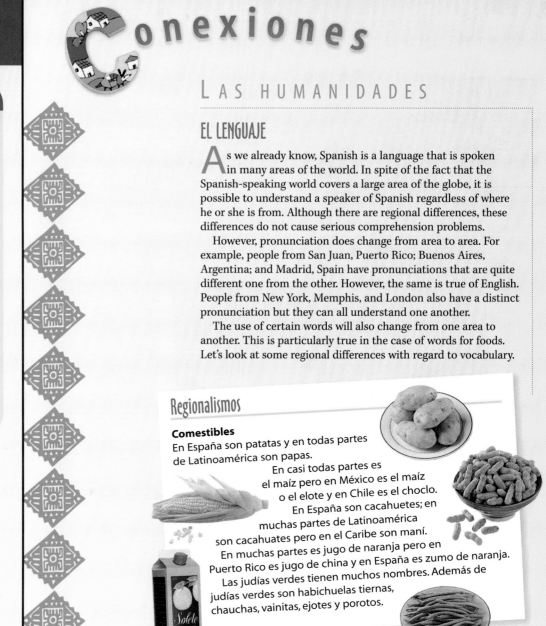

Regionalismos

Comestibles
En España son patatas y en todas partes de Latinoamérica son papas.

En casi todas partes es el maíz pero en México es el maíz o el elote y en Chile es el choclo.

En España son cacahuetes; en muchas partes de Latinoamérica son cacahuates pero en el Caribe son maní.

En muchas partes es jugo de naranja pero en Puerto Rico es jugo de china y en España es zumo de naranja.

Las judías verdes tienen muchos nombres. Además de judías verdes son habichuelas tiernas, chauchas, vainitas, ejotes y porotos.

Cosas que no son comestibles

Tomamos el autobús en España, el camión en México y la guagua en el Caribe y en las Islas Canarias.

En España todos duermen en el dormitorio o en la habitación. En México duermen en la recámara y, en muchas partes, en el cuarto o en el cuarto de dormir.

En España sacas un billete en la ventanilla y en Latinoamérica compras un boleto en la ventanilla o en la boletería.

~Después de leer~

A Hispanohablantes If any of your classmates are native speakers of Spanish, ask them to compare the way they say things. Have them share this information with you.

B El inglés There are variations in the use of English words. Discuss the following terms and where they might be heard.

1. bag, sack
2. soda, pop
3. elevator, lift
4. line, queue
5. pram, baby carriage
6. truck, lorry
7. traffic circle, rotary, roundabout
8. subway, underground

LAS HUMANIDADES
EL LENGUAJE

A. Have students read the introduction in English on page 48.

B. You may wish to have students skim this section for general interest.

C. For a more in-depth treatment, have students identify each illustrated item of food on page 48. Then have them give the additional regional names for each item. Now do the same with regard to the nonfood items in the photos on page 49.

~Después de leer~

B Ask students whether they know of additional examples in English. They might mention: purse/pocketbook.

For the Native Speaker

¿Cómo lo dices? Have native speakers make a list of at least 20 common items of food and clothing. Then have each student compare his or her list with those of the other native speakers in the class. Finally, have them make a list of the items that have different names.

ANSWERS

Después de leer

A Answers will vary. Have native speakers give a brief report to the class.

B Answers will include the following:
1. **bag:** U.S.
   sack: UK
2. **soda:** East and West Coasts, South
   pop: Midwest
3. **elevator:** U.S.
   lift: UK
4. **line:** U.S.
   queue: UK
5. **pram:** UK
   baby carriage: U.S.
6. **truck:** U.S.
   lorry: UK
7. **traffic circle:** U.S.
   rotary: New England states, Canada
   roundabout: UK
8. **subway:** US
   underground: UK

49

Actividades orales

¡OJO! Encourage students to say as much as possible when they do these activities. Tell them not to be afraid of making mistakes since the goal of the activities is real-life communication. If someone in the group makes an error, allow the others to politely correct him or her.

Let students choose the activities they would like to do.

A This activity is an excellent follow-up to the readings in Chapter 2, pages 44–47.

B **TECHNOLOGY OPTION** In the Chapter 2 Internet activity, students visit the Web sites of Spanish restaurants and "order" a meal. You may want to do this activity prior to your field trip. This activity will help familiarize students with restaurant food vocabulary. (See the Internet Connection, page 53.)

National Standards

Communities
Actividad B allows students to use their knowledge of Spanish beyond the school setting to order a meal in a Spanish restaurant.

JUEGO This is a good activity to use when students need a "break" during the class period, or as an opening or closing activity.

50

Culminación

Actividades orales

A Fuimos al restaurante. Get together with a classmate and describe some dishes from different areas of the Spanish-speaking world. Then decide what kind of restaurant or restaurants you want to go to. Tell why.

B ¡A comer! You and your classmates, accompanied by your teacher, go to a Spanish restaurant in your community and order your meal in Spanish. Try to speak only Spanish during your meal.

JUEGO La comida Mention a food category, such as meat, seafood, fruit, vegetable. Your partner will give the name of a food that belongs in that category. Take several turns each. Try to use as much of the food vocabulary you've learned as possible.

ANSWERS

Actividades orales
A Answers will vary. Students might use the names of foods and dishes from the readings on pages 44–47.

B Answers will vary, depending on the type of restaurant and its menu selections.

Student Portfolio
Have students keep a notebook containing their best written work from each chapter. These selected writings can be based on assignments from the Student Textbook and the Writing Activities Workbook. The activities on page 51 are examples of writing assignments that may be included in each student's portfolio.

See the Teacher's Manual for more information on the Student Portfolio.

Actividad escrita

A **Comidas buenas y ricas** Prepare the menu for several Spanish meals—**el desayuno, el almuerzo,** and **la cena.** Then present your menus to the class. Have the class vote on whether or not they would order your meals. Then decide who in the class should open a restaurant.

Writing Strategy

Writing a letter of complaint

When you write a letter of complaint, you must clearly identify the problem and suggest solutions; you should use a businesslike tone. You might be angry when you write a letter of complaint. But to be effective, you must control your emotions since your goal is to get the problem corrected. Your tone of voice is reflected in writing as much as it is in speech; your results will be better if you address the situation calmly and reasonably. In addition, it is important that the letter be addressed to the person who has the most authority.

¡Qué desastre!

Pretend you went to a restaurant where you had a very bad experience. The waiter didn't serve you what you ordered nor the way you ordered it. Write a letter to the management complaining about the food and the service.

CULMINACIÓN

Culminación

Actividad escrita

A Students can use the food items taught in **¡Buen viaje! Level 1,** as well as those taught in this chapter. Encourage students to list only those foods that they know how to say in Spanish.

Writing Strategy

Writing a letter of complaint

A. Have students do the Writing Strategy activity on page 51. Based on the strategy, ask students which statement in the Critical Thinking Activity below would be most effective when writing a letter of complaint.

Critical Thinking Activity

Drawing conclusions

1. **Tuvimos que esperar cinco minutos para la mesa y no pudimos leer el menú en español.**
2. **Nos gustó la comida, pero hay un problema con el servicio.**
3. **¡Su restaurante es horrible!**

TECHNOLOGY OPTION

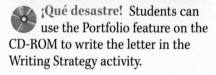

¡Qué desastre! Students can use the Portfolio feature on the CD-ROM to write the letter in the Writing Strategy activity.

Independent Practice

Assign any of the following:
1. Activities, pages 50–51
2. Workbook, **Mi autobiografía,** page 22
3. Situation Cards
4. CD-ROM, Disc 1, Chapter 2, **Juego de repaso**

ANSWERS

Actividad escrita

A Answers will vary. The selections for each meal should be logical.

Writing Strategy

Answers will vary depending on the creativity and imagination of each student. The illustration on page 51 gives clues as to what students could say in their letter.

51

VOCABULARY REVIEW

The words and phrases in the **Vocabulario** have been taught for productive use in this chapter. They are summarized here as a resource for both students and teacher. This list also serves as a convenient resource for the **Culminación** activities on pages 50 and 51. There are approximately eight cognates in this vocabulary list. Have students find them.

Teacher Notes

Vocabulario

GETTING ALONG AT A RESTAURANT

el restaurante	el menú
la mesa	la cuenta
el/la mesero(a),	la tarjeta de crédito
el/la camarero(a)	la propina
el/la cocinero(a)	el dinero

IDENTIFYING A PLACE SETTING

el vaso	el cuchillo
la taza	la cucharita
el platillo	la cuchara
el plato	el mantel
el tenedor	la servilleta

DESCRIBING SOME RESTAURANT ACTIVITIES

poner la mesa	repetir
pedir	reservar
servir	tener hambre
freír	tener sed

DESCRIBING FOOD

rico(a), delicioso(a)

IDENTIFYING MORE FOODS

la carne	el ajo
la carne de res, el biftec	la berenjena
la ternera	la alcachofa
el cerdo	el arroz
el cordero	el maíz
el pescado	la sal
los mariscos	la pimienta
los camarones	el aceite
las almejas	el vinagre
la langosta	

TECNOTUR

VIDEO

¡Buen viaje!

EPISODIO 2 ▶ En el restaurante

Cristina, Isabel y Luis van a un restaurante.

Después del almuerzo los jóvenes miran los videos que reciben de España.

CD-ROM

Expansión cultural

interNET
CONNECTION

In this video episode, Cristina, Isabel, and Luis are having lunch at a restaurant in Mexico. To visit some restaurants in cities in the Spanish-speaking world, go to the **Capítulo 2** Internet activity at the **Glencoe Foreign Language Web site:**

http://www.glencoe.com/sec/fl

La Casa de los Azulejos en la Ciudad de México es un restaurante muy popular.

TECNOTUR

cincuenta y tres ◌◌ **53**

OVERVIEW

This page previews three key multimedia components of the **Glencoe Spanish** series. Each reinforces the material taught in Chapter 2 in a unique manner.

VIDEO

The Video Program allows students to see how the chapter vocabulary and structures are used by native speakers in an engaging story. For maximum reinforcement, show the video episode as a final activity for Chapter 2.

A. Before viewing this episode, have students read the video photo captions. Ask them the following questions: **En la primera foto, ¿qué hacen? ¿Leen el menú? Y en la segunda foto, ¿de quiénes son los videos que reciben de España?**

B. Now show the Chapter 2 video episode. See the Video Activities Booklet for detailed suggestions for using this resource.

CD-ROM

A. Have students read the **Expansión cultural** photo caption on page 53.

B. In the CD-ROM version of **Expansión cultural** (Disc 1, page 53), students can listen to additional recorded information about the **Casa de los Azulejos** in Mexico City.

INTERNET

Teacher Information and Student Worksheets for this activity can be accessed at the Web site.

Video Synopsis

While on vacation in Puerto Vallarta, Luis, Cristina, and Isabel go out to lunch at an international restaurant. The waiter shows them to a table, then returns a few minutes later to take their order. All three decide on typical Mexican dishes. Isabel makes some comments about the table setting.

During lunch, they decide to look at some of the video clips that Juan Ramón has sent from Spain. In these clips we see Juan Ramón and Teresa in various locations in Spain.

TOPICS	FUNCTIONS	STRUCTURE	CULTURE
◆ Computer terminology ◆ Fax terminology ◆ Telephone terminology ◆ Telephone etiquette	◆ How to use the computer ◆ How to send a fax ◆ How to make a telephone call ◆ How to use proper telephone etiquette ◆ How to talk about habitual past actions	◆ Imperfect tense of -ar verbs ◆ Imperfect tense of -er and -ir verbs ◆ Imperfect tense of the verbs ser and ir ◆ Uses of the imperfect tense	◆ Carmen Tordesillas, a future engineer ◆ The telephone card in Spain ◆ The cellular telephone in the Spanish-speaking world ◆ Advances in computer technology

CHAPTER 3 RESOURCES

PRINT	MULTIMEDIA

Planning Resources

Lesson Plans Block Scheduling Lesson Plans	Interactive Lesson Planner

Reinforcement Resources

Writing Activities Workbook Student Tape Manual Video Activities Booklet Web Site User's Guide	Transparencies Binder Audiocassette/Compact Disc Program Videocassette/Videodisc Program Online Internet Activities Electronic Teacher's Classroom Resources

Assessment Resources

Situation Cards Chapter Quizzes Testing Program Performance Assessment	**Maratón mental** Mindjogger Videoquiz Testmaker Computer Software (Macintosh/Windows) Listening Comprehension Audiocassette/Compact Disc Communication Transparency: C-3

Motivational Resources

Expansion Activities	Café Glencoe: **www.cafe.glencoe.com** Keypal Internet Activities

Enrichment

Spanish for Spanish Speakers	

SECTION	PAGES	SECTION RESOURCES
Vocabulario Palabras 1 **La computadora** **El fax, el facsímil**	56–59	Vocabulary Transparencies 3.1 Audiocassette 3A/Compact Disc 3 Student Tape Manual, TE, pages 23–25 Workbook, page 23 Chapter Quizzes, page 11 CD-ROM, Disc 1, pages 56–59
Vocabulario Palabras 2 **El teléfono**	60–63	Vocabulary Transparencies 3.2 Audiocassette 3A/Compact Disc 3 Student Tape Manual, TE, pages 26–28 Workbook, pages 24–25 Chapter Quizzes, page 12 CD-ROM, Disc 1, pages 60-63
Estructura **Imperfecto de los verbos** **en -ar** **Imperfecto de los verbos** **en -er e -ir** **Imperfecto de los verbos** **ser e ir** **Usos del imperfecto**	64–71	Workbook, pages 26–28 Audiocassette 3A/Compact Disc 3 Student Tape Manual, TE, pages 29–30 Chapter Quizzes, pages 13–15 Computer Testmaker CD-ROM, Disc 1, pages 64–71
Conversación **Una llamada internacional**	72–73	Audiocassette 3A/Compact Disc 3 Student Tape Manual, TE, page 31 CD-ROM, Disc 1
Lecturas culturales **Futura ingeniera** **La tarjeta telefónica—una** **innovación popularísima** ***(opcional)*** **La solución a un problema de** **comunicaciones *(opcional)***	74–77	Testing Program, pages 26–27 CD-ROM, Disc 1, pages 74–77
Conexiones **La computadora *(opcional)***	78–79	Testing Program, page 27 CD-ROM, Disc 1, pages 78–79
Culminación **Actividades orales** **Actividad escrita** **Vocabulario** **Tecnotur**	80–83	**¡Buen viaje!** Video, Episode 3 Video Activities, pages 69–75 Internet Activities www.glencoe.com/sec/fl Testing Program, pages 23–26; 126; 170; 192 CD-ROM, Disc 1, pages 80–83

OVERVIEW

In this chapter students will learn to talk about computers, e-mail, and the Internet. They will also learn how to send a fax and make a telephone call in a Spanish-speaking country. Students will also learn the formation and uses of the imperfect tense. The cultural focus of the chapter is on a comparison of telephone service of yesterday and today in the Spanish-speaking world and on modern telecommunications technology.

National Standards

In Chapter 3, students will communicate in spoken and written Spanish on the following topics:
- computers, e-mail, and the Internet
- using the telephone and fax machine
- activities that they used to do

Students will provide and obtain information, express opinions, and participate in conversations dealing with computers and the telephone as they fulfill the chapter objectives listed on this page.

Pacing

Chapter 3 will require approximately six to eight days. Pacing will vary according to the length of the class, the age of your students, and student aptitude.

Block Scheduling

See the Block Scheduling Lesson Plans Booklet for suggestions on how to present the chapter material within a block scheduling framework.

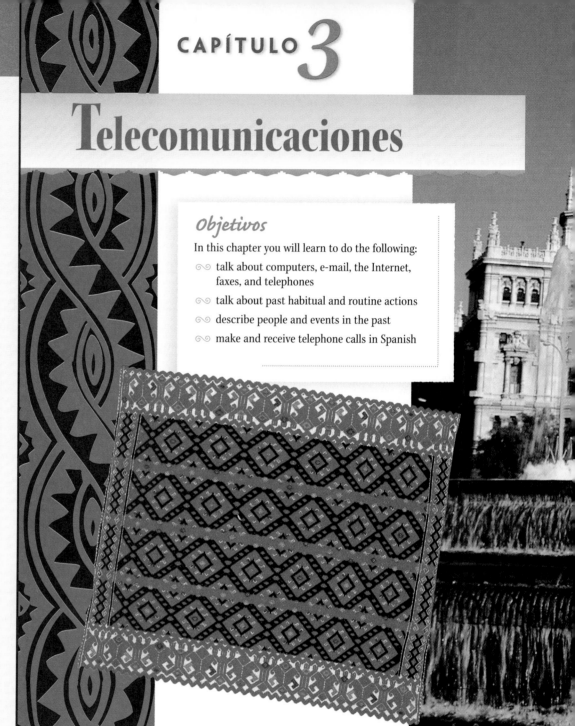

Telecomunicaciones

Objetivos

In this chapter you will learn to do the following:
- talk about computers, e-mail, the Internet, faxes, and telephones
- talk about past habitual and routine actions
- describe people and events in the past
- make and receive telephone calls in Spanish

*inter*NET
CONNECTION

The **Glencoe Foreign Language Web site** (http://www.glencoe.com/sec/fl) offers three options that enable you and your students to experience the Spanish-speaking world via the Internet:
- The online **Actividades** are correlated to the chapters and utilize Hispanic Web sites around the world. For the Chapter 3 activity, see student page 83.

- The **Correspondencia electrónica** section provides information on how to set up a key pal (pen pal) exchange between your class and a class in the Spanish-speaking world.
- At **Café Glencoe**, the interactive "after-school" section of the site, you and your students can access a variety of additional online resources, including interactive games.

cincuenta y cinco 55

Spotlight On Culture

Fotografía The photo on pages 54 and 55 shows the **Plaza de la Cibeles** with the **Fuente de la Cibeles** as its centerpiece. **La Cibeles** is to Madrid what the Eiffel Tower is to Paris and Big Ben is to London. It is the symbol of the city. The plaza is situated at the intersection of two major arteries, the Paseo del Prado and the Calle de Alcalá. The fountain was designed by the architects who designed the Paseo del Prado, Ventura Rodríguez and José Hermosilla, and was intended to be the terminus of their grand promenade.

 La Cibeles is the Cybele of Greek and Roman mythology. Cybele was primarily a nature goddess, responsible for maintaining and reproducing the wild things of the earth. She was also the guardian of cities and nations and was entrusted with the general welfare of the people. She is usually represented, as she is here, in a chariot drawn by lions.

 Behind **La Cibeles** is the main post office building, **El Palacio de Comunicaciones** (1918), designed by the architects Antonio Palacios and Joaquín Otamendi. The cathedral-like design of the building led **madrileños** to jokingly call it **Nuestra Señora de los Correos.**

Chapter Projects

Correo electrónico Your students may enjoy corresponding via e-mail with students from a Spanish-speaking country. For information on how to set up this type of project and a list of e-mail activities that correspond to each chapter of the book, go to the **Correspondencia electrónica** section of the **Glencoe Foreign Language Web site.** (See page 54 for the address.)

Postales electrónicas Your students may also send electronic postcards and greeting cards from **Café Glencoe** (www. cafe.glencoe.com).

Vocabulario

Bell Ringer Review

Use BRR Transparency 3-1, or write the following on the board:
Answer the following:
1. **¿Sabes usar una computadora?**
2. **¿Para qué usas la computadora?**
3. **¿Tienes una computadora en casa?**

TEACHING VOCABULARY

A. Have students close their books. Introduce the **Palabras 1** vocabulary using Vocabulary Transparencies 3.1 (A & B). Have students repeat each word after you or the recording on Cassette 3A/ Compact Disc 2 two or three times as you point to the appropriate illustration on the transparencies.

B. When presenting the sentences, intersperse questions to enable students to use the new words immediately. Build from simple to more complex questions. **¿Es un disquete? ¿Es la ranura? ¿Mete la muchacha un disquete en la ranura? ¿Qué mete en la ranura? ¿Dónde mete el disquete?**

La computadora

la computadora, el ordenador

el monitor, la pantalla

la impresora

el disquete

el disco compacto

el ratón

el teclado

La muchacha prende la máquina.

Ella mete un disquete en la ranura.

Ella usa la computadora para hacer las tareas. Ella entra los datos.

La muchacha no pierde los datos porque los guarda.

Después se comunica con los amigos. Usa el correo electrónico.

Cuando termina, ella apaga la máquina y saca el disquete.

56 ᕫᕍᕬ *cincuenta y seis*

Pantomime

Getting ready
If you don't have a computer in your classroom students will pantomime the actions. However, if you do have a computer, you may wish to have students actually perform the actions on the computer as you call them out.
Begin
___, levántate.
Ve a la computadora.
Indica el monitor.
Indica el teclado.

Indica el ratón.
Prende la máquina.
Mete un disquete en la ranura.
Entra los datos.
Guarda los datos.
Apaga la máquina y saca el disquete.
Gracias, ___. Puedes volver a tu asiento.

El fax, el facsímil

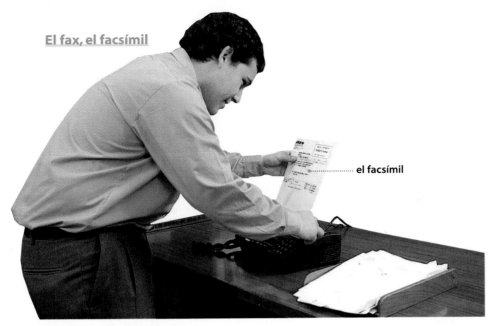

el facsímil

El señor manda el documento por fax.

Él mete el documento boca arriba.
No lo mete boca abajo.

el botón

Él pulsa el botón.

Él transmite el documento.

VOCABULARIO

57

⊹Práctica⊹

¡OJO! **Práctica** When students are doing the **Práctica** activities, accept any answer that makes sense. The purpose of these activities is to have students use the new vocabulary. They are not factual recall activities. Do not expect students to remember specific information from the vocabulary presentation when answering. If you wish, have students use the photos on this page as a stimulus, when possible.

Historieta Each time **Historieta** appears, the answers to the activity form a short story. Encourage students to look at the title of the **Historieta** since it can help them do the activity.

A It is suggested that you go over **Práctica A** orally in class with books closed. Then have students write the answers for homework and go over the activity once again the following day.

B Students can do **Práctica B** on their own and then read their answers.

C **Práctica C** can also be done as a paired activity. One student asks the question and another responds.

⊹Práctica⊹

A **¿Usas una computadora?**
Contesten personalmente.

1. ¿Sabes usar una computadora?
2. ¿Cuáles son tres partes de la computadora?
3. El monitor, ¿es de color o blanco y negro?
4. ¿Usas el correo electrónico?
5. ¿Con quién te comunicas por correo electrónico?
6. ¿Haces tus tareas en la computadora?
7. ¿Para qué clase o clases usas la computadora?
8. ¿Usas Internet?
9. ¿Tienes CD-ROM?
10. ¿Cuál es tu juego favorito en la computadora?

Caracas, Venezuela

Caracas, Venezuela

B **Los pasos a seguir** Pongan las oraciones en orden lógico.

1. Meto un disquete en la ranura.
2. Entro los datos.
3. Prendo la computadora.
4. Saco el disquete.
5. Apago la máquina.
6. Guardo los datos.

C **HISTORIETA** En la oficina

Contesten según la foto.

1. ¿Qué quiere hacer la señorita?
2. ¿Usa la señorita la máquina de fax o la computadora?
3. ¿Está prendida la máquina?
4. ¿Cómo mete el documento, boca arriba o boca abajo?
5. ¿Qué pulsa ella?

ANSWERS

Práctica

A Answers will vary but may include:

1. Sí, (No, no) sé usar una computadora.
2. Tres partes de la computadora son el monitor o la pantalla, el teclado y la impresora (el ratón).
3. El monitor es de colores.
4. Sí, (No, no) uso el correo electrónico.
5. Me comunico con mis amigos por correo electrónico.
6. Sí, (No, no) hago mis tareas en la computadora.
7. Uso la computadora para la clase de ___.
8. Sí, (No, no) uso Internet.
9. Sí, (No, no) tengo CD-ROM.
10. Mi juego favorito en la computadora es ___. (No tengo un juego favorito.)

B 3, 1, 2, 6, 4 (5), 5 (4)

C 1. La señorita quiere enviar un fax.
2. Usa la máquina de fax.
3. Sí, la máquina está prendida.
4. Mete el documento boca abajo (arriba).
5. Pulsa el botón.

Actividades comunicativas

A **¿Cómo uso la computadora?** Un(a) alumno(a) de Latinoamérica quiere aprender a usar tu computadora. Explícale.

B **¿Cómo mando un fax?** Tú y tu compañero(a) están trabajando en una oficina. Tú sabes usar la máquina de fax, pero tu compañero(a), no. Explícale.

C **Programas de software** Con un(a) compañero(a), hablen de cómo pasan el tiempo en la computadora. ¿Juegan mucho o hacen las tareas? Discutan los programas de software que Uds. usan. ¿Son los mismos o no? Luego miren la pantalla de la computadora abajo. Discutan lo que ven en el monitor. Decidan si consideran útil tal programa.

Writing Development

Have students write the answers to **Práctica C** on page 58 in a paragraph to illustrate how all of the items tell a story.

ABOUT THE SPANISH LANGUAGE

The generic word for *office* is **oficina**. However, specific kinds of offices often have specific names. The office of a lawyer is **un bufete** and a doctor's office is **una consulta**. The actual office room, especially in a business, is usually called **un despacho.**

Actividades comunicativas

¡OJO! Permit students to select the activity or activities they wish to take part in. When students do these free, unguided activities it is quite possible that they will make some structural errors just as they would when speaking on their own in the real world.

ANSWERS

Actividades comunicativas
A, B, and **C** Answers will vary.

59

Bell Ringer Review

Use BRR Transparency 3-2, or write the following on the board: Answer the following:
1. ¿Te gusta hablar por teléfono?
2. ¿Con quién hablas por teléfono?
3. ¿Hablas mucho por teléfono?
4. Cuando hablas por teléfono, ¿en qué lengua hablas generalmente?

TEACHING VOCABULARY

A. For the initial presentation of the new vocabulary, have students close their books and repeat the words orally as you point to the appropriate illustration on Vocabulary Transparencies 3.2 (A & B).
B. After the oral presentation, have students open their books and read aloud for reinforcement.

Learning From Realia

Una guía telefónica The phone book is for Málaga y Melilla. Melilla is one of two Spanish enclaves in Morocco; the other is Ceuta. Melilla was conquered by Spanish forces under the Duque de Medina Sidonia in 1496.

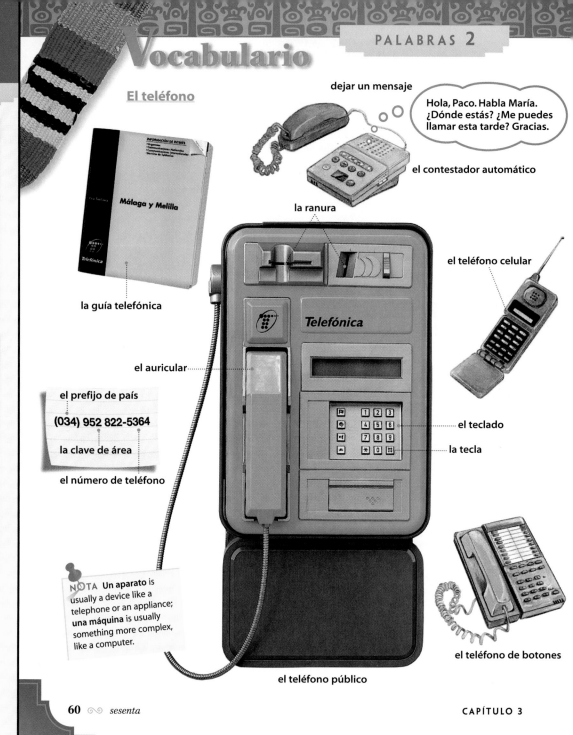

Vocabulario
PALABRAS 2

El teléfono

dejar un mensaje

Hola, Paco. Habla María. ¿Dónde estás? ¿Me puedes llamar esta tarde? Gracias.

el contestador automático

la ranura

Málaga y Melilla

la guía telefónica

el teléfono celular

el auricular

el prefijo de país

(034) 952 822-5364

la clave de área

el número de teléfono

Telefónica

el teclado

la tecla

NOTA Un aparato is usually a device like a telephone or an appliance; una máquina is usually something more complex, like a computer.

el teléfono de botones

el teléfono público

Pantomime

Begin
___, levántate.
Ven acá, por favor.
Toma la guía telefónica.
Abre la guía telefónica.
Mira adentro.
Busca un número.
Ve al teléfono público.
Descuelga.
Introduce la tarjeta telefónica.
Espera el tono.

Marca el número.
Habla.
Cuelga.
Gracias, ___. Puedes regresar a tu asiento ahora.

Rafael va a hacer una llamada telefónica.

Él descuelga el auricular.

Él introduce la tarjeta telefónica.
No introduce una moneda.

Él espera el tono.

Cuando oye el tono,
él marca el número.

El teléfono suena.

Cuando yo estaba en Madrid, vivía en una residencia para estudiantes.

¿Está Alicia?

De Rafael.

Sí, está. ¿De parte de quién?

Un momento, por favor.

La hermana de su amiga contesta.

Yo llamaba a mis padres a menudo (con frecuencia).
Yo siempre quería hablar mucho. Pero las llamadas largas costaban mucho. Eran muy caras.

C. Have students act out the short telephone conversation.

Note The sentences in this **Vocabulario** section introduce students to the forms of the imperfect. The imperfect tense will be taught in the **Estructura** section of this chapter.

Did You Know?

Residencias y colegios mayores Student **residencias**, unlike our college or university dorms, are not run directly by the universities. They are more like student hotels, although there is university oversight and students are under a certain degree of supervision. Another option for students in Spain is a **colegio mayor**, another type of student residence. Some **colegios mayores** are actually run by the universities. Others are run privately, usually by religious orders.

❖Práctica❖

A Go over **Práctica A** orally with books closed. Ask each question and call on a student to respond.

EXPANSION After going over **Práctica A**, have one student (or two) provide all the answers. The answers will give coherent directions on how to make a telephone call.

B Go over **Práctica B** with books open. You may wish to assign it first.

Writing Development

Students can write the answers to **Práctica A** in paragraph form. The answers will form a coherent story.

❖Práctica❖

A **HISTORIETA** Una llamada telefónica

Contesten.

1. ¿El muchacho hace la llamada desde un teléfono público o con un teléfono celular?
2. ¿Es un teléfono de disco o de botones?
3. ¿Qué tiene que esperar antes de marcar el número?
4. Si no sabe el número, ¿dónde puede buscar el número?
5. Si no es un número local, ¿qué tiene que marcar primero?
6. Y si es una llamada a un país extranjero, ¿qué tiene que marcar?

Lima, Perú

B **Aparatos y máquinas** Escojan.

1. Las computadoras y los teléfonos públicos tienen _____.
   a. ranuras **b.** teclas **c.** monitores
2. Si una persona no está en casa cuando llamas, puedes dejar un mensaje en el _____.
   a. teclado **b.** auricular **c.** contestador automático
3. Cuando estás en un automóvil o cuando no estás cerca de un teléfono público, puedes usar un teléfono _____.
   a. automático **b.** celular **c.** electrónico
4. Para usar cualquier máquina eléctrica, primero tienes que _____ la máquina.
   a. prender **b.** apagar **c.** marcar
5. Y cuando terminas, tienes que _____ la máquina.
   a. esperar **b.** meter **c.** apagar

ANSWERS

Práctica

A 1. **El muchacho hace la llamada desde un teléfono público.**
2. **Es un teléfono de botones.**
3. **Tiene que esperar el tono antes de marcar el número.**
4. **Si no sabe el número, puede buscar el número en la guía telefónica.**
5. **Si no es un número local, tiene que marcar la clave de área primero.**
6. **Si es una llamada a un país extranjero tiene que marcar el prefijo de país.**

B 1. **b**
2. **c**
3. **b**
4. **a**
5. **c**

C **HISTORIETA** Linda, la americanita en Madrid

Contesten.

1. ¿Dónde vivía Linda cuando era alumna en Madrid? (en una residencia para estudiantes)
2. ¿Cuándo llamaba a sus padres? (a menudo)
3. ¿Quién siempre contestaba el teléfono? (su madre)
4. ¿Quería hablar mucho Linda? (sí, siempre)
5. ¿Hablaban mucho Linda y su madre? (sí)
6. ¿Costaban mucho las llamadas cortas? (no, largas)
7. ¿Cómo eran las llamadas largas? (caras)

Una residencia para estudiantes, Madrid

Puerta del Sol, Madrid

Actividades comunicativas

A **Un número equivocado** Llamas a un(a) amigo(a) por teléfono, pero otra persona (tu compañero[a]) contesta y dice que tu amigo(a) no vive allí. Dile a la persona el número que marcaste. La persona va a decir que el número es correcto, pero la clave de área, no, y te va a dar la clave de área correcta.

1. (201) 899–6645 Felipe / (301)
2. (513) 371–8302 Andrea / (313)
3. (917) 356–3223 Tomás / (817)
4. (516) 384–1475 Inés / (517)

B **¿Cómo lo hago?** Estás en Madrid y quieres hacer una llamada telefónica. No sabes usar el teléfono público que está en la calle. Le pides ayuda a una persona en la calle (tu compañero[a]). Le preguntas a la persona cómo hacer la llamada. Él o ella te va a explicar lo que tienes que hacer.

VOCABULARIO

sesenta y tres **63**

CAPÍTULO 3
Vocabulario

C This activity has students use the imperfect tense in the third person. They can answer these questions without making any ending changes. They will learn how to manipulate the forms of the imperfect in the **Estructura** section of this chapter.

Actividades comunicativas

¡OJO! The **Actividades comunicativas** allow the students to use the vocabulary and structures of the chapter in open-ended, real-life situations. They also give students another opportunity to use words and structures from previous chapters.

Have students work on as many activities as you wish. You may also allow them to select those activities they want to do. Different groups can work on different activities.

Learning From Photos

Una residencia para estudiantes, Madrid This typical **residencia para estudiantes** is located in the city close to, but not on, the campus of the university. A **residencia** will usually provide meals, laundry facilities, reading and T.V. rooms, and a number of other amenities in addition to a bedroom.

Puerta del Sol, Madrid This telephone at Puerta del Sol has slots for coins, telephone cards, and credit cards.

ANSWERS

Práctica

C 1. **Linda vivía en una residencia para estudiantes cuando era alumna en Madrid.**
2. **Llamaba a sus padres a menudo.**
3. **Su madre siempre contestaba el teléfono.**
4. **Sí, siempre quería hablar mucho.**
5. **Sí, hablaban mucho.**
6. **No, las llamadas largas costaban mucho.**
7. **Las llamadas largas eran caras.**

Actividades comunicativas

A and B Answers will vary.

Estructura

RESOURCES

- 📁 Workbook, pages 26–28
- 📁 Student Tape Manual, TE, pages 29–30
- 🎧 Audiocassette 3A/CD2
- 📁 Quizzes 3–5, pages 13–15
- 💾 Computer Testmaker
- 💿 CD-ROM, Disc 1, pages 64–71

🔔 Bell Ringer Review

Use BRR Transparency 3-3, or write the following on the board:
Answer personally.

1. ¿A qué escuela vas ahora?
2. ¿Cuántos cursos estás tomando este semestre?
3. ¿Quién es tu profesor(a) de español?
4. ¿Te gusta la clase de español?

TEACHING STRUCTURE

✦ Talking about habitual past actions

A. Have students open their books to page 64. Read Step 1 to them aloud.

B. Read to students the definition of the imperfect in Step 2.

C. Write the **-ar** verb forms on the board. Underline the endings and have students read all forms aloud.

D. Read the model sentences aloud. Tell students to concentrate on the fact that these are things Carlos always did. Read the sentences once and then have students repeat them.

(continued on page 65)

 Talking about habitual past actions
Imperfecto de los verbos en -ar

1. In Spanish there are two simple past tenses. The preterite tense, which you have already learned, is used to state an action that began and ended at a specific time in the past. The other simple past tense is the imperfect.

2. The imperfect tense is used to describe a habitual or repeated action in the past. The exact times when the action began and ended are not important. These are the forms of regular **-ar** verbs in the imperfect.

INFINITIVE	tomar	llamar	
STEM	tom-	llam-	ENDINGS
yo	tomaba	llamaba	-aba
tú	tomabas	llamabas	-abas
él, ella, Ud.	tomaba	llamaba	-aba
nosotros(as)	tomábamos	llamábamos	-ábamos
vosotros(as)	tomabais	llamabais	-abais
ellos, ellas, Uds.	tomaban	llamaban	-aban

Carlos siempre se levantaba temprano.
Él tomaba el bus escolar a las siete.
El bus llegaba a la escuela a las siete y media.
Algunos muchachos caminaban a la escuela.
Todos los alumnos entraban a clase a las ocho.

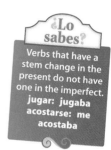

¿Lo sabes?
Verbs that have a stem change in the present do not have one in the imperfect.
**jugar: jugaba
acostarse: me acostaba**

La Ciudad de México

Learning From Photos

La Ciudad de México The students in the photo are wearing uniforms to school. Student uniforms are very common for both elementary and secondary school students in Spain and Latin America. Ask students to express their opinions regarding the pros and cons of school uniforms.

64

❖Práctica❖

A HISTORIETA Carlota iba a la escuela.

Contesten.

1. ¿Carlota se levantaba tarde o temprano todos los días?
2. ¿Carlota caminaba a la escuela o tomaba el bus?
3. ¿A qué hora llegaba a la escuela?
4. ¿Todos los alumnos caminaban a la escuela?
5. ¿A qué hora entraban todos a clase?

B HISTORIETA En el primer grado

Contesten.

1. En el primer grado, ¿tú caminabas a la escuela?
2. ¿Cómo se llamaba tu maestro(a) de primer grado?
3. ¿Qué estudiabas en el primer grado?
4. ¿Tomabas el almuerzo en casa o en la escuela?
5. ¿Dónde estaba tu escuela?
6. ¿A qué hora terminaban las clases?
7. ¿Qué te gustaba hacer por la tarde?
8. ¿Con quién jugabas?

C HISTORIETA La oficina de Carmen

Completen con el imperfecto.

Todos los veranos Carmen _____ (trabajar) en una oficina.
La oficina _____ (estar) en la ciudad. Más de treinta
personas _____ (trabajar) allí. Carmen _____ (tomar) el tren
para ir a la ciudad. El tren _____ (llegar) a las ocho. Carmen
_____ (caminar) de la estación a la oficina. Carmen _____
(usar) una computadora. Ella _____ (entrar) datos y los
_____ (revisar). Ella también _____ (mandar) copias de
documentos por fax. A las doce, Carmen y sus amigas _____
(tomar) el almuerzo. A las cinco, ellas _____ (terminar) de
trabajar. Entonces Carmen _____ (apagar) las máquinas y
_____ (regresar) a su casa.

La Ciudad de México

ESTRUCTURA

sesenta y cinco 〰 **65**

¡OJO! It is strongly recommended that you do not
give students the English equivalents
for the imperfect tense. Students
must grasp the concept that the imperfect is used to express an ongoing, continuing action. Its beginning
and end points are unimportant.
When students hear that *used to* is
an English equivalent of the imperfect, it confuses them and interferes
with the concept because *used to* implies *but no longer*, suggesting an end
at a given point in time.

❖Práctica❖

A and **B** **Práctica A** and
Práctica B can be done first orally
with books closed.

B Once students have done this
activity orally, they can open their
books and read the questions and
then answer orally for additional reinforcement.

PAIRED ACTIVITY One student
reads the question and calls on a
classmate to respond.

C Have students prepare **Práctica C** before going over it in class.

EXPANSION

After going over all the **Práctica** activities, students can retell the story
of each one in their own words.

ANSWERS

Práctica

A 1. Carlota se levantaba
temprano (tarde) todos
los días.
2. Carlota caminaba
(tomaba el bus) a la
escuela.
3. Llegaba a la escuela a
las ___.
4. Sí (No), todos los
alumnos (no)
caminaban a la escuela.
5. Todos entraban a clase
a las ___.

B Answers will vary but may
include:
1. Sí (No), en el primer
grado (no) caminaba a
la escuela.
2. Mi maestro(a) de primer
grado se llamaba ___.
3. En el primer grado
estudiaba ___.

4. Tomaba el almuerzo en
casa (en la escuela).
5. Mi escuela estaba en la
calle ___.
6. Las clases terminaban
a las ___.
7 Me gustaba ___ por la
tarde.
8. Jugaba con ___.

C 1. trabajaba
2. estaba

3. trabajaban
4. tomaba
5. llegaba
6. caminaba
7. usaba
8. entraba
9. revisaba
10. mandaba
11. tomaban
12. terminaban
13. apagaba
14. regresaba

TEACHING STRUCTURE

Talking about habitual past actions

A. Have students open their books to page 66. Read Step 1 to them.

B. Write the infinitives of the verbs **comer** and **vivir** on the board. Then cross out the infinitive endings, leaving just the stems.

C. Then write the forms of **comer** and **vivir** on the board. Underline the endings.

D. Have students read all the verb forms aloud.

E. Write all the imperfect forms of **querer** and **volver** on the board and have students repeat them.

F. Now go over Step 2. Explain to students that it is always **había**. It never changes.

Note It is better not to mention the **n** to English-speaking students because it may just confuse them. If you have native speakers in class, however, you may have to explain that **había** is also used when followed by a plural. **Habían** is wrong. This is a very common error made by native speakers.

Práctica

A After going over **Práctica A**, let students say anything they can about things they often did **cuando tenían doce años.**

Actividad comunicativa

A **El verano pasado** Mira la lista de palabras. Escoge una y pregúntale a tu compañero(a) si hacía eso con frecuencia durante el verano. Luego cambien de rol. Sigan hasta terminar con la lista.

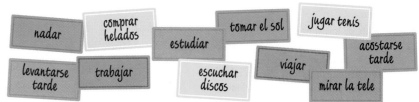

nadar | comprar helados | estudiar | tomar el sol | jugar tenis
levantarse tarde | trabajar | escuchar discos | viajar | acostarse tarde | mirar la tele

Talking about habitual past actions
Imperfecto de los verbos en -er e -ir

1. The imperfect tense forms of regular **-er** and **-ir** verbs are identical.

INFINITIVE	leer	comer	escribir	vivir	
STEM	le-	com-	escrib-	viv-	ENDINGS
yo	leía	comía	escribía	vivía	-ía
tú	leías	comías	escribías	vivías	-ías
él, ella, Ud.	leía	comía	escribía	vivía	-ía
nosotros(as)	leíamos	comíamos	escribíamos	vivíamos	-íamos
vosotros(as)	leíais	comíais	escribíais	vivíais	-íais
ellos, ellas, Uds.	leían	comían	escribían	vivían	-ían

2. The imperfect of **hay** is **había**.

No había papel en el fax.
No había mensajes en el contestador automático.

> ¿Te acuerdas?
> Remember that verbs that have a stem change in the present do not have one in the imperfect.
> **querer: quería**
> **volver: volvía**

Práctica

A **Cuando yo tenía doce años...** Contesten.

1. Cuando tenías doce años, ¿dónde vivías?
2. ¿A qué escuela asistías?
3. ¿Tenías muchos amigos?
4. ¿Podías hablar español?
5. ¿Sabías usar una computadora?
6. ¿Leías muchos libros?
7. ¿Tenías que estudiar mucho?

ANSWERS

Actividad comunicativa
A Answers will vary.

Práctica
A Answers will vary but may include:
1. Cuando tenía doce años vivía en ___.
2. Asistía a la Escuela ___.
3. Sí, (No, no) tenía muchos amigos.
4. Sí, (No, no) podía hablar español.
5. Sí, (No, no) sabía usar una computadora.
6. Sí, (No, no) leía muchos libros.
7. Sí, (No, no) tenía que estudiar mucho.

B ¿Qué hacía la gente en la oficina? Contesten según los dibujos.

1. ¿Qué hacía la señorita Flores?
2. ¿Qué hacían los señores?
3. ¿Qué hacía Eugenio?

4. ¿Qué hacía Teresita?
5. ¿Qué hacían Uds.?
6. ¿Qué hacías tú?

C HISTORIETA Las amiguitas de Ramona

Completen.

Cuando Ramona ____ (tener) cuatro años, ella ____ (vivir) en el
                    1   2
campo. Los padres de Ramona ____ (tener) una hacienda con muchos
                              3
animales. Ramona ____ (divertirse)
                  4
mucho en el campo. Ella ____
                         5
(tener) muchas amiguitas
imaginarias. Ella les ____
                       6
(servir) café a sus amiguitas. Las
amigas la ____ (querer) mucho
           7
a Ramona. Los padres no ____
                          8
(poder) ver a las amiguitas,
pero ellos ____ (saber) que,
            9
para Ramona, las amiguitas sí
____ (existir). Y Ramona nunca
 10
____ (aburrirse).
 11

En el campo, cerca de Cuzco, Perú

ESTRUCTURA

B Point out to students that questions with **hacer** are often answered with another verb.

Writing Development

Have students write **Práctica C** as a unified paragraph.

Additional Practice

Las amiguitas In **Práctica C** the word **amiguitas** appears a number of times. Ask the students why there is a **u** in **amiguitas**. Ask students what they think the diminutive of **amigo** would be.

GEOGRAPHY CONNECTION

Cuzco, la capital del imperio incaico You may wish to remind students that Cuzco is at an altitude of over 11,000 feet and that the Andes in the background are always snow-covered. Legend has it that Cuzco was founded by Manco Capac, the first of the Inca rulers.

ANSWERS

Práctica

B 1. La señorita Flores escribía.
2. Los señores leían.
3. Eugenio comía.
4. Teresita trabajaba (mandaba un fax).
5. Nosotros nos divertíamos.
6. Yo dormía.

C 1. tenía
2. vivía
3. tenían
4. se divertía
5. tenía
6. servía
7. querían
8. podían
9. sabían
10. existían
11. se aburría

Bell Ringer Review

Use BRR Transparency 3-4, or write the following on the board:
¿Sí o no?
1. Necesito una tarjeta telefónica para hacer una llamada telefónica.
2. Hoy día es posible marcar muchos números directamente.
3. Dejo un mensaje en el contestador automático.
4. Los teléfonos celulares son relativamente recientes.

Actividad comunicativa

A If there are any other Spanish-speaking teachers at your school, students may enjoy interviewing them and reporting back to the class.

TEACHING STRUCTURE

Talking about habitual past actions

A. Write the infinitives of the verbs **ser** and **ir** on the board.
B. Write all the forms on the board in paradigm order. Have students repeat all the forms after you.
C. When going over the verbs **ser** and **ir**, stress the importance of learning these verbs since they are used very often.

Práctica

A After going over **Práctica A** call on an individual student to do the exercise in its entirety, retelling the story in his or her own words.

Actividad comunicativa

A **Entrevista** Prepara una entrevista con tu profesor o profesora de español (tu compañero[a]). Entre otras cosas, tú quieres saber algo de su vida cuando asistía a la escuela secundaria. ¡Usen la imaginación!

Talking about habitual past actions
Imperfecto de los verbos **ser** e **ir**

The verbs **ser** and **ir** are irregular in the imperfect tense.

INFINITIVE	ser	ir
yo	era	iba
tú	eras	ibas
él, ella, Ud.	era	iba
nosotros(as)	éramos	íbamos
vosotros(as)	érais	íbais
ellos, ellas, Uds.	eran	iban

¿Lo sabes?

Ver is also considered irregular in the imperfect tense.
veía, veías...

Práctica

A **HISTORIETA** En la primaria

Contesten.
1. ¿Quiénes eran tus amigos?
2. ¿Adónde iban tus amigos por la tarde?
3. ¿Adónde iban Uds. los sábados?
4. ¿Quién era tu profesor(a) de español?
5. ¿Cómo ibas a la escuela?
6. ¿Quiénes eran tus maestros favoritos?

La Ciudad de Guatemala

ANSWERS

Actividad comunicativa
A Answers will vary.

Práctica
A Answers will vary but may include:
1. Mis amigos eran ___.
2. Mis amigos iban ___ por la tarde.
3. Nosotros íbamos ___ los sábados.
4. Mi profesor(a) de español era ___. (No tenía profesor[a] de español en la primaria.)
5. Iba a la escuela a pie (en carro, en el bus escolar, etc.).
6. Mis maestros favoritos eran ___.

B HISTORIETA Buenos amigos

Completen con la forma correcta de **ser** o **ir.**

Cuando Maribel y Paco ___(1)___ jóvenes, ___(2)___ muy buenos amigos. Ellos ___(3)___ a la escuela juntos. Ellos ___(4)___ a comer juntos. Maribel no ___(5)___ muy buena alumna, pero ella ___(6)___ excelente atleta. Y Paco no ___(7)___ buen atleta, pero ___(8)___ excelente alumno. Maribel ___(9)___ a casa de Paco para hacer la tarea con él. Los dos muchachos ___(10)___ al gimnasio donde Maribel le enseñaba a Paco a hacer los ejercicios. Todo el mundo decía que los dos ___(11)___ a ser buenos amigos para siempre.

Málaga, España

Actividad comunicativa

A **Los maestros de cuarto y quinto** Dile a tu compañero(a) cómo eran tus maestros(as) de cuarto y quinto grado. Tu compañero(a) va a hacer lo mismo. Después digan quiénes eran y cómo eran sus buenos(as) amigos(as) en esos grados.

Una clase de primaria

Writing Development

Have students write **Práctica B** as a unified paragraph.

Actividad comunicativa

A You may wish to have some groups present their conversations to the entire class.

Learning From Photos

Mariposa Ask the students to read the poem in the photo. You may want to help them by providing the meaning of a few unfamiliar words such as **miel**. The art on the chart should help them figure out what the poem is about.

VOCABULARY EXPANSION

The soccer ball shown in the photo on page 68 is **un balón.** A basketball is also called **un balón.** But a smaller ball such as a baseball or a jai-alai ball is **una pelota.** And just to confuse things a bit, while a golf ball is referred to as **una pelota** in Spain, it's **una bola** in most of Latin America. A billiard ball is **una bola** and so is a bowling ball.

ANSWERS

Práctica

B 1. eran   7. era
  2. eran   8. era
  3. iban   9. iba
  4. iban   10. iban
  5. era   11. iban
  6. era

Actividad comunicativa
A Answers will vary.

TEACHING STRUCTURE

Describing things in the past

A. Emphasize the fact that the imperfect is used for description in the past.

B. Ask students to open their books to page 70. Read the sentences as if they were part of an ongoing story in the past.

 **Práctica**

A Go over **Práctica A** once in class. Call on a different student to respond to each question. Then give students a couple of minutes to think about the answers and make up their own story.

B After going over **Práctica B**, call on students to give a description of don Quijote and another one of Sancho Panza.

 ## Writing Development

Have students write a description of don Quijote and Sancho Panza based on their answers to **Práctica B**.

 ## Describing things in the past
Usos del imperfecto

In addition to expressing repeated, habitual actions or events in the past, the imperfect is used to describe persons, places, objects, events, weather, and time in the past.

APPEARANCE	Victoria era alta y fuerte.
AGE	Tenía dieciséis años.
PHYSICAL CONDITION	Estaba cansada.
EMOTIONAL STATE	Pero estaba muy contenta.
ATTITUDES AND DESIRES	Ella quería ganar el campeonato.
LOCATION	Todos los equipos estaban en la cancha.
DATE	Era el ocho de octubre.
TIME	Eran las cuatro de la tarde.
WEATHER	Hacía un poco de frío.

 Práctica

A **Victoria la victoriosa** Contesten.

1. ¿Cómo era Victoria?
2. ¿Tenía veinte años?
3. ¿Estaba enferma o cansada?
4. ¿Estaba triste?
5. ¿Qué quería Victoria?
6. ¿Dónde estaban todos los atletas?
7. ¿Cuál era la fecha?
8. Y, ¿qué hora era?
9. ¿Qué tiempo hacía?

El Quijote interactivo
para toda la familia

La inmortal obra de Cervantes, ahora adaptada para niños y en CD-ROM. Supone un primer acercamiento, el niño podrá observar cómo el texto escrito y hablado da pie a secuencias animadas y posteriormente a animaciones ocultas. Contiene diccionario animado, juegos educativos y la posibilidad de seleccionar castellano / inglés.

SOFTWARE EDUCATIVO

 B **Don Quijote y Sancho Panza** Contesten.

1. ¿Quién era alto? (Don Quijote)
2. ¿Quién era bajo? (Sancho Panza)
3. ¿Quién tenía un asno? (Sancho Panza)
4. ¿Quién tenía un caballo? (Don Quijote)
5. ¿Quién era idealista? (Don Quijote)
6. ¿Quién era realista? (Sancho Panza)
7. ¿Quién quería viajar? (Don Quijote)
8. ¿Quién quería volver a casa? (Sancho Panza)
9. ¿Quién quería conquistar los males del mundo? (Don Quijote)
10. ¿Quién estaba loco? (Don Quijote)

70 ⌒ *setenta*

ANSWERS

Práctica

A 1. Era alta y fuerte.
2. No, tenía dieciséis años.
3. Estaba cansada.
4. No, estaba muy contenta.
5. Quería ganar el campeonato.
6. Estaban en la cancha.
7. Era el ocho de octubre.
8. Eran las cuatro de la tarde.
9. Hacía un poco de frío.

B 1. Don Quijote era alto.
2. Sancho Panza era bajo.
3. Sancho Panza tenía un asno.
4. Don Quijote tenía un caballo.
5. Don Quijote era idealista.
6. Sancho Panza era realista.
7. Don Quijote quería viajar.
8. Sancho Panza quería volver a casa.
9. Don Quijote quería conquistar los males del mundo.
10. Don Quijote estaba loco.

Actividades comunicativas

A **El año pasado en la escuela** Dile a tu compañero(a) las cosas que tú hacías a menudo en la escuela el año pasado. Tu compañero(a) te va a decir las cosas que él o ella hacía.

B **Eventos culturales** Tú asististe a uno de los siguientes eventos culturales. Descríbelo en detalle a un(a) compañero(a). Incluye el local, el día, la hora, etc. Di por qué querías asistir. Luego cambien de rol.

A Give students some other expressions that mean **a menudo: con frecuencia, frecuentemente, muchas veces.**

TECHNOLOGY OPTION In the CD-ROM version of this activity (Disc 1, page 71), students can interact with an on-screen native speaker and record their voices.

Learning From Realia

El Quijote interactivo (page 70) You may wish to ask students the following questions about the **software educativo:**
¿Cómo se llama el programa?
¿Quién es el autor de *El Quijote*?
¿Para quiénes fue adaptada la obra?
¿Qué contiene el programa?
¿En qué idiomas está el programa?
Eventos culturales (page 71) Have students look at the ticket to the Teatro de la Zarzuela. Two **zarzuelas** are being offered, **Gigantes y cabezudos** and **La viejecita.** The **zarzuela** is a cross between an American musical and an opera. There is spoken dialogue, song, and dance. What is unique, however, is that the setting of every **zarzuela** is Spain, and most often Madrid. The **zarzuela** is a uniquely Spanish art form.

¡**OJO**! There is no more new material to present in this chapter. The sections that follow recombine and reinforce the vocabulary and structures that have already been introduced.

RESOURCES

🎧 Audiocassette 3A/CD2

💿 CD-ROM, Disc 1, page 72

📖 Bell Ringer Review

Use BRR Transparency 3-6, or write the following on the board: You want to tell a friend something but he or she isn't home. Write a short message for your friend.

TEACHING THE CONVERSATION

A. 🎧 Have students listen to the conversation on Cassette 3A/Compact Disc 2.

B. Now have them open their books. Call on one student to read the part of Teresita and another to read the part of **la operadora**.

C. As students are reading aloud, you may wish to intersperse questions from the **Después de conversar** section.

D. Have students retell the information from the **Conversación** in their own words.

TECHNOLOGY OPTION

💿 On the CD-ROM (Disc 1, page 72), students can watch a dramatization of this conversation. They can then play the role of either one of the characters and record themselves in the conversation.

Conversación

Una llamada internacional

TERESITA:	Operadora, quiero hacer una llamada a los Estados Unidos.
OPERADORA:	¿Cómo va a pagar la llamada?
TERESITA:	Con tarjeta telefónica. ¿La puedo usar?
OPERADORA:	Claro que sí, si hay bastante dinero en la tarjeta.
TERESITA:	Sí, hay bastante. ¿Puedo marcar directamente, o tiene Ud. que poner la llamada?
OPERADORA:	Puede llamar directamente. Sólo tiene que meter la tarjeta en la ranura, marcar el «uno», que es el prefijo de los Estados Unidos, y ya está. Ud. sabe la clave de área y el número que desea, ¿no?
TERESITA:	Sí, sí. Ah, si el número está ocupado o si no contestan, no me cuesta nada, ¿verdad?
OPERADORA:	Claro que no.

Después de conversar

Contesten.

1. ¿A dónde quiere llamar Teresita?
2. ¿Qué le pregunta la operadora?
3. ¿Qué tiene Teresita?
4. ¿Hay bastante dinero en la tarjeta?
5. ¿La operadora tiene que poner la llamada?
6. ¿Dónde tiene que meter la tarjeta Teresita?
7. ¿Por qué tiene que marcar el «uno»?
8. Si nadie contesta, ¿le cuesta algo a Teresita?

72 〜 *setenta y dos*

ANSWERS

Después de conversar

1. Teresita quiere llamar a los Estados Unidos.
2. La operadora le pregunta cómo va a pagar la llamada.
3. Tiene una tarjeta telefónica.
4. Sí, hay bastante dinero en la tarjeta.
5. No, la operadora no tiene que poner la llamada.
6. Teresita tiene que meter la tarjeta en la ranura.

7. Tiene que marcar el «uno» porque es el prefijo de los Estados Unidos.
8. No, no le cuesta nada.

Actividades comunicativas

A **Los abuelos cuando eran jóvenes** Dile a tu compañero(a) todo lo que sabes de tus abuelos cuando ellos eran jóvenes: cómo eran, dónde vivían y trabajaban, qué hacían con tus padres, etc. Tu compañero(a) va a hacer lo mismo.

B **El/La operador(a) internacional** Tú eres el/la operador(a) internacional. Una persona (tu compañero[a]) llama para saber los prefijos de país y las claves de área para las ciudades a donde quiere llamar. Después cambien de rol.

PAÍS	PREFIJO DE PAÍS	CIUDAD	CLAVE DE ÁREA
Chile	56	Valparaíso	32
Ecuador	593	Quito	2
España	34	Sevilla	5
México	52	Acapulco	74
Perú	51	Lima	1
Uruguay	598	Paysandú	722

C **Las cosas que nos gustaban** Habla con tu compañero(a) de las cosas que les gustaba hacer cuando eran pequeños, pero que no les gusta hacer ahora.

 ¿Para qué lo (la) uso? With a partner, look at the following photos. One of you will make up a sentence describing something you do with one of the items in the photos. The other will guess which item you need. Take turns. Use the model as a guide.

> Quiero buscar el número de teléfono de mi tía.

> Ah, necesitas la guía telefónica.

CONVERSACIÓN *setenta y tres* 73

Actividades comunicativas

Allow students to choose the activities they would like to participate in.

JUEGO This is a good end-of-class activity.

Learning From Realia

Claves de área You may wish to ask students these questions about the area codes: **¿Qué ciudad tiene una clave de área de tres dígitos? ¿Qué ciudades tienen claves de área de un solo dígito? ¿Qué países tienen prefijos de país de tres dígitos?**

ANSWERS

Actividades comunicativas
A, B, and **C** Answers will vary.

Lecturas CULTURALES

TEACHING THE READING

Pre-reading

Give students a brief oral summary (in Spanish) of the reading.

Reading

A. Call on an individual to read two or three sentences.

B. Ask questions about the sentences just read and call on volunteers to answer them.

C. Continue in this way until the entire selection has been read and discussed.

Post-reading

Assign the reading selection and the **Después de leer** activities for homework. Go over the activities the following day.

TEACHING TIP

Call on students other than the reader to answer your comprehension questions. Most students have difficulty comprehending what they are reading when reading aloud, since they tend to concentrate on their pronunciation.

TECHNOLOGY OPTION

Students may listen to a recording of the **Lectura** on the CD-ROM, Disc 1, page 74.

Reading Strategy

Asking questions
There are several types of questions you can ask about a reading selection. A specific question is one that is answered by the information presented in just one sentence in the reading. A combined question is one that can only be answered by the information presented in several sentences or in a paragraph. An inference question is one that is not answered explicitly in the reading but can be answered by logical reasoning from the information given. You can also ask questions involving an opinion or thought—one not necessarily based on information in the reading but rather dealing with an interaction between the author and the reader. Asking any number of these different types of questions will usually aid comprehension.

FUTURA INGENIERA

Carmen Tordesillas es estudiante de ingeniería[1] en Madrid. El año que viene va a trabajar para la Compañía de Teléfonos, «la Telefónica». Ella nos habla.

—Cuando yo era niña siempre quería ser ingeniera. Los aparatos electrónicos me fascinaban, especialmente el teléfono. Mi papá me permitía hacer llamadas a casa desde los teléfonos públicos. Era una aventura. Él me levantaba. Me daba unas monedas. Yo las metía en la ranura. Cuando mami contestaba, las monedas caían[2] y empezábamos a hablar. Después de unos minutos sonaba un tono que decía que iba a terminar la conexión. Yo le pedía más monedas a papá. Cuando me daba las monedas, yo estaba contenta; si no, yo protestaba.

Hoy no necesitamos monedas, porque tenemos tarjetas telefónicas y teléfonos celulares que son muy convenientes.

Y van a ver lo que el futuro nos trae. Yo voy a trabajar en «la Telefónica». ¡Voy a crear una revolución en las telecomunicaciones!

[1]ingeniería *engineering*
[2]caían *dropped*

ESPAÑA DIRECTO →

LA MEJOR FORMA DE LLAMAR A CASA DESDE EL EXTRANJERO.

GUÍA DE CÓDIGOS

Telefónica

CAPÍTULO 3

Did You Know?

España directo Telefónica was the Spanish national telephone service until 1998 when the government monopoly ended and the company was privatized. Today Telefónica is one of the most important international telecommunications companies. It owns or has a major interest in many telephone systems in Latin America.

Después de leer

A. **Carmen Tordesillas**   Contesten.

1. Actualmente, ¿Carmen trabaja o estudia?
2. ¿Dónde quiere Carmen trabajar?
3. ¿Qué quería ser Carmen cuando era pequeña?
4. ¿Qué le interesaba mucho a la pequeña Carmen?
5. ¿Qué le permitía hacer su padre?
6. Cuando alguien contestaba, ¿qué pasaba con las monedas?
7. ¿Por qué le pedía más monedas a su padre?
8. ¿Su padre siempre le daba monedas a Carmen?
9. ¿Por qué no necesitamos monedas para llamar hoy?
10. ¿Qué va a hacer Carmen en el futuro?

Madrid, España

El Palacio Real, Madrid, España

LECTURAS CULTURALES

setenta y cinco 〜 **75**

ANSWERS

Después de leer

A 1. Actualmente, Carmen estudia.
2. Carmen quiere trabajar para la Compañía de Teléfonos.
3. Quería ser ingeniera.
4. Le interesaban mucho los aparatos electrónicos.
5. Su padre le permitía hacer llamadas a casa desde los teléfonos públicos.
6. Cuando alguien contestaba las monedas caían.
7. Porque después de unos minutos sonaba un tono que decía que iba a terminar la conexión.
8. No, su padre no siempre le daba monedas a Carmen.
9. Hoy no necesitamos monedas porque tenemos tarjetas telefónicas y teléfonos celulares.
10. Carmen va a trabajar en «la Telefónica».

LECTURA OPCIONAL 1

National Standards

Cultures
This reading and the related activity on this page familiarize students with the use of telephone cards in Spain.

Comparisons
In this selection students learn that phone cards were introduced in Spain earlier than in the United States.

TEACHING TIPS

¡OJO! This reading is optional. You may skip it completely, have the entire class read it, have only several students read it, or assign it for extra credit.

INFORMAL ASSESSMENT

You may want to give the following quiz to those students who read this selection.

Contesten.
1. ¿Dónde usaban primero la tarjeta telefónica? ¿En España o en los Estados Unidos?
2. ¿Se puede usar la tarjeta telefónica con un teléfono público?
3. ¿Qué tienen las tarjetas?
4. ¿Qué registra el microchip?
5. ¿En dónde introduces la tarjeta cuando quieres hacer una llamada?

LECTURA OPCIONAL 1

LA TARJETA TELEFÓNICA — UNA INNOVACIÓN POPULARÍSIMA

La introducción de la tarjeta telefónica ocurrió en España antes que en los Estados Unidos. Allí usan este conveniente método de hacer llamadas con teléfonos públicos. Las tarjetas tienen un microchip que registra la cantidad de dinero para llamadas. Introduces la tarjeta en la ranura del teléfono para hacer la conexión. Las tarjetas son muy convenientes. No tienes que llevar muchas monedas o ir a las tiendas para pedir cambio[1]. Y las compañías ahora tienen otro medio de propaganda. Muchas tarjetas llevan un anuncio[2] comercial. Y algunas compañías regalan tarjetas con sus anuncios a sus buenos clientes. La tarjeta telefónica es un invento muy popular.

[1]cambio *change*
[2]anuncio *advertisement, announcement*

Después de leer

A ¿Sí o no? Digan que sí o que no.
1. La introducción de la tarjeta telefónica ocurrió primero en los Estados Unidos.
2. Usan las tarjetas en los teléfonos públicos.
3. Hay un microchip en las tarjetas telefónicas.
4. Para usar las tarjetas necesitas muchas monedas.
5. Las compañías venden las tarjetas a todos sus clientes.
6. Algunas tarjetas llevan anuncios.

ANSWERS

Después de leer

A 1. No.
   2. Sí.
   3. Sí.
   4. No.
   5. No.
   6. Sí.

Learning From Realia

La tarjeta telefónica You may wish to ask students questions about the **tarjetas telefónicas:**
¿De qué país es la tarjeta de arriba?
¿Qué animal está representado en la tarjeta?
¿En qué parte de España se encuentra el animal?
¿Cuál es el valor (dinero) de la tarjeta española?
¿De qué país es la tarjeta de abajo?
¿Cuál es el valor de la tarjeta?

LECTURA OPCIONAL 2

LA SOLUCIÓN A UN PROBLEMA DE COMUNICACIONES

En los Estados Unidos y en España y las grandes ciudades de Latinoamérica, los teléfonos celulares son muy populares. Los hombres y las mujeres mantienen contacto con la oficina o con los clientes mientras viajan de casa al trabajo y viceversa. Pero en muchos pueblos de Latinoamérica el teléfono celular tiene otro rol.

Hay algunos pueblos y ciudades donde el sistema telefónico está en muy malas condiciones. Las familias tienen que esperar años para la instalación de un teléfono. Donde hay una necesidad, siempre hay una solución. En muchos pueblos y en algunas ciudades, empresarios[1] obtienen[2] teléfonos celulares y una conexión con el sistema telefónico. En las calles y las plazas hay mesitas donde un empleado se sienta con un teléfono celular. Si una persona quiere hacer una llamada, puede usar el teléfono celular y pagar al empleado. Así el pequeño empresario gana dinero y el público tiene acceso al servicio telefónico.

[1]empresarios *entrepreneurs, businesspeople*
[2]obtienen *obtain*

Lima, Perú

Después de leer

  A El teléfono celular Contesten.

1. ¿Quiénes usan mucho el teléfono celular?
2. ¿Para qué usan el teléfono celular?
3. ¿Cuál es el problema con el sistema telefónico en algunas partes de Latinoamérica?
4. ¿Qué problema tienen las familias?
5. ¿Dónde puedes ver los teléfonos celulares en partes de Latinoamérica?
6. ¿Qué puede hacer una persona que quiere hacer una llamada?

Cuzco, Perú

  B La solución a un problema Expliquen, en sus propias palabras, el uso de un teléfono celular que describen en la lectura.

LECTURAS OPCIONALES

setenta y siete ∽ **77**

CAPÍTULO 3
Lecturas

LECTURA OPCIONAL 2

National Standards

Cultures
This reading and the related activity on this page familiarize students with the use of cell phones in Latin America.

Comparisons
In this selection students learn that because of the poor condition of the phone system in some areas of Latin America, people who are otherwise without a phone can pay to make calls from cell phones provided on the street by enterprising business-people.

TEACHING TIPS

You may wish to explain to students that in some areas the phone is not necessarily a cellular phone. They actually have a regular phone installed and people line up to use it and pay for each call.

Learning From Photos

Cuzco, Perú The beautiful Cathedral of Cuzco was built between 1594 and 1654. It was designed by the Spanish architect Francisco Becerra.

ANSWERS

Después de leer

A 1. los hombres y las mujeres que trabajan en oficinas
2. para mantenerse en contacto con la oficina o con los clientes mientras viajan de casa al trabajo y viceversa
3. El sistema telefónico está en muy malas condiciones.
4. Las familias tienen que esperar años para la instalación de un teléfono.

5. en mesitas en calles y plazas
6. Puede usar el teléfono celular y pagar al empleado en las mesitas.

B Answers will vary.

77

¡OJO! This reading on computers is optional. You may choose any of the following ways to do it with your students.

Independent reading Have students read the selection and do the post-reading activities as homework, which you collect. This option is least intrusive on class time and requires a minimum of teacher involvement.

Homework with in-class follow-up Assign the reading and post-reading activities as homework. Review and discuss the material in class the next day.

Intensive in-class activity This option includes a pre-reading vocabulary presentation, in-class reading and discussion, assignment of the activities for homework, and a discussion of the assignment in class the following day.

Conexiones

LA TECNOLOGÍA

LA COMPUTADORA

It's hard to imagine life before the computer and the fax machine. The computer has revolutionized travel, medicine, architecture, the military, banking, and commerce. Hardly a field has been unaffected by computers. Even agriculture and the arts make extensive use of the new technology. The changes have been tremendous. Because the United States has led the way in computer science, much of the vocabulary used worldwide is in English or derived from English. Let's read about some of these changes in technology and the prevalence of English in this field.

Los avances en las telecomunicaciones

Las computadoras de hace treinta años eran enormes. Una computadora antigua, como la original ENIAC de 1946, procesaba menos datos que un p.c. moderno y llenaba toda una sala. Hoy hay computadoras portátiles que pesan menos de 2 kilos. Lo que ha facilitado el progreso en las computadoras es la «miniaturización». Un solo microchip puede almacenar[1] miles y miles de datos. Los primeros aparatos de transmisión de facsímil también eran muy grandes y las copias que salían en el destino muchas veces no se podían leer.

[1]almacenar *store*

Computadora ENIAC

Learning From Photos

Computadora ENIAC ENIAC stood for *Electronic Numerical Integrator and Computer*. ENIAC, with its thousands of electron tubes, was the first electronic digital computer.

Laura Ballesteros trabaja en uno de los ministerios del gobierno chileno. Ella es recepcionista. El edificio es del siglo XIX, pero los aparatos que usa Laura son muy modernos. Ella tiene una computadora y un fax. En el colegio Laura estudiaba inglés. Buena idea, porque hay mucho inglés en el vocabulario de la informática². Por ejemplo, tienes que hacer «clic» en un «icono» para tener acceso a un programa de «software». Y un «virus» puede infectar los programas.

Aquí hay otros ejemplos del predominio del inglés en el mundo de las computadoras: monitor, datos, disquete, memoria, documentación, drive, formateo, site de Internet. ¿Sabes lo que son en inglés?

²**informática** *computer science*

Edificio del siglo XIX

Interior del mismo edificio

⤳Después de leer⤳

A **¿Cómo se llama… ?**
Den la palabra en español.

1. icon
2. access
3. memory
4. program
5. click
6. data

B **¿Qué es?** Identifiquen.

1. el proceso de hacer muy pequeño un aparato u otra cosa
2. una copia exacta y precisa
3. la pantalla como la de un televisor en donde proyectan la información de la computadora
4. el disco pequeño para guardar datos que pueden sacar de la computadora
5. el disco grande con mucha memoria dentro de la computadora
6. una computadora muy pequeña que pueden llevar de viaje

LA TECNOLOGÍA

LA COMPUTADORA

Since many students are interested in computers you may wish to have all students scan or read this selection quickly just to get some general information and acquaint themselves with some vocabulary for receptive purposes.

Additional Practice

¿Qué quiere decir? You may wish to ask students what the following computer terms mean in English:

- **procesar**
- **tarjeta de sonido**
- **micrófono sobremesa**
- **placa base**
- **salidas**

ANSWERS

Después de leer

A 1. **icono**
2. **acceso**
3. **memoria**
4. **programa**
5. **clic**
6. **datos**

B 1. **la «miniaturización»**
2. **un fax**
3. **el monitor**
4. **el disquete**
5. **el drive**
6. **una computadora portátil**

79

Actividades orales

 ¡OJO! These **Actividades** are cumulative. They encourage students to use any Spanish they have already learned but focus on the vocabulary and structures of this particular chapter.

Allow students to select the activity or activities they wish to participate in.

 JUEGO You may wish to do this game as a whole-class activity.

Student Portfolio

Have students keep a notebook containing their best written work from each chapter. These selected writings can be based on assignments from the Student Textbook and the Writing Activities Workbook. The two activities on page 81 are examples of writing assignments that may be included in each student's portfolio.

In the Workbook, students will develop an organized autobiography **(Mi autobiografía).** These workbook pages may also become a part of their portfolio. See the Teacher's Manual for more information on the Student Portfolio.

# Culminación

⟡ Actividades orales ⟡

A **El contestador automático** Tú y tu compañero(a) tienen muchos amigos de habla española. Cada uno(a) de Uds. debe pensar en un mensaje en español para el contestador automático. Comparen sus mensajes y escojan uno para usar en el contestador automático.

B **Una persona famosa** Piensa en una persona famosa. Tú eres la persona. Dile a tu compañero(a) cómo eras y las cosas que hacías. Tu compañero(a) adivina quién eres. Luego, tu compañero(a) va a pensar en otra persona y va a hacer lo mismo.

C **¿Qué pasa?** Con un(a) compañero(a), miren las fotos. Cada uno(a) va a escoger una y explicar lo que pasa.

a.

b.

c.

JUEGO **«El teléfono»** Divide the class into teams by rows. Using the imperfect, the last person in each row will whisper to the person in front of him or her one sentence about what he or she always did in the past. Each person will whisper the same sentence to the next person until the message reaches the front of the row. The first person in each row will say the sentence to the class. The team whose final sentence most clearly resembles the original wins.

Actividad escrita

A. **Correo electrónico** Tú recibes el siguiente mensaje por correo electrónico. Responde.

```
Message Composition                              eperez@anon.com
Subject: ¡Hola!
▽ Addressing                          Attachments
    Mail To: smith@anon.com
        Cc:

¡Hola! Yo soy Engracia Pérez Toral. Soy venezolana, de Caracas, la capital. En mi colegio no
tenemos fax ni computadoras. Te mando el correo electrónico desde la oficina de mi mamá.
¿Qué máquinas o aparatos electrónicos tienes en tu escuela? ¿Para qué los usas? ¿Qué aparatos
recomiendas? Aquí van a comprar algunas máquinas. Tus recomendaciones van a ser muy
importantes. Muchas gracias. Escribe pronto.

Engracia
```

Writing Strategy

Expository writing

Expository writing is writing that explains and informs. It helps one understand a topic. Two important expressions to think about while writing an expository piece are "how to" and "why." Use familiar terms in your definitions and descriptions. Be careful not to omit important facts and steps. Be certain not to present steps out of order. These measures will help you present a clear and concise explanation that readers will find interesting and informative.

Un trabajo interesante

You had a job this past summer with a service organization in the Hispanic community in your town. You got the job because you speak Spanish. Since you've never worked in an office before, you were excited about learning to use equipment that was all new to you. Write to Octavio, your Peruvian pen pal and explain some of the things you did in the office and what equipment you used. Since you know that Octavio has never worked in an office and is not familiar with office machines, be as clear and logical as you can in your explanation.

Actividad escrita

A Have students edit each others' e-mail messages.

Writing Strategy

Expository Writing

A. Have students read the Writing Strategy on page 81.
B. You may wish to give less able students a somewhat less inclusive topic. Some suggestions:
  · how to make a call from a public phone
  · how to send a fax
  · how to use a computer
C. Have each student exchange his or her letter with a classmate. The classmate can then provide feedback on whether the writing in the letter is clear and logical.

TECHNOLOGY OPTION

 For information on how to set up a keypal (pen pal) exchange between your class and a class in a Spanish-speaking country, go to the **Correspondencia electrónica** section at the **Glencoe Foreign Language Web site** (http://www. glencoe.com/sec/fl).

ANSWERS

Actividad escrita
A Answers will vary.

Writing Strategy
Answers will vary.

VOCABULARY REVIEW

The words and phrases in the **Vocabulario** have been taught for productive use in this chapter. They are summarized here as a resource for both student and teacher. This list also serves as a convenient resource for the **Culminación** activities on pages 80 and 81. There are approximately 15 cognates in this vocabulary list. Have students find them.

Teacher Notes

Vocabulario

DESCRIBING A COMPUTER

la computadora, el ordenador	el ratón
el teclado	la impresora
el monitor, la pantalla	la ranura
el disquete	el correo electrónico
el disco compacto	el CD-ROM
	Internet

DESCRIBING COMPUTER ACTIVITIES

prender la máquina	comunicarse
meter un disquete	terminar
entrar los datos	apagar
hacer las tareas	sacar
guardar	

DESCRIBING HOW TO SEND A FAX

el facsímil, el fax	boca abajo
el aparato	mandar, transmitir
el documento	meter
boca arriba	pulsar el botón

DESCRIBING A TELEPHONE

el teléfono público	la tecla
la ranura	el teléfono celular
el auricular	el contestador automático
el disco	dejar un mensaje
el teléfono de botones	

DESCRIBING TELEPHONE NUMBERS

la guía telefónica	la clave de área
el prefijo de país	el número de teléfono

MAKING A TELEPHONE CALL

hacer una llamada telefónica, llamar	marcar el número
descolgar el auricular	sonar
introducir la tarjeta telefónica	contestar
	¿Está... ?
oír el tono	¿De parte de quién?

OTHER USEFUL EXPRESSIONS

a menudo
con frecuencia

ABOUT THE SPANISH LANGUAGE

The Mazatlán, México telephone directory shown here is called a **Directorio telefónico**. Ask students if they remember what the Málaga and Melilla (page 60) phone book was called (**Guía telefónica**). This is a good opportunity to remind students that different terms are used in different Spanish-speaking countries. Ask them if they can think of any examples in English of different ways of saying things in different places.

Independent Practice

Assign any of the following:
1. Activities, pages 80–81
2. Workbook, page 32
3. Situation Cards
4. CD-ROM, Disc 1, Chapter 3, **Juego de repaso**

TECNOTUR

VIDEO

¡Buen viaje!

EPISODIO 3 ▶ Telecomunicaciones

Juan Ramón necesita reparar su computadora (ordenador).

Teresa le enseña a Juan Ramón cómo hacer una llamada telefónica a México.

CD-ROM

Expansión cultural

NUEVO CURSO DE...
Mantenimiento y
REPARACION de PC's

Sea su propio jefe. Iníciese en esta nueva carrera de gran porvenir estudiando sin salir de su casa o en sus ratos libres. No hay técnico más requerido por cualquier empresa que el experto en mantenimiento de PC's -la herramienta universal más importante e indispensable.

Hemphill Schools.
Primaria en Educación a Distancia

MARQUE SOLO UN CURSO

Las computadoras son un elemento importante en el mundo hispano.

 inter**NET** CONNECTION

In this video episode Juan Ramón and Teresa call their friends in Mexico from Spain and receive an answer by e-mail. To find out how to set up an e-mail correspondence with teens in the Spanish-speaking world, go to the **Capítulo 3 Internet** activity at the Glencoe Foreign Language Web site:

http://www.glencoe.com/sec/fl

TECNOTUR

ochenta y tres ∽ **83**

This page previews three key multimedia components of the **Glencoe Spanish** series. Each reinforces the material taught in Chapter 3 in a unique manner.

 VIDEO

The Video Program allows students to see how the chapter vocabulary and structures are used by native speakers in an engaging story. For maximum reinforcement, show the video episode as a final activity for Chapter 3.

A. Before viewing the episode ask students: **¿En qué ciudad están Teresa y Juan Ramón? ¿Cuál vive en Madrid? ¿Cuál es de los Estados Unidos? ¿Con quiénes van a hablar en México?**

B. Now show the episode. See the Video Activities Booklet for detailed suggestions for using this resource.

 CD-ROM

A. Have students read the ad in the **Expansión cultural** photo. You may wish to make photocopies of this page so students can fill out the form.

B. In the CD-ROM version of **Expansión cultural** (Disc 1, page 83), students can listen to additional recorded information about the importance of computers in the Spanish-speaking world.

 INTERNET

Teacher Information and Student Worksheets for this activity can be accessed at the Web site.

Video Synopsis

In this episode Teresa takes Juan Ramón to an electronics repair shop in downtown Madrid to get his computer fixed. The technician says he will have to leave the computer for about a week. On their way home, they decide to call Cristina, Luis, and Isabel at the de la Rosa home in Mexico City.

Teresa shows Juan Ramón how to make an international call from a pay phone, using a phone card. The call goes through, but they only succeed in leaving a message for their friends on the de la Rosa family's answering machine.

Chapter 4 Overview ◆◆◆◆◆◆◆◆◆◆◆◆◆◆◆◆◆◆◆◆

SCOPE AND SEQUENCE pages 84–113

TOPICS	FUNCTIONS	STRUCTURE	CULTURE
◆ Men's clothing and apparel ◆ Women's clothing and apparel ◆ Food ◆ Quantities, prices, and sizes	◆ How to shop for clothing ◆ How to shop for food ◆ How to differentiate between coninuous habitual past actions and those completed at a definite time ◆ How to express two past actions in the same sentence	◆ Preterite versus imperfect ◆ Two actions in the same sentence ◆ Verbs such as **querer** and **creer** in the past ◆ The passive voice with **se**	◆ Shopping in the Spanish-speaking world ◆ The traditional market at Chichicastenango ◆ The science of marketing ◆ **Vistas de Chile**

CHAPTER 4 RESOURCES

PRINT	MULTIMEDIA

Planning Resources

PRINT	MULTIMEDIA
Lesson Plans Block Scheduling Lesson Plans	Interactive Lesson Planner

Reinforcement Resources

PRINT	MULTIMEDIA
Writing Activities Workbook Student Tape Manual Video Activities Booklet Web Site User's Guide	Transparencies Binder Audiocassette/Compact Disc Program Videocassette/Videodisc Program Online Internet Activities Electronic Teacher's Classroom Resources

Assessment Resources

PRINT	MULTIMEDIA
Situation Cards Chapter Quizzes Testing Program Performance Assessment	**Maratón mental** Mindjogger Videoquiz Testmaker Computer Software (Macintosh/Windows) Listening Comprehension Audiocassette/Compact Disc Communication Transparency: C-4

Motivational Resources

PRINT	MULTIMEDIA
Expansion Activities	Café Glencoe: www.cafe.glencoe.com Keypal Internet Activities

Enrichment

PRINT	MULTIMEDIA
Spanish for Spanish Speakers	Fine Art Transparency: F-3

Chapter 4 Planning Guide

SECTION	PAGES	SECTION RESOURCES
Vocabulario Palabras 1 **La tienda de ropa para caballeros** **La tienda de ropa para señoras** **En la zapatería; En la joyería**	86–89	Vocabulary Transparencies 4.1 Audiocassette 3B/ Compact Disc 3 Student Tape Manual, TE, pages 35–38 Workbook, pages 33–34 Chapter Quizzes, page 16 CD-ROM, Disc 1, pages 86-89
Vocabulario Palabras 2 **La compra de comestibles**	90–93	Vocabulary Transparencies 4.2 Audiocassette 3B/ Compact Disc 3 Student Tape Manual, TE, pages 38–40 Workbook, pages 35–36 Chapter Quizzes, page 17 CD-ROM, Disc 1, pages 90-93
Estructura **El pretérito y el imperfecto** **Dos acciones en una oración** **Verbos como querer y creer en el pasado** **La voz pasiva con se**	94–101	Workbook, pages 37–41 Audiocassette 3B/Compact Disc 3 Student Tape Manual, TE, pages 41–42 Chapter Quizzes, pages 18–21 Computer Testmaker CD-ROM, Disc 1, pages 94–101
Conversación **Naranjas para abuelita**	102–103	Audiocassette 3B/Compact Disc 3 Student Tape Manual, TE, pages 42–43 CD-ROM, Disc 1
Lecturas culturales **De compras** **El mercado de Chichicastenango** *(opcional)*	104–107	Testing Program, page 32 CD-ROM, Disc 1, pages 104–107
Conexiones **El mercadeo** *(opcional)*	108–109	Testing Program, page 33 CD-ROM, Disc 1, pages 108–109
Culminación **Actividades orales** **Actividades escritas** **Vocabulario** **Tecnotur**	110–113	**¡Buen viaje!** Video, Episode 4 Video Activities, pages 76–80 Internet Activities **www.glencoe.com/sec/fl** Testing Program, pages 28–32; 127; 171; 193 CD-ROM, Disc 1, pages 110–113

OVERVIEW

In this chapter students will learn about shopping for clothing and jewelry, as well as about grocery shopping in different types of markets. Students will learn the difference between the preterite and imperfect, how to express feelings in the past, and how to talk in general terms using the passive voice. The cultural focus of the chapter is on grocery shopping in the Spanish-speaking world.

National Standards

In Chapter 4 students will learn to communicate in spoken and written Spanish on the following topics:
- buying clothing, jewelry, and food
- asking for sizes, amounts, and prices
- grocery shopping in Spanish-speaking countries

Students will obtain and provide information about these topics and engage in conversations that would typically take place in clothing stores and in grocery stores or traditional markets as they fulfill the chapter objectives listed on this page.

CAPÍTULO 4

De tiendas

Objetivos

In this chapter you will learn to do the following:

- ∽ shop for apparel and food in Spanish-speaking countries
- ∽ ask for the quantities and sizes you want
- ∽ find out prices
- ∽ talk about different types of past actions
- ∽ talk in general terms about what is done
- ∽ talk about shopping practices in Spanish-speaking countries

interNET CONNECTION

The **Glencoe Foreign Language Web site** (http://www.glencoe.com/sec/fl) offers three options that enable you and your students to experience the Spanish-speaking world via the Internet:
- The online **Actividades** are correlated to the chapters and utilize Hispanic Web sites around the world. For the Chapter 4 activity see student page 113.
- The **Correspondencia electrónica** section provides information on how to set up a keypal (pen pal) exchange between your class and a class in the Spanish-speaking world.
- At **Café Glencoe**, the interactive "after-school" section of the site, you and your students can access a variety of additional online resources.

Spotlight On Culture

Fotografía The Gucci store is at the corner of Amberes and Hamburgo streets in the Zona Rosa **colonia** or section of Mexico City. The Zona Rosa is one of the most elegant residential neighborhoods of Mexico City. The shops are very upscale, with the same international boutiques, such as Gucci, as are found in Beverly Hills or on Fifth Avenue. Many streets in the Zona Rosa are named after the major cities of other countries.

Pacing

Chapter 4 will require approximately eight to ten days. Pacing will vary according to the length of the class, the age of your students, and student aptitude.

Block Scheduling

The extended time frame provided by block scheduling affords you the opportunity to implement a greater number of activities and projects to motivate and involve your students. See the Block Scheduling Lesson Plans Booklet for suggestions on how to present the chapter material within a block scheduling framework.

Chapter Projects

Anuncios Have students prepare some magazine ads for clothing.

Mi comida favorita Tell students that, as they progress through the chapter, they are to keep track of the names of their favorite foods as they learn them. This vocabulary is important since these are the words students will probably use most when ordering in restaurants or food shopping. At the end of the chapter, have students make up their own personal grocery lists and ideal restaurant menus.

ochenta y cinco **85**

🔔 Bell Ringer Review

Use BRR Transparency 4-1 or write the following on the board: List the items of clothing you typically wear to school.

TEACHING VOCABULARY

A. Have students close their books. Use Vocabulary Transparencies 4.1 (A & B) for the initial presentation of vocabulary. Point to each item and have students repeat after you or the recording on Cassette 3B/Compact Disc 3.

B. After presenting the vocabulary orally, have students open their books and read for additional reinforcement.

C. When going over the sentences, intersperse with questions such as: **¿Fue José a la tienda de ropa? ¿Adónde fue? ¿Qué miró en el escaparate? ¿Dónde miró la ropa? ¿Qué había en el escaparate? A José, ¿le gustó el traje?**

D. Have students act out the mini-conversation on this page.

Vocabulario

La tienda de ropa para caballeros

la ropa interior

los calcetines

el pañuelo

el abrigo

el traje

el impermeable, la gabardina

el escaparate

José fue a una tienda de ropa.
Miró la ropa en el escaparate.
En el escaparate había un traje.
A José le gustó el traje.

José entró en la tienda.
Se probó el traje.
Se miró en el espejo.

La tienda de ropa para señoras

la manga corta

el saco, la chaqueta

la bufanda

el suéter

el bolsillo

la manga larga

la blusa

el cinturón

el vestido

el pantalón

los botones

María fue a la tienda de ropa.
Quería comprar un suéter.

¿En qué puedo servirle?

Quisiera un suéter gris.

Su tamaño, por favor.

Mediano. (38)

VOCABULARY EXPANSION

Students may wish to know the names of articles of **ropa interior**:

Hombres
los calzoncillos	*underpants*
la camiseta	*undershirt*

Mujeres
la lencería	*lingerie*
las bragas, los pantis, el calzón	*panties*
el sostén	*bra*

ABOUT THE SPANISH LANGUAGE

The names of articles of clothing vary from country to country. For example, *sport coat:* **la americana, el saco, la chaqueta;** *men´s suit:* **el traje, el terno;** *sweater:* **el jersey, el suéter, la chompa, el pulóver.**

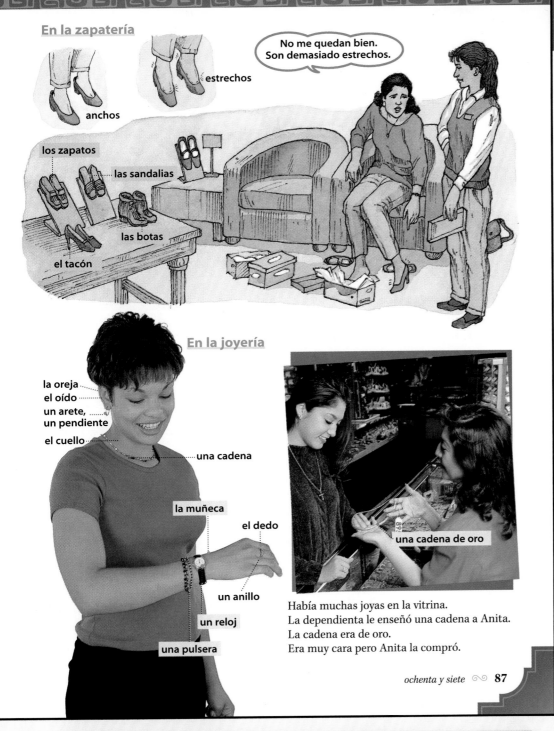

En la zapatería

estrechos

anchos

No me quedan bien.
Son demasiado estrechos.

los zapatos

las sandalias

las botas

el tacón

En la joyería

la oreja
el oído
un arete,
un pendiente
el cuello

una cadena

la muñeca

el dedo

un anillo

un reloj

una pulsera

una cadena de oro

Había muchas joyas en la vitrina.
La dependienta le enseñó una cadena a Anita.
La cadena era de oro.
Era muy cara pero Anita la compró.

ochenta y siete ∾ **87**

E. You can use gestures and facial expressions to help convey the meaning of **No me quedan bien. Son demasiado estrechos.**

F. You can also use a student or yourself to teach or reinforce: **la oreja (el oído), el cuello, la muñeca, el dedo.**

ABOUT THE SPANISH LANGUAGE

You may wish to remind students that **la oreja** is only the outer ear. The ear in the sense of the inner ear and/or the sense of hearing is **el oído**. An earache is **un dolor de oídos**.

Pantomime

Begin

Atención, todos.
Si Uds. llevan un artículo que yo digo, levanten la mano.
Veo un suéter.
Veo una blusa con mangas largas (cortas).
Veo un reloj.
Veo una pulsera.
Veo unas botas (sandalias).
Veo calcetines blancos (negros).
Veo un cinturón.

Veo aretes.
Veo una cadena.
Gracias. Bien hecho.

❖**Práctica**❖

 Práctica When students are doing the **Práctica** activities, accept any answer that makes sense. The purpose of these activities is to have students use the new vocabulary. They are not factual recall activities. Do not expect students to remember specific information from the vocabulary presentation when answering. If you wish, have students use the photos on this page as a stimulus, when possible.

Historieta Each time **Historieta** appears, it means that the answers to the activity form a short story. Encourage students to look at the title of the **Historieta** since it can sometimes help them do the activity.

A and **B** Do **Práctica A** and **Práctica B** with books open.

Did You Know?

La bufanda The **bufanda** is an important article of clothing in Hispanic countries. At the first sign of a chill, people will put on a scarf to protect against a cold or sore throat. It is very common to see men in a suit or sport coat with a scarf wrapped around their neck.

❖**Práctica**❖

A ¿Qué es? Identifiquen.

B La ropa que llevamos Escojan.

1. Es el verano y hace calor. Tadeo quiere comprar _____.
   a. un abrigo   b. una camisa de mangas largas
   c. una camisa de mangas cortas
2. Llevamos _____ cuando llueve.
   a. una bufanda   b. un impermeable   c. sandalias
3. _____ tiene botones.
   a. Un calcetín   b. Una blusa   c. Un pañuelo
4. Llevo _____ cuando voy a la playa.
   a. zapatos   b. sandalias   c. botas
5. Es necesario llevar _____ con algunos pantalones.
   a. corbata   b. calcetines   c. cinturón
6. Los zapatos que está llevando Elena tienen un tacón muy _____.
   a. largo   b. caro   c. alto
7. Isabel no compró los zapatos porque _____.
   a. le quedaban bien   b. eran un poco estrechos
   c. le gustaban
8. Uno puede llevar _____ en el dedo.
   a. una cadena   b. un arete   c. un anillo
9. Uno lleva una pulsera en _____.
   a. la oreja   b. la muñeca   c. el cuello

AJORICA
Joyas y Perlas

Colgante / Pendientes 14.500 Ptas.

ANSWERS

Práctica

A 1. un reloj
   2. unos calcetines
   3. una manga (larga)
   4. un cinturón
   5. unas botas
   6. un saco (una chaqueta)
   7. un botón
   8. una bufanda
   9. unos aretes (pendientes)
   10. un suéter

B 1. c
   2. b
   3. b
   4. b
   5. c
   6. c
   7. b
   8. c
   9. b

C HISTORIETA En la tienda de ropa

Contesten según se indica.

1. ¿Adónde fue Juan? (a la tienda de ropa)
2. ¿Qué vio en el escaparate? (un traje)
3. ¿Le gustó? (sí, mucho)
4. ¿De qué color era? (azul oscuro)
5. ¿Cuántos botones tenía la chaqueta? (tres)
6. ¿Entró Juan en la tienda? (sí)
7. ¿Con quién habló? (el dependiente)
8. ¿Qué le enseñó el dependiente? (el traje que vio en el escaparate)
9. ¿Qué hizo Juan? (se probó el traje)
10. ¿Cómo le quedó? (muy bien)

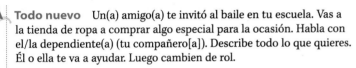

Málaga, España

D Preguntas personales   Contesten.

1. La última ropa que compraste, ¿dónde la compraste?
2. ¿Te atendió un dependiente?
3. ¿Viste el artículo que querías en una vitrina?
4. ¿Qué artículos de ropa te enseñó el dependiente?
5. ¿Tenían lo que querías en tu tamaño?
6. ¿Cuánto te costó?

Actividades comunicativas

A Todo nuevo   Un(a) amigo(a) te invitó al baile en tu escuela. Vas a la tienda de ropa a comprar algo especial para la ocasión. Habla con el/la dependiente(a) (tu compañero[a]). Describe todo lo que quieres. Él o ella te va a ayudar. Luego cambien de rol.

JUEGO   ¿Qué es?   Piensa en un artículo de ropa o en algo que ves en una joyería. Descríbelo a tu compañero(a). Él o ella va a adivinar lo que estás describiendo. Luego cambien de rol. Puedes usar el modelo como guía.

Lo llevo en la muñeca y lo uso para saber la hora.

¡Es un reloj!

C You can do **Práctica C** once giving the cues and a second time without the cues. When not giving cues, accept any answer that makes sense.

D You can do **Práctica D** as a paired activity. One student can ask the questions and another can respond.

EXPANSION   After going over **Práctica D,** have one student retell the story in his or her own words.

Writing Development

After going over **Práctica C,** have students write the answers in an organized paragraph.

Actividades comunicativas

A   TECHNOLOGY OPTION
Students may use the Portfolio feature on the CD-ROM to record their conversations.

JUEGO   You can alter this game and have students ask questions to guess the item the person is thinking of. Example: **¿Tiene mangas? No. ¿Es de oro? No. ¿Tiene un tacón? Sí. Es un zapato.**

ANSWERS

Práctica

C 1. Juan fue a la tienda de ropa.
2. Vio un traje en el escaparate.
3. Sí, le gustó mucho.
4. Era azul oscuro.
5. La chaqueta tenía tres botones.
6. Sí, Juan entró en la tienda.
7. Habló con el dependiente.
8. El dependiente le enseñó el traje que vio en el escaparate.
9. Juan se probó el traje.
10. Le quedó muy bien.

D Answers will vary but may include:
1. La última ropa que compré, la compré en ___.
2. Sí, (No, no) me atendió un dependiente.
3. Sí, (No, no) ví el artículo que quería en una vitrina.
4. El dependiente me enseñó ___.
5. Sí, (No, no) tenían lo que quería en mi tamaño.
6. Me costó ___.

Actividades comunicativas
A Answers will vary.

89

Vocabulario

La compra de comestibles

el puesto

el mercado

el colmado, la tienda de abarrotes, la tienda de ultramarinos

grocery store

el supermercado

el hipermercado

En la panadería se vende pan.

En la carnicería se vende carne.

En la pescadería se vende pescado. Se venden también mariscos.

En la pastelería se venden pasteles.

En la verdulería se venden legumbres (vegetales).

En la frutería se venden frutas.

RESOURCES

 Vocabulary Transparencies 4.2 (A & B)

📁 Student Tape Manual, TE, pages 38–40

🎧 Audiocassette 3B/CD3

📁 Workbook, pages 35–36

📁 Quiz 2, page 17

💿 CD-ROM, Disc 1, pages 90–93

🖌 Bell Ringer Review

Use BRR Transparency 4-2, or write the following on the board: List as many food items as you can under each of the following categories: **carnes, pescados y mariscos, legumbres, frutas.**

TEACHING VOCABULARY

A. After presenting the vocabulary using suggestions from previous chapters, you may wish to have a more able student come to the front of the room, play teacher, and ask questions about the illustrations on Vocabulary Transparencies 4.2 (A & B).

RECYCLING

♻ As they learn new vocabulary in this section, students are also reviewing many words from **¡Buen viaje! Level 1.**

VOCABULARY EXPANSION

Students have probably figured out that the ending **ería** usually refers to a place, especially a kind of shop. Ask them what they think the following places are:

· **una dulcería**
· **una heladería**
· **una camisería**
· **una sombrerería**
· **una perfumería**

Did You Know?

Hipermercados These giant markets have parking for thousands of cars. They sell food and a wide variety of other merchandise, from furniture to textbooks. There are chains of **hipermercados** in Spain and other countries (see page 105).

La señora iba de compras todos los días.
Compraba pan en la panadería.

¿A cuánto están los tomates hoy?

Están a cincuenta el kilo. Están muy frescos.

Sí, tienen muy buena pinta. Medio kilo, por favor.

Y compraba vegetales frescos en la verdulería.

el carrito

el pasillo

A veces la señora hacía sus compras en el
   supermercado.
Empujaba el carrito por los pasillos.
Hoy compró:
   seis tajadas (rebanadas) de jamón
   un paquete de guisantes congelados
   seis latas de refrescos
   una botella de agua mineral
   un frasco de mayonesa
   una caja de detergente

En el supermercado la señora
   siempre pagaba en la caja.
La empleada ponía sus compras en
   bolsas de plástico.

VOCABULARIO

B. Point out to students the following items in the **carrito:**
**seis tajadas de jamón
un paquete de guisantes
   congelados
seis latas de refrescos
una botella de agua mineral
un frasco de mayonesa
una caja de detergente**

Did You Know?

El pan Bread has enormous symbolic value in Hispanic culture. Someone who is very kind and good is called **un pedazo de pan.** Governments have often subsidized the cost of wheat to bakers so that reasonable prices could be maintained. Riots and civil unrest have often been the result of an increase in the price of bread.

Pantomime

Begin

___, levántate.
Ven acá, por favor.
Vas a ir de compras hoy. Vas al
   supermercado.
Toma un carrito.
Empuja el carrito por los pasillos.
Pon unas latas de refrescos en tu carrito.
Pon un frasco de mayonesa en tu carrito.
Mira los vegetales.
Toca los tomates.
Pon unos tomates en tu carrito.

Paga tus compras en la caja.
Toma la bolsa de plástico y sal del
   supermercado.
Gracias, ___. Puedes volver a tu asiento.

◆Práctica◆

A Do **Práctica A** orally with books closed. Then assign it for homework and go over it again quickly the following day.

B Do **Práctica B** orally with books closed. Then have students open their books and read the questions and give their answers again.

EXPANSION After going over **Práctica B**, have a student retell the entire story in his or her own words.

C You can have pairs of students do **Práctica C** together as if they were conducting an interview.

Learning From Photos

Una panadería, México Today in **una panadería** you can buy sweet rolls and other pastries. The traditional **panadería,** however, would sell only bread. Indeed, many traditional **panaderías** would open only in the morning and would close by noon.

◆Práctica◆

A De compras   Contesten.

1. Alicia necesitaba pan. ¿Adónde fue ella?
2. Ella quería comprar un biftec. ¿Adónde fue?
3. Quería ostras frescas y un filete de pescado. ¿Adónde fue?
4. Necesitaba una docena de naranjas. ¿Adónde fue?
5. Quería comprar un pastel delicioso. ¿Adónde fue?

B **HISTORIETA** **Al supermercado**

Contesten.

1. ¿Fue al mercado o al supermercado la señora Galdós?
2. ¿Empujó un carrito por los pasillos?
3. ¿Fue de un departamento a otro?
4. ¿Qué compró en la carnicería?
5. ¿Qué compró en el departamento de productos congelados?
6. Quería hacer un bocadillo de jamón y queso. ¿Cuántas rebanadas de jamón compró?
7. ¿Compró un frasco de mayonesa?
8. ¿Dónde pagó?
9. ¿En qué puso la señora sus compras?

Una panadería, México

Un supermercado, San José, Costa Rica

C **Preguntas personales**   Contesten.

1. ¿Quién en tu familia compra la comida?
2. ¿Hace las compras en un mercado o en un supermercado?
3. ¿Qué productos congelados compra con frecuencia?
4. ¿Compra la carne en una carnicería o en el supermercado?
5. En el supermercado donde Uds. compran, ¿usan bolsas de plástico o de papel?

ANSWERS

Práctica

A 1. Ella fue a la panadería
   2. Ella fue a la carnicería.
   3. Ella fue a la pescadería.
   4. Ella fue a la frutería.
   5. Ella fue a la pastelería.

B 1. La señora Galdós fue al supermercado (mercado).

2. Sí, (No, no) empujó un carrito por los pasillos.
3. Sí, (No, no) fue de un departamento a otro.
4. En la carnicería compró ___.
5. En el departamento de productos congelados compró un paquete de guisantes congelados.
6. Compró ___ rebanadas de jamón.

7. Sí, (No, no) compró un frasco de mayonesa.
8. Pagó en la caja.
9. La señora puso sus compras en bolsas de plástico.

C Answers will vary but may include:
   1. En mi familia, mi ___ compra la comida.

2. Hace las compras en un mercado (un supermercado).
3. Compra ___ con frecuencia.
4. Compra la carne en una carnicería (un supermercado).
5. En el supermercado donde nosotros compramos, usan bolsas de plástico (de papel).

92

D ¿A cuánto está?

Contesten según el anuncio.

1. la bolsa de patatas fritas
2. la lata de tomate
3. el jamón serrano
4. la caja de queso castellano
5. el frasco de mermelada

Actividades comunicativas

A ¿Cuánto? Tú eres el/la dependiente(a) en el mercado. El/La cliente (tu compañero[a]) pide uno de los siguientes productos y tú le preguntas la cantidad que quiere, en kilos, latas, paquetes, bolsas, botellas, etc. Luego cambien de rol.

> ternera
> atún
> zanahorias congeladas
> mayonesa
> Coca-Cola

B Los favoritos Prepara dos listas: una lista de los comestibles que te gustan y otra de los comestibles que no te gustan. Luego trabaja con un(a) compañero(a). Comparen sus listas y determinen los gustos que tienen en común.

C ¡Qué invitación! Estás viviendo con los Menéndez, una familia mexicana. ¡Qué coincidencia! Los «Dallas Cowboys» están en México y los señores Menéndez invitan a los «Cowboys» a cenar. Con el señor o la señora Menéndez (tu compañero[a]), planeen el menú para la comida que van a servir. Discutan las cantidades que van a necesitar. A propósito, *ton* en español es «una tonelada».

Guadalajara, México

Estructura

RESOURCES

- Workbook, pages 37–41
- Student Tape Manual, TE, pages 41–42
- Audiocassette 3B/CD3
- Quizzes 3–6, pages 18–21
- Computer Testmaker
- CD-ROM, Disc 1, pages 94–101

Bell Ringer Review

Use BRR Transparency 4-3, or write the following on the board: Write the following.
1. **cuatro cosas que hiciste ayer en la escuela**
2. **cuatro cosas que hiciste ayer después de las clases**

TEACHING STRUCTURE

Talking about past events

A. Have students open their books to page 94. Lead them through Steps 1–4.
B. For Step 2 draw a timeline on the board. Each time you give a verb in the preterite, draw an abrupt slash through the timeline to indicate completion or termination in the past.
C. As you go over the model sentences in Step 2, put another timeline on the board. Each time you give a verb in the imperfect, draw a long shaded box alongside it to indicate duration.

Talking about past events
El pretérito y el imperfecto

1. The choice of whether to use the preterite or imperfect depends upon whether the speaker is describing an action completed in the past or a continuous, recurring action in the past.

2. You use the preterite to express actions or events that began and ended at a specific time in the past.

   Anoche Carmen fue al supermercado.
   Compró una caja de detergente y unos productos congelados.
   El dependiente puso todo en una bolsa.

3. You use the imperfect to talk about a continuous, habitual, or repeated action in the past. The moment when the action began or ended is unimportant.

   Carmen iba al supermercado con frecuencia.
   Cada día compraba las cosas que necesitaba.
   Casi siempre pagaba con tarjeta de crédito.

4. Compare the following sentences.

REPEATED, HABITUAL ACTION	COMPLETED ACTION
Ellos iban al cine todos los sábados.	**Ellos fueron al cine el sábado pasado.**
Siempre se sentaban en la primera fila.	**Ayer se sentaron en la última fila.**
Todas las noches se acostaban tarde.	**Anoche se acostaron temprano.**

Caracas, Venezuela

ANSWERS (PAGE 95)

Práctica
A 1. **Sí, la señora fue al mercado ayer por la mañana.**
   Fue al mercado ayer por la mañana.
   Sí, la señora iba al mercado cada mañana.
   Iba al mercado cada mañana.
2. **Sí, jugué al tenis ayer por la tarde.**
   Jugué al tenis ayer por la tarde.
   Sí, jugaba al tenis cada tarde.
   Jugaba al tenis cada tarde.

94

❖Práctica❖

A **¿Una vez o frecuentemente?** Contesten.

1. ¿Fue la señora al mercado ayer por la mañana?
   ¿Cuándo fue la señora al mercado?
   ¿Iba la señora al mercado cada mañana?
   ¿Cuándo iba la señora al mercado?

2. ¿Jugaste al tenis ayer por la tarde?
   ¿Cuándo jugaste al tenis?
   ¿Jugabas al tenis cada tarde?
   ¿Cuándo jugabas al tenis?

3. Anoche, ¿se comunicaron por correo electrónico los amigos?
   ¿Cuándo se comunicaron por correo electrónico los amigos?
   ¿Se comunicaban por correo electrónico casi todas las noches?
   ¿Cuándo se comunicaban por correo electrónico los amigos?

B **¿Cuándo?** Sigan el modelo.

todas las semanas / la semana pasada
Bárbara, ¿ibas al cine todas las semanas?
Bárbara, ¿fuiste al cine la semana pasada?

1. todas las noches / anoche 2. todos los días / ayer 3. todas las mañanas / esta mañana

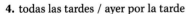

4. todas las tardes / ayer por la tarde 5. todos los sábados / el sábado pasado

ESTRUCTURA

noventa y cinco 〜 **95**

ANSWERS CONTINUED

3. Sí, los amigos se comunicaron por correo electrónico anoche.
   Se comunicaron por correo electrónico anoche.
   Sí, se comunicaban por correo electrónico casi todas las noches.
   Se comunicaban por correo electrónico casi todas las noches.

B 1. Bárbara, ¿mirabas televisión todas las noches?
   Bárbara, ¿miraste televisión anoche?

2. ¿Te ponías (Llevabas) aretes todos los días?
   ¿Te pusiste (Llevaste) aretes ayer?

3. ¿Tomabas el desayuno todas las mañanas?
   ¿Tomaste el desayuno esta mañana?

4. ¿Ibas de compras todas las tardes?
   ¿Fuiste de compras ayer por la tarde?

5. ¿Te levantabas tarde todos los sábados?
   ¿Te levantaste tarde el sábado pasado?

⟨Práctica⟩

C You may wish to give students a few minutes to prepare this activity before going over it in class.

Actividades comunicativas

A You may wish to have different pairs of students present their conversations to the class.

B Tell students to take a look at the realia before trying to do **Actividad B.**

C **HISTORIETA** Los sábados de Juan Antonio

Cambien **Todos los sábados** a **El sábado pasado.** Hagan los cambios necesarios.

Todos los sábados Juan Antonio se levantaba muy temprano. Bajaba a la cocina y él mismo preparaba el desayuno. Después de comer, subía a su cuarto y prendía su computadora. Cuando hacía la conexión entonces entraba la dirección de un buen amigo en España. En pocos minutos se comunicaba con su amigo. Los dos hablaban de muchas cosas durante horas.

Actividades comunicativas

A **Entrevista** Vas a entrevistar *(interview)* a un(a) compañero(a). Pregúntale lo que le gustaba hacer cuando era joven y dos cosas que le impresionaron como niño(a). Luego cambien de rol.

B **Tu amigo(a) chileno(a)** Estás hablando con un(a) amigo(a) (tu compañero[a]) que antes vivía en Chile. Él o ella te está describiendo «Paseo estación central», donde siempre iba de compras. Te está explicando por qué le gustaba ir de compras allí. Luego explícale donde tú prefieres hacer las compras.

ANSWERS

Práctica

C **El sábado pasado Juan Antonio se levantó muy temprano. Bajó a la cocina y él mismo preparó el desayuno. Después de comer, subió a su cuarto y prendió su computadora. Cuando hizo la conexión, entonces entró la dirección de un buen amigo en España. En pocos minutos se comunicó con su amigo. Los dos hablaron de muchas cosas durante horas.**

Actividades comunicativas
A and B   Answers will vary.

Narrating a sequence of events
Dos acciones en una oración

1. Often a sentence may have two or more verbs in the past. The verbs may be in the same tense or in different tenses. In the sentence below, both verbs are in the preterite. Both describe simple actions that began and ended at a specific time in the past.

> **Laura llegó ayer y Pepe la vio.**

2. In the sentence below, the two verbs are in the imperfect because they both describe habitual or continuous actions. The moment when the actions began or ended is unimportant.

> **Durante los inviernos, Adela iba a las montañas a esquiar, pero yo trabajaba.**

3. In the sentence below, the verb **estudiaba** is in the imperfect; it describes the background—what was going on. The verb in the preterite, **entró**, expresses the action or event that interrupted the ongoing action.

> **Yo estudiaba cuando Julia entró.**

A

HISTORIETA ¿Qué hacías cuando...?

Contesten.

1. ¿Estabas en casa cuando sonó el teléfono?
2. ¿Mirabas un video cuando sonó?
3. ¿Contestaste el teléfono cuando sonó?
4. ¿Hablabas por teléfono cuando tu padre volvió a casa?
5. ¿Preguntó tu padre con quién hablabas?
6. ¿Con quién hablabas cuando tu padre entró?

EL IPHONE permite navegar por Internet y usar correo electrónico. Tiene una pantalla sensible al tacto. Con monitor en blanco y negro cuesta 500 dólares en E.U.

CENTRO DE INFORMACIÓN UNIVERSITARIA

UNIVERSIDAD DE ALCALÁ

Plaza de San Diego, s/n.
Teléfono: (91) 885 40 03/06
28801 ALCALÁ DE HENARES
(Madrid)

Bell Ringer Review

Use BRR Transparency 4-4, or write the following on the board:
Complete with the preterite.

1. Ayer yo ___ de compras. (ir)
2. Yo ___ al mercado solo(a). Mi hermano no ___. (ir, ir)
3. Yo ___ algunas frutas muy ricas. (comprar)
4. Cuando yo ___ a casa, ___ una naranja. (volver, comer)

Narrating a sequence of events

A. When explaining the difference between the preterite and the imperfect, you may wish to have students think of a play. Explain that the stage background, the description, and the scenery are in the imperfect. What the actors and actresses actually do on stage is in the preterite.

B. Give some examples and show the difference between background information and acting. Background: **Él era muy guapo. Había una fiesta. Todo el mundo se divertía. José y Elena bailaban.** Acting: **En ese momento Carlos entró. Dijo «Buenos días» a todo el mundo. Saludó a todos.**

C. Now use two verbs in one sentence to contrast the background information with the actions on stage. For example: **Ana y Paco bailaban cuando Carlos entró.**

Práctica

A When going over **Práctica A,** have students identify the background, descriptive activity, and the activity that intervened or interrupted.

ANSWERS

Práctica

A 1. Sí, (No, no) estaba en casa cuando sonó el teléfono.
2. Sí, (No, no) miraba un video cuando sonó.
3. Sí, (No, no) contesté el teléfono cuando sonó.
4. Sí, (No, no) hablaba por teléfono cuando mi padre volvió a casa.
5. Sí (No), mi padre (no) preguntó con quién hablaba.
6. Hablaba con ___ cuando mi padre entró.

98

B EXPANSION After going over **Práctica B**, have students look at the illustration and make up an original story about it.

C Tell students to be as creative as possible and make up as many statements as they can when doing **Práctica C**. It is recommended that you do this **Práctica** orally and written.

Actividades comunicativas

JUEGO This is a good end-of-class activity that students should enjoy doing.

ABOUT THE SPANISH LANGUAGE

Students know the greetings **Hola** and **Buenos días.** They may not realize that **Adiós** is a greeting as well as a way of saying good-bye. When two friends or acquaintances pass each other and do not intend to stop to talk, an appropriate greeting is **Adiós,** accompanied by a wave of the hand.

B HISTORIETA En la tienda de ropa

Contesten según los dibujos.

1. ¿Adónde fue Susana para hacer sus compras?
2. ¿Qué quería comprar?
3. ¿Qué tomó para subir al segundo piso?
4. Cuando ella llegó a la caja, ¿con quién hablaba la dependienta?
5. Cuando Susana pagaba, ¿quiénes la saludaron?

C Yo hacía esto cuando eso pasó.   Sigan el modelo.

Yo jugaba cuando sonó el teléfono.

leer   correr   jugar   beber   ver   bailar   hablar   sonar   subir   servir   llover   pagar   llamar   comer   mirar

Actividades comunicativas

A Lo que hacía cuando...   Habla con un(a) compañero(a). Dile algo que hacías ayer. Tu compañero(a) te va a decir algo que ocurrió e interrumpió lo que hacías. Luego en una sola oración, describe lo que hacías y lo que pasó (ocurrió). ¡Usen la imaginación!

JUEGO   **Vicente el vago**   Lazy Vicente needs excuses for not turning in his homework. Something always interferes with his studying, reading, writing, etc. Help him out. Give him half a dozen good excuses like: **¡Yo estudiaba cuando el Presidente me llamó!** You get the idea. See who can come up with the most original excuse in the class!

ANSWERS

Práctica

B 1. **Susana fue a una tienda de ropa para señoras para hacer sus compras.**
2. **Quería comprar un vestido.**
3. **Tomó el ascensor para subir al segundo piso.**
4. **Cuando ella llegó a la caja, la dependienta hablaba con una señora.**
5. **Cuando Susana pagaba, unas amigas la saludaron.**

C Answers will vary.

Actividades comunicativas
A Answers will vary.

Expressing feelings in the past
Verbos como **querer** y **creer** en el pasado

Since most mental processes involve duration or continuance, verbs that deal with mental activities or conditions are most often expressed in the imperfect tense in the past. The most common of these verbs are:

creer	**pensar** *(to think)*
desear	**preferir**
querer	**poder**
tener ganas de *(to feel like)*	**saber**

> **Él sabía lo que preferíamos.**
> **Yo tenía ganas de salir.**
> **Él creía que yo estaba enfermo.**

A Yo quería... Preparen una lista de las cosas que querían hacer.

B Yo sabía... Preparen una lista de las cosas que sabían hacer cuando eran niños(as).

C Y yo no podía... Preparen una lista de las cosas que no podían hacer cuando eran niños(as).

D Sabía y podía... Preparen una lista de las cosas que sabían hacer y que podían hacer.

Caracas, Venezuela

ANSWERS

Práctica
A, B, C, and **D** Answers will vary.

 ## Bell Ringer Review

Use BRR Transparency 4-5, or write the following on the board: Your best friend got into trouble. Use preterite forms to tell what happened: **levantarse tarde, no hacer la tarea, hablar mucho en clase, no estudiar para el examen, sacar una nota mala en el examen.**

TEACHING STRUCTURE

Expressing feelings in the past

Have students open their books to page 99 and lead them through the explanation. Provide and elicit additional examples.

 ## Práctica

¡OJO! You may wish to assign these activities for homework and go over them the following day in class.

INFORMAL ASSESSMENT

Have students make up as many original sentences as they can, using the preterite and the imperfect.

 ## Learning From Photos

Caracas, Venezuela You may wish to ask students to compare the young people in the photo to American students of the same age. They will probably see little if any difference. They may then discuss the idea of a "youth culture" that crosses borders.

99

100

 Talking in general terms
La voz pasiva con se

1. When we talk about something being done without saying who does it, we use the passive voice in English.

Fish is sold at the fish market.

2. In Spanish the pronoun **se** is used to express this idea.

Se vende pescado en la pescadería.
Se venden papas en la verdulería.

The verb is singular or plural depending on the subject.

3. You will often see the **se** construction used to express ideas such as:

They speak Spanish here.
Spanish is spoken here. ⎫
One speaks Spanish here. ⎬ **Aquí se habla español.**
People speak Spanish here. ⎭

Puerto Montt, Chile

«La vendimia» de Francisco de Goya

 Práctica

A **¿Dónde se venden?** Contesten.

1. ¿Se vende pan en la panadería?
2. ¿Se venden suéteres en la tienda de ropa?
3. ¿Se vende carne en la carnicería?
4. ¿Se venden guisantes en la verdulería?
5. ¿Se vende fruta en la frutería?
6. ¿Se venden productos congelados en el supermercado?
7. ¿Se vende pescado en la pescadería?
8. ¿Se venden bolígrafos en la papelería?

100 〰 *ciento*

B **¿Qué idioma se habla dónde?** Escojan.

francés	español	portugués
inglés	árabe	alemán

1. ¿Qué idioma se habla en México?
2. ¿Qué idioma se habla en el Brasil?
3. ¿Qué idioma se habla en Egipto?
4. ¿Qué idioma se habla en Irlanda?
5. ¿Qué idioma se habla en Alemania?
6. ¿Qué idiomas se hablan en Quebec?

Taxco, México

La Ciudad de México

Actividad comunicativa

A **El «Hipercor»** Tú estás en un hipermercado y no puedes encontrar las cosas que necesitas. Hablas con un(a) dependiente(a) (tu compañero[a]). Pídele a él o a ella los productos que necesitas. Tu compañero(a) te va a decir dónde se encuentran en la tienda. Luego cambien de rol.

> Busco el atún.

> Ah, sí. El atún se encuentra en el pasillo dos.

B If you have a world map or a globe in the classroom, you may wish to point to each location mentioned in **Práctica B.**

Learning From Photos

Puerto Montt, Chile (page 100) Puerto Montt is the major port of southern Chile and the country's most important fishing port. Chile is one of the world's major fishing nations. Chile farms and exports fish and fish products around the world.

La Ciudad de México (page 101) Here is another view of the elegant Zona Rosa. Note the pink hue of the buildings typical of the entire **colonia**, the color from which it derives its name.

Taxco, México (page 101) This is a photo of the Cathedral of Taxco. Taxco is a beautifully preserved colonial city. It is famous for the silver work of its artisans.

¡OJO! There is no more new material to present in this chapter. The sections that follow recombine and reinforce the vocabulary and structures that have already been introduced.

ANSWERS

B 1. Se habla español en México.
2. Se habla portugués en el Brasil.
3. Se habla árabe en Egipto.
4. Se habla inglés en Irlanda.
5. Se habla alemán en Alemania.
6. Se hablan inglés y francés en Quebec.

Actividad comunicativa
A Answers will vary.

101

Bell Ringer Review

Use BRR Transparency 4-6, or write the following on the board: Answer the following questions.
1. **¿Qué hiciste esta mañana?**
2. **¿A qué hora saliste de casa?**
3. **¿Adónde fuiste?**
4. **¿Con quién fuiste?**

TEACHING THE CONVERSATION

A. 🎧 Tell students they are going to hear a conversation between a young woman and her grandmother. Then have them listen to the recording on Cassette 3B/Compact Disc 3 with books closed.

B. Have them listen to the recording again as they follow along in their books.

C. Call on two students to read the conversation aloud. Intersperse their reading with questions from the **Después de conversar** activity.

D. After going over the **Después de conversar** activity, have students retell the story of the conversation in their own words.

TECHNOLOGY OPTION

On the CD-ROM (Disc 1, page 102), students can watch a dramatization of this conversation. They can then play the role of either one of the characters and record themselves in the conversation.

Conversación

Naranjas para abuelita

LEONOR: Abuelita, te compré unas naranjas preciosas en el supermercado.

ABUELITA: Ay, gracias, mi cielito. Pero, ¿por qué no fuiste a la frutería del mercado San Miguel? Es donde yo siempre iba.

LEONOR: Yo fui allí una vez y no me gustó. ¿Por qué tú siempre hacías tus compras allí, abuelita?

ABUELITA: Ay, niña. Allí todo el mundo me conocía. Y todo era tan fresco. Todo lo podías ver. No estaba en paquetes de plástico. A propósito, ¿a cuánto estaban las naranjas?

LEONOR: No sé, abuelita.

ABUELITA: Sí, sabes. Yo sé que son muy caras. Recuerdo cuando estaban a diez pesos la docena.

102 ⌒ *ciento dos*

Después de conversar

Contesten.
1. ¿Dónde hizo sus compras Leonor?
2. ¿Para quién compró las naranjas?
3. ¿Adónde iba la abuelita para hacer sus compras?
4. ¿Fue Leonor alguna vez al mercado? ¿Le gustó?
5. ¿Por qué le gustaba a la abuela comprar en San Miguel?
6. ¿Cómo era todo allí?
7. ¿Sabe Leonor a cuánto estaban las naranjas?
8. ¿Qué recuerda la abuelita?

Actividades comunicativas

A. Ropa nueva para una fiesta Hay una fiesta en casa de unos amigos el sábado. Habla con tu compañero(a). Decidan qué ropa van a llevar y, si necesitan algo nuevo, qué van a comprar y dónde.

B. De compras Tú trabajas en una tienda de abarrotes. Un cliente (tu compañero[a]) les va a servir una comida a algunos invitados. No sabe qué servir y te pide recomendaciones. Pregúntale el número de personas que va a servir. Vas a ser muy cortés con el cliente y le vas a dar muchas recomendaciones o sugerencias. Le vas a sugerir lo que puede servir y las cantidades que va a necesitar.

C. Un recuerdo de la niñez Piensa en unas cosas que te gustaba hacer de niño(a). Luego cuenta a tu compañero(a) de una ocasión en la que hiciste una de estas cosas. Luego tu compañero(a) te va a decir lo mismo.

Barcelona, España

CONVERSACIÓN

ciento tres **103**

Lecturas CULTURALES

Reading Strategy

Skimming

Skimming is the quickest way to find out what a reading selection is about. When you skim, look at the titles, subtitles, and any words in bold print. Also look at the photographs. All of these will indicate to you the topic of the reading and will help you understand it better.

Bell Ringer Review

Use BRR Transparency 4-7, or write the following on the board: You are planning lunch for a friend. Make a shopping list and note where you are going to buy each item.

National Standards

Cultures

The reading about markets on pages 104–105 and the related activities on page 105 familiarize students with both traditional and modern types of markets in Spanish-speaking countries.

TEACHING THE READING

Pre-reading

A. Have students read the Reading Strategy and then have them look at the title and subheads.
B. Give students a brief synopsis of the **Lectura** in Spanish.
C. Ask them some questions about your synopsis.

Reading

A. Have students open their books. Call on an individual to read three or four sentences.
B. After the student has read, ask other members of the class questions about the sentences just read.

DE COMPRAS

Mercados

En los países hispanos la gente tradicionalmente compraba la comida en el mercado. Los mercados municipales tenían puestos para los diferentes productos. Había pescaderías, carnicerías, fruterías, verdulerías, etc. La señora hacía sus compras todos los días— generalmente temprano por la mañana. En el mercado iba de un puesto a otro. Conocía a todos los vendedores y conversaba (charlaba) con ellos. Llevaba una bolsa o un capacho[1] para sus compras. Los vendedores no las ponían en bolsas de plástico.

Supermercados

En todas las ciudades hispanas hay supermercados también. Son modernos, limpios[2] y sobre todo convenientes. En el supermercado uno toma un carrito. Lo empuja por los pasillos y en un solo establecimiento puede comprar todo lo que necesita.

[1]capacho *a cloth shopping bag*
[2]limpios *clean*

Sant Felíu de Guixols, España

Caracas, Venezuela

Learning From Photos

Sant Felíu de Guixols, España This outdoor market is in the port town of Sant Felíu de Guixols in Cataluña. The name of the town is in **catalán**.

Caracas, Venezuela This supermarket is in Caracas, the capital of Venezuela. Caracas is a magnificent, modern city with a population of over 2,000,000. It was founded by the Spaniards in 1567.

Hipermercados

Recientemente llegó otra posibilidad para hacer las compras—el hipermercado. El hipermercado es un enorme establecimiento comercial, normalmente en las afueras[3] de la ciudad. El hipermercado tiene lugar para miles de automóviles.

En el hipermercado se puede comprar comida, obviamente. Pero también se puede comprar de todo: ropa, aparatos electrónicos, libros, casi cualquier[4] tipo de producto. El hipermercado tiene docenas de pasillos y cajas registradoras. Si uno quiere, puede pagar sus compras con tarjeta de crédito.

Hoy en día nadie tiene bastante tiempo. Todos estamos muy ocupados. El hipermercado ayuda a conservar tiempo. Podemos comprar todo lo que necesitamos sin tener que ir a más de una tienda.

Pero todavía hay muchos que prefieren el mercado donde todo es muy fresco y todo el mundo se conoce. Los mercados municipales todavía existen y muchas personas siguen haciendo sus compras allí.

[3]afueras *outskirts*
[4]cualquier *any*

La Ciudad de México

Después de leer

A De compras   Contesten.

1. ¿Dónde compraba la gente la comida?
2. ¿Cuáles son tres puestos que se encuentran en el mercado?
3. ¿Cuándo hacía sus compras la señora?
4. ¿Con quiénes conversaba en el mercado?
5. ¿Para qué llevaba ella un capacho?
6. ¿Dónde hay supermercados?
7. ¿Por qué prefieren algunas personas el supermercado?
8. ¿Qué es un hipermercado?
9. ¿Dónde están los hipermercados normalmente?
10. ¿Por qué prefieren algunas personas el hipermercado?

B El hipermercado y el mercado tradicional   Comparen el mercado tradicional y el hipermercado.

LECTURAS CULTURALES   *ciento cinco* **105**

Post-reading

A. After going over the entire **Lectura**, ask about six salient questions the answers to which provide a synopsis of the story. Call on several individuals to answer one question each.

B. Call on one student to answer all six questions. The answers will give an oral synopsis.

C. Have students do the **Después de leer** activities for homework. Go over them in class the next day.

TECHNOLOGY OPTION

Students may listen to a recording of the **Lectura** on the CD-ROM, Disc 1, page 104.

Critical Thinking Activity

Giving opinions Have two groups of students debate the following issue: **¿Cuál es preferible, el mercado tradicional o el hipermercado moderno?** Allow time for the students to develop their arguments and then present the debate to the class with a student moderator.

ANSWERS

Después de leer

A 1. La gente compraba la comida en el mercado.

2. Tres puestos que se encuentran en el mercado son: la pescadería, la carnicería y la frutería.

3. La señora hacía sus compras todos los días—generalmente temprano por la mañana.

4. Conversaba con todos los vendedores.

5. Llevaba un capacho para sus compras.

6. Hay supermercados en todas las ciudades hispanas.

7. Algunas personas prefieren el supermercado porque es moderno, limpio y sobre todo conveniente.

8. Un hipermercado es un enorme establecimiento comercial.

9. Los hipermercados están normalmente en las afueras de la ciudad.

10. Algunas personas prefieren el hipermercado porque se puede comprar todo allí y el hipermercado ayuda a conservar tiempo.

B Answers will vary.

LECTURA OPCIONAL

National Standards

Cultures
This reading about the open-air market and the dress of the indigenous women in Chichicastenango, Guatemala, and the related activities on page 107 familiarize students with a typical traditional market and the clothing of one group of indigenous people in Latin America.

TEACHING TIPS

¡OJO! This reading is optional. You may skip it completely, have the entire class read it, have only several students read it, or assign it for extra credit.

A. You may wish to have a student or students who read this optional selection present the material briefly to the class.

 LITERATURE CONNECTION

Punto de vista For any students interested in contemporary life and conditions of the Indians of Guatemala, you might recommend that they read **me llamo Rigoberta Menchú y así me nació la conciencia** by the Nobel Prize-winning author. The book is available in English.
Note There is an excerpt from this book in **¡Buen viaje! Level 3.**

EL MERCADO DE CHICHICASTENANGO

El mercado

Los jueves y los domingos son días de mercado en la plaza del pequeño pueblo de Chichicastenango en Guatemala. Antes de levantarse el sol[1], individuos y grupos de indígenas llegan al pueblo. Muchos llevan en la cabeza o en los hombros[2] los productos que van a vender. Antes la gente caminaba muchas horas por las montañas para llegar temprano al mercado. Todavía hay muchos que llegan a pie, pero hoy día hay muchos que toman el autobús para ir al mercado.

En el mercado hay puestos de verduras y carne. Además de comestibles también venden joyas, cajas decoradas y preciosas mantas[3] y huipiles. Los huipiles son las blusas que llevan las indígenas.

[1]levantarse el sol *the sun rises*
[2]hombros *shoulders*
[3]mantas *blankets*

Una señora de la aldea de Sololá, Guatemala

Iglesia de Santo Tomás, Chichicastenango

La ropa indígena

Las mujeres de cada grupo indígena llevan ropa que las identifica como miembros del grupo. Las mujeres de Chichicastenango llevan un huipil que tiene muchos diseños⁴ geométricos y figuras de flores y plantas. Su falda tiene rayas azules. Hoy la mayoría de los hombres no llevan el traje tradicional. Antes llevaban un pantalón de lana negra, una faja roja y una chaqueta negra con diseños rojos. En la cabeza llevaban un «tzut», un tipo de bufanda roja.

⁴diseños designs

Después de leer

A La palabra, por favor.   Completen.

1. Los dos días de mercado en Chichicastenango son _____ y _____.
2. El mercado está en la _____ del pueblo pequeño.
3. Los _____ llegan al pueblo muy temprano por la mañana.
4. Llevan en la cabeza o en los _____ los productos que van a vender.
5. Algunos llegan al mercado a pie pero hoy en día muchos toman el _____.
6. Además de comestibles, en el mercado venden _____.
7. Un huipil es una _____ que llevan las mujeres de Chichicastenango.
8. Las mujeres llevan _____ que las identifica como miembros del grupo.
9. En el pasado, los hombres de Chichicastenango llevaban un tipo de _____ roja en la cabeza.

B El mercado de Chichicastenango

Describan la foto del mercado de «Chichi».

Chichicastenango

LECTURAS OPCIONALES

ciento siete 107

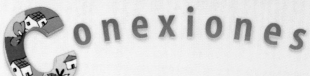

Conexiones

¡OJO! This reading on marketing is optional. You may choose any of the following ways to do it with your students.

Independent reading Have students read the selections and do the post-reading activities as homework, which you collect. This option is least intrusive on class time and requires a minimum of teacher involvement.

Homework with in-class follow-up Assign the readings and post-reading activities as homework. Review and discuss the material in class the next day.

Intensive in-class activity This option includes a pre-reading vocabulary presentation, in-class reading and discussion, assignment of the activities for homework, and a discussion of the assignment in class the following day.

EL COMERCIO

EL MERCADEO

A. You may wish to have only those students interested in a career in business or merchandising read this selection. However, since marketing and advertising affect everyone's life, this information could be of interest to all students.

B. Have students give a list of products that they know in Spanish that are really **necesidades.**

C. Have them give another list of products that are luxury items.

108

EL COMERCIO

EL MERCADEO

One of the most important subjects for business students is marketing. **Mercadeo** is the Spanish word for *marketing*, but the English word is more often used all over the Spanish-speaking world—**el marketing**. A major focus of marketing is the promotion and advertising of a product or service.

El mercado

Antes de definir el término «marketing», es necesario dar una definición de la palabra «mercado». El mercado es el conjunto de todos los posibles compradores (los consumidores) de un producto o de un servicio. Ejemplos de un producto son un coche o un pantalón. Ejemplos de un servicio son un banco o una agencia de viajes.

El marketing

En términos generales, el marketing es la creación de un mercado para un producto o servicio antes de comenzar a producir el producto o servicio. Es la responsabilidad del departamento de marketing de informar a los posibles compradores sobre la existencia del producto y las características del producto.

Learning From Realia

Tarjeta de crédito Citibank You may wish to ask questions about the realia:
¿Qué ofrece Citibank?
¿Es realmente «gratis» la tarjeta?
¿Por qué o por qué no?

La promoción

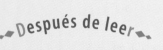

Para informar al público de la existencia y de las características de un producto, un aspecto muy importante del marketing es la promoción. Y la propaganda[1] juega un rol primordial, muy importante, en la promoción. Para lanzar[2] un buen programa de promoción, el personal de marketing tiene que emplear muchos medios de comunicación como la radio, la televisión, los anuncios en los periódicos y en las revistas.

Diferentes productos y mercados

Hay algunos productos y servicios que la gente necesita. Hay otros que la gente no necesita pero que quiere. No es necesario convencer a la gente de comprar comida o gasolina. ¡Pero otra cosa es el perfume!

La industria de la ropa es un caso muy interesante. La gente necesita ropa porque todos tenemos que vestirnos. Pero hay también ropa que la gente no necesita pero que quiere. Uno puede comprar un pantalón que cuesta treinta dólares. O puede comprar un pantalón que cuesta trescientos dólares. Los dos satisfacen la necesidad de vestirse. Pero la persona que paga trescientos dólares no compra solamente algo que necesita—un artículo de ropa. Compra algo que quiere—prestigio. Y la propaganda tiene que convencer a los clientes que la belleza, la calidad y el prestigio valen el precio que les ponen.

[1] propaganda *advertising*
[2] lanzar *to launch*

HERMÈS. ALL FOR SILK.

Corbata de seda natural
12.000 Ptas.

Pañuelo de seda natural
28.000 Ptas.

~Después de leer~

A El mercadeo   Digan que sí o que no.

1. El coche es un producto.
2. El banco es otro producto.
3. Los consumidores compran sólo productos que necesitan.
4. Los consumidores no tienen que conocer las características de un producto.
5. El perfume se considera una necesidad.
6. El prestigio es una necesidad.

B Definiciones   Den una definición de las siguientes palabras.

1. el consumidor
2. el comprador
3. el mercado
4. el producto
5. el servicio
6. la necesidad

C Un anuncio   Prepara un anuncio para un artículo de ropa.

CONEXIONES

ciento nueve 109

Additional Practice

Más preguntas   You may wish to ask additional comprehension questions such as:

¿Para qué sirve la promoción?
¿Cuáles son algunos medios de comunicación?
¿Cuáles son ejemplos de productos que son una necesidad?
¿Cuáles son algunos productos que no son una necesidad?

~Después de leer~

C   When students create their ads, you may wish to have them prepare them for the different media mentioned in the reading—print, radio, or television.

ANSWERS

Después de leer

A 1. Sí.
2. No.
3. No.
4. No.
5. No.
6. No.

B and C   Answers will vary.

Culminación

Actividades orales

iOJO! Encourage students to say as much as possible when they do these activities. Tell them not to be afraid of making mistakes since the goal of the activities is real-life communication.

Allow students to choose the activities they would like to take part in.

B **TECHNOLOGY OPTION** In the CD-ROM version of this activity (Disc 1, page 110), students can interact with an on-screen native speaker and record their voices.

Student Portfolio

Have students keep a notebook containing their best written work from each chapter. These selected writings can be based on assignments from the Student Textbook and the Writing Activities Workbook. The activities on page 111 are examples of writing assignments that may be included in each student's portfolio.

See the Teacher's Manual for more information on the Student Portfolio.

Actividades orales

A Liquidación *(The big sales event)* You and your partner have been asked to prepare a radio announcement for Galerías Sampere's annual sale. Select a number of products, give their prices, the days and times of the sale and add some "hype." If the sale is a success, you two will get a bonus.

B Mi juventud Pregúntale a un(a) compañero(a) si él o ella hacía las siguientes cosas cuando era joven. Toma apuntes y prepara un informe sobre las actividades de tu compañero(a).

> hablar por teléfono
> escribir cartas
> escuchar los CDs
> jugar fútbol
> ir a fiestas
> visitar a los abuelos
> recibir buenas notas

C Ayer Trabaja con un(a) compañero(a) de clase. Ayer Uds. hacían muchas cosas. Pero siempre había interrupciones. Hablen de todo lo que hacían y todo lo que interrumpió lo que hacían.

D En la tienda de ropa Con un(a) compañero(a), miren el dibujo de la tienda de ropa. Describan todo lo que ven en el dibujo.

ANSWERS

Actividades orales
A, B, C, and D Answers will vary.

For the Native Speaker

En español, por favor After the students have prepared and reviewed their "radio announcements" for **Actividad A,** ask the native speakers in the class to perform the radio ads.

Actividades escritas

A **Un viaje interesante** Tú viajabas por México y fuiste a un mercado interesante. Escríbele una tarjeta postal a un(a) amigo(a). Descríbele el mercado y todo lo que pasó allí.

B **¡Gran apertura!** Un supermercado americano quiere abrir sucursales *(branches)* en España. Prepara un anuncio para el nuevo supermercado. Incluye en el anuncio lo que se puede comprar, los precios, las ventas *(sales)* especiales, etc.

Writing Strategy

Writing with graphics

Sometimes words alone do not convey adequate information about a topic. Including maps, diagrams, tables, or graphs can help illustrate your expository writing. Pictures and text work well together. Often the graphic will show quickly what might take many paragraphs to describe. In using graphics, be sure to label clearly and accurately to help readers recognize and understand information.

Las compras en distintos países

You have read about shopping habits in Spanish-speaking countries. List the kinds of shops and the products people buy in each in one column. Now think about your family and the places where you do your shopping. List those stores and products in the second column.

In a Venn Diagram like this one, put those shopping practices that are exclusive to Spanish-speaking countries in the left; those of your family on the right, and those common to both in the middle, overlapping section of the diagram. Now write a paragraph, comparing your family's buying habits with those of families in Spanish-speaking countries.

Las tiendas y los productos

Los países hispanos — Mi familia

A **TECHNOLOGY OPTIONS**
Students may use the Portfolio feature on the CD-ROM to write their postcards.

Students may send electronic postcards from **Café Glencoe** (www.cafe.glencoe.com).

Writing Strategy

Writing with graphics

A. Have students read the Writing Stategy and the directions to the activity on page 111.

B. You may wish to work with the class in preparing their graphics. It can be done as a group effort.

C. Have students read aloud their paragraphs, displaying their Venn Diagrams to the class as they do so. Students can compare their family's shopping habits with those of others in the class. When everyone has finished, students can make a more general comparison (including another Venn Diagram) of their shopping habits with those in Spanish-speaking countries.

National Standards

Communities and Comparisons

Have students bring in Spanish-language newspapers available in the community and read the advertisements. They should discuss the content of the ads, the differences between the products advertised in the Spanish ads and those advertised in English-language newspapers, and any other similarities and differences they find.

ANSWERS

Actividades escritas
A and **B** Answers will vary.

Writing Strategy
Answers will vary.

111

ASSESSMENT RESOURCES

- 📁 Chapter Quizzes
- 📁 Testing Program
- 💾 Computer Testmaker
- 📁 Situation Cards
- ✍ Communication Transparency C-4
- 📁 Performance Assessment
- 📼 **Maratón mental** Videoquiz

VOCABULARY REVIEW

The words and phrases in the **Vocabulario** have been taught for productive use in this chapter. They are summarized here as a resource for both students and teacher. This list also serves as a convenient resource for the **Culminación** activities on pages 110 and 111. Have the students look at the list. If there are any words they do not know, have them find them in the **Vocabulario** sections on pages 86–87 and 90–91. If absolutely necessary, students can look up some words in the end vocabulary.

There are approximately four cognates in this vocabulary list. Have students find them.

Teacher Notes

Vocabulario

IDENTIFYING MORE STORES

la zapatería	la joyería

SHOPPING FOR CLOTHES AND JEWELRY

mirar en el escaparate (la vitrina)	¿En qué puedo servirle?
probarse la ropa	Quisiera...
	No me (le) queda(n) bien.

IDENTIFYING MORE CLOTHING

el bolsillo	el vestido	los botones
el saco, la chaqueta	el cinturón	las sandalias
el abrigo	el pañuelo	las botas
el impermeable, la gabardina	la ropa interior	el tacón
el suéter	la bufanda	
la camisa de mangas cortas (largas)		

IDENTIFYING JEWELRY

las joyas	una cadena	un arete,
una pulsera	un anillo	un pendiente
		un reloj

IDENTIFYING MORE PARTS OF THE BODY

la muñeca	el dedo
el cuello	la oreja, el oído

DESCRIBING CLOTHING AND JEWELRY

mediano(a)	estrecho(a)
ancho(a)	de oro

IDENTIFYING MORE FOOD STORES

el colmado, la tienda de abarrotes, la tienda de ultramarinos	el hipermercado	la pastelería
	la panadería	la verdulería
el puesto	la carnicería	la frutería
el supermercado	la pescadería	

FOODS

el pan	los mariscos
la carne	los pasteles
el pescado	las legumbres, los vegetales

SHOPPING FOR FOOD

hacer las compras, ir de compras	fresco(a)	un frasco
¿A cuánto están... ?	la bolsa de plástico	una caja
tener buena pinta	una tajada,	una docena
empujar el carrito	una rebanada	

For the Native Speaker

¿Cómo se dice... ? If there are native speakers in the class, ask them to tell the words they use where there are choices in the vocabulary, for example: **colmado, tienda de abarrotes, tienda de ultramarinos;** or **saco, chaqueta; impermeable, gabardina**, and any others they may come up with.

Independent Practice

Assign any of the following:
1. Activities, pages 110–111
2. Workbook, **Mi autobiografía**, page 44
3. Situation Cards
4. CD-ROM, Disc 1, Chapter 4, **Juego de repaso**

TECNOTUR

VIDEO

¡Buen viaje!

EPISODIO 4 ▶ De tiendas

Cristina acaba de hacer un video sobre Puerto Vallarta.

Luis le da un regalo muy sentimental a Cristina.

CD-ROM

Expansión cultural

Las artesanías mexicanas son muy populares entre los turistas, y sus precios son una verdadera ganga.

interNET CONNECTION

In this video episode Cristina, Luis, and Isabel run errands in Puerto Vallarta. During the course of the day, they explore the local shops, including an open-air market and a bookstore. To do some cyber-shopping of your own in the Spanish-speaking world, go to the **Capítulo 4** Internet activity at the **Glencoe Foreign Language** Web site:

http://www.glencoe.com/sec/fl

TECNOTUR

ciento trece ∾ **113**

OVERVIEW

This page previews three key multi-media components of the **Glencoe Spanish** series. Each reinforces the material taught in Chapter 4 in a unique manner.

VIDEO

The Video Program allows students to see how the chapter vocabulary and structures are used by native speakers in an engaging story. For maximum reinforcement, show the video episode as a final activity for Chapter 4.

A. These two photos show highlights from the Chapter 4 video episode. Ask students: **¿Por qué están Cristina, Isabel y Luis en Puerto Vallarta? ¿Dónde están Cristina y Luis en la primera foto? ¿Y en la segunda foto?**

B. See the Video Activities Booklet for detailed suggestions for using this resource.

CD-ROM

A. In the video episode Cristina says she needs to buy some souvenirs for her family. The **Expansión cultural** photo displays some typical Mexican folk art that Cristina might like to purchase. Have students read the caption on page 113.

B. In the CD-ROM version of **Expansión cultural** (Disc 1, page 113), students can listen to additional recorded information about Mexican folk art.

INTERNET

Teacher Information and Student Worksheets for this activity can be accessed at the Web site.

Video Synopsis

In this episode Cristina, Luis, and Isabel meet in a small plaza in downtown Puerto Vallarta. Cristina has been shopping and videotaping scenes for the Web page. The trio discuss the best places to buy food (for a picnic) and souvenirs for Cristina to take back to her family in Los Angeles. While Isabel shops for the food, Luis and Cristina visit a bookstore. Cristina purchases two travel books about Puerto Vallarta. As they leave, Luis surprises Cristina with a gift of his favorite book of poetry by Pablo Neruda.

113

OVERVIEW

This section reviews the salient points from Chapters 1–4. In the **Conversación** students will review train, restaurant, and shopping vocabulary and the preterite of some regular and irregular verbs. In the **Estructura** section, they will review the conjugations of irregular verbs in the preterite and the imperfect tense. They will practice these structures as they talk about train travel, eating in a restaurant, and a trip to Chichicastenango.

TEACHING THE CONVERSATION

A. Have students open their books to page 114. Call on two students to read the conversation aloud.

B. Go over the activities in the **Después de conversar** section.

Learning From Photos

Gran Vía, Madrid La Gran Vía was, for many years, Madrid's 5th Avenue. Here were the city's most elegant shops, first-run movie theaters, and luxury hotels. Today, the Gran Vía has lost some of its glamour.

114

Repaso CAPÍTULOS 1-4

Conversación

¿Cuándo volviste?

Gran Vía, Madrid

TADEO: ¿A qué hora llegaste?

ANITA: Pues, el tren llegó a tiempo, a las 18:10.

TADEO: ¿Viniste en tren?

ANITA: Sí, no quería tomar el avión. Tarda mucho tiempo el viaje del aeropuerto al centro.

TADEO: Con el tráfico, no hay duda. ¿Comiste en el tren?

ANITA: No. Fui a un restaurante cerca de la estación antes de salir. Pedí una tortilla y una ensalada. La tortilla estaba muy buena. Me gustó.

TADEO: ¿Qué hiciste desde que llegaste? Papá quería saber dónde estabas.

ANITA: ¿Te preguntó dónde estaba? Pues, fui a la Gran Vía. Le compré un regalo para su cumpleaños.

TADEO: Yo le compré un par de zapatos. Y tú, ¿qué le compraste?

ANITA: Una camisa blanca y azul. Tiene mangas cortas. Creo que le va a quedar muy bien y que le va a gustar.

Después de conversar

 Anita hizo mucho.   Contesten.

1. ¿A qué hora llegó Anita a Madrid?
2. ¿Cómo vino?
3. ¿Por qué no quería tomar el avión?
4. ¿Dónde comió?
5. ¿Qué pidió?
6. ¿Qué tal le gustó?
7. ¿Adónde fue cuando llegó a Madrid?
8. ¿Qué compró?

REPASO DE CAPÍTULOS 1-4

Estructura

El pretérito

1. Review the following irregular verbs in the preterite.

ESTAR	estuve	PONER	puse	HACER	hice
TENER	tuve	PODER	pude	VENIR	vine
ANDAR	anduve	SABER	supe	QUERER	quise

2. The preceding irregular verbs all take the same endings in the preterite. Review the following.

TENER	tuve	tuviste	tuvo	tuvimos	*tuvisteis*	tuvieron
PONER	puse	pusiste	puso	pusimos	*pusisteis*	pusieron
VENIR	vine	viniste	vino	vinimos	*vinisteis*	vinieron

3. Note that verbs with a **j** in the preterite have the ending **-eron**, not **-ieron**.

dijeron   **trajeron**

4. Review the verbs with the stem change **e → i** and **o → u** in the preterite.

SERVIR	serví	serviste	sirvió	servimos	*servisteis*	sirvieron
DORMIR	dormí	dormiste	durmió	dormimos	*dormisteis*	durmieron

Other verbs conjugated like **servir** are **pedir, repetir, freír,** and **seguir. Morir** is conjugated like **dormir.**

Práctica

A HISTORIETA Un viaje en tren

Contesten.

1. ¿Hiciste el viaje en tren?
2. ¿Viniste con tu hermano?
3. ¿Estuvieron Uds. mucho tiempo en la estación de ferrocarril?
4. ¿Tuvieron Uds. que hacer cola delante de la ventanilla para comprar sus billetes?
5. ¿Quién hizo las maletas? ¿Tú o tu hermano?
6. ¿Pudieron Uds. llevar las maletas o tuvieron que buscar ayuda?
7. ¿Le pidieron ayuda a un mozo?

El ferrocarril Pacífico, México

TEACHING STRUCTURE

El pretérito

A. Have students open their books to page 115. Lead them through Steps 1–4.

B. You may have them repeat the verb forms aloud.

Práctica

A After students do **Práctica A,** you may have them retell the story in their own words.

ANSWERS

Práctica

A 1. Sí, (No, no) hice el viaje en tren.
2. Sí, (No, no) vine con mi hermano.
3. Sí, (No, no) estuvimos mucho tiempo en la estación de ferrocarril.
4. Sí, (No, no) tuvimos que hacer cola delante de la ventanilla para comprar nuestros billetes.
5. Yo hice (Mi hermano hizo) las maletas.

6. Nosotros pudimos llevar las maletas. (Tuvimos que buscar ayuda.)
7. Sí, (No, no) le pedimos ayuda a un mozo.

115

✦Práctica✦

B If students have problems doing **Práctica B,** review the irregular preterite forms in the **Estructura** sections of Chapters 1 and 2.

TEACHING STRUCTURE

El imperfecto

A. Lead students through Steps 1–4 on page 116. Model the verb forms and have students repeat them after you.

B. For a more complete review of the imperfect, refer students to the **Estructura** sections in Chapters 3 (pages 64–71) and 4 (pages 94–99).

Note You may wish to do the first literary selection (pages 430–433) with students at this time.

B **HISTORIETA** En el restaurante

Completen.

El viernes pasado yo ____ (ir) a un restaurante con mi amiga Julia. Ella ____ (pedir) la especialidad de la casa. Yo ____ (pedir) un plato con camarones y langosta. Nosotros dos ____ (pedir) una ensalada de tomate y lechuga.

La comida estaba deliciosa. Julia ____ (decir) que le gustaba mucho. Yo le ____ (repetir) al mesero lo que ella ____ (decir). El mesero nos ____ (servir) muy bien.

Yo ____ (pedir) la cuenta. El mesero la ____ (traer) y nos ____ (invitar) a tomar un postre. Yo ____ (pedir) un helado y Julia ____ (pedir) flan—un tipo de pudín español.

Sevilla, España

El imperfecto

1. Review the forms of the imperfect tense of regular verbs.

TOMAR	tomaba	tomabas	tomaba	tomábamos	*tomabais*	tomaban
COMER	comía	comías	comía	comíamos	*comíais*	comían
VIVIR	vivía	vivías	vivía	vivíamos	*vivíais*	vivían

2. Review the forms of the irregular verbs **ir** and **ser.**

| IR | iba | ibas | iba | íbamos | *ibais* | iban |
| SER | era | eras | era | éramos | *erais* | eran |

¿Te acuerdas?
Ver is also considered irregular.
ver: veía

3. The imperfect tense is used to express an action in the past that is continuous or repeated. The time the action began and ended is not important. The preterite tense is used to express an action that began and ended at a definite time in the past. A sentence will often have both types of past action. The action that was going on is expressed by the imperfect, and the action that intervened or interrupted is expressed by the preterite.

> **Su hermano iba allí cada año pero Roberto fue solamente una vez.**
> **Él miraba en el escaparate cuando vio a su amigo.**

4. The imperfect is used for description in the past.

> **Él tenía ocho años y era muy inteligente.**

ANSWERS

Práctica
B 1. fui
2. pidió
3. pedí
4. pedimos
5. dijo
6. repetí
7. dijo
8. sirvió
9. pedí
10. trajo
11. invitó
12. pedí
13. pidió

✦Práctica✦

C **Cuando yo era niño(a)** Contesten personalmente.

1. Cuando tú eras niño(a), ¿dónde vivías?
2. ¿Cuántos cuartos tenía la casa donde vivía tu familia?
3. ¿A qué escuela ibas?
4. ¿A qué hora salías de casa para ir a la escuela?
5. ¿Quién hacía las compras en tu familia?
6. ¿Tenían Uds. una computadora?

D **HISTORIETA** *Un viaje estupendo*

Completen.

1. El año pasado mis amigos y yo _____ (hacer) un viaje estupendo.
2. Nosotros _____ (ir) a Guatemala.
3. Yo _____ (tomar) un curso de español en Antigua.
4. Mis amigos _____ (estudiar) el español también.
5. Un día nosotros nos _____ (levantar) temprano y _____ (ir) a Chichicastenango.
6. Nosotros _____ (andar) por el mercado de Chichi.
7. Nosotros _____ (ver) a los indígenas.
8. Las mujeres de Chichicastenango _____ (llevar) una blusa y una falda de colores vivos.
9. En el mercado los indios _____ (vender) los productos que _____ (cultivar) o _____ (hacer) en casa.
10. Con el dinero que _____ (recibir) por las cosas que _____ (vender), ellos _____ (comprar) todas las provisiones que _____ (necesitar).

Actividades comunicativas

A **Cuando era niño(a)** Con un(a) compañero(a), discutan todo lo que hacían con frecuencia cuando eran niños(as) y asistían a la escuela primaria.

B **Un regalo** Estás en una tienda de ropa. Tienes que comprar un regalo para un(a) pariente. Conversa con el/la dependiente(a) (tu compañero[a]). Cambien de rol.

C **¿Usas mucho la computadora?** Con un(a) compañero(a), hablen de todo lo que Uds. hacen con la computadora. Luego decidan quién se sirve más de (usa más) la computadora.

Antigua, Guatemala

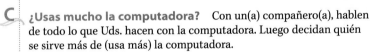

✦Práctica✦

C If students have problems doing **Práctica C**, review some of the **Práctica** activities in Chapter 3.

D After going over **Práctica D**, have students retell the story in their own words.

Actividades comunicativas

A Have students first make a list of things they did in elementary school.

B Students may want to review the vocabulary from Chapter 4 as they prepare to do this activity.

C Students may want to review the vocabulary from Chapter 3 as they prepare to do this activity.

GEOGRAPHY CONNECTION

Antigua, Guatemala Antigua is a beautiful colonial city founded in 1524. It was the original capital of Guatemala, but after it suffered a number of earthquakes, the worst in 1773, the Spanish governors decided to move the capital to Guatemala City in 1776.

Independent Practice

Assign any of the following:
1. Activities, pages 114–117
2. Workbook, pages 45–49
3. CD-ROM, Disc 1, pages 114–117
4. CD-ROM, Disc 1, Chapters 1–4, **Juegos de repaso**

ANSWERS

Práctica

C 1. **Cuando era niño(a) vivía en ___.**
2. **La casa donde vivía mi familia tenía ___ cuartos.**
3. **Iba a la Escuela ___.**
4. **Salía de casa a las ___ para ir a la escuela.**
5. **Mi ___ hacía las compras en mi familia.**
6. **Sí, (No, no) teníamos una computadora.**

D 1. **hicimos**
2. **fuimos**
3. **tomé**
4. **estudiaron**
5. **levantamos, fuimos**
6. **anduvimos**
7. **vimos**
8. **llevaban**
9. **vendían, cultivaban, hacían**
10. **recibían, vendían, compraban, necesitaban**

Actividades comunicativas
A, B, and **C** Answers will vary.

117

VISTAS DE CHILE

OVERVIEW

The **Vistas de Chile** were prepared by National Geographic Society. Their purpose is to give students greater insight, through these visual images, into the culture and people of Chile. Have students look at the photographs on pages 118–121 for enjoyment. If they would like to talk about them, let them say anything they can, using the vocabulary they have learned to this point.

National Standards

Cultures
The **Vistas de Chile** photos, and the accompanying captions, allow students to gain insights into the people and culture of Chile.

Learning From Photos

1. Lago Pehoé, Parque Nacional Torres del Paine Torres del Paine, located at the far south of the Cordillera de los Andes, is one of the newest nature preserves in South America. It was created in 1959. Mostly uninhabited, the area has unique physical formations, numerous glaciers and lakes, such as Pehoé, and many animals, such as guanacos, flamingos, condors, swans, hares, and foxes. Much of the park is lushly forested.

2. Cerro Santa Lucía, Santiago Here on a rocky outcropping, called **Huelén** by the Indians, Pedro de Valdivia decided to found the city of Santiago. Benjamín Vicuña Mackenna, the great historian and **intendente (jefe de servicios municipales)** began to transform the hill into the maze of pathways, gardens, fountains, and squares that it is today. *(continued)*

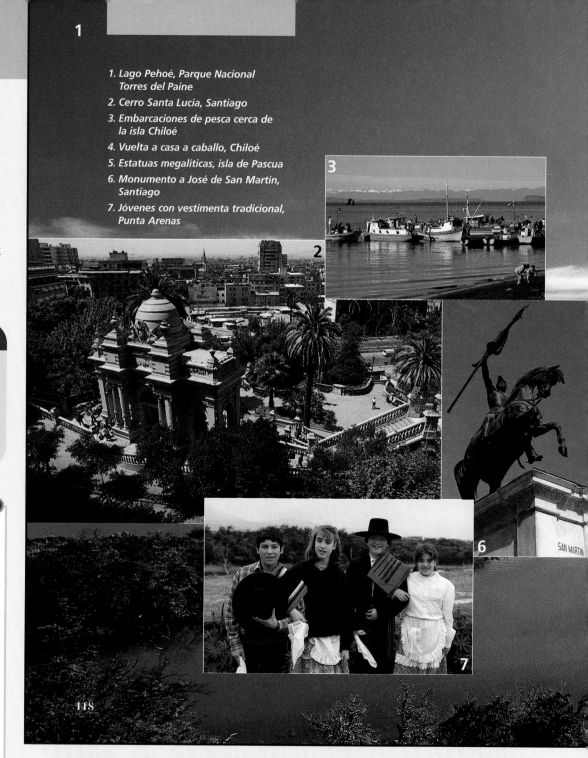

1
1. Lago Pehoé, Parque Nacional Torres del Paine
2. Cerro Santa Lucía, Santiago
3. Embarcaciones de pesca cerca de la isla Chiloé
4. Vuelta a casa a caballo, Chiloé
5. Estatuas megalíticas, isla de Pascua
6. Monumento a José de San Martín, Santiago
7. Jóvenes con vestimenta tradicional, Punta Arenas

118

Learning From Photos

3. Embarcaciones de pesca cerca de la isla Chiloé Chiloé is an archipelago with one main island, Isla Grande, surrounded by small groups of islands. Chiloé is often fogbound, and suffers very harsh winters. Chiloé holds a special place in the heart of Chileans. Many of Chile's traditions, its folk music and dance, crafts, and mythology have their origin in Chiloé. Many **chilotes** still try to eke out a living by fishing from rowboats and the small motor launches shown in the photo.

4. Vuelta a casa a caballo, Chiloé These horsemen in their rain-slicked ponchos and wide-brimmed sombreros are returning from a day at the **Festival Costumbrista** held in February in Castro, the capital city of Chiloé. The weather is typical of Chiloé, *(continued)*

NATIONAL GEOGRAPHIC

VISTAS
DE CHILE

Learning From Photos

González claimed the island for Spain and Carlos III in 1770. In 1888, after winning its independence from Spain, Chile annexed the island. Today, almost all 2,500 Easter Islanders live in the one town on the island, Hanga Roa.

6. Monumento a José de San Martín, Santiago In 1817 the Argentine general José de San Martín and the Chilean national hero, Bernardo O'Higgins with their 3,600 man **Ejército de los Andes**, made up of Chileans and Argentines, crossed the **Cordillera** from Argentina. They defeated Royalist troops at Chacabuco, then entered Santiago in triumph.

This equestrian statue of San Martín is in the center of the Alameda Libertador Bernardo O'Higgins, a broad avenue that has been Santiago's main thoroughfare since before independence. People refer to it simply as **la Alameda.**

7. Jóvenes con vestimenta tradicional, Punta Arenas While the girls are in traditional white aprons and embroidered skirts, the boys are dressed in the time-honored clothing of the **huaso,** Chile's cowboy. His hat is a broad-brimmed sombrero. The summer sombrero is made of tightly woven straw; the winter version is made of felt. Thrown over one shoulder is a brightly-colored, striped, **poncho de huaso.** The **huaso** wears this costume when participating in one of Chile's national sports, **el rodeo.**

Learning From Photos

(continued from page 118)
damp, overcast, drizzly. Various towns of Chiloé are well known for their woven wool products, especially blankets and ponchos. The riders in the photo are probably wearing ponchos from Quellón. Quellón is famous for its soft, grey ponchos, very resistant to the rain because the wool used for them is raw and therefore still full of natural oils.

5. Estatuas megalíticas, isla de Pascua
Covering only 130 square kilometers (50 square miles), Easter Island is 3,200 kilometers (2,000 miles) off the west coast of South America. The mysterious, monolithic basalt statues (**moai**) that are everywhere on the island, some of them up to 9 meters (30 feet) tall, are believed by most archeologists to be figures of dead chiefs or gods. Don Felipe
(continued)

VISTAS DE CHILE

Learning From Photos

1. Vista panorámica de Santiago Founded by the **conquistador** Valdivia in 1541, the capital of Chile, a city of five million, is situated on the banks of the Río Mapocho with the Cordillera de los Andes in the background. Home to the Universidad Nacional, the Museo de Bellas Artes, the Teatro Municipal, and many beautiful parks, Santiago has a very European atmosphere.

2. Turistas admiran un iceberg, sur de Chile In far southern Chile is the National Park of Laguna San Rafael with its magnificent glacier. When the sun is shining, the glacier is an extraordinary spectacle of light streaming through blue ice. Cruise ships take tourists south from Puerto Montt. Near the point where the glacier meets the sea, they are transferred to rowboats where they can reach out and touch the giant icebergs that float by.

3. Deportes acuáticos en el lago Villarrica, Pucón The area around Lake Villarrica in the exceptionally beautiful southern Lake District is one of the most visited holiday resorts in Chile. The snow-capped **volcán Villarrica** dominates the lake.

4. Observatorio del Cerro Tololo y remolina de estrellas, La Serena The Cerrro Tololo Observatory is located in north central Chile, the southern hemisphere's chosen spot for observatories because of the exceptionally clear mountain air. Conditions are right for sky photography 300 nights a year.

(continued)

1. Vista panorámica de Santiago
2. Turistas admiran un iceberg, sur de Chile
3. Deportes acuáticos en el lago Villarrica, Pucón
4. Observatorio del Cerro Tololo y remolino de estrellas, La Serena
5. Centro de Santiago
6. Bolsa de valores, Santiago
7. Viñedo, valle central

NATIONAL GEOGRAPHIC SOCIETY — TEACHER'S CORNER

Index to NATIONAL GEOGRAPHIC MAGAZINE

The following articles may be used for research relating to this chapter:

- "Chile's Uncharted Cordillera Sarmiento," by Jack Miller, April 1994.
- "Chile: Acts of Faith," by Allen A. Boraiko, July 1988.
- "The High Andes: South America's Islands in the Sky," by Loren McIntyre, April 1987.
- "Guanacos: Wild Camels of South America," by William L. Franklin, July 1981.
- "Chile, Republic on a Shoestring," by Gordon Young, October 1973.

NATIONAL GEOGRAPHIC

VISTAS
DE CHILE

Learning From Photos

(continued from page 120)

5. Centro de Santiago Here on this pedestrian thoroughfare, Ahumada, one can find a major cross-section of Santiago's population. Shoppers and business people stand and talk in the street, stop in for **un expreso** or **un cortado** (with milk) with a glass of mineral water on the side. On Ahumada there are banks and shops, department stores, and, everywhere, street vendors. The vendor in the photo is selling his wares from a traditional **barquito** mounted on bicycle wheels.

6. Bolsa de valores, Santiago The Stock Exchange, **La Bolsa,** is located, appropriately, on the **Calle de la Bolsa** in downtown Santiago. Chile's economy boomed in the 1980's and 90's. Exports of Chilean agricultural products, fish, and wine have increased manyfold. The Chilean **peso** has been very stable.

7. Viñedo, valle central The Spanish **conquistadores** planted the first grapes in Chile and produced the **vino del país.** These wines still account for three quarters of Chile's production.

Products available from
GLENCOE/MCGRAW-HILL

To order the following products, call Glencoe/McGraw-Hill at 1-800-334-7344.

CD-ROMs
· Picture Atlas of the World
· The Complete National Geographic: 109 Years of National Geographic Magazine

Software
· ZingoLingo: Spanish Diskettes

Transparency Set
· NGS PicturePack: Geography of South America

Videodisc
· STV: World Geography (Volume 3: "South America and Antarctica")

Products available from
NATIONAL GEOGRAPHIC SOCIETY

NATIONAL GEOGRAPHIC SOCIETY

To order the following products, call National Geographic Society at 1-800-368-2728.

Books
· Exploring Your World: The Adventure of Geography
· National Geographic Satellite Atlas of the World

Video
· South America ("Nations of the World" Series)

Chapter 5 Overview ◆◆◆◆◆◆◆◆◆◆◆◆◆◆◆◆◆◆◆◆◆

SCOPE AND SEQUENCE   pages 122–149

TOPICS	FUNCTIONS	STRUCTURE	CULTURE
◆ Board games and hobbies ◆ Activities in the park	◆ How to talk about leisure time activities ◆ How to talk about going to the amusement park and the zoo ◆ How to talk about future events ◆ How to compare people and things	◆ The future tense ◆ Comparatives and superlatives	◆ Sunday in the park in Spanish-speaking countries ◆ Chapultepec Park, Mexico, D.F. ◆ Palermo Park, Buenos Aires ◆ Game arcades in the Spanish-speaking world ◆ Domino ◆ Literary genres in Spanish ◆ Isabel Allende

CHAPTER 5 RESOURCES

PRINT	MULTIMEDIA

Planning Resources

Lesson Plans Block Scheduling Lesson Plans	Interactive Lesson Planner

Reinforcement Resources

Writing Activities Workbook Student Tape Manual Video Activities Booklet Web Site User's Guide	Transparencies Binder Audiocassette/Compact Disc Program Videocassette/Videodisc Program Online Internet Activities Electronic Teacher's Classroom Resources

Assessment Resources

Situation Cards Chapter Quizzes Testing Program Performance Assessment	**Maratón mental** Mindjogger Videoquiz Testmaker Computer Software (Macintosh/Windows) Listening Comprehension Audiocassette/Compact Disc Communication Transparency: C-5

Motivational Resources

Expansion Activities	Café Glencoe: www.cafe.glencoe.com Keypal Internet Activities

Enrichment

Spanish for Spanish Speakers	

SECTION	PAGES	SECTION RESOURCES
Vocabulario Palabras 1 **Los pasatiempos y hobbys** **¿Cómo pasarán el tiempo mañana?**	124–127	Vocabulary Transparencies 5.1 Audiocassette 4A/Compact Disc 4 Student Tape Manual, TE, pages 47–49 Workbook, pages 50–51 Chapter Quizzes, page 22 CD-ROM, Disc 2, pages 124–127
Vocabulario Palabras 2 **El parque**	128–131	Vocabulary Transparencies 5.2 Audiocassette 4A/Compact Disc 4 Student Tape Manual, TE, pages 50–51 Workbook, pages 51–52 Chapter Quizzes, page 23 CD-ROM, Disc 2, pages 128–131
Estructura **Futuro de los verbos regulares** **Comparativo y superlativo**	132–137	Workbook, pages 53–56 Audiocassette 4A/Compact Disc 4 Student Tape Manual, TE, pages 51–54 Chapter Quizzes, pages 24-25 Computer Testmaker CD-ROM, Disc 2, pages 132–137
Conversación **Una diferencia de opinión**	138–139	Audiocassette 4A/Compact Disc 4 Student Tape Manual, TE, page 55 CD-ROM, Disc 2
Lecturas culturales **El domingo en el parque** **Las salas de juegos** (opcional) **El dominó** (opcional)	140–143	Testing Program, pages 40–41 CD-ROM, Disc 2, pages 140–143
Conexiones **La literatura** (opcional)	144–145	Testing Program, pages 41–42 CD-ROM, Disc 2, pages 144–145
Culminación **Actividades orales** **Actividades escritas** **Vocabulario** **Tecnotur**	146–149	¡**Buen viaje!** Video, Episode 5 Video Activities, pages 81–83 Internet Activities **www.glencoe.com/sec/fl** Testing Program, pages 37–40; 129; 173; 194 CD-ROM, Disc 2, pages 146–149

OVERVIEW

In this chapter students will learn to talk about their favorite indoor leisure activities as well as activities in a park. In addition to learning the formation of the future tense, students will learn how to compare people and things. The cultural focus of the chapter is on typical park activities and pastimes in the Spanish-speaking world.

National Standards

In Chapter 5 students will learn to communicate in spoken and written Spanish on the following topics:
- playing games and pursuing hobbies
- participating in activities in a park

Students will obtain and provide information and engage in conversations dealing with indoor and outdoor leisure activities as they fulfill the chapter objectives listed on this page.

Teacher Notes

Los pasatiempos

Objetivos

In this chapter you will learn to do the following:
- talk about popular hobbies and games
- talk about activities in the park
- give details about location
- talk about what will happen in the future
- compare objects and people
- describe your favorite pastime
- talk about pastimes in Spanish-speaking countries

interNET CONNECTION

The **Glencoe Foreign Language Web site** (http://www.glencoe.com/sec/fl) offers three options that enable you and your students to experience the Spanish-speaking world via the Internet:
- The online **Actividades** are correlated to the chapters and utilize Hispanic Web sites around the world. For the Chapter 5 activity, see student page 149.
- The **Correspondencia electrónica** section provides information on how to set up a keypal (pen pal) exchange between your class and a class in the Spanish-speaking world.
- At **Café Glencoe,** the interactive "after-school" section of the site, you and your students can access a variety of additional online resources.

ciento veintitrés 123

Spotlight On Culture

Fotografía The **Parque María Luisa** is in Sevilla on the banks of the Guadalquivir. The sunken gardens with pools, fountains, and ceramic tiles, are magnificent. The elaborate buildings in the park were built for the **Exposición Ibero-americana** of 1929. Near the park is the old **Fábrica de tabacos,** built from 1750 to 1766. Today it houses the **Universidad de Sevilla.** In the photo is one of four bridges crossing the ornamental lake. Each bridge represents one of the four medieval kingdoms of the Iberian Peninsula.

Pacing

Chapter 5 will require approximately six to eight days. Pacing will vary according to the length of the class, the age of your students, and student aptitude.

Block Scheduling

The extended time frame provided by block scheduling affords you the opportunity to implement a greater number of activities and projects to motivate and involve your students. See the Block Scheduling Lesson Plans Booklet for suggestions on how to present the chapter material within a block scheduling framework.

Chapter Projects

Una partida de Scrabble You may wish to reserve a class period for your students to play Scrabble in Spanish. Allow the students to use dictionaries as they play. **Parques de atracciones** Have students write to their favorite amusement park and ask for information in Spanish about the park. Have them use this material to make posters advertising the amusement park.

Vocabulario

RESOURCES

 Vocabulary Transparencies 5.1 (A & B)

📁 Student Tape Manual, TE, pages 47–49

🎧 Audiocassette 4A/CD3

📁 Workbook, pages 50–51

📁 Quiz 1, page 22

💿 CD-ROM, Disc 2, pages 124–127

🔔 Bell Ringer Review

Use BRR Transparency 5-1, or write the following on the board: Write down your favorite team sport and in two or three sentences explain why it is your favorite.

TEACHING VOCABULARY

A. Have students close their books. Show Vocabulary Transparencies 5.1 (A & B) for the initial presentation of vocabulary. Point to individual items and have students repeat each word or expression two or three times after you or the recording on Cassette 4A/ Compact Disc 3.

B. After presenting the vocabulary orally, have students open their books and read for additional reinforcement.

C. You may wish to ask the following questions as you present the new vocabulary: **¿Juegas (al) dominó? ¿Te gusta el dominó? Y el ajedrez, ¿te gusta? ¿Se usa un tablero para jugar (al) ajedrez? ¿Se usa un tablero para jugar (a las) damas?**

Los pasatiempos y hobbys

el ajedrez

el dominó

el tablero

la ficha

las damas

el crucigrama

los sellos

las monedas

Luisa es coleccionista.
Colecciona sellos y monedas.

Mañana irá al centro.
Comprará unas monedas antiguas.

124 〰️ *ciento veinticuatro*

CAPÍTULO 5

VOCABULARY EXPANSION

For the chess players in your class:

el rey	*king*
la reina/la dama	*queen*
el alfil	*bishop*
el caballo	*knight*
la torre	*rook/castle*
el peón	*pawn*

¿Cómo pasarán el tiempo mañana?

Mañana Ramona jugará al ajedrez con
un amigo.
Ella es más lista que su rival.
Ramona ganará. Será la campeona.

A Tomás le gustan los crucigramas.
Él llenará un crucigrama.

los juegos de video

el futbolín

la sala de juegos

¡OJO! The future tense is introduced in the **Vocabulario** section in the third person only. Students can immediately use this form to answer questions without having to change endings.

ABOUT THE SPANISH LANGUAGE

In Spain the word is **vídeo** with a written accent on the **i**. In Latin America the word is **video** with the stress on the **e**.

✦Práctica✦

¡OJO! **Práctica** When students are doing the **Práctica** activities, accept any answer that makes sense. The purpose of these activities is to have students use the new vocabulary. They are not factual recall activities. Thus, do not expect students to remember specific information from the vocabulary presentation when answering. If you wish, have students use the photo as a stimulus, when possible.
Historieta Each time **Historieta** appears, it means that the answers to the activity form a short story. Encourage students to look at the title of the **Historieta** since it can sometimes help them do the activity.

A Have students refer to the illustrations as they do **Práctica A.**

B Do **Práctica B** orally with books closed. Then have students retell the story in their own words.

Writing Development

After going over **Práctica B** have students write the answers in an organized paragraph to illustrate how all of the items tell a story.

126

✦Práctica✦

A Los pasatiempos   Contesten según los dibujos.

1. ¿A qué juegan las muchachas?

2. ¿Qué hay en el periódico?

3. ¿A qué juegan los señores?

4. ¿A qué juegan los niños?

5. ¿Dónde están los muchachos?

B **HISTORIETA** Un juego de ajedrez

Contesten según se indica.
1. ¿Jugará Tomás a las damas o al ajedrez? (al ajedrez)
2. ¿Con quién jugará? (un amigo)
3. ¿Quién es el jugador más listo? (su amigo)
4. ¿Tomás ganará o perderá el juego? (perderá)
5. ¿Quién será el campeón? (su amigo)

Barcelona, España

ANSWERS

Práctica

A 1. Las muchachas juegan a las damas.
2. Hay un crucigrama en el periódico.
3. Los señores juegan al ajedrez.
4. Los niños juegan al futbolín.
5. Los muchachos están en la sala de juegos.

B 1. Tomás jugará al ajedrez.
2. Jugará con un amigo.
3. Su amigo es el jugador más listo.
4. Tomás perderá el juego.
5. Su amigo será el campeón.

C ¿Qué será? Adivinen.

1. Para completar uno de estos necesitas un lápiz o un bolígrafo.
2. Puedes participar en una carrera de automóviles, una aventura con monstruos, un viaje por las galaxias.
3. Hay juegos que duran horas. Los jugadores piensan mucho antes de mover una pieza.
4. Juegas con un tablero, como el ajedrez, y usas fichas, pero el juego es más fácil que el ajedrez.
5. Es un juego como el fútbol en miniatura. Puedes jugar con un amigo o con tres amigos más.

D Preguntas personales Contesten.

1. ¿Te gustan los juegos de video? ¿Juegas en casa?
2. ¿Cuáles son los juegos más populares?
3. ¿Tú sabes jugar al ajedrez? ¿Es difícil?
4. ¿Quién es el/la mejor jugador(a) entre tus amigos?
5. ¿Alguien en tu familia llena los crucigramas?
6. ¿A ti te gustan los crucigramas o crees que son aburridos?
7. ¿Eres coleccionista?
8. ¿Qué coleccionas?

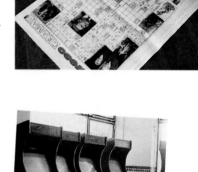

Actividades comunicativas

A Juegos de video Con un(a) compañero(a), preparen un cuestionario para determinar:

▶ cuántos alumnos en tu clase usan juegos de video
▶ cuántos juegan con los juegos de video en casa y cuántos en salas de juegos
▶ cuáles son los tres juegos de video más populares

Luego preparen un informe sobre los resultados de su encuesta *(survey)* para la clase.

Una sala de juegos

B Los gemelos con gustos distintos Eugenio y Eugenia son gemelos *(twins)*. Ellos tienen la misma apariencia pero no los mismos gustos. Con un(a) compañero(a), hagan el papel de los gemelos. Digan lo que cada uno hace después de las clases y en los fines de semana con su tiempo libre. Usen la imaginación.

VOCABULARIO

ciento veintisiete 127

CAPÍTULO 5
Vocabulario

C You can have students do **Práctica C** together as a game.

D Students can come to the front of the room and go over **Práctica D** in pairs, as if it were an interview.

Actividades comunicativas

B **TECHNOLOGY OPTION** Students can use the Portfolio feature on the CD-ROM to record this conversation.

EXPANSION After completing **Actividad B,** you may wish to ask students the following questions:
¿Conoces a algunos gemelos? ¿Quiénes son?
¿Hay gemelos en tu familia?
Los gemelos que conoces, ¿tienen los mismos intereses o no? ¿Son muy diferentes o son idénticos?

ABOUT THE SPANISH LANGUAGE

Twins are **gemelos** in most places, but in Mexico they are **cuates.** Mexicans also use the word **cuate** to mean *pal* or *buddy.*

Independent Practice

Assign any of the following:
1. Workbook, pages 50–51
2. Activities, pages 126–127
3. CD-ROM, Disc 2, pages 124–127

- Vocabulary Transparencies 5.2 (A & B)
- Student Tape Manual, TE, pages 50–51
- Audiocassette 4A/CD3
- Workbook, pages 51–52
- Quiz 2, page 23
- CD-ROM, Disc 2, pages 128–131

Bell Ringer Review

Use BRR Transparency 5-2, or write the following on the board: Tell where you go to do the following activities.
1. ver un partido de fútbol
2. ir de compras
3. tomar el sol y nadar
4. ver una película
5. dar una caminata

TEACHING VOCABULARY

A. Have students close their books. Then model the new vocabulary using Vocabulary Transparencies 5.2 (A & B). Have students repeat each word or expression two or three times after you or the recording on Cassette 4A/ Compact Disc 3.

B. After presenting the vocabulary, have students open their books and read the new vocabulary aloud. You can have the class read in chorus, or call on individuals to read.

Vocabulario

PALABRAS 2

El parque

el bote — remar por el lago — el lago

el mono — la jaula

El Zoológico

el payaso

el (parque) zoológico — el mimo

128 ∞ *ciento veintiocho*

CAPÍTULO 5

Pantomime

Begin
___, levántate.
Ven acá.
Vas a ir al parque hoy.
Da un paseo por el parque.
Compra una piragua.
Come la piragua.
Ahora rema por el lago en un bote.
Rema a la derecha.

Rema a la izquierda.
Baja del bote.
Gracias, ___. Regresa a tu asiento.

la senda

Mucha gente da un paseo por el parque.
Ellos caminan por las sendas bonitas.

el globo

una piragua

un helado

García y Molino

Los niños quieren una piragua.
Mamá les comprará una piragua.
Les comprará un globo también.

la montaña rusa

la noria

el caballito

a la izquierda

a la derecha

la boletería

el tiovivo

Entrada →

el parque de atracciones

Los jóvenes irán al parque de atracciones.
Están haciendo cola delante de la boletería.
En la cola (fila) Alberto está detrás de
Alejandra.

Y Alejandra está delante de Alberto.
La entrada al parque está al lado de la
boletería.

Learning From Photos

El Retiro, Madrid The park in
the photo on page 128 is the
Parque del Buen Retiro in the
heart of Madrid. Atop the pavillion overlooking the lake is an
equestrian statue of Alfonso XII
(1857–1885). The statue, by the
famous sculptor Mariano Benlli-
ure, was dedicated in 1922.

Did You Know?

¿Quieres una piragua? The
piragüero is a summertime fix-
ture, especially in the tropics.
From his little cart he sells paper
cupfuls of shaved ice over which
he pours syrup flavorings.

ABOUT THE SPANISH LANGUAGE

There are a number of words for
ticket. An airline, train, or bus
ticket is usually called **un boleto**
in Latin America. In Spain it's **un
billete**. A theater, movie, or other
admission ticket is **una entrada**.
However, **tique, tiquet**, and **ti-
quete** are becoming very common as generic terms for *ticket*.

⟨Práctica⟩

A Go over **Practica A** orally with books closed.

B After going over **Práctica B,** call on more able students to make up original sentences using the words that did not fit.

Writing Development

After going over **Práctica B,** have students write the answers in an organized paragraph to illustrate how all of the items tell a story.

⟨Práctica⟩

A HISTORIETA Al parque

Contesten.

1. ¿Irán los niños al parque mañana?
2. ¿Visitarán el zoológico?
3. ¿Verán los monos en el zoológico?
4. ¿Se divertirán los niños con los monos?
5. ¿Tomarán los niños una piragua?
6. ¿Les comprarán sus padres un globo?

B HISTORIETA Un día en el parque

Escojan la palabra apropiada.

1. La gente da un paseo por _____ del parque.
   a. las avenidas   **b.** los lagos   **c.** las sendas
2. Algunos _____ por el lago en un bote.
   a. compran   **b.** hacen   **c.** reman
3. Hay muchos animales en el _____.
   a. lago   **b.** zoológico   **c.** parque de atracciones
4. La gente hace cola _____ la boletería.
   a. detrás de   **b.** a la derecha de   **c.** delante de
5. Hay muchas _____ en un parque zoológico.
   a. jaulas   **b.** atracciones   **c.** norias
6. El _____ hace muchos gestos cómicos y extravagantes.
   a. tiovivo   **b.** payaso   **c.** caballito
7. A los niños les gusta tomar _____.
   a. lagos   **b.** atracciones   **c.** piraguas

El Retiro, Madrid

Parque de atracciones, Madrid

ANSWERS

Práctica

A 1. **Sí, los niños irán al parque mañana.**   **B** 1. **c**   5. **a**
2. **Sí, (No, no) visitarán el zoológico.**   2. **c**   6. **b**
3. **Sí, (No, no) verán los monos en el**   3. **b**   7. **c**
   zoológico.   4. **c**
4. **Sí (No), los niños (no) se divertirán**
   con los monos.
5. **Sí (No), los niños (no) tomarán una**
   piragua.
6. **Sí (No), sus padres (no) les**
   comprarán un globo.

C **¿Dónde está?**   Contesten según el plano.

1. ¿Qué hay en el centro del parque?
2. ¿Dónde está la boletería? ¿Delante del lago o al lado del lago?
3. ¿Dónde está la entrada al parque?
4. Y el parque zoológico, ¿dónde está?
5. Estás delante de la boletería. El parque de atracciones, ¿está a tu derecha o a tu izquierda?

EL PARQUE

Actividades comunicativas

A **En el parque**   Con un(a) compañero(a), miren el dibujo. Describan todo lo que ven en el dibujo. Tu compañero(a) te va a hacer preguntas. Contesta a sus preguntas. Entonces tú le puedes hacer preguntas y él o ella contestará.

B **Haciendo planes**   Habla con un(a) compañero(a). Uds. van a hacer algo el domingo. Tengan una conversación y decidan si van a ir al zoológico, al parque de atracciones o simplemente a un parque cerca de donde Uds. viven. Expliquen por qué prefieren ir adonde van.

VOCABULARIO   *ciento treinta y uno* **131**

C **EXPANSION** After going over **Práctica C**, have students make up sentences telling where things are located in relation to other things.

Actividades comunicativas

¡OJO! These **Actividades comunicativas** enable students to use the language creatively on their own as if they were communicating in real-life, survival situations. They are an excellent follow-up to the more controlled communicative activities in the **Práctica** section.

Let students choose the activities they wish to participate in. It is to be expected that students will make some errors as they communicate on their own.

A Encourage students to write as many sentences as possible to describe the illustration. You may wish to have a contest to see which pair comes up with the longest list.

B **TECHNOLOGY OPTION** Students can use the Portfolio feature on the CD-ROM to record their conversations.

Writing Development
Have students write a paragraph about what they see in the illustration that accompanies **Actividad A**.

ANSWERS

Práctica

C 1. **Hay un parque de atracciones.**
2. **La boletería está al lado del lago.**
3. **La entrada al parque está al lado de la boletería.**
4. **El parque zoológico está detrás del parque de atracciones.**
5. **El parque de atracciones está a mi izquierda.**

Actividades comunicativas
A and B Answers will vary.

Estructura

TEACHING STRUCTURE

◆ Talking about future events

A. Ask students to open their books to page 132. Read Steps 1 and 2 to them.
B. Have students repeat the verb forms after you.
C. Have students repeat the model sentences in Step 2 after you.

 You may wish to de-emphasize this structure point with some groups because it is a low-frequency structure in comparison to the periphrastic future **ir a** + infinitive. You may want to present this tense more for receptive purposes.

◆ Talking about future events
Futuro de los verbos regulares

1. The future tense is used to tell what will take place in the future. To form the future tense of regular verbs, you add the future endings to the infinitive. Study the following forms.

INFINITIVE	estudiar	leer	escribir	
STEM	estudiar-	leer-	escribir-	ENDINGS
yo	estudiaré	leeré	escribiré	-é
tú	estudiarás	leerás	escribirás	-ás
él, ella, Ud.	estudiará	leerá	escribirá	-á
nosotros(as)	estudiaremos	leeremos	escribiremos	-emos
vosotros(as)	*estudiaréis*	*leeréis*	*escribiréis*	-éis
ellos, ellas, Uds.	estudiarán	leerán	escribirán	-án

> **Mañana jugaré al ajedrez.**
> **Tú me verás jugar, ¿no?**
> **Yo seré el campeón.**

2. You have already learned the construction **ir a** + *infinitive* to express events that will take place in the near future. In everyday conversation, this construction is actually used more frequently than the future tense.

> **El año que viene voy a estudiar en Puerto Rico.**
> **Me vas a escribir, ¿no?**
> **Y yo voy a leer todas tus cartas.**

Universidad de Puerto Rico

Learning From Photos

Universidad de Puerto Rico This is the main campus of UPR in Río Piedras. The university was founded in 1903. A second campus was founded in 1911 in Mayagüez, followed later on by various others. The University of Puerto Rico is an accredited American university.

Práctica

A HISTORIETA Daniel viajará a España.

Contesten.

1. ¿Adónde irá Daniel el año que viene?
2. ¿Estudiará en Alcalá de Henares?
3. ¿Asistirá a clases en la universidad?
4. ¿Leerá muchos libros?
5. ¿Su amiga le escribirá con frecuencia?
6. ¿Recibirá las cartas en algunos días?
7. ¿Responderá a las cartas de su amiga?

Universidad de Alcalá, España

B ¡A divertirse esta noche!
Formen oraciones según el modelo.

los muchachos
Los muchachos verán la televisión.

1. Raúl

2. El señor Fornos

3. Los niños

4. Nosotros

5. Leonor

6. Los monos

7. Tú

8. Yo

ESTRUCTURA

ciento treinta y tres 133

Práctica

A Go over **Práctica A** orally with books closed.

EXPANSION Have a student or students retell the story in **Práctica A** in their own words.

B Allow students to prepare **Práctica B** before going over it in class.

HISTORY CONNECTION

Universidad de Alcalá, España
This university was founded in 1598 by Cardinal Cisneros. However, the oldest university in Spain is **la Universidad de Salamanca,** founded in 1230. Salamanca served as the model for the first universities of the Americas: Santo Domingo (1538), México (1553), and Lima (1553).

ANSWERS

Práctica

A 1. **Daniel irá a España el año que viene.**
2. **Sí, estudiará en Alcalá de Henares.**
3. **Sí, asistirá a clases en la universidad.**
4. **Sí, leerá muchos libros.**
5. **Sí, su amiga le escribirá con frecuencia.**
6. **Sí, recibirá las cartas en algunos días.**
7. **Sí, responderá a las cartas de su amiga.**

B 1. **Raúl leerá un libro.**
2. **El señor Fornos llenará un crucigrama.**
3. **Los niños jugarán a las damas.**
4. **Nosotros jugaremos con un juego de video.**
5. **Leonor dará un paseo por el parque.**
6. **Los monos dormirán.**
7. **Tú hablarás por teléfono.**
8. **Yo escribiré una carta.**

133

❖Práctica❖

C You may wish to have students prepare **Práctica C** before going over it in class.

D Have students do **Práctica D** with books open.

E **Práctica E** is somewhat difficult, going from preterite to future, but it is a very natural exchange since we so often tell someone what we didn't do but will do.

Writing Development
You may wish to have students write **Práctica D** as a unified paragraph.

C **HISTORIETA** El coleccionista

Sigan el modelo.

> **Mañana voy a ir al centro.**
> **Mañana iré al centro.**

1. Mañana Carlos va a ir al centro.
2. Yo voy a ir con él.
3. Vamos a visitar los puestos de los coleccionistas.
4. Sé que Carlos va a comprar monedas.
5. Él cree que va a encontrar unas monedas raras.
6. Y yo voy a buscar sellos.
7. Yo sé quien me va a vender los sellos.
8. Y no voy a pagar mucho.

Una casa de campo, Mucuchíes, Venezuela

D **HISTORIETA** El sábado que viene

Completen con el futuro.

El sábado que viene yo _____ (viajar) al campo. Allí _____ (visitar) a mis abuelos. Ellos _____ (estar) muy contentos. Ellos me _____ (esperar) en la estación. Entonces me _____ (llevar) a su casa. Mi tía María Luisa _____ (preparar) una comida deliciosa. Después de comer todos nosotros _____ (jugar) al dominó. Abuelita _____ (ganar) como siempre. Yo _____ (pasar) dos o tres días con ellos. Yo _____ (volver) a casa un poco triste. Me gusta mucho visitar a los abuelos.

E **Ayer no, pero mañana, sí** Contesten según el modelo.

> ¿Fuiste a la sala de juegos ayer?
> No, pero iré mañana.

1. ¿Fuiste al parque ayer?
2. ¿Viste al payaso ayer?
3. ¿Visitaste el zoológico?
4. ¿Caminaste por las sendas del parque?
5. ¿Te divertiste?

ANSWERS

Práctica

C 1. Mañana Carlos irá al centro.
2. Yo iré con él.
3. Visitaremos los puestos de los coleccionistas.
4. Sé que Carlos comprará monedas.
5. Él cree que encontrará unas monedas raras.
6. Y yo buscaré sellos.
7. Yo sé quién me venderá los sellos.
8. Y no pagaré mucho.

D 1. viajaré
2. visitaré
3. estarán
4. esperarán
5. llevarán
6. preparará
7. jugaremos
8. ganará
9. pasaré
10. volveré

E 1. No, pero iré mañana.
2. No, pero veré al payaso mañana.
3. No, pero visitaré el zoológico mañana.
4. No, pero caminaré por las sendas del parque mañana.
5. No, pero me divertiré mañana.

Actividades comunicativas

A **Tengo mucho que hacer.** Prepara una lista de todo lo que piensas hacer mañana. Por ejemplo, **Mañana escribiré una composición para la clase de español.** Puedes escoger algunas palabras de la lista. Entonces compara tu lista con la lista de un(a) compañero(a). ¿Cuáles son las actividades que Uds. dos van a hacer mañana?

B **Mi rutina** Prepara tu rutina para mañana. Luego prepara un informe para la clase. Incluye las siguientes actividades en tu informe.

Colegio Santa Teresita, Santurce, Puerto Rico

Actividades comunicativas

Allow students to choose the activities that they would like to participate in.

Learning From Photos

Colegio Santa Teresita, Santurce, Puerto Rico You may wish to ask questions about the photo such as:
¿Qué son los muchachos?
¿En qué escuela son alumnos?
¿Dónde está la escuela?
¿Qué hacen los alumnos?

ANSWERS

Actividades comunicativas
A and **B** Answers will vary.

135

Bell Ringer Review

Use BRR Transparency 5-4, or write the following on the board:
Answer.
1. ¿Cuál es una pintura que tú consideras muy bonita?
2. ¿Cuál es tu libro favorito?
3. ¿Cuál es una emisión de televisión que tú consideras muy interesante?
4. ¿Qué consideras aburrido?

TEACHING STRUCTURE

 Comparing people and things

A. Have students open their books to page 136. Lead them through Steps 1-6 and the model sentences.

B. Have students make lists of words they know which can be used to describe people.

C. Draw two stick figures on the board and name them. Using their list of adjectives, have students make up sentences comparing the two stick figures.

D. Provide additional examples by comparing objects or students in the room. For example: **Miren. ¿Es Fernando más alto que Alberto? (Sí, es más alto que Alberto.)**

E. Tell students that the superlative is followed by **de** in Spanish. Do not compare it to the *in* in English. When the comparison is made, students tend to get more confused.

 # Comparing people and things
Comparativo y superlativo

1. To compare people or things in English, you add *-er* to short adjectives and you use *more* before long adjectives. The word *than* follows.
   > *She is taller than her brother.*
   > *She is also more intelligent than her brother.*

   This construction is called the comparative.

2. To form the comparative in Spanish, you put **más** before the adjective or adverb and **que** after it.
   > Ella es **más** alta **que** su hermano.
   > Y también es **más** inteligente **que** su hermano.

3. The superlative is used to describe "the most." To form the superlative in English, you add *-est* to short adjectives and place *most* before long adjectives.
   > *She is the nicest person of all.*
   > *She is the most intelligent person in the world.*

4. In Spanish, the superlative is formed by using the appropriate definite article (**el, la, los, las**) plus **más** with the adjective. The preposition **de** follows the superlative.
   > Ella es **la** persona **más** simpática **de** todas.
   > Ella es **la** persona **más** inteligente **del** mundo.

5. The adjectives **bueno** and **malo** have irregular comparative and superlative forms.

   | bueno(a) | mejor | el/la mejor |
   | malo(a) | peor | el/la peor |

6. The adjectives **mayor** and **menor** most often refer to age.
   > Yo soy mayor que mi hermana.
   > Mi hermana es la menor de la familia.

¿**Lo sabes**?

The comparative is often followed by nadie.
Él sabe más que nadie.
Tiene más paciencia que nadie.

¿**Te acuerdas**?

Remember to add –es to an adjective that ends in a consonant.
mi mejor amigo
mis mejores amigos

Learning From Realia

Foto familiar This family portrait provides a good opportunity to practice **a la derecha** and **a la izquierda**.
¿Quién está a la derecha de la madre?
¿Quién está a la derecha del padre?
¿Quién está a la izquierda del padre?
¿Quién está a la izquierda de la madre?

Práctica

A Compararemos. Sigan el modelo.

Luis / Pablo / Andrés
Luis es alto.
Pablo es más alto que Luis.
Andrés es el más alto de todos.

1. graciosa

Susana / Lola / Anita

2. ricos

los Gómez / los García / los Ramos

3. cómicos

los mimos / los monos / los payasos

4. popular

el ajedrez / el futbolín / los juegos de video

B ¿Cuál es más... ? Sigan el modelo.

grande   la Ciudad de México / Nueva York
La Ciudad de México es más grande que
**   Nueva York.**

1. caro   el avión / el tren
2. rápido   el tren / el bus
3. difícil   el ajedrez / las damas
4. largo   un kilómetro / un metro
5. pequeña   una habichuela / una papa

C ¿Y tú? Contesten.

1. ¿Quién es tu mejor amigo(a)?
2. ¿En qué clase recibes las mejores notas?
3. ¿Quién es el (la) mayor de tu familia?
4. ¿Y el (la) menor? ¿Quién es?
5. ¿Eres mayor o menor que tu padre?

La Ciudad de México

ESTRUCTURA

ciento treinta y siete 137

Práctica

A and **B** Have students prepare **Práctica A** and **Práctica B** before going over them in class.

C **EXPANSION** After going over **Práctica C,** have students give a description of their **mejor amigo(a)**, **el/la mayor de su familia**, and **el/la menor de su familia.**

¡OJO! There is no more new material to present in this chapter. The sections that follow recombine and reinforce the vocabulary and structures that have already been introduced.

ANSWERS

Práctica

A 1. Susana es graciosa.
Lola es más graciosa que Susana.
Anita es la más graciosa de todas.
2. Los Gómez son ricos.
Los García son más ricos que los Gómez.
Los Ramos son los más ricos de todos.

3. Los mimos son cómicos.
Los monos son más cómicos que los mimos.
Los payasos son los más cómicos de todos.
4. El ajedrez es popular.
El futbolín es más popular que el ajedrez.
Los juegos de video son los más populares de todos.

B 1. El avión es más caro que el tren.
2. El tren es más rápido que el bus.
3. El ajedrez es más difícil que las damas.
4. Un kilómetro es más largo que un metro.
5. Una habichuela es más pequeña que una papa.

C Answers will vary but may include:
1. Mi mejor amigo(a) es ___.
2. Recibo las mejores notas en la clase de ___.
3. El/La mayor de mi familia es ___.
4. El/La menor de mi familia es ___.
5. Soy menor que mi padre.

🖌 Bell Ringer Review

Use BRR Transparency 5-5, or write the following on the board: Make a list of things you can do at the park in your hometown in the summer.

TEACHING THE CONVERSATION

A. 🎧 With books closed, have students listen and repeat as you read the conversation aloud or play Cassette 4A/ Compact Disc 3.

B. Have students open their books. Call on volunteers to read the conversation in parts with as much expression as possible.

C. Call on individual students to retell the information in the conversation in their own words. This activity gives students important practice in going from dialogue to narrative form.

TECHNOLOGY OPTION

💿 On the CD-ROM (Disc 2, page 138), students can watch a dramatization of this conversation. They can then play the role of either one of the characters, and record themselves in the conversation.

Conversación

Una diferencia de opinión

CLARITA: ¿Qué vamos a hacer mañana?
EUGENIO: No sé. Quizás iremos a casa de Felipe.
CLARITA: ¿A casa de Felipe? ¿Para qué?
EUGENIO: Jugaremos ajedrez.
CLARITA: ¿Jugar ajedrez? Estás loco. A mí no me gusta nada. Es el juego más aburrido…
EUGENIO: ¡Vale! ¡Vale! Pero te sentarás enfrente de una pantalla de video durante horas.
CLARITA: Tengo una idea. No jugaremos ajedrez y no miraremos videos. Iremos al cine.

Después de conversar

Contesten según la conversación.

1. ¿Adónde quiere ir mañana Eugenio?
2. Según Eugenio, ¿qué jugarán?
3. ¿Quiere ir Clarita?
4. ¿Le gusta a Clarita jugar ajedrez?
5. ¿Qué dice Clarita del ajedrez?
6. ¿Qué prefiere hacer Clarita?
7. Según Clarita, ¿adónde irán?

138 〜 *ciento treinta y ocho*

ANSWERS

Después de conversar

1. **Mañana Eugenio quiere ir a casa de Felipe.**
2. **Según Eugenio, jugarán ajedrez.**
3. **No, Clarita no quiere ir.**
4. **No, a Clarita no le gusta jugar ajedrez.**
5. **Dice que el ajedrez es el juego más aburrido.**
6. **Clarita prefiere ver un video.**
7. **Según Clarita, irán al cine.**

ABOUT THE SPANISH LANGUAGE

Eugenio says **¡Vale! ¡Vale!** It is the equivalent of *OK! OK!* in English. The expression **vale** is much more common in Spain than in Latin America, where people will often say **OK.**

Actividades comunicativas

A **Los pasatiempos favoritos** Un(a) estudiante de Colombia (tu compañero[a]) quiere saber cuál es tu pasatiempo favorito. Contéstale y explícale por qué te gusta tanto. Luego cambien de rol.

B **Al parque con tu hermanito(a)** Estás en el parque con tu hermanito(a) de cinco años (un[a] compañero[a]). Él o ella quiere hacer muchas cosas. Tú le dices lo que sí puede hacer y lo que no puede hacer y por qué. Después cambien de rol.

C **¡Qué exagerado!** Vas a crear una persona ficticia. Tu persona ficticia es la más _____ de todos; tiene más _____ que nadie. Al hablar de la persona, exagera todo lo posible. Luego trabaja con unos compañeros. Presenten sus descripciones y decidan quién ha creado la persona más increíble.

Cartagena, Colombia

D **No, de ninguna manera** Con un(a) compañero(a), miren esta foto. Los dos amigos están hablando de unos planes. Parece que a uno de ellos no le interesa nada el proyecto. Entablen la conversación entre los dos.

San Miguel de Allende, México

CONVERSACIÓN

ciento treinta y nueve ⁓ **139**

139

TEACHING THE READING

Pre-reading

Have students open their books and do the Reading Strategy on page 140. Then ask them what genre they think this passage will most closely resemble—a novel, a short story, a poem, or an essay.

Reading

A. To vary the presentation of the reading, you may wish to have students read this selection silently.
B. Have them tell something about what they read.

Post-reading

Assign the **Después de leer** activities on page 141 for homework and go over them the following day.

TECHNOLOGY OPTION

Students may listen to a recorded version of the **Lectura** on the CD-ROM, Disc 2, page 140.

Writing Development

You may wish to have some students write a summary of the **Lectura**.

Lecturas CULTURALES

EL DOMINGO EN EL PARQUE

Casi todas las ciudades hispanas tienen uno o más parques bonitos. Los parques son un centro de recreo[1] para jóvenes y viejos, especialmente los domingos.

Si vas a un parque como el Retiro en Madrid o Chapultepec en México, verás a los viejos jugando al dominó hora tras hora. Y los niños estarán en fila delante del vendedor de helados o piraguas.

En algunos parques, como Palermo en Buenos Aires, hay un zoológico. El domingo que viene los Rodríguez llevarán a los niños al zoológico. Se divertirán mucho mirando a los cómicos monos. Pero se asustarán[2] un poco al ver los leones y tigres en sus jaulas grandes.

A veces hay también un parque de atracciones. A los niños les gusta subir al tiovivo. Los caballitos suben y bajan al acompañamiento del organillo.

El parque no es sólo para viejos y niños. En el parque verás a muchos jóvenes. Los jóvenes se encuentran y dan un paseo por el parque. Charlan (Hablan) con otros jóvenes que conocen en el parque y hacen nuevos amigos. A veces alquilan (rentan) un bote y reman por el lago del parque.

También veremos en el parque a las personas que demostrarán su arte: caricaturistas que te dibujarán[3] en un momento; fotógrafos que te tomarán una foto; mimos y payasos que te van a hacer reír[4] y vendedores ambulantes vendiendo de todo: globos, dulces, refrescos, camisetas.

[1] recreo *recreation*
[2] se asustarán *they will be frightened*
[3] dibujarán *will draw*
[4] reír *laugh*

Bosque de Chapultepec, México

Palermo, Buenos Aires, Argentina

Learning From Photos

Bosque de Chapultepec This is Mexico City's greatest park. On Sunday afternoons it is filled with strollers and picnickers.
Palermo Palermo is the main park of Buenos Aires, Argentina.

HISTORY CONNECTION

El Castillo de Chapultepec Within the Bosque de Chapultepec in Mexico City is the Castillo de Chapultepec. During the 19th century it was the residence of the Emperor Maximilian. In the early 1500's the grounds of the park were the favorite gardens of the Aztec emperor Montezuma.

Después de leer

A **En el parque** Contesten.

1. ¿Quiénes van a los parques en las ciudades hispanas?
2. ¿Cuándo van?
3. ¿Qué juegan los viejos?
4. ¿Qué compran los niños?
5. ¿Qué hay en el zoológico?
6. ¿Qué hay en el parque de atracciones?
7. ¿Qué hacen los jóvenes en el parque?
8. ¿Qué venden los vendedores ambulantes?

B **Personajes interesantes** Contesten.

1. ¿Qué hacen los caricaturistas?
2. ¿Qué hacen los mimos y los payasos?
3. ¿Qué hacen los fotógrafos?

C **¿Qué es?** Adivinen.

1. un tipo de helado que es en realidad hielo con sirope
2. cualquier lugar adonde va la gente a divertirse
3. un animal bastante gracioso o cómico
4. personas que andan por las calles o parques vendiendo cosas
5. lugar donde exhiben muchos animales
6. dos animales salvajes de la misma familia que el gato

Buenos Aires, Argentina

Sevilla, España

LECTURAS CULTURALES   *ciento cuarenta y uno* **141**

ANSWERS

Después de leer

A 1. Los jóvenes y los viejos van a los parques en las ciudades hispanas.
2. Van especialmente los domingos.
3. Los viejos juegan dominó.
4. Los niños compran helados o piraguas.
5. En el zoológico hay monos, leones y tigres.
6. En el parque de atracciones hay un tiovivo.
7. Los jóvenes se encuentran y dan un paseo por el parque. Charlan con otros jóvenes que conocen y hacen nuevos amigos. A veces alquilan un bote y reman por el lago del parque.
8. Los vendedores ambulantes venden de todo: globos, dulces, refrescos, camisetas.

B 1. Los caricaturistas dibujan a la gente.
2. Los mimos y los payasos hacen reír a la gente.
3. Los fotógrafos toman fotos de la gente.

C 1. una piragua
2. un parque
3. un mono
4. vendedores ambulantes
5. un (parque) zoológico
6. un león y un tigre

LECTURA OPCIONAL 1

National Standards

Cultures
This reading and the related activities on this page familiarize students with game arcades and games, both traditional and modern, in Spanish-speaking countries.

Comparisons
In this selection students learn that, despite the advent of video games of the kind that are so popular in the United States, the time-honored game of table soccer remains for many Spanish-speaking teens the game of choice.

TEACHING TIPS

¡OJO! This reading is optional. You may skip it completely, have the entire class read it, have only several students read it, or assign it for extra credit.

A. You may tell students that if they are interested in video games or games such as dominos, they can read one of these selections and do the **Después de leer** activities for extra credit.

ABOUT THE SPANISH LANGUAGE
Video games are called either **juegos de video** or **videojuegos.** Remember, in Spain the word is **vídeo** with an accent on the **í,** while in Latin America it is **video** with the stress on the **e.**

El futbolín

LAS SALAS DE JUEGOS

Las salas de juegos son muy populares en muchos países hispanos. No son nuevas. Hace muchos años que los jóvenes van a las salas de juegos para jugar al tenis de mesa y al futbolín.

Hoy las salas tienen los más modernos juegos de video. Los jóvenes meten una moneda en la ranura. Pulsan un botón y salen en la pantalla monstruos, guerras intergalácticas y carreras de automóviles. Color, sonido, moción. Para los juegos de video se necesita buena coordinación de ojo y mano y excelentes reflejos[1].

Pero de todos los juegos antiguos y modernos, el juego que siempre gusta mucho a los jóvenes hispanos es el futbolín. Pueden jugar dos o cuatro y hasta seis muchachos a la vez. El juego es sencillo (fácil). Hay que meter el baloncito en la portería opuesta[2]. Los jugadores humanos mueven los jugadores de madera[3] o plástico para lanzar o bloquear el balón. Un partido entre buenos jugadores puede durar mucho tiempo.

[1]reflejos *reflexes*
[2]opuesta *opposite*
[3]madera *wood*

Una sala de juegos, Caracas, Venezuela

Después de leer

A **¿Qué es?** Describan.
1. el juego de video
2. el tenis de mesa
3. el futbolín

B **Las salas de juegos** Contesten.
1. ¿Dónde son populares las salas de juegos?
2. ¿A qué jugaban los jóvenes en las salas en el pasado?
3. ¿Qué juegos hay en las salas modernas que no había en las salas antiguas?
4. ¿Dónde salen los monstruos y las guerras intergalácticas?
5. ¿Qué tienes que tener para ser buen jugador de juegos de video?
6. ¿Cuáles son algunas características de los juegos de video?

C **El futbolín** Explica el objetivo del futbolín y cómo se juega.

ANSWERS

Después de leer
A Answers will vary.

B
1. Las salas de juegos son populares en muchos países hispanos.
2. En el pasado los jóvenes jugaban al tenis de mesa y al futbolín.
3. En las salas modernas hay juegos de video.
4. Los monstruos y las guerras intergalácticas salen en la pantalla.
5. Tienes que tener buena coordinación de ojo y mano y excelentes reflejos.
6. Color, sonido y moción son algunas características de los juegos de video.

C Answers will vary.

EL DOMINÓ

El juego es antiguo. Jugaban al dominó en Venecia en el siglo XVIII. Las reglas[1] del juego son las mismas del siglo XVIII. Pero las veintiocho fichas modernas serán de plástico. Las antiguas eran de madera[2], o las más elegantes de marfil[3].

En las plazas de pueblos y ciudades en todo el mundo hispánico podemos oír el «cli, cli» de las fichas que los jugadores golpean contra la mesa. Grupos de jugadores pasan horas jugando partida tras partida de dominó. Alrededor de la mesa siempre hay un grupo de «mirones».

Pero, ¿quiénes son los jugadores? Generalmente son señores mayores. Todos los días van a las mismas mesas, a la misma hora, con los mismos compañeros. Los señores son muy serios. Y juegan casi siempre sin expresión en la cara. Para ellos, el dominó es más que un pasatiempo, es un rito[4].

[1] reglas *rules*
[2] madera *wood*
[3] marfil *ivory*
[4] rito *ritual*

Estepona, España

Después de leer

A El dominó Completen.

1. El dominó es un juego muy _____.
2. En Venecia jugaban al dominó en el siglo _____.
3. Las _____ para jugar al dominó son las mismas del siglo XVIII.
4. Hay _____ fichas en el dominó.
5. Las fichas más elegantes eran de _____.
6. Las fichas modernas generalmente son de _____.
7. Los jugadores _____ las fichas contra la mesa.
8. Los jugadores se sientan a la mesa y los _____ están de pie alrededor de la mesa.
9. Los jugadores generalmente son señores _____.
10. Ellos son muy _____; no tienen _____ en la cara.

B Los mirones La lectura habla de «los mirones». ¿Sabes quiénes son?

National Standards

Cultures
This reading, and the related activities on this page, familiarize students with the popularity of the game of dominos in Spanish-speaking countries.

Comparisons
In this selection students learn that, unlike in the United States, where dominos is regarded for the most part as a child's game, in Spanish-speaking countries it is played chiefly by adults in a very competitive fashion.

ABOUT THE SPANISH LANGUAGE

Both **partido** and **partida** mean a game or a match. However, **un partido** is a sports competition, **un partido de fútbol**, for example, while **una partida** is a match or game of chess, checkers, dominos, or a similar, nonathletic pastime.

ANSWERS

Después de leer

A
1. **antiguo**
2. **XVIII**
3. **reglas**
4. **veintiocho**
5. **marfil**
6. **plástico**
7. **golpean**
8. **mirones**
9. **mayores**
10. **serios, expresión**

B Answers will vary.

Conexiones

LAS BELLAS ARTES

LA LITERATURA

The literary genres that we learn about in our English classes are the same ones that students in Spain and Latin America study: the novel, the short story, and poetry. People everywhere enjoy reading for pleasure. It is a very worthwhile pastime during one's leisure hours.

Casa de García Lorca

Los géneros literarios

La literatura les interesa a los jóvenes y a los viejos. Hay personas que pasan horas leyendo novelas, cuentos y poesía.

La novela
La novela es una obra[1] literaria en prosa bastante larga que narra eventos ficticios. La primera novela importante en español es *El Quijote* (1605), obra de Miguel de Cervantes. Hay diferentes tipos de novela. Hay novelas de amor y novelas de aventura. Hoy las novelas policíacas y las novelas de ciencia-ficción son especialmente populares.

El cuento
El cuento, como la novela, es una narración de eventos ficticios. Pero el cuento es mucho más corto que la novela. El cuento, igual que la novela, tiene uno o más protagonistas. El protagonista es el personaje más importante de la obra. El argumento es una narración de lo que pasa o lo que sucede en la novela o en el cuento.

[1]obra *work*

Isabel Allende, novelista chilena

La poesía

El cuento y la novela son obras en prosa. La prosa es el tipo de lenguaje que la gente usa en su habla diaria. La poesía, los poemas, son obras en verso, no en prosa. El poeta usa imágenes, métrica, ritmo y sonidos[2] para crear una reacción emocional en la persona que lee el poema.

A la gente de habla española le gusta mucho la poesía. Muchas veces, en una fiesta familiar, alguien se levanta y recita un poema. Y no es raro encontrar a un dentista o a una profesora que es también poeta.

[2]sonidos *sounds*

❧ Después de leer ❧

A **La literatura**   Contesten.

1. ¿Cuáles son tres géneros literarios?
2. ¿Qué escribió Miguel de Cervantes?
3. ¿Cuáles son cuatro tipos de novela?
4. ¿Cuál es la mayor diferencia entre una novela y un cuento?
5. ¿Qué recitan algunas personas en fiestas familiares?

B **¿Verso o prosa?**   Digan si es verso o prosa.

1. una poesía
2. un poema lírico
3. una novela de ciencia-ficción
4. un cuento corto
5. un poema épico
6. un artículo de periódico

C **Un cuento**   Vas a escribir un cuento. Para escribir el cuento, haz lo siguiente.

▸ **Protagonista** El o la protagonista es el personaje más importante del cuento. Le vas a dar un nombre y explicar quién es. Tienes que describir a tu protagonista. Explica cómo es físicamente y da algunos detalles sobre su personalidad.

▸ **Lugar o ambiente** Tienes que indicar de dónde es el o la protagonista. Indica también dónde tiene lugar la acción de tu cuento. Es necesario dar una descripción del lugar. Puedes describir la casa del protagonista, su pueblo o su ciudad. Incluye todo lo necesario o importante para el desarrollo *(development)* de la acción de tu cuento.

▸ **Argumento** Di lo que hace el o la protagonista. Escribe todo lo que sucede. Explica a los lectores (a los que leen tu cuento) cómo es la actuación del (de la) protagonista.

▸ **Desenlace** Explica lo que pasa al final y cómo termina la acción.

CAPÍTULO 5
Conexiones

LAS BELLAS ARTES
LA LITERATURA

A. Although this material is optional, you may wish to go over it with all students. This information will be beneficial to them in their future study of Spanish.

B. Ask students if they read the story about *El Quijote* in ¡Buen Viaje! **Level 1.** Call on students to tell as much as they remember about the story.

❧ Después de leer ❧

A and **B**   Quickly go over these activities with the class.

C   You may wish to give students time in class to write their short story or you may have them write it at home. If they write it at home, it is suggested that you tell them not to use a bilingual dictionary because, more often than not, they will choose the wrong word. Tell them to use only words they know and if once in a while they must use an unknown word, tell them to leave a space and you will fill it in.

ANSWERS

Después de leer

A 1. **Tres géneros literarios son la novela, el cuento y la poesía.**
2. **Escribió *El Quijote*.**
3. **Cuatro tipos de novela son la novela de amor, la novela de aventura, la novela policíaca y la novela de ciencia-ficción.**
4. **El cuento es mucho más corto que la novela.**
5. **Recitan un poema.**

B 1. **verso**
2. **verso**
3. **prosa**
4. **prosa**
5. **verso**
6. **prosa**

C Answers will vary.

Culminación

Actividades orales

A **El parque de atracciones** Con un(a) compañero(a), miren este anuncio para un parque de atracciones. Discutan sus planes para visitar el parque. Decidan cuándo irán, cómo llegarán y lo que verán.

Buenos Aires, Argentina

B **A un restaurante** Vas a estar libre el viernes por la noche. Quieres ir a un restaurante. Llama a un(a) amigo(a) por teléfono para ver si él o ella quiere ir también. Dile a tu amigo(a) a qué restaurante irás, lo que pedirás, si tomarás postre, cuánto costará, etc. Explica a tu amigo(a) como es que conoces el restaurante y por qué te gusta tanto que volverás a comer allí.

C **Somos muy cultos.** Tú y dos compañeros de la clase de español son miembros de un comité que hace planes para actividades culturales para su escuela. Preparen una lista de los eventos que están planeando para el año escolar que viene.

Actividad escrita

A. **Los pasatiempos en tu comunidad**
Prepara un e-mail para una alumna hispanoamericana que viene a tu escuela el semestre que viene. Pregúntale cuáles son los pasatiempos que le interesan; dile también lo que hay en tu comunidad para pasar el tiempo libre.

Message Composition

eperez@anon.com

Subject:
▽ Addressing
Mail To:
Cc:
Attachments

Writing Strategy

Writing about dreams and wishes—the future

To imagine the future, it is helpful to look at yourself as you are now. One way to do that is to use clusters to record your likes, interests, feelings, and reactions and how they relate to one another. These connections may help you learn more about yourself and help you see yourself years from now as you begin to think about the future. You can also use clusters to evaluate things as they are now and how you think they will be in the future. Evaluating these changes may help you understand how changes in the world may affect the way your own personal dreams are fulfilled.

Algunas predicciones para el futuro

Vas a escribir una composición sobre el tema **Algunas predicciones para el futuro.** Primero escoge algunas áreas para incluir en tus predicciones, por ejemplo: el transporte, la familia, los pasatiempos y las diversiones, las comunicaciones, la educación, la medicina y la higiene, la casa, las vacaciones. Si quieres, puedes incluir «yo» en la lista de áreas. Después, prepara dos listas: una con el título **El presente** y la otra con el título **El futuro.** Para cada área escribe cómo es ahora y cómo crees que será en el futuro. Al terminar las dos listas, escribe tu composición usando la información de las dos listas.

CULMINACIÓN

ciento cuarenta y siete 〜 **147**

A. Have students edit each others' e-mail messages.
TECHNOLOGY OPTION Students can use the Portfolio feature on the CD-ROM to write their e-mail messages.

Writing Strategy

Writing about dreams and wishes—the future

A. Have students read the Writing Stategy on page 147.
B. Since their essays will cover a variety of areas, encourage students to use as much vocabulary as possible that they have learned so far in their study of Spanish.

National Standards

Communities
For information on how to set up a keypal (pen pal) exchange between your class and a class in a Spanish-speaking country, go to the **Correspondencia electrónica** section at the **Glencoe Foreign Language Web site** (http://www.glencoe.com/sec/fl).

ANSWERS

Actividad escrita
A Answers will vary.

Writing Strategy
Answers will vary.

ABOUT THE SPANISH LANGUAGE

A number of terms are used to describe the regions and peoples of the Americas south of the United States. The most common terms are **Latinoamérica** and **latinoamericanos**. Some Spanish speakers feel that this is too broad since it includes Portuguese-speaking Brazil and French-speaking Haiti and Martinique. **Iberoamérica** and **iberoamericanos** exclude the French speakers but still include Brazil. **Hispanoamérica** and **hispanoamericanos** would be the appropriate terms for just the Spanish-speaking countries of the Americas and their people.

VOCABULARY REVIEW

The words and phrases in the **Vocabulario** have been taught for productive use in this chapter. They are summarized here as a resource for both students and teacher. This list also serves as a convenient resource for the **Culminación** activities on pages 146 and 147. There are approximately five cognates in this vocabulary list. Have students find them.

📌 *Teacher Notes*

Vocabulario

TALKING ABOUT PASTIMES AND HOBBIES

el pasatiempo	el campeón
el hobby	la campeona
el ajedrez	la sala de juegos
el tablero	el juego de video
las damas	el futbolín
el dominó	pasar el tiempo
la ficha	coleccionar sellos (monedas)
el/la coleccionista	llenar un crucigrama

TALKING ABOUT ACTIVITIES IN THE PARK

el parque	el caballito
el bote	la montaña rusa
el (parque) zoológico	la noria
el mono	el mimo
la jaula	el payaso
la boletería	el globo
el parque de atracciones	el helado
el tiovivo	la piragua

DISCUSSING WHAT ONE DOES IN THE PARK

dar un paseo
caminar por la senda
remar por el lago
hacer cola

GIVING LOCATION

delante de
detrás de
al lado de
a la derecha
a la izquierda

OTHER USEFUL EXPRESSIONS

listo(a)
la fila
la entrada

Independent Practice

Assign any of the following:
1. Activities, pages 146–147
2. Workbook, **Mi autobiografía,** page 59
3. Situation Cards
4. CD-ROM, Disc 2, Chapter 5, **Juego de repaso**

Learning From Photos

En el parque You may wish to ask students these questions about the photo:
¿Dónde está el grupo de personas en la foto?
¿Qué es el señor?
¿Qué tiene una de las muchachas en la mano?
¿Por qué lleva la niña un largo vestido blanco?

TECNOTUR

VIDEO

¡Buen viaje!

EPISODIO 5 ▸ Los pasatiempos

Luis y Cristina se divierten con un juego de ajedrez.

También juegan en la piscina del hotel.

CD-ROM

Expansión cultural

El Zoológico de Madrid tiene muchas atracciones para todos.

interNET CONNECTION

In this video episode Cristina and Luis discuss what they like to do in their free time. To find out what Spanish-speaking teenagers do in their free time, go to the **Capítulo 5** Internet activity at the Glencoe Foreign Language Web site:

http://www.glencoe.com/sec/fl

TECNOTUR

ciento cuarenta y nueve ∞ **149**

OVERVIEW

This page previews three key multimedia components of the **Glencoe Spanish** series. Each reinforces the material taught in Chapter 5 in a unique manner.

VIDEO

The Video Program allows students to see how the chapter vocabulary and structures are used by native speakers in an engaging story. Show the video episode as a final activity for Chapter 5.

A. Before watching the video, ask students the following about the photos: **¿Cuál es más serio, el juego de ajedrez o el polo acuático? ¿Quién va a ganar en el juego de ajedrez? ¿Y en el polo acuático?**
B. See the Video Activities Booklet for detailed suggestions for using this resource.

CD-ROM

A. In the video episode we find out what Cristina and Luis like to do in their free time. The **Expansión cultural** photo shows a popular destination for families in Madrid. Have students read the caption on page 149.
B. In the CD-ROM version of **Expansión cultural** (Disc 2, page 149), students can listen to additional recorded information regarding how Spanish-speaking people relax during their leisure time.

INTERNET

Teacher Information and Student Worksheets for this activity can be accessed at the Web site.

Video Synopsis

This episode begins with a game of water polo between Luis and Cristina at the hotel pool in Puerto Vallarta. Cristina tires of the game, so they check out the board games that the hotel offers. Cristina chooses chess and Luis reluctantly allows her to teach him how to play. As they play, Luis and Cristina discuss their favorite pastimes and the reasons why they enjoy them.

149

Chapter 6 Overview ◆●◆●◆●◆●◆●◆●◆●◆●◆●◆●◆

TOPICS	FUNCTIONS	STRUCTURE	CULTURE
◆ Hotel terminology	◆ How to check into and out of a hotel ◆ How to ask for things you need at a hotel ◆ How to express future actions ◆ How to refer to previously mentioned people or things	◆ Irregular verbs in the future ◆ Indirect and direct object pronouns in the same sentence	◆ Inns (paradors) in Spain ◆ Youth hostels in the Spanish-speaking world ◆ Hotel de la Reconquista, Oviedo, Spain ◆ Physical fitness

CHAPTER 6 RESOURCES

PRINT	MULTIMEDIA

Planning Resources

Lesson Plans Block Scheduling Lesson Plans	Interactive Lesson Planner

Reinforcement Resources

Writing Activities Workbook Student Tape Manual Video Activities Booklet Web Site User's Guide	Transparencies Binder Audiocassette/Compact Disc Program Videocassette/Videodisc Program Online Internet Activities Electronic Teacher's Classroom Resources

Assessment Resources

Situation Cards Chapter Quizzes Testing Program Performance Assessment	**Maratón mental** Mindjogger Videoquiz Testmaker Computer Software (Macintosh/Windows) Listening Comprehension Audiocassette/Compact Disc Communication Transparency: C-6

Motivational Resources

Expansion Activities	Café Glencoe: www.cafe.glencoe.com Keypal Internet Activities

Enrichment

Spanish for Spanish Speakers	

Chapter 6 Planning Guide

SECTION	PAGES	SECTION RESOURCES
Vocabulario Palabras 1 **La llegada al hotel** **La salida del hotel**	152–155	Vocabulary Transparencies 6.1 Audiocassette 4B/Compact Disc 4 Student Tape Manual, TE, pages 59–60 Workbook, pages 60–61 Chapter Quizzes, page 26 CD-ROM, Disc 2, pages 152–155
Vocabulario Palabras 2 **En el cuarto** **En el baño**	156–159	Vocabulary Transparencies 6.2 Audiocassette 4B/Compact Disc 4 Student Tape Manual, TE, pages 61–62 Workbook, pages 62–63 Chapter Quizzes, page 27 CD-ROM, Disc 2, pages 156–159
Estructura **Futuro de los verbos** **irregulares** **Me lo, te lo, nos lo**	160–165	Workbook, pages 64–66 Audiocassette 4B/Compact Disc 4 Student Tape Manual, TE, pages 62–64 Chapter Quizzes, pages 28–29 Computer Testmaker CD-ROM, Disc 2, pages 160–165
Conversación **La llegada al hotel**	166–167	Audiocassette 4B/Compact Disc 4 Student Tape Manual, TE, pages 64–65 CD-ROM, Disc 2, pages 166–167
Lecturas culturales **Los paradores de España** **Los albergues** *(opcional)*	168–171	Testing Program, page 46 CD-ROM, Disc 2, pages 168–171
Conexiones **El ejercicio** *(opcional)*	172–173	Testing Program, page 47 CD-ROM, Disc 2, pages 172–173
Culminación **Actividades orales** **Actividades escritas** **Vocabulario** **Tecnotur**	174–177	**¡Buen viaje!** Video, Episode 6 Video Activities, pages 84–87 Internet Activities www.glencoe.com/sec/fl Testing Program, pages 43–46; 130; 174; 195 CD-ROM, Disc 2, pages 174–177

OVERVIEW

In this chapter students will learn vocabulary associated with making a hotel reservation, checking in and out, identifying features of a hotel room, and requesting various hotel services. They will continue to narrate in the future and to talk about people and things already mentioned. The cultural focus of the chapter is on the different types of hotel accommodations available in the Spanish-speaking world.

National Standards

 In Chapter 6 students will learn to communicate in spoken and written Spanish on the following topics:
- making a reservation and checking into and out of a hotel
- requesting various hotel services
- discussing basic hotel features and facilities

Students will obtain and provide information about these topics and engage in conversations that would typically take place in a hotel as they fulfill the chapter objectives listed on this page.

CAPÍTULO 6

En el hotel

Objetivos

In this chapter you will learn to do the following:
- check into and out of a hotel
- ask for things you may need while at a hotel
- talk about future events
- refer to previously mentioned people or things
- talk about lodging in the Hispanic world

interNET CONNECTION

The **Glencoe Foreign Language Web site** (http://www.glencoe.com/sec/fl) offers three options that enable you and your students to experience the Spanish-speaking world via the Internet:
- The online **Actividades** are correlated to the chapters and utilize Hispanic Web sites around the world. For the Chapter 6 activity, see student page 177.

- The **Correspondencia electrónica** section provides information on how to set up a keypal (pen pal) exchange between your class and a class in the Spanish-speaking world.
- At **Café Glencoe**, the interactive "after-school" section of the site, you and your students can access a variety of additional online resources, including interactive games.

Spotlight On Culture

Fotografía You may wish to ask these questions about the photo of the Hotel Residencia La Casa Grande in Guatemala City:

¿Está el hotel en una ciudad o en el campo?

¿Cuántos pisos tiene el hotel?

¿Es un hotel muy moderno o de estilo tradicional?

Pacing

Chapter 6 will require approximately eight to ten days. Pacing will vary according to the length of the class, the age of your students, and student aptitude.

Block Scheduling

The extended time frame provided by block scheduling affords you the opportunity to implement a greater number of activities and projects to motivate and involve your students. See the Block Scheduling Lesson Plans Booklet for suggestions on how to present the chapter material within a block scheduling framework.

ciento cincuenta y uno ∽ **151**

Chapter Projects

Planes de viaje Have students plan hotel stays in different Hispanic cities. If possible have them collect, or provide them with, pictures and travel brochures of these places.

TECHNOLOGY OPTION In the Chapter 6 Internet activity, students choose a hotel in a Spanish-speaking country for their family vacation. Students can download and print out photos of the hotels and rate information from the hotel Web sites. For the address of

the **Glencoe Foreign Language Web site,** see page 150.

Un hotel imaginario Have groups create their own imaginary hotel and describe it to the class. The class can rate each different hotel as to quality, value-for-price, and cuisine.

Compartir experiencias Invite a native Spanish-speaker or a North American who has traveled in Hispanic countries to share hotel experiences with the class.

Vocabulario
PALABRAS 1

La llegada al hotel

RESOURCES

- Vocabulary Transparencies 6.1 (A & B)
- Student Tape Manual, TE, pages 59–60
- Audiocassette 4B/CD4
- Workbook, pages 60–61
- Quiz 1, page 26
- CD-ROM, Disc 2, pages 152–155

🔔 Bell Ringer Review

Use BRR Transparency 6-1, or write the following on the board: Write a list of things you have to pack when you go on a trip.

TEACHING VOCABULARY

A. Have students close their books. Present **Palabras 1** by using Vocabulary Transparencies 6.1 (A & B). Lead students through the new vocabulary by asking: **¿Qué es esto?** or **¿Quién es?** Model the response and have students repeat after you. For example:
¿Qué es? Es un hotel.

B. Now have students open their books and repeat in unison as you model the entire **Palabras 1** vocabulary, or play the recording on Cassette 4B/Compact Disc 4.

Did You Know?

Su pasaporte, por favor. When checking into a hotel in Spain and other countries you are required to leave your passport at the desk. Passport information is then submitted to the police.

el recepcionista

el cliente, el huésped

la recepcionista

la recepción

el cuarto, la habitación

un cuarto sencillo

Diego ya reservó un cuarto.
Reservó un cuarto sencillo, no un cuarto doble.

la llave

Diego llena la ficha.

la ficha, la tarjeta

PINOS

No. de Registro
Fecha

Cuarto
Sencillo
Doble
Nombre
Dirección   Estado   Código
Ciudad
Cuarto
( ) Empleo   ( ) Extra
( ) Casa
Referencias
No. de Licencia   Edad   No. Personas
Su firma
Fecha

Pantomime

Pantomime 1
Getting ready
Set up places in the classroom in order to create a hotel. As props you might use a room key and a small suitcase.
Begin
(Estudiante 1) y (Estudiante 2), vengan Uds., por favor.
(Estudiante 1), llegas al hotel.
(Estudiante 2), eres el/la recepcionista.
(Estudiante 1), ve a la recepción. Pide una habitación.

(Estudiante 2), dale la ficha.
(Estudiante 1), llena la ficha.
Dale la ficha al/a la recepcionista.
(Estudiante 2), dale la llave al/a la cliente.
(Estudiante 1), toma tu equipaje. Sube la escalera.
Gracias, (Estudiante 1) y (Estudiante 2).

el ascensor, el elevador

el botones,
el mozo

El mozo le subirá el equipaje.
Subirá el equipaje en el ascensor.

El mozo le abrirá la puerta al cliente.
Él le pondrá el equipaje en el cuarto.

La salida del hotel

Diego saldrá del hotel hoy.
Tendrá que abandonar el cuarto antes del
mediodía.

Él pedirá la cuenta y la pagará en la caja.
Pagará su factura con una tarjeta de crédito.

VOCABULARIO

ciento cincuenta y tres **153**

C. Project Vocabulary Transparencies 6.1 (A & B) again. Ask for volunteers to read the new words or phrases from their books in random order while other volunteers go to the screen and point out the corresponding images.

D. Make true/false statements about the material and have students respond. For example: **La recepción está en el jardín del hotel. (falso) La recepción está en el pasillo. (falso) El cliente llena la ficha. (verdad)**

TEACHING TIP

For additional practice in true/false activities, have students correct false statements.

ABOUT THE SPANISH LANGUAGE

◆ The traditional term for an elevator is **ascensor,** and that is the term used in Spain. The word **elevador** is more common in Latin America, as can be seen in the photo.

◆ A bellman is often called a **botones**. The term comes from the rows of brass buttons on the uniforms of old-time bellboys.

Pantomime

Pantomime 2
Begin
___, ven acá, por favor.
Tú eres un(a) turista. Estás en un hotel, delante de la puerta de tu habitación.
Toma tu llave.
Abre la puerta con la llave.
Toma tu equipaje.
Entra en la habitación.
Pon tu equipaje sobre la cama.
Cierra la puerta.

Mira bien la habitación.
Indica que estás contento(a) con la habitación.
Gracias, ___. Bien hecho.

CAPÍTULO 6
Vocabulario

✦Práctica✦

¡OJO! **Práctica** When students are doing the **Práctica** activities, accept any answer that makes sense. The purpose of these activities is to have students use the new vocabulary. They are not factual recall activities. Do not expect students to remember specific information from the vocabulary presentation when answering. If you wish, have students use the photos as a stimulus, when possible.

Historieta Each time **Historieta** appears, it means that the answers to the activity form a short story. Encourage students to look at the title of the **Historieta** since it can sometimes help them do the activity.

A Have students refer to the illustrations as you go over **Práctica A**.

B Go over **Práctica B** orally with books closed. Then have students read all the answers to the **Práctica** activity for reinforcement.

EXPANSION After going over **Práctica B**, have one or more students retell the story in their own words.

C Have students prepare the activity before going over it in class.

Writing Development

Have students write out **Práctica C** as though these were definitions in a dictionary. For example:

El/La recepcionista: la persona que saluda a los clientes y busca la reservación.

Have students put the entries in alphabetical order. This is a good copying exercise in disguise. As we know, many students do not copy accurately.

154

✦Práctica✦

A **¿Qué o quién será?** Identifiquen.

1. ¿Es una llave o una tarjeta de crédito?

2. ¿Es el mozo o el recepcionista?

3. ¿Es la caja o la recepción?

4. ¿Es la ficha o el equipaje?

5. ¿Es el equipaje o la cuenta?

B **HISTORIETA** Una visita al hotel

Contesten.

1. ¿Reservó un cuarto el señor?
2. ¿Tiene él una reservación?
3. ¿Quién lo saludó en la recepción?
4. ¿Qué tendrá que llenar el señor?
5. ¿Quién le subirá el equipaje?
6. ¿Quién le abrirá la puerta?
7. ¿Cuándo tendrá que abandonar el cuarto el señor?
8. ¿Qué pedirá y dónde la pagará?
9. ¿Cómo pagará su cuenta el señor?

C **¿Cómo se llama... ?** Identifiquen.

1. la persona que saluda a los clientes y busca la reservación
2. la persona que sube y baja las maletas
3. lo que se usa para abrir la puerta
4. un cuarto para una persona
5. un cuarto para dos personas
6. lo que se puede usar para pagar la cuenta
7. donde uno paga su cuenta

Fiesta Inn, Aguascalientes, México

154 ⚬⚬ *ciento cincuenta y cuatro*   CAPÍTULO 6

ANSWERS

Práctica

A
1. Es una llave.
2. Es el mozo.
3. Es la recepción.
4. Es la ficha.
5. Es la cuenta.

B
1. Sí, el señor reservó un cuarto.
2. Sí, tiene una reservación.
3. El/La recepcionista lo saludó en la recepción.
4. El señor tendrá que llenar una ficha.
5. El mozo (botones) le subirá el equipaje.
6. El mozo (botones) le abrirá la puerta.
7. El señor tendrá que abandonar el cuarto antes del mediodía.
8. Pedirá la cuenta y pagará en la caja.
9. Pagará su cuenta con una tarjeta de crédito.

C
1. el/la receptionista
2. el mozo (el botones)
3. la llave
4. un cuarto sencillo
5. un cuarto doble
6. una tarjeta de crédito
7. la caja

D HISTORIETA Al hotel

Contesten.

1. Cuando el cliente llega al hotel, ¿va primero a la caja?
2. ¿Lleva el mozo el equipaje al cuarto?
3. ¿Hay que llenar una ficha o tarjeta al llegar al hotel?
4. Un cuarto sencillo, ¿es para dos personas?
5. ¿Abandona el cuarto el cliente cuando llega al hotel?
6. Cuando uno paga la cuenta, ¿le da el dinero al botones?

Hotel Princess Reforma, Guatemala

Actividades comunicativas

A Una reservación Tu clase de español está pensando en hacer un viaje a España. Todos están muy entusiasmados y todos tienen una tarea para ayudar a planear el viaje. Tú y un(a) compañero(a) tienen la responsabilidad de reservar las habitaciones (los cuartos). Van a llamar al Hotel Regente. Uno(a) de Uds. será el/la alumno(a) y el/la otro(a) será el/la empleado(a) del Hotel Regente. Discutan las fechas, el número de alumnos, el número de habitaciones, las comidas, los precios.

B El huésped abandona su cuarto. Eres el/la cajero(a) en el Hotel Regente. Un(a) compañero(a) es un(a) huésped. Está abandonando su cuarto. Preséntale al huésped su factura y explícale los cargos *(charges)*. Tu compañero(a) te hará algunas preguntas sobre los cargos. Después tú le preguntarás cómo quiere pagar la cuenta. Él o ella te dirá.

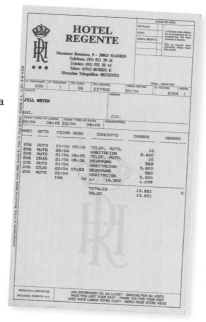

VOCABULARIO

ciento cincuenta y cinco 155

PALABRAS 2

Vocabulario

RESOURCES

 Vocabulary Transparencies 6.2 (A & B)

📁 Student Tape Manual, TE, pages 61–62

🎧 Audiocassette 4B/CD4

📁 Workbook, pages 62–63

📁 Quiz 2, page 27

💿 CD-ROM, Disc 2, pages 156–159

🔔 Bell Ringer Review

Use BRR Transparency 6-2, or write the following on the board: Write a list of all the rooms in a typical three-bedroom house.

TEACHING VOCABULARY

A. Have students close their books. Model the **Palabras 2** vocabulary using Vocabulary Transparencies 6.2 (A & B). Have students repeat the new material after you or the recording on Cassette 4B/ Compact Disc 4. Have them repeat each word or expression twice.

ABOUT THE SPANISH LANGUAGE

◆ Another word for blanket is **la frisa**.

◆ Another word for closet is **el ropero**. In a number of countries the closet is **el clóset**. The original **armario** was a piece of furniture, a wardrobe.

156

En el cuarto

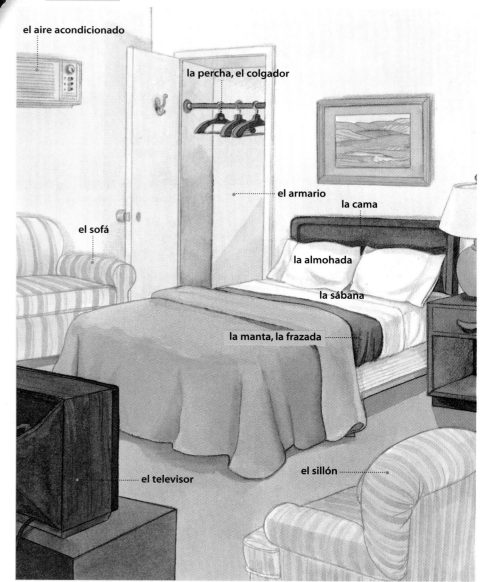

el aire acondicionado

la percha, el colgador

el armario

la cama

el sofá

la almohada

la sábana

la manta, la frazada

el televisor

el sillón

Pantomime

Begin

___, ven acá, por favor.
Estás en un hotel.
Estás en tu cuarto.
Abre la puerta del armario.
Toma una percha.
Cuelga tu abrigo.
Ponlo en el armario.
Cierra la puerta del armario.
Ve al baño.
Mírate en el espejo.
Toma el jabón. Lávate la cara.

Toma una toalla.
Sécate la cara con la toalla.
Gracias, ___. Bien hecho.
Ahora, vuelve a tu asiento, por favor.

En el baño

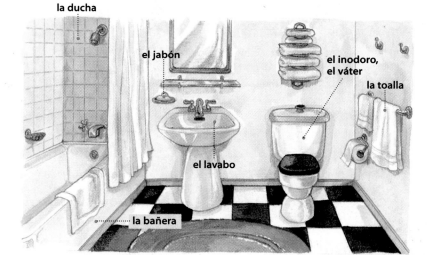

la ducha

el jabón

el inodoro, el váter

la toalla

el lavabo

la bañera

La camarera limpiará el cuarto.
Ella hará la cama.
Y cambiará las toallas.

B. Point to the appropriate illustration on page 157 and ask questions beginning with yes/no and either/or and then progressing to more open-ended ones such as: **¿Qué hará la camarera? ¿Quién hará las camas?**

C. Use props such as a pillow, soap, a hanger, etc., as cues. Ask students what one needs in order to do various things. For example: **Va a tomar una ducha. Va a bañarse. Se lava la cara. Va a dormir. Pone la ropa en el armario.**

Cooperative Learning

Comparaciones Allow time to prepare. Two team members are having a great time in an expensive hotel. The other two are having a terrible time in a cheap hotel. The four meet at a café and take turns describing their experiences. For example: **¡Nuestra habitación es enorme! ¡Nuestra habitación es como un armario! ¡Las camas son muy cómodas! ¡Nuestras camas son horribles!**, etc.

157

❖Práctica❖

A Have students refer to the illustrations as they do **Práctica A**. They can use the future tense in their responses.

B You can go over **Práctica B** without having students prepare it beforehand.

C Have students prepare **Práctica C** before going over it in class.

Did You Know?

Jabón español Some of the world's finest soaps come from Spain. The term *castile soap* comes from the Spanish soaps, fine, hard, bland soaps made from olive oil and sodium hydroxide.

❖Práctica❖

A **HISTORIETA** ¿Qué hará nuestra camarera?

Expliquen las cosas que hará la camarera según los dibujos.

1.

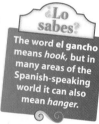
3.

2.

4.

B ¿En el baño, en el armario o en el cuarto? Digan si las cosas se encuentran en el baño, el armario o el cuarto.

1. la ducha
2. el jabón
3. las sábanas
4. la percha
5. el lavabo
6. las toallas
7. la cama
8. el inodoro
9. el aire acondicionado
10. la manta

¿Lo sabes?

The word **el gancho** means *hook*, but in many areas of the Spanish-speaking world it can also mean *hanger*.

C ¿Qué necesitarás? Pareen.

a.
b.
c.
d.

e.
f.
g.

1. Tienes que lavarte las manos.
2. Después de lavar las manos, tienes que secarlas.
3. Hace mucho frío esta noche.
4. Quieres ver tu programa favorito.
5. Hace calor en el cuarto.
6. Tienes que poner tu chaqueta en el armario.
7. Estás cansado(a) y quieres sentarte.

ANSWERS

Práctica

A 1. La camarera hará la cama.
2. Cambiará las toallas.
3. Limpiará el cuarto.
4. Pondrá las perchas en el armario.

B 1. La ducha se encuentra en el baño.

2. El jabón se encuentra en el baño.
3. Las sábanas se encuentran en el cuarto.
4. La percha se encuentra en el armario.
5. El lavabo se encuentra en el baño.
6. Las toallas se encuentran en el baño.

7. La cama se encuentra en el cuarto.
8. El inodoro se encuentra en el baño.
9. El aire acondicionado se encuentra en el cuarto.
10. La manta se encuentra en el cuarto.

C 1. e
2. g
3. b
4. a
5. f
6. c
7. d

Actividades comunicativas

A **Un hotel bueno** Con un(a) compañero(a), discutan lo que les importa cuando se quedan en un hotel. Usen las siguientes expresiones en su discusión.

clase de hotel · tipo de habitación · servicio · cama · precio · baño · aire acondicionado · cerca del centro · restaurante · piscina · gimnasio · desayuno

B **Un desastre de hotel** Pasaste unas vacaciones en San Juan de Puerto Rico. Lo pasaste muy bien y te gustó todo menos el hotel. ¡Qué horror! Fue un desastre total. Un(a) compañero(a) quiere saber todo lo que pasó. Dile. Usa tu imaginación y exagera todo lo posible. Luego cambien de rol y decidan quién tuvo la experiencia más desastrosa.

Hotel El Olivar de San Isidro, Lima, Perú

VOCABULARIO

ciento cincuenta y nueve 〰 **159**

Actividades comunicativas

 These activities encourage students to use the chapter vocabulary and structures in open-ended situations. It is not necessary to have them do all the activities. Choose the ones you consider most appropriate.

A **TECHNOLOGY OPTION**
In the CD-ROM version of this activity (Disc 2, page 159), students can interact with an on-screen native speaker and record their voices.

B You may wish to have students present their "experience" to the entire class.

GEOGRAPHY CONNECTION

Hotel El Olivar de San Isidro, Lima, Perú The hotel is in the San Isidro section of Lima, one of the city's most important commercial districts. Lima is the capital and major city of Peru with close to four million inhabitants. The city was founded in 1535 by Francisco Pizarro, the **conquistador**, who gave it the name **Ciudad de los Reyes.**

ANSWERS

Actividades comunicativas
A and **B** Answers will vary.

Estructura

 Bell Ringer Review

Use BRR Transparency 6-3, or write the following on the board: Rewrite the following in the future.

1. **Los Gómez van al parque.**
2. **Llegan al parque en carro.**
3. **Los niños dan un paseo por el lago.**
4. **En el parque ven a sus amigos.**
5. **Venden piraguas y globos en el parque.**

TEACHING STRUCTURE

◆ **Expressing more future actions**

A. Ask students to open their books to page 160. Lead them through the explanation and have them repeat the verb forms after you.

B. You may wish to write some of the verbs on the board and underline the endings.

 Although you will want to familiarize students with the forms of these irregular verbs in the future, you may remind students that the **ir a** + infinitive construction is a simple and valid way to express future action, and that it is more frequently used than the future tense in informal speech.

◆ **E**xpressing more future actions
Futuro de los verbos irregulares

> **¿Te acuerdas?**
> Regular verbs in the future use the infinitive as the stem.
> **hablaré, comeré, escribiré**

1. Study the following forms of verbs that have an irregular stem in the future tense. Note that the endings for all irregular verbs are the same as those for the regular verbs.

INFINITIVE	tener	salir	venir	
STEM	tendr-	saldr-	vendr-	ENDINGS
yo	tendré	saldré	vendré	-é
tú	tendrás	saldrás	vendrás	-ás
él, ella, Ud.	tendrá	saldrá	vendrá	-á
nosotros(as)	tendremos	saldremos	vendremos	-emos
vosotros(as)	tendréis	saldréis	vendréis	-éis
ellos, ellas, Uds.	tendrán	saldrán	vendrán	-án

2. Other verbs that follow the same pattern are **poner, saber,** and **poder.**

> **poner → pondré   saber → sabré   poder → podré**

3. The verbs **decir, hacer,** and **querer** also have an irregular future stem.

INFINITIVE	decir	hacer	querer	
STEM	dir-	har-	querr-	ENDINGS
yo	diré	haré	querré	-é
tú	dirás	harás	querrás	-ás
él, ella, Ud.	dirá	hará	querrá	-á
nosotros(as)	diremos	haremos	querremos	-emos
vosotros(as)	diréis	haréis	querréis	-éis
ellos, ellas, Uds.	dirán	harán	querrán	-án

✦Práctica✦

A **HISTORIETA** La huésped llegará mañana.

Contesten según se indica.

1. ¿Cuándo vendrá la huésped? (mañana)
2. ¿Quién sabrá si tiene una reservación? (el recepcionista)
3. ¿Qué tendrá que llenar la huésped? (una ficha)
4. ¿Quién podrá abrirle la puerta? (el mozo)
5. ¿Dónde le pondrá su equipaje? (en el cuarto)
6. ¿Cuándo saldrá la huésped? (en dos días)

B Y mañana, ¿qué? Contesten según el modelo.

Teresa no vino hoy.

No, pero vendrá mañana.

1. Ella no salió de casa a tiempo.
2. Yo no sabía la hora de su llegada.
3. Ella no nos puso un fax.
4. Nosotros no pudimos ir a buscarla.

C **HISTORIETA** Las vacaciones de Ricardo

Completen.

El invierno que viene Ricardo Valbuena _____ (tener)
1
dos semanas de vacaciones. Él y su familia _____ (hacer)
2
un viaje a México. Allí ellos _____ (poder) pasar unos
3
días con sus parientes. El padre de Ricardo _____
4
(llamar) a México y les _____ (decir) a sus parientes la
5
hora de su llegada. Todos los parientes de Ricardo _____
6
(querer) ir al aeropuerto a recibirlos. Ricardo y sus
padres _____ (salir) en el vuelo de las once. El vuelo
7
_____ (hacer) escala en Dallas antes de llegar a México.
8

POR FAVOR
NO MOLESTAR

Acapulco, México

ESTRUCTURA

ciento sesenta y uno 161

✦Práctica✦

A Go over **Práctica A** orally first
with books closed.
EXPANSION After going over **Práctica A**, call on a student to retell the
story in his or her own words.

B **Práctica B** is a bit difficult, but
the logical sequence of past to future
is used often in free communication:
"No, I didn't, but I will …"

C Have students prepare **Práctica C** and then read it aloud.

> ## Writing Development
> After going over **Práctica C**,
> give students a few minutes in
> class to rewrite the information from the story in their
> own words.

Learning From Realia

Por favor, no molestar You
may wish to ask students what
the meaning of the message is on
the piece of realia. Remind students that the hotel industry is
truly international. Marriott is
an American chain with hotels
worldwide. There are also Spanish chains such as Meliá with hotels throughout Latin America.

ANSWERS

Práctica

A 1. La huésped vendrá mañana.
2. El recepcionista sabrá si tiene una reservación.
3. La huésped tendrá que llenar una ficha.
4. El mozo podrá abrirle la puerta.
5. Le pondrá su equipaje en el cuarto.
6. La huésped saldrá en dos días.

B 1. No, pero saldrá de casa a tiempo mañana.

2. No, pero sabrás la hora de su llegada mañana.
3. No, pero ella nos pondrá un fax mañana.
4. No, pero nosotros podremos ir a buscarla mañana.

C 1. tendrá
2. harán
3. podrán
4. llamará
5. dirá
6. querrán
7. saldrán
8. hará

✦Práctica✦

D Have students prepare **Práctica D** before going over it in class. Then have two students read the conversation to the class.

EXPANSION Call on two very able students to ad lib and present their own conversation to the class based on the information from **Práctica D.**

E Have students prepare **Práctica E** before going over it in class.

Learning From Photos

Una reservación You may wish to ask students questions about the photos:

¿Qué tipo de teléfono usa la señorita?

¿Qué es la señora a la derecha?

¿Dónde está ella?

VOCABULARY EXPANSION

The stand of cubbyholes behind the desk clerk is called **un casillero** and each of the boxes is **una casilla.** In some places a **casilla** is also a post office box.

D **HISTORIETA** Una reservación

Completen la conversación con el futuro.

CLIENTE: Buenos días. Soy Elena Sánchez. ¿Quién ____₁ (poder) confirmar mi reservación?

RECEPCIONISTA: Pues, yo, señorita. ¿Cuándo ____₂ (venir) Ud. al hotel?

CLIENTE: El jueves. Yo ____₃ (saber) la hora exacta más tarde.

RECEPCIONISTA: Un momentito y le ____₄ (decir) si tiene reservación. Sí, sí, aquí está. Ud. ____₅ (venir) el jueves y ____₆ (salir) el domingo, ¿verdad?

CLIENTE: Así es. Yo ____₇ (tener) que salir a primera hora el domingo. Yo ____₈ (querer) transporte al aeropuerto.

RECEPCIONISTA: No hay problema. El conserje le ____₉ (hacer) una reservación en la limusina.

CLIENTE: Muchas gracias.

E **El pronóstico del tiempo para mañana** Completen.

1. Hoy hace calor pero mañana ____ frío.
2. Hoy no tienen que llevar abrigo, pero mañana sí que ____ que llevar abrigo.
3. Hoy no pueden esquiar, pero mañana ____ esquiar.
4. Hoy yo no quiero ir a clase, pero mañana ____ ir.
5. Hoy no me pongo el suéter, pero mañana me lo ____.
6. Hoy todo el mundo sale a la calle, pero mañana nadie ____ a la calle.

ANSWERS

Práctica

D 1. **podrá**
2. **vendrá**
3. **sabré**
4. **diré**
5. **vendrá**
6. **saldrá**

7. **tendré**
8. **querré**
9. **hará**

E 1. **hará**
2. **tendrán**
3. **podrán**
4. **querré**
5. **pondré**
6. **saldrá**

Actividades comunicativas

A **Un trabajo para el verano** Este verano trabajarás en un hotel o motel cerca de donde tú vives. El hotel tiene muchos clientes de Latinoamérica. Por eso, el director del hotel (un[a] compañero[a]) te da una entrevista (una interviú) en español. Pregúntale al director todo lo que tendrás que hacer. El modelo les servirá de guía.

> ¿Tendré que venir al hotel temprano?

> Sí, vendrás al hotel temprano.

B **El fin de semana que viene** No sabes por qué pero no hay duda que siempre tienes mucho que hacer. Con un(a) compañero(a), hagan planes para el próximo fin de semana. Discutan todo lo que harán. Dividan sus actividades en las siguientes categorías.

trabajo estudios pasatiempos obligaciones

Talking about things already stated
Me lo, te lo, nos lo

1. Many sentences have both a direct and an indirect object pronoun. In these sentences the indirect object pronoun always precedes the direct object pronoun in Spanish. Both pronouns precede the conjugated form of the verb.

Ella **nos** sirvió **el helado**.	Ella **nos** **lo** sirvió.
El mozo **me** dio **la llave**.	El mozo **me** **la** dio.
Él **me** vendió **los libros**.	Él **me** **los** vendió.
Papá **te** hizo **las reservaciones**.	Papá **te** **las** hizo.

2. Note that the indirect object **me, te,** or **nos** comes before the direct object **lo, la, los, las.**

Actividades comunicativas

A **TECHNOLOGY OPTION**
Students may use the Portfolio feature on the CD-ROM to record their conversations.

TEACHING STRUCTURE

Talking about things already stated

A. Have students open their books. Lead them through Steps 1 and 2 on page 163.
B. Call on volunteers to read the model sentences aloud.
C. You may wish to write the model sentences on the board. Circle and box in the objects as is done on page 163. Draw an arrow from the pronoun to the noun it replaces. Have students note that the second pronoun comes after the one that was already there.

ANSWERS

Actividades comunicativas
A and **B** Answers will vary.

163

⬩Práctica⬩

¡OJO! All the **Práctica** activities on pages 164 and 165 can be gone over orally in class with books closed. They can then be read for additional reinforcement.

Note You can decide to what extent you wish to emphasize this particular point. Students should be able to recognize the double object pronouns, but when speaking on their own (producing language) they could say, for example, **Mi tío Lucas me regaló la computadora.**

HISTORY CONNECTION

Visita al Alcázar The original Alcázar de Toledo was heavily damaged during the Spanish Civil War and subsequently reconstructed. In 1936 Nationalist forces withstood a Republican siege of over two months within the ruins of the fortress. The tour of the Alcázar focuses on the siege.

Learning From Realia

Una tarjeta llave The keycard is exactly that in Spanish, **una tarjeta llave.**

⬩Práctica⬩

A El generoso tío Lucas Contesten según el modelo.

¿Quién te regaló las entradas?

Mi tío Lucas me las regaló.

1. ¿Quién te regaló la computadora?
2. ¿Quién te regaló los videos?
3. ¿Quién te regaló el balón?
4. ¿Quién te regaló las damas?
5. ¿Quién te regaló los esquís?
6. ¿Quién te regaló el televisor?
7. ¿Quién te regaló las botas?

B El mozo del hotel

Contesten con pronombres.

1. ¿Te subió las maletas?
2. ¿Te abrió la puerta?
3. ¿Te dio la llave el mozo?
4. ¿Te prendió el aire acondicionado?

C ¿Quién te compró todo eso?

Formen preguntas según el modelo.

 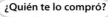

Es mi video nuevo. ¿Quién te lo compró?

1. Son mis zapatos nuevos.
2. Es mi equipaje nuevo.
3. Es mi computadora nueva.
4. Son mis revistas nuevas.
5. Es mi bufanda nueva.

ANSWERS

Práctica

A 1. Mi tío Lucas me la regaló.
2. Mi tío Lucas me los regaló.
3. Mi tío Lucas me lo regaló.
4. Mi tío Lucas me las regaló.
5. Mi tío Lucas me los regaló.
6. Mi tío Lucas me lo regaló.
7. Mi tío Lucas me las regaló.

B 1. Sí, (No, no) me las subió.
2. Sí, (No, no) me la abrió.

3. Sí, (No, no) me la dio.
4. Sí, (No, no) me lo prendió.

C 1. ¿Quién te los compró?
2. ¿Quién te lo compró?
3. ¿Quién te la compró?
4. ¿Quién te las compró?
5. ¿Quién te la compró?

D **Doña Flor, la profesora** Contesten con pronombres según el modelo.

> Doña Flor nos explicó el sistema.

> Doña Flor nos lo explicó.

1. Doña Flor nos enseñó los poemas.
2. Doña Flor nos explicó la teoría.
3. Doña Flor nos enseñó el vocabulario.
4. Doña Flor nos dio la interpretación.
5. Doña Flor nos explicó las diferencias.

E **No oigo bien.** Usen dos pronombres en cada oración.

1. Carlos me hizo la reservación
   Perdón, ¿quién _____?
2. Carlos. Y él me confirmó la reservación ayer.
   Perdón. ¿cuándo _____?
3. Ayer. Y también me dio las direcciones.
   Perdón, ¿Carlos _____?
4. Sí, Carlos. Y me envió las direcciones por fax.
   Perdón, ¿cómo _____?

Hotel Cortés, Ciudad de México

D **Práctica D** can be done in pairs. One student says the sentences with rising intonation, making them questions, and the other responds using double object pronouns.

Learning From Photos

Hotel Cortés, Ciudad de México The Hotel Cortés is in a colonial building dating from 1780. The hotel is of traditional architecture and has one of the last preserved colonial patios in Mexico City.

¡OJO! All new material in the chapter has been presented. The sections that follow recombine and reintroduce the vocabulary and structures that have already been introduced.

ANSWERS

Práctica
D **1.** Doña Flor nos los enseñó.
2. Doña Flor nos la explicó.
3. Doña Flor nos lo enseñó.
4. Doña Flor nos la dio.
5. Doña Flor nos las explicó.

E **1.** te la hizo
2. te la confirmó
3. te las dio
4. te las envió

165

🔔 Bell Ringer Review

Use BRR Transparency 6-4, or write the following on the board: Match the word in the first column with a related word in the second column.

1. reservar   a. la cuenta
2. limpiar   b. la llegada
3. bañar   c. la reservación
4. contar   d. la bañera
5. llegar   e. la limpieza

TEACHING THE CONVERSATION

A. 🎧 Tell students they are going to hear a conversation between a hotel clerk and a guest.

B. Have students open their books to page 166 and follow along as you play the recording on Cassette 4B/ Compact Disc 4.

C. Have pairs of students create hotel-centered skits based on the conversation. Then have them present their skits to the class. They can make any changes they wish.

D. Now go over the **Después de conversar** activity. If students can answer the questions with relative ease, move on. Students should not be expected to memorize the conversation.

TECHNOLOGY OPTION

💿 On the CD-ROM (Disc 2, page 166), students can watch a dramatization of this conversation. They can then play the role of either one of the characters and record themselves in the conversation.

166

Conversación

La llegada al hotel

RECEPCIONISTA: Buenas tardes, señor. ¿Tiene Ud. una reservación?

CLIENTE: Sí, a nombre de Sorolla, Ramón Sorolla. Un cuarto sencillo para tres noches.

RECEPCIONISTA: Aquí está. Ud. saldrá el jueves, día doce. Querrá un baño privado, ¿no?

CLIENTE: Sí, claro.

RECEPCIONISTA: Le daré el tres cero dos. Es un cuarto muy bonito. Da al patio. Tendrá que llenar la ficha. ¿Y su pasaporte, por favor?

CLIENTE: ¿A qué hora tendré que abandonar el cuarto el día doce?

RECEPCIONISTA: Al mediodía.

CLIENTE: De acuerdo.

RECEPCIONISTA: Aquí tiene Ud. la llave. Samuel le subirá el equipaje. ¡Samuel!

Después de conversar

Contesten.

1. ¿Cómo se llama el cliente?
2. ¿Cuántos días estará en el hotel?
3. ¿Qué día saldrá del hotel?
4. ¿Qué tipo de cuarto reservó?
5. ¿Qué tendrá que llenar el cliente y qué le dará a la recepcionista?
6. ¿A qué hora tendrá que abandonar el cuarto?
7. ¿Quién es Samuel y qué hará él?

166   *ciento sesenta y seis*   CAPÍTULO 6

ANSWERS

Después de conversar

1. El cliente se llama Ramón Sorolla.
2. Estará tres noches en el hotel.
3. Saldrá del hotel el jueves
4. Reservó un cuarto sencillo.
5. Tendrá que llenar la ficha y le dará su pasaporte a la recepcionista.
6. Tendrá que abandonar el cuarto al mediodía.
7. Samuel es el mozo y le subirá el equipaje.

Learning From Photos

La llegada al hotel You may wish to ask students questions about the scene:
¿Cómo se viste la señorita?
¿Dónde están ellos?
¿Qué hay en el mostrador?
¿Qué hace el señor?

Actividades comunicativas

A **Un hotel en Madrid** Tú y tu familia estarán en Madrid este verano. Aquí hay folletos de dos hoteles madrileños que ofrecen muchos servicios a sus clientes. Dile a un(a) compañero(a) en cuál de los dos hoteles quieres quedarte. Explica por qué. Luego tu compañero(a) te dirá su preferencia y te dirá por qué. Discutan por qué se quedarán o no se quedarán en el mismo hotel.

MADRID
HOTEL ORENSE
★★★★

DIRECCION
Pedro Teixeira, 5 (esq. Orense)
28020 Madrid
Tel. (91) 597 15 68
Fax. (91) 597 12 95

CAPACIDAD
• 140 habitaciones todas dobles (incluye 10 suites estilo)

SERVICIOS GENERALES
• Restaurante
• Bar Cafetería
• Comedor privado
• Salón social
• Fax
• Amplio garaje propio
• Desayuno Buffet
• Circuito cerrado de T.V.

SERVICIOS HABITACIONES
• Todas exteriores e insonorizadas
• Teléfono directo
• T.V. color con mando a distancia
• Antena parabólica / Canal +
• Hilo musical
• Radio
• Aire acondicionado
• Climatizador individual
• Cuarto de baño en dos volúmenes
• Secador de pelo
• Caja de seguridad
• Mini-bar
• Room service
• Línea de fax opcional

SITUACION
El Hotel está situado en el corazón de Azca (zona de negocios y centro financiero), junto al Palacio de Congresos, el Paseo de la Castellana y el Estadio Santiago Bernabeu. A 5 minutos de la estación de Chamartín. Acceso directo a la M-40, a 10 minutos del aeropuerto e Ifema.

MADRID
GRAN HOTEL COLON
★★★★

DIRECCION
Pez Volador, 11 (semiesquina con Dr.Ezguerdo)
28007 Madrid
Tel. (91) 573 59 00 / 573 86 00
Fax. (91) 573 08 09
Telex 22984 COLON E

CAPACIDAD
• 380 habitaciones (incluidas suites)

SERVICIOS GENERALES
Restaurante, Bar, Cafetería / Hall, Terraza con jardín, Sauna / Masajes, Peluquería, Rayos uva, Gimnasio panorámico (próxima apertura), Solarium, Agencia de viajes, Alquiler de coches, Garaje privado.

SERVICIOS HABITACIONES
Todas exteriores, Habitaciones con Terraza, Teléfono directo, T.V. color con mando a distancia, Antena parabólica, Radio / Hilo musical, Mini-bar, Caja de seguridad, Aire acondicionado, Servicio de habitaciones.

INSTALACIONES PARA CONFERENCIAS Y REUNIONES
El hotel permite la posibilidad de múltiples transformaciones, debido a que dispone de grandes espacios dedicados a salones. Todo ello contando con retroproyectores de transparencias, traducción simultánea, pantallas, vídeos, T.V., Megafonía y azafatas.

SITUACION
Ubicado en una zona céntrica y residencial, junto al Parque del Retiro. A 5 minutos de la estación de Atocha, del Centro Comercial de Goya y, del Triángulo del Arte. Acceso directo a la M-30 y M-40, (por la nueva prolongación O'Donnell) a 10 minutos del aeropuerto y del Parque Ferial Juan Carlos I.

B **¿Cómo podré hacerlo todo?** Vas a preparar un *skit* muy cómico y divertido con un(a) compañero(a). Uno de Uds. será el ama de llaves *(head housekeeper)* de un hotel y el otro será una camarera nueva. Dentro de poco estarán llegando unos clientes. La pobre camarera no sabe qué hacer. Te hará muchas preguntas. Contesta a sus preguntas. Explícale todo lo que tendrá que hacer y cómo.

CONVERSACIÓN

ciento sesenta y siete 〰 **167**

Actividades comunicativas

¡OJO! These **Actividades comunicativas** enable students to use the language creatively on their own as if they were communicating in real-life situations. Let students choose the activities they wish to participate in.

A Tell students working on **Actividad A** to take a look at the brochures before getting started.

B You may wish to have some groups present their skits to the entire class, especially if they are comical.

Learning From Realia

Hotel Orense y Gran Hotel Colon You may wish to ask students questions about the two hotels:

¿Cuál de los hoteles es más grande?
¿En cuál te quedarás si quieres ver un partido de fútbol?
Si tienes un coche, ¿en cuál de los hoteles puedes aparcar?
¿Cuál de los hoteles ofrece más servicios?

National Standards

Cultures
The reading on pages 168–169 and the related activities on page 169 familiarize students with the attractive, culturally interesting chain of government-run hotels known as **paradores** in Spain.

TEACHING THE READING

Pre-reading

A. Before starting the reading, give students some information about **paradores. En España hay paradores. Los paradores son hoteles. Son muy buenos. Y son del gobierno. Hay paradores en todas partes de España. Algunos son muy grandes y otros son muy pequeños. Vamos a leer ahora sobre unos planes que tiene una familia americana. Ellos piensan pasar algunas noches en un parador.**

B. Ask some questions in Spanish about what you just told the students.

Reading

Have students open their books. Call on individuals to read several sentences aloud.

Lecturas CULTURALES

LOS PARADORES DE ESPAÑA

El verano que viene Sandra, Roberto y sus padres harán un viaje a España. Saldrán el 28 de junio. Al llegar a España alquilarán un coche. Viajarán por todas partes del país. Pasarán una semana en el norte y otra en Madrid y sus alrededores. Pasarán la última semana en el sur, en Andalucía.

La señora White, la madre de Sandra y Roberto, está planeando el viaje. Dice que podrán pasar varias noches en algunos paradores.

Hay unos setenta paradores en España. Algunos son muy pequeños como el Parador de Villalba en Lugo, Galicia. Tiene sólo seis habitaciones. Otros son bastante grandes. El Parador de Cádiz tiene 147 habitaciones. Pero lo importante no es el tamaño. Lo más atractivo de los paradores es que son únicos. No son todos iguales. Cada uno tiene su carácter propio.

Algunos paradores son antiguos castillos[1] o monasterios. La madre de Sandra y Roberto dice que hará una reservación en el Parador San Francisco en Granada. Antes era un convento fundado por los Reyes Católicos, Fernando e Isabel. El parador está dentro de las murallas[2] y los jardines de la famosa Alhambra. Pero el Parador San Francisco es tan popular que los White tendrán que reservar una habitación con unos seis meses de anticipación.

[1]castillos *castles*
[2]murallas *walls*

Parador de Cádiz

PARADOR HOTEL DE LOS REYES CATOLICOS
Plaza del Obradoiro 1 15705 SANTIAGO DE COMPOSTELA (LA CORUÑA)

Parador San Francisco, Granada

Learning From Photos

Paradores Ask students to study the photos on this page of the two **paradores**, then ask them to contrast one with the other.

ANSWERS (PAGE 169)

Después de leer
A 1. Sandra, Roberto y sus padres harán un viaje a España.
2. Saldrán el 28 de junio.
3. Alquilarán un coche.
4. Pasarán una semana en Madrid y sus alrededores.
5. La señora White está planeando el viaje.
6. Podrán pasar algunas noches en algunos paradores.

Los paradores nacionales son del gobierno[3] español. Los restaurantes de muchos paradores son muy buenos. Sirven platos típicos de las regiones donde se encuentran. Muchos turistas dicen que pasar una noche en un parador es como pasar una noche en un museo—pero un museo con todas las comodidades de un hotel de cuatro estrellas[4]. A ver lo que dirán Sandra, Roberto y sus padres al volver de su viaje a España.

[3]gobierno *government*
[4]estrellas *stars*

Parador de Cardona, España

Después de leer

A **Un viaje a España** Contesten.

1. ¿Quiénes harán un viaje a España?
2. ¿Qué día saldrán?
3. ¿Qué alquilarán?
4. ¿Cuánto tiempo pasarán en Madrid y sus alrededores?
5. ¿Quién está planeando el viaje?
6. ¿Dónde podrán pasar algunas noches?
7. ¿Cómo son los paradores?
8. ¿De quién son los paradores?
9. ¿Qué sirven en los restaurantes de los paradores?

B **¿Cómo es?** Describan.

1. Describe el Parador de Villalba en Lugo, Galicia.
2. Describe el Parador San Francisco en Granada, Andalucía.

C **Lo magnífico de los paradores** Expliquen.

1. Lo más atractivo de los paradores es que son únicos.
2. Pasar una noche en un parador es como pasar una noche en un museo—pero un museo con todas las comodidades de un hotel de cuatro estrellas.

Parador San Francisco, Granada

Post-reading

A. After a student has read, ask questions such as: **¿Cuándo harán un viaje a España Sandra, Roberto y sus padres? ¿Cuándo saldrán?**

B. After completing the **Lectura** as suggested above, have students prepare the **Después de leer** activities at home. Go over them the following day in class.

TECHNOLOGY OPTION

Students may listen to a recorded version of the **Lectura** on the CD-ROM, Disc 2, pages 168–169.

Después de leer

A **B** and **C** Allow students to refer to the reading to look up the answers, or you may use these activities as testing devices for factual recall.

Independent Practice

Assign any of the following:
1. **Después de leer** activities, page 169
2. Workbook, pages 67–69
3. CD-ROM, Disc 2, pages 168–169

ANSWERS   CONTINUED

7. Los paradores son únicos. No son todos iguales.
8. Los paradores son del gobierno español.
9. Sirven platos típicos de las regiones donde se encuentran.

B 1. El Parador de Villalba en Lugo, Galicia, es muy pequeño. Tiene sólo seis habitaciones.
2. El Parador San Francisco en Granada, Andalucía, era un convento fundado por los Reyes Católicos, Fernando e Isabel. Está dentro de las murallas y los jardines de la famosa Alhambra.

C Answers will vary but may include:
1. Los paradores no son todos iguales. Cada uno tiene su carácter propio.
2. Algunos paradores son antiguos castillos o monasterios. Es porque se pueden comparar con un museo. Los cuartos son muy bonitos, y los restaurantes de muchos paradores son muy buenos, como los restaurantes de los hoteles de cuatro estrellas.

169

LECTURA OPCIONAL 1

LECTURA OPCIONAL 1

TEACHING TIPS

¡OJO! This reading is optional. You may skip it completely, have the entire class read it, have only several students read it, or assign it for extra credit.

A. You may wish to have a student or students who read this optional selection present the material briefly to the class.

Did You Know?

Hostal Lope de Vega Hotels in Spain are rated by the government, from five stars, for luxury hotels, to no stars. An **hostal** is a simple hotel without amenities such as a restaurant. The card says: **Hostal R.** The **R** stands for **Residencia**. This **hostal** is named for the great Spanish playwright, Lope de Vega (1562–1635).

LOS ALBERGUES

En España y en algunos países de Latinoamérica hay albergues juveniles. Los albergues ofrecen cuartos limpios y económicos para jóvenes. La mayoría de los jóvenes que se hospedan (pasan la noche) en un albergue son estudiantes. Les gustan mucho los albergues porque no cuestan mucho y allí pueden conocer a otros estudiantes de todas partes del mundo. En los albergues hay casi siempre un salón central donde todos se reúnen para charlar (hablar) y hacer amigos nuevos.

LOPE DE VEGA
V.
★ ★ ★
HOSTAL R.
GRAN VIA, 59
28013 **MADRID** ☎ **247 70 00**

Cuartos en albergues juveniles, España

Después de leer

 A **Los albergues juveniles** Digan que sí o que no.
1. Todos los países latinoamericanos tienen albergues juveniles.
2. Un albergue juvenil es para viejos o ancianos.
3. Los albergues son bastante caros.
4. La mayoría de los jóvenes que se hospedan en un albergue juvenil son estudiantes.

 B **Para pensar** Contesten.
¿Por qué a los estudiantes les gustan mucho los albergues juveniles?

ANSWERS

Después de leer
A 1. No.
2. No.
3. No.
4. Sí.

B A los estudiantes les gustan mucho los albergues juveniles porque no cuestan mucho y pueden conocer a otros estudiantes de todas partes del mundo.

El Hotel de la Reconquista, construido sobre la traza de un singular edificio del Siglo XVIII, antiguo Hospicio y Hospital del Principado de Asturias, Monumento Nacional, está situado en la zona más céntrica, residencial y comercial de la ciudad de Oviedo.

El Hotel dispone de un total de 142 habitaciones, incluyendo Junior suites y suites, algunas de ellas con preciosas vistas sobre el Patio de la Reina. Todas las habitaciones están perfectamente equipadas con hilo musical y TV vía satélite.

El Hotel le ofrece la oportunidad de disfrutar de la mejor cocina en su Restaurante.

El Hotel ofrece una amplia gama de instalaciones para Reuniones, congresos y Banquetes. Cuenta con una sala de proyecciones, con servicio de traducción simultánea disponible, ocho espléndidas salas de reuniones de 25 a 550 m² y encantadores patios para la celebración de todo tipo de conferencias y acontecimientos sociales como congresos, certámenes, exposiciones, banquetes y comidas de empresa con capacidad para albergar hasta 800 personas.

Después de leer

 ¿Dónde nos dice... ?

Busquen la información en el folleto.

1. el nombre del hotel
2. de qué siglo data el edificio
3. dónde está ubicado (situado)
4. el número de habitaciones
5. algunos servicios que ofrece el hotel

ANSWERS

Después de leer

A 1. Hotel de la Reconquista
2. del siglo XVIII
3. en la zona más céntrica, residencial y comercial de la ciudad de Oviedo
4. 142 habitaciones

5. salas para reuniones, congresos, banquetes y conferencias con capacidad para albergar hasta 800 personas

---

LECTURA OPCIONAL 2

National Standards

Cultures
This reading and the related activity on page 171 familiarize students with the upscale accommodations offered by a hotel in Spain.

TEACHING TIPS

¡OJO! This optional reading is an actual brochure from the Hotel de la Reconquista in Oviedo, Spain. You may wish to have students take a look at it just to get an idea of what the hotel is like, exactly as if they were perusing a brochure in a travel agency.

A. Have students read the brochure to themselves.
B. After they have read it, have them do the **Después de leer** activity on this page.

Después de leer

A Students can quickly scan the brochure to get the information.

HISTORY CONNECTION

Hotel de la Reconquista The Hotel de la Reconquista is in Asturias. The **Reconquista,** or reconquest of Spain from the Moors, began in the mountains of Asturias. Tradition has it that don Pelayo began the reconquest from Covadonga in Asturias in 722.

Conexiones

¡OJO! This reading is optional. You may choose any of the following ways to do it with your students.

Independent reading Have students read the selection and do the post-reading activities as homework, which you collect. This option is least intrusive on class time and requires a minimum of teacher involvement.

Homework with in-class follow-up Assign the reading and post-reading activities as homework. Review and discuss the material in class the next day.

Intensive in-class activity This option includes a pre-reading vocabulary presentation, in-class reading and discussion, assignment of the activities for homework, and a discussion of the assignment in class the following day.

LA EDUCACIÓN FÍSICA

EL EJERCICIO

Since students are probably familiar with most of the information in this reading from their health and physical education classes, you may wish to have all students scan the selection quickly. They should have little trouble understanding it.

LA EDUCACIÓN FÍSICA

EL EJERCICIO

Physical fitness is a concern for everyone. Our health depends upon our fitness. Maintaining muscle tone and cardiovascular health and avoiding overweight are important to our well-being and to our enjoyment of life. Sometimes it's difficult to stay in shape when traveling. For this reason, many hotels in major cities in Spain and Latin America provide exercise rooms or temporary membership in healthclubs for their guests.

El ejercicio

Los hombres y las mujeres que viajan mucho quieren mantenerse en forma. Por eso, muchos hoteles tienen un gimnasio para el uso de sus clientes donde pueden hacer ejercicio. Hay dos tipos de ejercicio, el ejercicio aeróbico o cardiovascular y el ejercicio de fortaleza muscular.

Ejercicios aeróbicos

Los ejercicios aeróbicos como el jogging, el caminar, la natación y los «steps» lineal y coreográfico aumentan temporalmente la respiración. Aumentan también el ritmo del corazón. Hacen más fuertes el corazón y todo el sistema cardiovascular. Algunos ejercicios aeróbicos son muy entretenidos[1] como, por ejemplo, el patinaje lineal[2] y el ciclismo.

[1] entretenidos *entertaining*
[2] patinaje lineal *roller blading*

EL ARTE DE VIVIR

YOGA

CALISTENIA ENERGÉTICA

ESTIRAMIENTOS

RELAJACIÓN

MEDITACIÓN

HATHA YOGA

EJERCICIOS RESPIRATORIOS

MARTES Y JUEVES DE 19,00 A 20,30

C/ Cabeza,15 - 2°
(Tirso de Molina)
MADRID
Tels. 539 98 60
y 939 152923

MANDALA

172

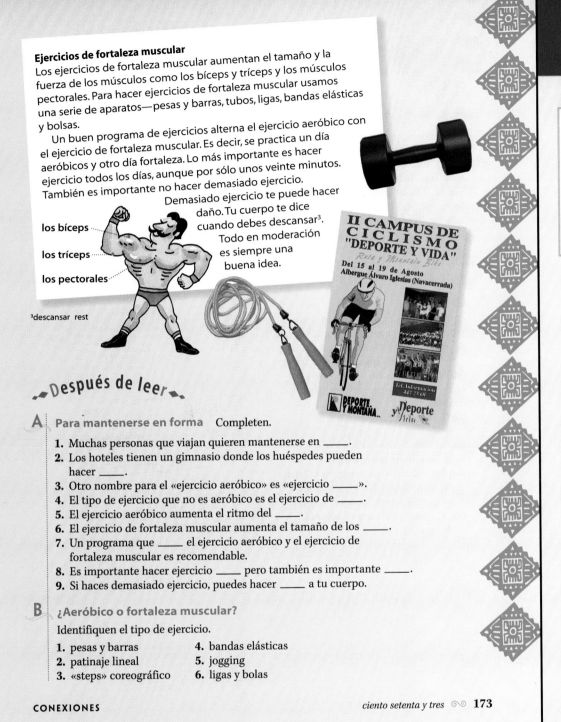

Ejercicios de fortaleza muscular

Los ejercicios de fortaleza muscular aumentan el tamaño y la fuerza de los músculos como los bíceps y tríceps y los músculos pectorales. Para hacer ejercicios de fortaleza muscular usamos una serie de aparatos—pesas y barras, tubos, ligas, bandas elásticas y bolsas.

Un buen programa de ejercicios alterna el ejercicio aeróbico con el ejercicio de fortaleza muscular. Es decir, se practica un día aeróbicos y otro día fortaleza. Lo más importante es hacer ejercicio todos los días, aunque por sólo unos veinte minutos. También es importante no hacer demasiado ejercicio.

Demasiado ejercicio te puede hacer daño. Tu cuerpo te dice cuando debes descansar[3]. Todo en moderación es siempre una buena idea.

los bíceps

los tríceps

los pectorales

[3]descansar rest

II CAMPUS DE CICLISMO "DEPORTE Y VIDA"
Ruta y Mountain Bike
Del 15 al 19 de Agosto
Albergue Álvaro Iglesias (Navacerrada)

Tel. Información
447 23 68

DEPORTE Y MONTAÑA...

y Deporte Girls

Learning From Realia

Deporte y vida Bicycle racing is a very popular sport in Spain and Latin America, especially Colombia. The famous **Tour de France** has been won often by Spaniards. There is also a **Vuelta a España** that is held every year.

Después de leer

A **Para mantenerse en forma** Completen.

1. Muchas personas que viajan quieren mantenerse en _____.
2. Los hoteles tienen un gimnasio donde los huéspedes pueden hacer _____.
3. Otro nombre para el «ejercicio aeróbico» es «ejercicio _____».
4. El tipo de ejercicio que no es aeróbico es el ejercicio de _____.
5. El ejercicio aeróbico aumenta el ritmo del _____.
6. El ejercicio de fortaleza muscular aumenta el tamaño de los _____.
7. Un programa que _____ el ejercicio aeróbico y el ejercicio de fortaleza muscular es recomendable.
8. Es importante hacer ejercicio _____ pero también es importante _____.
9. Si haces demasiado ejercicio, puedes hacer _____ a tu cuerpo.

B **¿Aeróbico o fortaleza muscular?**

Identifiquen el tipo de ejercicio.

1. pesas y barras
2. patinaje lineal
3. «steps» coreográfico
4. bandas elásticas
5. jogging
6. ligas y bolas

CONEXIONES

ciento setenta y tres 🌀 **173**

Culminación

Actividades orales

A. You may call on one group of students to present their conversation for **Actividad A** to the class.

B. **Actividad B** could be a fun activity to have pairs of students perform for the entire class.

GEOGRAPHY CONNECTION

Dos hoteles The Mesón del Cid is in Burgos, the home of the legendary hero **el Cid Campeador.** The Hotel Alfonso VIII is in Plasencia, in the province of Cáceres. Ask students to find the two cities on the map of Spain on page 451 and to find out why the two historical figures **el Cid** and Alfonso VIII are important.

Actividades orales

A. **Una habitación, por favor.** Tú has llegado a Burgos. Necesitas una habitación en un hotel. Llama al Hotel Mesón del Cid. Habla con el/la recepcionista (un[a] compañero[a]). Quieres saber si tienen una habitación disponible *(available).* Necesitas saber el precio. Como no conoces a Burgos, no sabes dónde está el hotel. El/La recepcionista te ayudará y contestará cortésmente a todas tus preguntas.

B. **La buenaventura** Trabaja con un(a) compañero(a). Él o ella te hará muchas preguntas porque quiere saber todo lo que le pasará en el futuro. Tú contestarás a todas sus preguntas y le dirás lo que crees que le pasará. Tendrás que usar tu imaginación. Después de terminar con las preguntas de tu compañero(a), cambien de rol y tú harás preguntas sobre tu futuro.

C. **La cuenta** Estás saliendo del Hotel Alfonso VIII. El cajero (un[a] compañero[a]) te presenta esta factura. Pero hay un error. Tú no has tenido carro durante tu visita aquí. Tengan una conversación para resolver el problema.

Vista tomada desde la fachada principal de la Catedral

Plaza Santa María, 8
Frente Fachada Principal Catedral
Tels. (947) 20 59 71 - 20 87 15
09003 BURGOS

ANSWERS

Actividades orales
A, B, and C Answers will vary.

Independent Practice

Assign any of the following:
1. Activities, pages 174–175
2. Workbook, **Mi autobiografía,** page 70
3. Situation Cards
4. CD-ROM, Disc 2, Chapter 6, **Juego de repaso**

Actividades escritas

A **Un fax para el Hotel Excelsior** Los padres de uno de tus amigos van a México. Quieren quedarse (hospedarse, alojarse) en el Hotel Excelsior. Saben que tú estás estudiando el español y te piden ayuda. Tú les vas a preparar un fax para el Hotel Excelsior. Para preparar el fax, escribe una lista de toda la información que necesitan los padres de tu amigo. Luego prepara todas las preguntas que tienes que incluir en el fax. Al terminar tus dos listas, prepara la copia final para el fax que vas a enviar.

B **A los veinticinco años de edad** Prepara un cuestionario corto. El tema de tu cuestionario es «A los veinticinco años de edad». Sírvete de (Usa) tu cuestionario para entrevistar (dar una interviú) a un(a) compañero(a). En tu cuestionario incluye preguntas sobre su educación, su familia, su trabajo y sus pasatiempos.

Writing Strategy

Creating an advertisement

The purpose of an advertisement is to persuade people to buy a product or service. An effective ad will attract attention, arouse interest, and create desire. You can use a striking design to draw readers in. You can use facts and opinions to explain the product's features and to show why readers should be interested in your product—why it is better than the competition. And you can appeal to your readers' reason and emotion to make them want your product.

Un anuncio

A hotel in your community wants to encourage Spanish-speaking guests to stay there. They have asked you to prepare an advertisement describing the hotel and listing its best features. Use the advertisement for the Parador Reyes Católicos in Santiago de Compostela, Galicia, as a guide, but be as original as you can. Be sure your ad reflects services offered by the hotel as well as activities and events in your community.

Actividades escritas

A Tell students that in preparing their list of the information they need, they can very often use just one word.

B **Actividad B** makes students actively use question words and interrogative word order.

Writing Strategy

Creating an advertisement
Have students read the Writing Strategy on page 175.

TECHNOLOGY OPTION

You may wish to have students do the Chapter 6 Internet activity about choosing a hotel in the Spanish-speaking world before they create their ads. They can use the information from the hotel Web sites as additional models for their ads.

HISTORY CONNECTION

Santiago, centro de peregrinación Santiago de Compostela was one of the major sites of Christian pilgrimage during the Middle Ages, along with Rome and Jerusalem.

ANSWERS

Actividades escritas
A and B Answers will vary.

Writing Strategy
Answers will vary.

175

VOCABULARY REVIEW

The words and phrases in the **Vocabulario** have been taught for productive use in this chapter. They are summarized here as a resource for both students and teacher. This list also serves as a convenient resource for the **Culminación** activities on pages 174 and 175. Have the students look at the list. If there are any words they do not know, have them find them in the **Vocabulario** sections on pages 152–153 and 156–157. If absolutely necessary, students can look up some words in the end vocabulary.

There are at least nine cognates in this vocabulary list. Have students find them.

📌 *Teacher Notes*

Vocabulario

MAKING A HOTEL RESERVATION

reservar	un cuarto sencillo
la reservación	un cuarto doble
el cuarto, la habitación	

CHECKING INTO A HOTEL

el hotel	la llave
la recepción	la puerta
el/la recepcionista	el botones, el mozo
el/la cliente, el/la huésped	el equipaje
la ficha, la tarjeta	el ascensor, el elevador

CHECKING OUT OF A HOTEL

abandonar el cuarto
bajar las maletas
pedir la cuenta
pagar la factura

TALKING ABOUT A HOTEL ROOM

la puerta	el aire acondicionado
la cama	el armario
la sábana	la percha, el colgador
la almohada	el sillón
la manta, la frazada	el sofá
el televisor	

TALKING ABOUT A BATHROOM

la bañera
la ducha
el inodoro, el váter
el lavabo
el jabón
la toalla

TALKING ABOUT CLEANING A HOTEL ROOM

la camarera
limpiar el cuarto
hacer la cama
cambiar las toallas

TECNOTUR

VIDEO

¡Buen viaje!

EPISODIO 6 ▶ En el hotel

Cristina e Isabel hacen sus maletas porque las vacaciones ya se acaban y tienen que abandonar el hotel.

La única queja del señor de la Rosa es que ya se acabaron las vacaciones.

CD-ROM

Expansión cultural

Pronóstico del clima

El pronóstico de México es muy variado.

interNET CONNECTION

In this video episode Cristina and the de la Rosa family are checking out of their hotel after their vacation in Puerto Vallarta. To find the perfect hotel in a Spanish-speaking country for your family vacation, go to the **Capítulo 6 Internet** activity at the **Glencoe Foreign Language Web site:**

http://www.glencoe.com/sec/fl

TECNOTUR

ciento setenta y siete ∿ **177**

OVERVIEW

This page previews three key multimedia components of the **Glencoe Spanish** series. Each reinforces the material taught in Chapter 6 in a unique manner.

VIDEO

The Video Program allows students to see how the chapter vocabulary and structures are used by native speakers in an engaging story. For maximum reinforcement, show the video episode as a final activity for Chapter 6.

A. These two photos show highlights from the episode. Before watching it, ask students the following: **¿Cómo es el cuarto de Cristina e Isabel? En la segunda foto, ¿dónde está el Sr. de la Rosa? ¿Qué hace en la recepción? ¿Adónde van todos cuando salen de Puerto Vallarta?**

B. See the Video Activities Booklet for detailed suggestions for using this resource.

CD-ROM

A. The **Expansión cultural** photo shows a weather map of Mexico. Have students read the caption.

B. In the CD-ROM version of **Expansión cultural** (Disc 2, page 177), students can listen to additional recorded information about Mexico's weather and climate.

INTERNET

Teacher Information and Student Worksheets for this activity can be accessed at the Web site.

Video Synopsis

As the episode begins, we see Cristina and Isabel in their Puerto Vallarta hotel room as they pack their bags to return to Mexico City. In the next scene, we see them at the front desk of the hotel, making arrangements to have the bill ready for Isabel's father. They also have the hotel clerk call Luis' room to make sure he is prepared to leave. Mr. and Mrs. de la Rosa then join the girls, and Mr. de la Rosa pays the hotel bill.

SCOPE AND SEQUENCE pages 178–207

TOPICS	FUNCTIONS	STRUCTURE	CULTURE
◆ Airplane terminology ◆ Airport terminology ◆ Geographical terms	◆ How to talk about air travel ◆ How to talk about geographical features ◆ How to express conditions ◆ How to talk about things stated earlier	◆ The conditional of regular verbs ◆ The conditional of irregular verbs ◆ Two object pronouns with **se**	◆ El Alto Airport and La Paz, Bolivia ◆ La Paz, El Alto, and Lake Titicaca ◆ Capitán Emilio Carranza: A Mexican hero ◆ The geography of Spain ◆ **Vistas de Costa Rica**

CHAPTER 7 RESOURCES

PRINT	MULTIMEDIA

Planning Resources

Lesson Plans
Block Scheduling Lesson Plans

Interactive Lesson Planner

Reinforcement Resources

Writing Activities Workbook
Student Tape Manual
Video Activities Booklet
Web Site User's Guide

Transparencies Binder
Audiocassette/Compact Disc Program
Videocassette/Videodisc Program
Online Internet Activities
Electronic Teacher's Classroom Resources

Assessment Resources

Situation Cards
Chapter Quizzes
Testing Program
Performance Assessment

Maratón mental Mindjogger Videoquiz
Testmaker Computer Software (Macintosh/Windows)
Listening Comprehension Audiocassette/Compact Disc
Communication Transparency: C-7

Motivational Resources

Expansion Activities

Café Glencoe: www.cafe.glencoe.com
Keypal Internet Activities

Enrichment

Spanish for Spanish Speakers

SECTION	PAGES	SECTION RESOURCES
Vocabulario Palabras 1 **En el avión** **La cabina**	180–183	Vocabulary Transparencies 7.1 Audiocassette 5A/Compact Disc 5 Student Tape Manual, TE, pages 71–72 Workbook, pages 71–72 Chapter Quizzes, page 30 CD-ROM, Disc 2, pages 180–183
Vocabulario Palabras 2 **En el aeropuerto** **Un poco de geografía**	184–187	Vocabulary Transparencies 7.2 Audiocassette 5A/Compact Disc 5 Student Tape Manual, TE, pages 73–74 Workbook, pages 73–74 Chapter Quizzes, page 31 CD-ROM, Disc 2, pages 184–187
Estructura **Modo potencial o condicional de verbos regulares** **Modo potencial de verbos irregulares** **Dos complementos con se**	188–195	Workbook, pages 75–77 Audiocassette 5A/Compact Disc 5 Student Tape Manual, TE, pages 74–77 Chapter Quizzes, pages 32–34 Computer Testmaker CD-ROM, Disc 2, pages 188–195
Conversación **En el avión**	196–197	Audiocassette 5A/Compact Disc 5 Student Tape Manual, TE, pages 77–78 CD-ROM, Disc 2, pages 196–197
Lecturas culturales **El aeropuerto que se llama «El Alto»** **Los alrededores de La Paz (opcional)** **Un héroe de la aviación latino- americana (opcional)**	198–201	Testing Program, pages 50–51 CD-ROM, Disc 2, pages 198–201
Conexiones **La geografía (opcional)**	202–203	Testing Program, page 52 CD-ROM, Disc 2, pages 202–203
Culminación **Actividades orales** **Actividades escritas** **Vocabulario** **Tecnotur**	204–207	¡Buen viaje! Video, Episode 7 Video Activities, pages 88–91 Internet Activities www.glencoe.com/sec/fl Testing Program, pages 48–51; 131; 175; 196 CD-ROM, Disc 2, pages 204–207

CAPÍTULO 7

OVERVIEW

In this chapter students will learn to talk about air travel in-flight services, and geography. They will learn the formation of the conditional and the use of **se** when combining direct and indirect object pronouns. The cultural focus of the chapter is on air travel in Latin America and how it is influenced by geographical features of the land.

National Standards

In Chapter 7 students will learn to communicate in spoken and written Spanish on the following topics:
- air travel
- services aboard a flight
- geography

Students will obtain and provide information about these topics and engage in conversations that would typically take place aboard a plane as they fulfill the chapter objectives listed on this page.

Teacher Notes

El vuelo

Objetivos

In this chapter you will learn to do the following:

- talk about air travel
- discuss the influence of geography on travel in Latin America
- talk about things that would happen under certain conditions
- talk about air travel in Hispanic countries

interNET CONNECTION

The **Glencoe Foreign Language Web site** (http://www.glencoe.com/sec/fl) offers three options that enable you and your students to experience the Spanish-speaking world via the Internet:

- The online **Actividades** are correlated to the chapters and utilize Hispanic Web sites around the world. For the Chapter 7 activity, see student page 207.

- The **Correspondencia electrónica** section provides information on how to set up a keypal (pen pal) exchange between your class and a class in the Spanish-speaking world.

- At **Café Glencoe,** the interactive "after-school" section of the site, you and your students can access a variety of additional online resources, including interactive games.

ciento setenta y nueve **179**

Spotlight On Culture

Fotografía The airplane is descending for a landing at the **Aeropuerto Internacional Mariscal Sucre** in Quito, the capital of Ecuador. The setting of Quito is spectacular. The city lies at the foot of the Pichincha volcano in the hollow of a gently sloping fertile valley. Although Quito is only a short distance below the equator, its elevation of 2,850 meters (9,350 feet) provides it with a pleasant, balmy climate. Quito is, however, subject to earthquakes and has been damaged several times. Quito is the educational, political, and cultural center of Ecuador. Much of the population of the city is Indian. The airport is named for Antonio José de Sucre, who liberated the city from Spain's control in 1822.

Pacing

Chapter 7 will require approximately six to eight days. Pacing will vary according to the length of the class, the age of your students, and student aptitude.

Block Scheduling

The extended time frame provided by block scheduling affords you the opportunity to implement a greater number of activities and projects to motivate and involve your students. See the Block Scheduling Lesson Plans Booklet for suggestions on how to present the chapter material within a block scheduling framework.

Chapter Projects

Visita a una agencia de viajes Have students visit a travel agency and obtain brochures on Bolivia and other countries in the Andes region of South America. Have them write captions for the brochures in Spanish and design a bulletin board display.
Informes turísticos Have groups prepare reports on Lake Titicaca and the Aymara and Quechua peoples.

Algo sobre la historia Have individuals or groups prepare reports on different aspects of the history of the Andean countries, such as Bolivia, Perú, Chile, or Ecuador.
La actualidad Have groups research modern-day Bolivia, compiling their findings for a class bulletin board display on that country.

Vocabulario

RESOURCES

- Vocabulary Transparencies 7.1 (A & B)
- Student Tape Manual, TE, pages 71–72
- Audiocassette 5A/CD4
- Workbook, pages 71–72
- Quiz 1, page 30
- CD-ROM, Disc 2, pages 180–183

Bell Ringer Review

Use BRR Transparency 7-1, or write the following on the board: List all the words and expressions you can remember that have to do with air travel.

TEACHING VOCABULARY

A. Project Vocabulary Transparencies 7.1 (A & B) and have students repeat the new words, phrases, and sentences after you or the recording on Cassette 5A/ Compact Disc 4.

B. Model the new vocabulary again, calling out vocabulary words in random order. Have volunteers point to the appropriate image on the screen as you say the words.

C. Use the usual questioning techniques to present the material on page 181. Begin with simple yes/no and either/or questions.

D. When students have produced the new vocabulary several times, progress to open-ended questions such as: **¿Qué estaba haciendo el asistente de vuelo? ¿Qué les estaba dando a los pasajeros? ¿Qué estaba distribuyendo la asistente de vuelo? ¿Qué estaban sirviendo los asistentes de vuelo?**

180

Vocabulario

En el avión

la tripulación

el comandante, el piloto

el co-piloto

la cabina de mando, la cabina de vuelo

los asistentes de vuelo

La cabina

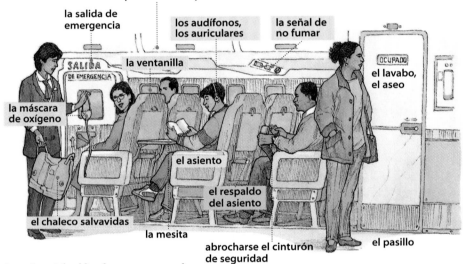

el compartimiento sobre la cabeza, el compartimiento superior

la salida de emergencia

los audífonos, los auriculares

la señal de no fumar

la ventanilla

el lavabo, el aseo

la máscara de oxígeno

el asiento

el respaldo del asiento

el chaleco salvavidas

la mesita

abrocharse el cinturón de seguridad

el pasillo

La señora iría al lavabo, pero no puede. Está ocupado.

Pantomime

Begin

___, ven acá. Estás en el avión.

Busca tu asiento.

Abre el compartimiento superior.

Pon tu equipaje en el compartimiento.

Cierra el compartimiento superior.

Siéntate.

Abróchate el cinturón de seguridad.

Pon el respaldo de tu asiento en posición vertical.

El asistente de vuelo llega. Va a darte los auriculares. Tómalos.

Pónte los auriculares.

Escoge un canal de música.

Gracias, ___. Bien hecho. Regresa a tu asiento.

El asistente de vuelo hizo algunos anuncios.
Dijo que los asistentes de vuelo:

pasarían por la cabina con los
  audífonos;
distribuirían los audífonos;
se los distribuirían a los pasajeros;

servirían bebidas y una
comida durante el vuelo;

También dijo que el equipaje
de mano tendría que caber
debajo del asiento o en el
compartimiento superior.

y que en el caso de una emergencia
  las máscaras de oxígeno caerían
  automáticamente.

la bandeja

el carrito

Durante el vuelo los asistentes de vuelo
sirvieron una comida a los pasajeros.

Se la sirvieron de un carrito.
Se la sirvieron en una bandeja.

VOCABULARIO

ciento ochenta y uno 〰 **181**

❖Práctica❖

¡OJO! **Práctica** When students are doing the **Práctica** activities, accept any answer that makes sense. The purpose of these activities is to have students use the new vocabulary. They are not factual recall activities. Thus, do not expect students to remember specific information from the vocabulary presentation when answering. If you wish, have students use the photos as a stimulus, when possible.

Historieta Each time **Historieta** appears, it means that the answers to the activity form a short story. Encourage students to look at the title of the **Historieta** since it can sometimes help them do the activity.

A Have students refer to the illustrations as they do **Práctica A**.

B **Práctica B** can be done first orally with books closed.

C and **D** Have students prepare **Práctica C** and **Práctica D** before you go over them in class.

182

❖Práctica❖

A ¿Qué es o quién es? Identifiquen.

1. ¿Es el lavabo o la cabina de mando?

2. ¿Es la máscara de oxígeno o la señal de no fumar?

3. ¿Es el asistente de vuelo o el comandante?

4. ¿Es el chaleco salvavidas o el cinturón de seguridad?

5. ¿Es el pasillo o el compartimiento superior?

6. ¿Es el asiento o la mesita?

B HISTORIETA A bordo del avión

Contesten según se indica.
1. ¿Dónde en el avión está el piloto? (en la cabina de vuelo o en la cabina de mando)
2. ¿Quiénes componen la tripulación? (el piloto o el comandante, el co-piloto y los asistentes de vuelo)
3. ¿Quiénes sirven a los pasajeros durante el vuelo? (los asistentes de vuelo)
4. ¿De qué se responsabilizan los asistentes de vuelo? (de la seguridad de los pasajeros)
5. En el caso de una emergencia, ¿por dónde salen los pasajeros? (por las salidas de emergencia)

C A bordo del avión Pareen.
1. donde uno va para lavarse las manos en el avión
2. donde se pone el equipaje de mano
3. lo que se usa para oír música o ver una película
4. la persona que sirve a los pasajeros en el avión
5. en la que sirve el asistente de vuelo la comida
6. donde pone el asistente de vuelo la comida que le sirve al pasajero

a. el lavabo
b. la bandeja
c. el asistente de vuelo
d. la mesita
e. el compartimiento superior
f. los audífonos

D **Algunas reglas a bordo del avión** Contesten.

1. ¿Qué abrocharías durante el despegue y el aterrizaje?
   a. el cinturón de seguridad
   b. el respaldo del asiento
   c. la máscara de oxígeno
2. Durante el despegue y el aterrizaje, ¿dónde pondrías tu equipaje de mano?
   a. debajo del asiento
   b. en el pasillo
   c. en el lavabo
3. En caso de un cambio en la presión del aire en el avión, ¿qué usarías?
   a. el cinturón de seguridad
   b. los audífonos
   c. la máscara de oxígeno
4. ¿Cómo pondrías el respaldo de tu asiento durante el despegue y el aterrizaje?
   a. en posición vertical
   b. debajo del asiento
   c. en el compartimiento sobre la cabeza
5. En caso de un aterrizaje de emergencia en el mar, ¿qué te pondrías?
   a. el lavabo
   b. la señal de no fumar
   c. el chaleco salvavidas

La aerolínea Avensa

Actividades comunicativas

A **Antes del despegue** Tú eres un(a) asistente de vuelo. Un(a) pasajero(a) (tu compañero[a]) está haciendo su primer viaje en avión. No tiene idea de lo que tiene que hacer. Explícale todo lo que tiene que hacer antes del despegue.

B **A bordo del avión** Con un(a) compañero(a), mira el dibujo. Juntos describan todo lo que ven en el dibujo. Luego decidan si quieren hacer un viaje en avión. Expliquen por qué.

CAPÍTULO 7
Vocabulario

Actividades comunicativas

¡OJO! Práctica versus Actividades comunicativas
All activities which provide guided practice are labeled **Práctica.** The more open-ended communicative activities are labeled **Actividades comunicativas.**

Allow students to select the activity they wish to take part in.

Learning From Photos

La aerolínea Avensa AVENSA is a Venezuelan airline serving a dozen destinations in Venezuela and offering flights to another dozen destinations in Europe and North and South America.

Did You Know?

Sociedad Anónima The **SA** in AVENSA and in the names of many companies in Spain and Latin America—VIASA, ATESA, etc.—stands for **Sociedad Anónima,** the Spanish equivalent of *incorporated.*

Independent Practice

Assign any of the following:
1. Workbook, **Palabras 1,** pages 71–72
2. Activities, pages 182–183
3. CD-ROM, Disc 2, pages 180–183

ANSWERS

Práctica

D **1. a**
2. a
3. c
4. a
5. c

Actividades comunicativas

A and B Answers will vary.

Vocabulario

En el aeropuerto

la avioneta

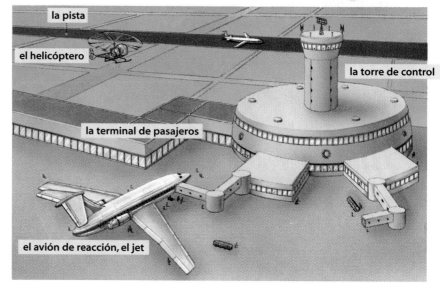

la pista

el helicóptero

la torre de control

la terminal de pasajeros

el avión de reacción, el jet

el despegue

el aterrizaje

RESOURCES

- Vocabulary Transparencies 7.2 (A & B)
- Student Tape Manual, TE, pages 73–74
- Audiocassette 5A/CD4
- Workbook, pages 73–74
- Quiz 2, page 31
- CD-ROM, Disc 2, pages 184–187

Bell Ringer Review

Use BRR Transparency 7-2, or write the following on the board: Match the word in the first column with a related word in the second column.

1. llegar   a. el asiento
2. aterrizar   b. el despegue
3. despegar   c. el aterrizaje
4. asistir   d. la comida
5. beber   e. la bebida
6. comer   f. la llegada
7. salir   g. la salida
8. sentar   h. el asistente

TEACHING VOCABULARY

A. Have students close their books. Project Vocabulary Transparencies 7.2 (A & B). Point to each item and have students repeat each word two or three times after you or the recording on Cassette 5A/Compact Disc 4.

B. Now point to items at random on the transparencies as you ask **¿Qué es?** and call on individuals to respond.

Did You Know?

Dos aerolíneas hispanas Iberia is the national airline of Spain. It was founded in 1927, with flights between Madrid and Barcelona. In 1946 Iberia began service between Madrid and Buenos Aires and in 1954 between Madrid and New York. The Iberia plane taking off is a DC10.

Avianca is the national airline of Colombia and one of the oldest airlines in Latin America. It began in collaboration with Pan American World Airways. Today it flies to dozens of cities in North and South America and Europe. The Avianca plane landing is a Boeing 767.

¿Dijo el piloto a qué hora llegaríamos?

No, sólo dijo que saldríamos a tiempo.

El comandante les habló a los pasajeros.
Les anunció que:
despegarían a tiempo.
el avión volaría a una altura de 10.000 metros.
sería un vuelo directo; no harían escala.
sobrevolarían los Andes.
habría muy poca turbulencia durante el vuelo.

C. You may wish to ask the following questions about the sentences on this page:
¿Dijo el piloto que despegarían a tiempo?
¿Dijo que despegarían a tiempo o con retraso?
¿A qué altura volaría?
¿Dijo que sería un vuelo directo?
¿Harían escala o no?

Un poco de geografía

la altura, la altitud
la cordillera
la montaña
el pico
el altiplano
la meseta
el lago
el valle
la llanura

ABOUT THE SPANISH LANGUAGE

Explain to students that the term **altiplano** is used to refer to the entire Andean region in general.

185

¡OJO! It is recommended that you go over the **Práctica** activities orally in class before assigning them for homework.

A Go over **Práctica A** orally with books closed. Then have students read the activity aloud for additional reinforcement.

B **Práctica B** can be done without prior preparation but with books open.

Did You Know?

Más pista a más altura Planes taking off from airports at high altitudes such as this Aeroperú aircraft in Cuzco need longer runways because of the lower air density at high altitudes. (The same thing is true at the airport **El Alto** in La Paz, Bolivia. See the **Lectura,** page 198.)

Caracas, Venezuela

❖Práctica❖

A HISTORIETA A bordo del avión

Contesten según se indica.

1. ¿De dónde hizo el comandante algunos anuncios? (de la cabina de vuelo)
2. ¿Dijo que despegarían con una demora? (no, a tiempo)
3. ¿Dijo que habría mucha turbulencia durante el vuelo? (no, poca)
4. ¿Dijo que el tiempo de vuelo sería de tres horas? (no, de tres horas y treinta minutos)
5. ¿Dijo que sobrevolarían los Andes? (sí)
6. ¿Qué dijo que podrían ver los pasajeros? (los picos de las montañas)

B En el aeropuerto Escojan.

1. El avión va a llegar en pocos momentos. Esperamos _____.
   a. el despegue   **b.** el aterrizaje   **c.** la salida
2. Los controladores le dan instrucciones al piloto. Se las dan desde la _____.
   a. cabina de mando   **b.** terminal   **c.** torre de control
3. Los amigos y parientes de los pasajeros los esperan en la _____.
   a. terminal   **b.** torre de control   **c.** pista
4. Otro avión ya va a salir. En pocos minutos veremos _____.
   a. la llegada   **b.** el despegue   **c.** el aterrizaje
5. _____ despega y aterriza verticalmente.
   a. La avioneta   **b.** El avión de reacción   **c.** El helicóptero

Cuzco, Perú

ANSWERS

Práctica

A 1. El comandante hizo algunos anuncios de la cabina de vuelo.
2. No, dijo que despegarían a tiempo.
3. No, dijo que habría poca turbulencia durante el vuelo.
4. No, dijo que el tiempo de vuelo sería de tres horas y treinta minutos.
5. Sí, dijo que sobrevolarían los Andes.
6. Dijo que los pasajeros podrían ver los picos de las montañas.

B 1. b
2. c
3. a
4. b
5. c

C Definiciones   Pareen.

1. parte superior de una montaña
2. extensión de tierra que no tiene altos ni bajos
3. espacio de tierra entre montañas
4. agua que comienza en la tierra y va al mar
5. serie de montañas, una tras otra
6. elevación de tierra que termina en un pico

a. río
b. cordillera
c. pico
d. llanura
e. valle
f. montaña

D ¿Qué son... ?   Contesten.

1. los Andes, los Apalaches, las Rocosas
2. el Amazonas, el Misisipí, el Nilo
3. Aconcagua, Everest, McKinley
4. Huron, Ontario, Michigan, Erie, Superior

Los Andes

Actividades comunicativas

A **Soy el/la comandante.**   Trabaja con un(a) compañero(a). Uno(a) de Uds. es el/la comandante a bordo de un avión de una compañía americana. El vuelo que estás haciendo es el vuelo entre Miami y Guayaquil, Ecuador. Como hay muchos pasajeros a bordo que hablan español, tú vas a hacer algunos anuncios en español. Tu compañero(a) escuchará tus anuncios. Luego cambien de rol y tu compañero(a) será el/la comandante y tú escucharás.

B **Donde vivimos**   Trabaja con un(a) compañero(a). Den una descripción de la geografía de la región donde viven. Pueden usar las siguientes palabras.

la montaña   el río   el tiempo
el pico   el mar   el nivel
el lago   la altura   el valle

VOCABULARIO

C You may wish to have students prepare **Práctica C** before going over it in class.

Actividades comunicativas

¡OJO!   The **Actividades comunicativas** allow students to use the vocabulary and structures of the chapter in open-ended situations. They also give students another opportunity to use words and structures from previous chapters.

Have students work on as many activities as you wish. You may also allow them to select those activities they want to do. Different groups can work on different activities.

A and **B**
TECHNOLOGY OPTION Students may use the Portfolio feature on the CD-ROM to do these activities.

Critical Thinking Activity

Identifying causes Read the following to the class or write it on the board:
¿Por qué razones se cancela o se anula un vuelo?

Learning From Photos

Los Andes The Andes are among the highest mountains in the world. They extend the entire length of South America, 8,500 kilometers (5,000 miles), from Cape Horn in the south to the Caribbean in the north. The average height of the mountains is 4,500 meters (14,763 feet). The highest peak is Aconcagua in Argentina at 6,960 meters (22,834 feet).

ANSWERS

Práctica
C
1. c
2. d
3. e
4. a
5. b
6. f

D
1. **Son cordilleras.**
2. **Son ríos.**
3. **Son montañas.**
4. **Son lagos.**

Actividades comunicativas
A and B Answers will vary.

187

Estructura

CAPÍTULO 7
Estructura

RESOURCES

- 📁 Workbook, pages 75–77
- 📁 Student Tape Manual, TE, pages 74–77
- 🎧 Audiocassette 5A/CD4
- 📁 Quizzes 3–5, pages 32–34
- 💾 Computer Testmaker
- 💿 CD-ROM, Disc 2, pages 188–195

Bell Ringer Review

Use BRR Transparency 7-3, or write the following on the board:
Rewrite the following sentences in the future.
1. Yo voy en tren.
2. Felisa compra los boletos.
3. Yo espero aquí con las maletas.
4. El tren llega a las dieciséis.
5. ¿Comen Uds. en el tren?
6. Sí, tomamos el almuerzo en el tren.

TEACHING STRUCTURE

Expressing conditions

A. Have students open their books to page 188. Lead them through Steps 1–3.
B. Have them repeat the verb forms after you.
C. Call on individuals to read the model sentences or have the class read them in unison.

 This structure point should not prove difficult for students. They are already familiar with the verb stems from the future tense and with the endings from the imperfect. The uses of the conditional are the same in Spanish and English.

188

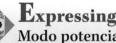

Expressing conditions
Modo potencial o condicional de verbos regulares

¿Te acuerdas?
Remember that the stem for the future tense of regular verbs is the infinitive.
volaré comeré serviré

1. As with the future, the infinitive is used as the stem for the conditional of regular verbs. Study the following forms.

INFINITIVE	llegar	ver	servir	
STEM	llegar-	ver-	servir-	ENDINGS
yo	llegaría	vería	serviría	-ía
tú	llegarías	verías	servirías	-ías
él, ella, Ud.	llegaría	vería	serviría	-ía
nosotros(as)	llegaríamos	veríamos	serviríamos	-íamos
vosotros(as)	llegaríais	veríais	serviríais	-íais
ellos, ellas, Uds.	llegarían	verían	servirían	-ían

Note that the endings for the conditional are the same as those for the imperfect of -**er** and -**ir** verbs.

2. You use the conditional, as you do in English, to tell what would take place under certain circumstances.

> **El avión despegaría ahora pero no puede porque hace mal tiempo.**
> **Nosotros viajaríamos a Europa pero no tenemos suficiente dinero.**

3. The conditional is also used to soften requests.

> **¿Me pasaría Ud. los audífonos, por favor?**
> **¿Se abrocharía el cinturón de seguridad, por favor, señor?**

La aerolínea LACSA, Costa Rica

Learning From Photos

La aerolínea LACSA, Costa Rica You may wish to ask students the following questions about the photo:
¿Dónde está el asiento del muchacho, al lado de la ventanilla o del pasillo?
¿Qué está haciendo el muchacho?
¿Está el respaldo de su asiento en posición vertical?
¿Qué lleva el muchacho?

Tell students that LACSA stands for **Líneas Aéreas Centroamericanas SA.** It is based in Costa Rica. Ask the students what the SA stands for. (**Sociedad Anónima.**) Recently LACSA formed an alliance with Aviateca, Nica, and Taca, all Central American airlines, to create a Central American airline consortium.

Práctica

A HISTORIETA Imaginándome millonario(a)

Contesten.

1. ¿Vivirías en la ciudad o en el campo?
2. ¿Viajarías mucho?
3. ¿Adónde irías?
4. ¿Cómo irías?
5. ¿Con quién irías?
6. ¿Comprarías una casa grande?
7. ¿Cómo sería la casa?
8. ¿Trabajarías?

B HISTORIETA Las vacaciones del muchacho

Contesten.

1. ¿Adónde iría el muchacho para las vacaciones?
2. ¿Cómo viajaría?
3. ¿Cuánto pagaría?
4. ¿Dónde nadaría él?
5. ¿A qué jugaría?
6. ¿Qué subiría él?
7. ¿Qué comería?
8. ¿Dónde dormiría?

En una agencia de viajes, España

Lima, Perú

ESTRUCTURA   *ciento ochenta y nueve* 189

CAPÍTULO 7
Estructura

Práctica

A **Práctica A** can be done orally with books closed. Tell students to be as original as possible when they respond.

B **Práctica B** can also be done orally with books closed.

EXPANSION Call on a student or students to tell in his or her own words all about the vacation described in this activity.

PAIRED ACTIVITY Have students ask one another questions about what they would do on vacation.

Learning From Photos

En una agencia de viajes, España You may wish to ask students these questions:
En la foto de arriba, ¿quiénes son las dos personas?
¿Qué usa el agente?
¿Qué querrá hacer el cliente?
Describe todo lo que ves en la foto.
Lima, Perú You may wish to ask these questions about the bottom photo:
¿De qué es la foto de abajo?
¿Es la torre de control o la terminal?
¿Qué serán las personas en la foto?

ANSWERS

Práctica

A 1. **Viviría en la ciudad (en el campo).**
2. **Sí, (No, no) viajaría mucho.**
3. **Iría a ___.**
4. **Iría en ___.**
5. **Iría con ___.**
6. **Sí, (No, no) compraría una casa grande.**
7. **La casa sería ___.**
8. **Sí, (No, no) trabajaría.**

B Answers will vary but may include:
1. **El muchacho iría a ___ para las vacaciones.**
2. **Viajaría en ___.**
3. **Pagaría ___.**
4. **Nadaría ___.**
5. **Jugaría a ___.**
6. **Subiría ___.**
7. **Comería ___.**
8. **Dormiría ___.**

189

C **No, no.** Contesten según el modelo.

Ellos piensan ir. ¿Y tú?

No, yo no iría.

1. Ellos piensan llamar. ¿Y tú?
2. Yo pienso escribir. ¿Y Uds.?
3. Carolina piensa visitar a sus primos. ¿Y su hermano?
4. Nosotros pensamos ir. ¿Y Uds.?
5. Ellos piensan viajar por avión. ¿Y Uds.?
6. Teresa piensa manejar. ¿Y tú?

D **HISTORIETA** **Un viaje con unos amigos**

Contesten según se indica.

1. ¿Irían tus amigos a la playa o a las montañas? (a las montañas)
2. ¿Los acompañarías? (sí)
3. ¿Cómo irían Uds., en tren o en carro? (en carro)
4. ¿Quién manejaría? (Teresa)
5. ¿Cuánto tiempo pasarían Uds. en las montañas (unos cinco días)
6. ¿Dónde se quedarían Uds.? (en un hotel económico)

San Carlos de Bariloche, Argentina

190

Expressing more conditions
Modo potencial de verbos irregulares

The same verbs that are irregular in the future tense are irregular in the conditional. Study the following.

INFINITIVE	FUTURE	CONDITIONAL
tener	tendré	tendría
poner	pondré	pondría
salir	saldré	saldría
venir	vendré	vendría
poder	podré	podría
saber	sabré	sabría
hacer	haré	haría
decir	diré	diría
querer	querré	querría

 **Práctica**

A HISTORIETA ¿Vendrá tu hermana o no?

Contesten según el modelo.

¿Estará tu hermana?

Dijo que estaría.

1. ¿Vendrá tu hermana?
2. ¿Hará el viaje?
3. ¿Podrá pagar el viaje?
4. ¿Saldrá el viernes?
5. ¿Tendrá bastante tiempo?

ESTRUCTURA

ciento noventa y uno 191

❖Práctica❖

B and **C** These activities must be done with books open. You can go over them without prior preparation or have students prepare them first.

D **Práctica D** can be done orally with books closed.

EXPANSION Call on a student or students to give a summary of the information the pilot and the flight attendant gave in **Práctica D**.

B **Uno sí y el otro no** Completen con el condicional.

1. Él sabría la dirección pero su hermano no la _____.
2. Yo te lo diría pero ellos nunca te lo _____.
3. Nosotros lo haríamos pero ellos no lo _____ nunca.
4. Yo podría ir pero mis amigos no _____.
5. Uds. lo pondrían en orden pero él no lo _____.
6. Yo tendría que volver pero tú no _____.

C **Ahora lo hará pero antes no lo haría.**

Completen con el condicional.

1. Carlos podrá pero antes no _____.
2. Los muchachos vendrán pero antes no _____.
3. Tú lo harás pero antes no lo _____.
4. Uds. saldrán pero antes no _____.
5. Ud. me lo dirá pero antes no me lo _____.

D **HISTORIETA** **A bordo del avión**

Contesten con **sí**.

1. ¿Dijo el comandante que el avión podría despegar a tiempo?
2. ¿Dijo que saldrían dentro de cinco minutos?
3. ¿Dijo el asistente de vuelo que los pasajeros tendrían que poner su equipaje de mano en el compartimiento superior?
4. ¿Dijo que no podríamos fumar cigarrillos durante el vuelo?
5. ¿Dijo que yo podría usar mi teléfono celular durante el vuelo?
6. ¿Dijo el comandante que nos diría la hora exacta de nuestra llegada?
7. ¿Dijo que haríamos escala en Bogotá?

ANSWERS

Práctica

B 1. sabría
2. dirían
3. harían
4. podrían
5. pondría
6. tendrías

C 1. podría
2. vendrían
3. harías
4. saldrían
5. diría

D 1. Sí, el comandante dijo que el avión podría despegar a tiempo.
2. Sí, el comandante dijo que saldrían dentro de cinco minutos.
3. Sí, el asistente de vuelo dijo que los pasajeros tendrían que poner su equipaje de mano en el compartimiento superior.
4. Sí, dijo que no podríamos fumar cigarrillos durante el vuelo.
5. Sí, dijo que tú podrías usar tu teléfono celular durante el vuelo.
6. Sí, el comandante dijo que nos diría la hora exacta de nuestra llegada.
7. Sí, dijo que haríamos escala en Bogotá.

Actividades comunicativas

A **Una encuesta** Trabaja con un(a) compañero(a). Van a hacer una encuesta *(survey)*. Ésta es la situación. Hay un billete de cien dólares en la calle. Cada uno(a) de Uds. preguntará a cinco compañeros qué harían al encontrar los cien dólares. Luego organicen las respuestas para informar a la clase sobre los resultados.

B **Lo que haría pero no puedo** ¿No es verdad que hay muchas cosas que te gustaría hacer pero que no puedes porque tienes otras obligaciones? Ten una conversación con un(a) compañero(a). Discutan todo lo que les gustaría hacer pero que no pueden. Expliquen por qué no pueden.

 Talking about things stated before
Dos complementos con se

1. The indirect object pronouns **le** and **les** change to **se** when used in the same sentence with either **lo, la, los,** or **las.**

> El asistente de vuelo les sirvió la comida a los pasajeros .
> El asistente de vuelo se la sirvió.
>
> El joven le dio los audífonos a su mamá .
> El joven se los dio.

2. Because the pronoun **se** can refer to many different people, it is often clarified with a prepositional phrase.

> El asistente se la pasó a él (a ella, a Ud., a ellos, a ellas, a Uds.)

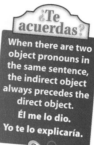

¿Te acuerdas?

When there are two object pronouns in the same sentence, the indirect object always precedes the direct object.

Él me lo dio.
Yo te lo explicaría.

Para volar a Australia y Nueva Zelanda desde Sudamérica, sólo hay que dar media vuelta. No veinte mil.

Ahora, 3 veces por semana con nuestro exclusivo vuelo Transpolar.

AEROLÍNEAS ARGENTINAS

ESTRUCTURA

ciento noventa y tres 193

 Bell Ringer Review

Use BRR Transparency 7-5, or write the following on the board: Make a list of clothing that you would buy right away if you had enough money.

Actividades comunicativas

Allow students to choose the activities they would like to participate in.

TEACHING STRUCTURE

Talking about things stated before

A. Have students open their books to page 193. Lead them through Steps 1 and 2.
B. You may want to write the model sentences on the board to reinforce this concept. Draw an arrow from the pronoun to the noun it replaces.

 GEOGRAPHY CONNECTION

Aerolíneas Argentinas Have students read the Aerolíneas Argentinas ad. They should look at a world map and determine the distance between Buenos Aires and Auckland, New Zealand. Buenos Aires is much closer to New Zealand and Australia than New York is, for example.

ANSWERS

Actividades comunicativas
A and **B** Answers will vary.

¡OJO! You may decide to what extent you wish to emphasize the practice of this particular structure point. Although students should recognize the **se lo** construction, it is less necessary for them to produce it since they could respond with nouns: **El asistente le dio la manta a la señora**. It takes students quite a bit of time to use the **se lo** construction actively.

A **Práctica A** can be done orally with books closed. Students can then write the answers for additional reinforcement.

B Students can present **Práctica B** as a series of mini-conversations.

Learning From Photos

Viña del Mar, Chile Viña del Mar, on Chile's Pacific Coast not far from Santiago, is Chile's premier summer resort. Viña del Mar and Valparaíso, Chile's major port, are located next to each other but are very different from one another. Valparaíso is a busy port plagued with pollution while Viña is a tourist city that lives for the summer months when thousands of Chileans and foreigners flock to its gorgeous beaches.

◈Práctica◈

A HISTORIETA **Durante el vuelo**

Contesten según el modelo.

> ¿Quién le dio la revista al pasajero?
> El asistente se la dio.

1. ¿Quién le dio la manta a la señora?
2. ¿Quién le pasó la bandeja a la señorita?
3. ¿Quién le ofreció los audífonos al pasajero?
4. ¿Quién les explicó las reglas de seguridad a los pasajeros?
5. ¿Quién les sirvió la comida a los pasajeros?
6. ¿Quién les anunció la hora de llegada a los viajeros?

Ciudad de México

B **Su abuelita se lo compró.** Contesten según el modelo.

¿Quién le compró el regalito?

Su abuelita se lo compró.

1. ¿Quién le compró la bicicleta?
2. ¿Quién le compró el billete?
3. ¿Quién le compró las entradas?
4. ¿Quién le compró los periódicos?

Viña del Mar, Chile

ANSWERS

Práctica

A 1. El asistente se la dio.
   2. El asistente se la pasó.
   3. El asistente se los ofreció.
   4. El asistente se las explicó.
   5. El asistente se la sirvió.
   6. El asistente se la anunció.

B 1. Su abuelita se la compró.
   2. Su abuelita se lo compró.
   3. Su abuelita se las compró.
   4. Su abuelita se los compró.

C **A mí, no. A Carlos.** Sigan el modelo.

¿Ramona te daría el regalo?

A mí, no. Se lo daría a Carlos.

1. ¿Tu papá te regalaría las entradas?
2. ¿Te darían la computadora?
3. ¿Tus abuelos te enviarían el dinero?
4. ¿Los muchachos te darían los esquís?
5. ¿Maribel te compraría los periódicos?

D **HISTORIETA** Tomás se los llevó.

Sigan el modelo.

> **Tomás le llevó los vegetales a su mamá.**
> **Tomás se los llevó a ella.**

1. Tomás le llevó los vegetales a su mamá.
2. Tomás le pidió dinero a su mamá.
3. Su madre le dio el dinero a Tomás.
4. Tomás le dio las legumbres congeladas a su mamá.
5. Tomás le devolvió el cambio a su mamá.

El Corte Inglés, Sevilla

Actividad comunicativa

A **Yo no se lo daría.** Trabaja con un(a) compañero(a). Él o ella te menciona algo que le daría a alguien. Tú le contestas que no se lo darías nunca. Usen el modelo como guía.

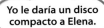

Yo le daría un disco compacto a Elena.

Yo nunca se lo daría a ella.

ESTRUCTURA

ciento noventa y cinco 〰 **195**

C Have students work in pairs to do this activity.

D You may wish to have students prepare **Práctica D** before going over it in class.

Actividad comunicativa

A **TECHNOLOGY OPTION**
In the CD-ROM version of this activity (Disc 2, page 195), students can interact with an on-screen native speaker and record their voices.

Learning From Photos

El Corte Inglés, Sevilla
El Corte Inglés is Spain's major department store chain with large stores in all major cities. Most include a food section, as does this one in Seville. You may wish to ask students to identify as many produce items as they can.

By the way, **El Corte Inglés** literally means *the English cut* (or style of clothing).

ANSWERS

Práctica

C 1. **A mí, no. Se las regalaría a Carlos.**
2. **A mí, no. Se la darían a Carlos.**
3. **A mí, no. Se lo enviarían a Carlos.**
4. **A mí, no. Se los darían a Carlos.**
5. **A mí, no. Se los compraría a Carlos.**

D 1. **Tomás se los llevó a ella .**
2. **Tomás se lo pidió a ella.**
3. **Su madre se lo dio a él.**
4. **Tomás se las dio a ella.**
5. **Tomás se lo devolvió a ella.**

Actividad comunicativa

A Answers will vary.

195

RESOURCES

🎧 Audiocassette 5A/CD4
💿 CD-ROM, Disc 2, page 196

🔔 Bell Ringer Review

Use BRR Transparency 7-6, or write the following on the board: Indicate whether it's a train trip or a flight.

1. **Aquí viene el revisor.**
2. **Hay asientos para 40 personas en cada coche.**
3. **Los pasajeros se abrochan el cinturón de seguridad.**
4. **Despega y aterriza.**
5. **Sale del andén número cuatro.**

TEACHING THE CONVERSATION

A. Tell students they will hear a conversation between Adela and Víctor, two passengers on a commercial airliner.

B. 🎧 Have students close their books and listen as you read the conversation or play Cassette 5A/Compact Disc 4.

C. Now have students open their books. Allow pairs a few minutes to practice reading the conversation.

D. Call on one or two pairs of volunteers to read the conversation to the class with as much expression as possible.

E. Then go over the **Después de conversar** activity.

F. After going over the conversation, have a student retell all the information in his or her own words in narrative form.

196

En el avión

ADELA: No pude oír el anuncio. ¿Qué dijo el asistente de vuelo?
VÍCTOR: Que el vuelo sería de tres horas y que llegaríamos a La Paz a tiempo.
ADELA: ¡Qué bien! La comida es bastante buena, ¿no?
VÍCTOR: Sí. No sabía que nos servirían una comida. Es un vuelo bastante corto.
ADELA: ¿Qué piensas? ¿Habrá una película?
VÍCTOR: No. Me dijeron que no podrían presentar una película porque no habría tiempo.

Después de conversar

Contesten.

1. ¿Dónde están Adela y Víctor?
2. ¿Adónde van ellos?
3. ¿Qué dijo el asistente de vuelo?
4. ¿Cuánto tiempo dura el vuelo?
5. Según Adela, ¿cómo es la comida?
6. ¿Qué no sabía Víctor?
7. ¿Habrá una película?
8. ¿Por qué le dijeron a Víctor que no podrían presentar una película?

196 〜 *ciento noventa y seis*

CAPÍTULO 7

ANSWERS

Después de conversar

1. **Adela y Víctor están en el avión.**
2. **Ellos van a La Paz.**
3. **El asistente de vuelo dijo que el vuelo sería de tres horas y que llegarían a La Paz a tiempo.**
4. **El vuelo dura tres horas.**
5. **Según Adela la comida es bastante buena.**
6. **Víctor no sabía que les servirían una comida.**

7. **No, no habrá una película.**
8. **Le dijeron a Víctor que no podrían presentar una película porque no habría tiempo.**

Actividades comunicativas

A ¿Te interesaría el trabajo o no? Trabaja con un(a) compañero(a). Describan el trabajo de los asistentes de vuelo. Después de describir el trabajo, den sus opiniones. ¿Les gustaría ser asistentes de vuelo o no? ¿Les interesaría el trabajo o no? ¿Por qué?

B ¡Qué problema! Estás en el aeropuerto de Jorge Chávez en Lima, Perú. Perdiste tu boleto para el vuelo de regreso a los Estados Unidos. Explica tu problema al (a la) agente (tu compañero[a]). Traten de resolver el problema.

Lima, Perú

C ¡Por favor! Trabaja con un(a) compañero(a). Uno(a) de Uds. será pasajero(a) y el/la otro(a) será asistente de vuelo. Preparen una conversación basada en lo que ven en cada dibujo.

CONVERSACIÓN

TECHNOLOGY OPTION

On the CD-ROM (Disc 2, page 196), students can watch a dramatization of the conversation on page 196. They can then play the role of either one of the characters, and record themselves in the conversation.

Did You Know?

La Paz de Ayacucho The full name of **La Paz** is **La Paz de Ayacucho**, so named for a Bolivian victory over the Spaniards at Ayacucho, Peru, in the War for Independence (1809–25).

Actividades comunicativas

¡OJO! Although the communicative activities are based on the chapter vocabulary and structures, encourage students to use any language they have learned up to this point.

Learning From Photos

En el avión (page 196) Have students say as much as they can about the photo. They may describe the two passengers, tell who they might be, and tell where they are seated.

Lima, Perú (page 197) The airport in Lima is named for a famous Peruvian, Jorge Chávez. You may wish to ask students:
¿Qué otros aeropuertos conoces con el nombre de una persona famosa?
¿Dónde está el aeropuerto?
¿Por qué es famosa la persona?

ANSWERS

Actividades comunicativas
A, B, and **C** Answers will vary.

197

Bell Ringer Review

Use BRR Transparency 7-7, or write the following on the board: Make up questions about an airplane flight using the following expressions: **¿cuándo? ¿cuánto tiempo? ¿de dónde? ¿a qué hora?**

National Standards

Cultures

The reading about the El Alto airport on pages 198–199 and the related activities on page 199 familiarize students with Bolivian geography and some interesting aspects of the world's highest airport.

TEACHING THE READING

Pre-reading

Tell students that they are going to read about a very interesting airport. Tell them that as they read they should concentrate on why it is so interesting.

Reading

A. Read the selection to the students. You may have them just listen as you read or have them follow along in their books.

B. Have students open their books. Call on an individual to read a few sentences. Then stop and ask questions about what the student read.

Post-reading

Have students read the **Lectura** at home and prepare the **Después de leer** activities. Go over them the next day in class.

198

Lecturas CULTURALES

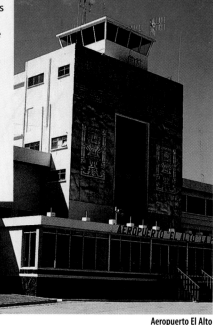

Reading Strategy

Distinguishing between fact and opinion

When writing, an author will sometimes include his or her opinions among facts. It is important to distinguish between facts and the author's opinions. You must watch for expressions that indicate when an author is expressing an opinion rather than a fact. Some of these expressions in Spanish are: **creo que, prefiero, pienso, en mi opinión.**

EL AEROPUERTO QUE SE LLAMA «EL ALTO»

El aeropuerto El Alto en La Paz, Bolivia, está en una llanura del altiplano andino. Es el aeropuerto comercial más alto del mundo. Está a 13.450 pies o 4.100 metros sobre el nivel del mar[1]. A estas alturas del altiplano hay menos oxígeno en el aire que al nivel del mar. Por esta razón cuando un viajero baja del avión en El Alto, puede tener dificultad en respirar[2]. En el aeropuerto hay botellas de oxígeno para los pasajeros que lo necesitan.

¿Te gustaría hacer un viaje a La Paz algún día? Te aseguro[3] que sería una experiencia maravillosa. Al aterrizar tendrías una vista magnífica de la ciudad de La Paz. La Paz, la capital del país, está a una altura 1.000 pies más abajo del aeropuerto. La ciudad parece estar en un cráter. Y encima de la ciudad el cielo es claro, limpio y muy azul—sobre todo en el invierno.

[1] nivel del mar *sea level*
[2] respirar *breathing*
[3] Te aseguro *I assure you*

Aeropuerto El Alto

El altiplano, Bolivia

Critical Thinking Activity

Drawing conclusions Read the following to the class or write it on the board: **¿Por qué es muy apropiado darle el nombre «El Alto» al aeropuerto de La Paz?**

GEOGRAPHY CONNECTION

El altiplano, Bolivia The **altiplano** is the great high plateau of South America. It is 4,000 meters high and covers an area of 100,000 square kilometers. The **altiplano** falls between the two **cordilleras** of the Andes, the Oriental and the Occidental, and is located primarily in Bolivia, with parts extending into Peru, Chile, and Argentina.

Al terminar tu viaje y salir de La Paz, el avión despegará de una de las pistas más largas del mundo. A esta altura el aire tiene muy poca densidad y no puede sostener el peso⁴ del avión. Por consiguiente el avión tiene que alcanzar una gran velocidad antes de poder despegar. Y para poder alcanzar esta velocidad la pista tiene que ser muy larga.

⁴sostener el peso *support the weight*

La Paz, Bolivia

Después de leer

A Un aeropuerto interesante   Contesten.
1. ¿Cómo se llama el aeropuerto que sirve a La Paz, Bolivia?
2. ¿Por qué puede tener un pasajero dificultad en respirar al bajar de un avión en La Paz?
3. ¿Qué tienen en el aeropuerto para su uso?
4. Al aterrizar en El Alto, ¿qué tendrías?
5. ¿Cómo es la pista del aeropuerto El Alto?
6. ¿Por qué es tan larga?

B ¿Sí o no?   Digan que sí o que no.
1. El aeropuerto El Alto está en la Sierra Nevada.
2. El aeropuerto de La Paz es el aeropuerto comercial más alto del mundo.
3. A esta altura el aire contiene más oxígeno que al nivel del mar.
4. La ciudad de La Paz está a una altura aún más alta que el aeropuerto.
5. En el verano el cielo sobre La Paz es claro, limpio y muy azul.
6. A esta altura el aire no puede sostener el peso del avión si no alcanza una gran velocidad antes de despegar.

LECTURAS CULTURALES   *ciento noventa y nueve* ∽ **199**

LECTURA OPCIONAL 1

LECTURA OPCIONAL 1

TEACHING TIPS

¡OJO! This reading is optional. You may skip it completely, have the entire class read it, have only several students read it, or assign it for extra credit.

You may wish to have students who read this selection present some information about the interesting area around Lake Titicaca to the class.

Learning From Photos

India aymará The Aymarás live in the Titicaca basin of Bolivia and Peru. Though subjugated by the Incas in the 15th century after a long struggle, they still dominate the region and continue to speak their own languages. Conquered by Hernando and Gonzalo Pizarro in 1538, their civilization survived. Contemporary Aymara and Quechua cultures are related.

El lago Titicaca High in the Andes, Titicaca is the world's highest large lake, at 3,810 meters (12,500 ft.) above sea level and has been a center of Indian cultures from pre-Incan times. The islands of Titicaca and Coati, the legendary birthplace of the Incas, are in the lake.

Cuzco, Perú Related to the camel, the llama thrives in the cold climate of the Andean foothills. Its wool is highly regarded.

200

LOS ALREDEDORES DE LA PAZ

Antiguamente la ciudad de La Paz estaba situada donde hoy está el aeropuerto. En este lugar siempre había mucho viento. A los conquistadores españoles no les gustaba el viento fuerte y decidieron trasladar la ciudad a un valle más abajo donde haría menos viento. Es por esta razón que el aeropuerto está a una altura más elevada que la ciudad. Para ir del aeropuerto a la ciudad el viajero tiene que bajar unos 1.000 pies.

En la carretera que enlaza la ciudad con el aeropuerto se ven muchos anuncios para aerodeslizadores. Estos aerodeslizadores o hidrofoils cruzan el lago Titicaca. El lago Titicaca está entre Bolivia y el Perú. Igual que el aeropuerto El Alto es el aeropuerto comercial más alto del mundo, el lago Titicaca es el lago navegable más alto del mundo. Cruzar el lago Titicaca es una experiencia extraordinaria. Al cruzar el lago verías los pueblos de los indios aymarás y quechuas. Verías también muchas alpacas, llamas, vicuñas y chinchillas. ¿Te interesan los animales y la naturaleza? ¿Sí? Pues, te encantaría un viaje por esta región interesante de la cordillera andina.

India aymará

Indios quechuas

El lago Titicaca

Después de leer

A **Los alrededores de La Paz** Contesten.

1. ¿Qué se ve en la carretera que enlaza la ciudad de La Paz con el aeropuerto?
2. ¿Por qué hay muchos aerodeslizadores?
3. ¿Dónde está el lago Titicaca?
4. ¿Cuál es una característica interesante del lago Titicaca?
5. ¿Quiénes viven a orillas del lago?
6. ¿Cuáles son algunos animales de esta región andina?

B **Análisis** Expliquen.

Expliquen cómo y por qué el aeropuerto está a una altura más elevada que la ciudad de La Paz.

Cuzco, Perú

200 doscientos

ANSWERS

Después de leer

A 1. **Se ven muchos anuncios para aerodeslizadores.**
2. **Hay muchos aerodeslizadores porque el lago Titicaca está cerca del aeropuerto.**
3. **El lago Titicaca está entre Bolivia y el Perú.**
4. **El lago Titicaca es el lago navegable más alto del mundo.**
5. **Los indios aymarás y quechuas viven a orillas del lago.**

6. **Algunos animales de esta región andina son las alpacas, llamas, vicuñas y chinchillas.**

B Answers will vary but may include:
El aeropuerto está a una altura más alta que la ciudad de La Paz porque a los conquistadores españoles no les gustaba el viento fuerte y decidieron trasladar la ciudad—que estaba situada donde hoy está el aeropuerto—a un valle más abajo donde haría menos viento.

LECTURA OPCIONAL 2

UN HÉROE DE LA AVIACIÓN LATINOAMERICANA

En 1928 Charles Lindbergh, «El Águila[1] Solitaria», voló de Wáshington a México D.F. en el mismo avión con el que cruzó el Atlántico. Los mexicanos querían responder a tan fino gesto. El 11 de junio de 1928 Emilio Carranza, de 22 años de edad, capitán de las Fuerzas Aéreas Mexicanas y sobrino del ex-presidente Venustiano Carranza, salió de México en su avión Excelsior. Llegó a Wáshington como héroe.

El joven piloto pasó un mes en los Estados Unidos. A las 7:05 de la noche del 12 de julio de 1928 despegó del aeropuerto Roosevelt de Nueva York para volver a México. Nunca llegó a México. Cerca de Chatsworth, Nueva Jersey, encontraron los restos del Excelsior y el cuerpo del valiente capitán.

Diez mil soldados y marinos norteamericanos marcharon con el cuerpo del héroe mexicano a la Pennsylvania Station donde un tren lo llevaría a México.

En las escuelas de México hicieron una colecta para levantar un monumento en el lugar de la tragedia. Allí está todavía. Y cada año, en el aniversario de su muerte, militares y representantes de las dos repúblicas dejan flores en honor de Emilio Carranza.

[1]Águila *Eagle*

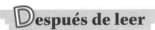
Emilio Carranza enfrente de su avión Excelsior

Venustiano Carranza (a la izquierda)

Después de leer

A **Dos aviadores**   Completen.

1. A Charles Lindbergh se le llamaba _____.
2. En 1928 Lindbergh voló de _____ a la Ciudad de México.
3. Emilio Carranza era _____ en las Fuerzas Aéreas mexicanas.
4. Su tío fue _____.
5. Carranza voló en su avión de _____ a Wáshington.
6. El avión cayó del cielo cerca de _____ en el estado de Nueva Jersey.
7. Los soldados y marinos americanos llevaron su cuerpo a la _____.
8. Los alumnos mexicanos hicieron una colecta para levantar un _____ en Nueva Jersey.
9. Todos los años representantes norteamericanos y mexicanos ponen _____ en el monumento.

National Standards

Cultures
This reading and the related activities on this page familiarize students with an authentic Mexican hero of aviation, Emilio Carranza.

TEACHING TIPS

Ask student if they know anything about Charles Lindbergh. Have them tell in Spanish what they know.

HISTORY CONNECTION

La revolución mexicana   The period from 1911 through the 1920's was one of the most turbulent periods in Mexican history. Francisco I. Madero, Emiliano Zapata, Francisco (Pancho) Villa, and Venustiano Carranza were major players in the Mexican Revolution that began with the overthrow of Porfirio Díaz in 1911.

Cooperative Learning

Venustiano Carranza   The historical figure of Venustiano Carranza is very interesting, especially his relations with the United States during World War I. Have a pair of students prepare a brief biography of Venustiano Carranza and report to the class.

ANSWERS

Después de leer
A 1. «El Águila Solitaria»
2. Wáshington
3. capitán
4. el ex-presidente, Venustiano Carranza
5. la Ciudad de México
6. Chatsworth
7. Pennsylvania Station
8. monumento
9. flores

¡OJO! The readings in the **Conexiones** section are optional. They focus on some of the major disciplines taught in schools and universities. The vocabulary is useful for discussing such topics as history, literature, art, economics, business, science, etc.

You may choose any of the following ways to do this reading on geography with your students.

Independent reading Have students read the selections and do the post-reading activities as homework, which you collect. This option is least intrusive on class time and requires a minimum of teacher involvement.

Homework with in-class follow-up Assign the readings and post-reading activities as homework. Review and discuss the material in class the next day.

Intensive in-class activity This option includes a pre-reading vocabulary presentation, in-class reading and discussion, assignment of the activities for homework, and a discussion of the assignment in class the following day.

Conexiones

LAS CIENCIAS NATURALES

La península ibérica

LA GEOGRAFÍA

Geography, the science, deals with the description, distribution, and interaction of the various physical, biological, and cultural features of the Earth's surface. However, for most people, geography is simply "physical geography" that studies the world's surface, the distribution and description of its land and water areas. The climate and the physical features of a country or region obviously have a great influence on the economy and even on the culture of a people.

The geography of Spain has affected its people enormously. The Pyrenees, separating Spain from the rest of Europe—the French have said that "Africa begins at the Pyrenees"—have often insulated Spain from European influence. Spain was a maritime nation in part because of its unique situation as a peninsula with coasts on the Atlantic and the Mediterranean. As you read, you will find out some things you probably did not know about Spain's geography.

Andalucía, España

La geografía de España

España, con Portugal, forman la península ibérica. La meseta central cubre más de la mitad del país con una altura media de 600 a 800 metros. Una serie de sierras cruza el país de este a oeste. En el extremo norte están los Pirineos, en el centro, no lejos de Madrid, la Sierra de Guadarrama, y continuando hacia el sur, la Sierra Morena y la Sierra Nevada.

De todos los países de Europa, sólo Suiza es más montañosa que España. Aunque mucha gente no lo cree, hay importantes estaciones de esquí en la Sierra Nevada y la Sierra de Guadarrama.

La península ibérica se divide en dos, la Iberia seca[1] y la Iberia húmeda. La Iberia húmeda es la región de los Pirineos, el noroeste de España y casi todo Portugal. La mayor parte de España está en la Iberia seca. Por eso, en el verano, si vuelas sobre España, verás un paisaje mayormente árido y pardo[2]. Los ríos, en el verano, llevan poca agua. Los ríos importantes que desembocan[3] en el Atlántico son el Duero, el Tajo, el Guadiana y el Guadalquivir. El río más importante que desemboca en el Mediterráneo es el Ebro. El agua tiene una importancia enorme. Sin agua, no se podría cultivar nada. Y España, hasta años recientes, era un país agrícola, y la agricultura sigue siendo un importante factor económico.

Sierra Nevada, España

[1]seca *dry*
[2]pardo *brown*
[3]desembocan *empty into*

Toledo, España

➤ Después de leer ➤

A Un poco de geografía

Completen según la lectura.

1. Los países que constituyen la península ibérica son _____ y _____.
2. Las montañas que están entre Francia y España son los _____.
3. Las sierras importantes van de este a _____.
4. La sierra más cerca de Madrid es la _____.
5. Portugal está en la Iberia húmeda, y la mayor parte de España está en la Iberia _____.
6. Muchos ríos en España desembocan en el _____.
7. Pero el Ebro desemboca en el _____.

B ¿Lo saben? Contesten.

1. Nombra tres ríos importantes de España.
2. Nombra dos sierras donde hay estaciones de esquí.
3. Di lo que uno vería desde un avión volando sobre la meseta central en verano.

CONEXIONES

doscientos tres ∽ **203**

LAS CIENCIAS NATURALES

LA GEOGRAFÍA

A. Since this geography selection is very specific to Spain, you may wish to have all students read it, at least quickly, as an additional cultural reading.

B. You may wish to have students locate all the places mentioned in the reading on the map of Spain on page 451 or on the Map Transparency.

HISTORY CONNECTION

Toledo, España Toledo, known in ancient times as **Toletum,** was conquered by the Romans in 193 B.C. Later, it became the capital of Visigothic Spain. During Moorish domination it was part of the Caliphat of Córdoba until reconquered in 1085. Pictured here is the Roman bridge over the Río Tajo. The Cathedral of Toledo and its ancient synagogues are world-famous. Toledo is also closely connected with El Greco and his art.

ANSWERS

Después de leer

A 1. España, Portugal
2. Pirineos
3. oeste
4. Sierra de Guadarrama
5. seca
6. Atlántico
7. Mediterráneo

B 1. el Ebro, el Duero, el Tajo (el Guadiana, el Guadalquivir)
2. La Sierra Nevada y la Sierra de Guadarrama
3. un paisaje mayormente árido y pardo

Culminación

Actividades orales

A **Yo conozco la América Latina.** Tú y tu compañero(a) ya saben mucho sobre varios países hispanos. Cada uno(a) de Uds. va a seleccionar el país que te gustaría visitar. Dile a tu compañero(a) por qué te gustaría viajar a ese país. Dile también todo lo que harías allí. Luego cambien de rol.

B **¡Qué suerte!** Tú y tu compañero(a) acaban de recibir medio millón de dólares. Cada uno(a) de Uds. va a hacer una lista de las cosas que harían con el dinero. Comparen sus listas. Luego decidan quién haría las cosas más interesantes.

C **Algo de geografía** Tu compañero(a) es un(a) alumno(a) de intercambio. Es de la Argentina. Él o ella te va a preguntar sobre la geografía de tu estado; si hay lagos, dónde están, cómo se llaman; los nombres de las montañas y dónde están, etc. Contesta a sus preguntas. Después, cambien de rol.

Patagonia, Argentina

Actividades escritas

A **¿Excelente o terrible?** Tú acabas de volver de un viaje a Costa Rica. Tu vuelo de regreso fue tan excelente (o terrible) que decides escribir una carta a la línea aérea. Describe el vuelo y diles lo que piensas de la tripulación y los servicios que ofrecen. Da ejemplos de lo que pasó (ocurrió) durante el vuelo.

● Visite San José con conexiones a Guatemala.
Salidas los jueves y lunes 8:20 a.m.
Tels. 724-3330/3444. Consulte a su agente de viajes
Desde $289.00 a San José y $299.00 a Panamá*
*ciertas restricciones aplican
Infórmese sobre nuestro exclusivo servicio de carga a través del
Tel. 723-3160

Con el estilo de... **LACSA**
Líneas Aéreas de Costa Rica/The Airline of Costa Rica
¡NOS ENCANTA LA GENTE!

B **¡A planear un viaje!** Quieres información. Prepara un fax o un e-mail a la línea aérea Iberia. Te interesa viajar a España. Pregúntales sobre los destinos a donde vuelan, de qué aeropuertos de EE.UU salen, las tarifas y los servicios que ofrecen durante el vuelo.

IBERIA
LINEAS AEREAS DE ESPAÑA

Writing Strategy

Identifying sources for a research paper

To write a research paper, you must plan, set goals, and gather information. When you find a source, skim it to see whether it has any useful information. If it does, record the publication information on an index card so you can find the source easily when you begin your research. Be sure to use all resources available to you—both print and nonprint. Your school library will be an excellent place to begin looking for sources for your research paper.

La geografía del estado de...

You have been asked to write a brief description of the geography of your state for a Spanish-speaking audience. Your school librarian will help you select the most appropriate print resources—encyclopedias, almanacs, and, of course, geography books. The Internet will be an excellent nonprint resource. Log in and go to your state's web sites. Once you have assembled your resources, scan them for the essential information you will need for your report. Jot down the information you need. Remember to include references at the end of your report. Prepare a draft of your report in Spanish and ask your Spanish teacher to review it for you. After you have seen your teacher's recommendations, prepare the final version of your report.

CULMINACIÓN

doscientos cinco **205**

Actividades escritas

A You may wish to call on a few students to read their letters to the class.

TECHNOLOGY OPTION
Students may use the Portfolio feature on the CD-ROM to write their letters.

Writing Strategy

Identifying sources for a research paper

A. You may wish to have students work in groups to research and write this report, or assign it for extra credit to more able students.

B. When students have prepared their drafts, you may wish to have them review each other's work before handing the reports in to you.

For the Native Speaker

En busca de un puesto Have pairs of students compose a letter to a Latin American airline inquiring about possible positions. The letters should request the following information:
- what positions are available
- the training needed and where it can be obtained
- the salary and benefits
- what positions require knowledge of both English and Spanish

---

Learning From Realia

Con el estilo de... LACSA You may wish to ask questions such as:
¿Qué es LACSA?
¿Qué días tiene vuelos?
¿A qué hora son los vuelos?
¿Cuál de los destinos cuesta más?
¿Quién llamaría al 723-3160?

ANSWERS

Actividades escritas
A and **B** Answers will vary.

Writing Strategy
Answers will vary.

VOCABULARY REVIEW

The words and phrases in the **Vocabulario** have been taught for productive use in this chapter. They are summarized here as a resource for both students and teacher. This list also serves as a convenient resource for the **Culminación** activities on pages 204 and 205. There are approximately ten cognates in this vocabulary list. Have students find them.

Teacher Notes

Vocabulario

DESCRIBING AN AIRPLANE

el avión de reacción, el jet	el asiento
la avioneta	el respaldo del asiento
el helicóptero	el cinturón de seguridad
la cabina de mando, la cabina de vuelo	el chaleco salvavidas
la ventanilla	la máscara de oxígeno
el compartimiento sobre la cabeza, el compartimiento superior	el carrito
	la mesita
	la bandeja
la señal de no fumar	el equipaje de mano
la salida de emergencia	el lavabo, el aseo
el pasillo	

IDENTIFYING SOME CREW MEMBERS

la tripulación	el/la co-piloto
el/la comandante, el/la piloto	el/la asistente de vuelo

DESCRIBING A FLIGHT AND ON-BOARD SERVICES

el vuelo	aterrizar
el anuncio	anunciar
el/la pasajero(a)	pasar por la cabina
el aterrizaje	distribuir audífonos (auriculares)
el despegue	servir bebidas
la escala	servir una comida
la altura	abrochar
la turbulencia	caber
volar	a tiempo
sobrevolar	con una demora
despegar	

DESCRIBING SOME THINGS AT AN AIRPORT

la pista	la torre de control
la terminal de pasajeros	

TALKING ABOUT GEOGRAPHY

la geografía	la meseta
la altura, la altitud	la llanura
el pico	el valle
la montaña	el río
la cordillera	el lago
el altiplano	

Independent Practice

Assign any of the following:
1. Activities, pages 204–205
2. Workbook, **Mi autobiografía,** page 81
3. Situation Cards
4. CD-ROM, Disc 2, Chapter 7, **Juego de repaso**

TECNOTUR

VIDEO

¡Buen viaje!

EPISODIO 7 ▶ El vuelo

Los amigos vuelven a la Ciudad de México.

La asistente de vuelo le habla a Luis de su equipaje.

CD-ROM

Expansión cultural

En las sierras de México hay volcanes y picos altos.

interNET
CONNECTION

In this video episode Cristina, Isabel, and Luis are at the Puerto Vallarta airport waiting to board their flight to Mexico City. To take a virtual flight on a Latin American or Iberian airline, go to the **Capítulo 7** Internet activity at the Glencoe Foreign Language Web site:

http://www.glencoe.com/sec/fl

TECNOTUR

doscientos siete ◈ **207**

OVERVIEW

This page previews three key multimedia components of the **Glencoe Spanish** series. Each reinforces the material taught in Chapter 7 in a unique manner.

VIDEO

The Video Program allows students to see how the chapter vocabulary and structures are used by native speakers in an engaging story. Show the video episode as a final activity for Chapter 7.

A. Before watching the episode, you may want to ask these questions about the photos: **¿Qué hicieron los tres amigos durante sus vacaciones en Puerto Vallarta? En la segunda foto, ¿crees que ya despegó el avión? ¿Por qué? ¿Dónde tiene que guardar su equipaje Luis?**

B. See the Video Activities Booklet for detailed suggestions for using this resource.

CD-ROM

A. The **Expansión cultural** photo shows an example of the mountainous terrain Cristina, Isabel, and Luis will fly over en route to Mexico City. Have students read the **Expansión cultural** photo caption on page 207.

B. In the CD-ROM version of **Expansión cultural** (Disc 2, page 207), students can listen to additional recorded information about the geography of Mexico.

INTERNET

Teacher Information and Student Worksheets for this activity can be accessed at the Web site.

Video Synopsis

Cristina, Isabel, and Luis are at the airport, waiting to leave Puerto Vallarta to return to Mexico City. They chat about their childhood aspirations—Luis thought of becoming a pilot, and Cristina, a flight attendant. Aboard the plane, Isabel gives her brother a hard time about his over-sized, carry-on bag. He retaliates by teasing Isabel about her need to check her appearance frequently in the plane's lavatory. The flight attendant announces the plane's departure. En route to Mexico City, the trio discuss the sights they will be able to see from the plane.

CAPÍTULOS 5-7
Repaso

OVERVIEW

This section reviews the salient points from Chapters 5–7. In the **Conversación** students will review forms of the future tense and direct and indirect object pronouns. In the **Estructura** section, they will review the regular and irregular forms of the future and the conditional. They will also review direct and indirect object pronouns used in the same sentence. They will practice these structures as they talk about air travel and hotel situations.

TEACHING THE CONVERSATION

A. Have students open their books to page 208. Ask two students to read the conversation aloud using as much expression as possible.

B. Go over the questions in the **Después de conversar** section.

Learning From Photos

En el aeropuerto You may wish to ask these questions about the top photo:

¿Dónde está la gente?
¿Por qué están en fila?
¿Qué harán ellos?
¿Quiénes están detrás de los mostradores?

Caracas, Venezuela Caracas is Venezuela's capital and major city. At 950 meters (3,100 feet) above sea level, the climate is spring-like. Caracas is the economic and cultural hub of the nation. Caracas was founded in 1567 by Diego de Losada and called Santiago de Léon de Caracas.

208

Conversación

En el aeropuerto

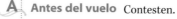

DIEGO:	¿De cuántas horas será el vuelo?
SUSANA:	Llegaremos a Caracas a las diez. Es un vuelo de cuatro horas.
DIEGO:	No sé lo que está pasando. Me parece que no saldremos a tiempo.
SUSANA:	Entonces podré hacer un crucigrama más.
DIEGO:	A ti te gusta mucho pasar el tiempo llenando tus crucigramas.
SUSANA:	¿Me darías mi maletín?
DIEGO:	Te lo doy con mucho placer. ¿Qué quieres? ¿Tus crucigramas?
SUSANA:	No. Quiero ver si la confirmación para el hotel está en el maletín.
DIEGO:	Yo la tenía pero te la di en el taxi.
SUSANA:	Sí, sí. La tengo. Aquí está.
DIEGO:	A propósito, ¿cuántas noches vamos a estar en el Hotel Tamanaco?
SUSANA:	Cuatro. Es bastante caro el cuarto, ¿sabes?

Después de conversar

A **Antes del vuelo** Contesten.

1. ¿Dónde están Diego y Susana?
2. ¿A qué hora llegarán a Caracas?
3. ¿De cuántas horas será el vuelo?
4. ¿Parece que saldrá a tiempo?
5. Si tiene más tiempo, ¿qué podrá hacer Susana?
6. ¿Por qué quería Susana su maletín?
7. ¿Dónde le dio la confirmación Diego?
8. ¿Cuántas noches estarán en el Hotel Tamanaco?

Caracas, Venezuela

ANSWERS

Después de conversar

A 1. Diego y Susana están en el aeropuerto.
2. Llegarán a Caracas a las diez.
3. El vuelo será de cuatro horas.
4. Parece que no saldrá a tiempo.
5. Si tiene más tiempo Susana podrá hacer un crucigrama más.
6. Susana quería su maletín para buscar la confirmación para el hotel.
7. Diego le dio la confirmación en el taxi.
8. Estarán cuatro noches en el Hotel Tamanaco.

Estructura

El futuro y el condicional

1. Review the following forms of the future and conditional of regular verbs.

FUTURE						
MIRAR	miraré	mirarás	mirará	miraremos	*miraréis*	mirarán
COMER	comeré	comerás	comerá	comeremos	*comeréis*	comerán
VIVIR	viviré	vivirás	vivirá	viviremos	*viviréis*	vivirán

CONDITIONAL						
MIRAR	miraría	mirarías	miraría	miraríamos	*miraríais*	mirarían
COMER	comería	comerías	comería	comeríamos	*comeríais*	comerían
VIVIR	viviría	vivirías	viviría	viviríamos	*viviríais*	vivirían

2. Review the stems for irregular verbs in the future and conditional. The endings for irregular verbs are the same as those for the regular verbs.

INFINITIVE	STEM	FUTURE	CONDITIONAL
TENER	tendr-	tendré	tendría
SALIR	saldr-	saldré	saldría
VENIR	vendr-	vendré	vendría
PONER	pondr-	pondré	pondría
SABER	sabr-	sabré	sabría
PODER	podr-	podré	podría
DECIR	dir-	diré	diría
HACER	har-	haré	haría
QUERER	querr-	querré	querría

Ciudad de México

❖Práctica❖

A **HISTORIETA** A México

Contesten.
1. ¿Irá Catalina a México?
2. ¿La acompañarás?
3. ¿Tomarán Uds. el avión?
4. ¿Leerás durante el vuelo o llenarás un crucigrama?
5. ¿Buscarán Uds. un taxi para ir al hotel?

El futuro y el condicional

A. Quickly review the verb paradigms on page 209. You may want to have students repeat the forms after you.

B. Write the regular future and conditional verb forms on the board. Underline the endings.

C. Remind students that all of the irregular verbs in Step 2 are verbs that are used frequently.

❖Práctica❖

A This activity gives students practice with regular verbs in the future. Ask for volunteers to continue the **Historieta.**

Note: You may wish to do the second literary selection (pages 434–437) with students at this time.

Did You Know?

Un escarabajo The Volkswagen "Beetle" is known as **un escarabajo.** It is the most popular taxi in Mexico City. The front passenger seat is removed to allow easier access for the customers. All the Volkswagen taxis are painted green and white. In some Latin American countries the "Beetle" is called **un volky.**

ANSWERS

Práctica

A 1. Sí (No), Catalina (no) irá a México.
2. Sí (No, no) la acompañaré.
3. Sí (No), nosotros (no) tomaremos el avión.
4. Leeré (Llenaré un crucigrama) durante el vuelo.
5. Sí, (No, no) buscaremos un taxi para ir al hotel.

209

◆Práctica◆

B **Práctica B** reviews regular forms of the conditional.

C **Práctica C** reviews irregular forms of the future.

D **Práctica D** reviews irregular forms of the conditional.

TEACHING STRUCTURE

Los complementos

A. Lead students through Steps 1 and 2 on page 210.

B. When reviewing Step 2, write the example on the board. Ask a volunteer to come to the board and explain to the class how **Se** and **las** take the place of the direct and indirect objects.

Learning From Photos

Miraflores, Perú Miraflores is one of Lima's more elegant neighborhoods and the site of many international hotels. There are also numerous art galleries as well as sidewalk art exhibits in Miraflores.

Learning From Realia

Una toalla refrescante You may wish to ask students questions about the moist towelette:
¿Qué es LanChile?
¿Qué será una toalla refrescante?
You may wish to tell the students that the **LAN** in **LanChile** means **Línea Aérea Nacional.**

210

B **Pasatiempos**   Sigan el modelo.

> **leer una novela o una revista**
> **Nosotros leeríamos una novela pero él leería una revista.**

1. jugar ajedrez o dominó
2. ir al zoológico o al parque de atracciones
3. comer en casa o en un restaurante
4. coleccionar sellos o monedas antiguas
5. mirar al mimo o al payaso

Miraflores, Perú

C **Unas vacaciones**   Completen con el futuro.

PEPE: Sandra, ¿por qué no me dices tú lo que

  ___ (hacer) durante tus vacaciones?
       1

SANDRA: No te ___ (poder) decir nada hasta la semana que viene.
               2

PEPE: ¿No ___ (saber) hasta entonces?
            3

SANDRA: No, porque yo ___ (tener) que hablar con Maripaz. Yo sé que
                          4

  ella ___ (querer) hacer algo y yo lo ___ (hacer) con ella.
       5   6

PEPE: ¿___ (Hacer) Uds. un viaje?
        7

D **Uno sí y el otro no**   Completen con el condicional.

1. Él sabría el número del vuelo pero su hermano no lo ____.
2. Yo te lo diría pero ellos nunca te lo ____.
3. Nosotros lo haríamos pero ellos no lo ____.
4. Yo podría ir pero tú no ____.
5. Uds. lo pondrían en orden pero él no lo ____.
6. Yo tendría que volver pero tú no ____.

Los complementos

1. When both a direct and an indirect object pronoun are used in the same sentence, the indirect object pronoun always precedes the direct object pronoun.

> **El agente me devolvió el billete .**
> **El agente me lo devolvió.**

2. The indirect object pronouns **le** and **les** change to **se** when used with the direct object pronouns **lo, la, los,** or **las.** Because **se** can mean **a él, a ella, a Ud., a ellos, a ellas,** or **a Uds.,** the prepositional phrase is often added for clarity.

> **¿A quién le diste las llaves del cuarto?**
> **Se las di a Teresa.**

ANSWERS

Práctica

B 1. **Nosotros jugaríamos al ajedrez pero él jugaría al dominó.**
2. **Nosotros iríamos al zoológico pero él iría al parque de atracciones.**
3. **Nosotros comeríamos en casa pero él comería en un restaurante.**
4. **Nosotros coleccionaríamos sellos pero él coleccionaría monedas antiguas.**
5. **Nosotros miraríamos al mimo pero él miraría al payaso.**

C 1. **harás**
2. **podré**
3. **sabrás**
4. **tendré**

D 1. **sabría**
2. **dirían**
3. **harían**
4. **podrías**
5. **pondría**
6. **tendrías**

5. **querrá**
6. **haré**
7. **Harán**

❖Práctica❖

E | A bordo del avión Contesten según el modelo.

¿Quién te sirvió la comida?
El asistente de vuelo me la sirvió.

1. ¿Quién te sirvió los refrescos?
2. ¿Quién te dio los audífonos?
3. ¿Quién te buscó la manta?
4. ¿Quién te explicó las reglas de seguridad?
5. ¿Quién te mostró el chaleco salvavidas?

F | En el hotel Contesten según el modelo.

¿Quién le dio la tarjeta al cliente? (la recepcionista)
La recepcionista se la dio.

1. ¿Quién le dio la llave al cliente? (el recepcionista)
2. ¿Quién le abrió la puerta? (el mozo)
3. ¿Quién le subió las maletas? (el mozo)
4. ¿Quién le limpió el cuarto? (la camarera)
5. ¿Quién le cambió las toallas? (la camarera)

Hotel Monasterio,
Cuzco, Perú

❖Actividades comunicativas❖

A | En el hotel Trabaja con un(a) compañero(a). Están en la recepción de un hotel. Uno de Uds. será el recepcionista y el otro será el cliente. Discutan el precio, el número de noches, el cuarto, etc.

B | Un vuelo Trabaja con un(a) compañero(a) de clase. Dentro de poco Uds. van a hacer un viaje juntos. Van a ir en avión. Discutan todo lo que tienen que hacer y todo lo que pasará o sucederá en el aeropuerto y durante el vuelo.

E **Práctica E** practices using two object pronouns together.

EXPANSION After dong this activity, ask students to imagine they were in a restaurant last week with a group of friends. Now ask them: **¿Quién les trajo el menú? ¿Quién les sirvió los refrescos? ¿Quién les sirvió la comida? ¿Quién les trajo la cuenta?**

F **Práctica F** uses the **se la, se los,** etc. combination.

Actividades comunicativas

A This activity reviews the vocabulary presented in Chapter 6.

B This activity reviews the vocabulary presented in Chapter 7.

ABOUT THE SPANISH LANGUAGE

¿Cuzco o Cusco? Although the traditional spelling of the city has been Cuzco, it is more often spelled Cusco in Peru.

Learning From Photos

Hotel Monasterio, Cuzco, Perú The Hotel Monasterio was once the Seminario de San Antonio Abad, founded over 300 years ago. The hotel has maintained the Capilla de San Antonio Abad with its gold leaf and colonial paintings.

Independent Practice

Assign any of the following:
1. Activities, pages 208–211
2. Workbook, pages 82–86
3. CD-ROM, Disc 2, pages 208–211
4. CD-ROM, Disc 2, Chapters 5-7, **Juegos de repaso**

ANSWERS

Práctica

E 1. El asistente de vuelo me los sirvió.
2. El asistente de vuelo me los dio.
3. El asistente de vuelo me la buscó.
4. El asistente de vuelo me las explicó.
5. El asistente de vuelo me lo mostró.

F 1. El recepcionista se la dio.
2. El mozo se la abrió.
3. El mozo se las subió.
4. La camarera se lo limpió.
5. La camarera se las cambió.

Actividades comunicativas
A and **B** Answers will vary.

OVERVIEW

The **Vistas de Costa Rica** were prepared by National Geographic Society. Their purpose is to give students greater insight, through these visual images, into the culture and people of Costa Rica. Have students look at the photographs on pages 212–215 for enjoyment. If they would like to talk about them, let them say anything they can, using the vocabulary they have learned to this point.

National Standards

Cultures
The **Vistas de Costa Rica** photos, and the accompanying captions, allow students to gain insights into the people and culture of Costa Rica.

Learning From Photos

1. Tucán The National Park System of Costa Rica embraces most of the country's ecosystems. Every imaginable climate, environmental region, and type of natural treasure lies within these protected areas, from desolate moon-like Irazú to evergreen Poás, and the rumbling and fiery Arenal (one of nine active volcanoes in Costa Rica).

2. Niñas indias Bri Bri, Reservación Amistad The Bri Bri from the Talamanca area are one of three major tribes in Costa Rica that have survived as distinct communities. Many Bri Bri live on the 22 reservations designed to protect their land and culture. The large extension of protected land in the giant Reservación Amistad covers 193,929 hectares. *(continued)*

1. Tucán
2. Niñas indias Bri Bri, Reservación Amistad
3. Parque Nacional Tortuguero
4. Baile folklórico, San José
5. Estatua de Coronado, San José
6. Iglesia de Zararo, cerca de San José
7. Parque Nacional Volcán Arenal

Learning From Photos

3. Parque Nacional Tortuguero This popular park on the northern Caribbean coast was created to protect an important nesting area for the green turtle, hence its name. The park also encompasses a stretch of the canals which are called Costa Rica's Amazon, as well as surrounding rain forest. Wildlife abounds within the park: birds, crocodiles, sloths, river otters and, the occasional manatee. Tortuguero has beautiful palm-lined beaches as well.

4. Baile folklórico, San José These dancers in their colorful costumes perform traditional folk dances. Art, music, and dance are encouraged and supported by the Ministry of Culture, Youth and Sports. A National *(continued)*

NATIONAL GEOGRAPHIC

VISTAS
DE COSTA RICA

Learning From Photos

especially during religious holidays, such as August 2nd, when thousands of Costa Ricans pay homage to **la Virgen de los Ángeles.**

7. Parque Nacional Volcán Arenal The national park surrounds the Arenal Volcano and includes beautiful Lake Arenal. The volcano erupted in 1998, spewing huge ash columns and hot rocks into the air. This massive explosion caused the crater to crack, and red-hot lava flows emerged from underground. Lake Arenal, very popular with windsurfers, is one of the world's premier windsurfing locations. Hiking, mountain biking, rafting, horseback riding, water skiing, and kayaking are all sports practiced in the national park.

Learning From Photos

(continued from page 212)
Theater Company and a National Dance Company are state-funded.

5. Estatua de Coronado, San José Juan Vázquez de Coronado (1523–1565) distinguished himself in the conquest of Costa Rica. He founded Cartago, which was the capital until Costa Rica won its independence from Spain.

6. Iglesia de Zarcero This lovely colonial church in the little town of Zarcero is the center of village life. Costa Ricans are predominantly Catholic, but freedom of religion is protected by the constitution, and the Protestant community is quite large. There is a Catholic church in every village and town. Fiestas, dances, and other cultural events take place around the church,

(continued)

VISTAS DE COSTA RICA

Learning From Photos

1. Cabalgata por la playa, Tamarindo The beaches of Tamarindo, on the Pacific Coast of Costa Rica, are among the most beautiful in the world. The Tamarindo estuary, more than 1,200 acres of saltwater jungle, is home to a great variety of plants and wildlife, including caimans, iguanas, and the American crocodile.

2. Vista panorámica, San José San José, the capital, has a population of about half a million, and is the economic, political, and social center of Costa Rican life. Founded in 1738, it became the capital in 1823, after independence was won from Spain. It is a modern city, with parks and fine public buildings, including the elaborate National Theater.

3. Rana con ojos en forma de rubi sobre planta haleconia, Parque Nacional Cahuita This tiny ruby-eyed frog is one of the many species found in the tropical forest of Cahuita National Park located on the Caribbean Sea south of Puerto Limón. Other animals found there include howler and white face monkeys, coatis, snakes, and butterflies.

4. Puesto de frutas, San José The street vendor in San José sells a wide variety of tropical fruit, including pineapples, papayas, guavas, and tamarinds from his colorfully decorated stand. Costa Rica has a long tradition of folk decoration of stands and, most famously, carts. The hand-decorated wooden oxcarts are a long-standing tradition and miniatures of these carts are a tourist shop staple.

(continued)

1. Cabalgata por la playa, Tamarindo
2. Vista panorámica, San José
3. Rana con ojos en forma de rubi sobre planta haleconia, Parque Nacional Cahuita
4. Puesto de frutas, San José
5. Estudiantes en descanso, San José
6. Balneario, San José
7. Niñas compartiendo una bicicleta, Tamarindo

214

NATIONAL GEOGRAPHIC SOCIETY — TEACHER'S CORNER

Index to NATIONAL GEOGRAPHIC MAGAZINE

The following articles may be used for research relating to this chapter:

- "Rain Forest Canopy: The High Frontier," by Edward O. Wilson, December 1991.
- "Teeming Life of a Rain Forest," by Carol Hughes, January 1983.
- "Costa Rica Steers the Middle Course," by Kent Britt, July 1981.
- "Nature's Living, Jumping Jewels," by Paul A. Zahl, July 1973.

Learning From Photos

(continued from page 214)

5. Estudiantes en descanso, San José These uniformed students are in a **colegio** in San José. Costa Rica boasts one of the highest literacy rates in the Americas, over 94%. The University of Costa Rica enjoys a reputation as an outstanding educational center. Costa Rica is one of the few countries in the world whose education budget far exceeds its defense budget.

6. Balneario, San José Resorts of all kinds abound in Costa Rica. The weather in the San José area is always pleasant and spring-like. Coastal areas are much hotter. Costa Rica, like many tropical countries, has only two seasons, a wet season and a dry season. The dry season is from late December to April—**verano** for Costa Ricans; the wet season—**invierno**—is from May to December.

7. Niñas compartiendo una bicicleta, Tamarindo The cyclists are enjoying a ride through one of the varied areas of Tamarindo, located 200 miles from San José.

Products available from
GLENCOE/MCGRAW-HILL

To order the following products, call Glencoe/McGraw-Hill at 1-800-334-7344.

CD-ROMs
· Picture Atlas of the World
· The Complete National Geographic: 109 Years of National Geographic Magazine

Poster
· Rain Forests

Software
· ZingoLingo: Spanish Diskettes

Transparency Set
· NGS PicturePack: Geography of North America

Videodisc
· STV: Rain Forest

Products available from
NATIONAL GEOGRAPHIC SOCIETY

NATIONAL GEOGRAPHIC SOCIETY

To order the following products, call National Geographic Society at 1-800-368-2728.

Books
· Destination: Rain Forest
· Exploring Your World: The Adventure of Geography
· National Geographic Satellite Atlas of the World

TOPICS	FUNCTIONS	STRUCTURE	CULTURE
◆ Minor accidents ◆ Parts of the body ◆ Emergency hospital care	◆ How to talk about minor accidents and medical procedures ◆ How to refer to parts of the body ◆ How to talk about emergency medical care ◆ How to talk about recent events ◆ How to compare people and things	◆ The present perfect ◆ Irregular participles ◆ Making comparisons of equal value	◆ Medical practitioners in remote areas of the Spanish-speaking world ◆ Buena Vista Hospital ◆ Contemporary medical problems ◆ Medical terms in Spanish

CHAPTER 8 RESOURCES

PRINT	MULTIMEDIA

Planning Resources

Lesson Plans Block Scheduling Lesson Plans	Interactive Lesson Planner

Reinforcement Resources

Writing Activities Workbook Student Tape Manual Video Activities Booklet Web Site User's Guide	Transparencies Binder Audiocassette/Compact Disc Program Videocassette/Videodisc Program Online Internet Activities Electronic Teacher's Classroom Resources

Assessment Resources

Situation Cards Chapter Quizzes Testing Program Performance Assessment	**Maratón mental** Mindjogger Videoquiz Testmaker Computer Software (Macintosh/Windows) Listening Comprehension Audiocassette/Compact Disc Communication Transparency: C-8

Motivational Resources

Expansion Activities	Café Glencoe: www.cafe.glencoe.com Keypal Internet Activities

Enrichment

Spanish for Spanish Speakers	

SECTION	PAGES	SECTION RESOURCES

Vocabulario Palabras 1
  Un accidente
  Más partes del cuerpo
  Una picadura
  La cara
  ¡A la sala de emergencia!
	218–221	Vocabulary Transparencies 8.1
		Audiocassette 5B/Compact Disc 5
		Student Tape Manual, TE, pages 82–84
		Workbook, pages 87–88
		Chapter Quizzes, page 35
		CD-ROM, Disc 3, pages 218–221

Vocabulario Palabras 2 **En el hospital**	222–225	Vocabulary Transparencies 8.2 Audiocassette 5B/Compact Disc 5 Student Tape Manual, TE, pages 85–86 Workbook, pages 88–89 Chapter Quizzes, page 36 CD-ROM, Disc 3, pages 222–225

Estructura
  El presente perfecto
  Los participios irregulares
  Comparación de igualdad
	226–231	Workbook, pages 89–91
		Audiocassette 5B/Compact Disc 5
		Student Tape Manual, TE, pages 87–89
		Chapter Quizzes, pages 37–39
		Computer Testmaker
		CD-ROM, Disc 3, pages 226–231

Conversación **Una fractura**	232–233	Audiocassette 5B/Compact Disc 5 Student Tape Manual, TE, pages 89–90 CD-ROM, Disc 3, pages 232–233

Lecturas culturales
  Practicantes
  El hospital Buena Vista
  (opcional)
  Problemas médicos de hoy
  (opcional)
	234–237	Testing Program, pages 60–61
		CD-ROM, Disc 3, pages 234–237

Conexiones **La medicina** *(opcional)*	238–239	Testing Program, pages 61–62 CD-ROM, Disc 1, pages 238–239

Culminación
  Actividades orales
  Actividades escritas
  Vocabulario
  Tecnotur
	240–243	**¡Buen viaje!** Video, Episode 8
		Video Activities, pages 92–96
		Internet Activities
		www.glencoe.com/sec/fl
		Testing Program, pages 57–60; 133; 177; 197
		CD-ROM, Disc 3, pages 240–243

CAPÍTULO 8

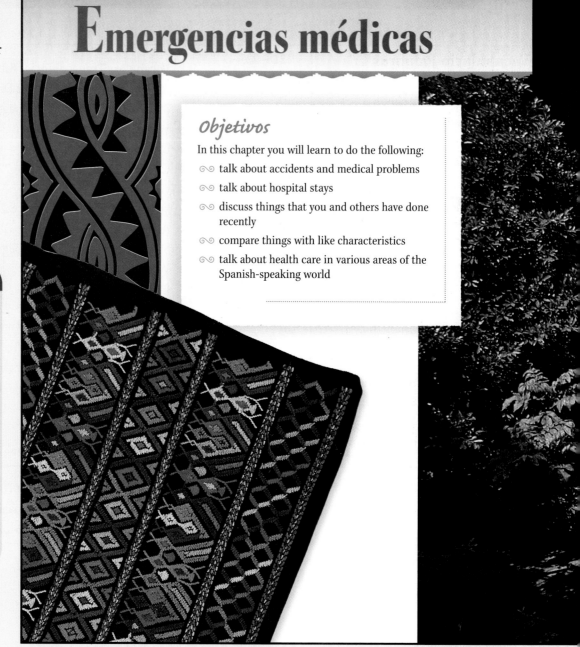

Emergencias médicas

OVERVIEW

In this chapter students will learn to describe certain accidents and minor injuries and to talk about emergency hospital treatment.

Students will learn how to speak about recent events in the past using the present perfect tense. They will also learn how to make comparisons of equality between people and things.

The cultural focus of the chapter is on health practitioners and services in the Spanish-speaking world.

National Standards

In Chapter 8 students will learn to communicate in spoken and written Spanish on the following topics:
- accidents and injuries
- emergency room treatment
- health issues in Spanish-speaking countries

Students will obtain and provide information about these topics and engage in conversations that would typically take place at the scene of an accident or in a hospital emergency room as they fulfill the chapter objectives listed on this page.

Objetivos

In this chapter you will learn to do the following:

- talk about accidents and medical problems
- talk about hospital stays
- discuss things that you and others have done recently
- compare things with like characteristics
- talk about health care in various areas of the Spanish-speaking world

interNET CONNECTION

The **Glencoe Foreign Language Web site** (http://www.glencoe.com/sec/fl) offers three options that enable you and your students to experience the Spanish-speaking world via the Internet:

- The online **Actividades** are correlated to the chapters and utilize Hispanic Web sites around the world. For the Chapter 8 activity, see student page 243.

- The **Correspondencia electrónica** section provides information on how to set up a keypal (pen pal) exchange between your class and a class in the Spanish-speaking world.

- At **Café Glencoe,** the interactive "after-school" section of the site, you and your students can access a variety of additional online resources, including interactive games.

Spotlight On Culture

Fotografía This is the famous **Hospital de Jesús** in Mexico City. It is one of the oldest hospitals in Mexico. The hospital is built in traditional Spanish style surrounding a central patio.

Pacing

Chapter 8 will require approximately eight to ten days. Pacing will vary according to the length of the class, the age of your students, and student aptitude.

Block Scheduling

The extended time frame provided by block scheduling affords you the opportunity to implement a greater number of activities and projects to motivate and involve your students. See the Block Scheduling Lesson Plans Booklet for suggestions on how to present the chapter material within a block scheduling framework.

doscientos diecisiete 〜 **217**

Chapter Projects

Un accidente Have students select one of the accidents or injuries that they will learn about in this chapter and have them write a paragraph about it.

La ciencia y la medicina In **¡Buen viaje! Level 1,** students read about the contributions of Hispanics to the world of medicine. Have those students interested in science and medicine do a report on one of the following: Miguel Servet, Carlos Juan Finlay y Barres, or Santiago Ramón y Cajal.

Vocabulario

RESOURCES

- Vocabulary Transparencies 8.1 (A & B)
- Student Tape Manual, TE, pages 82–84
- Audiocassette 5B/CD5
- Workbook, pages 87–88
- Quiz 1, page 35
- CD-ROM, Disc 3, pages 218–221

Bell Ringer Review

Use BRR Transparency 8-1, or write the following on the board: Write as many words and expressions as you remember related to health or health care.

TEACHING VOCABULARY

A. In addition to using Vocabulary Transparencies 8.1 (A & B) in your presentation, you may use gestures or dramatization to introduce many of these terms. Those which lend themselves to easy dramatizations are: **caerse, hacerse daño (lastimarse), torcerse el tobillo**, and **cortarse el dedo.**

B. Refer to yourself or a student model to demonstrate the parts of the body.

C. Have students repeat the vocabulary after you or the recording on Cassette 5B/Compact Disc 5.

D. Call on volunteers to read the sentences from **Palabras 1** with as much expression as possible.

(continued on page 219)

Un accidente

Más partes del cuerpo

hacerse daño, lastimarse

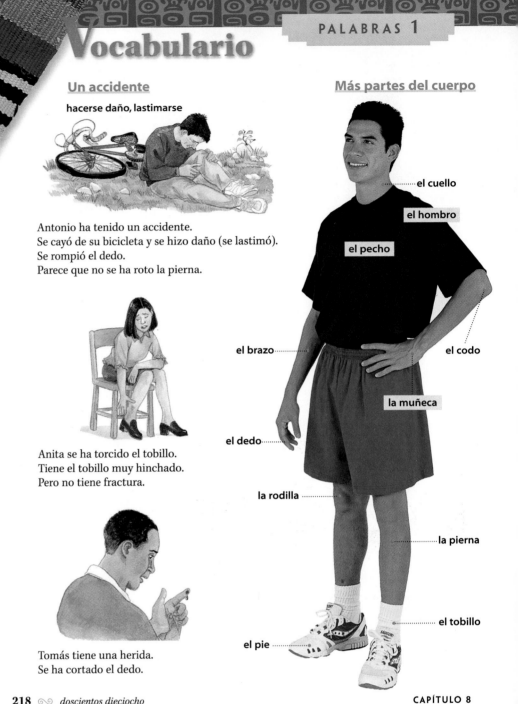

Antonio ha tenido un accidente.
Se cayó de su bicicleta y se hizo daño (se lastimó).
Se rompió el dedo.
Parece que no se ha roto la pierna.

Anita se ha torcido el tobillo.
Tiene el tobillo muy hinchado.
Pero no tiene fractura.

Tomás tiene una herida.
Se ha cortado el dedo.

el cuello
el hombro
el pecho
el brazo
el codo
la muñeca
el dedo
la rodilla
la pierna
el pie
el tobillo

Pantomime

Pantomime 1
Begin
___, levántate.
Ven acá, por favor.
Muéstrame el brazo.
Muéstrame el dedo.
Muéstrame el hombro.
Muéstrame el tobillo.
Muéstrame la rodilla.
Muéstrame la muñeca.
Gracias, ___. Siéntate.

Pantomime 2
___, levántate.
Ven acá, por favor.
Ve al teléfono.
Descuelga.
Marca el número.
Habla. Di lo que pasó.
Gracias, ___. Siéntate.

Una picadura

Una abeja le ha picado a Tere.
Le ha picado en el hombro.
Ella no se siente bien. Le duele mucho.

La cara

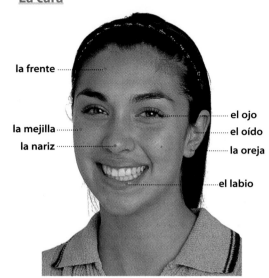

la frente

la mejilla
la nariz

el ojo
el oído
la oreja

el labio

¡A la sala de emergencia!

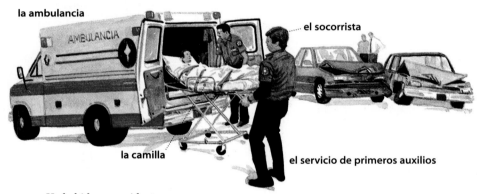

la ambulancia

el socorrista

la camilla

el servicio de primeros auxilios

Ha habido un accidente.
El accidente acaba de tener lugar.
Ha llegado el servicio de primeros auxilios.
Los socorristas han ayudado a la víctima.
La van a llevar al hospital en una ambulancia.

E. Have students look at the Vocabulary Transparencies again and ask them questions to elicit the new vocabulary. For example:
¿Es la pierna o el brazo?
¿Qué ha tenido Antonio?
¿Se cayó él?
¿De qué se cayó?
¿Se hizo daño o no?
¿Se ha roto la pierna?
¿Qué se rompió?

TEACHER TIP

When introducing **El accidente acaba de tener lugar,** repeat **acaba de tener lugar—acaba de—no en el pasado—sólo hace dos minutos.**

INFORMAL ASSESSMENT

Call on volunteers to draw human figures on the board. Ask other students to supply labels of as many parts of the body as they can.

ABOUT THE SPANISH LANGUAGE

◆ You may wish to remind students of the difference between **oreja** and **oído.** **La oreja** refers to the external ear only, and **el oído** refers to the inner ear and also means *hearing* in general. An earache is **un dolor de oídos.**

◆ The **camilla** *(gurney)* shown in the illustration is **una camilla de ruedas.** A **camilla** is a stretcher.

219

Práctica

¡OJO! **Práctica** When students are doing the **Práctica** activities, accept any answer that makes sense. The purpose of these activities is to have students use the new vocabulary. They are not factual recall activities. Thus, do not expect students to remember specific information from the vocabulary presentation when answering. If you wish, have students use the photos as a stimulus, when possible. **Historieta** Each time **Historieta** appears, it means that the answers to the activity form a short story. Encourage students to look at the title of the **Historieta** since it can sometimes help them do the activity.

It is recommended that you go over the Práctica before assigning them for homework.

B **Práctica B** can be done orally with books open.

EXPANSION Have a student retell the story from **Práctica B** in his or her own words.

Writing Development
Have students write the information in **Práctica B** as if it were a newspaper article.

220

Práctica

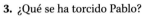

A **Unas heridas** Contesten según los dibujos.

1. ¿Qué se ha roto Carlos?   3. ¿Qué se ha torcido Pablo?

2. ¿Qué se ha cortado Elena?   4. ¿Qué se ha cortado Diana?

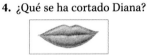

B **HISTORIETA** Un accidente

Contesten con **sí**.

1. ¿Ha habido un accidente?
2. ¿Acaba de tener lugar el accidente?
3. ¿Se ha caído de su bicicleta un niño?
4. ¿Se ha lastimado?
5. ¿Parece que se ha roto la pierna?
6. ¿Ha llegado el servicio de primeros auxilios?
7. ¿Han ayudado los socorristas al niño?
8. ¿Lo van a llevar al hospital en la ambulancia?
9. ¿Lo ponen en una camilla?

Cali, Colombia

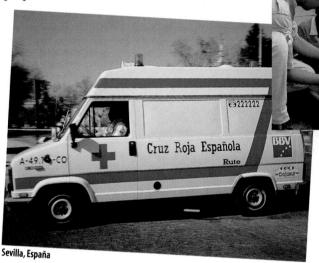

Sevilla, España

ANSWERS

Práctica

A 1. Carlos se ha roto la pierna.
2. Elena se ha cortado el dedo.
3. Pablo se ha torcido el tobillo.
4. Diana se ha cortado el labio.

B 1. Sí, ha habido un accidente.
2. Sí, el accidente acaba de tener lugar.
3. Sí, un niño se ha caído de su bicicleta.
4. Sí, se ha lastimado.
5. Sí, parece que se ha roto la pierna.

6. Sí, el servicio de primeros auxilios ha llegado.
7. Sí, los socorristas han ayudado al niño.
8. Sí, lo van a llevar al hospital en la ambulancia.
9. Sí, lo ponen en una camilla.

C HISTORIETA Una picadura

Contesten.

1. ¿Tiene Anita una picadura?
2. ¿Qué le ha picado?
3. ¿Dónde le ha picado?
4. ¿Le duele mucho la picadura?
5. ¿Tiene Anita alergia a las picaduras?

D Partes del cuerpo Completen.

1. La niña se ha torcido el ____; así no puede andar bien.
2. ____, ____ y ____ son partes del brazo.
3. ____, ____ y ____ son partes de la pierna.
4. Tenemos cinco ____ en cada mano.
5. Vemos con los ____.
6. Y oímos con los ____.

Granada, España

Actividades comunicativas

A Un accidente en el extranjero Tú y un(a) amigo(a) están viajando por España. Van en bicicleta. Tu amigo se ha caído de la bicicleta y tú crees que se ha roto el brazo. Llega un(a) socorrista (un compañero[a]). Explícale lo que ha pasado y contesta a todas sus preguntas.

Asturias, España

JUEGO Trabaja con un(a) compañero(a) de clase. Dibujen un monstruo. Luego describan su monstruo a otros miembros de la clase.

B and **C** **Práctica B** and **Práctica C** have students use the third-person forms of the present perfect. They will learn the other forms to express themselves in the present perfect in the **Estructura** section of this chapter.

D Have students prepare **Práctica D** before going over it in class.

Actividades comunicativas

¡OJO! **Práctica versus Actividades comunicativas** All activities which provide guided practice are labeled **Práctica**. The more open-ended communicative activities are labeled **Actividades comunicativas.**

Learning From Photos

Cali, Colombia You may wish to ask students the following questions about the top photo on page 220:

¿Es la víctima un niño o una persona mayor?
¿Quiénes ayudan al niño?
¿Cómo se llama el servicio de primeros auxilios?
¿Está el niño en una camilla?
Granada, España Ask students to describe what is happening in the top photo on this page. You might ask them:
¿Quiénes son las personas en la foto?
¿Dónde están ellas?
¿Cuál será el problema?
Asturias, España Have students say as much as they can about the bottom photo.

ANSWERS

Práctica

C 1. Sí, Anita tiene una picadura.
2. **Una abeja le ha picado.**
3. **Le ha picado en el brazo (el hombro, etc.)**
4. **Sí, (No, no) le duele mucho la picadura.**
5. **Sí (No), Anita (no) tiene alergia a las picaduras.**

D 1. tobillo
2. **La muñeca, el codo, el hombro**
3. **El tobillo, la rodilla, el pie**
4. **dedos**
5. **ojos**
6. **oídos**

Actividades comunicativas
A Answers will vary.

🖌 Bell Ringer Review

Use BRR Transparency 8-2, or write the following on the board: Choose.

1. **José abre la boca porque el médico le examina ___.**
   a. la cabeza
   b. la cara
   c. la garganta
2. **La farmacéutica despacha ___.**
   a. medicamentos
   b. recetas
   c. alergias
3. **Los medicamentos vienen en forma de ___**
   a. ejercicios
   b. pastillas
   c. carbohidratos
4. **El médico examina a la mayor parte (el número más grande) de sus pacientes en ___.**
   a. la ambulancia
   b. la farmacia
   c. su consultorio

TEACHING VOCABULARY

A. To present the vocabulary, you may wish to follow some suggestions presented in previous chapters, using Vocabulary Transparencies 8.2 (A & B) and Cassette 5B/Compact Disc 5.

222

Vocabulario

En el hospital

las muletas

el formulario

la recepción

la silla de ruedas

José ha llenado un formulario.
Lo ha llenado en la recepción.

222 〰 *doscientos veintidós*

ABOUT THE SPANISH LANGUAGE

The word **muleta** is also used to refer to the red cloth used by a matador during a bullfight.

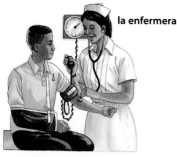

la enfermera

La enfermera le ha tomado la tensión (presión) arterial.

Le ha tomado el pulso también.

los rayos equis

El técnico le ha tomado una radiografía.
El joven tiene una fractura.

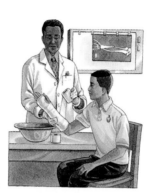

El cirujano ortopédico le ha reducido el hueso.
Ha puesto el brazo en un yeso.

 un vendaje

Paco tiene una herida.
La médica le ha cerrado la herida.
La ha cerrado con unos puntos.
Y le ha puesto un vendaje.

Los dos jóvenes están enfermos.
El uno está tan enfermo como el otro.
José tiene tantos dolores como Paco.

VOCABULARIO

doscientos veintitrés ∾ **223**

❖Práctica❖

A and **B** **Práctica A** and **Práctica B** can be done orally with books closed. After the oral presentation, students can write the answers to these activities as a homework assignment.

EXPANSION Call on a student or students to retell the information from either **Práctica A** or **Práctica B** in their own words.

Learning From Realia

OMRON You may wish to ask students to say as much as they can about the OMRON pamphlet.

Learning From Photos

Hospital Santrix, Caracas You may wish to ask the following questions about the photo:
¿Dónde están estas personas?
¿Quién será la señora?
¿Qué hace ella?
¿Quién será el señor?

❖Práctica❖

A **HISTORIETA** El pobre Joselito

Contesten con **sí**.

1. ¿Acaba de tener un accidente Joselito?
2. ¿Le duele mucho la pierna?
3. ¿Lo han puesto en una camilla los socorristas?
4. ¿Lo han llevado a la sala de emergencia del hospital municipal?
5. ¿Le ha tomado una radiografía un técnico?
6. ¿Se ha roto la pierna Joselito?
7. ¿Le ha reducido la fractura el cirujano ortopédico?
8. ¿Tendrá que andar con muletas Joselito?

B **HISTORIETA** Andrea va al hospital.

Contesten según se indica.

1. ¿Qué tiene que llenar Andrea cuando llega al hospital? (un formulario)
2. ¿Dónde lo llena? (en la recepción)
3. ¿Qué le toma un enfermero? (la tensión arterial y el pulso)
4. ¿Ha tenido Andrea un accidente? (no)
5. ¿Qué le duele mucho a Andrea? (el estómago)
6. ¿Qué le ha tomado un técnico? (una radiografía)
7. ¿De qué sufre Andrea? (un ataque de apendicitis)

OMRON

Por qué razón debería Ud. controlar su tensión arterial

Me siento bien

Informaciones imprescindibles sobre las causas y los riesgos de las enfermedades de la tensión arterial.
Incluye consejos para tomarse la tensión uno mismo.

Hospital Santrix, Caracas

ANSWERS

Práctica

A 1. Sí, Joselito acaba de tener un accidente.
2. Sí, le duele mucho la pierna.
3. Sí, los socorristas lo han puesto en una camilla.
4. Sí, lo han llevado a la sala de emergencia del hospital municipal.

5. Sí, un técnico le ha tomado una radiografía.
6. Sí, Joselito se ha roto la pierna.
7. Sí, el cirujano ortopédico le ha reducido la fractura.
8. Sí, Joselito tendrá que andar con muletas.

B 1. Andrea tiene que llenar un formulario cuando llega al hospital.
2. Lo llena en la recepción.
3. Un enfermero le toma la tensión arterial y el pulso.
4. No, Andrea no ha tenido un accidente.

5. A Andrea le duele mucho el estómago.
6. Un técnico le ha tomado una radiografía.
7. Andrea sufre de un ataque de apendicitis.

224

C **El hospital** Digan que sí o que no.

1. Al llegar al hospital, el enfermo o paciente tiene que llenar o completar un formulario.
2. La enfermera le ha tomado la tensión arterial al paciente en la cara.
3. La enfermera le ha tomado el pulso en la muñeca.
4. Los rayos equis son fotografías.
5. El joven ha tenido que andar con muletas porque se ha cortado el dedo.
6. El médico le ha puesto unos puntos porque se cortó la mejilla.
7. Han puesto al herido en una camilla porque lo tienen que llevar al hospital en la ambulancia.
8. Lo han puesto en una silla de ruedas porque no puede caminar.

D **Sinónimos** Pareen.

1. la sala de emergencia
2. los rayos equis
3. la tensión arterial
4. los puntos
5. se lastimó

   a. la presión arterial
   b. la sala de urgencias
   c. las suturas
   d. se hizo daño
   e. la radiografía

Actividades comunicativas

A **¡Socorro!** Tú estás en la Calle Sol en Ponce, Puerto Rico. Acaba de ocurrir un accidente de tráfico. No es muy grave, pero las víctimas necesitan ayuda. Desde un teléfono público, llama al 911. Explícale al/a la operador(a) (tu compañero[a]) lo que pasó y contesta a cualquier pregunta.

B **En el hospital** Tú eres el/la recepcionista del hospital. Tu compañero(a) es el/la paciente. Tienes que hacerle una serie de preguntas, por ejemplo, su nombre y dirección, el problema médico que tiene, etc. Después cambien de rol.

Ponce, Puerto Rico

C After going over **Práctica C** you may wish to call on more able students to correct the false statements.

D **Práctica D** can be done in class with or without prior preparation.

Actividades comunicativas

¡OJO! These activities encourage students to use the chapter vocabulary and structures in open-ended situations. It is not necessary to have them do all the activities. Choose the ones you consider most appropriate.

Learning From Photos

Ponce, Puerto Rico Ponce is Puerto Rico's second city, located on the south coast of the island. It was named for the first governor of Puerto Rico, Ponce de Leon. Ponce is noted for its colonial architecture, its fine art museum, and its charming plaza.

ANSWERS

Práctica

C 1. Sí.
2. No.
3. Sí.
4. Sí.
5. No.
6. Sí.
7. Sí.
8. Sí.

D 1. b
2. e
3. a
4. c
5. d

Actividades comunicativas
A and **B** Answers will vary.

RESOURCES

- 📁 Workbook, pages 89–91
- 📁 Student Tape Manual, TE, pages 87–89
- 🎧 Audiocassette 5B/CD5
- 📁 Quizzes 3–5, pages 37–39
- 💾 Computer Testmaker
- 💿 CD-ROM, Disc 3, pages 226–231

Bell Ringer Review

Use BRR Transparency 8-3, or write the following on the board:
Complete in the present.

1. Nosotros ___ al hotel. (llegar)
2. Nosotros ___ a la recepción. (ir)
3. El recepcionista nos ___ y nos ___ la llave. (hablar, dar)
4. El botones nos ___ con las maletas. (ayudar)
5. Él nos ___ las maletas. (subir)
6. Nosotros ___ en el ascensor. (subir)
7. Yo ___ la puerta con la llave. (abrir)
8. Yo ___ en el hotel pero mis amigos ___ a comer en un restaurante. (comer, salir)

TEACHING STRUCTURE

Talking about recent events

A. Go over the formation of the past participle as you write the examples on the board.

B. As you go over Step 2, you may wish to give students just the forms of the verb **haber.** Then go over the present perfect forms in the book. Have students read them aloud in unison.

(continued on page 227)

226

Estructura

 Talking about recent events
El presente perfecto

1. The present perfect tense in Spanish is formed by using the present tense of the verb **haber** and the past participle. The past participle of regular verbs is formed by adding **-ado** to the infinitive stem of **-ar** verbs and **-ido** to the infinitive stem of **-er** and **-ir** verbs.

llamar	llamado	comer	comido	sufrir	sufrido
cortar	cortado	tener	tenido	subir	subido

2. The present perfect is called a compound tense because it is made up of two verb forms. They are the present tense of the verb **haber** and the past participle.

INFINITIVE	llegar	comer	salir
yo	he llegado	he comido	he salido
tú	has llegado	has comido	has salido
él, ella, Ud.	ha llegado	ha comido	ha salido
nosotros(as)	hemos llegado	hemos comido	hemos salido
vosotros(as)	habéis llegado	habéis comido	habéis salido
ellos, ellas, Uds.	han llegado	han comido	han salido

3. The present perfect tense is used to describe an action completed very recently in the past. Some time expressions frequently used with the present perfect are:

ya	*already, yet*	jamás	*ever, never*
todavía no	*not yet*	nunca	*never*

En tu vida, ¿has tenido un accidente?
No, nunca he tenido un accidente.
Todavía no has tenido un accidente. ¡Qué suerte!
Y yo ya he tenido tres.

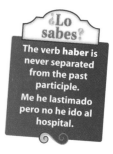

¿Lo sabes?

The verb **haber** is never separated from the past participle.
Me he lastimado pero no he ido al hospital.

For the Native Speaker

¿Te acuerdas? For those students who learned their grammar in a Spanish-speaking country, you may wish to remind them that the present perfect is also called **el pretérito perfecto compuesto.**

❖Práctica❖

A HISTORIETA El accidente

Contesten.

1. ¿Ha tenido un accidente Diego?
2. ¿Se ha caído de la bicicleta?
3. ¿Se ha lastimado?
4. ¿Ha llegado la ambulancia?
5. ¿Lo han atendido los socorristas?
6. ¿Adónde lo han llevado?

B Sí, ya la he llamado. Contesten según el modelo.

¿Has llamado a Rita?

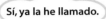
Sí, ya la he llamado.

1. ¿Has hablado con ella?
2. ¿Le has preguntado qué le pasó?
3. ¿Le has mandado unas flores?
4. ¿Has buscado sus libros?
5. ¿Los has llevado a su casa?

C HISTORIETA En el hospital

Completen con el presente perfecto.

Adela ____(llegar) al hospital. Ella
____(presentarse) en la recepción y
____(llenar) unos formularios. Una
abeja le ____(picar) en el brazo. Los
socorristas la ____(llevar) al hospital
porque ella ____(tener) una reacción
a la picadura. La médica la ____
(examinar) y le ____(permitir) volver
a casa.

Alergias

La alergia respiratoria se produce cuando una persona reacciona al contacto con determinadas sustancias (alergenos), como el polvo, polen, alimentos, algunos medicamentos o la pelusa de animales. Estas reacciones pueden variar, pues es posible que afecten órganos importantes como ojos, nariz, pulmones y piel.

ESTRUCTURA
doscientos veintisiete 227

C. As students read the model sentences in Step 3, you may want to draw a timeline on the board. Put a line through the past and bring the line right up to the present. Have a student read the information in the **¿Lo sabes?** box.

❖Práctica❖

A **Práctica A** can be done orally with books closed.

B Have students present **Práctica B** as a series of mini-conversations.

C Call on students to read **Práctica C** aloud.

Writing Development
After going over **Práctica C**, have students rewrite the information in their own words.

Learning From Realia

Alergias You may wish to call on a native speaker or one of the more able students to explain the content of the **Alergias** article in simpler Spanish.

You may also wish to ask students:
1. ¿Quién sufre de alergias?
2. ¿A qué tienes alergia?
3. ¿Qué síntomas tienes?
4. ¿Tomas algún medicamento para la alergia?

ANSWERS

Práctica

A 1. Sí, Diego ha tenido un accidente.
2. Sí, se ha caído de la bicicleta.
3. Sí, se ha lastimado.
4. Sí, la ambulancia ha llegado.
5. Sí, los socorristas lo han atendido.
6. Lo han llevado al hospital.

B 1. Sí, ya he hablado con ella.
2. Sí, ya le he preguntado qué le pasó.
3. Sí, ya le he mandado unas flores.
4. Sí, ya he buscado sus libros.
5. Sí, ya los he llevado a su casa.

C 1. ha llegado
2. se ha presentado
3. ha llenado
4. ha picado
5. han llevado
6. ha tenido
7. ha examinado
8. ha permitido

⟡Práctica⟡

 D **Práctica D** can be done orally with books closed.

EXPANSION After going over **Práctica D**, have any student who wishes, tell a story in his or her own words about a hospital experience.

A **TECHNOLOGY OPTION**
Students may use the Portfolio feature on the CD-ROM to record their conversations.

 Bell Ringer Review

Use BRR Transparency 8-4, or write the following on the board:
Rewrite in the preterite.
1. Él hace un viaje.
2. Ellos van a México.
3. Yo los veo.
4. Ellos salen el día 20.
5. Y vuelven el día 28.

TEACHING STRUCTURE

◈ **Talking about recent events**

Have students read these participles aloud several times. The more they hear them and practice them, the easier it will be for them to produce them.

⟡Práctica⟡

A **Práctica A** can be done as a series of mini-conversations.

D **Preguntas personales** Contesten.
1. ¿Has tenido un accidente alguna vez?
2. ¿Te han examinado los socorristas?
3. ¿Te han metido en una ambulancia?
4. ¿Te han llevado al hospital?
5. ¿Has tenido que pasar unos días en el hospital?

Actividad comunicativa

A **Un accidente** Un amigo se ha lastimado y lo han llevado al hospital. Tú llamas por teléfono y hablas con el/la enfermero(a) (tu compañero[a]). Quieres saber lo que le ha pasado a tu amigo, si lo han examinado, etc. Después cambien de rol.

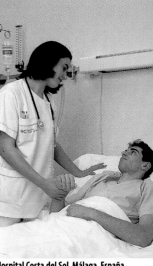

Hospital Costa del Sol, Málaga, España

Talking about recent events
Los participios irregulares

The following verbs have irregular past participles.

decir	dicho	volver	vuelto
hacer	hecho	devolver	devuelto
ver	visto	morir	muerto
escribir	escrito	abrir	abierto
poner	puesto	cubrir	cubierto
romper	roto		

⟡Práctica⟡

A **Ya lo han hecho.** Contesten según el modelo.

¿Verlo?
Pero ya lo han visto.

1. ¿Abrirlo?
2. ¿Ponerlo?
3. ¿Devolverlo?
4. ¿Escribirlo?
5. ¿Decirlo?
6. ¿Hacerlo?

ANSWERS

Práctica
D 1. **Sí, he tenido un accidente una vez. (No, no he tenido un accidente nunca.)**
2. **Sí, (No, no) me han examinado los socorristas.**
3. **Sí, (No, no) me han metido en una ambulancia.**
4. **Sí, (No, no) me han llevado al hospital.**
5. **Sí, (No, no) he tenido que pasar unos días en el hospital.**

Actividad comunicativa
A Answers will vary.

Práctica
A 1. **Pero ya lo han abierto.**
2. **Pero ya lo han puesto.**
3. **Pero ya lo han devuelto.**
4. **Pero ya lo han escrito.**
5. **Pero ya lo han dicho.**
6. **Pero ya lo han hecho.**

B **HISTORIETA** Pobre Antonio

Contesten.

1. ¿Antonio se ha hecho daño?
2. ¿Se ha roto el brazo?
3. ¿Ha ido Andrés a la sala de emergencia?
4. ¿Lo ha visto un médico?
5. ¿Le han puesto un vendaje en el hospital?
6. ¿Ha dicho algo Antonio?
7. ¿Ha vuelto a casa Antonio?

Actividades comunicativas

A **He estado muy ocupado(a).** Siempre estás muy ocupado(a). Siempre tienes algo que hacer. Trabaja con un(a) compañero(a). Cada uno(a) de Uds. va a preparar una lista de las cosas que ya han hecho hoy. Luego comparen sus listas. Determinen cuáles son las actividades que Uds. dos han hecho. Y decidan quién en realidad ha estado más ocupado(a).

Barcelona, España

B **Algún día** Hay tantas cosas que nos gustaría hacer algún día que hasta ahora no hemos hecho. Trabaja con un(a) compañero(a). Hablen de las cosas que quieren hacer algún día pero que hasta ahora no han hecho nunca. Si es posible, expliquen por qué no las han hecho.

ESTRUCTURA

doscientos veintinueve 229

CAPÍTULO 8

Estructura

B **Práctica B** can be done orally with books closed.

Actividades comunicativas

Allow students to select the activity they wish to take part in.

Learning From Photos

Hospital Costa del Sol, Málaga, España You may wish to ask students the following questions about the photo on page 228:
¿Quiénes son estas personas?
¿Por qué está el hombre en la cama?
¿Qué hace la médica?

Did You Know?

Barcelona, España The Barcelona subway was inaugurated in 1924 by combining two private companies, **El Gran Metro** and **El Metro Transversal**. Today there are five subway lines with 111 stations in the city and nearby suburbs.

For the Native Speaker

Más participios irregulares Students will often try to make irregular past participles into *regular* past participles. You may hear "**rompido,**" "**ponido,**" and "**cubrido.**" Remind them that verbs derived from verbs with irregular past participles maintain that irregularity:

prever	previsto
describir	descrito
posponer	pospuesto
descubrir	descubierto
revolver	revuelto

ANSWERS

Práctica

B 1. Sí (No), Antonio (no) se ha hecho daño.
2. Sí, (No, no) se ha roto el brazo.
3. Sí (No), Andrés (no) ha ido a la sala de emergencia.
4. Sí, (No, no) lo ha visto un médico.
5. Sí, (No, no) le han puesto un vendaje en el hospital.
6. Sí (No), Antonio (no) ha dicho algo (nada).

7. Sí (No), Antonio (no) ha vuelto a casa.

Actividades comunicativas

A and **B** Answers will vary.

229

230

Bell Ringer Review

TEACHING STRUCTURE

Comparing people and things

A. Have students open their books to page 230. Lead them through the explanation.
B. Have them repeat all the model sentences after you.

✤Práctica✤

  After going over the **Práctica** activities, have students make up their own sentences using the comparative structures they just learned.

National Standards

✿ Comparisons
Students develop an insight into their own language as they learn that the subject pronoun always follows a comparison in Spanish: **Ella es más alta que yo.** It is the same as the English construction: *She is taller than I.* English speakers often erroneously use the object pronoun: *She is taller than "me."*

Comparing people and things
Comparación de igualdad

1. To compare equal quantities in English you use *as much . . . as* or *as many . . . as.*
   > He has as much money as I.
   > He has as many problems as I.

   In Spanish you use **tanto... como.** Because **tanto** is an adjective it has to agree with the noun it modifies.
   > **Elena tiene tanta energía como yo.**
   > **Pero ella no tiene tantos accidentes como yo.**

2. To compare equal qualities in English you use *as . . . as.*
   > I am as smart as he is.

   In Spanish you use **tan... como** with either the adjective or adverb.
   > **Él está tan enfermo como su amigo.**
   > **Él se va a curar tan rápido como ella.**

✤Práctica✤

 A **Dos hospitales** Contesten.
1. ¿Tiene el hospital en la ciudad tantas camas como el hospital en las afueras?
2. ¿Tiene el doctor López tanta experiencia como el doctor Salas?
3. ¿Tienen tantos pacientes aquí como en el hospital nuevo?
4. ¿Tiene el hospital nuevo tantas enfermeras como el otro?
5. ¿Tienen tantos técnicos aquí como en el otro?
6. ¿Pagan tanto dinero aquí como en el otro hospital?

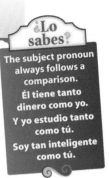

DIAGNOSTICO INTEGRAL

HOSPITAL DE MEXICO

• Laboratorios
  • Clínicos
  • Radiodiagnóstico e Imagenología
• Electrocardiograma, en reposo y con esfuerzo
• Espirometría
• Diagnóstico odontológico
• Diagnóstico oftalmológico
• Detección oportuna de cáncer

• Directo: 273 • 2521
• Conmutador: 516• 9900 Ext. 1411

HOSPITAL DE MEXICO

EXPERIENCIA
Que da vida
25

ANSWERS

Práctica
A 1. Sí (No), el hospital en la ciudad (no) tiene tantas camas como el hospital en las afueras.
2. Sí (No), el doctor López (no) tiene tanta experiencia como el doctor Salas.
3. Sí, (No, no) tienen tantos pacientes aquí como en el hospital nuevo.
4. Sí (No), el hospital nuevo (no) tiene tantas enfermeras como el otro.
5. Sí, (No, no) tienen tantos técnicos aquí como en el otro.
6. Sí, (No, no) pagan tanto dinero aquí como en el otro hospital.

B HISTORIETA Los dos son buenos.

Completen con **tanto... como** o **tan... como.**

1. El Hospital San José es _____ bueno _____ el Hospital Municipal.
2. Pero el Hospital San José no es _____ grande _____ el Hospital Municipal.
3. Y el Hospital Municipal no tiene _____ enfermeros _____ el Hospital San José.
4. Pero el Hospital San José tiene _____ pacientes _____ el Municipal.
5. La sala de emergencia del San José es _____ moderna _____ la sala de emergencia del Municipal.
6. El Hospital San José está _____ cerca de nuestra casa _____ el Hospital Municipal.

Hospital Costa del Sol,
Málaga, España

Actividad comunicativa

A **Son muy parecidas.** Trabaja con un(a) compañero(a). Piensen en algunas personas que Uds. conocen que, en su opinión, tienen mucho en común o que tienen las mismas características físicas. Comparen a estas personas.

LAS GEMELAS

ESTRUCTURA

doscientos treinta y uno ⚬ **231**

B Do this activity with books open.

Actividad comunicativa

A **TECHNOLOGY OPTION** In the CD-ROM version of this activity (Disc 3, page 231), students can interact with an on-screen native speaker and record their voices.

¡OJO! All new material in the chapter has been presented. The sections that follow recombine and reintroduce the vocabulary and structures that have already been introduced.

Learning From Realia

Experiencia que da vida You may wish to ask students questions about the **Hospital de México** pamphlet on page 230:

¿Qué clases de laboratorios tiene?

¿Cuál es la diferencia entre los dos electrocardiogramas?

¿Cuáles son dos diagnósticos que hacen?

¿Qué quiere decir detección «oportuna»?

ANSWERS

Práctica
B 1. tan, como
2. tan, como
3. tantos, como
4. tantos, como
5. tan, como
6. tan, como

Actividad comunicativa
A Answers will vary.

RESOURCES

- Audiocassette 5B/CD5
- CD-ROM, Disc 3, page 232

Bell Ringer Review

Use BRR Transparency 8-6, or write the following on the board: Write the names of three rooms of your house. For each room write one sentence telling what you do there.

TEACHING THE CONVERSATION

A. Have students close their books. Ask them to listen and repeat as you read the conversation aloud or play Cassette 5B/Compact Disc 5.

B. Open books and call on volunteers to read the conversation in parts with as much expression as possible.

C. Call on individual students to answer the questions that follow the conversation.

D. Call on a student to retell the information from the conversation in his or her own words. This activity gives students important practice in going from dialogue to narrative form.

TECHNOLOGY OPTION

On the CD-ROM (Disc 3, page 232), students can watch a dramatization of this conversation. They can then play the role of either one of the characters and record themselves in the conversation.

Conversación

Una fractura

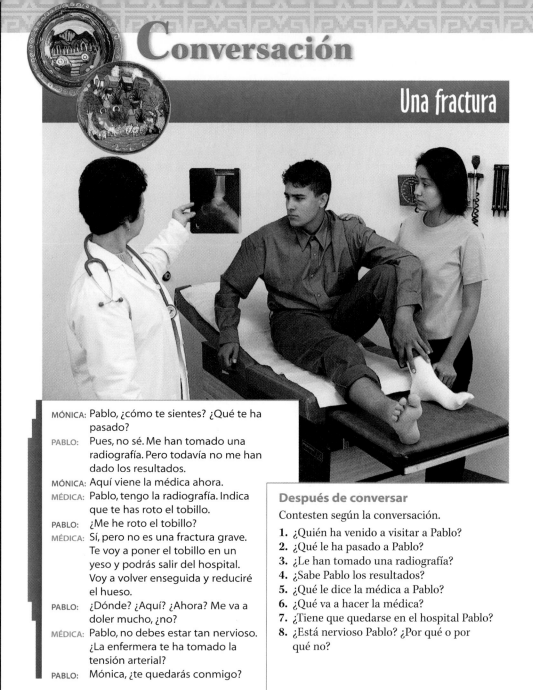

MÓNICA: Pablo, ¿cómo te sientes? ¿Qué te ha pasado?

PABLO: Pues, no sé. Me han tomado una radiografía. Pero todavía no me han dado los resultados.

MÓNICA: Aquí viene la médica ahora.

MÉDICA: Pablo, tengo la radiografía. Indica que te has roto el tobillo.

PABLO: ¿Me he roto el tobillo?

MÉDICA: Sí, pero no es una fractura grave. Te voy a poner el tobillo en un yeso y podrás salir del hospital. Voy a volver enseguida y reduciré el hueso.

PABLO: ¿Dónde? ¿Aquí? ¿Ahora? Me va a doler mucho, ¿no?

MÉDICA: Pablo, no debes estar tan nervioso. ¿La enfermera te ha tomado la tensión arterial?

PABLO: Mónica, ¿te quedarás conmigo?

Después de conversar

Contesten según la conversación.

1. ¿Quién ha venido a visitar a Pablo?
2. ¿Qué le ha pasado a Pablo?
3. ¿Le han tomado una radiografía?
4. ¿Sabe Pablo los resultados?
5. ¿Qué le dice la médica a Pablo?
6. ¿Qué va a hacer la médica?
7. ¿Tiene que quedarse en el hospital Pablo?
8. ¿Está nervioso Pablo? ¿Por qué o por qué no?

232 ⁕ *doscientos treinta y dos*

ANSWERS

Después de conversar

1. Mónica ha venido a visitar a Pablo.
2. Él no sabe qué le ha pasado.
3. Sí, le han tomado una radiografía.
4. No, él no sabe los resultados.
5. La médica le dice que se ha roto el tobillo.
6. La médica le va a poner el tobillo en un yeso y reducirá el hueso.
7. No, Pablo no tiene que quedarse en el hospital.

8. Sí, Pablo está nervioso porque piensa que le va a doler mucho.

Actividades comunicativas

A **Estoy nervioso(a).** Tu amigo(a) ha tenido un pequeño accidente. Tú estabas con él/ella cuando ocurrió. Han tenido que llevar a tu amigo(a) al hospital. Y eres tú quien tiene que llamar a sus padres para decirles lo que ha pasado. Sabes que los padres tendrán muchas preguntas. Llama a sus padres. Un(a) compañero(a) será el padre o la madre de tu amigo(a).

B **Un examen médico** Tú has recibido una beca *(scholarship)* para estudiar en Costa Rica. Antes de entrar en la universidad tienes que presentarte para un examen médico. Tu compañero(a) es el/la recepcionista y te va a hacer una serie de preguntas sobre tu salud. Después cambien de rol.

Universidad de Costa Rica

C **¿Qué te ha pasado?** Tú vas a ser el/la médico(a). Un(a) compañero(a) es el/la paciente. Él/Ella ha tenido un accidente. Házle preguntas sobre su accidente: dónde, cuándo, cómo ha ocurrido. Pregúntale dónde le duele. Luego dale una diagnosis y explícale el tratamiento—es decir, lo que vas a hacer.

Actividades comunicativas

¡OJO! The **Actividades comunicativas** allow students to use the chapter vocabulary and structures in open-ended situations. You may select those you consider most appropriate.

You may also allow students to select the activity or activities they wish to take part in.

A Students may have fun working on this activity in groups and presenting their conversations to the entire class.

B Have students make a list of questions before they begin the activity.

C **TECHNOLOGY OPTION** Students may use the Portfolio feature on the CD-ROM to record their conversations.

Learning From Photos

Universidad de Costa Rica The forerunner of the university was the **Casa de Enseñanza de Santo Tomás;** founded in 1814, which, in 1843, became the **Universidad de Santo Tomás;** 45 years later it was forced to close due to political and economic problems. In 1941 it reopened as the **Universidad de Costa Rica.**

Cooperative Learning

Un(a) herido(a) Have team members take turns being "injured." The other members will ask questions to determine the symptoms and to figure out what the "injured" student needs.

ANSWERS

Actividades comunicativas
A, B, and **C** Answers will vary.

233

234

National Standards

Cultures
The reading about **practicantes** on page 234 and the related activities on page 235 familiarize students with a type of traditional medical professional in Latin American countries.

Comparisons
Students learn that, unlike in the United States, where few areas today are inaccessible, many villages in Latin America are isolated owing to certain rugged features of the geography there. The need for **practicantes,** such as the one described in this reading, is therefore especially urgent.

TEACHING THE READING

Pre-reading
A. Give students a brief synopsis of the reading selection in Spanish.
B. Ask questions about the brief synopsis.

Reading
A. Have students open their books and repeat several sentences after you or call on individuals to read.
B. Ask questions about what was just read.
C. Have students read the selection at home and write the answers to the activities that accompany the **Lectura**.

Lecturas CULTURALES

Reading Strategy

Using context to determine meanings of words

Sometimes when reading you will come across words that you do not know. In this situation it is best to attempt to guess the most general meaning of the word or its category. To do this, it is helpful to rely on the words and sentences around the word. By doing this, you will probably be able to accurately guess those words you do not know.

PRACTICANTES

Estefanía Reyes es practicante. Ella vive en un pueblo pequeño cerca de Puno en los Andes del Perú. Vamos a ver lo que ha hecho Estefanía esta mañana. Ha estado muy ocupada. Son las once de la mañana y ya ha visto a muchos pacientes.

Le ha tomado la tensión arterial a un señor mayor. Tiene la tensión bastante elevada y Estefanía le ha recomendado una dieta.

Una niña de tres años se ha cortado el pie. Su mamá estaba muy nerviosa. Pero Estefanía le ha puesto cinco puntos para cerrar la herida. Y le ha puesto una inyección contra el tétano.

Ha visto a un señor que tiene dolores abdominales muy fuertes. Le duele tanto el estómago que Estefanía cree que está sufriendo de un ataque de apendicitis. Puede ser algo muy serio. Estefanía lo ha mandado al hospital para ver a un médico.

Pero, ¿qué es Estefanía? Es una practicante. En los países hispanos siempre ha habido practicantes. Son profesionales en el campo de la medicina. El o la practicante es un(a) diplomado(a) en enfermería. Puede poner inyecciones y practicar curas médicas simples y rutinarias. En caso de heridas o enfermedades serias, el practicante manda al paciente a un médico.

En muchos pueblos pequeños de áreas remotas, el practicante es muy importante. A veces es el único profesional médico que tienen los habitantes.

Un pueblo andino del Perú

Independent Practice

Assign any of the following:
1. **Después de leer** activities, page 235
2. Workbook, **Un poco más,** pages 92–93
3. CD-ROM, Disc 3, pages 234–235

Learning From Photos

Estefanía Reyes You may wish to ask students to describe the top photo on this page. Ask questions such as:
¿Quién será la señora?
¿Quiénes son los niños?
¿Hay más niños o niñas en el grupo?
¿Qué tiene el niño en la mano?
Un pueblo andino del Perú The houses in this village are made of stone. Trees are uncommon high in the Andes and timber is not abundant for building. Stone houses are the norm.

Después de leer

A **Un trabajo interesante** Contesten.

1. ¿Qué es Estefanía Reyes?
2. ¿De dónde es?
3. ¿Qué es un(a) practicante?
4. ¿En qué es diplomado(a)?
5. ¿Cuándo manda al paciente a ver al médico el practicante?
6. ¿Por qué es muy importante el practicante en muchas áreas?

B **Pacientes** Expliquen.

Son las once de la mañana y Estefanía ya ha visto a muchos pacientes. Identifiquen a todos los pacientes que ella ha examinado y describan lo que ha hecho a cada uno.

C **Palabras** Empleen las siguientes palabras en una oración.

1. el practicante
2. la tensión arterial
3. le ha puesto puntos
4. el tétano
5. un ataque de apendicitis

SERVICIO DE
A.T.S. / PRACTICANTE
A DOMICILIO

"TODO MADRID"

INYECCIONES
SONDAS
SUEROS
PRESIÓN ARTERIAL
CURAS QUIRÚRGICAS
(ÚLCERAS, HERIDAS, QUEMADURAS...)
SUTURAS
ETC.

Para comunicar su aviso llame al teléfono:
☎ 908 – 72 88 83

(Este teléfono móvil sustituye al anterior servicio de "busca"
450 28 12, abonado nº 3516)

Una zona rural en Bolivia

LECTURAS CULTURALES

doscientos treinta y cinco 〰 **235**

Post-reading

A. Go over the **Después de leer** activities in class the next day.

B. Call on a student to give a summary of the reading in his or her own words. If necessary, ask five or six questions to review the salient points of the reading selection in order to enable him or her to do this more easily. After the oral summary, the more able students can write a synopsis of the **Lectura** in their own words.

Learning From Realia

Servicio de A.T. S. Ask students to tell as much as they can about the **Servicio de A.T.S. / Practicante a domicilio.**

For the Native Speaker

Los servicios médicos In many Hispanic countries medical services are paid for by the government. Yet many people who can afford it prefer to get private medical care. Ask students to write a short paragraph addressing the following issue: **¿Cuáles son algunas ventajas y desventajas del servicio médico totalmente pagado por el gobierno? ¿Para quiénes es un beneficio? ¿Para quiénes no lo es?**

ANSWERS

Después de leer

A 1. Es una practicante.
2. Es del Perú.
3. Es un(a) profesional en el campo de la medicina.
4. Es diplomado(a) en enfermería.
5. El practicante manda al paciente a ver al médico en caso de heridas o enfermedades serias.
6. Es muy importante en muchas áreas porque a veces es el único profesional médico que tienen los habitantes.

B Answers will vary but may include:
1. **Un señor mayor:** Estefanía le ha tomado la tensión arterial y le ha recomendado una dieta.
2. **Una niña de tres años que se ha cortado el pie:** Estefanía le ha puesto cinco puntos para cerrar la herida y le ha puesto una inyección contra el tétano.
3. **Un señor que tiene dolores abdominales muy graves:** lo ha mandado al hospital para ver a un médico.

C Answers will vary.

LECTURA OPCIONAL 1

National Standards

Cultures
This reading about the opening of a new hospital and the related activities on this page familiarize students with the existence of modern medical services in the Spanish-speaking world.

TEACHING TIPS

¡OJO! This reading is optional. You may skip it completely, have the entire class read it, have only several students read it, or assign it for extra credit.

This reading is an actual newspaper article about the opening of a new hospital.

Did You Know?

Influencia griega **Quirófano, cirugía, cirujano** are all derived from the Greek word for *hand*. The English words "surgery" and "surgeon" have the same root. Ask students why they think this is so.

EL HOSPITAL BUENA VISTA

La mañana del jueves de esta semana se han abierto por primera vez las puertas del nuevo Hospital Buena Vista. La alcadesa de la ciudad, doña Emilia Porras Narváez, ha cortado la cinta ceremonial en frente de la entrada principal.

Este modernísimo hospital cuenta con doscientas camas, un quirófano[1] con un equipo técnico muy avanzado, salas de recuperación, una unidad de cuidado intensivo, y departamentos especializados, entre ellos los de cardiología, ginecología, ortopedia, y pediatría. El director del hospital, el doctor Elías Maldonado, ha dicho que la primera responsabilidad del hospital es la salud de la comunidad. Después de la ceremonia de apertura, los invitados fueron a la cafetería del hospital para una recepción.

[1]quirófano *operating room*

Después de leer

A **¿Cómo se dice en inglés... ?** Pareen.
1. la alcaldesa
2. la cinta
3. avanzado
4. cuidado intensivo
5. salas de recuperación

a. ribbon
b. advanced
c. intensive care
d. recovery rooms
e. the mayor (female)

B **Especialidades médicas** Contesten.
1. ¿Cuáles son cuatro especialidades médicas que mencionan en el artículo?
2. ¿Cómo se llaman esas cuatro especialidades en inglés?

C **El hospital nuevo** Contesten según el artículo.
1. ¿Cuándo inauguraron el nuevo hospital?
2. ¿Cuántos pacientes pueden dormir en el hospital?
3. ¿Qué hay en el quirófano?
4. ¿Qué ha dicho el doctor Maldonado?
5. ¿Por qué fueron los invitados a la cafetería?

ANSWERS

Después de leer

A 1. e   4. c
  2. a   5. d
  3. b

B 1. La cardiología, la ginecología, la ortopedia y la pediatría
  2. *Cardiology, gynecology, orthopedics* and *pediatrics*

C 1. Inauguraron el nuevo hospital la mañana del jueves de esta semana.
  2. Doscientos pacientes pueden dormir en el hospital.
  3. En el quirófano hay un equipo técnico muy avanzado.
  4. Ha dicho que la primera responsabilidad del hospital es la salud de la comunidad.
  5. Los invitados fueron a la cafetería para una recepción.

LECTURA OPCIONAL 2

DI NO A LAS DROGAS

* VENDER
* REGALAR
* TRANSPORTAR
* CONSUMIR
* COMERCIAR
* POSEER

DROGAS
Y ENERVANTES

Está altamente penado por la ley y se sanciona con CÁRCEL.

PGR
PROCURADURÍA
GENERAL DE LA REPÚBLICA

SONORA
TURISMO SECTUR

Alianza social contra el NARCOTRÁFICO

PROBLEMAS MÉDICOS DE HOY

Al hablar de la salud y la medicina hay tres problemas graves que todos tenemos que confrontar. Son la adicción a las drogas, el abuso del alcohol y el SIDA.

En todos los países hispanos, igual que en los Estados Unidos, verás anuncios que dicen «No a las drogas».

En España y en otros países hispanos hay campañas de castigos[1] rigurosos contra los conductores de automóviles que manejan (conducen) bajo la influencia del alcohol. El número de muertes[2] causadas por accidentes vehiculares excede la tasa[3] de mortalidad de muchas enfermedades.

Se considera el SIDA la plaga de nuestro siglo. Esta enfermedad contagiosa está matando[4] a miles de personas cada día en todos los continentes del mundo. En todas partes hay programas y campañas para educar a la gente sobre los peligros[5] del uso de las drogas y la promiscuidad sexual, las dos causas principales del SIDA.

La drogadicción, el alcoholismo y el SIDA son problemas que todos tenemos que confrontar, resolver y vencer.

[1]castigos *punishments*
[2]muertes *deaths*
[3]tasa *rate*
[4]matando *killing*
[5]peligros *dangers*

Después de leer

A. Problemas de hoy Digan que sí o que no.

1. Actualmente hay tres problemas médicos que son muy graves.
2. El SIDA es una enfermedad venérea contagiosa.
3. El número de muertes causadas por conductores de automóviles bajo la influencia del alcohol es muy bajo.
4. El SIDA no existe en muchas partes del mundo.

LECTURAS OPCIONALES

doscientos treinta y siete **237**

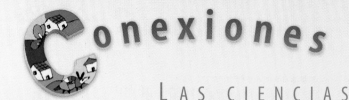

Conexiones

LAS CIENCIAS

LA MEDICINA

As you know, many English and Spanish words are cognates. They are similar in form and mean the same thing because both have the same source, usually Latin. Much medical terminology comes directly from Latin. Therefore the number of English/Spanish cognates is particularly great in this field. You will also note a pattern in the endings. The **ía** ending in Spanish is usually *y* in English. The **ólogo(a)** ending is usually *ogist* in English. Let's go over a few of these cognates.

ESPECIALIDADES MÉDICAS	MÉDICOS ESPECIALISTAS
la cardiología	**el/la cardiólogo(a)**
la ginecología	**el/la ginecólogo(a)**
la psiquiatría	**el/la psiquiatra**
la pediatría	**el/la pediatra**
la oncología	**el/la oncólogo(a)**
la oftalmología	**el/la oftalmólogo(a)**
la urología	**el/la urólogo(a)**
la dermatología	**el/la dermatólogo(a)**

It shouldn't be too hard to figure out what the names of these specialties and specialists are in English. If you don't know what they are in English, check with your science teacher or the school nurse. Here are a few hints.

la cardiología *cardiology*
el cardiólogo *the cardiologist*

Una pediatra,
Estepona, España

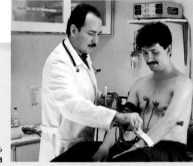

Un cardiólogo,
Caracas, Venezuela

National Standards

✿ *Connections*
This reading about medical specialties and diseases in the Spanish-speaking world establishes a connection with another discipline, allowing students to reinforce and further their knowledge of science, specifically medicine, through the study of Spanish.

Comparisons
This reading illustrates the prevalence of English/Spanish cognates, thereby giving students a better understanding of the nature of language.

¡OJO! The readings in the **Conexiones** section are optional. They focus on some of the major disciplines taught in schools and universities. The vocabulary is useful for discussing such topics as history, literature, art, economics, business, science, etc.

You may choose any of the following ways to do this reading on medicine with your students.
Independent reading Have students read the selections and do the post-reading activities as homework, which you collect. This option is least intrusive on class time and requires a minimum of teacher involvement.
Homework with in-class follow-up Assign the readings and post-reading activities as homework. Review and discuss the material in class the next day.
Intensive in-class activity This option includes a pre-reading vocabulary presentation, in-class reading and discussion, assignment of the activities for homework, and a discussion of the assignment in class the following day.

Learning From Photos

Una pediatra, Estepona, España Ask students the following questions about this photo: **¿Quién es el paciente, el niño o su madre? ¿Qué tratan los pediatras? ¿Qué opinas? ¿Al niño le duele el estómago? Un cardiólogo, Caracas, Venezuela** You may wish to ask students what the **cardiólogo** in the photo is doing to the patient. **¿Qué le está haciendo el cardiólogo al paciente?**

Now see whether you can guess the meaning of these diseases or illnesses:

LAS ENFERMEDADES

la tuberculosis	**la artritis**
el cáncer	**la meningitis**
la apendicitis	**la esquizofrenia**
la hepatitis	**las úlceras**

See whether you can answer these questions.

1. ¿Cómo se llama el especialista que trata las enfermedades de los niños?
2. ¿Quién es el especialista que trata las enfermedades mentales?
3. ¿A qué médico deben ir las personas que sufren de cáncer?
4. Si tienes un problema con los ojos, ¿a qué especialista debes consultar?

Now let's see how much you can understand about certain diseases.

1. La esquizofrenia es una enfermedad _____.
   a. de los ojos   **b.** mental   **c.** de niños
2. Los médicos les ponen a dieta a las víctimas de _____.
   a. úlceras   **b.** artritis   **c.** esquizofrenia
3. Esta enfermedad afecta más a las personas viejas. Se les hace difícil usar las manos. La enfermedad es _____.
   a. la artritis   **b.** la tuberculosis   **c.** la hepatitis
4. Si una persona come mariscos contaminados puede sufrir de _____.
   a. apendicitis   **b.** tuberculosis   **c.** hepatitis

BÉSAME

YA NO FUMO!

Al dejar de fumar su respiración se hace más fácil porque los pulmones están libres de humo y nicotina y los riesgos de desarrollar enfermedades relacionadas con el cigarro disminuyen. Unas de estas enfermedades son cáncer del **pulmón, enfisema, ataque cardíaco y embolio cerebral**.

Un cuerpo sano es uno de los beneficios que se gana al dejar de fumar. Se sentirá mejor física y mentalmente, dándole más energía para sí mismo, la familia y amigos.

CENTRO DE OFTALMOLOGIA

BARRAQUER

L AS CIENCIAS

LA MEDICINA

A. You may wish to have students interested in medicine do this reading along with the accompanying activities.

B. Students who are not particularly interested in medicine can take a quick look at the terms to familiarize themselves with them. They are all cognates.

Learning From Realia

Ya no fumo Have students look at the ad with the frog and ask them: **¿De qué trata el anuncio?** Then ask them to list all the benefits mentioned that come from stopping smoking.
Centro de oftalmología Ask students:
¿Cuál es la especialización de los médicos en el Centro Barraquer? ¿Quiénes tienen que ir al Centro Barraquer?

ANSWERS

Note These are the answers to the questions in the reading above.

1. el/la pediatra
2. el/la psiquiatra
3. el/la oncólogo(a)
4. el/la oftalmólogo(a)

1. b
2. a
3. a
4. c

Culminación

Actividades orales

A **Servicios médicos de tu comunidad** Hay un(a) estudiante de intercambio en tu escuela (tu compañero[a]). Es de Panamá. Tiene algunas preguntas sobre los servicios médicos que ofrece tu comunidad. Descríbele el hospital local. Si no sabes nada del hospital que sirve a tu comunidad, ve a buscar un folleto sobre el hospital para poder contestar a las preguntas del/de la estudiante de intercambio.

Canal de Panamá

B **Voy a ser intérprete.** El hospital local tiene un problema. Su intérprete de español ha estado enfermo. Tú vas a ayudar. Vas a trabajar a tiempo parcial en el hospital. Vas a ayudar a los pacientes hispanohablantes. Tu compañero(a) va a ser tu primer(a) paciente. Ayúdale a llenar el formulario en la recepción.

C **Una comedia** Van a divertirse. Trabajando en grupos de cuatro o cinco personas, preparen un «skit». Su «skit» se llama «Un día en la sala de emergencia». No va a ser muy serio. Va a ser muy cómico. Presenten su comedia a la clase.

Actividades escritas

A **Un formulario** Escribe, en una hoja de papel por separado, la información que te pide el formulario.

HOSPITAL ABC

Apellidos _____ Nombre _____

Dirección _____ Edad _____

Problema médico que tiene _____
_____

Nombres y dirección de padres
u otros parientes _____

Nombre de la compañía
de seguros _____

B **Un anuncio** Les han pedido a ti y a tu compañero(a) preparar un anuncio para el nuevo Hospital Buena Vista. Preparen un breve anuncio para el periódico. Deben incluir información sobre el tamaño del hospital y otros detalles importantes.

Writing Strategy

Writing a feature article

When writing a feature article, writers have two challenges: first, they must identify current topics that will be of interest; they must gather the information that will bring the topic to life and give readers the background they need. An important aspect of feature writing is the use of an effective "lead" to describe the opening of the story. This will catch the readers' attention and draw them in.

Las noticias

Your local Spanish language newspaper has asked you to write a feature story on a person or place in your community. Your parents recently had an accident and had to go to the emergency room. They were transported there by the First Aid Squad in your community. You were extremely pleased with the quality of service, beginning with the paramedics who arrived promptly and administered treatment at the scene. The care your parents received in the emergency room from the staff was equally as good. Write an article about this experience to share with the Spanish-speaking members of your community and to perhaps offer a refreshing perspective to an otherwise unpleasant event.

Actividades escritas

A You may wish to photocopy this form for your students.

B If Spanish-language newspapers are available in your area, you may wish to bring some to class so that your students can use real ads for hospitals as models for their ads.

Writing Strategy

Writing a feature article

A. Have students read the Writing Stategy on page 241.
B. In order to help them understand what a "lead" is, bring in Spanish-language newspapers and have them read the lead sentences of several articles.

TECHNOLOGY OPTION

Online Spanish-language newspapers are available to you and your students at the **Glencoe Foreign Language Web site** at **Café Glencoe** (www.cafe.glencoe.com).

Independent Practice

Assign any of the following:
1. Activities, pages 240–241
2. Workbook, **Mi autobiografía,** page 94
3. Situation Cards
4. CD-ROM, Disc 3, Chapter 8, **Juego de repaso**

ANSWERS

Actividades escritas
A and **B** Answers will vary.

Writing Strategy
Answers will vary.

ASSESSMENT RESOURCES

- 📁 Chapter Quizzes
- 📁 Testing Program
- 💾 Computer Testmaker
- 📁 Situation Cards
- 🎧 Communication Transparency C-8
- 📁 Performance Assessment
- 📼 **Maratón mental** Videoquiz

VOCABULARY REVIEW

The words and phrases in the **Vocabulario** have been taught for productive use in this chapter. They are summarized here as a resource for both students and teacher. This list also serves as a convenient resource for the **Culminación** activities on pages 240 and 241. Have the students look at the list. If there are any words they do not know, have them find them in the **Vocabulario** sections on pages 218–219 and 222–223. If absolutely necessary, students can look up some words in the end vocabulary. There are approximately eight cognates in this vocabulary list. Have students find them.

Teacher Notes

Vocabulario

TALKING ABOUT AN ACCIDENT

tener un accidente	cortarse
hacerse daño, lastimarse	picar
caerse	ocurrir
romperse	tener lugar
torcerse	acabar de

TALKING ABOUT MEDICAL EMERGENCIES AND A HOSPITAL

el servicio de primeros auxilios	la recepción
la ambulancia	la silla de ruedas
la camilla	las muletas
el hospital	la víctima
la sala de emergencia, la sala de urgencias	llenar el formulario

TALKING ABOUT MEDICAL PROFESSIONALS

el/la médico(a)	el/la técnico(a)
el/la cirujano(a) ortopédico(a)	el/la socorrista
el/la enfermero(a)	

TALKING ABOUT MEDICAL PROBLEMS

una fractura	el dolor
una herida	hinchado(a)
una picadura	

TALKING ABOUT MEDICAL CARE

ayudar	reducir el hueso
doler	poner en un yeso
sentirse	poner un vendaje
tomar la tensión (presión) arterial	cerrar la herida
tomar el pulso	poner puntos (suturas)
tomar una radiografía	parecer
tomar unos rayos equis	

IDENTIFYING PARTS OF THE BODY

el cuerpo	el pecho	la pierna
el hombro	el codo	la rodilla
el brazo	la muñeca	el tobillo
el cuello	el dedo	el pie

IDENTIFYING PARTS OF THE FACE

la cara	la nariz	el oído, la oreja
la frente	el labio	el ojo
la mejilla		

242 ◦◦ *doscientos cuarenta y dos*   CAPÍTULO 8

For the Native Speaker

Lo que digo yo Have students write down any words they know from their own experience in the categories listed on the **Vocabulario** page. They could define their words and share them with the class.

VIDEO

¡Buen viaje!

EPISODIO 8 ▶ Emergencias médicas

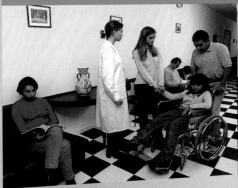

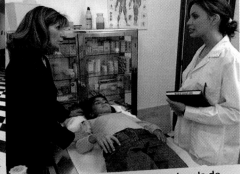

Pilar tuvo un accidente.

Su madre llegó inmediatamente a la sala de emergencia.

CD-ROM

Expansión cultural

Las ambulancias son un servicio esencial en todos los centros urbanos. Madrid, España

interNET CONNECTION

In this video episode Pilar has a bicycle accident and is taken to the emergency room. To find out what you need to know in case you have a medical emergency in a Spanish-speaking country, go to the Capítulo 8 Internet activity at the Glencoe Foreign Language Web site:
http://www.glencoe.com/sec/fl

TECNOTUR

doscientos cuarenta y tres ∞ **243**

OVERVIEW

This page previews three key multi-media components of the **Glencoe Spanish** series. Each reinforces the material taught in Chapter 8 in a unique manner.

VIDEO

The Video Program allows students to see how the chapter vocabulary and structures are used by native speakers in an engaging story. Show the video episode as a final activity for Chapter 8.

A. Before watching the episode, ask students these questions about the photos: **¿En qué está sentada Pilar? ¿Dónde están Pilar, Teresa y Juan Ramón? ¿Qué piensas que le ha pasado a Pilar? En la segunda foto, ¿con quién habla la mamá de Pilar?**

B. See the Video Activities Booklet for detailed suggestions for using this resource.

CD-ROM

A. Have students read the **Expansión cultural** photo caption on page 243. Then ask students what number they would call if they needed an ambulance in Madrid.

B. In the CD-ROM version of **Expansión cultural** (Disc 3, page 243), students can listen to additional recorded information about medical emergency services in the Spanish-speaking world.

INTERNET

Teacher Information and Student Worksheets for this activity can be accessed at the Web site.

Video Synopsis

This episode takes place in a hospital in Madrid where Teresa and Juan Ramón have taken Pilar, Teresa's ten-year-old sister, following a bicycle accident. In the emergency room, they discuss her injuries with an intake nurse. We then see the nurse filling out the forms necessary to admit Pilar. Teresa calls her mother, who rushes to the scene. In the emergency room, Pilar asks her mother to tell Juan Ramón that this time she is really sick, in contrast to her feigned illness in **¡Buen viaje! Level 1,** Chapter 8.

Chapter 9 Overview ◆◆◆◆◆◆◆◆◆◆◆◆◆◆◆◆◆

SCOPE AND SEQUENCE pages 244–271

TOPICS	FUNCTIONS	STRUCTURE	CULTURE
◆ Life in the city ◆ Life in the country	◆ How to get around in the city ◆ How to talk about common agricultural topics ◆ How to describe what was going on ◆ How to refer to things already mentioned ◆ How to point out people and things	◆ The imperfect progressive ◆ Placement of object pronouns ◆ Demonstrative adjectives and pronouns	◆ Buenos Aires, Argentina ◆ Lima, Peru ◆ Santa Fe, New Mexico ◆ The demography of Latin America

CHAPTER 9 RESOURCES

PRINT	MULTIMEDIA

Planning Resources

Lesson Plans
Block Scheduling Lesson Plans

Interactive Lesson Planner

Reinforcement Resources

Writing Activities Workbook
Student Tape Manual
Video Activities Booklet
Web Site User's Guide

Transparencies Binder
Audiocassette/Compact Disc Program
Videocassette/Videodisc Program
Online Internet Activities
Electronic Teacher's Classroom Resources

Assessment Resources

Situation Cards
Chapter Quizzes
Testing Program
Performance Assessment

Maratón mental Mindjogger Videoquiz
Testmaker Computer Software (Macintosh/Windows)
Listening Comprehension Audiocassette/Compact Disc
Communication Transparency: C-9

Motivational Resources

Expansion Activities

Café Glencoe: www.cafe.glencoe.com
Keypal Internet Activities

Enrichment

Spanish for Spanish Speakers

Chapter 9 Planning Guide

SECTION	PAGES	SECTION RESOURCES
Vocabulario Palabras 1 **En la ciudad** **La estación del metro**	246–249	Vocabulary Transparencies 9.1 Audiocassette 6A/Compact Disc 6 Student Tape Manual, TE, pages 96–98 Workbook, pages 95–96 Chapter Quizzes, page 40 CD-ROM, Disc 3, pages 246–249
Vocabulario Palabras 2 **En el campo**	250–253	Vocabulary Transparencies 9.2 Audiocassette 6A/Compact Disc 6 Student Tape Manual, TE, pages 98–100 Workbook, pages 97–98 Chapter Quizzes, page 41 CD-ROM, Disc 3, pages 250–253

Estructura
El imperfecto progresivo
Colocación de los pronombres
    de complemento
Adjetivos y pronombres
    demostrativos
	254–259	Workbook, pages 99–102
		Audiocassette 6A/Compact Disc 6
		Student Tape Manual, TE, pages 100–102
		Chapter Quizzes, pages 42–44
		Computer Testmaker
		CD-ROM, Disc 3, pages 254–259

Conversación **El campo y la ciudad**	260–261	Audiocassette 6A/Compact Disc 6 Student Tape Manual, TE, page 103 CD-ROM, Disc 3, pages 260–261

Lecturas culturales
Buenos Aires, Argentina
Lima, Perú *(opcional)*
Una ciudad norteamericana
    con profundas raíces his-
    panas *(opcional)*
	262–265	Testing Program, page 66
		CD-ROM, Disc 3, pages 262–265

Conexiones **La demografía** *(opcional)*	266–267	Testing Program, page 67 CD-ROM, Disc 3, pages 266–267
Culminación **Actividades orales** **Actividad escrita** **Vocabulario** **Tecnotur**	268–271	**¡Buen viaje!** Video, Episode 9 Video Activities, pages 97–100 Internet Activities **www.glencoe.com/sec/fl** Testing Program, pages 63–66; 134; 178; 198 CD-ROM, Disc 3, pages 268–271

OVERVIEW

In this chapter students will learn to compare and contrast city and country life. Students will learn how to describe an action as it was taking place in the past, using the imperfect progressive tense. They will also expand their knowledge of how to refer to people and things already mentioned. In addition, they will learn to point out people or things by using demonstrative adjectives and pronouns.

The cultural focus of the chapter is on urban life in the Spanish-speaking world, in particular in Buenos Aires, Argentina and Lima, Peru.

National Standards

In Chapter 9 students will learn to communicate in spoken and written Spanish on the following topics:
- city life
- country life
- cities in the Spanish-speaking world

Students will obtain and provide information about these topics and engage in conversations that would typically take place in urban or rural settings as they fulfill the chapter objectives listed on this page.

Ciudad y campo

Objetivos

In this chapter you will learn to do the following:
- talk about life in the city
- talk about life in the country
- describe things that were happening
- refer to things already mentioned
- indicate where things are located
- talk about some cities in the Spanish-speaking world

inter**NET** CONNECTION

The **Glencoe Foreign Language Web site** (http://www.glencoe.com/sec/fl) offers three options that enable you and your students to experience the Spanish-speaking world via the Internet:
- The online **Actividades** are correlated to the chapters and utilize Hispanic Web sites around the world. For the Chapter 9 activity, see student page 271.

- The **Correspondencia electrónica** section provides information on how to set up a keypal (pen pal) exchange between your class and a class in the Spanish-speaking world.
- At **Café Glencoe,** the interactive "after-school" section of the site, you and your students can access a variety of additional online resources, including interactive games.

Spotlight On Culture

Fotografía The photo on pages 244 and 245 shows **campesinos** returning to the village from the fields. Fewer and fewer **campesinos** are willing to remain in villages such as these, dedicating their lives to agriculture. The exodus to the cities is a major concern in almost all Latin American countries. Poor farmers flock to the cities in search of better economic opportunities, better health care, and better schooling for their children. Unfortunately, the quality of their life in the cities is often as bad as, or worse than, in the countryside. They are crowded into unsanitary living quarters and forced to work for minimum wages if they can find work at all.

Pacing

Chapter 9 will require approximately eight to ten days. Pacing will vary according to the length of the class, the age of your students, and student aptitude.

Block Scheduling

The extended time frame provided by block scheduling affords you the opportunity to implement a greater number of activities and projects to motivate and involve your students. See the Block Scheduling Lesson Plans Booklet for suggestions on how to present the chapter material within a block scheduling framework.

doscientos cuarenta y cinco ∞ **245**

Chapter Projects

¿Prefieres la ciudad o el campo? Have students choose a Spanish-speaking city or town that they would like to live in, according to whether they prefer urban or rural life. Have them prepare a report on their city or town and ask them to explain why they selected it. Students should include photos and maps of the city or town in their report, if possible. The Internet is a good source for this information.

Vocabulario
PALABRAS 1

Bell Ringer Review

Use BRR Transparency 9-1, or write the following on the board: On a piece of paper make two columns. Head the column on the left **el avión** and the one on the right **el tren.** Copy each of the following terms into the correct column.

el coche-comedor
el aterrizaje
el chaleco salvavidas
el andén
el comandante
el revisor
el cinturón de seguridad
la cabina
el asistente
la estación
la torre de control

TEACHING VOCABULARY

A. Have students close their books. Project Vocabulary Transparencies 9.1 (A & B) to present the **Palabras 1** vocabulary. Model each new word or expression and have students repeat two or three times after you or the recording on Cassette 6A/Compact Disc 5. *(continued on page 247)*

En la ciudad

el rascacielos

la oficina

En la zona comercial hay muchas oficinas y tiendas.
Eran las siete y media de la tarde y mucha gente estaba saliendo de sus oficinas.

la fábrica

La zona industrial está en las afueras de la ciudad.
Los obreros estaban trabajando todo el día en la fábrica.

el edificio alto

En la zona residencial hay muchos apartamentos (departamentos) y condominios.
Hay pocas casas privadas.

un plano de la ciudad

la plaza

la calle

la avenida, el bulevar

Muchas calles y avenidas desembocan en la plaza.
Las avenidas son anchas.

Esta calle o callecita angosta es muy pintoresca.
Está en el barrio viejo de la ciudad.

Pantomime

Begin
___, ven acá, por favor.
Estás en la ciudad hoy.
Camina en la acera.
Ve a la esquina.
Espera en la esquina. El semáforo está rojo.
El semáforo está verde ahora. Cruza la calle en el cruce de peatones.
Ve a la boca del metro.
Baja la escalera mecánica.

Mete tu tique en la ranura del torniquete.
Sube al metro.
Gracias, ___. Puedes regresar a tu asiento.

el semáforo
el cruce
la esquina
los peatones
la acera

Hay un semáforo en la esquina
Los peatones caminan en la acera.
Cruzan la calle en el cruce de peatones.

La gente estaba esperando en la parada del bus.

el autobús, la guagua, el camión

La estación del metro

la boca del metro

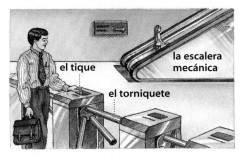

el tique
la escalera mecánica
el torniquete

La señorita estaba subiendo la escalera mecánica.
El señor estaba metiendo el tique en la ranura del torniquete.

VOCABULARIO

doscientos cuarenta y siete 247

B. When the new words are used in sentences, ask questions about each sentence: **¿Dónde hay muchas oficinas? ¿Qué más hay en una zona comercial? ¿Es alto un rascacielos?**

C. After presenting the vocabulary orally, have students open their books and read for additional reinforcement.

D. Call a student to the front of the room. Show the Vocabulary Transparencies again. Have the student play teacher and ask questions about what he or she sees in the illustrations.

Additional Practice

Palabras Give students the following definitions and have them supply the correct words.

1. un edificio muy alto, que tiene muchos pisos
2. donde trabajan los obreros para hacer o manufacturar productos
3. una calle pequeña y angosta
4. una casa donde vive sólo una familia
5. donde se encuentran dos calles
6. donde cruzan los peatones la calle
7. donde se puede subir a un autobús o bajar de un autobús
8. la entrada del metro

ABOUT THE SPANISH LANGUAGE

◆ **Un plano** is a map or diagram of a city or town, a fortress or park or similar area. **Un mapa** is a road map or map of a relatively large geographic area, a province or state, for example.

◆ **El semáforo** is also called **la luz roja** in many places.

◆ **Un torniquete** is, of course, a turnstile, but it is also the word for *tourniquet,* the bandage used to stop bleeding.

◆ In Mexico a bus is **un camión**, in Puerto Rico it's **una guagua**, in Spain it's **un autobús**. In other places it may be called **un bus, un ómnibus** or **un colectivo**. In Chile **una guagua** is a baby. In Spain, a long-distance bus is **un autocar**.

Learning From Photos

Una calle pintoresca The street scene pictured in the photo on the lower right, page 246, is from one of the picturesque **Pueblos Blancos** of Andalucía. What can be seen in the photo are:

macetas	*flower pots*
balcones	*balconies*
un escudo	*heraldic shield*
rejas	*iron grilles on the windows*

247

Práctica

¡OJO! **Práctica** When students are doing the **Práctica** activities, accept any answer that makes sense. The purpose of these activities is to have students use the new vocabulary. They are not factual recall activities. Thus, do not expect students to remember specific information from the vocabulary presentation when answering. If you wish, have students use the photos as a stimulus, when possible. **Historieta** Each time **Historieta** appears, it means that the answers to the activity form a short story. Encourage students to look at the title of **Historieta** since it can sometimes help them do the activity.

It is recommended that you go over the **Práctica** before assigning them for homework.

A **Práctica A** can be done first orally with books closed.

EXPANSION After going over **Prática A**, call on a student to tell all about **el señor Salas** in his or her own words.

B Have students refer to the illustration to do **Práctica B**.

Writing Development
Have students write the information in **Práctica B** in an organized paragraph, as a description of a city scene.

Práctica

A **HISTORIETA** El señor Salas de Caracas

Contesten.

1. ¿Estaba viviendo el señor Salas en Caracas?
2. ¿Tenía un apartamento en una zona residencial de la ciudad?
3. ¿Estaba su apartamento en un edificio alto?
4. ¿Trabajaba él en una oficina cerca de la Plaza Simón Bolívar?
5. ¿Estaba su oficina en un rascacielos?
6. ¿Tomaba el señor Salas el metro a su trabajo?
7. ¿Había una boca de metro cerca de su apartamento?
8. ¿Compraba el señor Salas tiques para el metro?

Caracas, Venezuela

B **El plano de la ciudad**

Contesten según el dibujo.

1. ¿Desembocan muchas calles en la Plaza San Martín?
2. ¿Es ancha o angosta la calle Ayacucho?
3. ¿Hay un semáforo en la esquina de Ayacucho y Cuzco?
4. ¿Hay una parada de bus en la plaza?
5. ¿Hay muchos coches en la plaza?
6. ¿Hay peatones en la acera?

ANSWERS

Práctica

A 1. Sí, el señor Salas estaba viviendo en Caracas.
2. Sí, (No, no) tenía un apartamento en una zona residencial de la ciudad.
3. Sí (No), su apartamento (no) estaba en un edificio alto.
4. Sí (No), él (no) trabajaba en una oficina cerca de la Plaza Simón Bolívar.
5. Sí (No), su oficina (no) estaba en un rascacielos.

6. Sí (No), el señor Salas (no) tomaba el metro a su trabajo.
7. Sí, (No, no) había una boca de metro cerca de su apartamento.
8. Sí (No), el señor Salas (no) compraba tiques para el metro.

B 1. Sí, muchas calles desembocan en la Plaza San Martín.
2. La calle Ayacucho es angosta.
3. No, no hay un semáforo en la esquina de Ayacucho y Cuzco.

(continued on page 249)

248

C En la ciudad Digan que sí o que no.

1. Frecuentemente el barrio viejo de una ciudad es también una zona histórica.
2. Una zona comercial de una ciudad tiene muchas fábricas.
3. La zona industrial siempre se encuentra en el centro mismo de la ciudad.
4. Un obrero trabaja en una oficina.
5. Hay muchas oficinas en la zona comercial de la ciudad.
6. Un rascacielos es un edificio muy alto que tiene muchos apartamentos u oficinas.
7. Los semáforos se encuentran por lo general en una esquina y ayudan a controlar el tráfico.
8. La gente espera el bus en la boca del metro.
9. Los peatones caminan en la calle.
10. Los peatones pueden cruzar la calle en el cruce de peatones.

La Habana, Cuba

D El transporte en la ciudad Contesten.

1. ¿Qué toman los pasajeros para bajar y subir de una estación de metro?
2. ¿Dónde meten los pasajeros el tique antes de abordar el metro?
3. ¿Dónde esperan los pasajeros el bus?
4. ¿Dónde caminan los peatones?
5. ¿Dónde pueden cruzar la calle los peatones?

Actividades comunicativas

A Una ciudad cercana Trabaja con un(a) compañero(a). Si Uds. viven en una ciudad, conversen juntos y describan su ciudad. Si no viven en una ciudad, hablen de una ciudad que han visitado cerca de donde viven.

B Opiniones Trabaja con un(a) compañero(a). Discutan lo que Uds. consideran las ventajas y las desventajas de la vida en una ciudad. ¿Están Uds. de acuerdo o no? ¿Quién preferiría vivir en la ciudad?

Madrid, España

VOCABULARIO

doscientos cuarenta y nueve **249**

Side teacher column:

CAPÍTULO 9
Vocabulario

C Whenever possible have students correct any false statements in **Práctica C.**

D **Práctica D** can be done first orally with books closed.

Writing Development
After going over **Práctica D**, have students write a short paragraph about urban transportation.

Actividades comunicativas

¡OJO! **Práctica versus Actividades comunicativas**
All activities which provide guided practice are labeled **Práctica.** The more open-ended communicative activities are labeled **Actividades comunicativas.**

A One student in each pair should take notes about the discussion and then report back to the class.

B You may wish to have students doing **Actividad B** share their opinions with the rest of the class.

Learning From Photos
La Habana, Cuba La Habana is the capital of Cuba and one of the oldest cities of the Americas. It was founded in 1514 and named **San Cristóbal de La Habana**. The colonial section of the city is particularly beautiful.
Madrid, España The metro stop is Serrano on the **Calle Serrano**, named after a general who served as Regent in 1869. The Serrano section of Madrid is one of the more elegant parts of the city.

ANSWERS CONTINUED

Práctica

B 4. No, no hay una parada de bus en la plaza.
5. No, no hay muchos coches en la plaza.
6. No, no hay peatones en la acera.

C 1. Sí.   6. Sí.
2. No.   7. Sí.
3. No.   8. No.
4. No.   9. No.
5. Sí.   10. Sí.

D 1. Toman la escalera mecánica.
2. Meten el tique en la ranura del torniquete.
3. Los pasajeros esperan el bus en la parada del bus.
4. Los peatones caminan en la acera.
5. Pueden cruzar la calle en el cruce de peatones.

Actividades comunicativas
A and B Answers will vary.

249

Bell Ringer Review

Use BRR Transparency 9-2, or write the following on the board: Write as many things as you can think of that you would see in a big city.

TEACHING VOCABULARY

A. To present the vocabulary, you may wish to follow some suggestions presented in previous chapters, using Vocabulary Transparencies 9.2 (A & B) and Cassette 6A/Compact Disc 5.

B. Point to the appropriate illustration on the Vocabulary Transparencies and begin by asking yes/no and either/or questions and then progress to more open-ended ones such as: **¿Qué está sembrando el campesino? ¿En qué estación va a cosechar los cereales? ¿Qué animales crían los agricultores?**

C. After presenting the vocabulary orally, have students open their books and read the sentences for additional reinforcement.

250

Vocabulario

PALABRAS 2

En el campo

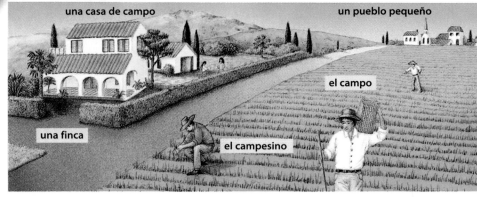

Los campesinos viven en el campo.
Ellos tienen una finca.
Ellos cultivan los campos.

El cultivo de los cereales es muy importante.

El campesino va a sembrar cereales.
No está sembrándolos ahora.
Va a sembrarlos en la primavera.

Y va a cosecharlos en el otoño.

250 〜 *doscientos cincuenta*

CAPÍTULO 9

Pantomime

Begin

___, ven acá, por favor.
Vas a ser campesino(a).
Da de comer a las gallinas.
Ve al campo.
Siembra los cereales.
Ve a la huerta.
Cosecha los vegetales.
Vuelve a tu casa de campo.
Gracias, ___. Bien hecho. Regresa a tu asiento ahora.

VOCABULARY EXPANSION

- **El campo** is both the country or the countryside and a field, **un campo de trigo**, for example.
- The people who work on farms are also called **labradores**.
- **Un pueblo pequeño** can also be called **una aldea**.
- In some parts of South America **el maíz** is called **el choclo**.

el ganado

las vacas

los cerdos

las gallinas

Los agricultores crían animales domésticos.

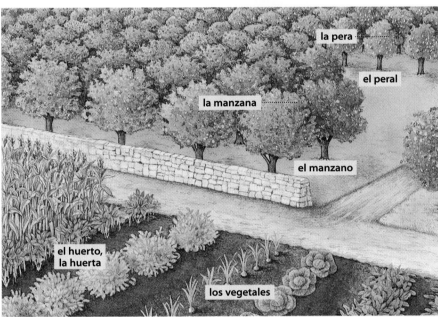

la pera

el peral

la manzana

el manzano

el huerto, la huerta

los vegetales

VOCABULARIO

doscientos cincuenta y uno 251

Learning From Photos

Los campesinos You may wish to ask students the following questions about the photos on pages 250 and 251:

¿Qué llevan en la cabeza el campesino en la foto de abajo en la página 250 y el campesino en la foto en la página 251? (una boina)

¿Qué animal tiene el campesino en la foto?

¿Qué ropa lleva el campesino?

251

✦Práctica✦

A **Práctica A** can be done first orally with books closed. Students can then write the answers for additional reinforcement.

EXPANSION After going over **Práctica A**, have students tell the story about **los Ayala** in their own words.

B **Práctica B** has students review and recall a great deal of previously learned vocabulary.

Learning From Photos

Echalar, España Echalar is a town in northern Spain in the region of Navarra in the province of Pamplona. The provincial capital, Pamplona, is famous for the yearly running of the bulls the week of July 7.

Andalucía, España Andalucía is one of Spain's most important agricultural regions. It is a major producer of olives and olive oil, wheat and other cereals, cotton, sugar cane, citrus fruits, and wine. Seville oranges are used in the world's best marmalades. The olive oils of Andalucía are valued everywhere, as is its unique sherry wine, **el vino de Jerez**.

Have students locate each of the areas shown in the photographs on the map of Spain on page 451 or on the Map Transparency.

✦Práctica✦

A **HISTORIETA** Los Ayala

Contesten según se indica.

1. ¿Dónde viven los Ayala? (en un pueblo pequeño en el campo)
2. ¿Qué tienen ellos? (una finca)
3. ¿Qué hay en la finca? (campos de cereales)
4. ¿Qué siembran los Ayala? (trigo y maíz)
5. ¿Cuándo siembran? (en la primavera)
6. ¿Cuándo es la cosecha? (en el otoño)
7. ¿Qué crían los Ayala en su finca? (animales domésticos)
8. ¿Qué animales tienen? (vacas y cerdos)

Echalar, España

B Ya sabemos mucho. Contesten.

1. ¿Cuáles son todos los vegetales o todas las legumbres que ya conoces en español?
2. ¿Cuáles son las frutas que ya conoces en español?
3. ¿Cuáles son los animales que ya conoces en español?
4. ¿Cuáles son las cuatro estaciones del año?

Andalucía, España

ANSWERS

Práctica

A 1. **Los Ayala viven en un pueblo pequeño en el campo.**
2. **Ellos tienen una finca.**
3. **En la finca hay campos de cereales.**
4. **Los Ayala siembran trigo y maíz.**
5. **Siembran en la primavera.**
6. **La cosecha es en el otoño.**
7. **Los Ayala crían animales domésticos en su finca.**
8. **Tienen vacas y cerdos.**

B Answers will vary.

C. Cosas del campo   Digan que sí o que no.

1. Las vacas nos dan leche.
2. Las gallinas ponen huevos.
3. El tomate es un vegetal.
4. Hay muchas fincas en la ciudad.
5. Los obreros son campesinos.
6. Los campesinos cultivan los campos en una fábrica.
7. El manzano es un árbol y la manzana es la fruta que da el árbol.
8. Una carne que nos da el cerdo es el jamón.
9. Los campesinos viven en una casa de campo.
10. Una huerta produce muchos vegetales.

Actividades comunicativas

A. En el campo   No importa si vives en el campo o no. A casi todos nosotros nos gusta de vez en cuando pasar un día tranquilo en el campo. Trabaja con un(a) compañero(a). Describan un día fabuloso en el campo. Hablen de lo que ven y lo que hacen.

B. Opiniones   Trabaja con un(a) compañero(a). Discutan lo que Uds. consideran las ventajas y las desventajas de la vida en el campo. ¿Están Uds. de acuerdo o no? ¿Quién preferiría vivir en el campo?

Oaxaca, México

Sinaloa, México

C Whenever possible, have students correct the false statements in **Práctica C**.

Actividades comunicativas

¡OJO!   These activities encourage students to use the chapter vocabulary and structures in open-ended situations. It is not necessary to have them do all the activities. Allow students to select the activity or activities they wish to take part in.

A **TECHNOLOGY OPTION**
Students may use the Portfolio feature on the CD-ROM to do this activity.

B   You may wish to have students share their opinions in **Actividad B** with the entire class.

Learning From Photos

Oaxaca, México Oaxaca is in southern Mexico. The villages surrounding Oaxaca are famous for their artisans, whose popular art is prized. Near Oaxaca are two extraordinary pre-Columbian sites, Monte Albán and Mitla.
Sinaloa, México This state is on the northern Mexican Pacific coast. Mazatlán is the major city as well the major seaport. The climate of Sinaloa is varied. Near the coast it is warm and wet most of the year. Nearer the mountains the weather is cooler. Near Sonora it's a semi-desert.

ANSWERS

Práctica

C 1. Sí.   6. No.
2. Sí.   7. Sí.
3. No.   8. Sí.
4. No.   9. Sí.
5. No.   10. Sí.

Actividades comunicativas
A and **B** Answers will vary.

253

RESOURCES

 Workbook, pages 99–102

Student Tape Manual, TE, pages 100–102

Audiocassette 6A/CD5

Quizzes 3–5, pages 42–44

Computer Testmaker

CD-ROM, Disc 3, pages 254–259

Bell Ringer Review

Use BRR Transparency 9-3, or write the following on the board: Rewrite the following in the present perfect.

1. **Los pasajeros abordaron el avión.**
2. **El asistente les dio la bienvenida a bordo.**
3. **El avión salió a tiempo.**
4. **El avión despegó a tiempo.**
5. **Roberto puso su equipaje de mano debajo del asiento.**

TEACHING STRUCTURE

Describing what was going on

A. Have students open their books to page 254. Lead them through Steps 1–3. Model the examples and have students repeat in unison.

B. Write the forms of the verb **estar** on the board in the present, imperfect, and future tenses, or make a transparency with these forms and project it.

C. Add the present participles to the forms of **estar** and have students repeat the now-completed forms of the progressive tenses.

254

Estructura

Describing what was going on
El imperfecto progresivo

1. The imperfect progressive is used to describe an action as it was taking place. It is formed by using the imperfect tense of **estar** and the present participle.

> **El obrero estaba trabajando en la fábrica.**
> **Los muchachos estaban comiendo las frutas del huerto.**

2. Most verbs that have a stem change in the preterite have the same stem change in the present participle.

E → I		O → U	
pedir	pidiendo	dormir	durmiendo
servir	sirviendo	morir	muriendo
repetir	repitiendo		
decir	diciendo		

3. The following verbs have a **y** in the present participle

caer	cayendo	distribuir	distribuyendo
leer	leyendo	construir	construyendo
traer	trayendo	contribuir	contribuyendo
oír	oyendo		

Práctica

A **HISTORIETA** Un día típico en la ciudad

Contesten con **sí.**

1. ¿Estaba circulando mucho tráfico por la ciudad?
2. ¿Estaba dirigiendo el tráfico un policía?
3. ¿Estaban caminando por las aceras muchos peatones?
4. ¿Estaban cruzando las calles?
5. ¿Estaban cruzando las calles en el cruce de peatones?
6. ¿Estaba haciendo cola mucha gente en la parada del bus?
7. ¿Estaba saliendo mucha gente de la boca del metro?
8. ¿Estaba subiendo mucha gente en la escalera mecánica?

Madrid, España

ANSWERS

Práctica

A 1. **Sí, mucho tráfico estaba circulando por la ciudad.**
2. **Sí, un policía estaba dirigiendo el tráfico.**
3. **Sí, muchos peatones estaban caminando por las aceras.**
4. **Sí, estaban cruzando las calles.**
5. **Sí, estaban cruzando las calles en el cruce de peatones.**
6. **Sí, mucha gente estaba haciendo cola en la parada del bus.**

7. **Sí, mucha gente estaba saliendo de la boca del metro.**
8. **Sí, mucha gente estaba subiendo en la escalera mecánica**

B HISTORIETA Durante el vuelo

Contesten según el modelo.

¿Trabajaban durante el vuelo los asistentes de vuelo?

Sí, estaban trabajando durante el vuelo.

1. ¿Servían refrescos los asistentes de vuelo?
2. ¿Servían una comida?
3. ¿Daban anuncios?
4. ¿Leían las reglas de seguridad?
5. ¿Oían música estereofónica los pasajeros?
6. ¿Leían revistas algunos pasajeros?
7. ¿Dormían otros?

C HISTORIETA El túnel nuevo

Completen con el imperfecto progresivo.

Los ingenieros ____ (construir) el túnel nuevo. El público ____1 (esperar) la apertura del túnel. Muchos hombres y mujeres ____2 (trabajar) en su construcción. Este proyecto les ____3 (pagar) un buen salario. Pero algunas personas ____4 (decir) que no era buena idea. Ellos ____5 (pensar) en el impacto ecológico del túnel. Pero nadie ____6 (escuchar) a los ecologistas. El público ____7 (ver) que con el túnel los viajes al centro serían más cortos.8

Actividades comunicativas

A Ayer a las...
Pregúntale a tu compañero(a) lo que estaba haciendo ayer a la hora indicada. Él o ella te contestará. Luego cambien de rol.

8:00 a.m. 5:00 a.m. 6:30 a.m. 6:30 p.m. 10:30 a.m.
3:00 p.m. 8:00 p.m. 12:00 p.m. 11:00 p.m. 4:00 p.m.

B Tienes un problema.
Un(a) compañero(a) va a ser tu padre o tu madre. Está muy enfadado(a) (angry) porque tú volviste a casa muy tarde anoche. Él o ella tiene muchas preguntas para ti. Tienes que decirle todo lo que estabas haciendo para explicar por qué no podías volver a casa más temprano. Luego cambien de rol.

Práctica

A **Práctica A** can be done first orally while books are closed.

B **Práctica B** can be done as a paired activity. One student asks the question and the other student answers.

C You may wish to have students prepare **Práctica C** before going over it in class.

Writing Development
After going over **Práctica C**, have students write it in paragraph form.

For the Native Speaker
Más práctica Ask your students to do **Práctica A** and **Práctica B**, changing the verbs in the **imperfecto progresivo** to the **futuro progresivo** and the **condicional progresivo**: ¿Estará circulando... ? ¿Estaría circulando... ?

Actividades comunicativas
A Encourage students to use all of the cues in the colored boxes.

B **EXPANSION** Students could prepare funny skits based on **Actividad B** and present them to the class.

ANSWERS

Práctica

B 1. Sí, estaban sirviendo refrescos.
2. Sí, estaban sirviendo una comida.
3. Sí, estaban dando anuncios.
4. Sí, estaban leyendo las reglas de seguridad.
5. Sí, los pasajeros estaban oyendo música estereofónica.
6. Sí, algunos pasajeros estaban leyendo revistas.
7. Sí, otros estaban durmiendo.

C 1. estaban construyendo
2. estaba esperando
3. estaban trabajando
4. estaba pagando
5. estaban diciendo
6. estaban pensando
7. estaba escuchando
8. estaba viendo

Actividades comunicativas
A and B Answers will vary.

255

TEACHING STRUCTURE

 Referring to things already mentioned

A. Ask students to open their books to page 256. Lead them through Steps 1–2.

B. Students should realize that the pronouns are often attached to the participle. For productive purposes, however, they need only place them before the auxiliary.

Práctica

A and **B**   It is recommended that **Práctica A** and **Práctica B** be done with books open. You may wish to have students prepare these activities before going over them in class.

Referring to things already mentioned
Colocación de los pronombres de complemento

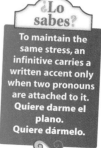

1. When the object pronouns are used with the present participle, they may precede the helping verb or they may be attached to the participle.

> Estaban comiendo **el maíz**.   **Me** estaba mostrando **la finca**.
> **Lo** estaban comiendo.   **Me la** estaba mostrando.
> Estaban comiéndo**lo**.   Estaba mostrándome**la**.

2. When the object pronouns are used with the infinitive, they may precede the helping verb that accompanies the infinitive or they may be attached to the infinitive.

> Voy a cruzar **la calle**.   Voy a dar **el plano** a José.
> **La** voy a cruzar.   **Se lo** voy a dar.
> Voy a cruzar**la**.   Voy a dárse**lo**.

Práctica

 **A HISTORIETA En la finca**

Contesten según el modelo.

> **¿Estaba mostrándote la finca el señor?**
> **Sí, estaba mostrándomela.**
> **Sí, me la estaba mostrando.**

1. ¿Estaba mostrándote la casa de campo el señor?
2. ¿Te estaba describiendo la casa?
3. ¿Estabas admirando la casa?
4. ¿Estabas mirando a los campesinos en la finca?
5. ¿Estaban ellos sembrando los campos?
6. ¿Estaban criando los animales también?

B Buena higiene   Sigan el modelo.

> **Me voy a lavar el pelo.**
> **Voy a lavármelo.**

1. Me voy a lavar *el pelo*.
2. Quiero comprarme *el nuevo champú* en la farmacia.
3. No puedo recordar *el nombre del champú*.
4. El farmacéutico podrá darme *el nombre*.
5. Tengo que lavarme *el pelo* esta noche.

ANSWERS

Práctica

A 1. Sí, estaba mostrándomela. Sí, me la estaba mostrando.
2. Sí, estaba describiéndomela. Sí, me la estaba describiendo.
3. Sí, estaba admirándola. Sí, la estaba admirando.
4. Sí, estaba mirándolos en la finca. Sí, los estaba mirando en la finca.
5. Sí, estaban sembrándolos. Sí, los estaban sembrando.
6. Sí, estaban criándolos también. Sí, los estaban criando también.

B 1. Voy a lavármelo.
2. Quiero comprármelo en la farmacia.
3. No puedo recordarlo.
4. El farmacéutico podrá dármelo.
5. Tengo que lavármelo esta noche.

(PAGE 257)

C 1. Sí (No), Marisol (no) quiere verla. Sí (No), Marisol (no) la quiere ver.
2. Sí, (No, no) va a verla. Sí, (No, no) la va a ver.
3. Sí, (No, no) las está comprando ahora. Sí, (No, no) está comprándolas ahora.
4. Sí, (No, no) las está comprando en la taquilla del cine. Sí, (No, no) está comprándolas en la taquilla del cine.

C HISTORIETA En el cine

Contesten con pronombres.

1. ¿Quiere ver la película Marisol?
2. ¿Va a ver la película?
3. ¿Está comprando las entradas ahora?
4. ¿Está comprando las entradas en la taquilla del cine?
5. ¿Quiere Marisol sentarse en la primera fila?
6. ¿Quiere ver la película desde la primera fila?
7. Desde la primera fila, ¿puede ver la película bien?

D ¿Acabas de hacerlo? Contesten según el modelo.

¿Acabas de hacer el crucigrama o vas a hacer el crucigrama?

Acabo de hacerlo.

¿Te acuerdas?

Acabar de means *to have just.*

Acabo de llegar.
I have just arrived.

1. ¿Acabas de leer el periódico o vas a leer el periódico?
2. ¿Acabas de escribir la carta o vas a escribir la carta?
3. ¿Acabas de tomar el examen o vas a tomar el examen?
4. ¿Acabas de hacer tus tareas o vas a hacer tus tareas?
5. ¿Acabas de llamar a tu amigo o vas a llamar a tu amigo?

E HISTORIETA Una carta

Contesten según se indica.

1. ¿Está escribiendo la carta Elena? (no)
2. ¿Cuándo va a escribírtela? (mañana)
3. ¿Está comprando los sellos ahora? (no)
4. ¿Ya los ha comprado? (sí)
5. ¿Cuándo va a enviarte la carta? (mañana)
6. ¿La vas a abrir enseguida? (sí)
7. ¿Cómo vas a leerla? (con mucho interés)
8. ¿La vas a contestar enseguida? (sí)
9. ¿Vas a enviarle la carta enseguida? (sí)

C **Práctica C** can be done orally with books closed.

D Have students present **Práctica D** as a series of mini-conversations.

E **Práctica E** can be done first orally with books closed.

257

258

Bell Ringer Review

Use BRR Transparency 9-4, or write the following on the board: Write answers to the following questions.

1. **¿Tu amigo(a) te espera en la parada del autobús?**
2. **¿Cuándo te esperan tus amigos?**
3. **¿La escalera mecánica te lleva de un piso al otro en la tienda?**
4. **¿Los agricultores te venden sus productos?**

TEACHING STRUCTURE

Pointing out people or things

A. Use a boy, a girl, a book, and a magazine to illustrate the meaning of **este, ese, aquel.** Have the boy stand near you as you say **este muchacho.** Have him stand near another student as you say **ese muchacho.** Have the boy stand in the back of the room away from everyone as you say **aquel muchacho.** Do the same with a girl, a book, and a magazine. Explain to students that the forms used for the demonstrative pronouns are the same as those used for the demonstrative adjectives.

B. Then have students open their books and read the explanation in Steps 1–3 aloud.

C. Write the forms of the demonstrative adjectives and pronouns on the board.

D. Have students read all the model sentences aloud.

Pointing out people or things
Adjetivos y pronombres demostrativos

1. You use the demonstrative adjectives *this, that, these,* and *those* to point out people or things. In Spanish, the demonstrative adjective, like all adjectives, agrees with the noun it modifies.

2. All forms of **este** indicate someone or something close to the speaker. They mean *this* or *these* in English.

   Este boleto que tengo aquí es para el metro.

   All forms of **ese** indicate someone or something close to the person being spoken to.

   Ese boleto que tú tienes allí es para el bus.

All forms of **aquel** indicate someone or something away from both the speaker and the listener. The forms of both **ese** and **aquel** mean **that, those** in English.

   Aquellos boletos en aquella mesa allá no son usados.

Note that the adverbs **aquí, allí,** and **allá** indicate relative position— *here, there, over there.*

3. The forms used for the demonstrative pronouns—*this one, that one, these, those*—are the same as those used for demonstrative adjectives.

   No me gusta este (aquí).
   Pero aquellos (allá), sí, me gustan.

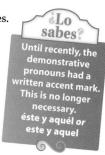
¿Lo sabes?
Until recently, the demonstrative pronouns had a written accent mark. This is no longer necessary. **éste y aquél** *or* **este y aquel**

ABOUT THE SPANISH LANGUAGE

◆ The **Real Academia** has ruled that it is no longer necessary to put a written accent on the demonstrative pronoun. It is only required when there would be ambiguity.

◆ Just as it was recently decided that the accent mark is no longer required with the demonstrative pronouns, so too was another important decision made in 1994 to no longer consider the **ch** and the **ll** as separate letters of the Spanish alphabet.

ANSWERS

Práctica (PAGE 259)

A 1. **¿Qué precio tienen los guantes? ¿Cuáles? ¿Estos guantes aquí? No, aquellos guantes en el escaparate.**
   2. **¿Que precio tiene la falda? ¿Cuál? ¿Esta falda aquí? No, aquella falda en el escaparate.**
   3. **¿Qué precio tiene el suéter? ¿Cuál? ¿Este suéter aquí? No, aquel suéter en el escaparate.**

(continued on page 259)

Práctica

A ¿Qué precio tienen? Sigan el modelo.

> el abrigo
> **¿Qué precio tiene el abrigo?**
> **¿Cuál? ¿Este abrigo aquí?**
> **No, aquel abrigo en el escaparate.**

1. los guantes
2. la falda
3. el suéter
4. las corbatas
5. el cinturón
6. los pantalones
7. la blusa
8. los calcetines
9. la chaqueta

Buenos Aires, Argentina

B El plano que tú tienes Completen con **este, ese** o **aquel**.

1. _____ plano de la ciudad que tú estás mirando es bueno pero _____ que tiene Felipe es malo. No sirve para nada.
2. _____ calle aquí es una calle peatonal pero _____ allá no es sólo para peatones. Y tiene mucho tráfico.
3. _____ estación de metro aquí en el centro de la ciudad es mucho más grande que _____ estación en las afueras.
4. _____ edificios aquí en el centro mismo de la ciudad son muy altos. _____ que están más lejos en las afueras no son tan altos.
5. _____ novela que yo estoy leyendo tiene lugar aquí en _____ ciudad. Pero _____ novela que tiene Pedro, no la conozco. No sé dónde tiene lugar.
6. En _____ esquina aquí no hay semáforo pero _____, donde está Felipe, tiene semáforo.

Actividades comunicativas

A Preferencias Trabaja con un(a) compañero(a). Miren esta foto de un escaparate de una tienda de ropa en Caracas. Discutan lo que a cada uno(a) de Uds. le gusta y no le gusta. Luego comparen sus preferencias.

JUEGO ¿Cuál? Trabaja con un(a) compañero(a). Haz una frase usando **este, ese** o **aquel**. Tu compañero(a) te dirá si hablas de algo **aquí, allí** o **allá**. Luego cambien de rol.

Caracas, Venezuela

ESTRUCTURA

Práctica

A Have students present **Práctica A** as a mini-conversation.

B The information in each sentence of **Práctica B** allows students to determine which demonstrative must be used. Have students prepare **Práctica B** before going over it in class.

Actividades comunicativas

JUEGO This is a good end-of-class activity.

Learning From Realia

Un plano callejero You may wish to ask students the following questions about the city map:
¿Qué es esto?
¿Quiénes necesitan un plano callejero?
¿Qué más tiene el plano?

¡OJO! All new material in the chapter has been presented. The sections that follow recombine and reintroduce the vocabulary and structures that have already been introduced.

259

🔔 Bell Ringer Review

Use BRR Transparency 9-5, or write the following on the board: Where would you find the following things, **¿en la ciudad o en el campo?**
1. **el huerto**
2. **las gallinas**
3. **la fábrica**
4. **la finca**

TEACHING THE CONVERSATION

A. Have two students with good pronunciation read the conversation to the class. One can take the part of Lupe, the other the part of Mónica or you can change the name(s) to boys' names.

B. 🎧 Have students listen to the recording on Cassette 6A/Compact Disc 5 once.

C. Call on individuals to read parts of the conversation aloud.

D. After a student reads you can intersperse some questions. You can make up questions or use those that are in the **Después de conversar** section.

E. After presenting the conversation in class, have students write answers to the **Después de conversar** questions for homework.

TECHNOLOGY OPTION

◉ On the CD-ROM (Disc 3, page 260), students can watch a dramatization of this conversation. They can then play the role of either one of the characters, and record themselves in the conversation.

Conversación

El campo y la ciudad

LUPE: ¿Te gusta vivir en el campo? ¿Qué haces? ¿No es aburrido?

MÓNICA: De ninguna manera. El otro día estaba hablando con mi amigo Miguel. Estaba diciéndole todo lo que podemos hacer aquí en este pueblo.

LUPE: Pero en la ciudad tenemos cines, museos. Tenemos de todo. Y puedes tomar el bus o el metro para ir de un lugar a otro. Todo es tan conveniente.

MÓNICA: Sí, pero aquí no tienes que esperar el semáforo para cruzar la calle. ¿Y sabes lo que es el automóvil? Tenemos uno y podemos usarlo sin pasar horas en el tráfico.

LUPE: Sí, lo sé. Pero yo nunca viviría en el campo.

MÓNICA: Y yo nunca viviría en la ciudad. No me gustaría vivir sin aire puro y mucho espacio. Voy a pasear a caballo. ¿Quieres acompañarme?

LUPE: ¿A caballo?

Después de conversar

Contesten.

1. ¿Qué le pregunta Lupe a Mónica?
2. ¿Con quién estaba hablando Mónica el otro día?
3. ¿Cree Mónica que el campo es aburrido?
4. ¿Por qué prefiere Lupe la ciudad?
5. ¿Por qué dice ella que todo es tan conveniente?
6. Según Mónica, ¿hay mucho tráfico en el campo?
7. ¿Quién no viviría nunca en el campo? ¿Por qué no?
8. ¿Qué va a hacer Mónica?
9. ¿Qué crees? ¿La va a acompañar Lupe?

260 〰 *doscientos sesenta*

ANSWERS

Después de conversar

1. Lupe le pregunta a Mónica si le gusta vivir en el campo.
2. Mónica estaba hablando con su amigo Miguel el otro día.
3. Mónica cree que el campo no es aburrido.
4. Lupe prefiere la ciudad porque todo es tan conveniente.
5. Dice que todo es tan conveniente porque en la ciudad puedes tomar el bus o el metro para ir de un lugar a otro.
6. No, según Mónica, no hay mucho tráfico en el campo.
7. Lupe nunca viviría en el campo porque prefiere la ciudad y cree que el campo es aburrido.
8. Mónica va a pasear a caballo.
9. Sí (No), Lupe (no) la va a acompañar.

Actividades comunicativas

A **Donde quiere vivir** Trabaja con un(a) compañero(a). Discutan si preferirían vivir en la ciudad o en el campo. Den sus razones.

El Alcázar, Segovia, España

Palacio de Bellas Artes, Ciudad de México

B **Explica por qué.** Trabaja con un(a) compañero(a). Él o ella te preguntará por qué no hiciste algo ayer. Explica que no lo hiciste ayer porque estabas haciendo otra cosa. Dile lo que estabas haciendo. Luego cambien de rol. Pueden usar el modelo como guía.

¿Por qué no me llamaste ayer?
No te llamé porque estaba leyendo un libro interesante.

CONVERSACIÓN

doscientos sesenta y uno 261

Actividades comunicativas

A With more able groups you can have students prepare a debate on the topic in **Actividad A**.

B **TECHNOLOGY OPTION** In the CD-ROM version of this activity (Disc 3, page 261), students can interact with an on-screen native speaker and record their voices.

Learning From Photos

El Alcázar, Segovia, España This storybook castle looks like a huge ship rising atop an 80 meter (262 ft.)-high rock. It was built during the time of **El Cid** by King Alfonso VI. You may wish to ask students these questions about the photo:
¿Qué animales hay en la foto?
¿Qué es el hombre?
¿Qué hace el perro?
Palacio de Bellas Artes, Ciudad de México Construction on the Palacio de Bellas Artes began in 1904 during the dictatorship of Porfirio Díaz. Work was interrupted by the revolution and was not resumed until 1932. In the building there are works by most of the great Mexican muralists: Rivera, Orozco, Siqueiros, and Tamayo. It is considered one of the world's great theaters.

ANSWERS

Actividades comunicativas
A and B Answers will vary.

261

National Standards

Cultures
The reading about Buenos Aires on pages 262–263 and the related activity on page 263 familiarize students with life in a vibrant Latin American city.

Comparisons
Students learn that, as in many cities in the United States, urban poverty is a persistent problem in Latin America.

TEACHING THE READING

Pre-reading

Before reading the **Lectura**, have students look at the photographs on these pages. Also have them scan the book quickly and look at all the photographs of Buenos Aires and Argentina. You might also wish to have them locate Buenos Aires on the map of South America on page 452 or on the Map Transparency.

Reading

A. Call on a student to read three or four sentences aloud. Then stop and ask other members of the class questions about the material that was just read.
(continued on page 263)

262

Lecturas CULTURALES

BUENOS AIRES, ARGENTINA

Buenos Aires, la capital de la Argentina, es una ciudad muy bonita. Se dice que esta ciudad es la más europea de todas las ciudades de Latinoamérica.

Recientemente Sandra Connors, una americana, estaba visitando a Buenos Aires. Un día, mientras estaba caminando por el centro de la ciudad, les dijo a algunos conocidos porteños[1] que no sabía si estaba en Buenos Aires, Londres o Madrid.

La calle Florida es una calle peatonal en la zona comercial de la ciudad. En esta calle no permiten carros. Si te gusta ir de compras tienes que caminar por esta calle con sus cientos de tiendas.

La avenida más ancha del mundo es la Avenida 9 de Julio. Aquí puedes sentarte en una confitería[2] y mirar a la gente que pasa. Si tienes hambre, puedes ir a uno de los carritos de la Costanera norte. Los verdaderos carritos del pasado se han transformado en una fila de restaurantes al borde del río de la Plata. Aquí sirven el delicioso bife argentino.

[1]porteños *inhabitants of Buenos Aires*
[2]confitería *café, tea room*

Calle Florida y Avenida Córdoba

Avenida 9 de Julio, Buenos Aires

ABOUT THE SPANISH LANGUAGE

In Argentina the slum communities of the poor mentioned in the **Lectura** are called **villas miseria.** In other countries they have other names: in Peru, **pueblos jóvenes;** in Chile, **callampas**; and in Brazil, **favelas.**

El bife argentino viene del ganado que cuidan los gauchos en las pampas argentinas. Muchos porteños ricos tienen estancias en las pampas. Una estancia es una finca grande donde crían ganado. Los ricos van a su estancia para divertirse en sus lujosas casas de campo.

Es imposible hablar de las ciudades de Latinoamérica sin mencionar el problema de los pobres que vienen a las ciudades desde el campo en busca de trabajo. Estos pobres viven en chabolas que se encuentran principalmente en las afueras. En Buenos Aires se llaman «villas miseria».

Una estancia, Argentina

Un gaucho en las pampas argentinas

Una villa miseria, Buenos Aires

Después de leer

 A **Buenos Aires** Identifiquen y describan.

1. la calle Florida
2. la Avenida 9 de Julio
3. los carritos de la Costanera norte
4. las pampas
5. una estancia
6. una «villa miseria»

LECTURAS CULTURALES

doscientos sesenta y tres ∾ **263**

B. If students have any trouble understanding the information about the **carritos**, explain the following to them. The Costanera norte is a street that runs along the Río de la Plata. Until recently there were many little carts where meats were grilled and people would come to feast. Slowly but surely, these little carts have given way to a whole series of barbecue restaurants that line the shore of the Río de la Plata. It is still a very popular family eating area.

C. Have students read the selection at home and write the answers to the **Después de leer** activity that accompanies the **Lectura**.

Post-reading

A. Go over the **Después de leer** activity in class the next day.

B. Call on a student to give a summary of the reading in his or her own words. If necessary, ask five or six questions to review the salient points of the reading selection in order to enable him or her to do this more easily. After the oral summary, the more able students can write a synopsis of the **Lectura** in their own words.

TECHNOLOGY OPTION

Students may listen to a recorded version of the **Lectura** on the CD-ROM, Disc 3, pages 262–263.

ANSWERS

Después de leer

A 1. **La Calle Florida es una calle peatonal en la zona comercial de la ciudad. Tiene cientos de tiendas.**

2. **La Avenida 9 de Julio es la avenida más ancha del mundo.**

3. **Los carritos de la Costanera norte se han transformado en una fila de restaurantes al borde del Río de la Plata.**

4. **Los gauchos crían ganado en las pampas y muchos porteños ricos tienen estancias allí.**

5. **Una estancia es una finca grande donde crían ganado.**

6. **Una «villa miseria» es un lugar en las afueras de la ciudad dónde viven en chabolas los pobres que vienen a las ciudades en busca de trabajo.**

Independent Practice

Assign any of the following:
1. **Después de leer** activity, page 263
2. Workbook, pages 103–105
3. CD-ROM, Disc 3, pages 262–263

LECTURA OPCIONAL 1

National Standards

Cultures

This reading about Lima and its surroundings, and the related activity on page 264, familiarize students with another important city in Latin America.

TEACHING TIPS

¡OJO! This reading is optional. You may skip it completely, have the entire class read it, have only several students read it, or assign it for extra credit.

A. Have students who are going to read the **Lectura** on Lima peruse the book and look at all the photographs of Lima or Peru that appear in it. You may also wish to have them find Lima on the map of South America on page 452 or on the Map Transparency.

RECYCLING

Have students give any information they remember about Peru. Some may have read the selections on Machu Picchu or the Nazca lines in **¡Buen viaje! Level 1.**

Did You Know?

La garúa **La garúa** is a curious weather phenomenon affecting Lima. The cold Peru current offshore helps maintain the stability of the atmosphere, but it gives rise to frequent fogs. During the months of June, July, and August, Lima's winter, the mist is constant. This constant fog is called **la garúa.**

264

Plaza de Armas, Lima

LIMA, PERÚ

Lima, la capital del Perú, es una ciudad muy hermosa. En el centro mismo de la ciudad hay un gran barrio histórico. Muchos de los edificios de este barrio datan de la época colonial.

Hay dos plazas importantes en el centro de Lima—la Plaza de Armas y la Plaza San Martín. El famoso Jirón de la Unión enlaza[1] estas dos plazas. El Jirón de la Unión es una calle peatonal con muchas tiendas y centros o galerías comerciales. Hoy día hay también muchos vendedores ambulantes. Estos vendedores ambulantes han venido a la capital de los pueblos pequeños del altiplano.

En los alrededores de Lima cerca de las playas del Pacífico hay muchas zonas residenciales muy bonitas. En las calles bordeadas de palmas hay edificios altos con apartamentos y condominios. Hay también casas lujosas[2].

Una vez más, es imposible hablar de las ciudades de Latinoamérica sin mencionar el problema de los pobres que vienen a las ciudades desde el campo en busca de trabajo. Como hemos aprendido, los barrios pobres donde viven se llaman «villas miseria» en Buenos Aires. En el Perú se llaman «pueblos jóvenes».

[1]enlaza *joins*
[2]lujosas *luxurious*

Después de leer

Jirón de la Unión, Lima

A **Lima** Contesten.

1. ¿Cuál es la capital del Perú?
2. ¿Cómo es el centro de Lima?
3. ¿De qué época datan muchos de los edificios?
4. ¿Cuáles son dos plazas importantes en el centro de Lima?
5. ¿Qué calle enlaza estas dos plazas?
6. ¿Qué es el Jirón de la Unión?
7. ¿Quiénes son los vendedores ambulantes?
8. ¿Qué hay en los alrededores de Lima?
9. ¿Por qué van los campesinos a la ciudad?
10. ¿Qué es un «pueblo joven»?

ANSWERS

Después de leer

A 1. La capital del Perú es Lima.
2. Hay un gran barrio histórico en el centro de Lima.
3. Muchos de los edificios datan de la época colonial.
4. Dos plazas importantes en el centro de Lima son la Plaza de Armas y la Plaza San Martín.
5. El Jirón de la Unión enlaza estas dos plazas.
6. El Jirón de la Unión es una calle peatonal con muchas tiendas y centros o galerías comerciales.
7. Los vendedores ambulantes han venido a la capital de los pueblos pequeños del altiplano.
8. En los alrededores de Lima hay muchas zonas residenciales muy bonitas.
9. Los campesinos van a la ciudad en busca de trabajo.
10. Un «pueblo joven» es una «villa miseria»—un lugar en las afueras de la ciudad donde viven los pobres.

264

Plaza Central, Santa Fe

UNA CIUDAD NORTEAMERICANA CON PROFUNDAS RAÍCES HISPANAS

Santa Fe, la capital de Nuevo México, está al pie de las montañas Sangre de Cristo. Esta ciudad fue fundada[1] por los españoles en 1609 sobre unas ruinas indígenas prehistóricas. Durante doscientos años Santa Fe fue un centro para el comercio entre los españoles y varios grupos indígenas. En 1680 los indios pueblos se levantaron contra los españoles. Querían echarlos[2] de Santa Fe y así hicieron. Pero doce años después, los españoles, bajo Diego de Vargas, volvieron a Santa Fe y restablecieron su dominio.

Si abres la guía telefónica o simplemente miras los nombres en las casas, verás que la influencia hispana todavía vive en Santa Fe. Sigue existiendo no solamente en los museos sino en carne y hueso. Las familias hispanas predominan en esta ciudad que es la capital más antigua de todos los Estados Unidos.

[1]fundada *founded*
[2]echarlos *throw them out*

Después de leer

A La geografía Busquen en un mapa dónde está la ciudad de Santa Fe y dónde están las montañas Sangre de Cristo.

B Santa Fe Contesten.

1. ¿Qué edad tiene Santa Fe?
2. Antes de la fundación de Santa Fe, ¿qué había en el mismo sitio?
3. ¿Para qué servía la ciudad durante dos siglos?
4. ¿Qué hicieron los indios pueblos en 1680?
5. ¿Qué hicieron los españoles en 1692?

Calle comercial, Santa Fe

C El significado En tus propias palabras, explica lo que dice el último párrafo de la lectura.

LECTURAS OPCIONALES · *doscientos sesenta y cinco* · **265**

National Standards

Cultures
This reading and the related activities on page 265 familiarize students with the Hispanic heritage of Santa Fe, New Mexico.

TEACHING TIPS

¡OJO! This reading is optional. You may skip it completely, have the entire class read it, have only several students read it, or assign it for extra credit.

Learning From Photos

Plaza Central, Santa Fe y Calle comercial, Santa Fe The city of Santa Fe is on the old Camino Real, the Royal Road that led from Mexico City to Spain's northern settlements in the American Southwest.

ANSWERS

Después de leer

B 1. Santa Fe tiene casi cuatrocientos años. (Fue fundada en 1609.)
2. Había unas ruinas indígenas prehistóricas en el mismo sitio.
3. Durante dos siglos la ciudad fue un centro para el comercio entre los españoles y varios grupos indígenas.
4. En 1680 los indios pueblos se levantaron contra los españoles. Los echaron de Santa Fe.

5. En 1692 los españoles volvieron a Santa Fe y restablecieron su dominio.

C Answers will vary but may include:
La influencia hispana todavía vive en Santa Fe, no solamente en los museos pero también con las familias hispanas que predominan en Santa Fe.

¡OJO! The readings in the **Conexiones** section are optional. They focus on some of the major disciplines taught in schools and universities. The vocabulary is useful for discussing such topics as history, literature, art, economics, business, science, etc.

You may choose any of the following ways to do this reading on demographics with your students.

Independent reading Have students read the selections and do the post-reading activities as homework, which you collect. This option is least intrusive on class time and requires a minimum of teacher involvement.

Homework with in-class follow-up Assign the readings and post-reading activities as homework. Review and discuss the material in class the next day.

Intensive in-class activity This option includes a pre-reading vocabulary presentation, in-class reading and discussion, assignment of the activities for homework, and a discussion of the assignment in class the following day.

Conexiones

LAS CIENCIAS SOCIALES

LA DEMOGRAFÍA

Demography is the study of human populations, of their distribution, density, and vital statistics. Demographics explain where people choose to live and why. They also explain population shifts—why people move around.

The demography of Latin America is particularly interesting. You will see some marked contrasts between the demographics of the two Americas.

La demografía de Latinoamérica

La demografía es el estudio de las poblaciones humanas. El demógrafo nos explica dónde decide vivir la gente y por qué decide vivir allí. Nos explica también cuándo y por qué la gente decide mudarse para establecerse en otro lugar. Es decir que el demógrafo explica las razones por la migración.

Algunas estadísticas

Si contrastamos las poblaciones de Latinoamérica y los Estados Unidos, lo primero que notamos es que Latinoamérica tiene una población mucho más numerosa. Durante muchos años Nueva York y Los Ángeles fueron las dos ciudades más grandes de las Américas. Ya no.

Lima, Perú

Nueva York	15.000.000	México D.F.	27.000.000
Los Ángeles	10.000.000	São Paulo, Brasil	25.000.000

Bogotá, Colombia

Learning From Photos

Lima, Perú You may wish to ask students the following questions about the photo: **¿Hay muchos peatones en la calle? ¿Hay tiendas en la calle? ¿Es una calle muy ancha? ¿Está la calle en la zona residencial de la ciudad? ¿En qué zona está?**
Bogotá, Colombia Ask students the following questions about the photo: **¿Es una foto de qué zona de la ciudad? ¿Hay rascacielos en la foto? ¿Hay muchas fábricas en esta zona de la ciudad? Y detrás de la ciudad, ¿qué ves?**

Patrones migratorios

En las últimas décadas los centros urbanos de Latinoamérica han crecido dramáticamente. Los campesinos se han ido del campo a la ciudad en busca de trabajo y mejores condiciones de vida. En muchos casos ellos no han encontrado mejor vida, sino miseria. Las ciudades no pueden acomodar a todos los que allí buscan mejor vida. No hay bastante trabajo. Y no hay viviendas adecuadas. Los pobres tienen que vivir en barrios sin agua corriente ni electricidad.

La edad

Otra estadística significativa es la de la edad de las poblaciones de las Américas. Latinoamérica es una región de jóvenes, mientras que los Estados Unidos es un país de envejecientes. Como ejemplo, vamos a comparar a México con los Estados Unidos.

	% menos de 5 años	% 5 a 14 años	% más de 65 años
EE.UU.	7.5	14.1	12.4
México	13.8	25.1	4.1

Después de leer

A **¿Cuál es la palabra?** Busquen la palabra cuya definición sigue.

1. el acto de trasladarse para establecerse en otro lugar
2. personas que se están poniendo viejos
3. el estudio de las poblaciones humanas
4. casas, residencias donde la gente vive
5. zona o parte de una ciudad

B **La demografía** Digan que sí o que no.

1. El demógrafo nos enseña dónde vive la gente y por qué decide vivir allí.
2. Las ciudades de los Estados Unidos son más grandes que las ciudades de Latinoamérica.
3. Las ciudades latinoamericanas siempre han sido más grandes que las ciudades de los Estados Unidos.
4. Los campesinos que se establecen en las ciudades de Latinoamérica siempre encuentran mejor vida.
5. No hay bastante trabajo para todos en el campo y no hay bastante trabajo en las ciudades.
6. Hay más viejos o ancianos en Latinoamérica que en los Estados Unidos.
7. La población latinoamericana es más vieja (mayor) que la población estadounidense.

LAS CIENCIAS SOCIALES

LA DEMOGRAFÍA

¡OJO! Even if you don't have students read this section in depth, you may have them scan it quickly or tell them some of the most important information. Many of the problems facing some Latin American nations are due to demographic changes.

A. Have students read the introduction in English on page 266.
B. Now have them read the selection quickly.
C. Suggest to students that they look for cognates and attempt to guess the meaning from context.
D. Now do the **Después de leer** activities on this page.

Después de leer

B After going over this activity have students correct the false statements.

ANSWERS

Después de leer

A 1. **la migración**
2. **envejecientes**
3. **la demografía**
4. **viviendas**
5. **barrio**

B 1 **Sí.**
2. **No.**
3. **No.**
4. **No.**
5. **Sí.**
6. **No.**
7. **No.**

267

Culminación

Actividades orales

¡OJO!   Encourage students to say as much as possible when they do these activities. Tell them not to be afraid of making mistakes since the goal of the activities is real-life communication. If someone in the group makes an error, allow the others to politely correct him or her.

Let students choose the activities they would like to participate in.

C   TECHNOLOGY OPTION
Students can use the Portfolio feature on the CD-ROM to do this activity.

Student Portfolio

Have students keep a notebook containing their best written work from each chapter. These selected writings can be based on assignments from the Student Textbook and the Writing Activities Workbook. The activities on page 269 are examples of writing assignments that may be included in each student's portfolio.

In the Workbook, students will develop an organized autobiography (**Mi autobiografía**). These workbook pages may also become a part of their portfolio. See the Teacher's Manual for more information on the Student Portfolio.

268

Actividades orales

A   La ciudad   Con un(a) compañero(a), miren esta foto de la ciudad de Madrid. Hablen juntos y describan todo lo que ven en la foto. Luego decidan si es una ciudad que les gustaría visitar.

Puerta del Sol

B   Transporte público   Tu compañero(a) es un(a) joven ecuatoriano(a) que está visitando tu pueblo o ciudad. Quiere saber algo sobre los medios de transporte público. Si no hay transporte público donde vives, describe los medios de transporte en una ciudad cercana.

C   Una ciudad hispana   Tú ya conoces muchas ciudades hispanas. Selecciona una que a ti te gusta y descríbela a un(a) compañero(a). Luego tu compañero(a) te describirá una ciudad que a él o a ella le gusta.

JUEGO   ¿Hablas de la ciudad o del campo?   Trabaja con un(a) compañero(a). Haz una frase que describe algún aspecto de la ciudad o del campo. Tu compañero(a) te dirá de qué hablas—ciudad o campo. Luego cambien de rol.

268 ❧ *doscientos sesenta y ocho*

ANSWERS

Actividades orales
A, B, and C   Answers will vary.

Learning From Photos

Puerta del Sol   The Puerta del Sol is the heart of Madrid. On the left of the photo is the Calle Mayor leading down to the Plaza Mayor. On the right is the Calle Arenal that goes to the Plaza de la Ópera. In the building between the two is **La Mallorquina,** a venerable establishment where **madrileños** have been buying their cakes and sweets for over a century.

Actividad escrita

A **Yo nunca viviría en...** Vas a escribir una composición titulada «Yo nunca viviría en... ». Tienes que completar el título con **la ciudad** o **el campo.**

Writing Strategy

Comparing and contrasting

Comparing and contrasting involves writing about similarities and differences between two or more related things. A Venn diagram will help you do this. First draw two intersecting circles; title the circles with the subject to be compared. List unique features of each subject. Then list the similarities of the two subjects in the area where the circles intersect. This tool, or any other similar one you can think of, will help you organize your thoughts so you can clearly and effectively write your comparison.

Dos ciudades

Think of two cities you have visited. Write a paper, comparing the two places. If you are not familiar with two different cities, compare the town where you live with a nearby city or other town. Be sure to organize your thoughts with a list or a graphic, showing the similarities and differences.

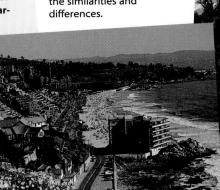

Viña del Mar

Santiago

CULMINACIÓN

Actividad escrita

A Encourage students to have fun with this activity and give as many reasons as possible why they would never live in either the city or the country.

Writing Strategy

Comparing and contrasting

A. Have students read the Writing Strategy on page 269.
B. Have students read aloud their papers, displaying their Venn Diagrams to the class as they do so. They can compare and contrast the cities or towns they wrote about with those that other students wrote about.

TEACHER TIP

You may wish to work with the class in preparing their graphic. It can be done as a group effort.

Learning From Photos

Santiago The photo of Santiago de Chile shows the **Cerro de Santa Lucía.** It was here that Pedro de Valdivia and his 150 men first encamped and he decided to found the city. He named the hill after the saint on whose day he reached it. Today on the hill you will find a baroque maze of fountains, pathways, and gardens.
Viña del Mar Viña del Mar is a lovely resort city on the coast of Chile, not far from Santiago. Its beautiful beaches attract many summer visitors.

ANSWERS

Actividad escrita
A Answers will vary.

Writing Strategy
Answers will vary.

269

VOCABULARY REVIEW

The words and phrases in the **Vocabulario** have been taught for productive use in this chapter. They are summarized here as a resource for both students and teacher. This list also serves as a convenient resource for the **Culminación** activities on pages 268 and 269. Have the students look at the list. If there are any words they do not know, have them find them in the **Vocabulario** sections on pages 246–247 and 250–251. If absolutely necessary, students can look up some words in the end vocabulary. There are approximately 12 cognates in this vocabulary list. Have students find them.

Teacher Notes

Vocabulario

TALKING ABOUT THE CITY

la ciudad	la fábrica
la zona comercial	el/la obrero(a)
el rascacielos	la zona residencial
el edificio	el apartamento
la oficina	(departamento)
la zona industrial	el condominio
las afueras	la casa privada

TALKING ABOUT THE LAYOUT OF A CITY

el plano	el semáforo
la plaza	el cruce de peatones
la avenida, el bulevar	caminar
la calle	cruzar
el barrio viejo	desembocar
la esquina	pintoresco(a)
la acera	ancho(a)
los peatones	angosto(a)

TALKING ABOUT PUBLIC TRANSPORTATION

la estación del metro	el torniquete
la boca del metro	la ranura
la escalera mecánica	la parada del bus
el tique	el autobús, la guagua, el camión

TALKING ABOUT THE COUNTRY

el campo	la casa de campo
el pueblo	el campesino
la finca	

TALKING ABOUT FARMING

la siembra	el huerto
la cosecha	el manzano
el maíz	el peral
el trigo	cultivar
los cereales	sembrar
la huerta	cosechar
los vegetales	criar los animales

IDENTIFYING SOME FARM ANIMALS

el ganado	el cerdo
la vaca	la gallina

Independent Practice

Assign any of the following:
1. Activities, pages 268–269
2. Workbook, **Mi autobiografía,** page 106
3. Situation Cards
4. CD-ROM, Disc 3, Chapter 9, **Juego de repaso**

TECNOTUR

VIDEO

¡Buen viaje!

EPISODIO 9 ▶ Ciudad y campo

Luis y Cristina visitan el centro histórico de la Ciudad de México.

También van al Palacio de Bellas Artes para ver una función del Ballet Folklórico, pero...

CD-ROM

Expansión cultural

La Ciudad de México fue construida sobre las ruinas de Tenochtitlán.

interNET CONNECTION

In this video episode Cristina and Luis spend the day exploring Mexico City. To visit other cities in the Spanish-speaking world, go to the **Capítulo 9** Internet activity at the Glencoe Foreign Language Web site:

http://www.glencoe.com/sec/fl

TECNOTUR

doscientos setenta y uno ∽ **271**

OVERVIEW

This page previews three key multimedia components of the **Glencoe Spanish** series. Each reinforces the material taught in Chapter 9 in a unique manner.

VIDEO

The Video Program allows students to see how the chapter vocabulary and structures are used by native speakers in an engaging story. Show the video episode as a final activity for Chapter 9.

A. You may wish to give students this information about the photos: **En la primera foto vemos el monumento a Benito Juárez, un presidente y héroe de México. En la segunda foto, Luis y Cristina no vieron el Ballet Folklórico. ¿Tienes alguna idea por qué no lo vieron?**

B. See the Video Activities Booklet for detailed suggestions for using this resource.

CD-ROM

A. In the video episode, Luis explains that Mexico City is built upon the ruins of Tenochtitlán. Have students read the **Expansión cultural** photo caption.

B. In the CD-ROM version of **Expansión cultural** (Disc 3, page 271), students can listen to additional recorded information about Tenochtitlán and the Aztec Empire.

INTERNET

Teacher Information and Student Worksheets for this activity can be accessed at the Web site.

Video Synopsis

In this episode, Luis gives Cristina a tour of the historic downtown area of Mexico City, beginning at the Parque de la Alameda. As they make their way to a performance of the Ballet Folklórico de México at the Palacio de Bellas Artes, Luis takes Cristina to see the Monument to Benito Juárez. The scene shifts to the Palacio de Bellas Artes where they are turned away because the performance is sold-out. Cristina is noticeably disappointed. After discussing what to do next, they decide to take the subway home.

Chapter 10 Overview ◆◆◆◆◆◆◆◆◆◆◆◆◆◆◆◆◆◆

TOPICS	FUNCTIONS	STRUCTURE	CULTURE
◆ Kitchen appliances ◆ Kitchen utensils ◆ Foods and food preparation	◆ How to talk about kitchen appliances ◆ How to talk about foods and food preparation ◆ How to give formal commands ◆ How to refer to things already stated	◆ Formal imperative: Regular forms ◆ Formal imperative: Irregular forms ◆ Placement of object pronouns	◆ A recipe for paella ◆ The tomato: Food or poison? ◆ The origin of corn and potatoes ◆ A healthy diet

CHAPTER 10 RESOURCES

PRINT	MULTIMEDIA

Planning Resources

Lesson Plans Block Scheduling Lesson Plans	Interactive Lesson Planner

Reinforcement Resources

Writing Activities Workbook Student Tape Manual Video Activities Booklet Web Site User's Guide	Transparencies Binder Audiocassette/Compact Disc Program Videocassette/Videodisc Program Online Internet Activities Electronic Teacher's Classroom Resources

Assessment Resources

Situation Cards Chapter Quizzes Testing Program Performance Assessment	**Maratón mental** Mindjogger Videoquiz Testmaker Computer Software (Macintosh/Windows) Listening Comprehension Audiocassette/Compact Disc Communication Transparency: C-10

Motivational Resources

Expansion Activities	Café Glencoe: www.cafe.glencoe.com Keypal Internet Activities

Enrichment

Spanish for Spanish Speakers	Fine Art Transparency: F-4

SECTION	PAGES	SECTION RESOURCES
Vocabulario Palabras 1 **La cocina** **¡A cocinar!** **Algunos comestibles**	274–277	Vocabulary Transparencies 10.1 Audiocassette 6B/Compact Disc 6 Student Tape Manual, TE, pages 108–110 Workbook, pages 107–108 Chapter Quizzes, page 45 CD-ROM, Disc 3, pages 274–277
Vocabulario Palabras 2 **¡A preparar la comida!** **Más comestibles**	278–281	Vocabulary Transparencies 10.2 Audiocassette 6B/Compact Disc 6 Student Tape Manual, TE, pages 111–112 Workbook, pages 109–111 Chapter Quizzes, page 46 CD-ROM, Disc 3, pages 278–281
Estructura **Imperativo formal: formas regulares** **Imperativo formal: formas irregulares** **Colocación de los pronombres de complemento**	282–287	Workbook, pages 112–114 Audiocassette 6B/Compact Disc 6 Student Tape Manual, TE, pages 113–115 Chapter Quizzes, pages 47–49 Computer Testmaker CD-ROM, Disc 3, pages 282–287
Conversación **¿Yo? ¿En la cocina?**	288–289	Audiocassette 6B/Compact Disc 6 Student Tape Manual, TE, page 116 CD-ROM, Disc 3, pages 288–289
Lecturas culturales **Una receta española** **El tomate, ¿comida o veneno?** *(opcional)* **El maíz y la papa, regalos de las Américas** *(opcional)*	290–293	Testing Program, pages 71-72 CD-ROM, Disc 3, pages 290-293
Conexiones **La nutrición** *(opcional)*	294–295	Testing Program, pages 72-73 CD-ROM, Disc 3, pages 294-295
Culminación **Actividades orales** **Actividad escrita** **Vocabulario** **Tecnotur**	296–299	**¡Buen viaje!** Video, Episode 10 Video Activities, pages 101-103 Internet Activities www.glencoe.com/sec/fl Testing Program, pages 68-71; 135;179; 199 CD-ROM, Disc 3, pages 296-299

OVERVIEW

In this chapter students will learn to talk about food and its preparation. Students will also increase their communication skills by learning the formal imperative forms as well as the placement of object pronouns with them. The cultural focus of this chapter is on the variety of foods and recipes available in the Spanish-speaking world, and the important role that cuisine plays in it.

National Standards

Communication

In Chapter 10 students will learn to communicate in spoken and written Spanish on the following topics:
- foods
- food preparation
- the origins of specific foods

Students will obtain and provide information about these topics and engage in conversations that would typically take place in a kitchen as they fulfill the chapter objectives listed on this page.

Pacing

Chapter 10 will require approximately eight to ten days. Pacing will vary according to the length of the class, the age of your students, and student aptitude.

Block Scheduling

See the Block Scheduling Lesson Plans Booklet for suggestions on how to present the chapter material within a block scheduling framework.

CAPÍTULO *10*

La cocina hispana

Objetivos

In this chapter you will learn to do the following:
- talk about foods and food preparation
- give commands
- refer to people and things previously mentioned
- prepare some regional specialties
- talk about the origin of several foods

interNET CONNECTION

The **Glencoe Foreign Language Web site** (http://www.glencoe.com/sec/fl) offers three options that enable you and your students to experience the Spanish-speaking world via the Internet:
- The online **Actividades** are correlated to the chapters and utilize Hispanic Web sites around the world. For the Chapter 10 activity, see student page 299.
- The **Correspondencia electrónica** section provides information on how to set up a keypal (pen pal) exchange between your class and a class in the Spanish-speaking world.
- At **Café Glencoe,** the interactive "after-school" section of the site, you and your students can access a variety of additional online resources, including interactive games.

doscientos setenta y tres ∞ **273**

Spotlight On Culture

Fotografía The photo on pages 272–273 shows an array of traditional Spanish foods. Pictured are varieties of **embutidos** (the generic word for sausages): **chorizos, salchichones,** and others. There is a whole **jamón serrano** in its stand ready for slicing. There are different cheeses, bread, and a bag of nuts. On the wall there is a **ristra** or string of hot peppers called **chiles picantes** in Mexico or **guindillas** in Spain.

   The poster is of the city of Trujillo in the province of Cáceres, region of Extremadura. Trujillo was the home of three of the greatest **conquistadores,** Francisco Pizarro and his brothers Gonzalo and Hernando. On the Plaza Mayor of Trujillo is the palace of the Marqueses de la Conquista, built with the treasure brought back from the New World. Sixteenth-century palaces surround the plaza with its equestrian statue of Francisco Pizarro.

Chapter Projects

Cocina hispana Make a paella using the recipe on page 290 or prepare another dish from a Spanish-speaking country with your class.

TECHNOLOGY OPTION

In the Chapter 10 Internet activity, students consult Hispanic recipe Web sites to create a menu for a three-course meal. You may wish to actually prepare the meal with your class.

Mi comida favorita   Have students make a list of their favorite foods. As they go through the chapter, have them observe and jot down differences between Hispanic and North American eating habits.

Vocabulario

La cocina

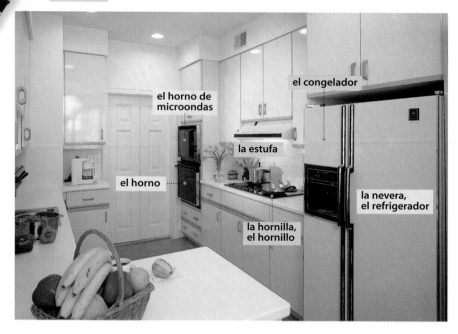

el horno de microondas

el congelador

la estufa

el horno

la nevera, el refrigerador

la hornilla, el hornillo

¡A cocinar!

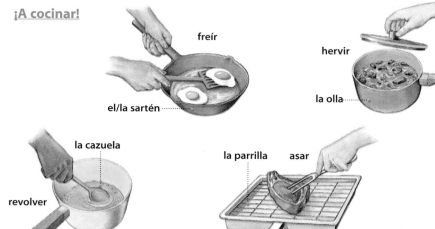

freír

el/la sartén

hervir

la olla

la cazuela

revolver

la parrilla   asar

🔔 Bell Ringer Review

Use BRR Transparency 10-1, or write the following on the board: Think of the last phone call you made. Tell where you were, whom you called, and what you talked about.

TEACHING VOCABULARY

A. Have students close their books. Project Vocabulary Transparencies 10.1 (A & B) and have them repeat the new words, phrases, and sentences after you or the recording on Cassette 6B/ Compact Disc 6. You may wish to use your own props, such as photos of kitchens or items from your own kitchen.

B. Intersperse the presentation with questions which elicit the new vocabulary.

C. After students have produced the new vocabulary several times, have them open their books to pages 274–275. Call on volunteers to read the new words, phrases, and sentences.

274

Pantomime

Begin

___, levántate.

Ven acá, por favor.

Vas a cocinar.

Pon el sartén en la hornilla.

Pon las papas en el sartén y fríelas.

Pon las habichuelas en la olla.

Revuelve las habichuelas.

Abre el horno.

Asa el pollo en el horno.

Ahora come.

Gracias, ___. Bien hecho. Regresa a tu asiento.

Algunos comestibles

la coliflor

la lechuga

la lima
la toronja

el limón

las uvas

las zanahorias

las cebollas

el pepino

las papas, las patatas

la pimienta

la sal

el azúcar

la salchicha, el chorizo

el cordero

el pollo

la chuleta de cerdo

la carne de res

la costilla

la ternera

Señor, ase Ud. el pollo en el horno.

Señorita, coma Ud. más.

Señora, fría Ud. las patatas.

Práctica

Práctica

A **HISTORIETA** En la cocina

Contesten.

1. ¿Está la señora en la cocina?
2. ¿Es una cocina moderna o anticuada?
3. ¿Cuántas hornillas tiene la estufa?
4. ¿Es una estufa eléctrica o de gas?
5. ¿Hay un refrigerador moderno en la cocina?
6. ¿Cuántas puertas tiene el refrigerador?
7. ¿Es del congelador la puerta izquierda del refrigerador?
8. ¿Qué haces tú en la cocina?

Restaurante El Sur, Estepona, España

B **¿Qué necesita el cocinero?** Completen.

1. El cocinero necesita una _____ porque va a freír algo.
2. El cocinero necesita una parrilla porque va a _____ algo.
3. El cocinero necesita una _____ porque va a hervir algo.
4. El cocinero va a _____ el agua.
5. El cocinero va a _____ las chuletas de cerdo.
6. El cocinero va a _____ los huevos.

C Lo que me gusta y lo que no me gusta

Contesten.

1. ¿Te gustan las uvas?
2. ¿Te gusta la ensalada de lechuga y tomates?
3. ¿Te gustan las papas asadas?
4. ¿Te gustan más las toronjas o las naranjas?
5. ¿Te gustan más las legumbres o las frutas?
6. ¿Te gusta el limón?
7. ¿Te gusta más el pollo frito o el pollo asado?
8. ¿Te gusta más la carne o el pescado?

276 doscientos setenta y seis

CAPÍTULO 10

D **¿A qué grupo pertenece?** Digan la categoría a la cual pertenece cada comestible.

legumbre   fruta   carne   especia

1. la cebolla
2. la toronja
3. la zanahoria
4. el cerdo
5. la papa
6. el cordero
7. el limón
8. las uvas
9. la pimienta

Mercado de San Miguel, Madrid, España

Actividades comunicativas

A **Nuestras comidas favoritas** Con un(a) compañero(a) hagan una lista de sus comidas favoritas. Luego decidan a cuál de los dos le gustan más las comidas que son buenas para la salud.

B **Una cocina** Trabaja con un(a) compañero(a). Miren esta foto de una cocina. Juntos describan la cocina. Indiquen si es una cocina moderna o anticuada.

D **Práctica D** can also be done without prior preparation.

Actividades comunicativas

¡OJO! **Práctica versus Actividades comunicativas**
All activities which provide guided practice are labeled **Práctica.** The more open-ended communicative activities are labeled **Actividades comunicativas.**

Let students say whatever they want when they do these **Actividades comunicativas.** If they make errors they can correct themselves but, following the proficiency guidelines, it is not realistic to expect students to perform with total accuracy. It is, therefore, not necessary to correct all errors. When doing the **Práctica,** however, all errors should be corrected.

Learning From Photos

Restaurante El Sur, Estepona, España Ask students to tell what the man in the photo on page 276 is and what he is doing.
Mercado de San Miguel, Madrid, España El Mercado de San Miguel is in Old Madrid, just off the Calle Mayor. It is a wonderfully preserved municipal market dating from the turn of the century.
Dos cocinas modernas You may wish to ask students to describe each of the two modern kitchens in the photos on pages 276–277.

ANSWERS

Práctica
D 1. legumbre
2. fruta
3. legumbre
4. carne
5. legumbre
6. carne
7. fruta
8. fruta
9. especia

Actividades comunicativas
A and B Answers will vary.

277

Vocabulario

¡A preparar la comida!

limpiar

pelar

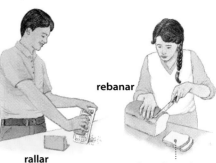
rebanar

rallar

las rebanadas

cortar

agregar, añadir

picar

los pedacitos,
los trocitos

tapar

Anita pone la cacerola al fuego.

Anita quita (retira) la cacerola del fuego.
Apaga el fuego.

278 ◊◊ *doscientos setenta y ocho*

CAPÍTULO 10

RESOURCES

- Vocabulary Transparencies 10.2 (A & B)
- Student Tape Manual, TE, pages 111–112
- Audiocassette 6B/CD6
- Workbook, pages 109–111
- Quiz 2, page 46
- CD-ROM, Disc 3, pages 278–281

Bell Ringer Review

Use BRR Transparency 10-2, or write the following on the board: Write the names of the equipment or cookware needed to do each of the following in a kitchen.

1. **freír**
2. **hervir**
3. **asar**
4. **congelar**

TEACHING VOCABULARY

A. Have students close their books. Model the **Palabras 2** vocabulary using Vocabulary Transparencies 10.2 (A & B). Have students repeat the new material after you or the recording on Cassette 6B/Compact Disc 6.

B. Dramatize the meaning of these words: **limpiar, pelar, rallar, rebanar, cortar, agregar, picar, tapar, retirar.**

C. When students have produced the new vocabulary several times, have them open their books to pages 278–279 and call on volunteers to read the words, phrases, and sentences. Model pronunciation as necessary.

278

Pantomime

Begin

___, ven acá, por favor.
Ve a la cocina.
Saca la carne del refrigerador.
Asa la carne en el horno.
Pela las papas.
Pon el aceite en la sartén.
Pica el ajo.
Agrega las papas y el ajo al aceite.
Fríe las papas y el ajo.
Limpia la lechuga.
Prepara la ensalada.

Pon la olla al fuego.
Pela las zanahorias y córtalas en rebanadas.
Agrega las zanahorias.
Gracias, ___. Vuelve a tu asiento.

Más comestibles

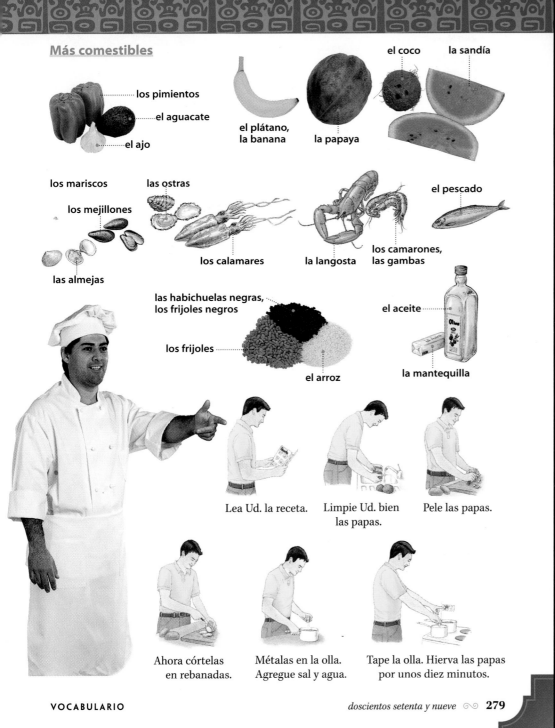

los pimientos

el aguacate

el ajo

el plátano,
la banana

la papaya

el coco

la sandía

los mariscos

las ostras

los mejillones

las almejas

los calamares

la langosta

los camarones,
las gambas

el pescado

las habichuelas negras,
los frijoles negros

los frijoles

el arroz

el aceite

la mantequilla

Lea Ud. la receta.

Limpie Ud. bien
las papas.

Pele las papas.

Ahora córtelas
en rebanadas.

Métalas en la olla.
Agregue sal y agua.

Tape la olla. Hierva las papas
por unos diez minutos.

**ABOUT THE
SPANISH LANGUAGE**

◆ In Mexico and some other
countries all peppers are called
chiles, not **pimientos.** Bell
peppers, in most Spanish-
speaking countries, are called
pimientos. Small hot peppers
are **ajíes**.

◆ In Puerto Rico sweet bananas
for eating are **guineos. Plá-
tanos** are big cooking bananas. In Venezuela a banana
is called **un cambur.**

◆ While in most places any lobster is called **una langosta,**
the word really refers to the
clawless, spiny lobster. The Atlantic lobster is called **un
bogavante.**

Práctica

A **Práctica A** can be done without prior preparation.

Note In **Práctica A** students hear the formal command form but they do not have to use it.

B Have students refer to the illustrations as they do **Práctica B**. This **Práctica** also reviews the present progressive.

Práctica

A **Una receta buena o mala** ¿Es algo que se hace o no?

1. Corte el pan en rebanadas para tostarlo.
2. Hierva el agua para preparar el té.
3. Fría bien la sandía.
4. Limpie la lechuga antes de comerla.
5. Pele las cebollas antes de comerlas.
6. Apague el fuego antes de empezar a cocinar.
7. Fría las papas en aceite.
8. Ponga la sartén al fuego para hervir el agua.

B **Preparando la comida**
Contesten según los dibujos.

Lima, Perú

1. ¿Qué está picando la señora?

3. ¿Qué está cortando la señorita?

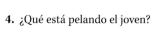

2. ¿Qué está rebanando el señor?

4. ¿Qué está pelando el joven?

5. ¿Qué está limpiando la muchacha?

C ¿Qué opinas? Digan si se puede o no.

1. ¿Se puede hervir o freír el arroz?
2. ¿Se puede rallar la lechuga?
3. ¿Se puede rallar el queso o el coco?
4. ¿Se puede rebanar la sandía?
5. ¿Se puede picar la carne de res?
6. ¿Se puede freír la chuleta?
7. ¿Se puede asar el arroz?
8. ¿Se puede tapar la olla?

D HISTORIETA Cocinando algo

Contesten según se indica.

1. ¿Qué estás preparando? (un pollo)
2. ¿Lo vas a asar o freír? (asar)
3. ¿Qué tienes que hacer con el pollo antes de asarlo? (lavarlo)
4. ¿Lo vas a asar entero? (no)
5. ¿Qué vas a hacer? (cortarlo en pedazos)
6. ¿Vas a sazonar el pollo? (sí, con ajo, sal y pimienta)
7. ¿Dónde lo vas a asar? (en el horno)
8. ¿Lo vas a asar a fuego lento? (sí)
9. ¿Qué vas a servir con el pollo? (una ensalada)
10. Y de postre, ¿qué hay? (frutas)

Le invitamos a conocer el mundo del arroz

Actividades comunicativas

A Una comida norteamericana Estás en Lima, Perú, con la familia Sandoval. Ellos quieren comer una comida típica norteamericana. La señora Sandoval (tu compañero[a]) te pide describir una comida típica norteamericana. Describe la comida y dile a la señora cómo prepararla. Después cambien de rol.

JUEGO ¿Qué categoría es? Trabaja con un(a) compañero(a). Miren las siguientes categorías. Tienen tres minutos. Trabajando independientemente, completen cada lista en español, dando los nombres de los comestibles que conocen que pertenecen a cada grupo. La persona que ha escrito el mayor número de comestibles en cada categoría gana.

marisco   fruta   pescado   vegetal   carne

VOCABULARIO

doscientos ochenta y uno 281

CAPÍTULO 10
Vocabulario

C Have students correct the false statements in **Práctica C**.

D **Práctica D** can be done first orally with books closed.

EXPANSION After going over **Práctica D**, have students retell the story in their own words.

Actividades comunicativas

¡OJO! The **Actividades comunicativas** allow students to use the vocabulary and structures of the chapter in open-ended, real-life situations. They also give students another opportunity to use words and structures from previous chapters.

Have students work on as many activities as you wish. You may also allow them to select those activities they want to do. Different groups can work on different activities.

Learning From Realia

El mundo del arroz Rice is an important staple in Spanish cuisine. It is the basis of the **paella** and many other traditional dishes. There are restaurants in Madrid and Valencia that specialize almost exclusively in rice-based dishes. Spain is a major rice producer.

ANSWERS

Práctica

C
1. Sí, se puede hervir o freír el arroz.
2. No, no se puede rallar la lechuga.
3. Sí, se puede rallar el queso o el coco.
4. Sí, se puede rebanar la sandía.
5. Sí, se puede picar la carne de res.
6. Sí, se puede freír la chuleta.
7. No, no se puede asar el arroz.
8. Sí, se puede tapar la olla.

D
1. Estoy preparando un pollo.
2. Lo voy a asar.
3. Tengo que lavarlo antes de asarlo.
4. No, no lo voy a asar entero.
5. Voy a cortarlo en pedazos.
6. Sí, voy a sazonar el pollo con ajo, sal y pimienta.
7. Lo voy a asar en el horno.
8. Sí, lo voy a asar a fuego lento.
9. Voy a servir una ensalada con el pollo.
10. De postre hay frutas.

Actividades comunicativas

A Answers will vary.

RESOURCES

- Workbook, pages 112–114
- Student Tape Manual, TE, pages 113–115
- Audiocassette 6B/CD6
- Quizzes 3–5, pages 47–49
- Computer Testmaker
- CD-ROM, Disc 3, pages 282–287

Bell Ringer Review

Use BRR Transparency 10-3, or write the following on the board: Make a list of foods you might eat for dinner tonight.

TEACHING STRUCTURE

Telling people what to do

A. Have students open their books to pages 282–283 and lead them through Steps 1 and 2.

B. Illustrate the difference between singular and plural imperatives by giving a command to an individual and then the same command to a group of students. For example: **María, tome Ud. su libro de español. María y José, tomen Uds. su libro de español.**

C. Practice negative forms by calling out affirmative commands and having students change them to the negative. Then reverse the procedure.

Estructura

Telling people what to do
Imperativo formal: formas regulares

1. You use the command form of the verb—the imperative—to tell someone what to do. To form the **Ud.** and **Uds.** commands, you drop the **o** from the present tense **yo** form and add the following endings.

INFINITIVE	YO—PRESENT	UD. COMMAND	UDS. COMMAND
preparar	preparø	prepare Ud.	preparen Uds.
leer	leø	lea Ud.	lean Uds.
abrir	abrø	abra Ud.	abran Uds.

You form the imperative of stem-changing verbs in the same way. The **yo** form of the present tense serves as the stem.

pensar	piensø	piense Ud.	piensen Uds.
volver	vuelvø	vuelva Ud.	vuelvan Uds.
hervir	hiervø	hierva Ud.	hiervan Uds.
pedir	pidø	pida Ud.	pidan Uds.

Note that the endings used for the formal commands have the vowel opposite to the vowel usually associated with the conjugation. The -**ar** verbs have **e** and the -**er** and -**ir** verbs have **a**.

¿Te acuerdas?

Remember the following spelling patterns.

busca — busque
agrega — agregue
empieza — empiece

2. To make these commands negative, simply place **no** before the verb.

prepare Ud.	no prepare Ud.	preparen Uds.	no preparen Uds.
pida Ud.	no pida Ud.	pidan Uds.	no pidan Uds.
abra Ud.	no abra Ud.	abran Uds.	no abran Uds.

ENCHILADAS DE CHILE ANCHO

Learning From Photos

Enchiladas de chile ancho The recipe is for **enchiladas** made with **chile ancho**. The **chile ancho** is a relatively mild, delicious pepper grown in Mexico and New Mexico.

You may wish to prepare this dish with your class.

✦Práctica✦

A La ensalada Contesten según el modelo.

¿Preparo la comida?

Sí, prepare Ud. la comida.

1. ¿Preparo la comida?
2. ¿Limpio la lechuga?
3. ¿Pelo los tomates?
4. ¿Pico el ajo?
5. ¿Hiervo el agua?
6. ¿Frío el pollo?
7. ¿Tapo la sartén?
8. ¿Retiro la sartén del fuego?

Gazpacho

Caracas, Venezuela

B ¿Preparamos la comida?
Contesten según el modelo.

¿Preparamos la comida?
No, no preparen Uds. la comida.
Yo la voy a preparar.

1. ¿Preparamos la comida?
2. ¿Limpiamos la lechuga?
3. ¿Pelamos los tomates?
4. ¿Picamos el ajo?
5. ¿Hervimos el agua?
6. ¿Freímos el pollo?
7. ¿Tapamos la sartén?
8. ¿Retiramos la sartén del fuego?

✦Práctica✦

A and **B** Have pairs of students present these activities as mini-conversations.

Learning From Photos

Gazpacho Gazpacho is often described as a liquid salad. It is made from tomatoes, olive oil, vinegar, and each of the ingredients surrounding it on the table, which also serve as garnishes. Gazpacho is always served cold.
Caracas, Venezuela You may wish to ask students to describe the kitchen pictured, the people in it, and the activities going on.

ESTRUCTURA

doscientos ochenta y tres ∞ **283**

ANSWERS

Práctica

A 1. Sí, prepare Ud. la comida.
2. Sí, limpie Ud. la lechuga.
3. Sí, pele Ud. los tomates.
4. Sí, pique Ud. el ajo.
5. Sí, hierva Ud. el agua.
6. Sí, fría Ud. el pollo.
7. Sí, tape Ud. la sartén.
8. Sí, retire Ud. la sartén del fuego.

B 1. No, no preparen Uds. la comida. Yo la voy a preparar.

2. No, no limpien Uds. la lechuga. Yo la voy a limpiar.
3. No, no pelen Uds. los tomates. Yo los voy a pelar.
4. No, no piquen Uds. el ajo. Yo lo voy a picar.
5. No, no hiervan Uds. el agua. Yo lo voy a hervir.
6. No, no frían Uds. el pollo. Yo lo voy a freír.
7. No, no tapen Uds. la sartén. Yo la voy a tapar.
8. No, no retiren Uds. la sartén del fuego. Yo la voy a retirar.

283

⟊Práctica⟊

**C** and **D** Have students work in pairs and present these activities as mini-conversations.

Actividad comunicativa

¡OJO! The **Actividades comunicativas** encourage students to use the chapter vocabulary and structures in open-ended situations.

🎨 **FINE ART CONNECTION**

«San Martín y el pordiosero» de El Greco El Greco (Domenikos Theotokópoulos) was born on the island of Crete in 1541. He studied in Italy, where he came in contact with the Venetian school: Titian, Tintoretto, and Bassano. He arrived in Spain around 1576 and established himself in Toledo. Among his most important works are: **«El Entierro del Conde de Orgaz»** (in the church of Santo Tomé), **«El Martirio de San Mauricio»** (El Escorial), **«El Caballero de la mano en el pecho»** (Museo del Prado), **«La Vista de Toledo»** (Metropolitan Museum, NY).

EXPANSION Show Fine Art Transparency F-4 of this painting by El Greco from the Transparency Binder. You may wish to have students read the background information accompanying this transparency and have them do the related activities. **Note** For «La Vista de Toledo» and related activities, see Fine Art Transparency F-1.

284

C **¿Qué debo hacer con la carta?** Contesten con el imperativo.

1. ¿Debo aceptar la carta?
2. ¿Debo abrir la carta?
3. ¿Debo leer la carta?
4. ¿Debo contestar la carta?
5. ¿Debo escribir la carta en inglés?

D **Debe hacer lo que quiere hacer.** Sigan el modelo.

Quiero viajar a España.

Entonces, ¡viaje Ud. a España!

1. Quiero viajar a España.
2. Quiero pasar un mes en Madrid.
3. Quiero tomar el tren a Toledo.
4. Quiero visitar la capital.
5. Quiero ver los cuadros de El Greco.
6. Quiero aprender el español.
7. Quiero comer una paella.
8. Quiero beber horchata.
9. Quiero vivir con una familia española.

«San Martín y el pordiosero» de El Greco

Actividad comunicativa

A **Soy yo el/la profesor(a).** Trabajen en grupos de tres. Uno(a) de Uds. va a ser el/la profesor(a). Los otros serán los alumnos. El/La profesor(a) les va a dar una orden. Los alumnos van a decir si quieren hacerlo o no. El/La profesor(a) puede usar las siguientes palabras.

hablar · escribir · abrir · estudiar · leer · cerrar · volver · trabajar · escuchar · jugar

---

ANSWERS

Práctica

C 1. Sí, acepte Ud. la carta.
2. Sí, abra Ud. la carta.
3. Sí, lea Ud. la carta.
4. Sí, conteste Ud. la carta.
5. Sí, escriba Ud. la carta en inglés.

D 1. Entonces, ¡viaje Ud. a España!
2. Entonces, ¡pase Ud. un mes en Madrid!
3. Entonces, ¡tome Ud. el tren a Toledo!
4. Entonces, ¡visite Ud. la capital!

5. Entonces, ¡vea Ud. los cuadros de El Greco!
6. Entonces, ¡aprenda Ud. el español!
7. Entonces, ¡coma Ud. una paella!
8. Entonces, ¡beba Ud. horchata!
9. Entonces, ¡viva Ud. con una familia española!

Actividad comunicativa

A Answers will vary.

Telling people what to do
Imperativo formal: formas irregulares

1. A verb that has an irregularity in the **yo** form of the present tense will keep the same irregularity in the command form, since the **yo** form of the present tense serves as the root for the command. Study the following.

INFINITIVE	YO—PRESENT	UD. COMMAND	UDS. COMMAND
hacer	hagø	haga Ud.	hagan Uds.
poner	pongø	ponga Ud.	pongan Uds.
salir	salgø	salga Ud.	salgan Uds.
venir	vengø	venga Ud.	vengan Uds.
decir	digø	diga Ud.	digan Uds.
introducir	introduzcø	introduzca Ud.	introduzcan Uds.

2. The following verbs are the only ones in Spanish that have irregular command forms.

INFINITIVE	UD. COMMAND	UDS. COMMAND
ir	vaya Ud.	vayan Uds.
ser	sea Ud.	sean Uds.
saber	sepa Ud.	sepan Uds.
estar	esté Ud.	estén Uds.
dar	dé Ud.	den Uds.

 Málaga, España

ꠣ Práctica ꠣ

A **Voy de compras.** Sigan el modelo.

> Quiero hacer las compras.

> Pues, haga Ud. las compras.

1. Quiero hacer las compras.
2. Quiero salir ahora.
3. Quiero ir al mercado de Santa Tecla.
4. Quiero poner mis compras en esta bolsa.
5. Quiero ir a pie.
6. No quiero manejar.

ESTRUCTURA

doscientos ochenta y cinco ꠣ **285**

 CAPÍTULO 10
Estructura

TEACHING STRUCTURE

 Telling people what to do

A. Have students open their books to page 285. Lead them through Steps 1 and 2.

B. Have them repeat the command forms after you.

ꠣPrácticaꠣ

A Have students present **Práctica A** as a series of mini-conversations.

ANSWERS

Práctica
A 1. **Pues, haga Ud. las compras.**
2. **Pues, salga Ud. ahora.**
3. **Pues, vaya Ud. al mercado de Santa Tecla.**
4. **Pues, ponga Ud. sus compras en esta bolsa.**
5. **Pues, vaya Ud. a pie.**
6. **Pues, no maneje Ud.**

285

◆Práctica◆

C RECYCLING **Práctica C** reintroduces vocabulary from Chapter 3.

EXPANSION After going over **Práctica C**, call on a student to explain how to use a public telephone.

Actividades comunicativas

A After students have done **Actividad A** in pairs, have them do it as a whole-class activity. One student describes a recipe and the class has to guess what the dish is.

JUEGO This is a good end-of-class activity that students will enjoy.

B ¿Podemos salir?   Sigan el modelo.

¿Podemos salir ahora?

¡Cómo no! ¡Salgan Uds. ahora!

1. ¿Podemos salir mañana?
2. ¿Podemos usar el carro?
3. ¿Podemos llevar a Anita?
4. ¿Podemos volver?
5. ¿Podemos poner las maletas en la maletera?

C Una llamada telefónica

Completen con el imperativo.

1. _____ (llamar) Ud. por teléfono.
2. _____ (hacer) Ud. la llamada esta noche.
3. _____ (ir) Ud. a una cabina telefónica.
4. _____ (descolgar) Ud. el auricular.
5. _____ (introducir) Ud. la tarjeta telefónica en la ranura.
6. _____ (esperar) Ud. el tono.
7. _____ (marcar) Ud. el número.
8. _____ (esperar) Ud. la contestación.
9. _____ (decir) Ud. quien es.
10. _____ (preguntar) Ud. por Antonio.
11. _____ (hablar) Ud. con él.

Buenos Aires, Argentina

◆Actividades comunicativas◆

A Dos recetas   Trabaja con un(a) compañero(a). Selecciona (Escoge) uno de tus platos favoritos—un plato no muy complicado. Luego dile a tu compañero(a) cómo se prepara el plato—es decir, le vas a dar la receta. Luego tu compañero(a) te dará la receta para su plato favorito.

JUEGO ¡Hágalo!   Have some fun. Get together in small groups and make up commands telling your teacher what to do. Now it's your turn because a teacher always tells you what to do. **¿Verdad?**

Referring to things already stated
Colocación de los pronombres de complemento

The object pronouns are attached to the affirmative command.
They come before, or precede, the negative command.

Lave los platos.	Lávelos.	No los lave Ud.
Coma la ensalada.	Cómala.	No la coma Ud.
Sirva el postre.	Sírvalo.	No lo sirva Ud.
Déme la receta.	Déme la.	No me la dé Ud.

¿Lo sabes?

To maintain the same stress, use a written accent with either one or two pronouns.
Diga. Dígame. Dígamelo.

 **Práctica**

A ¿Qué debo hacer? Contesten según el modelo.

¿Debo limpiar la lechuga?
Sí, límpiela.
No, no la limpie Ud.

1. ¿Debo lavar los cuchillos?
2. ¿Debo pelar las naranjas?
3. ¿Debo abrir la lata?
4. ¿Debo leer la receta?
5. ¿Debo picar el ajo?
6. ¿Debo rallar el queso?
7. ¿Debo revolver los huevos?
8. ¿Debo poner el pollo en la nevera?

B Ellos no lo hicieron. Sigan el modelo.

Ellos no cortaron la carne.
Pues, córtenla Uds.

1. Ellos no rebanaron el pan.
2. Ellos no hirvieron la sopa.
3. Ellos no frieron los huevos.
4. Ellos no taparon las ollas.
5. Ellos no añadieron azúcar.
6. Ellos no pusieron el pollo en el horno.

Una merienda, España

ESTRUCTURA

doscientos ochenta y siete 287

 Bell Ringer Review

Use BRR Transparency 10-4, or write the following on the board: Write the answers to the following questions.

1. ¿Quién te prepara la cena, tu mamá o tu papá?
2. ¿Quién te sirve la comida en el restaurante?
3. ¿Te la sirve pronto el mesero?
4. ¿Le das la propina al mesero?
5. ¿Se la das antes o después de comer?

TEACHING STRUCTURE

Referring to things already stated

A. Ask students to open their books to page 287. Lead them through the explanation.
B. Choose examples and write them on the board. Have students repeat the sentences.

Práctica

A and **B** Have students work in pairs and present these activities to the class as mini-conversations.

 All new material in the chapter has been presented. The sections that follow recombine and reintroduce the vocabulary and structures that have already been introduced.

ANSWERS

Práctica
A 1. Sí, lávelos.
No, no los lave Ud.
2. Sí, pélelas.
No, no las pele Ud.
3. Sí, ábrala.
No, no la abra Ud.
4. Sí, léala.
No, no la lea Ud.
5. Sí, píquelo.
No, no lo pique Ud.
6. Sí, rállelo.
No, no lo ralle Ud.
7. Sí, revuélvalos.
No, no los revuelva Ud.
8. Sí, póngalo en la nevera.
No, no lo ponga Ud. en la nevera.

B 1. Pues, rebánenlo Uds.
2. Pues, hiérvanla Uds.
3. Pues, fríanlos Uds.
4. Pues, tápenlas Uds.
5. Pues, añádanlo Uds.
6. Pues, pónganlo Uds. en el horno.

287

Bell Ringer Review

Use BRR Transparency 10-5, or write the following on the board: Choose a favorite dish of yours and write out the instructions for making it.

TEACHING THE CONVERSATIION

A. 🎧 To vary the procedure for presenting the conversation, don't tell the students what it's about. Have them listen to the recording on Cassette 6B/ Compact Disc 6. Now ask them questions to see how much they understood.

B. Have students open their books. Call on students to take parts and read the conversation to the class.

C. After every six to eight sentences, ask some comprehension questions from the **Después de conversar** section.

D. Have students ad lib and make up a conversation on the same theme—who does or doesn't like to cook.

Conversación

¿Yo? ¿En la cocina?

JAIME: David, ¿te gusta cocinar?

DAVID: A mí, ¿cocinar? ¿Hablas en serio? En la cocina soy un desastre. ¿A ti te gusta cocinar?

JAIME: Sí, bastante.

DAVID: ¿Qué sabes preparar?

JAIME: Muchas cosas, pero mi plato favorito es la paella.

DAVID: La paella, dices. ¿Qué es?

JAIME: Pues, es una especialidad española, de Valencia. Lleva muchos ingredientes—mariscos, arroz.

DAVID: Se comen muchos mariscos en España, ¿no?

JAIME: Sí, hombre. Y algún día te voy a preparar una buena paella.

Después de conversar

Contesten.

1. ¿A quién le gusta cocinar?
2. ¿Quién es un desastre en la cocina?
3. ¿Cuál es el plato que a Jaime le gusta mucho preparar?
4. ¿Dónde se come la paella?
5. ¿De qué región de España es la paella una especialidad?
6. ¿Qué opinas? ¿Te gustaría la paella o no?

288 〰 *doscientos ochenta y ocho*

CAPÍTULO 10

ANSWERS

Después de conversar

1. **A Jaime le gusta cocinar.**
2. **David es un desastre en la cocina.**
3. **A Jaime le gusta mucho preparar la paella.**
4. **La paella se come en España.**
5. **La paella es una especialidad de Valencia.**
6. **Sí, (No, no) me gustaría la paella.**

Actividades comunicativas

A **La cafetería de la escuela**
Tu compañero(a) es la persona responsable de la cafetería de tu escuela. Dile cuáles son los platos que sirven en la cafetería que te gustan y cuáles son los platos que no te gustan. Dale algunas sugerencias *(suggestions)*. Dile lo que debe preparar y servir en la cafetería. Luego cambien de rol.

Colegio Santa Teresita, Santurce, Puerto Rico

San José, Costa Rica

B **En un restaurante** Trabaja con un(a) compañero(a). Miren la foto de unas personas que están comiendo en un restaurante. Trabajando juntos, describan todo lo que ven en el restaurante. Decidan si a Uds. les gustaría comer en este restaurante.

C **Una comida española** Aquí ves una foto de un plato típico de Madrid—el cocido madrileño. Trabaja con un(a) compañero(a). Identifiquen todos los ingredientes que ven en el cocido. Luego expliquen cómo creen que se prepara el cocido.

CONVERSACIÓN

doscientos ochenta y nueve 〰 **289**

Actividades comunicativas

¡OJO! **Práctica versus Actividades comunicativas**
All activities which provide guided practice are labeled **Práctica.** The more open-ended communicative activities are labeled **Actividades comunicativas.**

Allow students to select the activity they wish to take part in.

A **TECHNOLOGY OPTION** In the CD-ROM version of this activity (Disc 3, page 289), students can interact with an on-screen native speaker and record their voices.

Learning From Photos

Colegio Santa Teresita, Santurce, Puerto Rico You may wish to ask these questions about the photo:
¿Qué son las dos personas?
¿Dónde están ellos?
¿Viven en una zona muy fría?
¿Qué ropa llevan ellos?
¿Qué están haciendo?
San José, Costa Rica Ask students:
¿Quiénes serán las cuatro personas?
¿Dónde están ellos?
¿Qué están haciendo?
Una comida española You may wish to ask students to look at the bottom photo on this page and do the following:
Describe el plato que vemos.

ANSWERS

Actividades comunicativas
A, B, and **C** Answers will vary.

Lecturas CULTURALES

UNA RECETA ESPAÑOLA

Como le dijo Jaime a David, la paella es un plato delicioso que es una especialidad de la cocina española. Quien no ha comido una paella no sabe lo que se ha perdido. La paella valenciana lleva muchos ingredientes. Aquí tiene Ud. una receta bastante sencilla para preparar una paella. Decida si a Ud. le gustaría comer este plato delicioso.

◈◇◈◇◈◇◈ LA PAELLA ◈◇◈◇◈◇◈

INGREDIENTES

3 tomates
2 cebollas grandes
2 pimientos
(uno verde y uno rojo)
4 dientes[1] de ajo
½ kilo de camarones

4 calamares
12 almejas
12 mejillones
langosta (opcional)
1 pollo en partes
3 chorizos

1 paquete de guisantes congelados
1 bote de pimientos morrones
1½ tazas de arroz
3 tazas de consomé de pollo
4 pizcas[2] de azafrán[3]
¼ taza de aceite de oliva

PREPARACIÓN

1. Pique los tomates, los pimientos, las cebollas y el ajo.
2. Lave las almejas y los mejillones en agua fría.
3. Limpie y pele los camarones.
4. Limpie y corte en rebanadas los calamares.
5. Corte en rebanadas los chorizos.
6. Fría o ase el pollo aparte.

COCCIÓN

Se usa una paellera o una olla.

1. Fría ligeramente[4] en el aceite los pimientos y las cebollas picadas.
2. Agregue el ajo y los tomates y fría ligeramente a fuego lento unos dos o tres minutos.
3. Agregue el arroz.
4. Revuelva el arroz con los tomates, las cebollas, los pimientos y el ajo.
5. Agregue el consomé de pollo y llévelo a la ebullición[5].
6. Baje el fuego y agregue los camarones, los calamares, el chorizo, el pollo, las almejas y los mejillones.
7. Agregue el azafrán.
8. Ponga sal y pimienta a su gusto.

Si se prepara la paella en una olla, tape la olla y cocine a fuego lento encima de la estufa unos 40 minutos. En una paellera, ase la paella en el horno sin tapa o cocine a fuego lento encima de la estufa. Al final agregue los guisantes y los pimientos y sirva. Ud. notará que el arroz tiene un bonito color amarillo. Es del azafrán.

[1]dientes *cloves*
[2]pizcas *pinches*
[3]azafrán *saffron*
[4]ligeramente *lightly*
[5]a la ebullición *to a boil*

Did You Know?

¡Qué deliciosa paella! The dish **paella** derives its name from the word **paella** in the Valencian language. In **valenciano, paella** means the special **sartén** or large flat pan in which it is prepared. In Spanish, the pan is called **una paellera.**

VIDEO CONNECTION

Paella In the Chapter 10 video episode Teresa's mother teaches Juan Ramón how to make **paella.** (See photos from the video, page 299.) You may wish to show this episode in connection with this reading. Also see the Video Activities Booklet for related activities on this topic.

Después de leer

A **¿Cuál es la palabra?** Completen según la receta.

1. una _____ para hacer la paella
2. medio _____ de camarones
3. un _____ de guisantes congelados
4. tres _____ de ajo
5. una _____ de sal
6. una _____ de consomé de pollo

B **La paella** Preparen una lista de los ingredientes que lleva una paella.

C **La cocción** Digan que sí o que no.

1. Se puede asar la paella en la parrilla.
2. La paella lleva muchas papas.
3. Hay muchas especias en una paella.
4. El arroz de una paella se pone amarillo.
5. El chorizo es un tipo de salchicha española.

D **Para pensar** Miren el mapa de España en la página 451 y expliquen por qué se comen muchos mariscos en España.

Valencia, España

LECTURAS CULTURALES   doscientos noventa y uno **291**

Post-reading

A. Have students re-read the recipe at home and write the answers to the accompanying **Después de leer** activities.

B. Go over the **Después de leer** activities in class the next day.

TECHNOLOGY OPTION

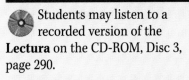 Students may listen to a recorded version of the **Lectura** on the CD-ROM, Disc 3, page 290.

Did You Know?

El azafrán Saffron, a basic ingredient of **paella,** is probably the world's most expensive spice. Only the stigma or the pistils of the flower are used. It is estimated that it takes the pistils of 4,000 plants to produce one ounce of saffron powder. (See photo, page 299.) Saffron gives the rice of **paella** its distinctive orange-yellow tint.

Critical Thinking Activity

Making inferences, drawing conclusions Read the following to the class or write it on the board or on an overhead transparency: **La paella viene de Valencia. La paella tradicional lleva muchos mariscos. Busca Valencia en el mapa en la página 451. ¿Por qué crees que hay muchos mariscos en la paella?**

ANSWERS

Después de leer

A 1. paellera
2. kilo
3. paquete
4. dientes
5. pizca
6. taza

B tomates, cebollas grandes, pimientos (verdes y rojos), ajo, camarones, calamares, almejas, mejillones, langosta, pollo en partes, chorizos, guisantes congelados, arroz, consomé de pollo, azafrán, aceite de oliva, sal y pimienta

C 1. No.
2. No.
3. No.
4. Sí.
5. Sí.

D Answers will vary but may include: **Se comen muchos mariscos en España porque hay muchas costas en España. Hay tres océanos o mares: el Atlántico, el Mediterráneo y el Mar Cantábrico.**

LECTURA OPCIONAL 1

National Standards

Cultures
This reading, and the related activities on this page, familiarize students with some interesting information about the tomato.

Comparisons
In this reading students learn that, although the Spaniards and Italians eventually realized tomatos were not poisonous and began to eat them, the English and North Americans avoided eating them until the 19th century.

TEACHING TIPS

¡OJO! This reading is optional. You may skip it completely, have the entire class read it, have only several students read it, or assign it for extra credit.

A. Even if students do not read this selection, you may wish to tell them this interesting bit of information about tomatoes.

ABOUT THE SPANISH LANGUAGE

◆ The word **tomate** comes from the Nahuatl word **tomatl.** The Nahuatl civilization at different times and places was known as Toltec, Chichimec, and Aztec.

◆ The potato is called **una papa** or **una patata.** Corn is called **el maíz** or **el choclo.**

LECTURA OPCIONAL 1

EL TOMATE, ¿COMIDA O VENENO?

¿Sabías que durante muchos años los ingleses y los norteamericanos no comían el tomate? Ellos creían que el tomate era venenoso[1]. Creían que al comer un tomate, uno se moriría[2]. Comer un tomate era fatal.

Cuando los españoles llevaron los primeros tomates de América a Europa, los usaban solamente como adorno, y no como comida. Pero en poco tiempo los españoles y los italianos descubrieron que el tomate era delicioso y no venenoso. Pero los ingleses, no. Hasta el siglo XIX, los ingleses y los norteamericanos seguían creyendo que el tomate era veneno.

[1]venenoso *poisonous*
[2]se moriría *would die*

Ica, Perú

Después de leer

A | **El tomate** Contesten según la lectura.

1. El tomate, ¿es de origen europeo o americano?
2. ¿Qué creían los ingleses que pasaría a la persona al comer un tomate?
3. ¿Para qué se usaban los tomates en Europa originalmente?
4. ¿Quiénes, en Europa, fueron los primeros en comer el tomate?
5. ¿Hasta cuándo creían los norteamericanos que el tomate era venenoso?

B | **La superstición** ¿Conoces tú alguna superstición acerca de alguna comida? ¿Cuál es? ¿Podrías decirnos?

292 ⌒ *doscientos noventa y dos*

ANSWERS

Después de leer

A 1. **El tomate es de origen americano.**
2. **Creían que la persona que comía un tomate se moriría.**
3. **Se usaban como adorno.**
4. **Los españoles y los italianos fueron los primeros en comer el tomate.**
5. **Los norteamericanos creían que el tomate era venenoso hasta el siglo XIX.**

B Answers will vary.

Santiago Atitlán, Guatemala

EL MAÍZ Y LA PAPA, REGALOS DE LAS AMÉRICAS

Los españoles llegaron a las Américas en el siglo XV. En Europa no había maíz ni papas. Los europeos no cultivaban estos vegetales. Los europeos no los conocían. La papa y el maíz tienen su origen en las Américas.

Los indios cultivaban el maíz en toda la América. El maíz era la base de la dieta de muchos indios. La tortilla de maíz sigue siendo muy importante en la cocina mexicana y centroamericana.

La papa tiene su origen en el altiplano sudamericano. Los incas cultivaban la papa en la región que hoy es el Perú y Bolivia. Los españoles llevaron la papa a Europa donde, en poco tiempo, llegó a ser la base de la dieta de varios países, como Irlanda y Polonia.

Después de leer

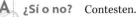

A ¿Sí o no? Contesten.

1. En el siglo XVIII los primeros españoles llegaron a las Américas.
2. Los europeos cultivaban la papa y el maíz antes del siglo XV.
3. La tortilla se hace de papa.
4. Los incas cultivaban la papa en el altiplano.
5. La tortilla es muy importante en la dieta del Perú y Bolivia.
6. La tortilla de maíz se come mucho en México.
7. La papa era muy importante en Irlanda y Polonia.

B ¿Qué país es? Identifiquen.

1. Irlanda está en Europa. Está cerca de Inglaterra. Su capital es Dublín. ¿Cómo se llama Irlanda en inglés?
2. Polonia está en el noreste de Europa. Está cerca de Rusia. Su capital es Varsovia. Los polacos son de Polonia. ¿Cómo se llama Polonia en inglés?

Urubamba, Perú

LECTURAS OPCIONALES

doscientos noventa y tres 〰 **293**

National Standards

Cultures
This reading, and the related activities on this page, familiarize students with information about the growing of corn and potatoes in the Americas.

Comparisons
Students learn that corn and potatoes were unknown in Europe prior to the Spanish exploration of the Americas.

TEACHING TIPS

¡OJO! This reading is optional. You may skip it completely, have the entire class read it, have only several students read it, or assign it for extra credit.

Did You Know?

Más productos de las Américas Other products unknown in Europe before the arrival of the Spaniards in the New World are:

tobacco	**tabaco**
peanuts	**maní, cacahuates, cacahuetes**
cacao (the bean from which cocoa and chocolate are made)	**cacao**

ANSWERS

Después de leer

A 1. No. 5. No.
2. No. 6. Sí.
3. No. 7. Sí.
4. Sí.

B 1. Ireland
2. Poland

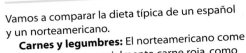
Conexiones

National Standards

Connections
This reading about diet and nutrition establishes a connection with another discipline, allowing students to reinforce and further their knowledge of science through the study of Spanish.

Comparisons
In this reading students learn how the consumption of certain categories of foods in the U.S. differs from that in Spain.

¡OJO! The readings in the **Conexiones** section are optional. They focus on some of the major disciplines taught in schools and universities. The vocabulary is useful for discussing such topics as history, literature, art, economics, business, science, etc. You may choose any of the following ways to do this reading on nutrition with your students.

Independent reading Have students read the selections and do the post-reading activities as homework, which you collect. This option is least intrusive on class time and requires a minimum of teacher involvement.

Homework with in-class follow-up Assign the readings and post-reading activities as homework. Review and discuss the material in class the next day.

Intensive in-class activity This option includes a pre-reading vocabulary presentation, in-class reading and discussion, assignment of the activities for homework, and a discussion of the assignment in class the following day.

LAS CIENCIAS

LA NUTRICIÓN

Everyone is aware of the importance of a healthy diet. What constitutes a healthy diet? What effect does diet have on our lives? How does the diet of Hispanic countries differ from ours?

Madrid, España

La dieta

Vamos a comparar la dieta típica de un español y un norteamericano.

Carnes y legumbres: El norteamericano come bastante carne, especialmente carne roja, como el biftec. También consume legumbres como los guisantes y las zanahorias y papas, pero casi siempre en pequeñas cantidades con la carne. El español come poca carne, y muy poca carne roja. Las carnes que consume, en pequeñas cantidades, son el pollo, la ternera y el cordero. Las legumbres que come son, muchas veces, el plato principal, basado en frijoles, garbanzos[1], lentejas[2], y similares. Una de las mayores diferencias es en el consumo de pescado y mariscos. El español come pescado y mariscos tres o cuatro veces a la semana. Muchos españoles consumen más pescado que carne. El norteamericano come poco pescado.

Frutas y verduras: El norteamericano come frutas con el cereal por la mañana y cuando tiene hambre entre comidas. Para el español las frutas son postre, y las come todos los días. Los norteamericanos y los españoles comen mucha ensalada. La ensalada de lechuga y tomate es tradicional en España.

[1]garbanzos *chick peas*
[2]lentejas *lentils*

Buenos Aires, Argentina

Learning From Photos

Madrid, España y Buenos Aires, Argentina You may wish to ask students to describe the two food stores pictured. Ask them to name as many of the foods in each photo as they can.

Productos lácteos (de la leche):
El norteamericano consume mucha mantequilla. El español come poquísima mantequilla y nunca cocina con mantequilla. El español consume menos mantequilla que cualquier otro europeo. El norteamericano toma leche. En España solamente los bebés y los niños pequeños toman leche. Pero el español consume bastante queso. El queso con frutas es un postre popular. Los españoles también toman yogur como postre. Al norteamericano le gusta mucho el helado. También les gusta a los españoles, pero ellos consumen mucho menos.

Pan y cereales: Los norteamericanos y los españoles comen mucho pan, pero el español casi nunca come pan con mantequilla. El norteamericano come cereales para el desayuno. El español come pan con su café con leche. Los espaguetis y otras pastas son más y más populares en los EE.UU. Pero el norteamericano, a diferencia del español, come poco arroz. El español consume grandes cantidades de arroz.

Es importante notar que muchos jóvenes, españoles y norteamericanos, tienen una dieta muy diferente a la dieta de la gente mayor. Muchos jóvenes son vegetarianos. Consumen poca grasa y muchas verduras, cereales y legumbres.

Después de leer

A **¿Es español o norteamericano?** Escojan.

1. Pide un plato de garbanzos.
2. Está comiendo un biftec grande.
3. No quiere mantequilla con su pan.
4. Come pescado tres veces a la semana.
5. Pide un vaso de leche.
6. Quiere camarones con arroz.
7. Para el desayuno toma cereal con fruta, pan con mantequilla y un vaso de leche.
8. Para el postre pide queso y fruta.
9. Usa aceite de oliva para freír, no mantequilla.

B **¿Qué opinas?** Contesten.

1. Para ti, ¿en qué consiste una dieta buena?
2. ¿Crees tú que los norteamericanos tienen una dieta buena? ¿Por qué o por qué no?

LAS CIENCIAS

LA NUTRICIÓN

A. You may wish to tell those students who are going to read this selection to take notes on a sheet of paper with a double column. The titles of the columns could be: **Comida hispana / Comida norteamericana.**

B. Have students read the introduction in English on page 294.

C. Now have them read the selection quickly.

D. Suggest to students that they look for cognates and attempt to guess the meaning from context.

E. Now do the **Después de leer** activities on this page.

ANSWERS

Después de leer

A **1.** Es español.
2. Es norteamericano.
3. Es español.
4. Es español.
5. Es norteamericano.
6. Es español.
7. Es norteamericano.
8. Es español.
9. Es español.

B Answers will vary but may include:
1. Para mí, una dieta buena consiste en ___.
2. Yo creo que los norteamericanos tienen una dieta buena (mala) porque ___.

295

The **Actividades orales** and the **Actividad escrita** allow students to use the vocabulary and structures from this chapter in open-ended, real-life settings.

Actividades orales

¡OJO! Encourage students to say as much as possible when they do these activities. Tell them not to be afraid of making mistakes since the goal of the activities is real-life communication.

Allow students to choose the activities they would like to take part in.

A and D
TECHNOLOGY OPTION
Students may use the Portfolio feature on the CD-ROM to record their conversations in these activities.

Student Portfolio

Have students keep a notebook containing their best written work from each chapter. These selected writings can be based on assignments from the Student Textbook and the Writing Activities Workbook. The activities on page 297 are examples of writing assignments that may be included in each student's portfolio.

In the Workbook, students will develop an organized autobiography **(Mi autobiografía).** These workbook pages may also become a part of their portfolio.

See the Teacher's Manual for more information on the Student Portfolio.

Culminación

Actividades orales

A En el mercado Tú estás en un mercado en México. Quieres comprar los ingredientes que necesitas para un plato favorito. Tu compañero(a) es el/la empleado(a) en el mercado. Dile todo lo que quieres y en qué cantidades. Dile también lo que vas a preparar.

Guanajuato, México

B Vegetarianos Hoy en día hay muchos vegetarianos. Los vegetarianos no comen carne. Trabaja con un(a) compañero(a). Discutan por qué Uds. creen que hay tantas personas que son vegetarianas. Discutan lo que comen y no comen. Si tú eres vegetariano(a), explica a tu compañero(a) por qué.

C Restaurantes étnicos ¿Hay restaurantes étnicos, restaurantes que sirven comida de otras partes del mundo, en tu comunidad? Si los hay, con un(a) compañero(a) preparen una lista de estos restaurantes y el tipo de comida que sirven. Luego describan un plato típico de uno de los restaurantes.

D ¿Te gusta comer? Mucha gente come sólo para vivir y mucha gente vive para comer. ¿Cómo te clasificarías tú? Explícale a un(a) compañero(a) por qué. Luego cambien de rol.

ANSWERS

Actividades orales
A, B, C, and D Answers will vary.

Actividad escrita

A **¡Qué comida más deliciosa!** Estás viajando por México. Anoche fuiste a cenar en un restaurante y pediste algo que salió delicioso, muy rico. Te gustó mucho. Escribe una tarjeta postal a tus padres. Descríbeles el restaurante y el plato que te gustó tanto. Si puedes, explícales cómo crees que el cocinero preparó el plato.

San Miguel de Allende, México

Writing Strategy

Writing about a process

When you write about a process or how to do something, you must remember to tell all the little details involved. Describe the process accurately and thoroughly. In this type of expository writing, be sure to define any terms you think your readers will not be familiar with and also to put the various steps of the process in logical order.

Un(a) americano(a) en Aranjuez

You are living with a Spanish family in Aranjuez, near Madrid. One day last week you prepared your favorite American dish for them. They loved it! They want you to write out the recipe for them before you leave to return to the United States. Since they don't speak much English, you will have to write the recipe in Spanish. Be sure to explain all the steps as clearly as possible so that they prepare something delicious rather than a disaster!

CULMINACIÓN

A **TECHNOLOGY OPTION**
Students may use the Portfolio feature on the CD-ROM to write their postcards.

Writing Strategy

Writing about a process

A. Have students read the Writing Strategy on page 297.
B. Have students translate the measures for their recipes into the metric system if necessary.

National Standards

Communities
You may wish to invite a Hispanic chef from a local restaurant or a member of the local Hispanic community to tell students about the favorite foods in his or her culture and how they are prepared. Encourage students to ask questions.

ANSWERS

Actividad escrita
A Answers will vary.

Writing Strategy
Answers will vary.

VOCABULARY REVIEW

The words and phrases in the **Vocabulario** have been taught for productive use in this chapter. They are summarized here as a resource for both students and teacher. This list also serves as a convenient resource for the **Culminación** activities on pages 296–297. There are approximately four cognates in this vocabulary list. Have students find them.

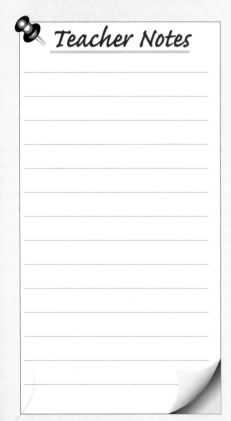

📌 *Teacher Notes*

Vocabulario

TALKING ABOUT SOME KITCHEN APPLIANCES AND UTENSILS

la cocina	la hornilla, el hornillo
el congelador	la cazuela, la cacerola
la nevera, el refrigerador	el/la sartén
la estufa	la parrilla
el horno	la olla
el horno de microondas	

TALKING ABOUT FOOD PREPARATION

limpiar	rebanar
pelar	agregar, añadir
rallar	tapar
picar	los pedacitos, los trocitos
cortar	las rebanadas

TALKING ABOUT SOME COOKING PROCEDURES

cocinar	hervir
revolver	poner al fuego
freír	quitar del fuego
asar	apagar el fuego

IDENTIFYING MORE FOODS

la coliflor	el cerdo
las cebollas	el cordero
el pepino	la salchicha, el chorizo
las zanahorias	la ternera
la lechuga	el pollo
las papas	la costilla
los pimientos	la chuleta
el aguacate	el pescado
el ajo	los mariscos
el arroz	la langosta
las habichuelas negras, los frijoles negros	los camarones, las gambas
	las almejas
la lima	los calamares
el limón	los mejillones
la toronja	las ostras
las uvas	la sal
la papaya	la pimienta
el coco	el azúcar
la sandía	el aceite
el plátano, la banana	la mantequilla
la carne de res	

Learning From Photos

Una paella completa The **paella** shown on page 299 contains, in addition to the **camarones,** some shellfish that students may not know. They are **langostinos** (the pink ones) and **cangrejos de río** (the red ones).

Independent Practice

Assign any of the following:
1. Activities, pages 296–297
2. Workbook, **Mi autobiografía,** page 118
3. Situation Cards
4. CD-ROM, Disc 3, Chapter 10, **Juego de repaso**

TECNOTUR

VIDEO

¡Buen viaje!

EPISODIO 10 ▶ La cocina hispana

Juan Ramón aprende a cocinar una paella.

La paella es un plato que se come mucho en España, sobre todo en Valencia.

CD-ROM

Expansión cultural

El azafrán se cultiva en la región de La Mancha.

interNET CONNECTION

In this video episode Teresa's mother, Señora de Hugo, shows Juan Ramón how to make a paella, as Teresa videotapes the "cooking class." To create your own menu for a three-course meal from a Spanish-speaking country, go to the **Capítulo 10** Internet activity at the Glencoe Foreign Language Web site:

http://www.glencoe.com/sec/fl

TECNOTUR

doscientos noventa y nueve ∾ **299**

OVERVIEW

This page previews three key multimedia components of the **Glencoe Spanish** series. Each reinforces the material taught in Chapter 10 in a unique manner.

VIDEO

The Video Program allows students to see how the chapter vocabulary and structures are used by native speakers in an engaging story. For maximum reinforcement, show the video episode as a final activity for Chapter 10.

A. Before watching the video episode, ask students: **¿Pueden Uds. identificar los ingredientes de la paella en estas fotos?** If they have trouble answering this question, refer them to the recipe on page 290.

B. See the Video Activities Booklet for detailed suggestions for using this resource.

CD-ROM

A. In the video episode, Mrs. de Hugo tells Juan Ramón that **el azafrán** is the secret ingredient for making delicious **paella.** The **Expansión cultural** photo shows the saffron flower from which the spice is made. Have students read the caption on page 299.

B. In the CD-ROM version of **Expansión cultural** (Disc 3, page 299), students can listen to recorded information about **paella.**

INTERNET

Teacher Information and Student Worksheets for this activity can be accessed at the Web site.

Video Synopsis

This episode takes place at the de Hugo residence in Madrid, where Teresa's mother teaches Juan Ramón how to prepare **paella.** Juan Ramón follows Mrs. de Hugo's instructions while Teresa has great fun recording the event for the Web page. Mrs. de Hugo eventually enlists Teresa's help in carrying out some of the cooking tasks in the kitchen so as not to distract Juan Ramón. The finished **paella** looks delicious!

Chapter 11 Overview ◆◆◆◆◆◆◆◆◆◆◆◆◆◆◆◆◆◆◆◆◆

SCOPE AND SEQUENCE   pages 300–327

TOPICS	FUNCTIONS	STRUCTURE	CULTURE
◆ Automobile terminology and driving ◆ Service station terminology ◆ Giving directions on the road and in the city	◆ How to talk about car models and parts of an automobile ◆ How to talk about routine services at a gas station ◆ How to talk about driving on the highway and in the city ◆ How to tell friends what to do and what not to do	◆ The familiar imperative: Regular forms ◆ The familiar imperative: Irregular forms ◆ Negative imperatives	◆ The Panamerican Highway ◆ Parking your car in Spanish-speaking countries ◆ Spanish traffic signs ◆ Pollution and the environment ◆ **Vistas del Perú**

CHAPTER 11 RESOURCES

PRINT	MULTIMEDIA

Planning Resources

Lesson Plans
Block Scheduling Lesson Plans

Interactive Lesson Planner

Reinforcement Resources

Writing Activities Workbook
Student Tape Manual
Video Activities Booklet
Web Site User's Guide

Transparencies Binder
Audiocassette/Compact Disc Program
Videocassette/Videodisc Program
Online Internet Activities
Electronic Teacher's Classroom Resources

Assessment Resources

Situation Cards
Chapter Quizzes
Testing Program
Performance Assessment

Maratón mental Mindjogger Videoquiz
Testmaker Computer Software (Macintosh/Windows)
Listening Comprehension Audiocassette/Compact Disc
Communication Transparency: C-11

Motivational Resources

Expansion Activities

Café Glencoe: www.cafe.glencoe.com
Keypal Internet Activities

Enrichment

Spanish for Spanish Speakers

Chapter 11 Planning Guide

SECTION	PAGES	SECTION RESOURCES
Vocabulario Palabras 1 **El coche** **La estación de servicio,** **La gasolinera**	302–305	Vocabulary Transparencies 11.1 Audiocassette 7A/Compact Disc 7 Student Tape Manual, TE, pages 121–122 Workbook, pages 119–120 Chapter Quizzes, page 50 CD-ROM, Disc 3, pages 302–305
Vocabulario Palabras 2 **En la carretera** **En la ciudad**	306–309	Vocabulary Transparencies 11.2 Audiocassette 7A/Compact Disc 7 Student Tape Manual, TE, pages 123–125 Workbook, pages 121–122 Chapter Quizzes, page 51 CD-ROM, Disc 3, pages 306–309

Estructura
Imperativo familiar: Formas
    regulares
Imperativo familiar: Formas
    irregulares
Imperativo negativo
	310–315	Workbook, pages 123–126
		Audiocassette 7A/Compact Disc 7
		Student Tape Manual, TE, pages 125–126
		Chapter Quizzes, pages 52–54
		Computer Testmaker
		CD-ROM, Disc 3, pages 310–315

Conversación **Un sitio para estacionar**	316–317	Audiocassette 7A/Compact Disc 7 Student Tape Manual, TE, page 127 CD-ROM, Disc 3, pages 316–317
Lecturas culturales **La carretera panamericana** **El estacionamiento** *(opcional)* **Las señales de tránsito** *(opcional)*	318–321	Testing Program, pages 76–77 CD-ROM, Disc 3, pages 318–321
Conexiones **La ecología** *(opcional)*	322–323	Testing Program, page 77 CD-ROM, Disc 3, pages 322–323
Culminación **Actividades orales** **Actividades escritas** **Vocabulario** **Tecnotur**	324–327	**¡Buen viaje!** Video, Episode 11 Video Activities, pages 104–108 Internet Activities **www.glencoe.com/sec/fl** Testing Program, pages 74–76; 136; 180; 200–201 CD-ROM, Disc 3, pages 324–327

OVERVIEW

In this chapter students will learn to talk about cars, roads, and driving. They will learn vocabulary associated with different types of cars, gas station services, and city and highway driving.

They will also learn both the affirmative and negative forms of the familiar imperative. The cultural focus of this chapter is on driving customs and highways in the Spanish-speaking world.

National Standards

Communication

In Chapter 11 students will learn to communicate in spoken and written Spanish on the following topics:
- cars and driving
- giving directions
- road travel in the Spanish-speaking world

Students will obtain and provide information about these topics and engage in conversations that would typically take place behind the wheel of a car as they fulfill the chapter objectives listed on this page.

CAPÍTULO *11*

El coche y la carretera

Objetivos

In this chapter you will learn to do the following:
- talk about cars and driving
- give directions on the road
- tell family and friends what to do and what not to do
- talk about highways in the Hispanic world

interNET CONNECTION

The **Glencoe Foreign Language Web site** (http://www.glencoe.com/sec/fl) offers three options that enable you and your students to experience the Spanish-speaking world via the Internet:
- The online **Actividades** are correlated to the chapters and utilize Hispanic Web sites around the world. For the Chapter 11 activity, see student page 327.
- The **Correspondencia electrónica** section provides information on how to set up a keypal (pen pal) exchange between your class and a class in the Spanish-speaking world.
- At **Café Glencoe,** the interactive "after-school" section of the site, you and your students can access a variety of additional online resources, including interactive games.

trescientos uno ◯◯ **301**

Spotlight On Culture

Fotografía The view is of the charming town of Casares, one of the famous **Pueblos Blancos** of Andalucía. There is a touristic **Ruta de los Pueblos Blancos** that connects these towns and villages from south to north: Castellar de la Frontera, Jimena de la Frontera, Gaucín, continuing on to Ronda and Arcos de la Frontera. Many of these towns have **de la Frontera** as part of their names. The **frontera** was the frontier between Christian and Moorish Spain. The **frontera** moved as territory was taken or lost by one side or the other. As is typical of many of the **Pueblos Blancos,** this town is dominated by a medieval castle set on high ground offering a clear view of the surrounding lands in case of attack. Some of the castles were built by the Christians, others by the Moors. Note the incongruity of a television antenna atop the castle.

Pacing

Chapter 11 will require approximately six to eight days. Pacing will vary according to the length of the class, the age of your students, and student aptitude.

Block Scheduling

See the Block Scheduling Lesson Plans Booklet for suggestions on how to present the chapter material within a block scheduling framework.

Chapter Projects

Mi coche favorito Have students bring in a large magazine photo of their favorite kind of car. Have them label all the parts of the car and elements from the setting, when appropriate.

RESOURCES

- Vocabulary Transparencies 11.1 (A & B)
- Student Tape Manual, TE, pages 121–123
- Audiocassette 7A/CD6
- Workbook, pages 119–120
- Quiz 1, page 50
- CD-ROM, Disc 3, pages 302–305

Bell Ringer Review

Use BRR Transparency 11-1, or write the following on the board: On a piece of paper make two columns. Head the column on the left **el avión** and the one on the right **el coche**. Copy each of the following terms into the correct column.

1. **el compartimiento superior**
2. **el chaleco salvavidas**
3. **la calle**
4. **el semáforo**
5. **el comandante**
6. **el cruce de peatones**
7. **la esquina**
8. **el aseo**
9. **el asistente de vuelo**
10. **la acera**

TEACHING VOCABULARY

¡OJO! More than the usual number of alternate words are presented in this vocabulary presentation. All the variants taught here are commonly used.

A. Have students close their books. Using Vocabulary Transparencies 11.1 (A & B), point to each illustration or photo and have students repeat the corresponding word or phrase two or three times.
(continued on page 303)

302

Vocabulario

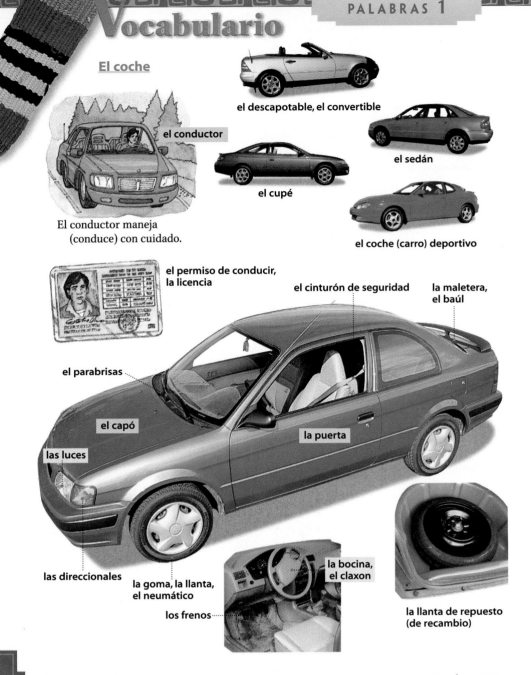

El coche

el descapotable, el convertible

el conductor

el sedán

el cupé

el coche (carro) deportivo

El conductor maneja (conduce) con cuidado.

el permiso de conducir, la licencia

el cinturón de seguridad

la maletera, el baúl

el parabrisas

el capó

la puerta

las luces

las direccionales

la goma, la llanta, el neumático

los frenos

la bocina, el claxon

la llanta de repuesto (de recambio)

302   *trescientos dos*

Pantomime

Getting ready

Set up a chair in the classroom as a driver's seat. Pieces of paper on the floor can serve as the accelerator and brake pedals.

Begin

(Estudiante 1), levántate, por favor. Ven acá. Es tu coche.
Abre la puerta de tu coche.
Sube.
Siéntate.
Cierra la puerta.
Pon el cinturón de seguridad.

Pon el pie en el acelerador.
Conduce con cuidado. Ve a la gasolinera. Pon los frenos. Necesitas gasolina.
(Estudiante 2), ven acá. Eres el empleado(a).
Llena el tanque de gasolina.
Limpia el parabrisas.
Pon aire en las llantas.
Gracias, (Estudiantes 1 y 2). Bien hecho. Pueden volver a su asiento.

Vocabulario

La estación de servicio, La gasolinera

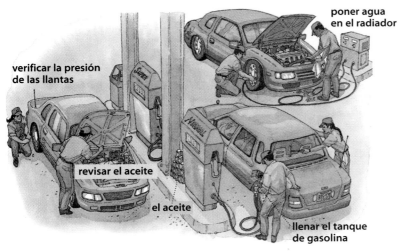

poner agua en el radiador

verificar la presión de las llantas

revisar el aceite

el aceite

llenar el tanque de gasolina

El empleado llenó el tanque de gasolina.
La empleada limpió el parabrisas.
El otro empleado puso aire en las llantas.

Sí, señor...

Favor de llenar el tanque.

¿Súper o normal?
¿Con plomo o sin plomo?

VOCABULARIO

trescientos tres ∽ **303**

B. Point to items at random and ask yes/no or either/or questions. After some practice, progress to more open-ended questions, such as **¿Qué es esto?**

C. Have students open their books to pages 302–303, and repeat the vocabulary after you or the recording on Cassette 7A/Compact Disc 6.

D. Call on volunteers to read the new words and sentences.

E. Show students a photo of your own car, or a magazine picture of one, and describe it, using as much of the new vocabulary as possible. For example: **Tengo un coche deportivo de color rojo. Es un descapotable americano. Es una marca americana, un Ford. Acelera rápidamente, pero siempre conduzco con cuidado.**

TEACHING TIP

When an individual cannot respond to a question, try getting the answer from a volunteer by gesturing silently to the class or asking **¿Quién sabe?** Always have the original student repeat the correct model, and come back to him or her soon with the same question.

Additional Practice

Favor de... Have students use the **favor de** expression with other words learned in this section that they could use at a service station.

Did You Know?

¿Cuánto cuesta la gasolina? Diesel powered cars are very popular in Spain because of their excellent gas mileage. Fuel is extremely expensive by American standards. A gallon of gasoline can cost the equivalent of $4.00 to $5.00 or more. The difference in price is attributable to very high taxes on fuel. For that reason large cars are far less common on the road in Spain than in the United States.

VOCABULARY EXPANSION

Additional vocabulary items related to cars include:

el retrovisor	*rear view mirror*
los parachoques	*bumpers*
el gato	*(tire) jack*

Remind students that the **para** in **parabrisas** and **parachoques** means *to stop*. Others words with this meaning of **para** are: **paracaídas** (*parachute*) and **paraguas** (*umbrella*).

CAPÍTULO 11
Vocabulario

❖Práctica❖

¡OJO! **Práctica** When students are doing the **Práctica** activities, accept any answer that makes sense. The purpose of these activities is to have students use the new vocabulary. They are not factual recall activities. Thus, do not expect students to remember specific information from the vocabulary presentation when answering. If you wish, have students use the photos as a stimulus, when possible.
Historieta Each time **Historieta** appears, it means that the answers to the activity form a short story. Encourage students to look at the title of the **Historieta** since it can sometimes help them do the activity.

A **Práctica A** can be done first orally with books closed.
EXPANSION After going over **Práctica A**, have students prepare the activity silently. Now call on individuals to give the information about themselves in their own words.

B Have students correct the false statements in **Práctica B**.

C **EXPANSION** Students can also make up questions about the illustrations in **Práctica C.** They can call on other members of the class to answer their questions.

❖Práctica❖

A **HISTORIETA** Mi coche

Contesten.
1. ¿Tienes un coche o quieres tener un coche algún día?
2. En el estado donde vives, ¿cuántos años tienes que cumplir para tener el permiso de conducir?
3. ¿Qué tipo de coche quieres?
4. ¿Tienes un modelo favorito? ¿Cuál es?
5. ¿Vas a manejar con cuidado?
6. ¿Vas a llevar tu coche a la estación de servicio con frecuencia?

Un coche clásico, La Habana, Cuba

B Coches   Digan que sí o que no.
1. El motor de un coche está en la maletera.
2. El motor del coche está debajo del capó.
3. Es una buena idea tener una llanta de repuesto en la maletera del carro.
4. Es necesario tocar la bocina cada vez que pasas por un hospital.
5. Es necesario tener el cinturón abrochado cuando estás en un asiento delantero del carro.
6. Es necesario poner los frenos para parar el coche.
7. Los automóviles tienen tres neumáticos.
8. Se limpia el parabrisas con gasolina.

C **HISTORIETA** En la gasolinera

Describan cada dibujo.

1.　　　　2.　　　　3.

4.　　　　5.

304 ∾ *trescientos cuatro*   CAPÍTULO 11

ANSWERS

Práctica

A 1. Sí, (No, no) tengo un coche. Sí, (No, no) quiero tener un coche algún día.
2. Tengo que cumplir ___ años para tener el permiso de conducir.
3. Quiero un ___.
4. Sí, (No, no) tengo un modelo favorito. Mi modelo favorito es ___.

5. Sí, (No, no) voy a manejar con cuidado.
6. Sí, (No, no) voy a llevar mi coche a la estación de servicio con frecuencia.

B 1. No.　　4. No　　7. No.
2. Sí.　　5. Sí.　　8. No.
3. Sí.　　6. Sí.

C Answers will vary but may include:
1. La empleada llena el tanque con gasolina sin plomo.
2. El empleado limpia el parabrisas.
3. El empleado verifica la presión de las llantas (los neumáticos, las gomas).
4. El empleado pone agua en el radiador.
5. La empleada pone aire en las llantas (los neumáticos, las gomas).

304

D En la gasolinera Escojan.

1. En la gasolinera el empleado llena el tanque de _____.
   a. agua   b. aceite   c. gasolina
2. El empleado revisa _____.
   a. el agua en los neumáticos   b. el tanque   c. el nivel del aceite
3. El empleado nunca pondría agua en _____.
   a. la batería   b. el radiador   c. el tanque
4. El empleado podría verificar _____.
   a. la presión de los neumáticos   b. el aire del radiador
   c. el parabrisas
5. El parabrisas está muy sucio. No puedo ver nada. ¿Me lo _____ Ud., por favor?
   a. llenaría   b. revisaría   c. limpiaría

Actividades comunicativas

A Mi carro ¿Tienes un carro (coche) o no? Si no tienes carro, ¿te comprarás uno algún día? Trabaja con un(a) compañero(a). Cada uno de Uds. describirá el carro de sus sueños.

B Un carro nuevo Estás pasando un año estudiando en Puerto Rico. Decides comprarte un carro. Como tienes muy poco dinero, tienes que comprar un carro usado (de ocasión). Visitas una agencia. Estás hablando con el/la vendedor(a) (tu compañero[a]). Él o ella te quiere vender un carro—cualquier carro, no importa la calidad ni la condición. Discutan juntos.

C Trabajo a tiempo parcial. Imagínate que trabajas en una gasolinera. Tu compañero(a) cree que a él o a ella le gustaría trabajar a tiempo parcial en una gasolinera para ganar unos dólares extra. Te va a hacer preguntas sobre el trabajo que haces. Contesta a sus preguntas.

Gerona, España

D Have students prepare **Práctica D** before going over it in class.

Actividades comunicativas

¡OJO! Práctica versus Actividades comunicativas
All activities which provide guided practice are labeled **Práctica.** The more open-ended communicative activities are labeled **Actividades comunicativas.**

A TECHNOLOGY OPTION
In the CD-ROM version of this activity (Disc 3, page 305), students can interact with an on-screen native speaker and record their voices.

Learning From Photos

Un coche clásico, La Habana, Cuba y Gerona, España You may wish to ask students to say as much as they can about the two photos on pages 304 and 305.

Independent Practice

Assign any of the following:
1. Workbook, **Palabras 1,** pages 119–120
2. Activities, pages 304–305
3. CD-ROM, Disc 3, pages 302–305

ANSWERS

Práctica
D 1. c
   2. c
   3. c
   4. a
   5. c

Actividades comunicativas
A, B, and C Answers will vary.

🔔 Bell Ringer Review

Use BRR Transparency 11-2, or write the following on the board: Write as many words and expressions as you can think of for giving directions.

TEACHING VOCABULARY

A. Have students act out the monologues in this vocabulary section.

B. As you present the vocabulary, you may wish to ask questions such as the following:

¿Se queda en qué carril para salir de la autopista? ¿En el carril derecho o en el carril izquierdo?

¿Indica un rótulo dónde está la salida de la autopista?

¿Se puede adelantar en una carretera donde hay solamente un carril en cada sentido?

¿Es necesario parar cuando hay una luz roja o una luz verde?

En una calle de sentido único, ¿puede el tráfico ir en dos direcciones?

En la carretera

la salida

la velocidad máxima

la garita de peaje

la autopista, la autovía

el peaje

el carril

el rótulo

la entrada

Alejandro, quédate en el carril derecho. Paga el peaje. Y luego, sal de la autopista en la próxima salida.

Donde está el rótulo, dobla a la derecha. Y luego sigue derecho.

¡Cuidado! Está prohibido adelantar. Hay solamente un carril en cada sentido.

En la ciudad

una cuadra

el semáforo

un cruce,
una bocacalle

la luz roja

Es necesario parar cuando hay una luz roja.

No podemos entrar. Es una calle de sentido único. Tenemos que ir en el sentido contrario.

de sentido único

el parquímetro

estacionar el coche, aparcar

You may wish to give students a few extra words that are useful on the road:

la flecha	*arrow*
virar	*to turn* (synonym of **doblar**)
dar la vuelta	*to turn around*
ceder el paso	*yield (right of way)*
el arcén	*shoulder (of the road)*

Both **coche** and **carro** are common words for *car*. **Coche** is more commonly used in Spain and southern South America, **carro** in most other places. The original **coche** was a horse-drawn coach designed to carry passengers, *a stagecoach*, for example. The **carro** was also a horse-drawn vehicle, *a cart*, but it was used for carrying produce or other goods, not people.

❧Práctica❧

A **Práctica A** can be done orally with books closed.

EXPANSION After going over **Práctica A**, have students describe some rules of the road in their own words.

B **Práctica B** can be done in class without prior preparation.
Note **Práctica B** has many informal commands but students do not have to use them actively.

Learning From Photos

Motril, España You may wish to ask these questions about the photo on page 308:

¿Dónde están estas personas?

¿Quién es el señor que está de pie?

¿Qué está haciendo él?

¿Quiénes son las otras personas?

¿Qué están haciendo ellos?

❧Práctica❧

A **HISTORIETA** En la carretera

Contesten según se indica.

1. ¿Qué vamos a tomar? (la autopista)
2. ¿Qué tendremos que pagar? (el peaje)
3. ¿Dónde lo tenemos que pagar? (en la garita)
4. ¿Cuántos carriles tiene la autopista en cada sentido? (tres)
5. ¿Cuál es la velocidad máxima? (ciento veinte kilómetros por hora)
6. ¿Está prohibido adelantar? (no)
7. ¿Está prohibido exceder la velocidad máxima? (sí)

B **Buenos o malos consejos** Digan que sí o que no.

1. Maneja con cuidado.
2. Estaciona el coche donde está prohibido el estacionamiento.
3. Excede la velocidad indicada en el rótulo.
4. Quédate en el carril derecho para adelantar un carro.
5. Mete una moneda en la ranura del parquímetro.
6. Paga el peaje en la garita.
7. Al llegar a un cruce, para y mira a la derecha y a la izquierda antes de seguir.
8. Cuando vas a parar, pon las direccionales.
9. Pon las direccionales porque vas a doblar a la izquierda.

Motril, España

ANSWERS

Práctica

A
1. Vamos a tomar la autopista.
2. Tendremos que pagar el peaje.
3. Lo tenemos que pagar en la garita.
4. La autopista tiene tres carriles en cada sentido.
5. La velocidad máxima es ciento veinte kilómetros por hora.
6. No, no está prohibido adelantar.
7. Sí, está prohibido exceder la velocidad máxima.

B
1. Sí.
2. No.
3. No.
4. No.
5. Sí.
6. Sí.
7. Sí.
8. No.
9. Sí.

C HISTORIETA Donde vivo yo

Contesten.

1. ¿Cuál es una autopista cerca de donde tú vives?
2. ¿Es una autopista de peaje?
3. ¿Cuánto es el peaje?
4. ¿Dónde tienes que pagar el peaje? ¿En la salida de la autopista?
   Si no, ¿a cada cuántos kilómetros hay garitas de peaje?
5. ¿Cuál es el número de la salida más cerca de tu casa?
6. ¿Cuál es la velocidad máxima en la autopista?
7. ¿Cuántos carriles tiene?
8. A la salida, ¿hay un rótulo que indica los pueblos cercanos?

Actividades comunicativas

A Las autopistas Estás viajando por el Ecuador. Un(a) amigo(a) ecuatoriano(a) (tu compañero[a]) te hace preguntas sobre las autopistas donde tú vives. Contesta a todas sus preguntas y descríbele las autopistas de tu estado.

B Ventajas En las autopistas es casi siempre necesario pagar peaje. En las carreteras secundarias no hay peaje. Con un(a) compañero(a), discutan por qué es mejor tomar la autopista y pagar el peaje. ¿Cuáles son las ventajas *(advantages)*?

Lima, Perú

En el sur de España

VOCABULARIO

trescientos nueve 309

C **Práctica C** can be done orally with books closed.

Writing Development
You can have students write a short paragraph about a super highway near where they live using the information in **Práctica C** as a guide.

Actividades comunicativas

¡OJO! The **Actividades comunicativas** allow students to use the vocabulary and structures of the chapter in open-ended, real-life situations. They also give students another opportunity to use words and structures from previous chapters.

Have students work on as many activities as you wish. You may also allow them to select those activities they want to do. Different groups can work on different activities.

GEOGRAPHY CONNECTION

En el sur de España The road signs in the right-hand photo on this page are in Málaga. This is the intersection of two major **autovías, Nacional 340** and **Nacional 321. Nacional 340** follows the coast from Cádiz to Almería and offers magnificent views of both the Atlantic and Mediterranean coasts, including the Straits of Gibraltar. **Nacional 340** is the highway of the Costa del Sol, traversing its entire length. **Nacional 321** goes inland from Málaga and leads to other highways that take the traveler to the major cities of Andalucía.

ANSWERS

Práctica
C 1. **Una autopista cerca de donde yo vivo es ___.**
2. **Sí, (No, no) es una autopista de peaje.**
3. **El peaje es ___.**
4. **Tengo que pagar el peaje en ___. Hay garitas de peaje cada ___ kilómetros.**
5. **El número de la salida más cerca de mi casa es ___.**
6. **La velocidad máxima en la autopista es ___.**
7. **Tiene ___ carriles.**
8. **Sí (No), a la salida (no) hay un rótulo que indica los pueblos cercanos.**

Actividades comunicativas
A and B Answers will vary.

RESOURCES

- 📁 Workbook, pages 123–126
- 📁 Student Tape Manual, TE, pages 125–126
- 🎧 Audiocassette 7A/CD6
- 📁 Quizzes 3–5, pages 52–54
- 💾 Computer Testmaker
- 💿 CD-ROM, Disc 3, pages 310–315

Bell Ringer Review

Use BRR Transparency 11-3, or write the following on the board:
Write the opposites of these words and expressions:
1. **la izquierda**
2. **detrás de**
3. **el este**
4. **la luz roja**

TEACHING STRUCTURE

 Telling friends what to do

A. Have students open their books to page 310. Lead them through the explanation. Have students repeat the imperative forms.
B. Provide and elicit additional examples.

 Students should not be expected to produce the command forms perfectly since one who is not very fluent seldom tells someone what to do. You may wish to present this point more for receptive purposes.

✦Práctica✦

 Have students present each item of **Práctica A** as a mini-conversation.

310

Estructura

 Telling friends what to do
Imperativo familiar: formas regulares

You use the **tú** command when speaking with friends, family, people you know well, and children. The regular **tú** form of the command is the same form as the **usted** form in the present tense.

PRESENT (UD.)	IMPERATIVE (TÚ)
Ud. maneja.	¡Maneja!
Ud. aprende.	¡Aprende!
Ud. escribe.	¡Escribe!
Ud. comienza.	¡Comienza!
Ud. vuelve.	¡Vuelve!
Ud sigue.	¡Sigue!

Estepona, España

✦Práctica✦

A. **¿Qué debo hacer?** Sigan el modelo.

¿Debo hablar?

Sí, Pepe, habla.

1. ¿Debo parar?
2. ¿Debo doblar?
3. ¿Debo dar la vuelta?
4. ¿Debo doblar a la derecha?
5. ¿Debo leer el rótulo?
6. ¿Debo seguir derecho?
7. ¿Debo volver?
8. ¿Debo pedir direcciones?

ANSWERS

Práctica
A 1. **Sí, Pepe, para.**
2. **Sí, Pepe, dobla.**
3. **Sí, Pepe, da la vuelta.**
4. **Sí, Pepe, dobla a la derecha.**
5. **Sí, Pepe, lee el rótulo.**
6. **Sí, Pepe, sigue derecho.**
7. **Sí, Pepe, vuelve.**
8. **Sí, Pepe, pide direcciones.**

B HISTORIETA El instructor

Completen con el imperativo.

Estepona, España

Luis, primero ___1___ (prender) el motor. ___2___ (Prestar) atención a la carretera. Ahora ___3___ (entrar) en la carretera. Bien. ___4___ (Adelantar) en el carril izquierdo. Ahora ___5___ (volver) al carril derecho. ___6___ (Seguir) derecho hasta la salida. ___7___ (Manejar) siempre con calma. ___8___ (Parar) aquí. ___9___ (Apagar) el motor. ___10___ (Tomar) este manual y ___11___ (leer). Es todo para hoy.

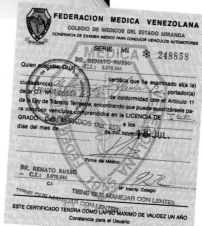

C Una visita a la Argentina   Sigan el ejemplo.

Quiero visitar a la Argentina.

Pues, visita a la Argentina.

1. Quiero viajar a la Argentina.
2. Quiero tomar un avión.
3. Quiero pasar un mes allí.
4. Quiero visitar a Buenos Aires.
5. Quiero subir a la cordillera.
6. Quiero esquiar en Bariloche.
7. Quiero comer un biftec allí.
8. Quiero nadar en los lagos.

ESTRUCTURA

trescientos once 〰 **311**

311

TEACHING STRUCTURE

 Telling friends what to do

Have students open their books to page 312 and have them repeat the irregular forms of the **tú** command after you.

 **Práctica**

A Have students present each item of **Práctica A** as a mini-conversation.

B Have students prepare **Práctica B** before going over it in class.

Did You Know?

Autopistas modernas The **autovías** in Spain are a series of modern highways inaugurated at the time of the Expo '92 international fair. The **autovías** do not charge tolls. The **autopistas** are a small number of superhighways on which there is no speed limit and which do require toll payments.

 # Telling friends what to do
Imperativo familiar: formas irregulares

The following verbs have irregular forms for the **tú** commands.

INFINITIVE	IMPERATIVE (TÚ)
decir	di
ir	ve
ser	sé
salir	sal
hacer	haz
tener	ten
venir	ven
poner	pon

 **Práctica**

A A casa del abuelo

Contesten con **sí** y el imperativo.

1. ¿Debo venir mañana?
2. ¿Debo salir temprano?
3. ¿Debo hacer el viaje en carro?
4. ¿Debo poner aire en las llantas?
5. ¿Debo decir adiós a mi hermano?
6. ¿Debo ir por la carretera vieja?
7. ¿Debo tener cuidado?

El camino a Otavalo, Ecuador

B HISTORIETA El mecánico experto y el mecánico nuevo

Completen con el imperativo.

____ (Oír), Paco. ____ (Venir) aquí. Hay aceite en el piso, así es que ____ (tener) cuidado. Bien, ____ (mirar) lo que yo hago, y tú, ____ (hacer) lo mismo. ____ (Poner) la luz aquí y ____ (ser) atento. Ahora, ____ (decir) todo lo que aprendiste hoy.

ANSWERS

Práctica

A
1. Sí, ven mañana.
2. Sí, sal temprano.
3. Sí, haz el viaje en carro.
4. Sí, pon aire en las llantas.
5. Sí, di adiós a tu hermano.
6. Sí, ve por la carretera vieja.
7. Sí, ten cuidado.

B
1. Oye
2. Ven
3. ten
4. mira
5. haz
6. Pon
7. sé
8. di

C **HISTORIETA** Tito el tímido.

Sigan el modelo.

> **No sé si debo manejar.**
> **¡Maneja, hombre!**

1. No sé si debo hacer el viaje.
2. No sé si debo salir de la ciudad.
3. No sé si debo manejar.
4. No sé si debo ir por la autopista.
5. No sé si debo pedir un día de vacación.
6. No sé si debo volver tarde.

Actividades comunicativas

A **Las direcciones**   Habla con un(a) compañero(a). Dale direcciones para ir de la escuela a tu casa. Luego tu compañero(a) te dirá cómo ir a su casa.

B **Una llamada telefónica**   Estás hablando con un(a) estudiante de intercambio de Buenos Aires, Argentina. Él o ella quiere hacer una llamada desde un teléfono público. Dile lo que tiene que hacer.

Calle Florida, Buenos Aires

C **A la capital**   Alicia acaba de recibir su permiso de conducir. Mañana sus padres le van a permitir usar el carro. Alicia tiene que ir a la capital y no conoce la ruta. Explícale cómo puede ir de tu pueblo a la capital de tu estado. Contesta a todas sus preguntas.

C   Have students present **Práctica C** as a mini-conversation.

Actividades comunicativas

Have students choose the activity or activities they wish to take part in.

ANSWERS

Práctica

C **1.** **¡Haz el viaje, hombre!**
2. **¡Sal de la ciudad, hombre!**
3. **¡Maneja, hombre!**
4. **¡Ve por la autopista, hombre!**
5. **¡Pide un día de vacación, hombre!**
6. **¡Vuelve tarde, hombre!**

Actividades comunicativas
A, B, and **C**   Answers will vary.

TEACHING STRUCTURE

Telling friends what not to do

A. Have students open their books to page 314 and lead them through Steps 1 and 2. Then have them repeat the forms after you.

B. Provide and elicit additional examples.

 The use of the commands, and particularly the placement of pronouns with commands, is extremely difficult for students. Since they do not have to produce these forms until they are quite fluent, it is recommended that you present them primarily for recognition only.

Práctica

A Have students do this activity in pairs. Have different pairs each present one item to the class.

Telling friends what not to do
Imperativo negativo

1. The negative **tú** commands are formed the same way as the formal **(Ud., Uds.)** commands. You drop the **o** of the **yo** form of the present tense and add **es** to **-ar** verbs and **as** to **-er** and **-ir** verbs.

INFINITIVE	PRESENT (YO)	NEGATIVE COMMAND (TÚ)
hablar	hablø	no hables
comer	comø	no comas
abrir	abrø	no abras
volver	vuelvø	no vuelvas
pedir	pidø	no pidas
hacer	hagø	no hagas
salir	salgø	no salgas

2. The same verbs that are irregular in the formal command are irregular in the negative **tú** command.

ir	no vayas
ser	no seas
saber	no sepas
estar	no estés
dar	no dés

¿Te acuerdas?

Object pronouns are attached to affirmative formal commands and precede negative commands. The same is true of familiar commands.
¡Levántate!
¡No te levantes!
¡Dámelo!
¡No me lo des!
¡Cómpramelo!
¡No me lo compres!
¡Mírame!
¡No me mires!
¡Díselo!
¡No se lo digas!

Práctica

A HISTORIETA *¿Hago el viaje o no?*
Contesten según modelo.

¿Voy temprano o no?

No, no vayas temprano.

1. ¿Voy temprano o no?
2. ¿Salgo a las nueve o no?
3. ¿Tomo la carretera vieja o no?
4. ¿Manejo el convertible o no?
5. ¿Excedo la velocidad máxima o no?
6. ¿Le digo la verdad a Pepe o no?
7. ¿Vuelvo tarde o no?
8. ¿Hago el viaje o no?

ANSWERS

Práctica

A
1. **No, no vayas temprano.**
2. **No, no salgas a las nueve.**
3. **No, no tomes la carretera vieja.**
4. **No, no manejes el convertible.**
5. **No, no excedas la velocidad máxima.**
6. **No, no le digas la verdad a Pepe.**
7. **No, no vuelvas tarde.**
8. **No, no hagas el viaje.**

B En la gasolinera

Contesten con **no** y el imperativo.

1. ¿Lleno el tanque?
2. ¿Abro el capó?
3. ¿Reviso el aceite?
4. ¿Pongo agua en el radiador?
5. ¿Limpio el parabrisas?
6. ¿Pongo aire en las llantas?

Ciudad de México

C ¡Qué dormilona es Marisa!

Practiquen la conversación.

MAMÁ: Marisa, levántate. Ya es hora.
MARISA: ¡Ay, mamá! Que no. ¡Déjame, por favor!
MAMÁ: Bien. No te levantes. Y no te laves ni te vistas. Quédate en cama.
MARISA: Perdóname, mami, pero estoy muy cansada.

D ¿Lo compro o no?   Sigan el ejemplo.

¿Compro el carro o no?
Sí, cómpralo.
No, no lo compres.

1. ¿Compro las baterías o no?
2. ¿Compro el aceite o no?
3. ¿Compro la gasolina o no?
4. ¿Compro el convertible o no?
5. ¿Compro los neumáticos o no?

Madrid, España

E Sí, dámelas.   Contesten según el modelo.

¿Te doy las direcciones?   Sí, dámelas.

1. ¿Te doy el mapa?
2. ¿Te doy las instrucciones?
3. ¿Te doy el dinero para el parquímetro?
4. ¿Te doy los tiques?
5. ¿Te doy la licencia?

ESTRUCTURA

trescientos quince 〰 **315**

B You can go over **Práctica B** without prior preparation.

EXPANSION Have two students present **Práctica B** as a conversation in a service station.

C Call on two students to read **Práctica C** with as much expression as possible.

D and **E** Call on more able students to answer when going over these activities.

Learning From Photos

Ciudad de México You may wish to ask these questions about the top photo on this page:
¿Dónde están ellos?
¿Qué será uno de los hombres?
¿Qué están mirando ellos?
¿Cuál será el problema?
Madrid, España CEPSA is the **Compañía Española de Petróleo**. Ask students if they remember what the SA stands for. ELF is a French oil company. The service station provides products from both companies.

¡OJO! There is no more new material to present in this chapter. The sections that follow recombine and reinforce the vocabulary and structures that have already been introduced.

ANSWERS

Práctica

B 1. No, no llenes el tanque.
2. No, no abras el capó.
3. No, no revises el aceite.
4. No, no pongas agua en el radiador.
5. No, no limpies el parabrisas.
6. No, no pongas aire en las llantas.

D 1. Sí, cómpralas. No, no las compres.
2. Sí, cómpralo. No, no lo compres.
3. Sí, cómprala. No, no la compres.
4. Sí, cómpralo. No, no lo compres.
5. Sí, cómpralos. No, no los compres.

E 1. Sí, dámelo.
2. Sí, dámelas.
3. Sí, dámelo.
4. Sí, dámelos.
5. Sí, dámela.

Bell Ringer Review

Use BRR Transparency 11-5, or write the following on the board: Define the following briefly in Spanish.

1. la entrada
2. la salida
3. la carretera
4. el rótulo

TEACHING THE CONVERSATON

A. 🎧 Have students listen to the conversation on Cassette 7A/Compact Disc 6.

B. Have the class repeat the conversation after you.

C. Call on two students to read the conversation aloud.

D. After students read a few lines, ask corresponding questions from the **Después de conversar** section.

TECHNOLOGY OPTION

💿 On the CD-ROM (Disc 3, page 316), students can watch a dramatization of this conversation. They can then play the role of either one of the characters, and record themselves in the conversation.

ABOUT THE SPANISH LANGUAGE

Two additional words that mean *to park* besides **estacionar** are **aparcar** and **parquear**.

Conversación

Un sitio para estacionar

MARÍA: Anita, ¿puedo estacionar aquí?
ANITA: Aquí, no. ¿No ves que es un cruce de peatones? Hay un estacionamiento municipal en la plaza.
MARÍA: ¿Cómo voy a la plaza?
ANITA: Toma la avenida Cisneros. Quédate en el carril derecho porque a dos cuadras de aquí vas a doblar a la derecha.
MARÍA: ¿En la esquina donde está la estación de servicio?
ANITA: Precisamente. Repito—dobla a la derecha y sigue derecho hasta el primer semáforo. Al primer semáforo, dobla a la izquierda y verás la plaza.
MARÍA: ¿Y puedo estacionar en la plaza?
ANITA: En la plaza misma, no. Pero hay un estacionamiento subterráneo. Hay un rótulo para indicar la entrada.

Después de conversar

Contesten.

1. ¿Qué quiere saber María?
2. Según Anita, ¿por qué no se puede estacionar allí?
3. ¿Dónde se puede estacionar?
4. ¿Sabe María ir allí?
5. ¿Por qué debe María quedarse en el carril derecho?
6. ¿Qué hay en la esquina donde debe doblar?
7. Después de doblar a la derecha, ¿qué debe hacer María?
8. ¿Cuándo debe doblar a la izquierda?
9. ¿Dónde se encuentra el estacionamiento?
10. ¿Qué hay para indicar la entrada?

ANSWERS

Después de conversar

1. **María quiere saber si puede estacionar allí.**
2. **Según Anita, no se puede estacionar allí porque es un cruce de peatones.**
3. **Se puede estacionar en un estacionamiento municipal en la plaza.**
4. **No, María no sabe cómo ir allí.**
5. **Debe quedarse en el carril derecho porque a dos cuadras de allí va a doblar a la derecha.**
6. **En la esquina donde debe doblar está la estación de servicio.**
7. **Después de doblar a la derecha María debe seguir derecho hasta el primer semáforo.**
8. **Debe doblar a la izquierda al primer semáforo.**
9. **El estacionamiento se encuentra en la plaza pero es un estacionamiento subterráneo.**
10. **Hay un rótulo para indicar la entrada.**

Actividades comunicativas

A **Las señales de tránsito** Trabaja con un(a) compañero(a). Tú escogerás una señal y explicarás a tu compañero(a) lo que significa. Tu compañero(a) tiene que adivinar cuál de las señales estás describiendo. Luego cambien de rol.

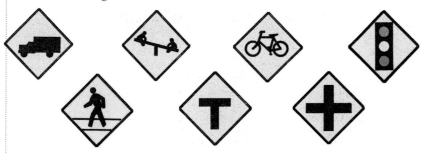

JUEGO **¿No lo hago?** Have some fun. Your parents and teachers are always telling you what not to do. Get together in small groups and in a nice way imitate your parents and teachers. State all those things they do indeed tell each of you not to do.

Santo Domingo, República Dominicana

Actividades comunicativas

¡OJO! These activities encourage students to use the chapter vocabulary and structures in open-ended situations. It is not necessary to have them do all the activities. Choose the ones you consider most appropriate.

HISTORY CONNECTION

Los dominicanos In what is today **La República Dominicana** Columbus established the first Spanish settlement in the Americas, La Isabela, on the island of **La Española** in 1493. The capital is Santo Domingo but most Spanish speakers refer to the entire island as Santo Domingo despite the fact that a third of the island constitutes the Republic of Haiti. Dominican immigration to the United States is significant. New York City has a large Dominican population.

ANSWERS

Actividades comunicativas
A • **Camiones**
• **Niños jugando**
• **Bicicletas**
• **Semáforo**
• **Cruce de peatones**
• **Fin del camino**
• **Cruce**

317

Cultures
The reading about the Pan American Highway on page 318, and the related activities on page 319, familiarize students with the longest highway system in the world.

Comparisons
In this reading students learn that, unlike in the United States, where roads are generally well-maintained, traveling on certain portions of the Pan American Highway may require caution and, often, a sense of adventure.

TEACHING THE READING

Pre-reading

Tell students that they are going to read about the longest and possibly most interesting highway in the world. If possible, show students on a map or maps the route the Pan American Highway takes.

Reading

A. Call on an individual to read several sentences aloud.

B. After two students have read aloud, stop and ask questions such as: **¿Qué es la carretera panamericana? ¿Dónde empieza (nace)? ¿Dónde termina (muere)? ¿Enlaza la carretera la costa oriental con la costa occidental?**

Lecturas CULTURALES

Reading Strategy

Summarizing
When you read informative passages, you must develop ways to try to remember what you read. This is most important if you are reading about a topic you know nothing about. Summarizing is a good way to do this. The easiest way to summarize is to take notes as you begin to read. From your notes, you can write a sentence about each section or paragraph of the reading. From your paragraph sentences, it will be easy to write one sentence describing the main idea of the selection. Use all your summary sentences to help trigger your memory about the contents of each part of the reading.

LA CARRETERA PANAMERICANA

La carretera panamericana es la carretera más larga del mundo—47.516 kilómetros. La panamericana es un sistema de carreteras y caminos que se extiende desde la frontera de los Estados Unidos y México hasta la ciudad de Puerto Montt en Chile. Además de extenderse del norte al sur de los continentes americanos, la carretera enlaza[1] la costa oriental con la costa occidental de la América del Sur. Enlaza[1] también las capitales de diecisiete países latinoamericanos. Esta carretera es una ruta importante para el transporte de materias primas y productos agrícolas.

En algunas partes la carretera panamericana es una carretera moderna con dos o más carriles en cada sentido. En su mayor parte la carretera está pavimentada—en algunos casos en buenas condiciones y en otros casos en malas condiciones. En muchos trayectos de la carretera la tierra es muy inhóspita. Se puede decir que la carretera también es inhóspita. Hay que manejar con mucho cuidado porque nunca sabes cuándo encontrarás un bache[2] muy profundo. A veces el pavimento desaparece repentinamente y te encuentras en un camino de rocas, piedras y lodo[3].

[1]enlaza *connects*
[2]bache *pothole*
[3]lodo *mud*

La carretera panamericana, México

¡Ten cuidado! Hay otro peligro. La mayor parte de la carretera no tiene borde. Por consiguiente cuando un carro o un camión tiene una avería⁴, el conductor pone unas ramas⁵ de árboles o plantas a unos metros detrás del carro. Estas ramas advierten⁶ a los conductores que se están acercando que hay un carro averiado. Pero al reparar el carro o cambiar la llanta pinchada⁷, el conductor sale y allí se quedan las ramas. Y de noche es difícil verlas.

Como ya hemos dicho, en muchas áreas la carretera panamericana es una carretera moderna y conveniente. Pero en las zonas remotas que recorre, tomar la panamericana es una verdadera aventura.

⁴avería *breakdown*
⁵ramas *branches*
⁶advierten *warn*
⁷pinchada *flat*

La carretera panamericana, Guatemala

Después de leer

A **La panamericana** Contesten.

1. ¿Cuál es la carretera más larga del mundo?
2. ¿Qué es la panamericana?
3. ¿Dónde empieza la panamericana y dónde termina?
4. ¿Enlaza a cuántas capitales?
5. ¿Cómo es la carretera en algunas partes?
6. ¿Cómo es en otras partes?

B **Palabras** Empleen las siguientes palabras en una oración.

1. carril
2. enlaza (hace enlace con)
3. bache
4. avería
5. llanta pinchada

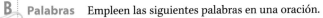

LECTURAS CULTURALES

trescientos diecinueve 〜 **319**

Post-reading

A. Go over the **Después de leer** activities.

B. Have a few students give a description of the Pan American Highway in their own words.

TECHNOLOGY OPTION

Students may listen to a recording of the **Lectura** on the CD-ROM, Disc 3, pages 318–319.

GEOGRAPHY CONNECTION

La carretera panamericana

Have students plot the entire length of the **Carretera Panamericana** on the maps on pages 452 and 453 or on the Map Transparencies. You may wish to ask the students:

¿Cuántos kilómetros tiene la carretera panamericana en total?

¿Por qué países pasa la carretera?

¿Qué montañas tiene que cruzar?

ANSWERS

Después de leer

A **1.** La carretera más larga del mundo es la carretera panamericana.

2. Es un sistema de carreteras y caminos que se extiende desde la frontera de los Estados Unidos y México hasta la ciudad de Puerto Montt en Chile.

3. Empieza en la frontera de los Estados Unidos y México y termina en Puerto Montt, en Chile.

4. Enlaza a diecisiete capitales.

5. En algunas partes es una carretera moderna con dos o más carriles en cada sentido.

6. En otras partes la carretera está en malas condiciones y es inhóspita. Hay que manejar con mucho cuidado.

B Answers will vary.

LECTURA OPCIONAL 1

National Standards

Cultures
This reading, and the related activities on this page, familiarize students with parking in the Spanish-speaking world.

TEACHING TIPS

¡OJO! This reading is optional. You may skip it completely, have the entire class read it, have only several students read it, or assign it for extra credit.

Note that this selection reintroduces quite a few familiar command forms.

A. Have a student who read this selection explain in his or her own words how to use a parking meter where he or she lives.

Learning From Realia

Un boleto de aparcamiento
Direct the students' attention to the blue ticket. You may wish to ask them:
¿Para qué es el tique?
¿Cuánto cuesta?
¿Para cuánto tiempo es válido?
¿Es obligatorio tener un tique?
¿Qué anuncios o propaganda lleva el tique?

Málaga, España

EL ESTACIONAMIENTO

En todas las grandes ciudades de España y Latinoamérica es difícil estacionar. En algunas calles donde no está prohibido el estacionamiento hay parquímetros donde uno puede meter una moneda. Entonces el parquímetro indicará el tiempo que puedes estacionar.

Hay también aparcamientos públicos y garajes privados donde es necesario pagar. En muchas ciudades hay aparcamientos municipales donde no hay parquímetros pero tienes que pagar.

—Dime lo que tengo que hacer si voy a uno de estos estacionamientos.

—Busca la (máquina) distribuidora de tiques. Introduce una o varias monedas en la distribuidora. Pon suficiente dinero para el tiempo deseado. Oprime el botón y saldrá un papelito o tique. Indicará el tiempo que puedes estacionar. Pon el papelito o el tique en el interior del parabrisas del coche donde lo pueden ver los guardias o policías. Si no lo ven, te darán una multa[1].

[1]multa *fine*

Después de leer

A **¿Qué es?** Identifiquen.

 1.

 2.

 3.

 4.

B **¿Qué hago para estacionar?** Explica a un(a) amigo(a) todo lo que tiene que hacer para estacionar el coche (aparcar el carro) en un aparcamiento público con una distribuidora de tiques.

ANSWERS

Después de leer

A 1. Es un parquímetro.
2. Es un estacionamiento (aparcamiento) municipal.
3. Es un garaje.
4. Es una (máquina) distribuidora de tiques.

B Answers will vary, but may include:
Busco una distribuidora de tiques. Pongo varias monedas en la distribuidora. Pongo suficiente dinero para el tiempo deseado. Oprimo el botón y sale un papelito o tique que indica el tiempo que puedo estacionar. Pongo el tique en el interior del parabrisas del coche donde lo pueden ver los policías.

LAS SEÑALES DE TRÁNSITO

Desde hace muchos años, en España, Latinoamérica y en otras partes del mundo, se han usado las señales de tránsito internacionales. En los Estados Unidos la introducción de estas señales fue más reciente, pero ahora se ven en todas partes. Lo bueno de las señales internacionales es que no es necesario saber el idioma del país, porque muchas de las señales no usan palabras.

Estas son las señales más comunes.

Después de leer

A ¿Qué quiere decir... ? Identifiquen las señales de tránsito.

LECTURAS OPCIONALES
trescientos veintiuno 🙢 **321**

LECTURA OPCIONAL 2

National Standards

Cultures
This reading, and the related activity on this page, familiarize students with international road signs and their use in the Spanish-speaking world.

Comparisons
Students learn that, unlike in Spain and the Latin American countries, international road signs were only recently introduced here in the United States.

TEACHING TIPS

A. Have students quickly read the selection. See how many of the signs they can identify.

B. Ask them if there are signs like these in your community.

Did You Know?

¡**Alto!** The stop signs in some Latin American countries say **Alto**, in others they say **Pare**, and in Spain they say **Stop**.

ANSWERS

Después de leer

A Answers will vary, but may include:
- **Parar**
- **No doblar a la izquierda**
- **Curva**
- **No exceder 40 km**
- **Sentido de tránsito**
- **En dos sentidos**
- **De sentido único**
- **No doblar a la derecha**
- **Ceder el paso**
- **Se permite adelantar**

Conexiones

LAS CIENCIAS

LA ECOLOGÍA

Ecology is a subject of great interest to people around the world. People are becoming more aware of the damage being done to our environment. Many of the ecological problems that exist in one area of the world are common in many other areas. People in Mexico City are as concerned about their polluted air as are the residents of Los Angeles.

Ciudad de México

La ecología

El problema de la contaminación del medio ambiente[1] ha dado lugar al movimiento ecologista. El término «ecología» significa el equilibrio entre los seres vivientes y la naturaleza.

La contaminación del aire
La contaminación del aire es un problema serio en muchas partes del mundo. España y Latinoamérica no son ninguna excepción. El aire de muchas ciudades de España y Latinoamérica está contaminado. Los gases que salen de los tubos de escape de los automóviles, camiones y buses son una causa principal de la contaminación.

[1]medio ambiente *environment*

Quito, Ecuador

322

Campañas ecológicas

Muchas ciudades están experimentando con programas para controlar o eliminar la contaminación. La Ciudad de México, que tiene uno de los problemas más serios en cuanto a la contaminación del aire, no permite a los autobuses de largo recorrido entrar en el centro de la ciudad.

En algunas ciudades los carros con placa² de número par circulan un día y los carros con placa de número impar circulan el otro. Es una manera de tratar de eliminar el número de vehículos y así reducir la emisión de gases que contaminan el aire.

Ciudad de México

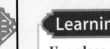

²placa *license plate*

⇜Después de leer⇝

A **¿Cuál es la palabra?** Busquen la palabra equivalente en la lectura.

1. pollution
2. environment
3. human beings
4. campaign

B **Donde vivimos** Contesten.

1. ¿Está muy contaminado el aire donde Uds. viven?
2. ¿Hay otros tipos de contaminación?
3. ¿Hay mucho o poco tráfico donde Uds. viven?
4. ¿Tiene su pueblo o ciudad un programa para controlar la contaminación?
5. En su ciudad o pueblo, ¿pueden circular todos los vehículos el mismo día?
6. ¿Sabes el número de la placa del carro de tu familia?
7. ¿Tiene un número par o impar?

Sea buen ciudadano: recicle las latas de aluminio.

Autoridad de Desperdicios Sólidos
Reciclando hoy para un mejor mañana
Tel. (809) 765-7575/1-800-981-RECI

CONEXIONES

trescientos veintitrés 〜 **323**

L A S   C I E N C I A S
LA ECOLOGÍA

You may wish to have all students scan this selection quickly. The topic is of great interest today and the reading selection is quite easy. Tell students that the word **contaminación,** as it is used here, does not mean "contamination." Ask them what it means. *(pollution)*

Learning From Realia

Una placa del DF You may wish to ask students the following about the Mexican license plate:

La placa que vemos, ¿es un número par o un número impar?

Reciclaje de aluminio You may wish to ask students the following questions about the poster:

¿Qué es la figura en la caricatura?

¿Qué pide él?

¿Quiénes son *buenos ciudadanos*?

¿Cuáles son algunos *desperdicios sólidos*?

¿Qué quiere decir *Reciclando hoy para un mejor mañana*?

National Standards

Communities
If there are exchange students from Spain or Latin America, ask them to report to the class on problems of pollution in their countries and what is being done or can be done about them. Encourage students to ask questions. If a student is unavailable, an adult member of the Hispanic community could be invited.

ANSWERS

Después de leer

A 1. la contaminación

2. el medio ambiente

3. los seres vivientes

4. la campaña

B Answers will vary but may include:

1. **Sí (No), el aire (no) está muy contaminado donde vivimos.**
2. **Sí ,(No, no) hay otros tipos de contaminación.**

3. **Hay mucho (poco) tráfico donde vivimos.**
4. **Sí (No), nuestro pueblo (nuestra ciudad) (no) tiene un programa para controlar la contaminación.**
5. **Sí (No), en nuestro pueblo (nuestra ciudad), (no) pueden circular todos los vehículos el mismo día.**
6. **Sí, (No, no) sé el número de la placa del carro de mi familia.**
7. **Tiene un número par (impar).**

323

Actividades orales

Let students choose the activities they would like to do.

Student Portfolio

Have students keep a notebook containing their best written work from each chapter. These selected writings can be based on assignments from the Student Textbook and the Writing Activities Workbook. The activities on page 325 are examples of writing assignments that may be included in each student's portfolio.

In the Workbook, students will develop an organized autobiography **(Mi autobiografía).** These workbook pages may also become a part of their portfolio. See the Teacher's Manual for more information on the Student Portfolio.

Culminación

Actividades orales

A. En la gasolinera Has alquilado un coche. En este momento estás en una gasolinera. Dile al/a la empleado(a) (tu compañero[a]) lo que necesitas. Y pregúntale cómo llegar a tu próximo destino.

B. El zoo aquarium Trabaja con un(a) compañero(a). Miren este anuncio sobre el zoo aquarium en la Casa de Campo en Madrid. Hay muchas opciones para llegar al zoo. Discútanlas y decidan cómo Uds. van a ir.

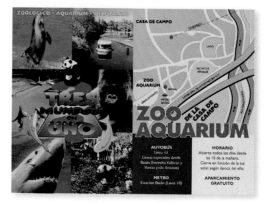

C. Leyendo el mapa Con un(a) compañero(a), miren el mapa de España. Han alquilado un coche y quieren ir de Madrid a otra ciudad que los dos escogen. Discutan cómo van a ir y las carreteras que van a tomar. ¡A ver si pueden adivinar cuánto tiempo durará *(will take)* el viaje!

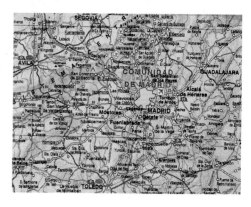

ANSWERS

Actividades orales
A, B, and C Answers will vary.

Independent Practice

Assign any of the following:
1. Activities, pages 324–325
2. Workbook, **Mi autobiografía,** page 130
3. Situation Cards
4. CD-ROM, Chapter 11, Disc 3, **Juego de repaso**

324

Actividades escritas

A **Del aeropuerto** Tú tienes un buen amigo que vive en Venezuela. Te va a visitar dentro de poco. Viene con su familia y al llegar al aeropuerto van a alquilar un carro. Escríbele a tu amigo(a) dándole direcciones para ir del aeropuerto a tu casa.

B **Instrucciones** Tus padres van a salir este fin de semana. Ellos te han escrito una lista de cosas que debes hacer y otra lista de cosas que no debes hacer. Escribe lo que dice la lista. Luego compara tu lista con la de un(a) compañero(a).

Writing Strategy

Developing a fictional narrative

Like any other narrative, a fictional narrative tells a story. A short story is one kind of fictional narrative, created in the writer's imagination. It tells about a made-up event built up around a complication. It has a plot, characters, and a setting, all of which are related from a certain point of view. For some writers, the hardest part is coming up with the idea, but once they do, they must be sure that their stories contain all these elements.

Tú y Antonio llegaron muy tarde

You were driving to school with Antonio, the high school exchange student living with you. You missed your first period class, which happens to be your Driver Education class. And to make matters worse, you had a test that day. You tried to explain to your teacher what happened but he asked you to write it down for him because it seemed so complicated. Write an imaginative story to tell why you and Antonio were late. It might be fun to use the road signs below to help you make up excuses. Be as humorous and creative as you can. Remember, you have to be convincing enough so your teacher will let you make up the exam rather than take a zero!

Actividades escritas

A **TECHNOLOGY OPTION**
Students may use the Portfolio feature on the CD-ROM to write their letters.

B Have individuals read their lists to the class. Have the other students raise their hands each time they have the same item on their lists. Then poll the class to see how many times each order was given.

Writing Strategy

Developing a fictional narrative

A. Have students read the Writing Strategy on page 325.
B. Have students work in pairs to write this story.

ANSWERS

Actividades escritas
A and **B** Answers will vary.

Writing Strategy
Answers will vary.

VOCABULARY REVIEW

The words and phrases in the **Vocabulario** have been taught for productive use in this chapter. They are summarized here as a resource for both students and teacher. This list also serves as a convenient resource for the **Culminación** activities on pages 324 and 325. There are approximately nine cognates in this vocabulary list. Have students find them.

📌 Teacher Notes

Vocabulario

TALKING ABOUT CARS

el descapotable, el convertible	el sedán
el coche (carro) deportivo	el cupé
el permiso de conducir, la licencia	el conductor

IDENTIFYING PARTS OF A CAR

el cinturón de seguridad	las direccionales
el capó	la bocina, el claxon
la puerta	la goma, la llanta, el neumático
la maletera, el baúl	la llanta de repuesto (de recambio)
las luces	el parabrisas
los frenos	

TALKING ABOUT SERVICES AT A GAS STATION

la estación de servicio, la gasolinera	sin plomo
el aceite	limpiar el parabrisas
la gasolina	llenar el tanque
súper	poner agua en el radiador
normal	revisar el aceite
con plomo	verificar la presión

TALKING ABOUT DRIVING ON THE HIGHWAY

la carretera	la entrada
la autopista, la autovía	la salida
el carril	el rótulo
el peaje	la velocidad máxima
la garita de peaje	

GIVING DIRECTIONS

seguir derecho	estar prohibido
quedarse en el carril	adelantar
doblar	entrar

TALKING ABOUT THE CITY

la cuadra	estacionar el coche, aparcar
el cruce, la bocacalle	el parquímetro
el semáforo, la luz roja	una calle de sentido único

OTHER USEFUL EXPRESSIONS

favor de

For the Native Speaker

¿Cómo se dice... ? If there are native speakers in the class, ask them to tell the words they use where there are choices in the vocabulary. For example: **¿el descapotable o el convertible? ¿El permiso de conducir o la licencia? ¿La bocina o el claxon? ¿La estación de servicio o la gasolinera?**, etc.

VIDEO

¡Buen viaje!

EPISODIO 11 ▶ El coche y la carretera

Cristina, Isabel y Luis van a visitar las ruinas de Tlatelolco.

Pero antes de salir, tienen que reparar su coche.

CD-ROM

Expansión cultural

El Tajín es uno de los sitios arqueológicos más interesantes de México.

interNET CONNECTION

In this video episode Isabel, Luis, and Cristina take a day trip by car. To be certain that you know what to do in case you have a car accident in a Spanish-speaking country, go to the **Capítulo 11** Internet activity at the Glencoe Foreign Language Web site:

http://www.glencoe.com/sec/fl

TECNOTUR

trescientos veintisiete ∞ **327**

OVERVIEW

This page previews three key multimedia components of the **Glencoe Spanish** series. Each reinforces the material taught in Chapter 11 in a unique manner.

VIDEO

The Video Program allows students to see how the chapter vocabulary and structures are used by native speakers in an engaging story. Show the video episode as a final activity for Chapter 11.

A. These two photos show highlights from the Chapter 11 video episode. Tell students: **En la primera foto vemos la Plaza de las Tres Culturas en la Ciudad de México. Es un lugar histórico. En la segunda foto, Luis, Isabel y Cristina están en una gasolinera. ¿Quién es el hombre a la izquierda?**

B. See the Video Activities Booklet for detailed suggestions for using this resource.

CD-ROM

A. The **Expansión cultural** photo shows another of the many archeological sites found throughout Mexico. Have students read the caption on page 327.

B. In the CD-ROM version of **Expansión cultural** (Disc 3, page 327), students can listen to additional recorded information about archeological sites in Mexico.

INTERNET

Teacher Information and Student Worksheets for this activity can be accessed at the Web site.

Video Synopsis

This episode continues Cristina's introduction to Mexican history and culture as Isabel and Luis show her Tlatelolco and the Plaza de las Tres Culturas in Mexico City. Then, on their way to Teotihuacán, they stop at a gas station to fill up the tank and check the oil and the tires. When Luis mentions that the turn signals are not working, the gas station attendant gives them directions to a mechanic in the next town. They drive off in search of the mechanic with hopes of still being able to get to Teotihuacán before the end of the day.

OVERVIEW

This section reviews the salient points from Chapters 8–11. In the **Lectura** students will review the present perfect and the present progressive in context. In the **Estructura** section, they will review the present perfect, irregular past participles, object pronouns that are attached to infinitives or participles, and comparisons of equality. They will practice these structures as they talk about the topics that were presented in Chapters 8–11.

TEACHING THE LECTURA

A. Have students open their books to page 328. Ask a student to read aloud using as much expression as possible.

B. Go over the questions in the **Después de leer** section.

Learning From Photos

Un accidente You may wish to ask these questions about the top photo on page 328.

¿Qué es la señora?

¿Cómo es el uniforme que lleva?

¿Quién se ha lesionado?

¿En qué le han puesto a ella?

Bogotá, Colombia You may wish to ask these questions about the photo at the bottom of page 328.

¿Es una calle o una carretera?

¿Cuántos carriles vemos?

¿Qué tipos de vehículos puedes identificar?

328

Repaso CAPÍTULOS 8–11

Lectura

Un accidente

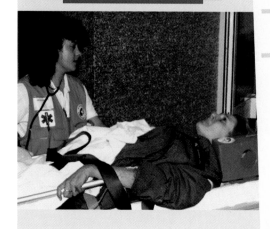

ACCIDENTE ENTRE UN CAMIÓN Y UN COCHE

Ha habido un accidente entre un camión y un coche privado en el pueblo de Mirasierra en el kilómetro 55 de la carretera nacional 3A. La policía local ha cerrado dos carriles de la carretera en dirección norte. Los socorristas han llegado al escenario y en este momento están administrando los primeros auxilios a los lesionados (heridos). Parece que la conductora del coche ha sufrido heridas más graves. Ha sido transportado en ambulancia al Hospital del Sagrado Corazón en la ciudad de San Cristóbal.

Bogotá, Colombia

Después de leer

A **En la carretera** Contesten.
1. ¿Dónde ha habido un accidente?
2. ¿Qué ha cerrado la policía?
3. ¿Quiénes han llegado al escenario?
4. ¿Qué están haciendo los socorristas?
5. ¿Quién ha sufrido lesiones o heridas más graves?
6. ¿Adónde la han transportado?
7. ¿Cómo la han transportado?

Estructura

El presente perfecto

1. The present perfect is used to express an action completed recently. The present perfect is formed by using the present tense of the verb **haber** and the past participle. Review the forms of regular verbs.

HABLAR	COMER	VIVIR
he hablado	he comido	he vivido
has hablado	has comido	has vivido
ha hablado	ha comido	ha vivido
hemos hablado	hemos comido	hemos vivido
habéis hablado	*habéis comido*	*habéis vivido*
han hablado	han comido	han vivido

2. The following verbs have irregular past participles.

DECIR	dicho	VOLVER	vuelto
HACER	hecho	MORIR	muerto
VER	visto	CUBRIR	cubierto
ESCRIBIR	escrito	ABRIR	abierto
PONER	puesto		

Práctica

A **HISTORIETA** Una comida deliciosa

Contesten.

1. ¿Ha preparado una comida buena Lucinda?
2. ¿La has ayudado?
3. ¿Han hecho Uds. una paella?
4. ¿La han cocinado en el horno?
5. ¿Han llegado los invitados?
6. ¿Ya han comido?

Hotel Jaragua, Santo Domingo

TEACHING STRUCTURE

El presente perfecto

A. Lead students through Steps 1 and 2 on page 329. Have them repeat the forms after you. Remind students that the initial **h** is silent.

B. Tell students that most of the irregular past participles in Step 2 are high-frequency verbs.

Práctica

A After doing **Práctica A,** have students retell the story in their own words.

Learning From Photos

Hotel Jaragua, Santo Domingo
You may wish to ask students:
¿Es la foto de la recepción o del comedor del hotel?
¿Qué hay en la foto, carnes o postres?

ANSWERS

Práctica

A 1. **Sí (No), Lucinda (no) ha preparado una comida buena.**
2. **Sí, (No, no) la he ayudado.**
3. **Sí, (No, no) hemos hecho una paella.**
4. **Sí, (No, no) la hemos cocinado en el horno.**
5. **Sí, (No, no) han llegado los invitados.**
6. **Sí, ya (No, todavía no) hemos comido.**

329

Pronombres con el participio y el infinitivo

When a sentence has an infinitive (**hablar**) or a present participle (**hablando**), the object pronouns can either be added to the infinitive or participle or they can precede the helping verb.

El médico quiere examinarlo.

El médico lo quiere examinar.

El técnico está tomándole los rayos equis.

Está tomándoselos en el hospital.

Él está tomándole los rayos equis.

San Juan, Puerto Rico

Práctica

A **En la sala de emergencia** Sigan el modelo.

¿Quiere el médico examinarle la garganta?
Sí, se la quiere examinar.
Sí, quiere examinársela.

1. ¿Quiere el médico tomarle una radiografía?
2. ¿Está dándole una inyección contra el tétano la enfermera?
3. ¿Están ayudando al paciente los socorristas?
4. ¿Quiere el cirujano reducirle la fractura?
5. ¿Le está poniendo el vendaje el enfermero?
6. ¿Tiene que ponerle puntos el médico?

B **HISTORIETA** Una visita a la ciudad

Sigan el modelo.

Él quiere ver el plano de la ciudad.
Él lo quiere ver.
Él quiere verlo.

1. Él está mirando el plano de la ciudad.
2. Quiere visitar la ciudad.
3. Tiene que cruzar la calle en el cruce para peatones.
4. Va a tomar el metro.
5. Está esperando el metro en la estación Plaza de España.
6. Muchos pasajeros están bajando la escalera mecánica.

Madrid, España

Comparación de igualdad

The comparative of equality means that two items being compared have equal characteristics. Remember that **tan... como** is used with adjectives and adverbs and **tanto... como** is used with nouns. **Tanto** must agree with the noun it modifies.

> **Él es tan rico como su hermano.**
> **Él tiene tanto dinero y tanta fortuna como su hermano.**

 **Práctica**

A **Comparaciones** Contesten según el modelo.

> **¿Hay más tráfico en Lima que en Caracas?**
> **No, hay tanto tráfico en Lima como en Caracas.**

1. ¿Es más alto el edificio Latar que el edificio Lamar?
2. ¿Tiene el edificio Latar más pisos que el edificio Lamar?
3. ¿Es la Plaza Simón Bolívar más bonita que la Plaza San Martín?
4. ¿Tiene la Plaza Simón Bolívar más estatuas que la Plaza San Martín?
5. ¿Es más larga la calle Luna que la calle Londres?
6. ¿Hay más tiendas en la calle Luna que en la calle Londres?
7. ¿Hay más gente en la boca del metro que en la parada del autobús?

Caracas, Venezuela

Actividades comunicativas

A **La ciudad o el campo** Trabaja con un(a) compañero(a). Van a hacer un viaje juntos. Discutan si prefieren ir a un lugar en el campo o a una ciudad. Den sus preferencias y expliquen por qué.

B **De aquí a mi casa** Habla con un(a) compañero(a). Dale direcciones para ir de la escuela a tu casa. Entonces tu compañero(a) te dirá cómo ir a su casa.

C **Un accidente** Has visto un accidente. Un(a) compañero(a) te va a hacer preguntas sobre el accidente. Contesta sus preguntas. Recuerda que es un accidente ficticio.

TEACHING STRUCTURE

Comparación de igualdad

A. Have students open their books to page 331. Lead students through the explanation.
B. Write the two examples on the board. Underline **tan... como** and **tanto... como** in the examples.

Práctica

A After doing **Práctica A,** ask volunteers to make up questions that compare anything they can think of. Have other students respond.

Actividades comunicativas

Allow students to select the activities that they want to participate in.

A This activity reviews vocabulary presented in Chapter 9.
B This activity reviews vocabulary presented in Chapter 11.
C This activity reviews vocabulary presented in Chapter 8.

Note: You may wish to do the third literary selection (pages 438–441) with students at this time.

Independent Practice

Assign any of the following:
1. Activities, pages 328–331
2. Workbook, pages 131–136
3. CD-ROM, Disc 3, pages 328–331
4. CD-ROM, Disc 3, Chapters 8-11, **Juegos de repaso**

ANSWERS

Práctica

A 1. **No, el edificio Latar es tan alto como el edificio Lamar.**
2. **No, el edificio Latar tiene tantos pisos como el edificio Lamar.**
3. **No, la Plaza Simón Bolívar es tan bonita como la Plaza San Martín.**
4. **No, la Plaza Simón Bolívar tiene tantas estatuas como la Plaza San Martín.**
5. **No, la calle Luna es tan larga como la calle Londres.**
6. **No, hay tantas tiendas en la calle Luna como en la calle Londres.**
7. **No, hay tanta gente en la boca del metro como en la parada del autobús.**

Actividades comunicativas
A, B, and **C** Answers will vary.

331

VISTAS DEL PERÚ

OVERVIEW

The **Vistas del Perú** were prepared by National Geographic Society. Their purpose is to give students greater insight, through these visual images, into the culture and people of Peru. Have students look at the photographs on pages 332–335 for enjoyment. If they would like to talk about them, let them say anything they can, using the vocabulary they have learned to this point.

National Standards

Cultures
The **Vistas del Perú** photos and the accompanying captions allow students to gain insights into the people and culture of Peru.

Learning From Photos

1. Río Manú, cuenca del Amazonas The view is of the Manú River as it flows through the National Park of Manú in southeastern Peru. The park, established in 1973, covers an enormous area of 15,328 square kilometers. The Amazon basin covers an area of seven million square kilometers. The rivers of the Amazon basin carry one-fifth of the world's running water. The headwaters of the Amazon are high in the Peruvian Andes.

2. Machu Picchu The ruins of this Inca city are situated on the saddle of a high mountain with terraced slopes falling away to the **río Urubamba** below. The ruins are well preserved because they were never found by the Spaniards. The American, Hiram Bingham, discovered the city in 1911. It was then explored by an *(continued)*

1. Río Manú, cuenca del Amazonas
2. Machu Picchu
3. Iglesia de San Francisco, Lima
4. Granja cerca del Cuzco
5. Niño con llama, Cuzco
6. Vendedor de hierbas en mercado al aire libre, Huancavelica
7. Hombre en embarcación de totora, Lago Titicaca

332

Learning From Photos

archeological expedition from Yale University. The ruins consist of staircases, temples, terraces, palaces, towers, fountains, and a famous sundial.

3. Iglesia de San Francisco, Lima This church has a facade of exceptional beauty. It was built between 1657 and 1674. It is considered an architectural masterpiece of the period.

4. Granja cerca del Cuzco Farming is carried out today in the area around Cuzco much as it has been for centuries. Motive power is still supplied by animals. Besides potatoes (**papas**), **quinoa** is a major crop. **Quinoa** is a grain of great nutritive value until recently virtually unknown outside the Andean region. *(continued)*

NATIONAL GEOGRAPHIC

VISTAS
DEL PERÚ

Learning From Photos

6. Vendedor de hierbas en mercado al aire libre, Huancavelica The marketplace is in Huancavelica high in the Cordillera Central. The road from Huancavelica to Ayacucho via Santa Inés averages 4,000 meters in altitude for 150 kilometers, making it the world's highest continuous road. The vendor is selling herbs.

7. Hombre en embarcación de tortora, Lago Titicaca Titicaca is high in the Andes on the border between Bolivia and Peru. It is the world's highest large lake at 3,810 meters (12,500 feet) above sea level. The lake covers 8,290 square kilometers (3,200 square miles). It has been a center of Indian life from pre-Incan times. In the lake are the islands of Titicaca and Coati, the legendary birthplace of the Incas. The **balsa** in the photo is a flat-bottomed reed boat.

Learning From Photos

(continued from page 332)
5. Niño con llama, Cuzco The llama is native to the Andes and is a relative of the camel. It is believed that it is descended from the guanaco, a wild, similar-looking, though smaller, animal (3½ ft. tall) found on the arid plains of the Andes. Llamas live in herds owned by indigenous peoples and can work at altitudes that most animals cannot tolerate. The llama carries loads up to 100 lbs. but is never ridden. The llama is valued for its wool and milk. The alpaca and the vicuña are cousins of the llama.

(continued)

VISTAS DEL PERÚ

Learning From Photos

1. Vista panorámica del Cuzco
According to legend, Cuzco was founded by the first of the Inca rulers, Manco Cápac. The city had massive palaces and temples, especially the Templo del Sol, that later became a Dominican convent. When Francisco Pizarro entered the city in 1533 it was plundered, and on the ruins the **conquistadores** built the colonial city, using the ancient walls as foundations for the new buildings. The population of the city is predominantly Indian. Cuzco stands at an altitude of 3,416 meters (11,207 feet).

2. Niño futbolista, Cordillera Blanca Tradition has it that a British ship anchored at a Latin American port late in the 19th century. The crew went to the dock and played a game of soccer. The onlookers were so fascinated by the game that they too began playing. Today soccer (**fútbol**) is Latin America's most popular sport. There are stadiums with capacity for over 100,000 spectators in various Latin American cities. Latin American teams have been World Cup champions various times. The Cordillera Blanca is in western Peru. It is a range of the Andes.

3. Mujer en el mercado, Pisac
The town of Pisac is high in the Andes, in the Departamento de Cuzco, not far from the city of Cuzco. Beneath her felt hat the woman wears her hair in a long **trenza**.

4. Mono marrón, Reserva Nacional de Paracas The park is located on the Paracas peninsula on the south coast of Peru.

(continued)

1. *Vista panorámica del Cuzco*
2. *Niño futbolista, Cordillera Blanca*
3. *Mujer en el mercado, Pisac*
4. *Mono marrón, Reserva Nacional de Paracas*
5. *Pescadores seleccionando la pesca, Cabo Blanco*
6. *Parque Central, Lima*
7. *Rascacielos modernos, Lima*

NATIONAL GEOGRAPHIC SOCIETY — TEACHER'S CORNER

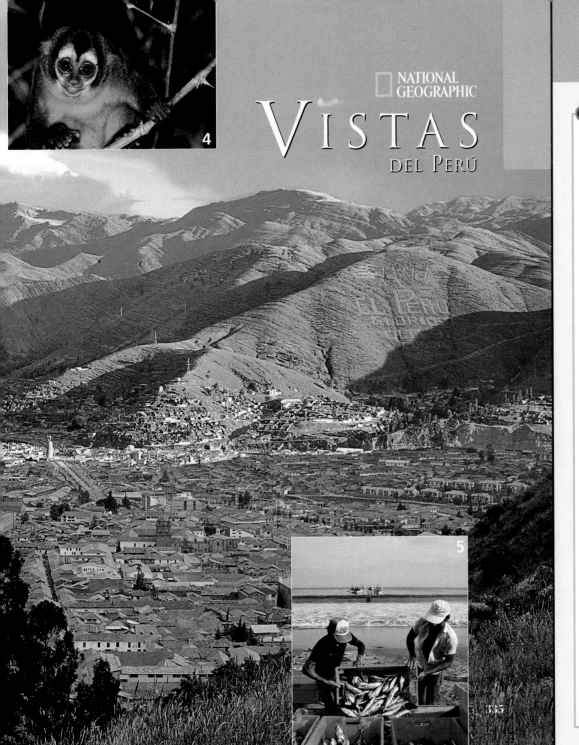

VISTAS DEL PERÚ

Learning From Photos

(continued from page 334)
Besides its rich fauna, the area is important as the home of one of the earliest indigenous cultures, the Paracas. Little is known of their way of life, but remains of their pottery and textiles have been found in the region.

5. Pescadores seleccionando la pesca, Cabo Blanco Cabo Blanco is on the Pacific coast of Peru not far from its border with Ecuador. Peru is one of the world's major fishing nations.

6. Parque Central, Lima This is one of the many public gardens, parks, and plazas in Lima. The largest and most famous is the Plaza de Armas, dominated by the huge Palacio de Gobierno and the cathedral. Lima was founded in 1535 by Francisco Pizarro and is the second oldest capital in South America.

7. Rascacielos modernos, Lima These high-rise buildings are typical of modern Lima. The city was rebuilt several times and so Lima reflects the architectural styles prevalent in various periods.

Products available from
GLENCOE/MCGRAW-HILL

To order the following products, call Glencoe/McGraw-Hill at 1-800-334-7344.

CD-ROMs
· Picture Atlas of the World
· The Complete National Geographic: 109 Years of National Geographic Magazine

Poster
· Rain Forests

Software
· ZingoLingo: Spanish Diskettes

Transparency Set
· NGS PicturePack: Geography of South America

Videodisc
· STV: World Geography (Volume 3: "South America and Antarctica")

Products available from
NATIONAL GEOGRAPHIC SOCIETY

NATIONAL GEOGRAPHIC SOCIETY

To order the following products, call National Geographic Society at 1-800-368-2728.

Books
· Exploring Your World: The Adventure of Geography
· National Geographic Satellite Atlas of the World

Video
· South America ("Nations of the World" Series)

TOPICS	FUNCTIONS	STRUCTURE	CULTURE
◆ Beauty salons and barber shops ◆ The dry cleaners ◆ The post office ◆ The bank	◆ How to talk about hairstyles and hair care ◆ How to have clothing dry-cleaned ◆ How to talk about common postal services ◆ How to conduct banking transactions ◆ How to tell what may or may not happen ◆ How to express wishes and orders ◆ How to express opinions	◆ The subjunctive ◆ The subjunctive in nominal clauses ◆ The subjunctive with impersonal expressions	◆ José Luis and his friends prepare for a trip to southern Spain ◆ La Alhambra, Granada ◆ La Mezquita, Córdoba ◆ El Alcázar, Sevilla ◆ La Moneda, Santiago, Chile ◆ Hairstyles

CHAPTER 12 RESOURCES

PRINT	MULTIMEDIA

Planning Resources

PRINT	MULTIMEDIA
Lesson Plans Block Scheduling Lesson Plans	Interactive Lesson Planner

Reinforcement Resources

PRINT	MULTIMEDIA
Writing Activities Workbook Student Tape Manual Video Activities Booklet Web Site User's Guide	Transparencies Binder Audiocassette/Compact Disc Program Videocassette/Videodisc Program Online Internet Activities Electronic Teacher's Classroom Resources

Assessment Resources

PRINT	MULTIMEDIA
Situation Cards Chapter Quizzes Testing Program Performance Assessment	**Maratón mental** Mindjogger Videoquiz Testmaker Computer Software (Macintosh/Windows) Listening Comprehension Audiocassette/Compact Disc Communication Transparency: C-12

Motivational Resources

PRINT	MULTIMEDIA
Expansion Activities	Café Glencoe: www.cafe.glencoe.com Keypal Internet Activities

Enrichment

PRINT	MULTIMEDIA
Spanish for Spanish Speakers	Fine Art Transparency: F-5

Chapter 12 Planning Guide

SECTION	PAGES	SECTION RESOURCES
Vocabulario Palabras 1 **En la peluquería** **En la tintorería**	338–341	Vocabulary Transparencies 12.1 Audiocassette 7B/Compact Disc 7 Student Tape Manual, TE, pages 133–135 Workbook, pages 137–139 Chapter Quizzes, page 55 CD-ROM, Disc 4, pages 338–341
Vocabulario Palabras 2 **El correo** **El banco; La casa de cambio**	342–345	Vocabulary Transparencies 12.2 Audiocassette 7B/Compact Disc 7 Student Tape Manual, TE, pages 135–137 Workbook, pages 140–141 Chapter Quizzes, page 56 CD-ROM, Disc 4, pages 342–345
Estructura **El subjuntivo** **El subjuntivo en cláusulas** **nominales** **El subjuntivo con expresiones** **impersonales**	346–353	Workbook, pages 142–146 Audiocassette 7B/Compact Disc 7 Student Tape Manual, TE, pages 137–139 Structure Transparency S-12 Chapter Quizzes, pages 57–59 Computer Testmaker CD-ROM, Disc 4, pages 346–353
Conversación **En la casa de cambio**	354–355	Audiocassette 7B/Compact Disc 7 Student Tape Manual, TE, page 140 CD-ROM, Disc 4, pages 354–355
Lecturas culturales **Muchos quehaceres** **La Moneda: Un edificio con** **mucha historia** *(opcional)* **El pelo y el peinado** *(opcional)*	356–359	Testing Program, pages 85–86 CD-ROM, Disc 4, pages 356–359
Conexiones **La banca** *(opcional)*	360–361	Testing Program, page 86 CD-ROM, Disc 4, pages 360–361
Culminación **Actividades orales** **Actividad escrita** **Vocabulario** **Tecnotur**	362–365	**¡Buen viaje!** Video, Episode 12 Video Activities, pages 109–112 Internet Activities www.glencoe.com/sec/fl Testing Program, pages 82–85; 138; 182; 202 CD-ROM, Disc 4, pages 362–365

CAPÍTULO *12*

OVERVIEW

In this chapter students will learn how to talk about going to the hair stylist, the post office, the bank, and the dry cleaner's. They will learn to use the subjunctive mood to express actions that may or may not happen, wishes and orders, and opinions introduced by impersonal expressions. The cultural focus of the chapter is on personal services in the Spanish-speaking world.

National Standards

Communication

In Chapter 12 students will learn to communicate in spoken and written Spanish on the following topics:
- hairstyling
- laundry and dry cleaning
- using the postal service
- personal banking

Students will obtain and provide information about these topics and engage in conversations that would typically take place in business establishments as they fulfill the chapter objectives listed on this page.

Pacing

Chapter 12 will require approximately eight to ten days. Pacing will vary according to the length of the class, the age of your students, and student aptitude.

Block Scheduling

See the Block Scheduling Lesson Plans Booklet for suggestions on how to present the chapter material within a block scheduling framework.

Los servicios al público

Objetivos

In this chapter you will learn to do the following:

- talk about going to the hairdresser/barber shop
- talk about having your clothes cleaned
- talk about using the services of the post office and bank
- talk about things that may or may not happen
- express what you would like, wish, or hope others would do

*inter*NET
CONNECTION

The **Glencoe Foreign Language Web site** (http://www.glencoe.com/sec/fl) offers three options that enable you and your students to experience the Spanish-speaking world via the Internet:
- The online **Actividades** are correlated to the chapters and utilize Hispanic Web sites around the world. For the Chapter 12 activity, see student page 365.

- The **Correspondencia electrónica** section provides information on how to set up a keypal (pen pal) exchange between your class and a class in the Spanish-speaking world.
- At **Café Glencoe,** the interactive "after-school" section of the site, you and your students can access a variety of additional online resources, including interactive games.

Spotlight On Culture

Fotografía The photo on pages 336 and 337 is of the **Plaza de Mayo**, in Buenos Aires. It is a beautiful open space with greenery and the monument to the 25th of May, 1810, the day on which armed citizens of the **cabildo**, or town council, demanded the resignation of the Spanish viceroy **(virrey)** and established a provisional representative government. This action marked the beginning of the Latin American revolt against Spanish rule. **El 25 de mayo** is a national holiday. In recent years the Plaza has been the scene of protests by **las Madres de la Plaza de Mayo** and **las Abuelas de la Plaza de Mayo** protesting the disappearance of many young people during the military repression of the 1970's and 80's. The **Banco Río,** also pictured here, is a major Argentine international bank.

Teacher Notes

Chapter Projects

Presupuesto Have students keep a diary of their expenditures as you do this chapter. At the chapter's end, have them tell or write what they learned about themselves by doing this.

Note You may also have them check the Internet for the exchange rates for the Spanish **peseta** or the Mexican **peso** and ask them to convert their expenses into one of these currencies.

337

RESOURCES

- Vocabulary Transparencies 12.1 (A & B)
- Student Tape Manual, TE, pages 133–135
- Audiocassette 7B/CD7
- Workbook, pages 137–139
- Quiz 1, page 55
- CD-ROM, Disc 4, pages 338–341

🔔 Bell Ringer Review

Use BRR Transparency 12-1, or write the following on the board: Make a list of words and expressions you might need when shopping for clothes.

TEACHING VOCABULARY

¡OJO! Note that many of the sentences introduce students to the use of the subjunctive. The subjunctive will be taught in this chapter. The subjunctive forms in the **Vocabulario** section are in the third person only.

A. Present the vocabulary by projecting Vocabulary Transparencies 12.1 (A & B).

B. Have students repeat the new words and phrases two or three times after you or the recording on Cassette 7B/Compact Disc 7.

C. Ask the following questions:
¿Quiere Paco que el barbero le corte el pelo?
¿Quiere Teresa que la peluquera le lave el pelo?
¿Quiere Paco que el barbero le corte el pelo con navaja?
¿Y quiere Teresa que la peluquera le corte el pelo con tijeras?

338

En la peluquería

Más corto por los lados, por favor.

la raya

una navaja

el peluquero, el barbero

el pelo, el cabello

el peine

Paco quiere un corte de pelo.
Quiere que el barbero le corte el pelo con navaja.

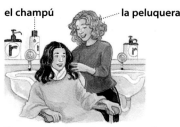

el champú · la peluquera

Teresa quiere que la peluquera le lave el pelo.
Quiere un champú.

las tijeras

Quiere que le corte el pelo con tijeras.

el secador

Quiere que le seque el pelo con el secador.

338 ∾ *trescientos treinta y ocho*

CAPÍTULO 12

Pantomime

Begin
___, ven acá, por favor.
Eres peluquero(a).
Lávale el pelo a tu cliente.
Córtale el pelo con tijeras.
Ahora córtale los lados con tijeras.
El/La cliente lo quiere más corto por los lados.
Córtale más los lados con tijeras.

Toma el peine y ponle la raya a la derecha.
Sécale el pelo con el secador.
Gracias, ___. Regresa a tu asiento.

En la tintorería

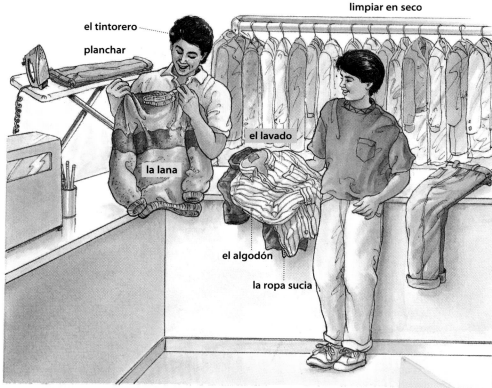

limpiar en seco

el tintorero

planchar

el lavado

la lana

el algodón

la ropa sucia

José tiene mucha ropa sucia.
Quiere que le laven las camisas.
Quiere que le planchen el pantalón.
El tintorero puede lavar las camisas.
Las puede lavar porque son de algodón.
Pero no puede lavar el suéter.
El suéter es de lana.
Es necesario que el tintorero limpie en seco el suéter.

la máquina de lavar

D. After presenting the vocabulary orally, have students open their books and read the words, expressions, and sentences for additional reinforcement.

E. Call a student to the front of the room. Show the Vocabulary Transparencies again. Have the student play teacher and ask questions about what he or she sees in the illustrations.

TEACHING TIP

Students may have trouble getting the meaning of **algodón**. Tell them: **La camisa no es de nilón. No es de poliéster. La camisa es de algodón. El algodón es una tela natural. ¿Qué es el algodón?** You can also point to some cotton shirts or blouses in the classroom.

VOCABULARY EXPANSION

A few more hairdressing terms are:

el espejo	*mirror*
el salón de belleza	*beauty salon*
la barbería	*barbershop*
el cepillo para el cabello	*hairbrush*
la maquinilla	*hair clippers*
la peluca	*wig*

Did You Know?

La peluquería y la tintorería The **peluquería** was originally the place where you got your **peluca** cleaned and repaired. The **tintorería** was the dyer's shop and the **tintorero** only dyed clothes.

❖Práctica❖

A Have students refer to the illustrations as they do **Práctica A**.

B **Práctica B** can be gone over orally with books closed.

Writing Development

After going over **Práctica B**, have students write their answers in a unified paragraph.

Learning From Photos

San Miguel de Allende, México
You may want to ask students:
¿Dónde están ellos?
¿Qué es la señorita en la foto?
¿Qué le da ella a su cliente?
¿En qué se mira el cliente?
Ciudad de México You may want to ask the following questions about the photo:
¿Qué hace el peluquero con su cliente?
¿Qué tiene ella debajo del cuello?
¿Qué hay en las botellas de plástico?

❖Práctica❖

A ¿Qué prefieren los clientes? Pareen.

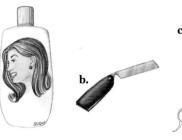

1. La señora quiere que le corten el pelo con tijeras.
2. Ella quiere que le laven el pelo.
3. Y después quiere que lo sequen.
4. El señor quiere que el barbero use la navaja.

B **HISTORIETA** A la peluquería

Contesten personalmente.
1. ¿Prefieres llevar el pelo largo o corto?
2. ¿A qué peluquería vas?
3. ¿Con qué frecuencia te cortas el pelo?
4. ¿Prefieres lavarte el pelo o que te lo laven en la peluquería?
5. ¿Prefieres que te corten el pelo con tijeras o con navaja?
6. Cuando te lavas el pelo, ¿prefieres secarlo con una toalla o con un secador?
7. ¿Cuántas veces al día te peinas?

San Miguel de Allende, México

Ciudad de México

ANSWERS

Práctica

A 1. c
2. a
3. d
4. b

B 1. Prefiero llevar el pelo largo (corto).
2. Voy a ___.
3. Me corto el pelo cada ___.
4. Prefiero lavarme el pelo (que me lo laven en la peluquería).

5. Prefiero que me corten el pelo con tijeras (con navaja).
6. Cuando me lavo el pelo, prefiero secarlo con una toalla (con un secador).
7. Me peino ___ veces al día.

C HISTORIETA En la tintorería

Contesten.

1. ¿Tiene el joven mucha ropa sucia?
2. ¿La lleva a la tintorería?
3. ¿Quiere que la tintorera le lave las camisas?
4. ¿De qué material son las camisas?
5. ¿Puede lavarlas la tintorera?
6. ¿De qué material es el saco?
7. ¿Puede lavar el saco la tintorera?
8. ¿Es necesario que lo limpie en seco?
9. ¿Quiere el joven que la tintorera le planche el pantalón?
10. ¿Quiere que le planche las camisas también?

Lima, Perú

D Preguntas personales   Contesten.

1. ¿Qué ropa llevas a la tintorería?
2. ¿Qué ropa lavas en casa?
3. ¿Prefieres que te planchen o que no te planchen las camisas?
4. ¿Planchas los blue jeans o no?
5. ¿Tienes mucho lavado cada semana?

Actividades comunicativas

A La peluquería   Trabaja con un(a) compañero(a). Dile con qué frecuencia vas a la peluquería. Descríbele todo lo que hace el/la peluquero(a). Luego cambien de rol.

B En la tintorería   Estás en la tintorería. Tienes mucha ropa sucia. Ten una conversación con el/la tintorero(a) (tu compañero[a]). Dile todo lo que necesitas. Luego cambien de rol.

C En una lavandería   Estás trabajando a tiempo parcial *(part time)* en una lavandería *(laundromat)* en tu comunidad donde hay muchos clientes hispanohablantes. Explícale a un(a) cliente (tu compañero[a]) cómo usar la máquina de lavar. Puedes usar las siguientes expresiones.

Lima, Perú

prender la máquina

escoger la temperatura

poner blanqueador

sacar el lavado

esperar media hora

introducir monedas

añadir detergente

poner la ropa sucia

CAPÍTULO 12
Vocabulario

C and **D**   You may wish to go over these activities orally in class with books closed before assigning them as written homework. Go over them once again the following day for additional reinforcement.

D   You can do **Practica D** as a paired activity. One student asks the questions and the other answers.

Actividades comunicativas

A TECHNOLOGY OPTION
In the CD-ROM version of this activity (Disc 4, page 341), students can interact with an on-screen native speaker and record their voices.

B TECHNOLOGY OPTION
Students may use the Portfolio feature on the CD-ROM to record their conversations.

Learning From Photos

Lima, Perú You may wish to ask students the following questions about the top photo:
¿Dónde están los dos?
¿Qué trae el joven?

Did You Know?

Me afeito **Una navaja** can be either a straight razor or a safety razor. In many countries a safety razor is called **una gilette**. You may wish to ask students why this is so.

Independent Practice

Assign any of the following:
1. Workbook, pages 137–139
2. Activities, pages 340–341
3. CD-ROM, Disc 4, pages 338–341

341

ANSWERS

Práctica

C 1. Sí, el joven tiene mucha ropa sucia.
2. Sí, la lleva a la tintorería.
3. Sí, quiere que la tintorera le lave las camisas.
4. Las camisas son de algodón.
5. Sí, la tintorera puede lavarlas.
6. El saco es de lana (algodón).
7. No, la tintorera no puede lavar el saco.
8. Sí, es necesario que lo limpie en seco.
9. Sí, el joven quiere que la tintorera le planche el pantalón.

10. Sí, quiere que le planche las camisas también.

D Answers will vary but may include:
1. Llevo ___ a la tintorería.
2. Lavo en casa mis ___.
3. Prefiero que (no) me planchen las camisas.
4. Sí, (No, no) plancho los blue jeans.
5. Sí, (No, no) tengo mucho lavado cada semana.

Actividades comunicativas
A, B, and **C**   Answers will vary.

Bell Ringer Review

Use BRR Transparency 12-2, or write the following on the board:
Answer the following:
1. ¿Te gusta escribir?
2. ¿En qué clase escribes mucho?
3. ¿Qué escribes?
4. Y, ¿qué lees?
5. ¿Les escribes cartas a los/las amigos(as)?
6. ¿A quiénes escribes?
7. ¿Cuándo les escribes?

TEACHING VOCABULARY

A. After presenting the vocabulary using any of the suggestions given in previous chapters, show Vocabulary Transparencies 12.2 (A & B) again.

B. Have students look at the Vocabulary Transparencies. Call on individuals to say as much as they can about what they see on them.

342

Vocabulario

El correo

la carta

el sobre

el sello, la estampilla

la tarjeta postal, la postal

El correo aéreo cuesta más que el correo ordinario.

el buzón

la ventanilla

La señora echa la carta en el buzón.

La empleada pesa el paquete.

342 ⮌ *trescientos cuarenta y dos*

CAPÍTULO 12

Pantomime

Begin

(Estudiante 1) y (Estudiante 2), vengan acá, por favor.

(Estudiante 1), eres un(a) empleado(a) de correo.

(Estudiante 2), tienes algo que mandar. Ve al correo. Dile «buenos días» al/a la empleado(a).

(Estudiante 1), contesta. Preguntale al/a la cliente qué quiere mandar.

(Estudiante 2), dile lo que quieres mandar. Dile adónde quieres mandarlo.

(Estudiante 1), dile cuánto va a costar.

(Estudiante 2), págale al/a la empleado(a). Dale el dinero.

(Estudiante 1), dale unos sellos.

(Estudiante 2), mira bien los sellos. Hay un problema. El/La empleado(a) no te dio bastantes sellos. Explícale el problema al/a la empleado(a).

El banco

la cuenta corriente

el cajero

la cajera

las monedas

el cheque de viajero

los billetes

BANCO DE MEXICO

el dinero en efectivo

endosar

La señorita quiere cobrar un cheque de viajero.
Ella endosa el cheque.
Ella firma el cheque.

La casa de cambio

¿Cuál es el tipo de cambio?

El cambio está a 130 pesos el dólar.

el cambista

el tipo de cambio, la tasa de cambio

CAMBIO

el suelto

El joven quiere que le cambien dólares en pesos.

El cajero le da muchos billetes grandes.
El joven quiere cambio de un billete de cinco mil. Quiere suelto también.

❖Práctica❖

A Students can work in pairs to do **Práctica A** as an interview.

B **Práctica B** can be prepared before going over it in class. You may wish to call on more able students to make up original sentences using the alternative words.

C **Práctica C** can be done orally with books closed. Then have students write the answers as a homework assignment.

Learning From Realia

Billetes You may wish to ask students to identify the historical figures depicted on the two banknotes and to find out something about each one.

❖Práctica❖

A **Tu experiencia personal**   Contesten.

1. ¿Tú escribes muchas cartas o prefieres hablar por teléfono?
2. Cuando viajas, ¿mandas tarjetas postales? ¿A quién?
3. ¿Quién te escribe a ti con frecuencia?
4. ¿Dónde está el buzón más cerca de tu casa?
5. ¿Cuánto cuesta un sello para una carta por correo ordinario?
6. ¿Cuándo fue la última vez que recibiste un paquete por correo?
7. ¿Qué había en el paquete?

Ciudad de México

B **La correspondencia**   Escojan.

1. Acabo de escribir esta carta, pero no tengo un _____ en que meterla.
   a. sello   **b.** sobre   **c.** buzón
2. Y ahora tengo que ponerle un _____ para correo aéreo.
   a. sello   **b.** sobre   **c.** buzón
3. Quiero echar la carta al correo. ¿Hay un _____ en esta calle?
   a. sello   **b.** sobre   **c.** buzón
4. El correo aéreo es caro. Es posible que sea mejor que yo la mande por correo _____.
   a. postal   **b.** ordinario   **c.** pesado

C **HISTORIETA** Cosas bancarias

Contesten.

1. ¿Tiene tu familia una cuenta en el banco?
2. ¿Quién en tu familia escribe cheques?
3. ¿Tú has recibido un cheque alguna vez?
4. ¿De quién o para qué?
5. ¿Dónde cobraste el cheque?
6. ¿Tuviste que endosar el cheque?
7. ¿Te dio billetes grandes el cajero?
8. ¿Le pediste cambio?

ANSWERS

Práctica

A 1. Yo escribo muchas cartas. (Yo prefiero hablar por teléfono.)
2. Sí (No), cuando viajo (no) mando tarjetas postales. Mando tarjetas postales a ___.
3. ___ me escribe con frecuencia.

4. El buzón más cerca de mi casa está ___.
5. Un sello para una carta por correo ordinario cuesta ___.
6. La última vez que recibí un paquete por correo fue ___.
7. En el paquete había ___.

B 1. b
2. a
3. c
4. b

C 1. Sí (No), mi familia (no) tiene una cuenta en el banco.
2. Mi ___ escribe cheques.
3. Sí, (No, no) he recibido un cheque (nunca).

4. De ___. Para ___.
5. Cobré el cheque en ___.
6. Sí, tuve que endosar el cheque.
7. Sí (No), el cajero (no) me dio billetes grandes.
8. Sí, (No, no) le pedí cambio.

D **Tipos de cambio** Contesten según la lista.

1. ¿Cuál de las monedas tiene el menor valor?
2. ¿Cuál tiene el mayor valor?
3. ¿Es mejor el tipo de cambio para billetes o para cheques de viajero?
4. ¿Recibirías más pesos por un dólar canadiense o un dólar estadounidense?
5. ¿Cuánto tienes que pagar en comisiones?

tasas de cambio

PAÍS (divisa)	DIVISA	SUS
Alemania (marco)	1.82	0.5498
Argentina (peso)	0.99	1.0002
Australia (dólar)	1.50	0.6665
Austria (chelín)	12.75	0.0784
Bélgica (franco)	37.21	0.0269
Brasil (real)	1.13	0.8857
Canadá (dólar)	1.42	0.7040
Chile (peso)	454.25	0.0022
Colombia (peso)	1340.92	0.0007
Dinamarca (corona)	6.87	0.1455
Ecuador (sucre)	4550.00	0.0002
Egipto (libra)	3.41	0.2933
España (peseta)	154.00	0.0065
Finlandia (marco)	5.49	0.1821
Francia (franco)	6.10	0.1641
Gran Bretaña (libra)	0.61	1.6431
Grecia (dracma)	287.49	0.0035
Holanda (florín)	2.03	0.4921
Hong Kong (dólar)	7.75	0.1291
India (rupia)	39.20	0.0255
Irlanda (punt)	0.73	1.3630
Israel (shekel)	3.60	0.2779
Italia (lira)	1793.75	0.0006
Japón (yen)	128.78	0.0078
México (peso)	8.57	0.1166
Noruega (corona)	7.54	0.1327
Perú (nuevo sol)	2.86	0.3498
Portugal (escudo)	186.09	0.0054
Suecia (corona)	8.05	0.1242
Suiza (franco)	1.47	0.6806
Uruguay (nuevo peso)	9.97	0.1003
Venezuela (bolívar)	517.00	0.0019

Actividades comunicativas

A **En el correo** Estás en el correo en Chosica, no muy lejos de Lima. Tienes unas tarjetas postales que quieres mandar a casa. No sabes cuántos sellos necesitas ni cuánto te costará mandarlas. Y quieres tener una idea de cuándo van a llegar tus tarjetas. Ten una conversación con el/la empleado(a) en el correo (tu compañero[a]). Luego cambien de rol.

B **Cambio** Estás viajando por Guatemala y te quedan muy pocos quetzales. Ve al banco para cambiar dinero. Tu compañero(a) será el/la cajero(a) en el banco.

Una lavandería pública, Antigua, Guatemala

D Have students refer to the chart as they do **Práctica D**.

Actividades comunicativas

¡OJO! The **Actividades comunicativas** allow students to use the vocabulary and structures of the chapter in open-ended, real-life situations. They also give students another opportunity to use words and structures from previous chapters.

Have students work on as many activities as you wish. You may also allow them to select those activities they want to do. Different groups can work on different activities.

B **TECHNOLOGY OPTIONS**

Students may use the Portfolio feature on the CD-ROM to record their conversations.

Students can use the Internet to find out how many **quetzales** there are to a dollar. (**Note** There is a currency converter link in the **¡Buen viaje! Level 1,** Chapter 6 activity at the **Glencoe Foreign Language Web site.** See page 336 for the address.)

Did You Know?

Una lavandería pública, Antigua, Guatemala There are fewer and fewer **lavanderías públicas** such as the one shown in the photo on page 345. In Hispanic countries these **lavanderías** served as a social gathering place for village women.

Learning From Photos

Tipo de cambio Refer students to the two listings of currency exchange rates on this page. Have them choose one of them and ask individual students to find the exchange rate for one of the countries listed. Continue until they've covered all the countries on both charts.

ANSWERS

Actividades comunicativas
A and **B** Answers will vary.

345

Bell Ringer Review

Use BRR Transparency 12-3, or write the following on the board: On a piece of paper make two columns. Head the column on the left **en la peluquería** and the one on the right **en el banco.** Copy each of the following terms into the correct column.

1. el cheque
2. el champú
3. el cabello
4. el suelto
5. la cajera
6. las tijeras
7. la cuenta corriente
8. la raya

TEACHING STRUCTURE

Telling what may or may not happen

The basic concept for students to understand is that the subjunctive is used when we do not know if the action will take place. If we know that it is or will be a reality, the indicative is used. If students understand this, it will not be necessary for them to memorize lists of phrases followed by the subjunctive. You may give students the following simple outline:

(continued on page 347)

346

Telling what may or may not happen
El subjuntivo

1. All verb forms you have learned so far are in the indicative. All tenses of the indicative mood are used to express actions that actually do, did, or will take place. They are used to express real events.

> **José tiene el pelo muy largo.**
> **No fue a la peluquería ayer.**
> **Irá mañana.**

All these statements express factual, real information.

> *José has long hair. He didn't go to the barber's yesterday, but he will go tomorrow.*

2. Now you will learn the subjunctive mood. The subjunctive is used to express that which is not necessarily true or real. It expresses things that might happen, that you hope or want to happen. Let's compare the following two sentences.

> **José tiene el pelo muy largo y va a la peluquería.**
> **Los padres de José no quieren que él tenga el pelo tan largo y esperan que él vaya a la peluquería.**

The first sentence tells you that José has long hair and that he goes to the barber's. The information is factual. For this reason you use the indicative. The second sentence tells you that José's parents don't want him to have long hair, but that doesn't mean that his hair will necessarily be short. The sentence also tells us that they hope he goes to the barber, but this doesn't mean that he will. The second sentence tells you things that may happen. It does not present facts and, for this reason, you use the subjunctive.

«El peinado» de Pablo Picasso

For the Native Speaker

Discusión La gente mayor muchas veces se queja de los estilos de pelo de los jóvenes, especialmente de los varones. ¿Qué es lo que les molesta de los estilos de pelo de los jóvenes? ¿Qué preferirían los mayores? ¿Hay algo más en esto que el mero estilo?

FINE ART CONNECTION

Pablo Picasso Ruiz (1881–1973) Picasso is one of the most important artists of the 20th century. Picasso was born in Málaga and studied in Barcelona and later in Paris. He spent most of his adult life in France. His art passed through various phases such as his blue period, rose period, and later on cubism. "**El peinado**" is one of the artist's earlier works.

EXPANSION Show Fine Art Transparency F-5 of this painting by Picasso from the Transparency Binder.

3. To form the present tense of the subjunctive of regular verbs, you drop the **o** of the **yo** form of the present indicative. This is true of verbs that also have an irregular form in the present tense of the indicative. Add **e** endings to all **-ar** verbs and **a** endings to all **-er** and **-ir** verbs.

INFINITIVE	PRESENT (YO)	STEM	PRESENT SUBJUNCTIVE (YO)
mirar	mirø	mir-	mire
comer	comø	com-	coma
vivir	vivø	viv-	viva
salir	salgø	salg-	salga
hacer	hagø	hag-	haga
decir	digø	dig-	diga
conducir	conduzcø	conduzc-	conduzca

4. Study the forms for the present tense of the subjunctive.

mirar	comer	vivir	salir
mire	coma	viva	salga
mires	comas	vivas	salgas
mire	coma	viva	salga
miremos	comamos	vivamos	salgamos
miréis	*comáis*	*viváis*	*salgáis*
miren	coman	vivan	salgan

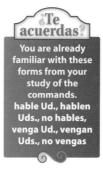

¿Te acuerdas?

You are already familiar with these forms from your study of the commands. hable Ud., hablen Uds., no hables, venga Ud., vengan Uds., no vengas

5. The following are the only verbs that do not follow the normal pattern for the formation of the present subjunctive.

dar	estar	ir	saber	ser
dé	esté	vaya	sepa	sea
des	estés	vayas	sepas	seas
dé	esté	vaya	sepa	sea
demos	estemos	vayamos	sepamos	seamos
deis	*estéis*	*vayáis*	*sepáis*	*seáis*
den	estén	vayan	sepan	sean

- **Indicative:** indicates or points something out; is factual; objective, stands alone; is independent.
- **Subjunctive:** is subjective, not objective; not factual; cannot stand alone; is dependent on something else.

A. Have students open their books to page 346. Go over Step 1 thoroughly and carefully. It is important for students to understand this concept.
B. Have students repeat the verb forms after you.
C. Have students repeat each verb in the charts in Steps 3–5.
D. Have students read the **¿Te acuerdas?** note to let them know that they are already familiar with the subjunctive verb forms from their study of the commands.

Learning From Realia

¿Para qué sirven? You may wish to ask students:
¿Para qué se usa cada uno de los productos y el aparato en la página 347?

✦Práctica✦

A The purpose of this **Práctica** activity is to give students initial practice with one form of the subjunctive.

Learning From Photos

Ciudad de Guatemala y Colegio Santa Teresita, Santurce, Puerto Rico Have students say as much as they can about both photos on this page.

✦Práctica✦

A ¿Qué quieren los padres de Adela? Quieren que ella haga muchas cosas. Sigan el modelo.

> **estudiar**
> **Los padres de Adela quieren que ella estudie.**

Ciudad de Guatemala

1. estudiar mucho
2. trabajar duro
3. tomar cursos avanzados
4. leer mucho
5. comer bien
6. escribir a sus abuelos
7. recibir buenas notas
8. asistir a la universidad
9. salir bien en sus exámenes
10. decir la verdad
11. ser generosa
12. ir a una universidad buena
13. conducir con cuidado

B Los profesores insisten Sigan el modelo.

> **estudiar**
> **Los profesores insisten en que estudiemos.**

1. trabajar
2. prestar atención
3. tomar apuntes
4. aprender
5. recibir buenas notas
6. hacer nuestras tareas
7. estar presentes
8. ser puntuales

Colegio Santa Teresita, Santurce, Puerto Rico

ANSWERS

Práctica

A All answers begin with **Los padres de Adela quieren que ella...**
1. ... estudie mucho.
2. ... trabaje duro.
3. ... tome cursos avanzados.
4. ... lea mucho.
5. ... coma bien.
6. ... escriba a sus abuelos.
7. ... reciba buenas notas.
8. ... asista a la unversidad.

9. ... salga bien en sus exámenes.
10. ... diga la verdad.
11. ... sea generosa.
12. ... vaya a una universidad buena.
13. ... conduzca con cuidado.

B All answers begin with **Los profesores insisten en que...**
1. ... trabajemos.
2. ... prestemos atención.
3. ... tomemos apuntes.

4. ... aprendamos.
5. ... recibamos buenas notas.
6. ... hagamos nuestras tareas.
7. ... estemos presentes.
8. ... seamos puntuales.

Expressing wishes and orders
El subjuntivo en cláusulas nominales

As you have seen, the subjunctive is used with the verbs **querer** and **insistir**. Even though someone wants or insists that something be done, it will not necessarily happen. The information in the clause introduced by either **querer** or **insistir** is not factual. It may or may not happen. Other verbs like **querer** and **insistir** that take the subjunctive are:

desear *to wish*	**mandar** *to order*
esperar *to hope*	**temer** *to fear*
preferir *to prefer*	**tener miedo de** *to be afraid*

Quiero que mis amigos vayan a la fiesta.
Y espero que no lleguen tarde.
Tengo miedo de que no sepan las direcciones.

Práctica

A HISTORIETA En la peluquería

Contesten.

1. ¿Quiere Antonio que el peluquero le corte el pelo?
2. ¿Quiere que le dé un champú?
3. ¿Quiere que use las tijeras?
4. ¿Quiere que le ponga la raya a la derecha o a la izquierda?
5. ¿Quiere que le seque el pelo con el secador?

B HISTORIETA Una carta

Sigan el modelo.

Tú le escribes.
Yo prefiero que tú le escribas.

1. Le escribes en español.
2. Le mandas una tarjeta.
3. Pones un sello para correo aéreo.
4. Vas al correo.
5. Pones la tarjeta en el buzón delante del correo.

Práctica

C **Práctica C** gives students practice using the **yo** form of the subjunctive.

D **Práctica D** elicits the **tú** and **Uds.** forms of the subjunctive.

E **Práctica E** has students use many forms of the subjunctive. You may have students prepare this activity before going over it in class.

C **HISTORIETA** ¿Qué temen ellos?

Sigan el modelo.

Yo no tengo bastante dinero.
Temen que yo no tenga bastante dinero.

1. Yo no voy al banco.
2. Yo no tengo bastante dinero en efectivo.
3. No compro cheques de viajero.
4. Cambio demasiados dólares en pesos.
5. No sé dónde firmar el cheque.

D **HISTORIETA** ¡Vamos todos!

Contesten.

1. ¿Quieres que vayamos a Sevilla?
2. ¿Prefieres que yo conduzca?
3. ¿Insistes en que yo no exceda el límite de velocidad?
4. ¿Prefieres que yo tome la autopista?
5. ¿Temes que yo no pague el peaje?
6. ¿Esperas que lleguemos a Sevilla antes de la hora de cenar?

Valladolid, España

E **HISTORIETA** Cada uno quiere otra cosa.

Completen.

Yo no sé lo que vamos a hacer esta noche. Pablo quiere que nosotros ____ (ir) al cine. Él insiste en que nosotros ____ (ver) la película en el cine Apolo. Carlota teme que mañana ____ (ser) el último día. Tiene miedo de que ellos ____ (cambiar) las películas los sábados. Y tú, ¿quieres que nosotros ____ (ir) al cine o que ____ (hacer) otra cosa? ¿Qué me dices? Que Felipe quiere que Uds. ____ (quedarse) en casa. ¿Por qué? Ah, él quiere que todo el grupo ____ (ir) a su casa. Él prefiere que nosotros ____ (escuchar) música y que ____ (bailar). ¡Buena idea!

ANSWERS

Práctica

C 1. Temen que yo no vaya al banco.
2. Temen que yo no tenga bastante dinero en efectivo.
3. Temen que yo no compre cheques de viajero.
4. Temen que yo cambie demasiados dólares en pesos.
5. Temen que yo no sepa dónde firmar el cheque.

D 1. Sí, (No, no) quiero que vayan a Sevilla.
2. Sí, (No, no) prefiero que tú conduzcas.
3. Sí, (No, no) insisto en que tú no excedas el límite de velocidad.
4. Sí, (No, no) prefiero que tú tomes la autopista.
5. Sí, (No, no) temo que tú no pagues el peaje.
6. Sí, (No, no) espero que lleguen a Sevilla antes de la hora de cenar.

E 1. vayamos
2. veamos
3. sea
4. cambien
5. vayamos
6. hagamos
7. se queden
8. vaya
9. escuchemos
10. bailemos

350

Actividades comunicativas

A **Lo que quieren mis padres** Dile a un(a) compañero(a) de clase lo que tus padres siempre quieren que hagas. Tu compañero(a) te dirá lo que sus padres quieren que él o ella haga. Luego pongan sus dos listas juntas y decidan cuáles son los mismos consejos *(advice)* que Uds. reciben de sus padres. ¿Están Uds. de acuerdo con los deseos de sus padres? Den sus opiniones sobre sus consejos o deseos.

B **Mi mejor amigo(a)** Trabaja con un(a) compañero(a). Cada uno(a) de Uds. va a preparar una lista de características que Uds. quieren que tenga su mejor amigo(a). Luego comparen sus listas y determinen las características que Uds. dos buscan en su mejor amigo(a).

Expressing opinions
El subjuntivo con expresiones impersonales

1. The subjunctive is also used after the following impersonal expressions.

es imposible	es probable
es posible	es necesario
es bueno	es fácil
es mejor	es difícil
es importante	

2. These expressions are followed by the subjunctive because it is uncertain whether the action of the verb will take place or not.

Es necesario que cambiemos el dinero mañana.
Es importante que sepas el tipo de cambio.
Es posible que el banco esté cerrado.

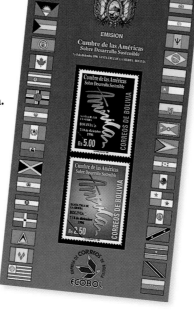

Actividades comunicativas

¡OJO! These activities encourage students to use the chapter vocabulary and structures in open-ended situations.

🖌 Bell Ringer Review

Use BRR Transparency 12-4, or write the following on the board: Write logical completions to these sentences:
1. **Yo quiero que mis padres___.**
2. **Yo prefiero que el/la profesor(a) de español ___.**
3. **Mis padres insisten en que yo ___.**
4. **Yo deseo que mi mejor amigo(a) ___.**
5. **Mi madre espera que yo ___.**

TEACHING STRUCTURE

Expressing opinions

Have students open their books to page 351 and lead them through the explanation. Then have them read the expressions and model sentences aloud.

¡OJO! You may emphasize here that even though an action is necessary (or important or good), it is not certain that it will occur. Therefore the subjunctive is used.

Learning From Realia

Cambio de moneda You may wish to ask students these questions about the **volante de billetes y monedas extranjeras:**
¿Cuánto dinero cambiaron?
¿Cuál fue el tipo de cambio?
¿Cuánto recibió el cliente en moneda nacional?
¿Cómo se llama el banco?

ANSWERS

Actividades comunicativas
A and **B** Answers will vary.

351

✦Práctica✦

A **B** and **C** You can go over these activities first orally with books closed. Then have students write them for homework and go over them again the following day.

Learning From Realia

Billetes mexicanos Each of the three Mexican banknotes features an important figure in Mexican history. You may wish to ask students, for each banknote, the 20, 50 and 100 **pesos**:

¿Quién es la persona en el billete?

¿Por qué es importante esta persona?

If students do not know who they are, you may have them look this information up for homework.

✦Práctica✦

A **¿Sí o no? ¿Cuál es tu opinión?** Contesten.

1. ¿Es importante que los jóvenes estudien lenguas?
2. ¿Es fácil que reciban buenas notas?
3. ¿Es bueno que hablen mucho?
4. ¿Es posible que visiten otros países?
5. ¿Es mejor que aprendan el español?

B **Voy a la ciudad. Pues, es importante que...**

Sigan el modelo.

> **tener cuidado**
> **Pues, es importante que tengas cuidado.**

1. desayunar antes
2. tener cuidado
3. tomar el tren
4. llevar bastante dinero
5. llamar a los abuelos

C **HISTORIETA** Finanzas

Contesten.

1. ¿Es importante que tú tengas dinero en el banco?
2. ¿Es posible que tengas una cuenta corriente?
3. ¿Es importante que todos pongamos dinero en el banco?
4. ¿Es necesario que endosemos un cheque antes de cobrarlo?
5. ¿Es mejor que paguemos con una tarjeta de crédito?

Benidorm, España

ANSWERS

Práctica

A 1. Sí, (No, no) es importante que los jóvenes estudien lenguas.
2. Sí, (No, no) es fácil que reciban buenas notas.
3. Sí, (No, no) es bueno que hablen mucho.
4. Sí, es posible que visiten otros países.
5. Sí, (No, no) es mejor que aprendan el español.

B 1. Pues, es importante que desayunes antes.
2. Pues, es importante que tengas cuidado.
3. Pues, es importante que tomes el tren.
4. Pues, es importante que lleves bastante dinero.
5. Pues, es importante que llames a los abuelos.

C 1. Sí, (No, no) es importante que yo tenga dinero en el banco.
2. Sí, (No, no) es posible que tenga una cuenta corriente.
3. Sí, (No, no) es importante que todos pongamos dinero en el banco.
4. Sí, es necesario que endosemos un cheque antes de cobrarlo.
5. Sí, (No, no) es mejor que paguemos con una tarjeta de crédito.

D Historieta ¿Dónde están los nietos?
Completen.

Abuelito está un poco nervioso. Es posible que sus nietos ___1___ (llegar) mañana por la mañana. Es importante que abuelito ___2___ (saber) cuándo van a llegar. Pero es difícil que abuelita le ___3___ (decir) la hora precisa de la llegada de los nietos. Es posible que mañana ___4___ (hacer) mal tiempo. Como los nietos vienen en carro será necesario que ___5___ (manejar) despacio y con mucho cuidado si hay mucha nieve. Es mejor que ellos ___6___ (llegar) un poco tarde. Abuelito no quiere que ellos ___7___ (tener) un accidente. Es mejor que ___8___ (llegar) tarde pero sanos y salvos.

Tolima, Colombia

Actividades comunicativas

A Cosas fáciles y difíciles Prepara una lista de cosas que es probable que tú hagas con frecuencia porque es fácil hacerlas. Prepara otra lista que indica las cosas que es difícil que tú hagas. Luego compara tus listas con las listas que ha preparado tu compañero(a).

JUEGO **No, no. Es imposible.** Work in a small group. Talk together and tell one another what you think is important, necessary, or a good idea that some other member of the group do. Whoever is told to do it will answer with a good excuse as to why it's impossible.

D Have students prepare **Práctica D** before going over it in class.

Actividades comunicativas

¡OJO! **Práctica versus Actividades comunicativas**
All activities which provide guided practice are labeled **Práctica.** The more open-ended communicative activities are labeled **Actividades comunicativas.**

Learning From Realia

Recibos You may wish to ask students what the papers on page 353 are. For the certified mail receipt you might ask:
¿Qué es el papel?
¿Quién manda la carta o paquete?
¿Dónde vive el remitente?
¿A quién o a quiénes manda la carta o paquete?
¿Dónde viven ellos?

¡OJO! There is no more new material to present in this chapter. The sections that follow recombine and reinforce the vocabulary and structures that have already been introduced.

ANSWERS

Práctica
D 1. lleguen   5. manejen
2. sepa   6. lleguen
3. diga   7. tengan
4. haga   8. lleguen

Actividades comunicativas
A Answers will vary.

353

RESOURCES

🎧 Audiocassette 7B/CD7
💿 CD-ROM, Disc 4, page 354

🔔 Bell Ringer Review

Use BRR Transparency 12-5, or write the following on the board: Complete each sentence with a different verb expressing a wish, preference, or demand.

1. Los estudiantes ___ que los profesores se rían más.
2. Ellos ___ que la comida de la cafetería sea mejor.
3. Ellos ___ que los profesores no les den las tareas el viernes.
4. Los profesores ___ que los estudiantes salgan bien en los exámenes.
5. Ellos ___ que los estudiantes miren la televisión menos.

TEACHING THE CONVERSATION

A. Tell students they will hear a conversation between a customer in an exchange bureau and a teller.
B. 🎧 Have students close their books and listen as you read the conversation on page 354 or play the recording on Cassette 7B/Compact Disc 7.
C. Divide the class into two groups, each of which assumes the role of one of the people in the conversation. Have each group repeat its part of the conversation in unison after you or the recording.
D. Choose a volunteer from each group to present the conversation to the class.
E. Supply substitutions for the amount of money exchanged and the rate of exchange. Call on pairs to present the conversation making these substitutions.

354

Conversación

En la casa de cambio

EMPLEADA: Sí, señor. ¿En qué puedo servirle?
FELIPE: Quiero cambiar dólares en pesos.
EMPLEADA: ¿Tiene Ud. dólares en efectivo o en cheque de viajero?
FELIPE: Cheque de viajero. ¿Cuál es el tipo de cambio hoy, por favor?
EMPLEADA: Para cheques de viajero 223 pesos por dólar. ¿Para cuánto es el cheque?
FELIPE: Cien dólares. ¿Quiere Ud. que yo lo endose?
EMPLEADA: Sí, claro. Y necesito su pasaporte también.
FELIPE: Aquí lo tiene.
EMPLEADA: Gracias.

Después de conversar

Contesten.

1. ¿Qué va a hacer Felipe?
2. ¿Quiere cambiar dinero en efectivo o un cheque de viajero?
3. ¿Cuántos pesos recibirá Felipe por un dólar?
4. ¿Cuántos dólares quiere cambiar?
5. ¿Qué tiene que hacer Felipe con el cheque?
6. ¿Qué más tiene que darle a la empleada?

354 ∾ *trescientos cincuenta y cuatro*

CAPÍTULO 12

ANSWERS

Después de conversar

1. Felipe va a cambiar dólares en pesos.
2. Quiere cambiar un cheque de viajero.
3. Felipe recibirá 223 pesos por un dólar.
4. Quiere cambiar cien dólares.
5. Tiene que endosar el cheque.
6. Tiene que darle su pasaporte.

Actividades comunicativas

A **En la peluquería** Estás en una peluquería en un país hispano. Habla con el/la peluquero(a) (tu compañero[a]). Dile cómo quieres el pelo. Dile todo lo que quieres que él o ella haga. Luego cambien de rol.

B **Sí, sí, pero...** Habla con un(a) compañero(a). Dile algunas cosas que quieres que él o ella haga. Tu compañero(a) te contestará que sabe que es bueno que él o ella haga lo que quieres pero en este momento es imposible que lo haga porque es importante que haga otra cosa. Luego cambien de rol.

Sevilla, España

Baños, Ecuador

Ávila, España

CONVERSACIÓN

trescientos cincuenta y cinco 〰 **355**

TECHNOLOGY OPTION

On the CD-ROM (Disc 4, page 354), students can watch a dramatization of the conversation on page 354. They can then play the role of either one of the characters and record themselves in the conversation.

Actividades comunicativas

A **TECHNOLOGY OPTION**
Students may use the Portfolio feature on the CD-ROM to do this activity.

Learning From Photos

Sevilla, España; Baños, Ecuador; Ávila, España You may wish to ask students to describe and tell as much as they can about each of the three photos on page 355.

GEOGRAPHY CONNECTION

¿Dónde están... ? Ask students to locate each of the three cities, Sevilla and Ávila, Spain and Baños, Ecuador, on the maps on pages 451 and 452.

ANSWERS

Actividades comunicativas
A and **B** Answers will vary.

National Standards

Cultures
The reading on pages 356–357 and the related activities on page 357 familiarize students with daily life in the Spanish-speaking world.

TEACHING THE READING

Pre-reading

Tell students: **Vamos a leer algo de un grupo de amigos de Madrid. Ellos van a hacer un viaje por el sur de España. Pero antes de salir de Madrid tienen muchas cosas que hacer.**

Reading

You may wish to follow some of the suggestions outlined in previous chapters for the presentation of the **Lectura.** Assign the **Despues de leer** activities on page 357 for homework.

356

Lecturas CULTURALES

MUCHOS QUEHACERES

José Luis y un grupo de amigos de su colegio en Madrid han decidido que van a hacer una gira por el sur de España—por Andalucía. Van a ir a Córdoba, Granada y Sevilla donde quieren visitar los famosos monumentos de los árabes. Los árabes o los moros estuvieron en España por casi ocho siglos—desde 711 hasta 1492.

En Córdoba van a visitar la Mezquita.

En Granada, la Alhambra.

Y en Sevilla, el Alcázar.

Saben que en agosto va a hacer mucho calor en estas ciudades. Por consiguiente van a pasar unos días en una playa de la Costa del Sol antes de volver a casa.

La Mezquita, Córdoba

La Alhambra, Granada

Learning From Photos

The photos on pages 356–357 are of three of the most famous Moorish monuments in Spain.

La Mezquita de Córdoba The Great Mosque of Córdoba was built during the reign of Abd er-Rahman in the 8th century upon the site of a Roman temple. The building is massive; 2,250 feet of wall surround it. Within are hundreds of columns and red and white-striped arches that we see in the photo. Córdoba was, during the time of Abd er-Rahman, a city without equal in the West as a center of learning.

La Alhambra This palace-fortress overlooks the city of Granada. In it lived the Nazarí monarchs. Its construction dates from the 13th and 14th centuries. The towers and patios are marvellous: **la torre de las Infantas, la torre de las Damas, el patio de los Leones, el patio de los Arrayanes.** The gardens and grounds are of exceptional beauty.

(**Note** See Learning From Photos, page 357 for information on **El Alcázar.**)

El Alcázar, Sevilla

Como les quedan sólo dos días antes de salir para Andalucía, todos tienen muchos quehaceres[1]. José Luis tiene que ir a la peluquería. Quiere que el peluquero le corte el pelo. Tiene el pelo bastante largo y es mejor que tenga el pelo corto para la playa. Piensa nadar mucho en el Mediterráneo.

Teresa tiene mucho lavado. Tiene que llevar su ropa sucia a la lavandería. No es necesario que ella vaya a la tintorería. No es necesario limpiar en seco la ropa que va a llevar durante el viaje. Sólo tiene algunas camisetas, blusas y pantalones. Y Teresa no va a planchar la ropa tampoco[2]. Va a poner todo en su mochila y sabe que se va a arrugar[3].

Elena quiere ir al correo para comprar sellos. Querrá enviar unas postales a sus amigos y parientes y no quiere perder tiempo haciendo cola en el correo de Córdoba o Sevilla.

Y, ¿adónde tienen que ir todos? ¡Al banco! Sí, todos tienen que ir al banco porque necesitan dinero. En el banco no tienen que cambiar dinero porque estarán viajando dentro de España. Pero tienen que cobrar un cheque porque es necesario que tengan algún dinero en efectivo. Es probable que no compren cheques de viajero porque si no pagan sus cuentas en efectivo, pueden usar una tarjeta de crédito.

Pues, ¡buen viaje a todos! Y esperamos que lo pasen bien en Andalucía—¡que se diviertan!

[1]quehaceres *chores* [2]tampoco *either* [3]arrugar *to wrinkle*

Después de leer

A Preparativos para un viaje
Contesten.

1. ¿Quiénes han decidido hacer una gira por el sur de España?
2. ¿Por qué van a pasar unos días en la Costa del Sol?
3. ¿Qué tienen que hacer todos?
4. ¿Adónde tiene que ir José Luis?
5. ¿Qué quiere él?
6. ¿Cómo quiere el pelo para la playa?
7. ¿Adónde tiene que ir Teresa?
8. ¿Por qué no es necesario que ella vaya a la tintorería?
9. ¿Qué quiere hacer Elena en el correo?
10. ¿Qué van a hacer todos en el banco?

B Una gira Identifiquen.

1. una región del sur de España
2. tres ciudades de esta región
3. un monumento de Córdoba
4. un monumento de Granada
5. un monumento de Sevilla
6. el año 711

LECTURAS CULTURALES

trescientos cincuenta y siete **357**

Post-reading

A. Go over the **Después de leer** activities in class the next day.

B. Call on a student to give a summary of the reading in his or her own words. If necessary, ask five or six questions to review the salient points of the reading selection in order to enable him or her to do this more easily. After the oral summary, the more able students can write a synopsis of the **Lectura** in their own words.

TECHNOLOGY OPTION

Students may listen to a recorded version of the **Lectura** on the CD-ROM, Disc 4, pages 356–357.

Learning From Photos

El Alcázar Despite its very Moorish look, a great part of the Alcázar was built for King Pedro el Cruel of Castilla in the 1360's, using Moorish artisans. The original Alcázar was the palace of the Moorish governors who began its construction in the 9th century. Almost all the decorative work in the Alcázar was done under Pedro. It is an outstanding example of **mudéjar** art.

ANSWERS

Después de leer

A
1. José Luis y un grupo de amigos de su colegio en Madrid han decidido hacer una gira por el sur de España.
2. Van a pasar unos días en la Costa del Sol porque saben que va a hacer mucho calor y quieren ir a la playa.
3. Todos tienen que hacer muchos quehaceres.
4. José Luis tiene que ir a la peluquería.
5. Quiere que el peluquero le corte el pelo.
6. Quiere el pelo corto para la playa.
7. Teresa tiene que ir a la lavandería.
8. No es necesario que ella vaya a la tintorería porque no es necesario limpiar en seco la ropa que va a llevar durante el viaje.
9. Elena quiere comprar sellos en el correo.
10. En el banco todos tienen que cobrar un cheque porque es necesario que tengan algún dinero en efectivo.

B
1. Andalucía
2. Córdoba, Granada y Sevilla
3. la Mezquita
4. la Alhambra
5. el Alcázar
6. el año que los árabes llegaron a España

LECTURA OPCIONAL 1

National Standards

Cultures
This reading, and the related activities on this page, familiarize students with some interesting information about the Moneda Palace in Santiago de Chile.

TEACHING TIPS

¡OJO! This reading is optional. You may skip it completely, have the entire class read it, have only several students read it, or assign it for extra credit.

Did You Know?

While the **peseta** and the **peso** are well known, there are other names for the national currencies of various Latin American countries.

- Venezuela: **el bolívar,** named for Simón Bolívar, **el Libertador**
- Guatemala: **el quetzal,** named for the national bird
- Panamá: **el balboa,** named for the explorer and **conquistador** Vasco Nuñez de Balboa
- Costa Rica y El Salvador: **el colón,** named for Cristóbal Colón
- Ecuador: **el sucre,** named for Antonio José de Sucre, an ally of Bolívar
- Nicaragua: **el córdoba,** named for the **conquistador** Francisco Hernández de Córdoba
- Honduras: **la lempira,** named for the Indian chief who fought the Spaniards

LECTURA OPCIONAL 1

LA MONEDA: UN EDIFICIO CON MUCHA HISTORIA

En pleno centro de Santiago, la capital de Chile, está el edificio de la Moneda. El edificio se construyó entre 1788 y 1805. Es un bello ejemplo de arquitectura colonial.

Desde 1846 hasta 1958 la Moneda sirvió de residencia a los presidentes de la República de Chile. Pero el edificio no se construyó para residencia presidencial. Era donde se acuñaba[1] la moneda en tiempos coloniales. Hasta 1929, los presidentes vivían en el edificio mientras se continuaba acuñando las monedas allí.

En 1973 el edificio de la Moneda apareció en los periódicos de todo el mundo. El 11 de septiembre durante un golpe[2] militar, unos aviones atacaron la Moneda y en las ruinas murió el presidente Salvador Allende.

La Moneda fue restaurada y hoy sirve de sede[3] al gobierno chileno.

[1]se acuñaba *they minted*
[2]golpe *a coup (the overthrow of a government)*
[3]sede *seat (of government)*

Palacio de la Moneda, Santiago de Chile

Después de leer

A **La Moneda** Completen según la lectura.

1. La Moneda es un _____.
2. Está en el _____ de la ciudad.
3. Los presidentes del país vivían en el edificio desde _____ hasta _____.
4. El año 1929 fue el último año en que _____ dinero en el edificio.
5. La construcción del edificio tomó _____ años.

B **Las noticias de 1973** Expliquen.

Expliquen lo que ocurrió de importancia en 1973.

ANSWERS

Después de leer

A 1. **edificio con mucha historia**
2. **centro**
3. **1846, 1958**
4. **se acuñó**
5. **diecisiete**

B Answers will vary but may include:
El 11 de septiembre de 1973, durante un golpe militar, unos aviones atacaron (el palacio de) la Moneda y en las ruinas murió el presidente Salvador Allende.

358

LECTURA OPCIONAL 2

EL PELO Y EL PEINADO

En muchas culturas del mundo el pelo y el peinado siempre han tenido un gran significado. Aún hoy los jueces[1] en Gran Bretaña siguen llevando peluca[2] en la corte.

En las Américas, entre los indígenas, el peinado, igual que el vestido, frecuentemente identifica al grupo o a la tribu. Y el pelo largo no tiene nada que ver con el sexo de la persona. En algunos grupos las mujeres tienen el pelo largo y llevan trenzas[3] que adornan con cintas[4] de colores vivos. En otros grupos, como los indios otavaleños del Ecuador, son los hombres quienes llevan trenzas.

Y, ¿quién se encarga[5] del cuidado del pelo y de la barba[6]? Los barberos o peluqueros, por supuesto. En la literatura hispana, el barbero es un personaje especial. Ha tenido fama de ser muy independiente—casi anarquista. Trabaja por sí mismo. No tiene jefe y conoce todos los secretos del pueblo. Y el hombre que pone el cuello bajo la navaja del barbero pone allí su vida. Este ha sido el tema o argumento de varios cuentos españoles y latinoamericanos.

[1]jueces *judges*
[2]peluca *wig*
[3]trenzas *braids*
[4]cintas *ribbons*
[5]se encarga *takes charge*
[6]barba *beard*

 Después de leer

A **Costumbres interesantes** Digan que sí o que no.

1. Los jueces en Gran Bretaña no tienen pelo.
2. Entre los indígenas de las Américas, el peinado identifica el grupo al que pertenecen.
3. Sólo las mujeres llevan el pelo largo.
4. En algunos grupos indígenas los señores llevan trenzas.
5. El barbero es un personaje especial en la literatura hispana.

LECTURAS OPCIONALES   *trescientos cincuenta y nueve* **359**

National Standards

Connections

This reading about banking and finance establishes a connection with another discipline, allowing students to reinforce and further their knowledge of business through the study of Spanish.

¡OJO! The readings in the **Conexiones** section are optional. They focus on some of the major disciplines taught in schools and universities. The vocabulary is useful for discussing such topics as history, literature, art, economics, business, science, etc.

You may choose any of the following ways to do this reading on banking with your students.

Independent reading Have students read the selections and do the post-reading activities as homework, which you collect. This option is least intrusive on class time and requires a minimum of teacher involvement.

Homework with in-class follow-up Assign the readings and post-reading activities as homework. Review and discuss the material in class the next day.

Intensive in-class activity This option includes a pre-reading vocabulary presentation, in-class reading and discussion, assignment of the activities for homework, and a discussion of the assignment in class the following day.

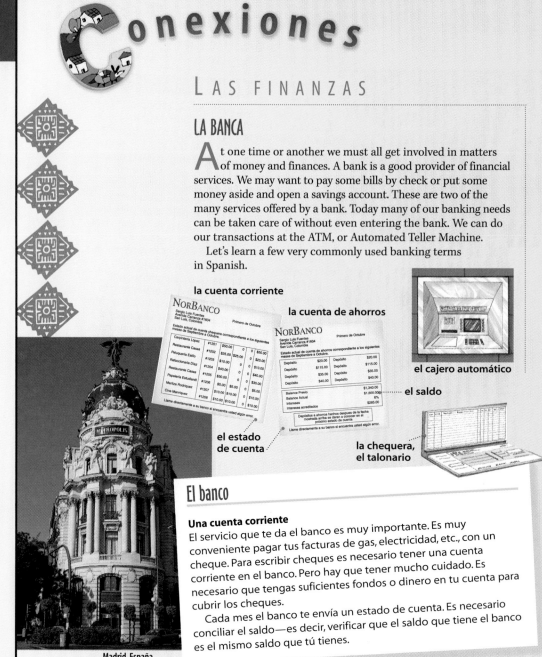

Conexiones

LAS FINANZAS

LA BANCA

At one time or another we must all get involved in matters of money and finances. A bank is a good provider of financial services. We may want to pay some bills by check or put some money aside and open a savings account. These are two of the many services offered by a bank. Today many of our banking needs can be taken care of without even entering the bank. We can do our transactions at the ATM, or Automated Teller Machine.

Let's learn a few very commonly used banking terms in Spanish.

la cuenta corriente

la cuenta de ahorros

el cajero automático

el saldo

el estado de cuenta

la chequera, el talonario

El banco

Una cuenta corriente

El servicio que te da el banco es muy importante. Es muy conveniente pagar tus facturas de gas, electricidad, etc., con un cheque. Para escribir cheques es necesario tener una cuenta corriente en el banco. Pero hay que tener mucho cuidado. Es necesario que tengas suficientes fondos o dinero en tu cuenta para cubrir los cheques.

Cada mes el banco te envía un estado de cuenta. Es necesario conciliar el saldo—es decir, verificar que el saldo que tiene el banco es el mismo saldo que tú tienes.

Madrid, España

ABOUT THE SPANISH LANGUAGE

El banco is a specific banking institution or building. **La banca** refers to the entire banking industry.

Una cuenta de ahorros

¿Te gusta ahorrar[1] dinero? Entonces puedes abrir una cuenta de ahorros. Ingresas dinero (haces un depósito) en la cuenta de ahorros y el banco te paga interés. Así va subiendo el saldo de tu cuenta y vas haciéndote más rico.

Préstamos

A veces es necesario pedir prestado[2] dinero. Es posible que quieras comprar un carro o una casa. Es posible que no tengas bastante dinero. El banco te hará un préstamo[3].

Una hipoteca es un préstamo para comprar una casa. Es un ejemplo de un préstamo a largo plazo[4]. Durante unos veinte o veinticinco años tendrás que hacer pagos. Cada pago incluye el interés que el banco te cobra[5]. La tasa de interés varía. Por ejemplo, la tasa de interés para un préstamo a corto plazo es generalmente más alta que la tasa de interés para un préstamo a largo plazo.

Hoy día puedes efectuar casi todas las funciones bancarias sin entrar en el banco. El banco te dará una tarjeta para el cajero automático. Introduces la tarjeta en el cajero automático y aparecen en la pantalla las instrucciones para cualquier función bancaria.

San Juan, Puerto Rico

[1]ahorrar *to save*
[2]pedir prestado *to borrow*
[3]préstamo *loan*
[4]a largo plazo *long-term*
[5]cobra *charges*

Después de leer

A Ahorros para el futuro Escojan.

1. Roberto quiere tener dinero para el futuro. Debe abrir _____.
   a. una cuenta corriente **b.** una cuenta de ahorros
   c. un banco
2. Si Roberto quiere ahorrar mucho dinero, tendrá que _____.
   a. retirar mucho dinero **b.** ingresar muchos fondos
   c. cobrar muchos cheques
3. Roberto no paga siempre con dinero en efectivo o con tarjeta de crédito. Él paga con _____.
   a. billetes **b.** libretas **c.** cheques
4. Roberto no tiene más cheques. Necesita _____.
   a. otra cuenta **b.** otro talonario **c.** otro estado
5. No se puede escribir otro cheque si no hay _____ en la cuenta corriente.
   a. fondos **b.** cheques **c.** depósitos
6. Una hipoteca es un préstamo _____.
   a. para un carro **b.** a largo plazo **c.** a corto plazo

---

LAS FINANZAS

LA BANCA

A. You may have students who are interested in finance, accounting, or banking read this selection.

B. You may wish to have all students look at the vocabulary words presented here since they are quite useful.

Career Connection

Yo hablo español Banking is an industry where knowledge of Spanish can be essential. Have the students write to one of the large banks in the area, asking about careers in international banking. Be sure to have them ask what courses are necessary to be qualified for the positions.

ANSWERS

Después de leer

A **1. b**
  2. b
  3. c
  4. b
  5. a
  6. b

361

Culminación

RECYCLING

The **Actividades orales** and the **Actividad escrita** allow students to use the vocabulary and structures from this chapter in open-ended, real-life settings.

Actividades orales

¡OJO! Encourage students to say as much as possible when they do these activites. Tell them not to be afraid of making mistakes since the goal of the activities is real-life communication. Let students choose the activities they would like to do.

Student Portfolio

Have students keep a notebook containing their best written work from each chapter. These selected writings can be based on assignments from the Student Textbook and the Writing Activities Workbook. The activities on page 363 are examples of writing assignments that may be included in each student's portfolio.

In the Workbook, students will develop an organized autobiography **(Mi autobiografía).** These workbook pages may also become a part of their portfolio. See the Teacher's Manual for more information on the Student Portfolio.

Actividades orales

A **Planes para un viaje** Trabaja con un(a) compañero(a). Dentro de poco los dos van a hacer un viaje. Hablen de todo lo que tienen que hacer antes de salir para el viaje.

B **Quehaceres** Habla con un(a) compañero(a). Describan todos los quehaceres que son parte de su rutina. Expliquen cuáles les gusta hacer y cuáles no les gusta hacer. Digan los que hacen durante la semana y los que hacen durante los fines de semana.

C **¡A mandar los regalos!** Con un(a) compañero(a), miren el anuncio para MBE. Vives en Madrid y quieres mandar unos regalos a tus padres en los Estados Unidos. Tú piensas ir al correo para enviar los paquetes, pero tu amigo(a) español(a) (tu compañero[a]) te explica que debes ir al MBE y no al correo. Discutan las ventajas *(advantages)* de ir al MBE. Discutan los servicios que los dos ofrecen y decidan si es necesario que vayas al MBE en vez de ir al correo.

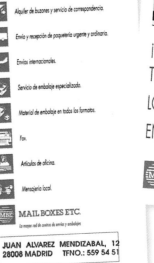

Alquiler de buzones y servicio de correspondencia.

Envío y recepción de paquetería urgente y ordinaria.

Envíos internacionales.

Servicio de embalaje especializado.

Material de embalaje en todos los formatos.

Fax.

Artículos de oficina.

Mensajería local.

MBE MAIL BOXES ETC.
La mayor red de centros de envíos y embalajes

JUAN ALVAREZ MENDIZABAL, 12
28008 MADRID   TFNO.: 559 54 51

¡NO PIERDAS EL TIEMPO! NOSOTROS LO EMBALAMOS Y ENVIAMOS POR USTED.

MBE MAIL BOXES ETC.
La mayor red de centros de envíos y embalajes

Actividades orales
A, B, and **C** Answers will vary.

Actividad escrita

A. Todo es fabuloso. Estás viajando por un país hispano. Te encanta. Te gusta mucho. Quieres que un(a) amigo(a) venga a visitar el mismo país. Escríbele una carta diciéndole por qué te gusta tanto y por qué quieres que él o ella lo visite también. Luego dile todas las cosas que es posible o importante que él o ella haga durante su estadía *(stay)* en el país.

Writing Strategy

Writing dialogue

Dialogue is the conversational element of a story—the written composition representing two or more people talking. Dialogue within a story can help bring characters and events to life. Good dialogue within a story can do several things. It can reveal things about characters, create a sense of time and place, and move the plot along. You can use dialogue for these purposes and for many more.

Un viaje con un(a) amigo(a)

You and a friend are going to Chile for a semester to study. Part of your credit for this coursework is writing about your entire trip, from beginning to end. This includes, of course, the planning stage as well. You are going to leave soon and your Spanish teacher would like you to submit a story about what it was like to prepare for this exciting upcoming adventure. Write about the meeting you and your friend had when you discussed everything you had to do to get ready. Use dialogue in your story to make it more lively. Be imaginative and creative.

Universidad de Chile

Actividad escrita

A. TECHNOLOGY OPTION

 Students may use the Portfolio feature on the CD-ROM to write their letters.

Writing Strategy

Writing dialogue

A. Have students read the Writing Strategy on page 363.
B. You may wish to have them work in pairs to do this activity.

Learning From Photos

Universidad de Chile La Universidad de Chile was founded in 1843 for research and debate. The building that we see in the photo was begun in 1863 by French architects in the neoclassical style. The statue in front of the building is of the founder of the university, the Venezuelan intellectual giant of the 19th century, Andrés Bello.

ANSWERS

Actividad escrita
A Answers will vary.

Writing Strategy
Answers will vary, depending on the imagination and creativity of each student.

Independent Practice

Assign any of the following:
1. Activities, pages 362–363
2. Workbook, page 150
3. Situation Cards
4. CD-ROM, Disc 4, Chapter 12, **Juego de repaso**

363

VOCABULARY REVIEW

The words and phrases in the **Vocabulario** have been taught for productive use in this chapter. They are summarized here as a resource for both students and teacher. This list also serves as a convenient resource for the **Culminación** activities on pages 362 and 363. There are two cognates in this vocabulary list. Have students find them.

Teacher Notes

Vocabulario

TALKING ABOUT THE HAIRDRESSER

la peluquería	las tijeras
el/la peluquero(a), el barbero	el secador
el pelo, el cabello	el champú
un corte de pelo	cortar
el lado	lavar
la raya	secar
la navaja	

TALKING ABOUT THE DRY CLEANERS

la tintorería	de algodón
el/la tintorero(a)	de lana
la ropa sucia	planchar
el lavado	limpiar en seco
la máquina de lavar	

TALKING ABOUT THE POST OFFICE

el correo	la tarjeta postal, la postal
el buzón	el correo aéreo
la ventanilla	el correo ordinario
la carta	pesar el paquete
el sobre	echar la carta
el sello, la estampilla	

TALKING ABOUT THE BANK

el/la cajero(a)
el dinero en efectivo
las monedas
los billetes
la cuenta corriente
el cheque de viajero
el suelto
endosar
firmar
cobrar

TALKING ABOUT CHANGING CURRENCY

la casa de cambio
el/la cambista
el tipo (la tasa) de cambio
cambiar
estar a

TECNOTUR

VIDEO

¡Buen viaje!

EPISODIO 12 ▶ Los servicios al público

Juan Ramón comienza a prepararse para su regreso a los Estados Unidos.

Teresa sugiere un nuevo estilo de corte para Juan Ramón.

CD-ROM

Expansión cultural

Los sellos revelan algo de la historia de un país.

interNET CONNECTION

In this video episode Juan Ramón does some last-minute errands in Madrid as he gets ready to return to Los Angeles. To do some virtual errands yourself, go to the **Capítulo 12** Internet activity at the Glencoe Foreign Language Web site:

http://www.glencoe.com/sec/fl

TECNOTUR

trescientos sesenta y cinco ∽ **365**

OVERVIEW

This page previews three key multi-media components of the **Glencoe Spanish** series. Each reinforces the material taught in Chapter 12 in a unique manner.

VIDEO

The Video Program allows students to see how the chapter vocabulary and structures are used by native speakers in an engaging story. Show the video episode as a final activity for Chapter 12.

A. Before watching the episode, ask students: **En la primera foto, ¿dónde están la Sra. de Hugo y Juan Ramón? ¿Qué lleva Juan Ramón en la mano? Y en la segunda foto, ¿dónde están Teresa y Juan Ramón ahora? ¿Pueden describirnos lo que está pasando en la foto?**

B. See the Video Activities Booklet for detailed suggestions for using this resource.

CD-ROM

A. In the video episode, Juan Ramón buys postage at the post office in Madrid. The **Expansión cultural** photo shows some Spanish stamps. Have students read the caption on page 365.

B. In the CD-ROM version of **Expansión cultural** (Disc 4, page 365), students can listen to additional recorded information about postage stamps.

INTERNET

Teacher Information and Student Worksheets for this activity can be accessed at the Web site.

Video Synopsis

In this episode, Mrs. de Hugo accompanies Juan Ramón to the post office where he sends some videocassettes to the Institute in Los Angeles. The two discuss some last-minute errands Juan Ramón needs to do before returning to the U.S. These include going to the cleaners, buying gifts for his family, and getting a haircut. Later that afternoon, Teresa goes with Juan Ramón to the barbershop. We discover that she has very specific ideas about what his hair should look like!

Chapter 13 Overview ◆◆◆◆◆◆◆◆◆◆◆◆◆◆◆◆◆◆◆◆◆◆◆

SCOPE AND SEQUENCE   pages 366–395

TOPICS	FUNCTIONS	STRUCTURE	CULTURE
◆ Birthdays ◆ Weddings ◆ Holidays	◆ How to talk about family celebrations ◆ How to discuss some important holidays ◆ How to tell what may or may not take place ◆ How to give advice and make suggestions ◆ How to express doubt or uncertainty ◆ How to express emotional reactions	◆ Radical-changing verbs in the subjunctive ◆ The subjunctive with verbs such as **pedir** and **aconsejar** ◆ The subjunctive with expressions of doubt ◆ The subjunctive with expressions of emotion	◆ New Year's Eve at Puerta del Sol, Madrid ◆ How Angel and Monica became married ◆ The Freyssiner-Parada wedding: A newspaper account ◆ Spanish artists: Bartolomé Murillo and Diego Velázquez

CHAPTER 13 RESOURCES

PRINT	MULTIMEDIA

Planning Resources

Lesson Plans Block Scheduling Lesson Plans	Interactive Lesson Planner

Reinforcement Resources

Writing Activities Workbook Student Tape Manual Video Activities Booklet Web Site User's Guide	Transparencies Binder Audiocassette/Compact Disc Program Videocassette/Videodisc Program Online Internet Activities Electronic Teacher's Classroom Resources

Assessment Resources

Situation Cards Chapter Quizzes Testing Program Performance Assessment	**Maratón mental** Mindjogger Videoquiz Testmaker Computer Software (Macintosh/Windows) Listening Comprehension Audiocassette/Compact Disc Communication Transparency: C-13

Motivational Resources

Expansion Activities	Café Glencoe: www.cafe.glencoe.com Keypal Internet Activities

Enrichment

Spanish for Spanish Speakers	Fine Art Transparency: F-6

Chapter 13 Planning Guide

SECTION	PAGES	SECTION RESOURCES
Vocabulario Palabras 1 **El cumpleaños** **La boda**	368–371	Vocabulary Transparencies 13.1 Audiocassette 8A/Compact Disc 8 Student Tape Manual, TE, pages 145–146 Workbook, pages 151–152 Chapter Quizzes, page 60 CD-ROM, Disc 4, pages 368–371
Vocabulario Palabras 2 **Navidad; Año Nuevo** **Los Reyes Magos**	372–375	Vocabulary Transparencies 13.2 Audiocassette 8A/Compact Disc 8 Student Tape Manual, TE, pages 147–149 Workbook, pages 153–154 Chapter Quizzes, page 61 CD-ROM, Disc 4, pages 372–375
Estructura **El subjuntivo de los verbos de cambio radical** **El subjuntivo con verbos como pedir y aconsejar** **El subjuntivo con expresiones de duda** **El subjuntivo con expresiones de emoción**	376–383	Workbook, pages 155–159 Audiocassette 8A/Compact Disc 8 Student Tape Manual, TE, pages 150–152 Chapter Quizzes, pages 62–65 Computer Testmaker CD-ROM, Disc 4, pages 376–383
Conversación **Año Nuevo**	384–385	Audiocassette 8A/Compact Disc 8 Student Tape Manual, TE, page 153 CD-ROM, Disc 4, pages 384–385
Lecturas culturales **Las doce uvas de la felicidad** **La boda** *(opcional)* **Una ceremonia nupcial** *(opcional)*	386–389	Testing Program, pages 89–90 CD-ROM, Disc 4, pages 386–389
Conexiones **Las artes plásticas** *(opcional)*	390–391	Testing Program, page 90 CD-ROM, Disc 4, pages 390–391
Culminación **Actividades orales** **Actividades escritas** **Vocabulario** **Tecnotur**	392–395	¡Buen viaje! Video, Episode 13 Video Activities, pages 113–117 Internet Activities www.glencoe.com/sec/fl Testing Program, pages 87–89; 139; 183; 203–204 CD-ROM, Disc 4, pages 392–395

CAPÍTULO 13

OVERVIEW

In this chapter students will learn how to talk about parties, weddings, and holidays. They will also expand their knowledge of the use of the subjunctive to express actions that may or may not happen, to give advice and offer suggestions, and to express doubt or uncertainty as well as emotional reactions to what others do.

The cultural focus of the chapter is on family and social events and significant holidays in the Hispanic world.

National Standards

Communication
In Chapter 13 students will learn to communicate in spoken and written Spanish on the following topics:
- family social events
- weddings
- holiday customs

Students will obtain and provide information about these topics, express feelings, and engage in conversations that would typically take place at celebrations or on important holidays as they fulfill the chapter objectives listed on this page.

Pacing

Chapter 13 will require approximately eight to ten days. Pacing will vary according to the length of the class, the age of your students, and student aptitude.

Block Scheduling

See the Block Scheduling Lesson Plans Booklet for suggestions on how to present the chapter material within a block scheduling framework.

¡Fiestas!

Objetivos

In this chapter you will learn to do the following:
- describe and talk about parties and weddings
- talk about some holidays
- give advice and make recommendations
- express doubt, uncertainty, or disbelief
- express emotional reactions to what others do
- talk about New Year's Eve in the Hispanic world

interNET CONNECTION

The **Glencoe Foreign Language Web site** (http://www.glencoe.com/sec/fl) offers three options that enable you and your students to experience the Spanish-speaking world via the Internet:
- The online **Actividades** are correlated to the chapters and utilize Hispanic Web sites around the world. For the Chapter 13 activity, see student page 395.

- The **Correspondencia electrónica** section provides information on how to set up a keypal (pen pal) exchange between your class and a class in the Spanish-speaking world.
- At **Café Glencoe,** the interactive "after-school" section of the site, you and your students can access a variety of additional online resources, including interactive games.

Spotlight On Culture

Fotografía The wedding pictured on pages 366 and 367 is being performed at a lovely old church in Buenos Aires. **Los novios** and **la comitiva** are arrayed before the altar. **La comitiva** consists of the **padrinos, el padrino y la madrina**, and any number of **damas** and ushers. **El sacerdote** or **cura** faces the members of the wedding party and officiates at the ceremony.

Teacher Notes

trescientos sesenta y siete ∞ **367**

Chapter Projects

Fiestas hispanas Have students prepare a report on either **el 2 de noviembre** or **el seis de enero.**

TECHNOLOGY OPTION In the Chapter 13 Internet activity, students visit holiday-related Web sites throughout the Spanish-speaking world. You may want students to do the activity as a chapter project. See page 366 for the address of the **Glencoe Foreign Language Web site.**

Feliz Navidad Have students select a holiday such as Christmas that is celebrated in the Spanish-speaking world and the United States. Ask them to prepare a report comparing and contrasting the ways in which the holiday is celebrated in the two different cultures.

Una boda Have students prepare a wedding invitation or a wedding announcement in Spanish.

¡Saludos! Students can send electronic greeeting cards in Spanish for various holidays from **Café Glencoe** (**www.cafe. glencoe.com**).

🔔 Bell Ringer Review

Use BRR Transparency 13-1, or write the following on the board: Imagine you are planning to open a checking account in a new bank. What are some words you would need to know?

TEACHING VOCABULARY

A. Have students close their books. Project Vocabulary Transparencies 13.1 (A & B) and have students repeat the new words, phrases, and sentences after you or the recording on Cassette 8A/ Compact Disc 7.

B. Have students open their books and read the new vocabulary for additional reinforcement.

Vocabulario

PALABRAS 1

El cumpleaños

¡Feliz cumpleaños!

las velas

el pastel, la torta, el bizcocho

Anita nació el ocho de abril.
Su familia y sus amigos celebran su cumpleaños con una fiesta.
No hay duda que todos se divierten.
Anita se alegra de que todos sus parientes vengan a la fiesta.

Pantomime

Getting ready
Dramatize the meaning of **encender** and **apagar** before beginning.
Begin
___, ven acá, por favor.
Es tu fiesta de cumpleaños hoy.
Pon las velas en la torta.
Enciende las velas.
Apaga las velas.
Ahora, come la torta.

Baila con tus amigos. ¡Diviértete!
Gracias, ___. Bien hecho. Puedes volver a tu asiento.

La boda

¡Felicitaciones!

la novia

el novio

¡Enhorabuena!

la dama de honor

el padrino

Los novios acaban de casarse.

la orquesta

el regalo

La recepción es en un salón elegante.
Los novios reciben muchos regalos.

RECYCLING

Remind students that they have already learned the word **padrino,** but its meaning was quite different. Ask them: **¿Quién es el padrino?** «**El padrino asiste al bebé durante el bautizo.**» Ask them the meaning of **padrino** in the context in which it is used in this chapter.

National Standards

Comparisons
Students will compare traditional celebrations in their culture with those in Hispanic cultures.

While most families celebrate a person's **cumpleaños** or birthday, many traditional families still celebrate the **santo,** the person's *name day* or *saint's day*. There is a saint for every day of the year. For example, every José and Josefina celebrates his or her **santo** on March 19th.

Did You Know?

El calendario Calendars in the Hispanic world usually have Monday, **lunes,** as the first day of the week.

✦Práctica✦

¡OJO! **Práctica** When students are doing the **Práctica** activities, accept any answer that makes sense. The purpose of these activities is to have students use the new vocabulary. They are not factual recall activities. Thus, do not expect students to remember specific information from the vocabulary presentation when answering. If you wish, have students use the photos as a stimulus, when possible. **Historieta** Each time **Historieta** appears, it means that the answers to the activity form a short story. Encourage students to look at the title of the **Historieta** since it can sometimes help them do the activity.

It is recommended that you go over all the **Práctica** in class before assigning them for homework.

A **Práctica A** can be done as an interview. One student asks the questions and the other responds.

A and **B** After going over these activities orally, have students write the answers for homework.

EXPANSION Call on students to give a summary in their own words about the stories in **Práctica A** and **Práctica B**.

Writing Development
Have students write the answers to **Práctica B** in a unified paragraph.

370

✦Práctica✦

A **HISTORIETA** Una fiesta

Contesten personalmente.

1. ¿Cuándo es tu cumpleaños?
2. ¿Cuándo naciste?
3. ¿Te preparan una torta para tu cumpleaños?
4. ¿Qué clase de torta te gusta?
5. ¿Cuántas velas tendrás en tu próxima torta?
6. ¿Te dan una fiesta para tu cumpleaños?
7. ¿Quiénes asisten a la fiesta?
8. ¿Recibes muchos regalos?
9. ¿Qué hacen Uds. en la fiesta?
10. ¿Qué regalo te gustaría recibir para tu próximo cumpleaños?

En Tu Cumpleaños, Querida Hija

*Que el día de tu cumpleaños
Celebres con alegría
Y que tu vida esté siempre
Llena de dicha, Hija mía.*

*Que Seas Muy
Feliz Siempre*

Buenos Aires, Argentina

B **HISTORIETA** La boda

Contesten.

1. ¿Dan la recepción en un salón elegante o en un cuarto pequeño?
2. ¿Acaba de casarse la pareja?
3. ¿La mujer vestida de blanco es la dama de honor o la novia?
4. ¿Los novios dan o reciben regalos?
5. La música, ¿es de discos o de una orquesta?
6. ¿Quién es la señora al lado de la novia?
7. ¿Quién es el señor al lado del novio?

ANSWERS

Práctica

A 1. **Mi cumpleaños es el ___.**
2. **Nací el ___.**
3. **Sí, (No, no) me preparan una torta para mi cumpleaños.**
4. **Me gusta la torta ___.**
5. **En mi próxima torta tendré ___ velas.**
6. **Sí, (No, no) me dan una fiesta para mi cumpleaños.**
7. **Mis amigos y mis parientes asisten a la fiesta.**
8. **Sí, (No, no) recibo muchos regalos.**
9. **En la fiesta nosotros comemos, bebemos y bailamos (nos divertimos).**
10. **Para mi próximo cumpleaños me gustaría recibir ___.**

B 1. **Dan la recepción en un salón elegante.**
2. **Sí, la pareja acaba de casarse.**
3. **La mujer vestida de blanco es la novia.**
4. **Los novios reciben regalos.**
5. **La música es de una orquesta.**

(continued on page 371)

C Preguntas personales Contesten.

1. ¿Has asistido a una boda alguna vez? ¿Quiénes se casaron?
2. ¿Cómo era la ropa de la novia?
3. ¿La ceremonia fue religiosa o civil?
4. ¿Quiénes fueron el padrino y la dama de honor?
5. ¿Fuiste a la recepción?
6. ¿Dónde tuvieron la recepción?
7. ¿Qué hiciste en la recepción?

Actividades comunicativas

A Una boda Trabaja con un(a) compañero(a). Cada uno(a) de Uds. va a describir una boda a la que ha asistido. Luego comparen las dos bodas. ¿Había algunas diferencias entre las dos? ¿Cuáles eran las diferencias?

B Fiestas de cumpleaños A muchas personas les gusta mucho tener fiestas en su honor. A otras no les gusta. Trabaja con un(a) compañero(a). Dile si a ti te gustan las fiestas en tu honor o no. Explica por qué. Luego tu compañero(a) te dará sus opiniones. ¿Están de acuerdo o no?

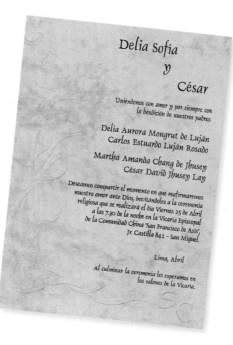

Delia Sofía
y
César

Uniéndonos con amor y por siempre con la bendición de nuestros padres:

Delia Aurora Mongrut de Luján
Carlos Estuardo Luján Rosado

Martha Amanda Chang de Jhusey
César David Jhusey Lay

Deseamos compartir el momento en que reafirmaremos nuestro amor ante Dios, invitándoles a la ceremonia religiosa que se realizará el día Viernes 25 de Abril a las 7.30 de la noche en la Vicaría Episcopal de la Comunidad China "San Francisco de Asís", Jr. Castilla 842 - San Miguel.

Lima, Abril

Al culminar la ceremonia les esperamos en los salones de la Vicaría.

C Students can do **Práctica C** on their own and then read their answers aloud to the class.

Actividades comunicativas

¡OJO! **Práctica versus Actividades comunicativas**
All activities which provide guided practice are labeled **Práctica.** The more open-ended communicative activities are labeled **Actividades comunicativas.**

A and **B** **TECHNOLOGY OPTION** Students may use the Portfolio feature on the CD-ROM to record their conversations.

Learning From Realia

Una invitación You may wish to ask questions about the wedding invitation on page 371:

¿Para qué ocasión es la tarjeta?
¿Quiénes son Delia Sofía y César?
¿Quiénes son las otras personas?
¿Qué va a ocurrir el 25 de abril?
¿Adónde deben ir las personas después de la ceremonia?

ANSWERS CONTINUED

Práctica

B 6. La señora al lado de la novia es la dama de honor.
7. El señor al lado del novio es el padrino.

C Answers will vary but may include:
1. Sí, (No, no) he asistido a una boda. ___ se casaron.
2. La ropa de la novia era ___.
3. La ceremonia fue religiosa (civil).

4. El padrino fue ___ y la dama de honor fue ___.
5. Sí, (No, no) fui a la recepción.
6. Tuvieron la recepción en ___.
7. En la recepción yo ___.

Actividades comunicativas
A and **B** Answers will vary.

Independent Practice

Assign any of the following:
1. Workbook, pages 151–152
2. Activities, pages 370–371
3. CD-ROM, Disc 4, pages 368–371

RESOURCES

- Vocabulary Transparencies 13.2 (A & B)
- Student Tape Manual, TE, pages 147–149
- Audiocassette 8A/CD7
- Workbook, pages 153–154
- Quiz 2, page 61
- CD-ROM, Disc 4, pages 372–375

Bell Ringer Review

Use BRR Transparency 13-2, or write the following on the board: Write down a suggestion you might make to a friend who is going with you to each of the following places. Use the **tú** form of the imperative.

1. **al restaurante o al café**
2. **a la clase**
3. **a la peluquería**
4. **al banco**

TEACHING VOCABULARY

A. Have students close their books. Model the **Palabras 2** vocabulary using Vocabulary Transparencies 13.2 (A & B). Have students repeat the new material two or three times after you or the recording on Cassette 8A/Compact Disc 7.

B. As you present the new vocabulary ask questions such as:
¿Cuándo es la Navidad?
¿Qué tiene la familia en la sala para Navidad?
¿Hay regalos debajo del árbol?

Vocabulario

Navidad

el árbol de Navidad

¡Feliz Navidad!

Diciembre

L	M	M	J	V	S	D
	1	2	3	4	5	6
7	8	9	10	11	12	13
14	15	16	17	18	19	20
21	22	23	24	(25)	26	27
28	29	30	31			

La Navidad es el veinticinco de diciembre.

Nochebuena es el veinticuatro de diciembre.

Año Nuevo

¡Próspero Año Nuevo!

La Víspera de Año Nuevo (Nochevieja) es el treinta y uno de diciembre.
La gente celebra cuando el reloj da las doce.

Diciembre

L	M	M	J	V	S	D
	1	2	3	4	5	6
7	8	9	10	11	12	13
14	15	16	17	18	19	20
21	22	23	24	25	26	27
28	29	30	(31)			

Enero

L	M	M	J	V	S	D
				(1)	2	3
4	5	6	7	8	9	10
11	12	13	14	15	16	17
18	19	20	21	22	23	24
25	26	27	28	29	30	31

Año Nuevo es el primero de enero, el primer día del año.

Los Reyes Magos

el camello

los Reyes Magos

la paja

El seis de enero es el Día de los Reyes.
Los padres les dicen a los niños que pongan paja para
  los camellos en sus zapatos.
Los niños esperan que los Reyes les traigan regalos.

¡Feliz Hanuka!

la menora

Hanuka es la fiesta de las luces.
Es una fiesta hebrea. La fiesta dura ocho días.
Durante la fiesta le piden al hijo mayor que encienda
  las velas de la menora.
La menora tiene nueve brazos.

Did You Know?

Los tres Reyes Magos Hispanic children know the names of each of the Three Wise Men: **Gaspar, Melchor y Baltasar.** Tradition has it that the Wise Men brought the baby Jesus gifts of gold **(oro),** frankincense **(olíbano),** and myrrh **(mirra).** Tradition also has it that Baltasar was African. Parents will often be very imaginative in creating the impression that the Wise Men and their animals have visited. They remove the straw from the shoes and leave signs leading to where gifts may be. Many families in Mexico give children toys and playthings on Christmas (**Navidad**) and practical gifts, such as clothing, on January 6th (**el Día de los Reyes**).

En Latinoamérica There are sizable Jewish populations in several countries in Latin America, in Mexico, Panama, and Argentina in particular.

VOCABULARY EXPANSION

You may wish to give students the names of a few Christmas carols in Spanish:

Noche de Paz *Silent Night*
Navidad *Deck the Halls*
Paz en la Tierra *Joy to the World*

VOCABULARIO

trescientos setenta y tres ∾ **373**

Práctica

A Have students refer to the illustrations while doing **Práctica A**.

B **Práctica B** can be done first orally with books closed.

EXPANSION Have a student retell all the information from **Práctica B** in his or her own words.

Writing Development
Have students write the answers to **Práctica B** in a unified paragraph.

Práctica

A **¿Qué celebran?** Identifiquen según se indica.

1.
2.
3.
4.
5.

B **HISTORIETA** Los regalos

Contesten.

1. En los Estados Unidos, ¿quién les trae regalos a los niños, San Nicolás o los Reyes?
2. ¿Quiénes traen regalos a los niños hispanos?
3. ¿Qué decoran para Navidad las familias norteamericanas?
4. ¿Cuándo reciben sus regalos los niños norteamericanos?
5. ¿Cuándo reciben sus regalos los niños hispanos?
6. ¿Para quiénes es la paja en los zapatos?
7. ¿Quiénes les dicen a los niños que pongan la paja en sus zapatos?
8. ¿Están contentos los niños que los Reyes les traigan regalos?

Paja para los camellos

ANSWERS

Práctica

A 1. Es Hanuka.
2. Es la Navidad.
3. Es un cumpleaños.
4. Es el Día de los Reyes.
5. Es una boda.

B 1. En los Estados Unidos San Nicolás les trae regalos a los niños.
2. Los Reyes (Magos) les traen regalos a los niños hispanos.
3. Las familias norteamericanas decoran el árbol de Navidad para Navidad.
4. Los niños norteamericanos reciben sus regalos el veinticinco de diciembre.
5. Los niños hispanos reciben sus regalos el seis de enero, el Día de los Reyes.
6. La paja en los zapatos es para los camellos.
7. Los padres les dicen a los niños que pongan la paja en sus zapatos.
8. Sí, los niños están contentos que los Reyes les traigan regalos.

C Algunas tradiciones Completen.

1. La «fiesta de las luces» se llama ____.
2. La menora lleva ____ brazos.
3. En cada brazo hay una ____.
4. La persona que enciende las velas es el ____.
5. Esta fiesta dura ____ días.

La Ciudad de Panamá

Actividades comunicativas

A Una fiesta de invierno El/La alumno(a) de intercambio (tu compañero[a]) quiere saber qué celebra tu familia en el invierno y cómo lo celebran. Descríbele las costumbres y tradiciones de tu familia para Navidad, Hanuka, Kwanza o cualquier otra fiesta de invierno. Después cambien de rol.

B Entrevista Si es posible, busca en tu comunidad a una persona mayor hispana. Prepara una entrevista con esta persona sobre las costumbres de Navidad o Reyes en su país. Luego prepara un reportaje y preséntalo a la clase.

Writing Development
After going over **Práctica C** in class, have students write a paragraph about **Hanuka** in their own words.

Actividades comunicativas

¡OJO! These activities encourage students to use the chapter vocabulary and structures in open-ended situations. It is not necessary to have them do all the activities. Choose the ones you consider most appropriate.

A TECHNOLOGY OPTION In the CD-ROM version of this activity (Disc 4, page 375), students can interact with an on-screen native speaker and record their voices.

ANSWERS

Práctica
C 1. Hanuka
   2. nueve
   3. vela
   4. hijo mayor
   5. ocho

Actividades comunicativas
A and B Answers will vary.

Bell Ringer Review

Use BRR Transparency 13-3, or write the following on the board: Using the present perfect, make a list of things you have done so far today.

TEACHING STRUCTURE

❖ Telling what may or may not take place

A. Have students open their books to page 376 and lead them through Steps 1–3.

B. Write the forms of one or two of the verbs on the board.

C. Have students repeat the verb forms.

D. With books closed, call on volunteers to write conjugations of other verbs, following the model(s) which you have provided. Have the class repeat these forms.

Estructura

❖ Telling what may or may not take place
El subjuntivo de los verbos de cambio radical

1. Verbs that have a stem change in the present indicative also have a stem change in the present subjunctive.

	E → IE		O → UE	
INFINITIVE	**cerrar**	**perder**	**encontrar**	**poder**
yo	cierre	pierda	encuentre	pueda
tú	cierres	pierdas	encuentres	puedas
él, ella, Ud.	cierre	pierda	encuentre	pueda
nosotros(as)	cerremos	perdamos	encontremos	podamos
vosotros(as)	*cerréis*	*perdáis*	*encontréis*	*podáis*
ellos, ellas, Uds.	cierren	pierdan	encuentren	puedan

Other verbs with the **e → ie** stem change like **cerrar** are:

   sentarse, comenzar, empezar, pensar.

Other **o → ue** verbs like **encontrar** are:

   acostarse, recordar, volver.

2. The verbs **sentir (e → ie)** and **dormir (o → ue)** have a stem change in every person of the present subjunctive.

   sentir: sienta, sientas, sienta, sintamos, *sintáis*, sientan

   dormir: duerma, duermas, duerma, durmamos, *durmáis*, duerman

3. The verb **pedir** has an **i** in every person of the present subjunctive.

   pedir: pida, pidas, pida, pidamos, *pidáis*, pidan

Other verbs like **pedir** are:

   repetir, freír, seguir, servir.

 **Práctica**

A HISTORIETA Yo quiero.

Sigan el modelo.

> **Él vuelve pronto.**
> **Yo quiero que él vuelva pronto.**

1. Él vuelve mañana.
2. Él nos encuentra en el restaurante.
3. Él se sienta a nuestra mesa.
4. Él pide algo bueno.
5. Él me recomienda un plato.
6. El mesero nos sirve atentamente.

Ciudad de México

B HISTORIETA Necesitamos a Luis.

Completen.

Espero que Luis _____ (volver) mañana. Quiero que él _____
                    1   2
(encontrar) un vuelo temprano. Esperamos que él _____ (poder) llegar
                                                 3
por la mañana. Es posible que el partido _____ (comenzar) a las dos de
                                          4
la tarde. Para nosotros, es mejor que el partido _____ (empezar) más
                                                  5
tarde. Temo que Luis no _____ (poder) jugar si llega tarde. Y sin Luis,
                        6
es probable que nosotros _____ (perder) el partido.
                         7

ESTRUCTURA

trescientos setenta y siete 377

Práctica

A Go over **Práctica A** first orally with books closed.

EXPANSION Call on a student to retell in his or her own words what he or she wants a friend to do at a restaurant based on the information in **Práctica A**.

B Have students prepare **Práctica B** before going over it in class.

Writing Development

After going over **Práctica B** orally, have students rewrite the story in their own words.

Learning From Realia

Una factura You may wish to ask students:
¿Para qué es la factura?
¿En qué ciudad está el restaurante?
¿Dónde en la ciudad está?
¿Quién recibe el original de la factura?
¿Qué comió el cliente?
¿Cuánto fue el total de la cuenta?

ANSWERS

Práctica

A 1. Yo quiero que él vuelva mañana.
2. Yo quiero que él nos encuentre en el restaurante.
3. Yo quiero que él se siente a nuestra mesa.
4. Yo quiero que él pida algo bueno.
5. Yo quiero que él me recomiende un plato.
6. Yo quiero que el mesero n___ a atentamente.

B 1. vuelva
2. encuentre
3. pueda
4. comience
5. empiece
6. pueda
7. perdamos

377

Use BRR Transparency 13-4, or write the following on the board: Make two columns on a piece of paper. Head one of the columns **La Navidad** and the other **Hanuka.** Copy each of the following into the appropriate column.

1. los camellos
2. las velas
3. la menora
4. los Reyes Magos
5. la paja
6. la Nochebuena
7. el árbol
8. la fiesta de las luces

TEACHING STRUCTURE

 Giving advice and making suggestions

A. Have students open their books to page 378 and lead them carefully through Steps 1–3.

B. Have students repeat the model sentences after you.

C. Re-emphasize that we use the subjunctive because we don't know if the action of the verb will take place or not.

 Práctica

A You may wish to have students prepare **Práctica A** before going over it in class.

EXPANSION Have students do the activity again with **Mi mamá me pide que...**

378

 Giving advice and making suggestions
El subjuntivo con verbos como **pedir** y **aconsejar**

1. The subjunctive is used with the following verbs because even though you may advise, recommend, suggest, ask, or order someone to do something, he or she may not do it.

pedir *to ask*	**rogar** *to beg, to plead*
aconsejar *to advise*	**exigir** *to demand*
sugerir *to suggest*	

Él pide que yo vaya.
Y yo le aconsejo que se quede aquí.
Mamá nos sugiere que salgamos ahora.

2. An indirect object pronoun often goes with these verbs. The pronoun serves as the subject of the dependent clause.

Él *me* pide que (yo) sirva de padrino.
Les ruego que (Uds.) no se casen en junio porque no voy a estar.

3. The verbs **decir** and **escribir** call for the subjunctive only when they imply a command or request, such as: "He writes me to come right away."

Ellos me dicen que no me case.
Yo le escribo que venga pronto.

 Práctica

A **Mamá te pide que...**
Completen según el modelo.

limpiar tu cuarto
Mamá te pide que limpies tu cuarto.

1. levantarte temprano
2. limpiar tu cuarto
3. bañarte
4. tomar el desayuno
5. no jugar hoy
6. dormir bastante
7. volver a casa en el bus

Coyoacán, México

Práctica
A All answers begin with **Mamá te pide que...**
1. ... te levantes temprano.
2. ... limpies tu cuarto.
3. ... te bañes.
4. ... tomes el desayuno.
5. ... no juegues hoy.
6. ... duermas bastante.
7. ... vuelvas a casa en el bus.

Learning From Photos

Para novias Have students say whatever they can about the magazine cover on page 378. You may wish to ask questions such as: **¿Con qué revista norteamericana se relaciona esta revista? ¿Para quiénes es la revista? ¿De qué trata el artículo principal de la revista? ¿Qué lugar para novios se describe en uno de los artículos?**

B **¿Qué te escribe tu primo?** Sigan el modelo.

ir a la fiesta
Mi primo me escribe que vaya a la fiesta.

1. ir al cine
2. tomar el tren
3. llegar un día antes de la fiesta
4. no ir a un hotel
5. quedarse en casa de mis tíos

C **El profesor exige que…** Sigan el modelo.

Estudiamos mucho.
El profesor nos exige que estudiemos mucho.

1. Llegamos temprano a clase.
2. Hacemos preguntas.
3. Estudiamos.
4. No perdemos el tiempo.
5. Pensamos antes de hablar.

D **Consejos de mis padres** Contesten.

1. ¿Tus padres te aconsejan que seas bueno?
2. ¿Tus padres te piden que ayudes un poco con las tareas domésticas?
3. ¿Te piden que les digas adónde vas y con quiénes?
4. ¿Tus padres te sugieren que hagas tus tareas antes de poner la televisión?
5. ¿Te dicen que te acuestes antes de las once?

Actividad comunicativa

A **Los consejos de don o doña Sabelotodo**
Tú vas a ser don o doña Sabelotodo—y no hay duda que tú lo sabes todo. Además sabes lo que todo el mundo debe hacer. Trabaja con un(a) compañero(a). Dale muchos consejos, sugerencias y recomendaciones. Tu compañero(a) te dirá si va a seguir tus consejos o no. Luego cambien de rol.

Santurce, Puerto Rico

Parking gratuito
Hasta 24 horas GRATIS con billete sencillo
Hasta 48 horas GRATIS con billete ida y vuelta

• Clase Club
• Clase Preferente

• TARJETA Club AVE ORO
• Coche Cama y Preferente de Trenes de Grandes Líneas

P

Nuevo Servicio
Sin Esperas
Ahora puede formalizar su plaza de aparcamiento al dejar su coche. Le evitará la espera al regreso.

AVE

CAPÍTULO 13
Estructura

B and **C** Before going over these activities in class, have students prepare them. Or if you prefer, do them orally with books open.

C **EXPANSION** Have students redo **Práctica C** with **Yo sé que el profesor siempre te exige que…**

D You may wish to have students prepare **Práctica D** before going over it in class.

Learning From Realia

Parking gratuito Ask students to tell you as much as they can about the ad on page 379. You may wish to remind them that the **AVE** is the Spanish high-speed train.

ANSWERS

Práctica

B All answers begin with **Mi primo me escribe que…**
1. … vaya al cine.
2. … tome el tren.
3. … llegue un día antes de la fiesta.
4. … no vaya a un hotel.
5. … me quede en casa de mis tíos.

C All answers begin with **El profesor nos exige que…**
1. … lleguemos temprano a clase.
2. … hagamos preguntas.
3. … estudiemos.
4. … no perdamos el tiempo.
5. … pensemos antes de hablar.

D 1. Sí, mis padres me aconsejan que sea bueno(a).
2. Sí (No), mis padres (no) me piden que ayude un poco con las tareas domésticas.
3. Sí, (No, no) me piden que les diga adónde voy y con quiénes.
4. Sí (No), mis padres (no) me sugieren que haga mis tareas antes de poner la televisión.
5. Sí, (No, no) me dicen que me acueste antes de las once.

Actividad comunicativa
A Answers will vary.

TEACHING STRUCTURE

◆ Expressing doubt or uncertainty

A. Have students open their books to page 380 and lead them through Steps 1–3.
B. Have students repeat the model sentences in Steps 1 and 2 after you.

 **Práctica**

A **Práctica A** can be done in class without prior preparation.

Learning From Realia

Este motor... Ask students to give their interpretation of **Este motor... no contamina** on the book cover on page 380.

 Expressing doubt or uncertainty
El subjuntivo con expresiones de duda

1. The subjunctive is always used after expressions that imply doubt or uncertainty.

> **Dudo que ellos se casen.**
> **No creo que ellos tengan una recepción.**

2. If the statement implies certainty, however, the indicative rather than the subjunctive is used. The verb is frequently in the future tense.

> **No dudo que ellos se casarán.**
> **Creo que tendrán una gran recepción.**

3. Study the following expressions of doubt and certainty.

SUBJUNCTIVE	INDICATIVE
dudar	no dudar
es dudoso	no es dudoso
no estar seguro(a)	estar seguro(a)
no creer	creer
no es cierto	es cierto

Parque del Amor, Lima, Perú

 **Práctica**

A **¿Lo crees o no lo crees?**
Introduzcan la oración con **creo** o **no creo.**

1. Los aviones vuelan a un millón de millas por hora.
2. Las bicicletas contaminan el aire.
3. Hace mucho calor en la Siberia.
4. Todos los españoles hablan inglés.
5. Todos los compañeros de clase bailan muy bien.
6. Sirven comida excelente en la cafetería.
7. Las muchachas son más inteligentes que los chicos.

ANSWERS

Práctica
A 1. **No creo que los aviones vuelen a un millón de millas por hora.**
2. **No creo que las bicicletas contaminen el aire.**
3. **No creo que haga mucho calor en la Siberia.**
4. **No creo que todos los españoles hablen inglés.**
5. **No creo que todos los compañeros de clase bailen bien.**
6. **No creo que sirvan comida excelente en la cafetería.**
7. **No creo que las muchachas sean más inteligentes que los chicos.**

B Martín nunca dice la verdad.
Sigan el modelo.

> **Yo soy el más inteligente de la clase.**
> **No, Martín. Dudo que seas el más**
> **inteligente de la clase.**

1. Yo tengo mucho talento.
2. También soy muy guapo.
3. Recibo las mejores notas de la clase.
4. Yo bailo como un profesional.
5. Mis padres son millonarios.
6. Las muchachas me adoran.
7. Voy a Madrid mañana.
8. Me quieren en Hollywood.

C **HISTORIETA** La boda de mi mejor amigo(a)

Contesten con **creo** o **dudo**.

1. Tu mejor amigo(a) se casa pronto.
2. Te invita a la recepción.
3. La recepción es en un gran hotel.
4. La orquesta toca música clásica.
5. Tú le regalas un coche.
6. Los novios viajan a Buenos Aires.

Actividad comunicativa

A **¿Pasará o no pasará?** Con un(a) compañero(a), determinen las cosas o los eventos que Uds. creen que van a pasar u ocurrir en su vida y cosas que no creen que pasen ni ocurran. Luego comparen sus dos listas para determinar lo que Uds. creen que tienen en común.

ESTRUCTURA

trescientos ochenta y uno 381

B Have students present each item of **Práctica B** as a mini-conversation. Insist that they use as much expression as possible.

C You may go over **Práctica C** with or without prior preparation.

Critical Thinking Activity

Giving opinions Read the following to the class or write it on the board.

Las bodas lujosas y elegantes, y muy caras, están otra vez de moda. Algunos dicen que esto representa un deseo de volver al formalismo y tradición del pasado. Otros dicen que es cuestión de «status» social. ¿Qué opinas tú? ¿Quiénes deben determinar el tipo de boda que tienen los novios, los novios o los padres de los novios? ¿Por qué?

ANSWERS

Práctica

B 1. No, Martín. Dudo que tengas mucho talento.
2. No, Martín. Dudo que seas muy guapo.
3. No, Martín. Dudo que recibas las mejores notas de la clase.
4. No, Martín. Dudo que bailes como un profesional.
5. No, Martín. Dudo que tus padres sean millonarios.
6. No, Martín. Dudo que las muchachas te adoren.
7. No, Martín. Dudo que vayas a Madrid mañana.
8. No, Martín. Dudo que te quieran en Hollywood.

C 1. Creo que tu mejor amigo(a) se casará pronto. Dudo que tu mejor amigo(a) se case pronto.
2. Creo que te invitará a la recepción. Dudo que te invite a la recepción.
3. Creo que la recepción será en un gran hotel. Dudo que la recepción sea en un gran hotel.
4. Creo que la orquesta tocará música clásica. Dudo que la orquesta toque música clásica.
5. Creo que tú le regalarás un coche. Dudo que tú le regales un coche.
6. Creo que los novios viajarán a Buenos Aires. Dudo que los novios viajen a Buenos Aires.

Actividad comunicativa
A Answers will vary.

Expressing emotional reactions

A. Have students open their books to page 382 and lead them through Steps 1 and 2.

B. Call on volunteers to read the model sentences aloud.

 The use of the subjunctive after these expressions does not fit the general rule that it be used when it is uncertain whether or not an event will take place. Emphasize here that the subjunctive is used due to the subjective nature of the statements, as explained in Step 1.

❖Práctica❖

A Have students prepare **Práctica A** before going over it in class. Call on three students and have them present each item.

Learning From Photos

Santiago de Chile y Santurce, Puerto Rico Ask students to describe and say as much as they can about the photos on pages 382 and 383. You may wish to prompt responses by asking questions such as: **¿Qué están haciendo las dos muchachas? ¿Para quién serán los regalos? ¿Dónde están los muchachos? ¿Qué hacen ellos? ¿Llevan uniforme? ¿Cómo es el uniforme?**

382

Expressing emotional reactions
El subjuntivo con expresiones de emoción

1. The subjunctive is used in a dependent clause that is introduced by a verb or expression of emotion.

> **Me alegro de que tú celebres tu cumpleaños.**
> **Siento que tu hermano no pueda asistir.**
> **Es una lástima que él tenga que trabajar.**

2. The following are verbs and expressions that convey emotion.

alegrarse de
estar contento
sorprender
gustar
sentir
ser una lástima

Santiago de Chile

❖Práctica❖

A **Sara, sí, y Nora, no.** Sigan el modelo.

> **Tenemos un examen mañana.**
> **Sara se alegra de que tengamos un examen mañana.**
> **Nora siente que tengamos un examen mañana.**

Sara   Nora

1. Tenemos clase mañana.
2. El profesor nos da un examen.
3. El examen es difícil.
4. No podemos usar los libros.

5. Escribimos una composición.
6. Hacemos una presentación oral.
7. El profesor lee las composiciones.

B **¿Se alegra o no se alegra Andrés?** Contesten. Empiecen las frases con **Andrés se alegra** o **Andrés no se alegra.**

1. La escuela cierra temprano.
2. Los chicos pueden jugar.
3. Va a llover.
4. Acaba de llover.
5. Su equipo pierde.
6. Los padres les compran pizza.
7. Juegan otra vez mañana.

C **HISTORIETA** El Día de los Reyes y Hanuka

Contesten.

1. ¿Están contentos los niños que llegue el seis de enero?
2. ¿Se alegran de que vengan los Reyes?
3. ¿Están alegres que los Reyes les traigan regalos?
4. ¿Les sorprende que los camellos coman la paja en los zapatos?
5. ¿Te sorprende que la fiesta de Hanuka dure ocho días?
6. ¿Los niños se alegran de que los padres les den un regalo cada uno de los ocho días?
7. ¿Se alegran los padres de que su hijo mayor encienda las velas de la menora?

Actividad comunicativa

A **Emociones** Trabaja con un(a) compañero(a). Van a hablar de su escuela y de su vida escolar. Es cierto que en la escuela hay cosas que les ponen contentos y hay otras cosas que les ponen tristes. Al hablar de su vida escolar usen las expresiones **Me alegro de que, Siento que, Estoy contento(a) que, Estoy triste que** y den sus opiniones.

Santurce, Puerto Rico

ESTRUCTURA

B **Práctica B** can be done orally in class with books closed.

C Because of the length of the sentences, it is recommended that you go over **Práctica C** with books open.

¡OJO! There is no more new material to present in this chapter. The sections that follow recombine and reinforce the vocabulary and structures that have already been introduced.

ANSWERS

Práctica

B 1. Andrés (no) se alegra de que la escuela cierre temprano.
2. Andrés (no) se alegra de que los chicos puedan jugar.
3. Andrés (no) se alegra de que vaya a llover.
4. Andrés (no) se alegra de que acabe de llover.
5. Andres (no) se alegra de que su equipo pierda.
6. Andrés (no) se alegra de que los padres les compren pizza.
7. Andrés (no) se alegra de que jueguen otra vez mañana.

C 1. Sí, los niños están contentos que llegue el seis de enero.
2. Sí, se alegran de que vengan los Reyes.
3. Sí, están alegres que los Reyes les traigan regalos.
4. No, no les sorprende que los camellos coman la paja en los zapatos.
5. Sí, (No, no) me sorprende que la fiesta de Hanuka dure ocho días.
6. Sí, los niños se alegran de que sus padres les den un regalo cada uno de los ocho días.
7. Sí, los padres se alegran de que su hijo mayor encienda las velas de la menora.

Actividad comunicativa

A Answers will vary.

RESOURCES

🎧 Audiocassette 8A/CD7

💿 CD-ROM, Disc 4, page 384

🔔 Bell Ringer Review

Use BRR Transparency 13-6, or write the following on the board: Complete the following sentences:

1. **Tengo miedo que ___.**
2. **Lucía está triste que ___.**
3. **¿Te sorprende que ___?**
4. **Estoy contento(a) que ___.**
5. **Siento que ___.**

TEACHING THE CONVERSATION

A. Tell students they are going to hear a conversation about plans for New Year's Eve. Something *interesting* comes out in the conversation. Tell them to listen for what it is.

B. 🎧 Have students listen to Cassette 8A/Compact Disc 7 or read the conversation aloud to the class.

C. Call on pairs of individuals to read the conversation aloud using as much expression as possible.

D. Go over the **Después de conversar** questions.

E. Have students write the answers to the **Después de conversar** questions for homework.

F. Call on a student to tell all about the conversation in his or her own words.

TECHNOLOGY OPTION

On the CD-ROM (Disc 4, page 384), students can watch a dramatization of this conversation. They can then play the role of either one of the characters and record themselves in the conversation.

384

Conversación

Año Nuevo

RAMÓN: ¿Qué vas a hacer para Año Nuevo?
YOLANDA: ¿Año Nuevo? Estaré durmiendo. Pero Nochevieja voy a una fiesta.
RAMÓN: Me alegro de que vayas a una fiesta. Yo me quedaré en casa.
YOLANDA: ¿Por qué? ¿Qué pasa?
RAMÓN: Pues, invité a Cristina a ir a la fiesta de Luis Miguel y ella me dijo que no podía.
YOLANDA: Claro que no podía. Ella no puede ir contigo porque va con Antonio.
RAMÓN: ¡Pero Antonio es tu novio! Es imposible que Cristina vaya con él.
YOLANDA: Pues, imposible o no, es verdad. Créeme. ¡Oye, tengo una idea!
RAMÓN: No es necesario que me digas. Ya lo sé. Y es excelente idea. ¡Vamos tú y yo a la fiesta!
YOLANDA: Muchas gracias por la invitación. Acepto.

384 ᗦ *trescientos ochenta y cuatro*

CAPÍTULO 13

Después de conversar

Contesten.

1. ¿Qué va a hacer Yolanda durante Año Nuevo?
2. ¿Cuándo va ella a una fiesta?
3. ¿Quién da la fiesta?
4. ¿Qué piensa hacer Ramón?
5. ¿A quién pensaba Ramón invitar a la fiesta?
6. ¿Qué le dijo ella?
7. ¿Por qué no puede Cristina ir a la fiesta con Ramón?
8. ¿Quién es Antonio?
9. ¿Cuál es la idea que tiene Yolanda?
10. ¿Qué van a hacer Yolanda y Ramón?

ANSWERS

Después de conversar

1. **Yolanda va a dormir durante Año Nuevo.**
2. **Ella va a una fiesta Nochevieja.**
3. **Luis Miguel da la fiesta.**
4. **Ramón piensa quedarse en casa.**
5. **Ramón invitó a Cristina.**
6. **Le dijo que no podía.**
7. **Cristina no puede ir a la fiesta con Ramón porque va con Antonio.**

8. **Antonio es el novio de Yolanda.**
9. **La idea que tiene Yolanda es de ir a la fiesta con Ramón.**
10. **Yolanda y Ramón van a ir a la fiesta juntos.**

Actividades comunicativas

A **¡Qué horror!**   Trabaja con un(a) compañero(a). Uno(a) de Uds. va a ser (tomar el papel de) Yolanda en la conversación en la página 384. El/La otro(a) tomará el papel de Antonio que va a salir con otra. Yolanda va a decirle a Antonio todo lo que ella piensa de él. Antonio va a tratar de defenderse.

Ciudad de México

B **La víspera de Año Nuevo**   Trabaja con un(a) compañero(a). Discutan todo lo que Uds. hacen o no hacen para celebrar el Año Nuevo.

Actividades comunicativas

Allow students to choose the activities that they would like to participate in.

Did You Know?

Ciudad de México Mexicans usually refer to their capital city simply as **México** if the context is clear. In print the capital city is usually just **México, D.F.**

In Spain, Mexico is often spelled with a «j»; **Méjico.** In most other countries, out of respect for the preference of the Mexicans, it is spelled **México.**

ANSWERS

Actividades comunicativas
A and **B** Answers will vary.

385

386

Bell Ringer Review

Use BRR Transparency 13-7, or write the following on the board: Put the following scrambled conversation into a logical order.

1. ¿De parte de quién?
2. ¿Puedo dejarle un mensaje?
3. ¿Está el Sr. Salas, por favor?
4. ¡Hola!
5. De acuerdo.
6. De Roberto Díaz.
7. Lo siento, pero no está.
8. Un momento. Favor de no colgar.

National Standards

Cultures
The reading on page 386 and the related activity on this page familiarize students with an interesting Spanish New Year's Eve custom.

Comparisons
Students learn that, as in New York, where crowds watch the ball descend in Times Square every New Year's Eve, the citizens of Madrid gather in the city center and eat the 12 "grapes of happiness" as a golden ball descends in the clock tower at the stroke of midnight.

TEACHING THE READING

Pre-reading

A. Tell students that they are going to learn how some **madrileños** spend New Year's Eve.
B. Have students read the Reading Strategy on this page. Have them look at the photos as well. Visualizing this New Year's Eve custom can help in understanding the **Lectura.**

Lecturas CULTURALES

LAS DOCE UVAS DE LA FELICIDAD

Madrid, la capital de España, está en el centro del país. Y en el mismo centro de Madrid está La Puerta del Sol. La Puerta del Sol es una plaza donde desembocan muchas calles. La Puerta del Sol tiene gran importancia histórica. Es allí donde los madrileños se reúnen cuando algo importante ha ocurrido o va a ocurrir.

Cada Nochevieja miles y miles de madrileños llenan la Puerta del Sol para esperar la llegada del Año Nuevo. Todos miran el reloj que está en la torre de la antigua Casa de Correos. Están contentos que llegue otro año. En los momentos antes de las doce de la noche, una bola dorada[1] comienza a bajar, segundo por segundo. Cuando baja completamente, el año ha terminado, y un año nuevo comienza. Mientras el reloj da las doce los madrileños tienen la costumbre de comerse doce uvas, una por una. Estas uvas se llaman las uvas de la felicidad. Comerlas es garantía de un año nuevo próspero y feliz.

[1]dorada *golden*

Puerta del Sol, Madrid

386 trescientos ochenta y seis

Learning From Photos

Puerta del Sol, Madrid The building shown on page 386 is the **Dirección General de Seguridad** or police headquarters. The building was originally the **Casa de correos** built during the reign of Carlos III in the 18th century. The clock tower, from which the golden ball descends on New Year's Eve, was added in 1866.

Did You Know?

El punto de partida All national highways in Spain have as 0 kilometers the **Puerta del Sol.** If you are on **Nacional V** and the marker says 220, you are 220 kilometers from the **Puerta del Sol.**

Después de leer

A **Nochevieja en Madrid** Contesten según la lectura.
1. ¿Qué tienen en común Madrid y la Puerta del Sol?
2. ¿Por qué es importante históricamente la Puerta del Sol?
3. ¿Qué día del año llenan los madrileños la Puerta del Sol?
4. ¿Qué hacen ellos allí?
5. ¿Qué hay en la antigua Casa de Correos?

B **¿Cómo es Nochevieja?** Expliquen en sus propias palabras las tradiciones de Nochevieja en España.

Puerta del Sol, Madrid

LECTURAS CULTURALES *trescientos ochenta y siete* ∾ **387**

Reading

A. Call on a student to read three or four sentences aloud. Then stop and ask other members of the class questions about the material that was just read.

B. Have students read the selection at home and write the answers to the **Después de leer** activities that accompany the **Lectura**.

Post-reading

A. Go over the **Después de leer** activities in class the next day.

B. Call on a student to give a summary of the reading in his or her own words. If necessary, ask five or six questions to review the salient points of the reading selection in order to enable him or her to do this more easily. After the oral summary, the more able students can write a synopsis of the **Lectura** in their own words.

TECHNOLOGY OPTION

Students may listen to a recorded version of the **Lectura** on the CD-ROM, Disc 4, page 386.

HISTORY CONNECTION

La Puerta del Sol La Puerta del Sol is regarded as the geographical center of Spain. It has also been the scene of great events in the history of Spain. One of the most significant was the uprising by the people of Madrid against Napoleon's Mamelukes and Imperial Guard on the 2nd of May, 1808. This event was immortalized by Goya in his painting «El dos de mayo».

ANSWERS

Después de leer

A 1. **Madrid está en el centro del país y la Puerta del Sol está en el centro de Madrid.**
2. **La Puerta del Sol es importante históricamente porque es allí donde los madrileños se reúnen cuando algo importante ha ocurrido o va a ocurrir.**
3. **Los madrileños llenan la Puerta del Sol la Nochevieja.**
4. **Esperan la llegada del Año Nuevo.**
5. **Hay un reloj en la torre de la antigua Casa de Correos.**

B Answers will vary but may include: **Los madrileños esperan el Año Nuevo en La Puerta del Sol. Miran el reloj y una bola dorada que baja en los momentos antes de las doce. Mientras el reloj da las doce, ellos comen doce uvas, las uvas de la felicidad. Comerlas es garantía de un año nuevo próspero y feliz.**

387

LECTURA OPCIONAL 1

LA BODA

Ángel y Mónica seguían saliendo juntos y cada mes se querían más. Sabían que querían casarse. Ángel fue a la casa de Mónica y le pidió al padre la mano de su hija. Poco después los padres anunciaron el compromiso[1] de sus hijos. Hubo un cóctel elegante en el que fijaron la fecha para sus bodas y todos los parientes de las dos familias y los amigos íntimos festejaron a los nuevos comprometidos. Estas fiestas y reuniones familiares son muy importantes porque el matrimonio es el enlace de las dos familias y durante las fiestas antenupciales las dos familias van conociéndose.

Se casaron un año después. El día de la boda hay generalmente dos ceremonias—la civil y la religiosa. Los novios van a la iglesia acompañados del padrino y de la madrina, de sus pajes de honor y de sus damas de honor. La madre de Mónica le sirvió de madrina y el padre de Ángel le sirvió de padrino. Después de la ceremonia Ángel y Mónica salieron de la iglesia como esposo y esposa y fueron a una recepción en donde sus familiares y sus amigos íntimos les dieron la enhorabuena.

Al terminar la recepción, Ángel y Mónica salieron para su viaje de novios. Fueron a Europa a pasar su luna de miel[2].

[1]compromiso *engagement*
[2]luna de miel *honeymoon*

Después de leer

A **Los novios** Contesten.

1. ¿Quiénes son Ángel y Mónica?
2. ¿Qué hizo Ángel cuando supo que él y Mónica iban a comprometerse?
3. ¿Qué hubo para anunciar su compromiso?
4. ¿Para qué sirven las fiestas antenupciales?
5. ¿Cuántas ceremonias hay para la boda?
6. ¿A quiénes escogieron Ángel y Mónica para su padrino y madrina?
7. ¿Adónde fueron los recién casados para su luna de miel?

National Standards

Cultures
This reading about wedding customs and the related activity on page 388 familiarize students with an important family and social event in the Spanish-speaking world.

Comparisons
Students learn that, in the Spanish-speaking world, it is very important for the young couple's families to get to know each other better during the engagement period. Also, the couple usually has both a religious and a civil wedding ceremony.

TEACHING TIPS

¡OJO! This reading is optional. You may skip it completely, have the entire class read it, have only several students read it, or assign it for extra credit.

Learning From Photos

Una boda hispana You may wish to ask students to describe what they see in the photo of the wedding on page 388.

ANSWERS

Después de leer

A 1. Ángel y Mónica son novios.
2. Fue a la casa de Mónica y le pidió al padre la mano de su hija.
3. Hubo un cóctel elegante.
4. Sirven para que las familias de los novios se conozcan.
5. Hay dos ceremonias—la civil y la religiosa.
6. Escogieron a la madre de Mónica para su madrina y al padre de Ángel para su padrino.
7. Los recién casados fueron a Europa para su luna de miel.

388

LECTURA OPCIONAL 2

Freyssiner-Parada

El reverendo Manuel Belman Robles, S.J., impartió la bendición nupcial a Sandra Freyssiner y César Parada, durante una ceremonia que tuvo lugar el pasado sábado por la tarde en la iglesia de Nuestra Señora del Socorro.

A la hora señalada llegaron los novios con su comitiva y en la puerta fueron recibidos por el sacerdote[1], quien les acompañó hasta el altar mayor, donde participaron del calvario de Cristo.

La iglesia fue profusamente iluminada y decorada con arreglos de flores naturales mientras el coro interpretó trozos de música sacra, lo que dio mayor lucimiento a la ceremonia.

El sacerdote oficiante pronunció un emotivo fervorín en donde dio consejos a los novios para su vida espiritual.

Estuvieron los padres de los contrayentes Jaime Freyssiner de la Barrera, Gloria Márquez Marrón, Francisco Javier Parra Jiménez y Amelia López de Parada.

Asimismo fueron madrinas Gloria Freyssiner Márquez, Karu Noval de Freyssiner, Amelia Parada de Hernández, Leticia Parada de Alba y Beatriz Alvarez.

Como pajes actuaron los niños Elvira Parada Dommarco y Cristina Hernández Parada.

Al finalizar el acto religioso, los nuevos esposos desfilaron[2] por el pasillo central y en el atrio[3] recibieron felicitaciones de amigos y parientes.

Más tarde se ofreció una recepción en su honor en donde se brindó[4] por la felicidad de la pareja, la que más tarde salió de viaje de bodas.

[1] sacerdote *priest*
[2] desfilaron *paraded*
[3] atrio *vestibule, entrance*
[4] se brindó *everyone toasted*

Después de leer

A La boda   Contesten.

1. ¿Cómo se llama el sacerdote que le dio la bendición nupcial a la pareja?
2. ¿Dónde tuvo lugar la ceremonia?
3. ¿Cuándo tuvo lugar?
4. ¿Dónde recibió a la pareja el sacerdote?
5. ¿Adónde los acompañó?
6. ¿Con qué fue decorada la iglesia?
7. Después de la ceremonia, ¿dónde recibieron felicitaciones los nuevos esposos?
8. ¿Qué se ofreció después de la ceremonia en la iglesia?
9. ¿Para dónde salió la pareja después de la recepción?

National Standards

Cultures This reading, and the related activity on this page, familiarize students with a typical wedding ceremony in the Hispanic world.

TEACHING TIPS

¡OJO! This reading is optional. You may skip it completely, have the entire class read it, have only several students read it, or assign it for extra credit.

A. Have any students who are interested in the topic of weddings do the reading and then discuss any differences they may have noted between the wedding described in this article and weddings they may themselves have attended.

B. **Note** This is an actual wedding announcement that appeared in a newspaper. Students could bring in a wedding announcement from the social pages of a local newspaper and compare it with the Spanish one.

Did You Know?

Un refrán popular In Madrid there was a refrain: **El que no pasa por la calle de la Pasa no se casa.** The church offices for registering marriages were on **la calle de la Pasa** in Old Madrid. The saying meant that if one didn't marry in the Church, one didn't marry.

ANSWERS

Después de leer

A 1. El sacerdote se llama Manuel Belman Robles, S.J.
2. La ceremonia tuvo lugar en la iglesia de Nuestra Señora del Socorro.
3. La boda tuvo lugar el sábado por la tarde.
4. El sacerdote recibió a la pareja en la puerta.
5. Los acompañó hasta el altar mayor.
6. La iglesia fue decorada con (arreglos de) flores naturales.

7. Después de la ceremonia los nuevos esposos recibieron felicitaciones en el atrio.
8. Después de la ceremonia en la iglesia se ofreció una recepción en honor de la pareja.
9. Después de la recepción la pareja salió de viaje de bodas.

¡OJO! The readings in the **Conexiones** section are optional. They focus on the major disciplines taught in schools and universities. The vocabulary is useful for discussing such topics as history, literature, art, economics, business, science, etc. You may choose any of the following ways to do this reading on Spanish painting with your students.

Independent reading Have students read the selections and do the post-reading activities as homework, which you collect. This option is least intrusive on class time and requires a minimum of teacher involvement.

Homework with in-class follow-up Assign the readings and post-reading activities as homework. Review and discuss the material in class the next day.

Intensive in-class activity This option includes a pre-reading vocabulary presentation, in-class reading and discussion, assignment of the activities for homework, and a discussion of the assignment in class the following day.

Conexiones

LAS BELLAS ARTES

LAS ARTES PLÁSTICAS

From earliest times, religion has had a profound influence on art. The temples of the Far East, the Gothic cathedrals of Europe, the pyramids of the Mayas, and the great mosques of Cordoba and Cairo are artistic expressions of profound religious feeling. Throughout the centuries, the painters of Europe, especially the Spaniards, often employed religious themes in their work. *The Adoration of the Magi* by Velazquez and *The Return of the Prodigal Son* by Murillo are two notable examples.

Diego Velázquez

Bartolomé Murillo

La escuela española

Como ya saben Uds., hay diferentes épocas y «escuelas» de arte y, en particular, de pintura. Velázquez y Murillo son representantes de la «escuela española». Pero también se puede decir que eran clásicos. Cuando hablamos de los clásicos en el arte, nos referimos a los artistas que se notan por su claridad, elegancia y atención a las formas de los griegos y romanos.

Los dos artistas nacieron[1] en Sevilla. Velázquez (1599–1660) era de una familia noble. Murillo (1617–1682) era de una familia pobre. Perdió a sus padres cuando tenía sólo diez años. Velázquez fue a Madrid a pintar para la corte donde su talento artístico fue reconocido enseguida. Murillo se quedó en Sevilla donde se ganó la vida pintando y vendiendo sus cuadros en el mercado. En poco tiempo ganó fama y fue reconocido como el pintor principal de la ciudad.

[1]nacieron *were born*

Did You Know?

Grandes maestros The statue of Velázquez is at the entrance to the Museo del Prado, one of the world's most important art museums. The collection began as the royal collections of both Hapsburg and Bourbon monarchs. The building was designed during the reign of Carlos III and opened in 1819 during the reign of Fernando VII. The museum possesses more than 5,000 pictures of which about 2,300 are on display to the public in 120 rooms on three floors. The Museo del Prado houses the finest collection of Spanish masters: El Greco, Velázquez, Murillo, Zurbarán, Ribera, and Goya.

«La adoración de los Magos»
de Diego Velázquez

Los temas favoritos de la escuela española eran la mitología y la religión. Este cuadro de Velázquez, «La adoración de los Magos», representa a los tres Reyes Magos—Melchor, Gaspar y Baltasar—ofreciendo sus regalos al Niño Jesús. Notarán Uds. los anacronismos en esta obra. Por ejemplo, la época del evento es del primer siglo. Las ropas son contemporáneas con la época del pintor del siglo XVII. Noten los colores que emplea el artista. Velázquez es maestro de colorido.

Este cuadro de Murillo, «El regreso del hijo pródigo», describe la historia bíblica del mismo nombre. Todos los personajes y objetos que aparecen[2] en la historia bíblica están incluidos en el cuadro. Vemos al padre que recibe a su hijo que regresa y los sirvientes que le traen zapatos y ropa nueva. El cuadro no tiene líneas definidas ni un fuerte contraste de colores. El pintor quería una composición sencilla y armoniosa. No hay nada en el cuadro que nos distraiga[3] de la contemplación de la alegría del padre.

[2]aparecen *appear*
[3]distraiga *distracts*

«El regreso del hijo pródigo» de Bartolomé Murillo

Después de leer

A **La escuela española** Contesten.

1. ¿Quiénes son representantes de la «escuela española»?
2. ¿Dónde nacieron?
3. ¿Quién era de una familia noble y rica?
4. ¿Quién era de una familia pobre?
5. ¿Dónde pintó Velázquez?
6. ¿Dónde pintó Murillo?
7. ¿Cuáles eran los temas favoritos de la «escuela española»?
8. ¿Cómo se llama el cuadro de Velázquez?
9. ¿Qué representa?
10. ¿Cómo se llama el cuadro de Murillo?

B **Tu preferencia** ¿Cuál de los dos cuadros te gusta más? ¿Por qué?

CONEXIONES   *trescientos noventa y uno*   **391**

CAPÍTULO 13
Conexiones

L AS BELLAS ARTES
LAS ARTES PLÁSTICAS

A. Even though this material is optional, you may wish to go over this selection at least quickly with the entire class.
B. Have students who read the reading on «**Las Meninas**» in ¡**Buen viaje! Level 1,** Chapter 6 retell any information they remember.
C. When discussing these paintings you may wish to show Fine Art Transparency F-6 for the painting by Murillo and Fine Art Transparency F-7 for the one by Velázquez from the Transparency Binder. In addition, you may wish to have students read the background information and do the related activities that accompany the Fine Art Transparencies.

Culminación

Actividades orales

A **Una situación delicada** Tu mejor amigo(a) (tu compañero[a]), iba a casarse. Pero ahora ha cambiado de idea. Él o ella no sabe qué hacer. Te pide consejos. Conversen juntos.

B **El pobre Manolo** Manolo nunca sabe qué hacer. Nunca ha asistido a una fiesta y acaba de recibir una invitación. Aconséjale a Manolo sobre cómo vestirse para la fiesta y cómo comportarse—es decir, lo que debe hacer durante la fiesta.

San José, Costa Rica

C **Mi fiesta favorita** Trabaja con un(a) compañero(a). Descríbele tu fiesta favorita. Explícale por qué te gusta tanto. Luego cambien de rol.

Actividades escritas

A Un correo electrónico Lee el siguiente correo electrónico. Después de leerlo, prepara una contestación. Incluye todos los detalles.

```
┌──────────────────── Message Composition ────────────────────┐
│ 📧 📋 ✏️ 🖼️ ⚫                              eperez@enon.com │
│ Subject: [                                            ]       │
│ ▽ Addressing                    Attachments                  │
│   Mail To:                    ┌──────────────────┐           │
│       Co:                     │                  │           │
│                               └──────────────────┘           │
│ ─────────────────────────────────────────────────────────── │
│ Hola, amigo:                                                 │
│ Anoche fue Nochevieja. Todos fuimos a la Puerta del Sol a celebrar. │
│ Había miles de personas allí.                               │
│ Hacía frío, pero no nos importaba. Cuando el reloj empezaba a dar las │
│ doce, empezamos a comer las doce uvas de la felicidad. Después fuimos a │
│ casa de unos amigos y seguimos en fiesta hasta las tres de la mañana. │
│ ¿Qué hiciste tú para Nochevieja? Ya tienes mi dirección para correo │
│ electrónico. Escríbeme pronto.                              │
└──────────────────────────────────────────────────────────────┘
```

B Una invitación Prepara una invitación para una fiesta de cumpleaños, una boda o cualquier fiesta. Da todos los detalles necesarios.

Writing Strategy

Classifying a subject

When writing, one way to effectively organize your material is to classify your subject. For example, if you are writing about clothing, there are several categories your subject could fit into: clothing for school, clothing for weekends, clothing for doing chores, and many more. By choosing a category and classifying your subject, you will be able to organize your information more appropriately and use this classification to construct a good paragraph or paper.

Las fiestas

Obviously you celebrate many holidays throughout the year. This does not mean, however, that you and your classmates celebrate the same ones. Write a paper about some of the holidays you celebrate and describe what these celebrations entail. It would be impossible to write about all the holidays you celebrate; therefore, narrow your list by selecting a category for your holidays: holidays I like best, religious holidays, winter holidays, summer holidays, or any other you can think of. Include an introduction and a conclusion.

Actividades escritas

A **TECHNOLOGY OPTION**
For information on setting up an e-mail correspondence between your class and a class in the Spanish-speaking world and for a list of e-mail activities for each chapter, go to the **Correspondencia electrónica** section of the **Glencoe Foreign Language Web site** (http://www.glencoe.com/sec/fl).

Writing Strategy

Classifying a subject

A. Have students read the Writing Strategy on page 393.
B. You may wish to have students do the Chapter 13 Internet activity on Hispanic holidays before you assign this composition. Students can do this writing activity as a follow-up to the Internet activity.

ANSWERS

Actividades escritas
A and B Answers will vary.

Writing Strategy
Answers will vary.

ASSESSMENT RESOURCES

- 📁 Chapter Quizzes
- 📁 Testing Program
- 💾 Computer Testmaker
- 📁 Situation Cards
- 🎙 Communication Transparency C-13
- 📁 Performance Assessment
- 📼 **Maratón mental** Videoquiz

VOCABULARY REVIEW

The words and phrases in the **Vocabulario** have been taught for productive use in this chapter. They are summarized here as a resource for both students and teacher. This list also serves as a convenient resource for the **Culminación** activities on pages 392 and 393. There are approximately three cognates in this vocabulary list. Have students find them.

📌 *Teacher Notes*

Vocabulario

TALKING ABOUT A BIRTHDAY PARTY

el cumpleaños	nacer
el pastel, la torta, el bizcocho	venir a la fiesta
las velas	divertirse
el regalo	¡Feliz cumpleaños!
los parientes	

TALKING ABOUT A WEDDING

la boda	la recepción
la novia	el salón
el novio	la orquesta
la dama de honor	casarse
el padrino	¡Felicitaciones!
la madrina	¡Enhorabuena!

TALKING ABOUT CHRISTMAS

la Navidad	los camellos
el árbol de Navidad	la paja
la Nochebuena	¡Feliz Navidad!
los Reyes Magos	

TALKING ABOUT HANUKA

la fiesta de las luces
la menora
hebreo
encender las velas
durar
¡Feliz Hanuka!

TALKING ABOUT NEW YEAR'S

el Año Nuevo
La Víspera de Año Nuevo (Nochevieja)
el reloj
dar las doce
celebrar
¡Feliz Año Nuevo!

OTHER USEFUL EXPRESSIONS

alegrarse

Independent Practice

Assign any of the following:
1. Activities, pages 392–393
2. Workbook, **Mi autobiografía,** page 164
3. Situation Cards
4. CD-ROM, Disc 4, Chapter 13, **Juego de repaso**

TECNOTUR

VIDEO

¡Buen viaje!

EPISODIO 13 ▶ ¡Fiestas!

Isabel y Luis hacen planes para celebrar el cumpleaños de una amiga muy especial.

¡Sorpresa!

CD-ROM

Expansión cultural

La fiesta de Navidad en la Ciudad de México

interNET CONNECTION

In this video episode Isabel and Luis help Cristina celebrate her November 1 birthday in a special way. To find out more about the Day of the Dead celebration in Mexico and other holidays in the Spanish-speaking world, go to the Capítulo 13 Internet activity at the Glencoe Foreign Language Web site:

http://www.glencoe.com/sec/fl

TECNOTUR

trescientos noventa y cinco ∽ **395**

This page previews three key multimedia components of the **Glencoe Spanish** series. Each reinforces the material taught in Chapter 13 in a unique manner.

VIDEO

The Video Program allows students to see how the chapter vocabulary and structures are used by native speakers in an engaging story. Show the video episode as a final activity for Chapter 13.

A. These two photos show highlights from the Chapter 13 video episode. Ask students: **En la primera foto, ¿dónde está Isabel? ¿Quiere comprar una torta o pan? ¿Quién es la amiga especial? Y en la segunda foto, ¿quiénes son los hombres detrás de Cristina y Luis (al fondo)? ¿Cuántos años cumple Cristina?**

B. See the Video Activities Booklet for detailed suggestions for using this resource.

CD-ROM

A. Have students read the **Expansión cultural** caption on page 395.

B. In the CD-ROM version of **Expansión cultural** (Disc 4, page 395), students can listen to additional recorded information about the numerous holidays celebrated in the Spanish-speaking world.

INTERNET

Teacher Information and Student Worksheets for this activity can be accessed at the Web site.

Video Synopsis

This episode focuses on Cristina's birthday celebration as well as on the end of her stay in Mexico. Isabel and Luis have planned a surprise birthday and going-away party at a local outdoor restaurant. Isabel goes to the bakery and selects an appropriate birthday cake while Luis and Cristina go for a walk.

All three then meet at the restaurant. Isabel and Luis encourage Cristina to stay longer, but she explains why she can't. Their conversation is interrupted when the birthday cake is presented and a group of mariachis make a surprise appearance.

SCOPE AND SEQUENCE pages 396–421

TOPICS	FUNCTIONS	STRUCTURE	CULTURE
◆ Professions and occupations ◆ Job interviews	◆ How to talk about professions and occupations ◆ How to prepare for job interviews ◆ How to say what you would like to do and what you would like others to do ◆ How to say "perhaps" or "maybe" ◆ How to describe indefinite persons or things	◆ Infinitive or subjunctive ◆ The subjunctive with **ojalá** and **quizá(s)**	◆ A young man named Bobby ◆ The importance of knowing a second language ◆ The science of economics ◆ **Vistas de Guatemala**

CHAPTER 14 RESOURCES

PRINT	MULTIMEDIA

Planning Resources

Lesson Plans Block Scheduling Lesson Plans	Interactive Lesson Planner

Reinforcement Resources

Writing Activities Workbook Student Tape Manual Video Activities Booklet Web Site User's Guide	Transparencies Binder Audiocassette/Compact Disc Program Videocassette/Videodisc Program Online Internet Activities Electronic Teacher's Classroom Resources

Assessment Resources

Situation Cards Chapter Quizzes Testing Program Performance Assessment	**Maratón mental** Mindjogger Videoquiz Testmaker Computer Software (Macintosh/Windows) Listening Comprehension Audiocassette/Compact Disc Communication Transparency: C-14

Motivational Resources

Expansion Activities	Café Glencoe: www.cafe.glencoe.com Keypal Internet Activities

Enrichment

Spanish for Spanish Speakers	

Chapter 14 Planning Guide

SECTION	PAGES	SECTION RESOURCES
Vocabulario Palabras 1 **La oficina, etc.**	398–401	Vocabulary Transparencies 14.1 Audiocassette 8B/Compact Disc 8 Student Tape Manual, TE, pages 157–159 Workbook, pages 165–166 Chapter Quizzes, page 166 CD-ROM, Disc 4, pages 398–401
Vocabulario Palabras 2 **En busca de un puesto**	402–405	Vocabulary Transparencies 14.2 Audiocassette 8B/Compact Disc 8 Student Tape Manual, TE, pages 159–160 Workbook, pages 166–167 Chapter Quizzes, page 67 CD-ROM, Disc 4, pages 402-405
Estructura **Infinitivo o subjuntivo** **El subjuntivo con ojalá y quizá(s)** **El subjuntivo en cláusulas relativas**	406–409	Workbook, pages 168–170 Audiocassette 8B/Compact Disc 8 Student Tape Manual, TE, pages 161–162 Chapter Quizzes, pages 68–70 Computer Testmaker CD-ROM, Disc 4, pages 406–409
Conversación **Planes para el futuro**	410–411	Audiocassette 8B/Compact Disc 8 Student Tape Manual, TE, pages 163–164 CD-ROM, Disc 4, pages 410–411
Lecturas culturales **Un muchacho que se llama Bobby** **La importancia de las lenguas extranjeras** *(opcional)* **Gerente de restaurante, gerente de tienda, gerente de ventas y un chef** *(opcional)*	412–415	Testing Program, pages 93–94 CD-ROM, Disc 4, pages 412–415
Conexiones **La economía** *(opcional)*	416–417	Testing Program, page 94 CD-ROM, Disc 4, pages 416–417
Culminación **Actividades orales** **Actividades escritas** **Vocabulario** **Tecnotur**	418–421	**¡Buen viaje!** Video, Episode 14 Video Activities, pages 118–121 Internet Activities **www.glencoe.com/sec/fl** Testing Program, pages 91–93; 140; 184; 205 CD-ROM, Disc 4, pages 418–421

OVERVIEW

In this chapter students will learn to talk about professions, occupations, and looking for work, including interviewing for a position. They will also expand their knowledge of the use of the subjunctive to say what they would like others to do, in contrast to the use of the infinitive to say what they would like to do. Additionally, they will learn to use the subjunctive to state *perhaps* or *maybe*.

The cultural focus of this chapter is on future careers, in particular those that may require knowledge of Spanish.

National Standards

Communication

In Chapter 14 students will learn to communicate in spoken and written Spanish on the following topics:
- professions and occupations
- looking for work
- interviewing for a job

Students will obtain and provide information about these topics and engage in conversations that would typically take place when discussing their future plans.

Pacing

Chapter 14 will require approximately eight to ten days. Pacing will vary according to the length of the class, the age of your students, and student aptitude.

Block Scheduling

See the Block Scheduling Lesson Plans Booklet for suggestions on how to present the chapter material within a block scheduling framework.

Profesiones y oficios

Objetivos

In this chapter you will learn to do the following:
- talk about professions and occupations
- interview for a job
- state work qualifications
- talk about future events
- talk about probable events

inter**NET** CONNECTION

The **Glencoe Foreign Language Web site** (http://www.glencoe.com/sec/fl) offers three options that enable you and your students to experience the Spanish-speaking world via the Internet:
- The online **Actividades** are correlated to the chapters and utilize Hispanic Web sites around the world. For the Chapter 14 activity, see student page 421.
- The **Correspondencia electrónica** section provides information on how to set up a keypal (pen pal) exchange between your class and a class in the Spanish-speaking world.
- At **Café Glencoe,** the interactive "after-school" section of the site, you and your students can access a variety of additional online resources, including interactive games.

Spotlight On Culture

Fotografía The photo on pages 396 and 397 was shot in a business office in an ultra-modern office building in the **Tikal Futura** district of Guatemala City. Tikal Futura is an enormous complex housing three office towers, theaters, a large variety of boutiques and specialty shops, and other attractions. You may wish to ask students questions about the photo, such as:

¿Quién es la señora detrás del escritorio?

¿Quién es la señorita?

¿Por qué estará allí la señorita?

¿Qué le está haciendo la señora a la señorita?

VOCABULARY EXPANSION

You may wish to give students the words for some of the things in the photo:

el escritorio	*large desk*
el archivo	*file cabinet*
la alfombra	*carpet/rug*
el florero	*vase*
el sillón de visita	*visitor's chair*
el cuadro	*picture*
la agenda de mesa	*desk calendar/ diary*

Teacher Notes

trescientos noventa y siete 397

Chapter Projects

Curriculum vitae Have students prepare their **curriculum vitae** in Spanish.

Tu futuro Have students prepare a report on what they think they would like to do when they complete their education, and how Spanish might help them in their careers.

Note You might like to do this project in conjunction with the **Lecturas,** pages 412–414.

Bell Ringer Review

Use BRR Transparency 14-1, or write the following on the board: Make a list of trades and professions you know in Spanish.

TEACHING VOCABULARY

A. Have students close their books. Project Vocabulary Transparencies 14.1 (A & B) and have students repeat the new words, phrases, and sentences after you or the recording on Cassette 8B/Compact Disc 8.

B. Have students open their books to pages 398–399 and ask them to read the new words, phrases, and sentences.

C. Using the Vocabulary Tansparencies, call on volunteers to point to various illustrations at random and name the professions.

Vocabulario

PALABRAS 1

La oficina

el secretario

la contable

la programadora de informática

el gerente

La tienda

la cajera

el comerciante

El gobierno municipal

el funcionario

el alcalde

la alcaldía

La corte

el juez

la abogada

el tribunal

el bufete del abogado

Otras profesiones

la ingeniera

el arquitecto

Pantomime

Begin

Write the following sentences on cards, one to a card, and distribute them for students to mime the actions. Have the rest of the class guess what profession each individual is miming.

Tú eres artista.
Tú eres juez.
Tú eres escultor(a).
Tú eres secretario(a).

Tú eres profesor(a).
Tú eres programador(a) de informática.
Tú eres carpintero(a).
Tú eres albañil.
Tú eres plomero(a).
Tú eres contable.

Algunos oficios

el electricista

el plomero, el fontanero

la carpintera

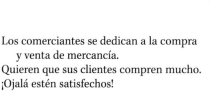

el albañil

Las profesiones son los trabajos que requieren un título universitario.
Es necesario que los profesionales tengan un título universitario.

Los oficios son los trabajos de especialistas como plomeros y carpinteros.
Estos especialistas tienen que tener (poseer) un talento.

Los comerciantes se dedican a la compra y venta de mercancía.
Quieren que sus clientes compren mucho.
¡Ojalá estén satisfechos!

CAPÍTULO 14
Vocabulario

National Standards

Comparisons
Students learn to understand the nature of language through comparisons of Spanish and English. Both **fontanero** and **plomero** mean *plumber*. **Plomero** is not an anglicism. The word comes from the same Latin root as the English word *plumber*: **plumbum**, meaning *lead*, the metal used by the ancient Romans in their plumbing.

Learning From Photos

Fotografías You may wish to ask students to describe the scenes in the two photos on page 399.

ABOUT THE SPANISH LANGUAGE

You may wish to tell students that the names of most professions have both masculine and feminine forms: **el/la ingeniero(a), el/la abogado(a), el/la doctor(a), el/la farmacéutico(a),** etc. Some change only in the article: **el/la contable, el/la juez,** etc. All those that end in **a** will change in the article only: **el/la artista, el/la electricista, el/la anestesista,** etc.

✦Práctica✦

✦Práctica✦

¡OJO! **Práctica** When students are doing the **Práctica** activities, accept any answer that makes sense. The purpose of these activities is to have students use the new vocabulary. They are not factual recall activities. Thus, do not expect students to remember specific information from the vocabulary presentation when answering. If you wish, have students use the photos on this page as a stimulus, when possible.

Historieta Each time **Historieta** appears, it means that the answers to the activity form a short story. Encourage students to look at the title of the **Historieta** since it can sometimes help them do the activity.

A Have students refer to the illustrations as they do **Práctica A.**

B **Práctica B** also reviews other professions learned in previous chapters.

EXPANSION You can do **Práctica B** a second time and not allow students to look at the illustrations.

A ¿Qué es y quiénes trabajan aquí?   Contesten.

 **1.**    **2.**    **3.**

 **4.**    **5.**

B ¿Quién trabaja dónde?   Escojan.

a. el mecánico

b. la funcionaria

c. el cocinero

d. la profesora

e. el mesero

f. el contable

g. la juez

h. el pintor

i. el campesino

j. la obrera

k. la veterinaria

l. el médico

1. ¿Quién trabaja en una fábrica?
2. ¿Quién trabaja en la sala de consulta?
3. ¿Quién cuida de los animales?
4. ¿Quién siembra los campos?
5. ¿Quién pinta cuadros?
6. ¿Quién enseña?
7. ¿Quién repara el carro?
8. ¿Quién prepara los platos en el restaurante?
9. ¿Quién les sirve a los clientes en el restaurante?
10. ¿Quién prepara cuentas y documentos financieros?
11. ¿Quién trabaja en la corte y decide quién es inocente o no?
12. ¿Quién trabaja para el gobierno municipal, estatal o federal?

ANSWERS

Práctica

A Answers will vary but may include:

1. Es una oficina. Los secretarios, los contables, los programadores de informática y los gerentes trabajan aquí.
2. Es una tienda. Los comerciantes y los empleados (dependientes) trabajan aquí.
3. Es un cuarto de baño. Los plomeros (fontaneros) trabajan aquí.
4. Es una corte (un tribunal). Los jueces y los abogados trabajan aquí.
5. Es un cuarto. Los electricistas trabajan aquí.

B
1. j   4. i   7. a   10. f
2. l   5. h   8. c   11. g
3. k   6. d   9. e   12. b

Práctica (PAGE 401)

C 1. Necesito un carpintero.
2. Necesito un abogado.
3. Necesito un farmacéutico.
4. Necesito un mozo.

C **¿A quién necesitas si... ?** Contesten.

1. quieres construir un garaje para tu casa
2. tienes un problema legal
3. necesitas medicina y tienes una receta del médico
4. quieres ayuda con tus maletas en el aeropuerto
5. quieres unos audífonos en el avión
6. estás buscando ayuda en una tienda

D **Una carrera que me interesaría** Sigan el modelo.

agente de policía
Sí, me gustaría ser agente de policía. Me interesaría.
No, no me gustaría ser agente de policía. No me
interesaría nada.

1. médico
2. arquitecto
3. gerente de una gran empresa o compañía
4. abogado
5. dentista
6. contable
7. electricista
8. programador
9. funcionario en una agencia del gobierno
10. veterinario

Un cocinero, Marbella

Una abogada, Ciudad de México

AMALIA ANAYA
Coordinadora General

Equipo Técnico de Apoyo a la Reforma Educativa - ETARE
MINISTERIO DE PLANEAMIENTO Y COORDINACION
Av. Sánchez Lima No. 2647-Tel. 376051-Fax 392399-Casilla 6406-La Paz - Bolivia

Actividades comunicativas

A **Una profesión** Trabaja con un(a) compañero(a). Hablen de las profesiones u oficios que les interesarían. Expliquen por qué les interesaría cierta profesión.

JUEGO Piensa en un oficio o profesión. Tu compañero(a) te puede hacer un máximo de cinco preguntas para adivinar o acertar el oficio o la profesión en que estás pensando. Luego cambien de rol.

C You may wish to have students prepare **Práctica C** before going over it in class.

D **Práctica D** reviews the verbs **interesar** and **gustar**.

Actividades comunicativas

¡OJO! **Práctica versus Actividades comunicativas**
All activities which provide guided practice are labeled **Práctica.** The more open-ended communicative activities are labeled **Actividades comunicativas.**

A **TECHNOLOGY OPTION**
Students may use the Portfolio feature on the CD-ROM to record their conversations.

Learning From Realia

Una tarjeta personal The card on page 401 is called **una tarjeta de visita.** You may wish to ask students to tell you as much as they can about it.

401

🔔 Bell Ringer Review

Use BRR Transparency 14-2, or write the following on the board:
Where would you find the following people?

1. **el cajero**
2. **el piloto**
3. **la juez**
4. **el botones**
5. **la enfermera**
6. **el mozo**
7. **la médica**
8. **el obrero**
9. **el cocinero**
10. **la farmacéutica**

TEACHING VOCABULARY

A. You may follow some of the suggestions given in previous chapters.

B. The following are questions you can ask when presenting the sentences:

¿Qué está buscando Jorge?

¿Qué tipo de puesto está buscando?

¿Quiere un puesto que le pague bien?

¿Dónde es posible que haya un anuncio?

Vocabulario

En busca de un puesto

Jorge está buscando un puesto que sea interesante.
Quiere que le paguen bien.
Es posible que vea un anuncio en el periódico.
¡Quizás encuentre algo que le interese!

Jorge no quiere trabajar a tiempo completo (cuarenta horas por semana).
Quizás le ofrezcan un trabajo a tiempo parcial.

Did You Know?

Los clasificados Jorge is looking in the **Anuncios clasificados**. He is probably looking under the heading of **Ofrezco**. Under this heading are listed the job offerings. The other heading is **Busco empleo**. The ads under **Busco empleo** are placed by people looking for jobs.

el departamento de recursos humanos (personal)

la solicitud de empleo

Catalina busca un puesto también.
Ella llena una solicitud de empleo.

la entrevistadora

el candidato, el aspirante

El candidato tiene una entrevista.
La entrevistadora le hace preguntas.
¡Ojalá (que) conteste bien a las preguntas!
Es posible que esté un poco nervioso.
Quizás esté nervioso durante la entrevista.

VOCABULARIO

cuatrocientos tres ∽ **403**

¿Quiere Jorge trabajar a tiempo completo o a tiempo parcial?

¿Y qué busca Catalina?

¿Qué llena ella?

¿Con quién tiene el candidato una entrevista?

¿Es posible que el candidato esté un poco nervioso durante la entrevista?

PAIRED ACTIVITY

Have students create a conversation between the **entrevistador(a)** and the **aspirante** based on the photo on page 403. Allow pairs time to practice their conversation then have them present it to the class.

Pantomime

Begin

(Estudiante 1) y (Estudiante 2), vengan acá.

(Estudiante 1), buscas trabajo.

(Estudiante 2), trabajas en el departamento de recursos humanos. Vas a ser entrevistador(a).

(Estudiante 1), toma el periódico. Lee los anuncios clasificados.

Ve al departamento de personal. Llena una solicitud de empleo.

(Estudiante 2), invita al/ a la aspirante a sentarse en el sillón en tu oficina.

Hazle preguntas.

(Estudiante 1), estás nervioso(a). Contesta a sus preguntas.

Gracias, (Estudiante 1) y (Estudiante 2), pueden regresar a su asiento.

Práctica

A B and **C** These activities can be done first orally with books closed. Students can then write answers to each **Práctica** for homework.

EXPANSION After going over the activities, call on a student or several students to retell all the information from each **Práctica** in their own words.

Learning From Realia

Anuncios clasificados You may wish to ask questions about the two want ads:

1. ¿Qué tipo de compañía es? ¿Qué tipo de profesional busca? ¿Cuáles son tres cosas que son importantes para el puesto? ¿Cuánto es el salario?

2. ¿Qué necesita esta empresa? ¿Cuándo debe presentarse el/la aspirante? ¿Dónde debe presentarse? ¿Qué debe llevar a la entrevista?

Práctica

A **HISTORIETA** Una entrevista

Contesten según la foto.

1. ¿Están entrevistando a la señorita?
2. ¿Estará buscando ella un puesto que sea interesante y que le pague bien?
3. ¿Tiene la candidata una carta de recomendación?
4. ¿Tiene que llenar una solicitud de empleo?
5. ¿Quiere la señorita que la entrevistadora lea su carta de recomendación?
6. ¿Es posible que la candidata esté un poco nerviosa?

B **HISTORIETA** Mi trabajo

Contesten.

1. ¿Trabajas?
2. ¿Dónde trabajas?
3. ¿Trabajas a tiempo completo o a tiempo parcial?
4. ¿Prefieres trabajar a tiempo completo o a tiempo parcial?
5. ¿Recibes un salario?
6. ¿Cuánto te pagan?

Caracas, Venezuela

Empresa de primer orden de INGENIERIA Y SISTEMAS DE CONTROL DE TRAFICO Y TRANSPORTE, con presencia consolidada en ámbitos internacionales, ofrece puesto de

ingeniero de compras y logística

- Buscamos un profesional, con formación de **Ingeniero Superior o Técnico**, dominio del **inglés** y disponibilidad para viajar por España y el extranjero.
- **Se valorará:**
  - La experiencia adquirida en el área de compras y logística en Empresa Industrial.
  - La formación específica sobre la materia.
  - La capacidad de negociación con proveedores nacionales y extranjeros.
- La remuneración es a convenir, en función de la formación y experiencia aportada por los candidatos.

Rogamos envíen Historial Profesional detallado, con pretensiones económicas, fotografía, señas y teléfono de contacto, indicando la Ref.: 22.229 a:

GM&A Selección

C/ Don Ramón de la Cruz, 33
28001 Madrid

SE SOLICITA RECEPCIONISTA

Para importante empresa. Presentarse de lunes a viernes, en Av. 20 de Octubre # 1743 (esq. Conchitas) de 9 a 10:30 con curriculum y referencias.

ANSWERS

Práctica

A
1. Sí, están entrevistando a la señorita.
2. Sí, estará buscando un puesto que sea interesante y que le pague bien.
3. Sí, la candidata tiene una carta de recomendación.
4. Sí, tiene que llenar una solicitud de empleo.
5. Sí, la señorita quiere que la entrevistadora lea su carta de recomendación.
6. Sí, es posible que la candidata esté un poco nerviosa.

B Answers will vary but may include:
1. Sí, (No, no) trabajo.
2. Trabajo en ___.
3. Trabajo a tiempo completo (parcial).
4. Prefiero trabajar a tiempo completo (parcial).
5. Sí, (No, no) recibo un salario.
6. Me pagan ___.

C HISTORIETA Él solicita trabajo.

Contesten según se indica.

1. ¿Juan busca trabajo? (sí)
2. ¿Qué ha leído? (un anuncio en el periódico)
3. ¿Qué compañía está buscando (reclutando) empleados? (Austral)
4. ¿Adónde va Juan? (al departamento de recursos humanos de Austral)
5. ¿Qué tiene que llenar? (una solicitud de empleo)
6. ¿A quién le da la solicitud? (a la recepcionista)
7. ¿Qué va a tener? (una entrevista)

Actividades comunicativas

A Una entrevista Eres un(a) empleado(a) en una agencia de empleos. Un(a) compañero(a) es un(a) candidato(a) para un empleo. Tú vas a darle una entrevista. Pregúntale sobre sus estudios, experiencia, aptitudes personales, talentos artísticos, etc. Luego cambien de rol.

B En la oficina del/de la consejero(a) de orientación El/La consejero(a) de orientación *(guidance counselor)* de tu escuela te ha pedido ayudar a un(a) estudiante hispanohablante que acaba de llegar de un país latinoamericano. Quiere que le hagas preguntas para determinar una carrera que le interesaría. Luego quiere que le expliques todo lo que tiene que hacer para prepararse para esa carrera.

Guadalajara, México

Writing Development

After going over **Práctica C**, have students write the story about Juan in a unified paragraph using **Práctica C** as their guide.

Actividades comunicativas

¡OJO! These activities encourage students to use the chapter vocabulary and structures in open-ended situations. It is not necessary to have them do all the activities. Choose the ones you consider most appropriate.

A TECHNOLOGY OPTION In the CD-ROM version of this activity (Disc 4, page 405), students can interact with an on-screen native speaker and record their voices.

ANSWERS

Práctica

C 1. Sí, Juan busca trabajo.
2. Ha leído un anuncio en el periódico.
3. Austral está buscando (reclutando) empleados.
4. Juan va al departamento de recursos humanos de Austral.
5. Tiene que llenar una solicitud de empleo.
6. Le da la solicitud a la recepcionista.
7. Va a tener una entrevista.

Actividades comunicativas
A and B Answers will vary.

Bell Ringer Review

Use BRR Transparency 14-3, or write the following on the board: Name four articles of clothing a young man would wear for a job interview. Do the same for a young woman.

TEACHING STRUCTURE

 Saying what you would like to do and what you would like others to do

A. Lead students through Steps 1 and 2 on page 406.
B. Call on volunteers to read the model sentences aloud.

Práctica

A and **B** Have students present each item in these activities as a mini-conversation. Students must do **Práctica A** and **Práctica B** with books open so they can read the first line of each mini-conversation.

Estructura

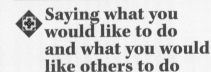 **Saying what you would like to do and what you would like others to do**
Infinitivo o subjuntivo

1. With any verbs or expressions that require the subjunctive, the subjunctive is used only when there is a change of subject. In other words, the subjunctive is used when the subject of the main clause is different from the subject of the dependent clause that follows **que**.

MAIN CLAUSE		DEPENDENT CLAUSE
Tú quieres	**que**	**yo vaya al banco.**
Nosotros preferimos	**que**	**Uds. cambien dinero.**
Es necesario	**que**	**alguien decida.**

2. If there is no change of subject, the infinitive is used.

> **Tú quieres ir al banco.**
> **Nosotros preferimos cambiar dinero.**
> **Es necesario decidir.**

Práctica

A HISTORIETA No. Yo quiero hacerlo.

Contesten según el modelo.

¿Quieres que yo vaya al banco?

No. Yo quiero ir al banco.

Caracas, Venezuela

1. ¿Quieres que yo vaya al banco?
2. ¿Quieres que yo endose el cheque?
3. ¿Quieres que yo cobre el cheque?
4. ¿Quieres que yo pida la tasa de cambio?
5. ¿Quieres que yo cambie dólares?
6. ¿Quieres que yo abra una cuenta?

Learning From Photos

Caracas, Venezuela Ask students to say all they can about the photo. Some questions you might ask are: **En la foto de Caracas, ¿qué tipo de zona es? ¿Son modernos o antiguos los edificios? ¿Hay rascacielos en la foto? ¿Hay muchos peatones?**

ANSWERS

Práctica
A 1. No, yo quiero ir al banco.
2. No, yo quiero endosar el cheque.
3. No, yo quiero cobrar el cheque.
4. No, yo quiero pedir la tasa de cambio.
5. No, yo quiero cambiar dólares.
6. No, yo quiero abrir una cuenta.

B HISTORIETA Nosotros también

Sigan el modelo.

> Yo espero que Uds. hagan el viaje.

> Nosotros también esperamos hacer el viaje.

1. Yo espero que Uds. hagan el viaje.
2. Espero que Uds. viajen en avión.
3. Espero que tomen un vuelo directo.
4. Espero que lleguen a tiempo.
5. Espero que visiten los museos.
6. Espero que vean los monumentos.
7. Espero que coman bien.
8. Espero que tengan bastante dinero.
9. Espero que vuelvan en una semana.

Ciudad de México

C HISTORIETA La ropa sucia

Contesten.

1. ¿Quieres lavar la ropa sucia?
2. ¿O prefieres que yo la lave?
3. ¿Quieres ir a la lavandería?
4. ¿O prefieres que yo vaya?
5. ¿Quieres que yo te lave el suéter?
6. ¿O es necesario limpiarlo en seco?
7. ¿Quieres que yo lo lleve a la tintorería?

Actividad comunicativa

A **Este fin de semana** Pregúntale a tu compañero(a) lo que él o ella quiere hacer este fin de semana. Después, pregúntale lo que quiere que sus padres hagan. Luego cambien de rol.

Museo de Arte Contemporáneo, Ciudad de México

C **Práctica C** can be done first orally with books closed.

Learning From Photos

Ciudad de México Ask students to say all they can about the photo. Some questions you might ask are: **¿Dónde están las personas en la foto de arriba en la página 407? ¿Qué están haciendo ellos?**

Museo de Arte Contemporáneo, Ciudad de México Ask students to do the following: **Describe lo que ves en la foto del Museo de Arte Contemporáneo.**

ANSWERS

Práctica

B 1. **Nosotros también esperamos hacer el viaje.**
2. **Nosotros también esperamos viajar en avión.**
3. **Nosotros también esperamos tomar un vuelo directo.**
4. **Nosotros también esperamos llegar a tiempo.**
5. **Nosotros también esperamos visitar los museos.**
6. **Nosotros también esperamos ver los monumentos.**
7. **Nosotros también esperamos comer bien.**
8. **Nosotros también esperamos tener bastante dinero.**
9. **Nosotros también esperamos volver en una semana.**

C 1. **Sí, (No, no) quiero lavar la ropa sucia.**
2. **Sí, (No, no) prefiero que tú la laves.**
3. **Sí, (No, no) quiero ir a la lavandería.**
4. **Sí, (No, no) prefiero que tú vayas.**
5. **Sí, (No, no) quiero que tú me laves el suéter.**
6. **Sí, (No, no) es necesario limpiarlo en seco.**
7. **Sí, (No, no) quiero que tú lo lleves a la tintorería.**

Actividad comunicativa
A Answers will vary.

TEACHING STRUCTURE

Stating *perhaps* or *maybe*

A. Have students open their books to page 408. Lead them through the explanation.

B. Have volunteers read the model sentences aloud.

A and **B** **Práctica A** and **Práctica B** can be done orally with books closed. Students can then write the answers at home. Have students use as much expression as possible when using **ojalá** and **quizás** in these activities.

Learning From Realia

Carlos Durán You may wish to ask these questions about the realia: **¿Para qué irías a *Carlos Durán*? ¿Qué será *Luisa Fernanda*?**

Stating *perhaps* or *maybe*
El subjuntivo con **ojalá** y **quizá(s)**

The expressions **ojalá** (*I wish* or *I hope*) and **quizás** (*perhaps* or *maybe*) are always followed by the subjunctive.

> **¡Ojalá que tengas una entrevista!**
> **¡Ojalá que te salga bien!**
> **¡Quizá te ofrezcan el puesto!**

A **HISTORIETA** ¡Ojalá que sí!

Contesten con **ojalá**.

1. ¿Él va a buscar un puesto?
2. ¿Va a ir al departamento de recursos humanos?
3. ¿Va a pedir una solicitud de empleo?
4. ¿Va a llenar la solicitud?
5. ¿Le van a dar una entrevista?
6. ¿No va a estar muy nervioso?
7. ¿Le van a ofrecer el puesto?
8. ¿Le va a pagar bien el trabajo?

Ciudad de México

B El corte de pelo   Contesten según el modelo.

> **¿Dónde estará Marta (la peluquería)?**
> **Quizás esté en la peluquería.**

1. ¿Dónde estará Marta? (la peluquería)
2. ¿Qué pedirá ella? (un corte de pelo)
3. ¿Qué usarán para cortarle el pelo? (tijeras)
4. ¿Qué más le darán? (un champú)
5. ¿Quién le cortará el pelo? (Nilda)
6. ¿Cuánto tiempo tomará? (media hora)
7. ¿Cuánto le cobrarán? (20 pesos)

CARLOS DURAN
PELUQUEROS
Luisa Fernanda, 6. 28008 Madrid. Tíno. 541 33 70

ANSWERS

Práctica

A 1. ¡Ojalá que él busque un puesto!
2. ¡Ojalá que vaya al departamento de recursos humanos!
3. ¡Ojalá que pida una solicitud de empleo!
4. ¡Ojalá que llene la solicitud!
5. ¡Ojalá que le den una entrevista!
6. ¡Ojalá que no esté muy nervioso!
7. ¡Ojalá que le ofrezcan el puesto!
8. ¡Ojalá que le pague bien el trabajo!

B 1. Quizás esté en la peluquería.
2. Quizás pida un corte de pelo.
3. Quizás usen tijeras para cortarle el pelo.
4. Quizás le den un champú.
5. Quizás Nilda le corte el pelo.
6. Quizás tome media hora.
7. Quizás le cobren 20 pesos.

Actividad comunicativa

A. **Quizá y ojalá** Habla con un(a) compañero(a). Usando **quizá,** dile algunas cosas que es posible que ocurran en el futuro. Si es algo que quieres que ocurra, sigue hablando usando **ojalá.** Por ejemplo, **¡Quizá seas rico(a)! ¡Ojalá sea rico(a)!** Luego cambien de rol.

 Describing indefinite persons or things
El subjuntivo en cláusulas relativas

A grouping of words that modifies a noun is called a relative clause. A relative clause can modify or describe a noun that refers to a specific, definite person or thing or an indefinite person or thing. When the clause describes a definite person or thing, the verb in the clause is in the indicative. If, however, it modifies an indefinite person or thing, the verb is in the subjunctive. Note too that the **a personal** is omitted when the object is indefinite.

> **Conocemos a una secretaria que habla bien el español.**
> **Buscamos una secretaria que hable bien el español.**

 **Práctica**

A. **Un conocido** Contesten según el modelo.

una persona que habla español
No necesito una persona que hable español.
Conozco a una persona que habla español.

1. una persona que es bilingüe
2. una persona que tiene experiencia
3. una persona que conoce el mercado
4. una persona que puede viajar

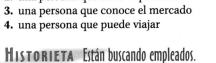

B. **HISTORIETA** Están buscando empleados.

Contesten.
1. ¿Está ofreciendo la compañía Avensa un puesto que paga bien?
2. ¿Buscan alguien que tenga experiencia en ventas?
3. ¿Quieren alguien que pueda viajar?
4. ¿Necesitan una persona que conozca más de un idioma?

ESTRUCTURA *cuatrocientos nueve* **409**

CAPÍTULO 14
Estructura

 Bell Ringer Review

Use BRR Transparency 14-5, or write the following on the board: Name four occasions for celebration in the Hispanic family.

TEACHING STRUCTURE

 Describing indefinite persons or things

A. Have students open their books to page 409. Lead them through the explanation.
B. Call on volunteers to read the model sentences aloud.

Práctica

A. Have students prepare **Práctica A** before going over it in class.

B. **Práctica B** can be done orally with books closed.

 Learning From Realia

Secretariado bilingüe de dirección You may wish to ask students the following questions about the ad:
¿Para qué es el anuncio? ¿Qué aprenderías allí? ¿Con qué máquinas podrías practicar?

¡**OJO!** There is no more new material to present in this chapter. The sections that follow recombine and reinforce the vocabulary and structures that have already been introduced.

ANSWERS

Práctica
A 1. **No necesito una persona que sea bilingüe. Conozco a una persona que es bilingüe.**
2. **No necesito una persona que tenga experiencia. Conozco a una persona que tiene experiencia.**
3. **No necesito una persona que conozca el mercado. Conozco a una persona que conoce el mercado.**

4. **No necesito una persona que pueda viajar. Conozco a una persona que puede viajar.**

B 1. **Sí (No), la compañía Avensa (no) está ofreciendo un puesto que paga bien.**
2. **Sí, (No, no) buscan alguien que tenga experiencia en ventas.**
3. **Sí, (No, no) quieren alguien que pueda viajar.**
4. **Sí, (No, no) necesitan una persona que conozca más de un idioma.**

409

TEACHING THE CONVERSATION

A. 🎧 Have students listen once to the recording on Cassette 8B/Compact Disc 8.

B. Call on two students to read. One can take the part of Lorenzo, the other the part of Alejandra.

C. After going over the entire conversation, do the **Después de conversar** activity.

D. Have students retell Alejandra's plans in their own words.

TECHNOLOGY OPTION

💿 On the CD-ROM (Disc 4, page 410), students can watch a dramatization of this conversation. They can then play the role of either of the characters and record themselves in the conversation.

Conversación

Planes para el futuro

LORENZO: ¿Piensas asistir a la universidad, Alejandra?

ALEJANDRA: Sí. Tengo muy buenas notas y me gustan los estudios académicos.

LORENZO: ¿Tienes una idea de lo que quieres hacer?

ALEJANDRA: No sé exactamente. Quizás me especialice en comercio o marketing.

LORENZO: Son dos campos interesantes.

ALEJANDRA: Creo que me gustaría trabajar con una empresa multinacional. Quiero un puesto que me permita viajar.

LORENZO: Entonces es importante que continúes con tus estudios del español. ¡Ojalá tengas mucha suerte en tu carrera!

ALEJANDRA: Gracias.

Después de conversar

Contesten.

1. ¿Qué piensa hacer en el futuro Alejandra?
2. ¿Por qué quiere asistir a la universidad?
3. ¿Sabe Alejandra lo que quiere hacer después?
4. ¿En qué campos piensa especializarse?
5. ¿Por qué dice que le gustaría trabajar con una empresa multinacional?
6. ¿Qué le aconseja Lorenzo?

ANSWERS

Después de conversar

1. **Alejandra piensa asistir a la universidad.**
2. **Tiene buenas notas y le gustan los estudios académicos.**
3. **No, Alejandra no sabe exactamente qué quiere hacer después.**
4. **Piensa especializarse en comercio o marketing.**
5. **Quiere un puesto que le permita viajar.**
6. **Lorenzo le aconseja que continúe con sus estudios del español.**

Actividades comunicativas

A **Un trabajo ideal** Piensa en lo que tú considerarías un trabajo ideal, algo que a ti te gustaría mucho hacer. Describe tu trabajo ideal a un(a) compañero(a). Luego cambien de rol.

B **Posibles carreras** Trabaja con un(a) compañero(a). Cada uno(a) de Uds. va a preparar una lista de las cosas que le interesan y de las materias o asignaturas que le gustan. Luego miren sus listas. Determinen los intereses que tienen en común. Luego discutan las profesiones o los oficios que les interesarían a los dos.

C **Buscando un puesto** Trabaja con un(a) compañero(a). Miren las fotos y describan lo que pasa en cada una.

a.

b.

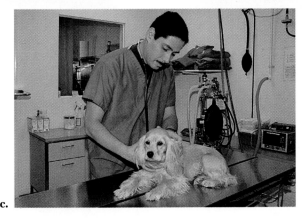

c.

CONVERSACIÓN

411

Lecturas CULTURALES

UN MUCHACHO QUE SE LLAMA BOBBY

Esta historia no es ficción. Bobby, a quien hoy le llaman don Roberto, es norteamericano. Asistió a una escuela pública donde estudió el español por cuatro años. Siguió con sus estudios del español en la universidad, aunque el español no era su campo de especialización. Se especializó en ciencias políticas.

Después de graduarse de la universidad Bobby entró al Cuerpo de Paz[1] como voluntario. Pasó unos meses de entrenamiento[2] en Puerto Rico. Después fue a Centroamérica donde trabajaba con campesinos en proyectos de irrigación y reforestación. Cuando terminó su período de voluntario, Bobby tomó el examen para el Departamento de Estado.

Bobby fue a trabajar con el Departamento de Estado y ascendió rápidamente. Fue cónsul en Costa Rica y agregado cultural en España. Él ha representado a los Estados Unidos en Centroamérica, Sudamérica y España. Y hoy Bobby es embajador.

[1]Cuerpo de Paz *Peace Corps*
[2]entrenamiento *training*

Bolivia

Ecuador

Bell Ringer Review

Use BRR Transparency 14-6, or write the following on the board: Write as many words as you can think of which are related to each of the following categories.

1. la peluquería
2. la tintorería
3. la gasolinera
4. el correo

National Standards

Cultures The reading on pages 412–413 and the related activity on page 413 allow students to see how, by combining Spanish with his college major, one young man was able to pursue a successful career in diplomacy.

TEACHING THE READING

Pre-reading

A. Have students read the Reading Strategy on page 412.
B. Then have them scan the selection and ask them to tell you in Spanish what they think it's about.

Reading

A. Have students open their books and call on individuals to read.
B. Ask questions about what was just read.

Post-reading

A. Ask students to answer the question posed in the last paragraph of the reading.
B. Have students read the selection at home and write the answers to the **Después de leer** activity. Go over it in class the next day.

412

Learning From Photos

Bolivia, Ecuador y Perú Ask students to describe what they see and to say all they can about the photos on pages 412 and 413.

Did You Know?

El Cuerpo de Paz The Peace Corps was founded in 1961 by executive order of President Kennedy. Volunteers serve for two-year periods. Volunteers serve in a number of countries in Latin America in areas such as agriculture; the teaching of languages, mathematics, and science; vocational training; business and public administration; and natural resource development.

¿Dónde y cómo comenzó esta ilustre carrera diplomática? Según don Roberto, «en el noveno grado, en mi clase de español uno».

¡Ojalá que tú también tengas una carrera tan interesante como la de Bobby! ¡Quizás seas nuestro embajador o embajadora en España o en México! ¿Qué opinas? ¿Te interesa la posibilidad de un puesto que te pague bien y que te permita ver el mundo al mismo tiempo?

Perú

Después de leer

A **Una carrera interesante** Contesten.
1. ¿Cómo le llaman a Bobby hoy?
2. ¿De qué nacionalidad es?
3. ¿Cuántos años estudió el español en la escuela secundaria?
4. ¿Dónde siguió con sus estudios del español?
5. ¿En qué se especializó?
6. ¿Qué hizo en el Cuerpo de Paz?
7. Al terminar su período con el Cuerpo de Paz, ¿adónde fue a trabajar Bobby?
8. ¿Qué ha sido él?

ANSWERS

Después de leer
A 1. Hoy le llaman don Roberto.
2. Es norteamericano.
3. Estudió el español cuatro años en la escuela secundaria.
4. Siguió con sus estudios del español en la universidad.
5. Se especializó en ciencias políticas.
6. Trabajó con campesinos en proyectos de irrigación y reforestación.
7. Fue a trabajar con el Departamento de Estado.
8. Fue cónsul en Costa Rica y agregado cultural en España. Ha representado a los Estados Unidos en Centroamérica, Sudamérica y España. Y hoy es embajador.

413

LECTURA OPCIONAL 1

LECTURA OPCIONAL 1

TEACHING TIPS

¡OJO! This reading is optional. You may skip it completely, have the entire class read it, have only several students read it, or assign it for extra credit.

ABOUT THE SPANISH LANGUAGE

The expression **¡Ojalá!** is used to indicate the fervent desire that something happen. The origin of the expression is **wa-sa'Allah** meaning *would that God will it*. This is another vivid example of the influence of the Arabic language and culture in Spain.

Career Connection

Empresas multinacionales
Have students research what American companies have offices in Spanish-speaking countries and what types of positions are available. Have them pool the information and decide which company they would like to work for and what type of job they would be interested in.

LA IMPORTANCIA DE LAS LENGUAS EXTRANJERAS

No hay duda que el conocimiento de un idioma extranjero como el español puede ser un beneficio en muchas carreras. Hoy en día el comercio internacional tiene más y más importancia. No es suficiente sólo exportar nuestros productos al extranjero. Hay que tener una presencia real en muchos países. Por consiguiente muchas grandes empresas norteamericanas han llegado a ser multinacionales. Quiere decir que tienen instalaciones o sucursales[1] y filiales[2] en el extranjero. ¡Imagínate! Es posible que algún día tú trabajes con una compañía americana y que tu oficina esté en Caracas, Lima o Madrid.

Quizás el español en sí[3] no sea una carrera. Pero el español con otra especialización le da a uno una ventaja incalculable. Si tú conoces la contabilidad, el marketing o la informática, por ejemplo, y además dominas bien el español, podrás trabajar con una empresa multinacional. El español y tu otra especialización te permitirán encontrar un trabajo que te pague bien, que te sea interesante y que te dé la oportunidad de viajar y ver el mundo. ¡Ojalá! ¿No?

[1] sucursales *branches*
[2] filiales *subsidiaries*
[3] en sí *in itself*

Caracas, Venezuela

Después de leer

A La importancia de una lengua extranjera
Discutan.

¿Por qué es importante estudiar una lengua extranjera?
¿Cómo te puede ayudar en tu vida?

Caracas, Venezuela

ANSWERS

Después de leer
A Answers will vary.

Learning From Realia

La UNESCO para América Latina y el Caribe You may wish to call students' attention to the calling card, then ask:
¿Cuáles son tres formas de comunicarse con la oficina de la UNESCO en Santiago de Chile?

LECTURA OPCIONAL 2

AHORA EN MADRID **PLANET HOLLYWOOD**
ABRE SUS PUERTAS

y para integrar su equipo profesional
te necesitamos en los puestos de

GERENTES DE RESTAURANTE, GERENTE DE TIENDA, GERENTE DE VENTAS Y UN CHEF

Requisitos para chef:
• Inglés (nivel medio).
• Edad no mayor de 40 años.
• Escolaridad mínima de BUP o Secundaria, con estudios de especialización en alimentos y bebidas.
• Experiencia mínima comprobable de 4 años como chef en restaurantes de medio o alto volumen, con conocimientos de control de costos, gastos y manejo de personal.
• Buena presencia.

Requisitos para gerentes de tienda, gerente de ventas y gerente de restauración:
• Inglés (dominio).
• Edad entre 28 y 35 años.
• Estudios en administración, turismo, mercadotecnia o comercio (requisito sustituible únicamente con experiencia comprobable).
• Experiencia mínima comprobable de dos años como responsable del área.
• Con excelente actitud de servicio y ventas.
• Excelente presentación.

Ofrecemos para todos los puestos:
• Sueldo a convenir.
• Bonificación semestral y otras ventajas sociales.

Los interesados deberán enviar *curriculum vitae,* con fotografía, por correo, a: C/ Antonio Maura, 12, 4.º derecha, 28014 MADRID, a la atención de Planet Hollywood Madrid. Fax 91 522 08 53.

La confirmación de los expedientes seleccionados se realizará telefónicamente para un proceso de entrevistas que se efectuará en Madrid.

LA FECHA LÍMITE PARA RECEPCIÓN DE DATOS ES EL 14 DE OCTUBRE

Málaga, España

Después de leer

A **El «Planet Hollywood»**
Contesten.

1. ¿Qué abre sus puertas en Madrid?
2. ¿Quién necesita saber más inglés, el chef o el gerente de ventas?
3. ¿Cuál es la edad máxima para el chef? ¿Y para los otros puestos?
4. ¿Cuántos años de experiencia tiene que tener el chef? ¿Y los otros?
5. ¿Dónde tendrán lugar las entrevistas?
6. ¿Qué deben enviar los interesados con su curriculum vitae?
7. ¿Cómo van a informar a las personas que seleccionan para presentarse para una entrevista?

National Standards

 Cultures
This reading and the related activity on this page familiarize students with a want ad that might be found in a typical newspaper in the Spanish-speaking world.

TEACHING TIPS

¡OJO! This reading is optional. You may skip it completely, have the entire class read it, have only several students read it, or assign it for extra credit.

Conexiones

LAS CIENCIAS SOCIALES

LA ECONOMÍA

Economics is the science that deals with the production, distribution, and consumption of goods and services for the welfare of humankind. It is an interesting and complex science. People need or desire all kinds of goods and services. However, we do not have at our disposal all the resources we would need to produce all that society would like to have. For this reason, economists provide the information necessary to those who must make crucial decisions as to what will and will not be produced.

National Standards

Connections

This reading about basic concepts in economics such as *opportunity costs* establishes a connection with another discipline, allowing students to reinforce and further their knowledge of the social sciences through the study of Spanish.

¡OJO! The readings in the **Conexiones** section are optional. They focus on some of the major disciplines taught in schools and universities. The vocabulary is useful for discussing such topics as history, literature, art, economics, business, science, etc.

You may choose any of the following ways to do this reading on economics with your students.

Independent reading Have students read the selections and do the post-reading activities as homework, which you collect. This option is least intrusive on class time and requires a minimum of teacher involvement.

Homework with in-class follow-up Assign the readings and post-reading activities as homework. Review and discuss the material in class the next day.

Intensive in-class activity This option includes a pre-reading vocabulary presentation, in-class reading and discussion, assignment of the activities for homework, and a discussion of the assignment in class the following day.

La economía

¿Qué es la economía?

Hay varias definiciones de economía. La economía es el estudio de las decisiones que tomamos en la producción, distribución y consumo de bienes y servicios[1]. Es el estudio de las maneras en que las sociedades deciden lo que van a producir y para quién. También es el estudio del uso y control de recursos[2] para satisfacer las necesidades y los deseos humanos. Este es un aspecto muy importante de la economía porque los deseos humanos no tienen límite. Las necesidades humanas pueden ser de primera necesidad como la comida y la ropa. Hay también bienes y servicios que no son de primera necesidad pero que son importantes para algunas personas—los diamantes y un chófer, por ejemplo. Si las necesidades y los deseos humanos no tienen límite, no es el caso con los recursos. Los recursos son limitados. La verdad es que hay una escasez[3] de recursos.

[1] bienes y servicios *goods and services*
[2] recursos *resources*
[3] escasez *shortage*

Barcelona, España

Critical Thinking Activity

Supporting statements with reasons
Have pairs of students work together to consider other examples of **costo de oportunidad** either from their own lives or on a wider scale. They should present their examples to the class.

Recursos económicos

Los recursos económicos son el total de los recursos naturales, fabricados[4] y humanos que se emplean en la producción de bienes y la provisión de servicios. Los recursos naturales son la materia prima[5], lo que viene de la Tierra. Los recursos fabricados incluyen las fábricas, los edificios comerciales y todo tipo de equipo mecánico y técnico. Los recursos humanos incluyen la mano de obra[6] de toda clase—profesional, técnica, gerencial y obrera.

Costo de oportunidad

Como todos los recursos son limitados, es imposible dar a la sociedad todos los bienes y servicios que desea. La escasez de materiales y recursos nos obliga a escoger lo que vamos a producir porque no podemos producir todo. Si usamos los recursos disponibles[7] para producir una cosa, perdemos la oportunidad de usar estos mismos recursos para producir otra cosa. Este sacrificio se llama «el costo de oportunidad». Si todos los trabajadores en una fábrica van a producir televisores, la fábrica no puede producir otro producto. Es el costo de oportunidad. Todo lo que hacemos tiene su costo de oportunidad. Si decides ir al cine en vez de estudiar para un examen, estás sacrificando la oportunidad de estudiar. Es el costo de oportunidad de ir al cine.

Una fábrica de Ford, México

[4]fabricados *manufactured*
[5]materia prima *raw material*
[6]mano de obra *workforce*
[7]disponibles *available*

FABRICA
DE INSTRUMENTOS MUSICALES
SUKAY
Pocho Barrientos
CHARANGOS - ZAMPOÑAS - QUENAS - WANKARAS
FABRICA Y REPARADORA DE
GUITARRAS, CHARANGOS Y MANDOLINAS

Quenas	Clavijas	Capodástros
Zampoñas	Cuerdas	Boquillas
Bombos	Métodos	Estuches
Tambores	Cancioneros	Fundas
Wankaras	Cassettes	Trastes

Calle Linares No. 850 ☎ 312789
La Paz - Bolivia - Sud América

❧ Después de leer ❧

A **Términos económicos** Contesten.
1. ¿Cuál es un ejemplo de una necesidad esencial?
2. ¿Cuál es un ejemplo de una necesidad que no es esencial?
3. ¿Cuáles son algunos recursos económicos?
4. ¿Cuál es un ejemplo de una materia prima?

B **Costo de oportunidad** Expliquen.
Explica lo que significa «el costo de oportunidad».

LAS CIENCIAS SOCIALES
LA ECONOMÍA

You may wish to have only students interested in economics do this reading, along with the accompanying activities.

Did You Know?

Maquiladoras Many American manufacturing companies have plants in Mexico near the border where final assembly is performed on a number of products ranging from VCRs to automobiles. These assembly plants are known as **maquiladoras**. After assembly, the products return to the United States for distribution and sale.

ANSWERS

Después de leer

A 1. la comida (la ropa)
2. diamantes (un chófer)
3. La materia prima, las fábricas, los edificios comerciales, todo tipo de equipo mecánico y técnico y la mano de obra de toda clase son algunos recursos económicos.
4. la madera, el algodón

B Answers will vary but may include:
El «costo de oportunidad» es el uso de los recursos disponibles para producir una cosa, perdiendo la oportunidad de producir otra.

417

Culminación

RECYCLING

The **Actividades orales** and the **Actividades escritas** allow students to use the vocabulary and structures from this chapter in open-ended, real-life settings.

Actividades orales

Let students choose the activities they would like to do.

Student Portfolio

Have students keep a notebook containing their best written work from each chapter. These selected writings can be based on assignments from the Student Textbook and the Writing Activities Workbook. The activities on page 419 are examples of writing assignments that may be included in each student's portfolio.

In the Workbook, students will develop an organized autobiography (**Mi autobiografía).** These workbook pages may also become a part of their portfolio. See the Teacher's Manual for more information on the Student Portfolio.

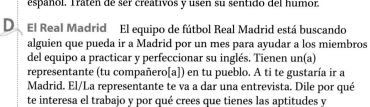

Actividades orales

A **Ventajas y desventajas**   Con un(a) compañero(a), piensen en varias carreras. Hablen de lo que consideran las ventajas y desventajas de cada una.

B **Líneas aéreas nacionales**   Una línea aérea está buscando (reclutando) asistentes de vuelo. A ti te interesa. Decides ir a tener una entrevista. Tu compañero(a) te va a dar la entrevista. Luego cambien de rol.

C **La importancia del español**   Tú y un(a) compañero(a) van a hablar a los alumnos en una clase del primer año de español. Les van a decir por qué deben continuar con sus estudios del español. Les van a explicar por qué es muy importante el estudio del español. Traten de ser creativos y usen su sentido del humor.

Lima, Perú

D **El Real Madrid**   El equipo de fútbol Real Madrid está buscando alguien que pueda ir a Madrid por un mes para ayudar a los miembros del equipo a practicar y perfeccionar su inglés. Tienen un(a) representante (tu compañero[a]) en tu pueblo. A ti te gustaría ir a Madrid. El/La representante te va a dar una entrevista. Dile por qué te interesa el trabajo y por qué crees que tienes las aptitudes y cualidades necesarias.

Madrid, España

ANSWERS

Actividades orales
A, B, C, and D   Answers will vary.

Learning From Photos

Fotografías Have students describe in as much detail as possible what they see in the photos on this page. Or you may wish to ask them the following:
Lima, Peru ¿Qué son las tres señoritas? ¿Dónde trabajan ellas? ¿Llevan uniforme? Describe su uniforme. ¿Por qué llevan equipaje?
Madrid, España ¿Es un estadio o un teatro? ¿A qué juegan los jugadores? ¿Hay muchos o pocos espectadores?

Actividades escritas

A. **El currículum vítae** Vas a preparar tu currículum vítae o resumen personal en español. En tu resumen incluye los siguientes detalles: nombre, dirección, preparación académica, título, talentos, intereses y hobbys.

B. **Unos anuncios** Estás trabajando con una agencia de empleos. Vas a preparar algunos anuncios clasificados para el periódico local. Escoge a lo menos tres puestos vacantes. En tus anuncios, da una descripción de cada puesto y los requisitos para el trabajo.

Una agente de viajes, Caracas

Writing Strategy

Using visuals

Well-organized writing that is clearly expressed is the key to good communication. However, visuals can help organize, clarify, and expand many different kinds of data. A visual can help you illustrate an important concept. Good visuals can portray at a glance an idea that might take several paragraphs to express in words.

¿Cuáles son los intereses de la clase?

It is likely that many of your classmates have varied opinions about and plans for the future. Prepare a survey to administer to your classmates, asking what they would like to do. After you have gathered the data, prepare a visual that gives an overview of the possible careers and job interests your class has. You may wish to use a computer to help you create your visual to convey your information to your readers.

CULMINACIÓN

cuatrocientos diecinueve ∾ **419**

Actividades escritas

A. **TECHNOLOGY OPTION**
Students may use the Portfolio feature on the CD-ROM to write their C.V.

Writing Strategy

Using visuals

A. Have students read the Writing Strategy on page 419.
B. Once students have completed the survey, you might have them enlist the help of the computer science or graphic arts teacher at your school to help them prepare their visuals.

Learning From Photos

Una agente de viajes, Caracas
You may wish to ask students:
¿En qué clase de oficina trabaja la señora? ¿Qué usa ella en su trabajo? ¿Quiénes son sus clientes? ¿De qué es la foto en la pared?

Independent Practice

Assign any of the following:
1. Activities, pages 418–419
2. Workbook, **Mi autobiografía,** page 174
3. Situation Cards
4. CD-ROM, Chapter 14, Disc 4, **Juego de repaso**

ANSWERS

Actividades escritas
A and B Answers will vary.

Writing Strategy
Answers will vary depending on the creativity and imagination of each student.

VOCABULARY REVIEW

The words and phrases in the **Vocabulario** have been taught for productive use in this chapter. They are summarized here as a resource for both students and teacher. This list also serves as a convenient resource for the **Culminación** activities on pages 418 and 419. There are approximately 10 cognates in this vocabulary list. Have students find them.

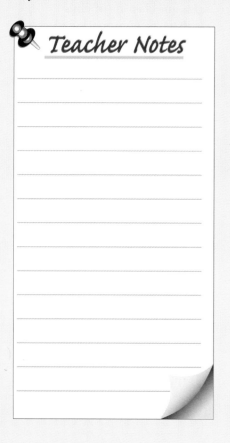

📌 *Teacher Notes*

Vocabulario

IDENTIFYING SOME OFFICE PERSONNEL

el/la programador(a) de informática
el/la secretario(a)

la oficina
el/la gerente
el/la contable

TALKING ABOUT MERCHANDISING

el/la comerciante
el/la cliente
el/la cajero(a)
la venta

la compra
la mercancía
satisfecho(a)

DISCUSSING SOME LEGAL PROFESSIONS

el tribunal
el/la juez

el/la abogado(a)
el bufete del abogado

IDENTIFYING SOME MUNICIPAL GOVERNMENT WORKERS

la alcaldía
el/la alcalde

el/la funcionario(a)

TALKING ABOUT SOME PROFESSIONS

la profesión
el título universitario

el/la ingeniero(a)
el/la arquitecto(a)

IDENTIFYING SOME TRADES

el oficio
el/la especialista
el/la electricista
el/la albañil

el/la plomero(a),
    el/la fontanero(a)
el/la carpintero(a)

TALKING ABOUT JOB OPPORTUNITIES

un puesto
el anuncio
el departamento de recursos
    humanos (personal)
el/la candidato(a),
    el/la aspirante

el/la entrevistador(a)
la entrevista
la solicitud de empleo
a tiempo completo
a tiempo parcial
ofrecer un trabajo

OTHER USEFUL EXPRESSIONS

ojalá
quizás

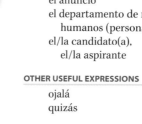

TECNOTUR

VIDEO

¡Buen viaje!

EPISODIO 14 ▶ Profesiones y oficios

Teresa

Luis

Isabel

Cristina

Juan Ramón

CD-ROM

Expansión cultural

¿Qué clase de trabajo buscas? Los anuncios clasificados del periódico te pueden ayudar.

interNET
CONNECTION

In this video episode Juan Ramón, Teresa, Luis, Isabel, and Cristina discuss their plans for the future. To find out more about career opportunities in the Spanish-speaking world, go to the **Capítulo 14** Internet activity at the Glencoe Foreign Language Web site:

http://www.glencoe.com/sec/fl

TECNOTUR

cuatrocientos veintiuno ∽ **421**

OVERVIEW

This page previews three key multimedia components of the **Glencoe Spanish** series. Each reinforces the material taught in Chapter 14 in a unique manner.

VIDEO

The Video Program allows students to see how the chapter vocabulary and structures are used by native speakers in an engaging story. Show the video episode as a final activity for Chapter 14.

A. This episode takes place one year after Juan Ramón's and Cristina's visits abroad. This is an excellent opportunity for students to summarize what they know about each of the video characters.

B. See the Video Activities Booklet for detailed suggestions for using this resource.

CD-ROM

A. In the video episode, each of the five characters talks about his or her plans for the future. Have students read the caption on page 421. Then have them mention other avenues for finding job and career opportunities.

B. In the CD-ROM version of **Expansión cultural** (Disc 4, page 421), students can listen to additional recorded information about various careers in which knowledge of a second language is beneficial.

INTERNET

Teacher Information and Student Worksheets for this activity can be accessed at the Web site.

Video Synopsis

This last episode takes place one year later, with the International Web Page up and running. Through the Web Page, Juan Ramón, Cristina, Teresa, Isabel, and Luis relate what has happened in each of their lives, what they are doing now, and their plans and aspirations for the future.

National Standards

✿ Students will develop insight into the nature of language through comparisons of Spanish and English. You may wish to remind students that there is a subjunctive in English although it is rarely used since we usually use the infinitive instead.

I insist that he go is an example of the subjunctive in English. *I want him to go* is the more typical infinitive construction.

The subjunctive is often encountered in more formal language:
It is imperative that they attend.
We demand that he surrender.

OVERVIEW

This section reviews the salient points from Chapters 12–14. In the **Conversación** students will review subjunctive forms as well as vocabulary having to do with public services. In the **Estructura** section, they will review the uses of the subjunctive.

TEACHING THE CONVERSATION

A. Have students open their books to page 422. Call on two students to read the conversation aloud.
B. Ask the questions from the **Después de conversar** section.

422

Repaso CAPÍTULOS 12–14

Conversación

La futura jefa de banquetes

ANTONIA: ¿Adónde vas, Isabel?
ISABEL: Voy a la peluquería. Tengo el pelo un poco largo. Necesito un corte. Y después voy al correo.
ANTONIA: ¿Por qué es necesario que vayas al correo?
ISABEL: Tengo que enviar las invitaciones. Quiero que lleguen a tiempo.
ANTONIA: ¿Qué invitaciones?
ISABEL: Pues, el día 13 voy a dar una gran fiesta.
ANTONIA: ¿Qué estás celebrando?
ISABEL: No te voy a decir. ¡Ya verás!
ANTONIA: Ay, pero siempre estás dando fiestas.
ISABEL: Pues, me gustan las fiestas y me gusta darlas.
ANTONIA: Algún día, ¡quizás seas una jefa de banquetes que planee fiestas y recepciones para bodas y bautizos.
ISABEL: ¡Tal vez! ¿Quién sabe?

Después de conversar

A **Un trabajo para Isabel** Contesten.
1. ¿Adónde va Isabel?
2. ¿Por qué va allí?
3. Y después, ¿adónde va?
4. ¿Por qué es necesario que ella vaya allí?
5. ¿Cuándo será la fiesta?
6. ¿Para qué es?
7. ¿Por qué da muchas fiestas Isabel?
8. Un día, ¿es posible que ella haga qué tipo de trabajo?

ANSWERS

Después de conversar

A 1. Isabel va a la peluquería.
2. Tiene el pelo un poco largo.
3. Después va al correo.
4. Es necesario que ella vaya porque tiene que enviar invitaciones para una fiesta.
5. La fiesta será el día 13.
6. Isabel no quiere decir para qué es la fiesta.

7. Le gustan las fiestas.
8. Algún día quizás sea jefa de banquetes.

422

Estructura

Usos del subjuntivo

The indicative mood of the verb is used to express events and actions that actually have, are, or will take place. The subjunctive, on the other hand, is used to express events that may or may not take place. Some introductory statement makes the actual event uncertain. The following are some expressions that are followed by the subjunctive.

querer	es posible	alegrarse de
esperar	es imposible	sentir
temer	es probable	estar contento
preferir	es necesario	estar triste
pedir	es importante	
sugerir	es bueno, es mejor	
aconsejar	es fácil	
exigir	es difícil	
mandar		
insistir		

Quiero que él vaya. Espero que él vaya. Le pido que vaya. La verdad es que insisto en que él vaya porque es importante que él vaya. Más que importante, es necesario que él vaya. Pero la verdad es que yo no sé si va a ir o no.

Práctica

A HISTORIETA En la peluquería

Contesten.

1. ¿Quiere José que el peluquero le corte el pelo?
2. ¿Prefiere que el peluquero use la navaja o las tijeras para cortarle el pelo?
3. ¿Le pide que le dé un champú también?
4. ¿Quiere el peluquero que José le diga cómo quiere el pelo?
5. ¿Insiste José en que el peluquero le ponga una raya?

TEACHING STRUCTURE

Usos del subjuntivo

A. Have students open their books to page 423. Lead students through the explanation of the subjunctive.

B. Have students repeat the sentences on page 423. Ask volunteers to make up additional sentences, choosing from the list of words and expressions. Write their sentences on the board.

Práctica

A After doing **Práctica A,** ask for volunteers to retell the story in their own words.

ANSWERS

Práctica

A 1. Sí (No), José (no) quiere que el peluquero le corte el pelo.

2. Prefiere que el peluquero use la navaja (las tijeras).

3. Sí, (No, no) le pide que le dé un champú también.

4. Sí (No), el peluquero (no) quiere que José le diga cómo quiere el pelo.

5. Sí (No), José (no) insiste en que el peluquero le ponga una raya.

423

Práctica

B After doing **Práctica B,** divide the class into pairs and do this activity again for additional practice with the subjunctive.

C After going over **Práctica C,** have students retell the story in their own words.

TEACHING STRUCTURE

Más usos del subjuntivo

A. Go over Steps 1–2 on page 424 with the students. You may want to write the examples on the board or on an overhead transparency in order to explain the concepts.

B. You may want to use additional examples from Chapter 13, pages 380–381, and Chapter 14, page 409.

B Consejos   Contesten.

1. ¿Quieren tus padres que escojas una buena carrera?
2. ¿Te aconseja tu profesor que sigas con tus estudios del español?
3. ¿Te sugiere que tomes un curso de informática?
4. ¿Están contentos tus padres que estudies mucho y que saques buenas notas?
5. ¿Es probable que tú vayas a la universidad?
6. ¿Es importante que tú sepas la carrera que vas a escoger antes de ir a la universidad?

C HISTORIETA En la estación de servicio

Sigan el modelo.

Yo quiero / él / llenar el tanque
Yo quiero que él llene el tanque.

1. Yo quiero / él / poner gasolina sin plomo
2. Le pido / revisar el aceite
3. Me alegro de que / él / limpiar el parabrisas
4. Es necesario / él / poner aire en las llantas
5. Es importante / nosotros / manejar con cuidado
6. El empleado prefiere / yo / pagar con cheque

San José, Costa Rica

Más usos del subjuntivo

1. The subjunctive is also used when introduced by a statement that conveys doubt. When the statement implies certainty, however, the indicative is used.

   Dudo que él asista a la boda.
   Pero creo que los novios van a recibir muchos regalos.

2. The subjunctive is also used in a clause that modifies an indefinite antecedent. If the antecedent refers to a specific person or thing, the indicative is used.

   La compañía está buscando un candidato que hable inglés.
   La compañía tiene un candidato que habla inglés.

INGLÉS
● Grupos reducidos. Método directo.
● Profesorado británico titulado.
● Niveles desde Principiantes a Proficiency.
● Biblioteca, vídeo.
Matrícula abierta
BRITISH LANGUAGE CENTRE
Bravo Murillo, 377
Esq. Plaza Castilla
Teléfono 733 07 39

ANSWERS

Práctica

B 1. Sí, mis padres quieren que escoja una buena carrera.
2. Sí, mi profesor me aconseja que siga con mis estudios de español.
3. Sí, (No, no) me sugiere que tome un curso de informática.
4. Sí, mis padres están contentos que estudie mucho y que saque buenas notas.

5. Sí, (No, no) es probable que vaya a la universidad.
6. Sí, (No, no) es importante que sepa la carrera que voy a escoger antes de ir a la universidad.

C 1. Yo quiero que él ponga gasolina sin plomo.
2. Le pido que revise el aceite.
3. Me alegro de que él limpie el parabrisas.

4. Es necesario que él ponga aire en las llantas.
5. Es importante que nosotros manejemos con cuidado.
6. El empleado prefiere que yo pague con cheque.

✦Práctica✦

A **HISTORIETA** Una carta

Contesten.

1. ¿Crees que José te ha escrito?
2. ¿Piensas que él ha puesto la carta en un buzón?
3. ¿Dudas que él vaya al correo para mandar la carta?
4. ¿Es dudoso que la carta llegue hoy?
5. ¿Es cierto que la carta tiene bastantes sellos?

B **Hay que tener ciertas calificaciones.** Completen.

1. La compañía Vensa está buscando alguien que ____ (tener) experiencia, que ____ (conocer) bien el español y el inglés y que ____ (poder) viajar.
2. El director del servicio de personal me dijo que necesitan alguien que ____ (estar) libre inmediatamente.
3. Han entrevistado a dos candidatos. Hay un candidato que ____ (tener) experiencia, que ____ (querer) y ____ (poder) trabajar enseguida.
4. Desgraciadamente él no habla inglés y la compañía sigue buscando alguien que ____ (hablar) inglés y que ____ (conocer) el mercado norteamericano.

Actividades comunicativas

A **Carreras** Trabaja con un(a) compañero(a). Identifiquen las carreras que creen que les interesarían. Identifiquen también las carreras que no les interesarían. Digan por qué. Decidan si tienen muchos intereses en común. ¿Es posible que sigan o escojan la misma carrera?

B **Fiestas** Trabaja con un(a) compañero(a). Planeen una gran fiesta. Discutan por qué van a dar la fiesta y todo lo que van a hacer durante la fiesta. Entonces decidan todo lo que tienen que hacer antes de la fiesta.

C **En la peluquería** Con un(a) compañero(a), entablen una conversación que tiene lugar en una peluquería. Uno(a) de Uds. será el/la peluquero(a) y el/la otro(a) será el/la cliente.

A Have students answer the items in **Práctica A** in the affirmative.
EXPANSION After doing this activity, have students retell the story in their own words.

B After doing this activity, have volunteers read all of the items together, in paragraph form.

Actividades comunicativas

A This activity reviews the vocabulary from Chapter 14.

B This activity reviews the vocabulary from Chapter 13. Have students share their ideas for a **fiesta** with the class. Everyone will be interested in hearing the details!

C This activity reviews vocabulary from Chapter 12. Students can view the Chapter 12 video episode as a model for their conversation.

Note You may wish to do the fourth literary selection (pages 442–447) with students at this time.

ANSWERS

Práctica

A
1. **Sí, creo que José me ha escrito.**
2. **Sí, pienso que él ha puesto la carta en un buzón.**
3. **Sí, dudo que el vaya al correo para mandar la carta.**
4. **Sí, es dudoso que la carta llegue hoy.**
5. **Sí, es cierto que la carta tiene bastantes sellos.**

B
1. **tenga, conozca, pueda**
2. **esté**
3. **tiene, quiere, puede**
4. **hable, conozca**

Actividades comunicativas
A, B, and **C** Answers will vary.

Independent Practice

Assign any of the following:
1. Activities, pages 422–425
2. Workbook, pages 175–178
3. CD-ROM, Disc 4, pages 422–425
4. CD-ROM, Disc 4, Chapters 12–14, **Juegos de repaso**

VISTAS DE GUATEMALA

OVERVIEW

The **Vistas de Guatemala** were prepared by National Geographic Society. Their purpose is to give students greater insight, through these visual images, into the culture and people of Guatemala. Have students look at the photographs on pages 426–429 for enjoyment. If they would like to talk about them, let them say anything they can, using the vocabulary they have learned to this point.

National Standards

Cultures
The **Vistas de Guatemala** photos, and the accompanying captions, allow students to gain insights into the people and culture of Guatemala.

Learning From Photos

1. Ruinas mayas, Seibal The famous Mayan ruins of Seibal or Ceibal, are in the central region of the department of Petén. The sculptured decorations on the exterior of the buildings, stairways, and terraces are notable. Many contain hieroglyphic inscriptions. A number of the buildings have sculpture in their interiors as well.

2. Celebración de Todos los Santos, poblado de Todos Santos Cuchumatán November 1st is an important date in Guatemala. People visit and decorate cemeteries in honor of their dead. On this day there is a major celebration in the village of Todos Santos Cuchumatán, in the department of Huehuetenango. Horse races are traditional. People look forward to these races all year long. In addition to the races, another part of *(continued)*

1. Ruinas mayas, Seibal
2. Celebración de Todos los Santos, poblado de Todos los Santos
3. Procesión de Semana Santa, Chichicastenango
4. Mercado, Chichicastenango
5. Iglesia de San Francisco, Antigua Guatemala
6. Tucán, Parque Nacional Tikal

Learning From Photos

the celebration is the eating of a traditional meal consisting of a black **tamal**.

3. Procesión de Semana Santa, Chichicastenango Women of the region, richly attired in traditional dress, attend the processions of Holy Week in the market town of Chichicastenango. There are processions throughout Holy Week culminating in the Easter Sunday celebrations. Chichicastenango has its own fair, celebrated between December 14th and 21st. The most spectacular event of the fair at Chichicastenango is **Palo volador**, where men dressed as monkeys fly over the plaza suspended by a rope from a tall pole.

(continued)

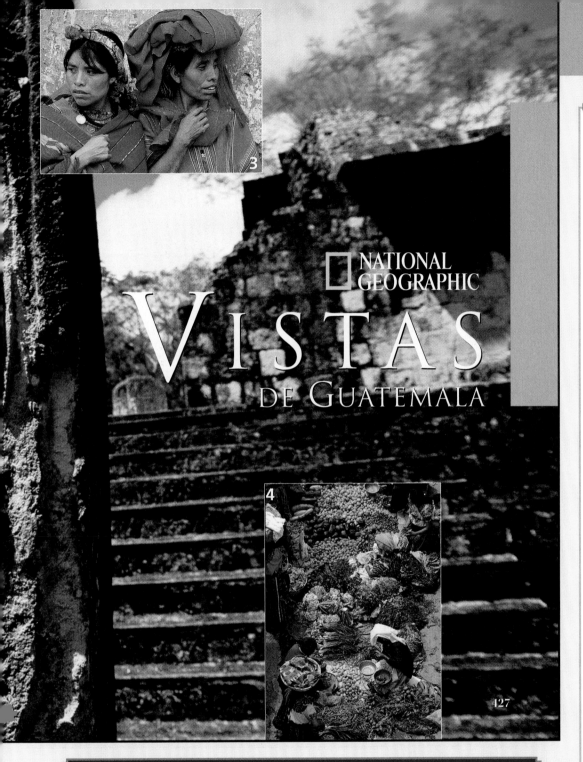

NATIONAL GEOGRAPHIC

VISTAS
DE GUATEMALA

5. Iglesia de San Francisco, Antigua Guatemala Only 45 kilometers from the modern capital of Guatemala City is the magnificent colonial town of Antigua Guatemala. Antigua was the capital of Guatemala in Spanish times, but after suffering enormous damage during a number of earthquakes, the capital was moved from Antigua to its present site in 1776. Antigua is the capital of the department of Sacatepéquez. Antigua was founded in 1524 by the conquistador Pedro de Alvarado and given the name of Santiago de los Caballeros de Guatemala. In addition to the Church of San Francisco, other notable colonial buildings are the Convento de la Merced, the cathedral, and the Palacio de los Capitanes Generales.

6. Tucán, Parque Nacional Tikal This toucan is but one of 333 species of birds to be found in the park. The park covers an area of 57,600 hectares and is situated in the department of Petén in northeastern Guatemala. The park is within the Maya Biosphere Reserve that covers over one million hectares and is a Natural/Cultural World Heritage Site established under UNESCO. In addition to the 333 species of birds, numbers of rare reptiles, amphibians, and mammals can be found in the park, including: pumas, jaguars, tapirs, crocodiles, and 38 species of snakes.

Learning From Photos

(continued from page 426)
4. Mercado, Chichicastenango Twice a week this highland town comes alive for market day. The people, carrying enormous loads on their heads or backs, arrive by dawn, walking from their mountain homes or arriving on rickety buses. Everyone congregates in the plaza in front of the church of Santo Tomás, built on the ruins of a Mayan temple. On the steps of the church, men swing tin cans filled with hot coals and an incense made of the resin of trees. The sellers will speak Spanish with the tourists, if necessary, but the language most heard is Quiché. *(continued)*

VISTAS DE GUATEMALA

Learning From Photos

1. Escolares, Antigua Guatemala These uniformed school girls are in Antigua, a colonial city with cobblestoned streets and architecture which has hardly changed since the days of the **conquistadores.** One of the first planned cities in the Americas, Antigua was designed as a traditional Spanish grid— eight by eight blocks. Antigua was declared a national monument in 1944.

2. Ciudad de Guatemala Guatemala City, the modern capital, was founded in 1776 and christened **Nueva Guatemala**, as opposed to **Antigua Guatemala,** the old capital. The largest city in Central America, it has a population of over two milllion. Because of its altitude (1,520 meters or 5,000 feet), it enjoys a spring-like climate year-round.

3. Cometas gigantes en el cielo, Sumpango The flying of these giant kites of more than two meters in diameter is part of the celebration of **el Día de los Muertos,** November 1st, in the villages of Sumpango and Santiago Sacatepéquez. People tie small messages to the tails of the kites as a way of communicating with their loved ones who have died.

4. Teatro Nacional, Ciudad de Guatemala This ultra-modern building is representative of the architecture of the *new* Guatemala.

5. Lago Atitlán y Volcán San Pedro Volcanic activity began in the Lake Atitlán area about 11–12 million years ago. The lake is the crater of an extinct *(continued)*

1. Escolares, Antigua Guatemala
2. Ciudad de Guatemala
3. Cometas gigantes en el cielo de Sumpango
4. Teatro Nacional, Ciudad de Guatemala
5. Lago Atitlán y Volcán San Pedro
6. Arco de Santa Catalina con vista del Volcán de Agua, Antigua
7. Amanecer con neblina cerca de Nebaj

428

NATIONAL GEOGRAPHIC SOCIETY **TEACHER'S CORNER**

Index to NATIONAL GEOGRAPHIC MAGAZINE

The following articles may be used for research relating to this chapter:

- "The Elusive Quetzal," by Steve Winter, June 1998.
- "The Violent Saga of a Maya Kingdom," by Arthur Demarest, February 1993.
- **"La Ruta Maya,"** by Wilbur E. Garrett, October 1989.
- "Guatemala: A Fragile Democracy," by Griffin Smith, Jr., June 1988.
- **"El Mirador:** An Early Maya Metropolis Uncovered," by Ray T. Matheny, September 1987.
- "Maya Art Treasures Discovered in Cave," by George E. Stuart, August 1981.
- "Troubled Times for Central America," by Wilbur E. Garrett, July 1981.

NATIONAL GEOGRAPHIC
VISTAS
DE GUATEMALA

Learning From Photos

(continued from page 428) volcano. From the top of the San Pedro volcano, pictured here, there is a magnificent view of the lake and of a whole line of volcanos. Every morning a mail boat crosses the lake to the charming village of Santiago Atitlán, located on an embankment of broken lava.

6. Arco de Santa Catalina con vista del Volcán de Agua, Antigua This view of the Volcán de Agua was taken through the Santa Catalina arch in Antigua. The volcano, located on the Pacific side of Guatemala, is part of a chain of volcanos, some of which are still active.

7. Amanecer con neblina cerca de Nebaj Nebaj is one of three areas that make up the departamento del Quiché, an area of tropical forests with the largest population of Mayan origin. The people are considered to be **no hispanizada** since owing to their isolation, they have conserved traditions predating the Spanish conquest. Their language, Ixil, is also the name of the indigenous group of Mayan descent that has populated the region since 200 B.C.

Products available from
GLENCOE/MCGRAW-HILL

To order the following products, call Glencoe/McGraw-Hill at 1-800-334-7344.

CD-ROMs
• Picture Atlas of the World
• The Complete National Geographic: 109 Years of National Geographic Magazine

Software
• ZingoLingo: Spanish Diskettes

Transparency Set
• NGS PicturePack: Geography of North America

Products available from
NATIONAL GEOGRAPHIC SOCIETY

NATIONAL GEOGRAPHIC SOCIETY

Books
• Exploring Your World: The Adventure of Geography
• Lost Kingdom of the Maya
• National Geographic Satellite Atlas of the World

Video
Central America ("Nations of the World" Series)

National Standards

❀ **Cultures**
Students experience, discuss, and analyze an expressive product of the culture, a selection from the poetic narrative *Platero y yo* by Juan Ramón Jiménez.

¡**OJO!** The exposure to literature early in one's study of a foreign language should be a pleasant experience. As students read these selections it is not necessary for them to understand every word. Explain to them that they should try to enjoy the experience of reading literature in a new language. As they read they should look for the following:

- who the main characters are
- what they are like
- what they are doing—the plot
- what happens to them—the outcome of the story

PLATERO Y YO (FRAGMENTO)

TEACHING VOCABULARY

A. Present the new vocabulary on pages 430 and 431 using the teaching suggestions given in the regular chapters in this textbook.

B. Quickly go over **Práctica A** and **Práctica B** with the class.

430

Literatura 1

PLATERO Y YO (FRAGMENTO)
de don Juan Ramón Jiménez

Vocabulario

el burro
el prado
la piedra
el hocico
los cascabeles
las flores
celesté
gualda
rosa

El burro anda por el prado.
Acaricia las florecitas con su hocico.

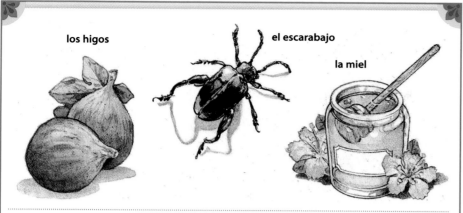

los higos

el escarabajo

la miel

el cascabeleo el sonido de los cascabeles
la pena algo triste
los gemelos dos cosas iguales o dos hermanos nacidos al mismo tiempo
el acero un metal muy duro
la plata un metal blanco, valioso; se usa para monedas

blando(a) lo contrario de «duro(a)»
suelto(a) libre
peludo(a) con mucho pelo
tibiamente suavemente
acariciar tocar suavemente
la abeja un insecto que produce la miel del néctar de las flores

Literatura 1

ABOUT THE SPANISH LANGUAGE

There are many names for colors in Spanish in addition to the basic ones. Here are a few: For yellow there is **gualda** (the yellow in the flag of Spain) in addition to **amarillo**.

azul marino	*navy blue*
celeste	*light blue*
rosa, color de rosa, rosado	*pink*
marrón, castaño, moreno, pardo	*brown*

Práctica

A **¿Sí o no?** Digan que sí o que no.

1. Los higos son una flor.
2. A veces un gato lleva un collar de cascabeles.
3. Las abejas son insectos.
4. Los escarabajos producen la miel del néctar de las flores.
5. Otro nombre para «celeste» es blanco.
6. Otro nombre para «gualda» es amarillo.
7. Se hacen monedas de la plata.

B **La palabra, por favor.** Completen.

1. Yo tengo un dólar, pero no es de papel; es de _____.
2. Los dos hermanos nacieron el mismo día; ellos son _____.
3. No es blando; es muy _____.
4. Pero el otro es duro, muy duro, duro como el _____.
5. El animal puede ir adonde quiera; siempre anda _____.
6. Está muy triste; tiene muchas _____.
7. El hombre pasa la mano sobre el burrito; lo _____.

LITERATURA

cuatrocientos treinta y uno 〰 **431**

ANSWERS

Práctica

A
1. No.
2. Sí.
3. Sí.
4. No.
5. No.
6. Sí.
7. Sí.

B
1. plata
2. gemelos
3. duro
4. acero
5. suelto
6. penas
7. acaricia

431

Literatura 1

DISCUSSING LITERATURE

INTRODUCCIÓN

A. You may go over the **Introducción** with the students or you may decide to omit it and just have them read the narrative.

B. You can ask the following questions about the **Introducción.** ¿Es *Platero y yo* una obra para niños? ¿Qué recibió Juan Ramón Jiménez en 1956? ¿En qué pueblo español vive Platero? ¿En qué región de España está Moguer? ¿Está en el norte o en el sur de España?

Platero y yo

A. Read the selection to the class. Use as much expression as you can.

B. Have students open their books to page 432. Have them read the selection silently. Then call on individuals to read a paragraph each.

C. Now go over the **Después de leer** activities.

TECHNOLOGY OPTION

Students can listen to a recording of this narrative on the CD-ROM, Discs 1, 2, 3, 4, page 432.

Andalucía, España

PLATERO Y YO
de Juan Ramón Jiménez

INTRODUCCIÓN Esta obra no es prosa, ni es poesía. Se puede decir que es prosa poética. Muchos creen que don Juan Ramón escribió la obra para niños, pero en su prólogo el autor dice: «Ese breve libro, en donde la alegría y la pena son gemelos, cual las orejas de Platero, estaba escrito para… qué sé yo para quien… para quien escribimos los poetas líricos». Juan Ramón Jiménez recibió el Premio Nóbel de Literatura en 1956.

El fragmento que sigue se titula «Platero», y es uno de 139 capítulos. Es una descripción del burrito, amigo y compañero constante de don Juan Ramón en el pequeño pueblo de Moguer en Andalucía, España.

Platero y yo

Platero es pequeño, peludo, suave; tan blando por fuera que se diría todo de algodón, que no lleva huesos. Sólo los espejos de azabache° de sus ojos son duros cual dos escarabajos de cristal negro.

Lo dejo suelto, y se va al prado, y acaricia tibiamente con su hocico, rozándolas° apenas, las florecillas rosas, celestes y gualdas. Lo llamo dulcemente: —¿Platero?— y viene a mí con un trotecillo alegre que parece que se ríe, en no sé qué cascabeleo ideal… Come cuanto le doy. Le gustan las naranjas mandarinas, las uvas moscateles°, todas de ámbar, los higos morados, con su cristalina gotita de miel…

Es tierno° y mimoso° igual que un niño, que una niña…; pero fuerte y seco por dentro, como de piedra. Cuando paso sobre él, los domingos, por las últimas callejas del pueblo, los hombres del campo, vestidos de limpio y despaciosos°, se quedan mirándolo: —Tien´ asero—… Tiene acero. Acero y plata de luna, al mismo tiempo.

espejos de azabache *black mirrors*

rozándolas *brushing against them*

uvas moscateles tipo de uva muy dulce

tierno *tender*
mimoso *pampered*

despaciosos con calma

Moguer, Andalucía

Ste. 300
200 Mansell Court
Roswell, GA 30076-4850

STAMP OUT HUNGER MAY 12

The National Association of Letter Carriers, in conjunction with the United States Postal Service, will be collecting non-perishable food items like canned soup, juice, pasta, vegetables, cereal and rice on Saturday, May 12, to help families in need in our community.

You can help by placing your food donation at your mailbox on May 12 before your letter carrier arrives. Your carrier will take it to the Post Office, and it will then be delivered to a local food bank or pantry. Please do not include any glass or perishable items.

Thank you for caring,
Your Letter Carrier

Co-Sponsored by:

PRIORITY MAIL
UNITED STATES POSTAL SERVICE

M0054

UNITED STATES POSTAL SERVICE

United Way

POSTAL CUSTOMER

BULK RATE
Postage & Fees Paid
USPS
Permit No. G-10

NATIONAL ASSOCIATION OF LETTER CARRIERS' FOOD DRIVE
HELP STAMP OUT HUNGER

Saturday, May 12, 2001

1 Collect and bag any non-perishable food items.

2 Place your food donation by your mailbox.

3 Your letter carrier will pick it up and deliver it to a local food bank!

PRIORITY MAIL
UNITED STATES POSTAL SERVICE.

Proud to Support "STAMP OUT HUNGER"

Después de leer

A **Platero** Completen.

1. Platero no es grande; es _____.
2. Y no es duro; es _____.
3. Las uvas moscateles son del color de _____.
4. Platero acaricia las florecillas con su _____.
5. El día de la semana que el autor pasa sobre su burro es el _____.

B **Platero** Contesten.

1. Cuando el autor suelta al burro, ¿adónde va el animalito?
2. ¿Con quiénes compara el autor a Platero?
3. ¿Qué le gusta comer a Platero?
4. ¿Quiénes miran a Platero cuando pasa por el pueblo?

C **Para pensar** Discutan.

1. El autor describe a Platero en formas contradictorias, especialmente cuando habla de lo exterior y de lo interior del animalito. Explica.
2. ¿Cómo describirías tú a Platero?
3. Los campesinos dicen que el burrito «Tien´ asero...» ¿Qué quiere decir esa frase, y por qué lo escribe de esa forma el autor?
4. Al final del capítulo don Juan Ramón dice: «Acero y plata de luna, al mismo tiempo». Interpreta esa frase.

D **Recursos literarios** Contesten.

A metaphor is a figure of speech in which a word that means one thing is substituted for another to indicate a similarity or likeness, for example, "In the springtime of life." A simile is a figure of speech in which two very different things are compared to each other, usually using the word "like" **(como),** for example, "eyes like stars, hands like hams," etc. What metaphors and similes can you identify in this selection?

Un campesino con su burro, Andalucía, España

LITERATURA

cuatrocientos treinta y tres **433**

ANSWERS

Después de leer

A 1. pequeño
2. blando
3. ámbar
4. hocico
5. domingo

B 1. El animalito se va al prado.
2. El autor compara a Platero con un niño, con una niña.
3. A Platero le gusta comer las naranjas mandarinas, las uvas moscateles, los higos morados.
4. Los hombres del campo miran a Platero cuando pasa por el pueblo.

C 1. Answers will vary.
2. Answers will vary but may include: **Platero es pequeño, suave, parece de algodón. Tiene ojos negros. Es tierno y mimoso, pero fuerte como la piedra.**
3. **Quiere decir que es fuerte como el acero. El autor lo dice de esa forma porque repite la forma de hablar de los campesinos.**
4. Answers will vary.

D Answers will vary but may include:
Espejos de azabache de sus ojos
Es fuerte y seco por dentro, como de piedra

National Standards

Cultures
Students experience, discuss, and analyze an expressive product of the culture, the poem ***La muralla*** by the Cuban poet Nicolás Guillén.

LA MURALLA

TEACHING VOCABULARY

A. Have students open their books to page 434. Have them repeat the new vocabulary words and sentences after you.

B. It is not necessary for students to become as thoroughly familiar with this vocabulary as with the vocabulary in a typical chapter. It is presented to help students understand the reading but it is not necessary for them to learn the vocabulary for productive purposes.

ABOUT THE SPANISH LANGUAGE

There are different words for different kinds of walls.

- ◆ **Una pared** is an interior wall in a house or other building.
- ◆ **Un muro** is a fortified outer wall such as that found on fortresses or around walled towns.
- ◆ **Una muralla** is a synonym of **un muro.**
- ◆ **Una verja** is another outer wall or fence.
- ◆ **Una tapia** is an outer wall, usually an earthen wall.

434

Literatura 2

LA MURALLA
de Nicolás Guillén

Vocabulario

Labels: el monte, la paloma, el laurel, el ruiseñor, el ciempiés, el horizonte, la muralla, la rosa, el alacrán, la serpiente, el clavel

Las dos niñas están cerca de la muralla.
Ellas juntaban las manos.

el veneno   una sustancia que puede matar, como el arsénico
el puñal   un tipo de cuchillo
alzar   levantar

❖Práctica❖

A Estudio de palabras   Pareen.

1. el horizonte   **a.** poison, venom
2. la serpiente   **b.** horizon
3. la rosa   **c.** mountain
4. el veneno   **d.** rose
5. el monte   **e.** serpent

B ¿Sabes?   Identifiquen.

1. dos flores   3. un reptil
2. dos pájaros   4. dos insectos

C ¿Cuál es?   Escojan.

1. Entre las flores había unos preciosos _____.
   a. claveles   **b.** puñales   **c.** venenos
2. La serpiente podría matar con su _____.
   a. flor   **b.** veneno   **c.** cuchillo
3. Sí, sí, el criminal tenía un cuchillo; era un _____.
   a. alacrán   **b.** clavel   **c.** puñal
4. No, no lo va a bajar; al contrario, lo va a _____.
   a. alzar   **b.** matar   **c.** abrir

Cañaverales, Cuba

Literatura 2

❖Práctica❖

A **B** and **C** Quickly go over these activities orally to be sure that students will understand the words in the reading.

Did You Know?

Cabo Cañaveral Cape Canaveral, the Florida launch site for the astronauts, was, in Spanish times, the location of large sugar cane fields.

ANSWERS

Práctica

A 1. b
   2. e
   3. d
   4. a
   5. c

C 1. a
   2. b
   3. c
   4. a

B Answers will vary, but may include:
1. **la rosa, el clavel**
2. **la paloma, el ruiseñor**
3. **la serpiente**
4. **el alacrán, el ciempiés**

Literatura 2

DISCUSSING LITERATURE

¡OJO! This reading is OPTIONAL. You may present the story thoroughly as a class activity or you may have some or all students merely read it on their own. If you present the story as a class activity you may wish to vary presentation procedures from section to section. Some options are:

- Students read silently.
- Students repeat after you in unison.
- Call on individuals to read aloud.
- When dialogue appears in the story, call on students to take parts.

With any of the above procedures, intersperse some comprehension questions. Call on a student or students to give a brief synopsis of a section in Spanish.

La muralla

A. Before reading this selection you may wish to review the symbols in the photos on page 436. For example: **¿Cómo son las manos en la foto? ¿Son manos blancas o negras? ¿Cómo se llaman las flores en la foto?**

B. If you are presenting the story as a class activity, you can use many gestures or expressions to help students with comprehension.

C. Have students close their books. Read the poem aloud to the class with as much expression as possible.

D. Now have students open their books. Have them read the poem silently to themselves.

E. Have students locate the line in the poem that corresponds to each photo on page 436.

436

LA MURALLA
de Nicolás Guillén

INTRODUCCIÓN El poeta cubano Nicolás Guillén presenta, en sus versos, elementos de folklore negro. Él es uno de los cultivadores de la poesía «afrocubana». En el poema que sigue, el poeta nos presenta un lindo mensaje de comprensión y tolerancia.

La muralla

Para hacer esta muralla,
tráiganme todas las manos:
los negros sus manos negras,
los blancos sus blancas manos.
Ay,
una muralla que vaya
desde la playa hasta el monte,
desde el monte hasta la playa, bien,
allá sobre el horizonte.
—¡Tun, tun!
—¿Quién es?
—Una rosa y un clavel...

¡Abre la muralla!
—¡Tun, tun!
—¿Quién es?
—El sable° del coronel°...
—¡Cierra la muralla!
—¡Tun, tun!
—¿Quién es?
—La paloma y el laurel...
—¡Abre la muralla!
—¡Tun, tun!
—¿Quién es?
—El alacrán y el ciempiés...
—¡Cierra la muralla!

sable *sword, saber*
coronel *colonel*

LITERATURA

Al corazón del amigo,
abre la muralla;
al veneno y al puñal,
cierra la muralla;
al mirto° y la yerbabuena°,
abre la muralla;
al diente de la serpiente,
cierra la muralla;
al ruiseñor en la flor,
abre la muralla...

Alcemos una muralla
juntando todas las manos;
los negros, sus manos negras,
los blancos sus blancas manos.
Una muralla que vaya
desde la playa hasta el monte,
desde el monte hasta la playa, bien,
allá sobre el horizonte...

mirto *myrtle*
yerbabuena *mint*

Después de leer

A La muralla Escojan.
1. Para hacer la muralla se necesitan muchas _____.
   a. flores   **b.** manos   **c.** palomas
2. La muralla estará entre el monte y _____.
   a. la playa   **b.** el coronel   **c.** el horizonte
3. Los primeros que llegan son _____.
   a. el coronel y el alacrán   **b.** la rosa y el clavel
   c. el ciempiés y el ruiseñor
4. El coronel lleva _____.
   a. un sable   **b.** una flor   **c.** un diente

B Cosas en común Contesten.
1. ¿Qué tienen en común la rosa, el clavel, el mirto y el laurel?
2. ¿Qué tienen en común el ruiseñor y la paloma?
3. ¿Qué tienen en común el alacrán y el ciempiés?
4. ¿Qué tienen en común el sable y el puñal?

C Rima ¿Qué rima con... ?
1. muralla   3. clavel
2. monte   4. quién es

LITERATURA

cuatrocientos treinta y siete **437**

Literatura 2

National Standards

Comparisons
Students will develop an understanding of the nature of language through comparisons of Spanish and English. Onomatopoeia is the use of words whose sound suggests the meaning. In this poem, **tun, tun** is an example of onomatopoeia. Ask students what the equivalent of **tun, tun** is in English. Ask them for other examples of onomatopoeia in English.

Después de leer

Note Students should read the entire poem on pages 436 and 437 before doing the **Después de leer** activities.

TECHNOLOGY OPTION

Students can listen to a recording of this poem on the CD-ROM, Discs 1, 2, 3, 4, pages 436–437.

ANSWERS

Después de leer

A 1. b
  2. a
  3. b
  4. a

B 1. Son plantas.
  2. Cantan.
  3. Pican.
  4. Cortan.

C 1. playa
  2. horizonte
  3. coronel
  4. ciempiés

RESOURCES

⚙ CD-ROM, Discs 1, 2, 3, 4,
pages 438–441

National Standards

Cultures
Students experience,
discuss, and analyze an expressive product of the culture, the
Puerto Rican legend *El cohítre,*
as re-told by the Puerto Rican
scholar Ester M. Feliciano
Mendoza.

EL COHÍTRE
UNA LEYENDA
PUERTORRIQUEÑA

TEACHING
VOCABULARY

A. Have students open their books
to page 438. Have them repeat the
new vocabulary words and sentences after you.

B. Students merely need to be familiar with the vocabulary to help
them understand the story. This
vocabulary does not have to be a
part of their active, productive
vocabulary. All high-frequency
words will be reintroduced in
¡Buen viaje! Level 3.

Literatura 3

EL COHÍTRE
UNA LEYENDA PUERTORRIQUEÑA
de Ester M. Feliciano Mendoza

Vocabulario

La niña hacía un castillo.   A lo lejos había un cerro.
Era muy feliz.   No lo podía ver bien porque era muy neblinoso.

La niña veía su reflejo en el agua.

438 ⌒ *cuatrocientos treinta y ocho*   LITERATURA

dorado
el tesoro

las lágrimas
arrodillarse
la tumba

El padre lloraba. Lloraba porque su hija murió.

liláceo(a)   del color de las lilas
el alma   el espíritu, no el cuerpo
el barro   la combinación de tierra y agua
reidor(a)   que se ríe
enjugar   secar, lavar

la súplica   la petición, el ruego
rogar, rezar   decir u ofrecer una oración a Dios
ofrendar   ofrecer
brotar   salir

A Otra manera de decirlo   Expresen la parte indicada de otra manera.

1. Los ojos de la niña eran *del color de las lilas*.
2. El padre y la hija subieron *el pequeño monte*.
3. Allí encontraron *muchas riquezas*.
4. En ese monte los indios *ofrecían* regalos a sus dioses.
5. Con los regalos también hacían *peticiones* a los dioses.

B La palabra, por favor.   Escojan.

1. El niño lloraba y su madre le _____ las lágrimas.
   a. enjugó   **b.** ofrendó   **c.** modeló
2. Donde cayeron las lágrimas pronto _____ unas flores de la tierra.
   a. ofrecieron   **b.** ofrendaron   **c.** brotaron
3. Era difícil ver el cerro claramente porque era muy _____.
   a. neblinoso   **b.** reidor   **c.** liláceo
4. Los religiosos creen que _____ es más importante que el cuerpo.
   a. el alma   **b.** la ofrenda   **c.** el reflejo
5. La niña vio _____ de su cara en el agua.
   a. el barro   **b.** el reflejo   **c.** la figurita
6. La familia puso flores en _____ del abuelo.
   a. la tumba   **b.** el alma   **c.** el caracol

❖Práctica❖

A and **B**   Quickly go over these activities orally to be sure that students will understand the words in the reading.

ANSWERS

Práctica
A 1. liláceos
   2. el cerro
   3. muchos tesoros
   4. ofrendaban
   5. súplicas

B 1. a
   2. c
   3. a
   4. a
   5. b
   6. a

Literatura 3

DISCUSSING LITERATURE

INTRODUCCIÓN

The **Introducción** on page 440 gives students a concise summary of the legend. Before doing the reading, go over the introduction with the students.

El cohítre

A. Tell students they are going to read a legend about a young girl who, during Spanish colonial times, lived on the island now known as Puerto Rico. The legend explains how the **cohítre** flower, native to Puerto Rico, came into being.

B. You may wish to have students take a few minutes to read the selection silently before going over it orally in class.

C. Call on a more able student to give a synopsis of each paragraph. This helps less able students understand the selection.

Los indios taínos

EL COHÍTRE
de Ester M. Feliciano Mendoza

INTRODUCCIÓN Ester Feliciano Mendoza (1918–1988) escribió en varios géneros, pero se destacó más como poeta. Esta selección viene de una de sus colecciones de leyendas. Esta leyenda nos habla de una flor típica de Puerto Rico y cómo llegó a ser. Los indios de Puerto Rico eran los taínos. La niña de la leyenda es hija de un español y una india. El padre de la niña quiere marcharse al Perú en busca de tesoro. La niña quiere quedarse en su isla amada.

Un cerro neblinoso

cemíes *clay figures made by Taíno Indians of Puerto Rico*
escurridizas *slippery*

El cohítre

Tenía los ojos azules y la piel dorada. Cuando nació, su padre creyó ver en sus pupilas los mismos reflejos liláceos de las tardes de Castilla. La amó por él y por la india que se murió rogando por su niña que no era ni india ni española.

La niña criolla fue tímida y amorosa. Amiga de los cerros neblinosos y las playas reidoras, conoció los secretos de las flores y de los caracoles. Aprendió a modelar cemíes° con la carne dócil del barro y a hacer castillos con las arenas escurridizas°. Amó al indio tanto como al español y a unos y otros enjugó las heridas del cuerpo y del alma. La niña criolla era feliz.

Un día el padre oyó hablar de las riquezas del Perú. Por primera vez la niña sintió el temor de la ausencia. Lloró los días que vendrían lejos de la isla querida. Se arrodilló ante la Virgen blanca y ofrendó flores y frutas a Yocahu, en una misma súplica: «No me dejen marchar». A los pies del altar cristiano rogaba también el padre español: «Dios nos lleve al Perú». Mirando a lo lejos el neblinoso monte Yukiyú, pensaba sin embargo: ¿Valdrá la pena marcharme?

Enfermó de angustia la niña criolla. Veía los cielos de Castilla en las pupilas azules, pero el padre no vio cómo la muerte lentamente las cubría de nubes... Y la niña, un día claro, se murió de pena.

Desde los brazos del padre voló a las regiones de Yocahu y de la virgencita blanca. Y pasaron los días... Sobre la tumba amada vio el padre español brotar, apretadita a la tierra, con sus florecitas azules reflejando el cielo de la isla, la yerba del cohítre... Y así fue para siempre en la tierra de Puerto Rico.

Puerto Rico

Después de leer

A **Estudio de palabras** Pareen.

1. las pupilas   a. absence
2. modelar   b. pupils (eyes)
3. dócil   c. tomb
4. la ausencia   d. to model
5. la tumba   e. reflections
6. los reflejos   f. docile, obedient

B **¿Sí o no?** Corrijan las oraciones incorrectas.

1. La niña tenía los ojos azules.
2. La piel de la niña era del color del oro.
3. El padre de la niña era indio.
4. La madre de la niña murió.
5. La madre rogaba por su marido.

C **¿Qué comprendieron?** Escojan.

1. La niña hacía figuritas de _____.
   a. arena   b. agua   c. barro
2. Para construir castillos usaba _____.
   a. arena   b. agua   c. barro
3. El padre de la niña se interesó en el Perú por sus _____.
   a. castillos   b. cerros   c. riquezas
4. La niña le ofreció a Yocahu _____.
   a. flores y frutas   b. riquezas   c. caracoles
5. La niña murió de _____.
   a. una herida   b. pena   c. temor

D **Según la leyenda...** Contesten.

1. ¿Por qué dice la leyenda «que la niña no era ni india ni española»?
2. ¿Por qué sintió la niña el temor de la ausencia?
3. ¿Por qué lloraba ella?
4. ¿A quiénes rogaba la niña?
5. ¿Qué quería la niña?
6. ¿Dónde rogaba el padre?
7. ¿Cuál era el conflicto entre padre e hija?
8. ¿Qué serán «las regiones de la Virgen blanca y Yocahu»?
9. ¿Qué será Yocahu?

E **Interpretación** Contesten.

1. ¿Qué significa que la niña «modelaba cemíes y hacía castillos»?
2. ¿Qué significa que la niña «rogaba a la Virgen blanca y a Yocahu»?
3. ¿Qué es lo que veía el padre cada vez que miraba los ojos de su hija?

ABOUT THE SPANISH LANGUAGE

The literal meaning of **criollo** is the child born in the Americas of European, especially Spanish, parents. In Puerto Rico, however, **criollo** means *native* Puerto Rican, regardless of ethnic background.

Después de leer

Note Students should read the entire selection on page 440 before doing the **Después de leer** activities.

TECHNOLOGY OPTION

Students can listen to a recording of this story on the CD-ROM, Discs 1, 2, 3, 4, page 440.

ANSWERS

Después de leer

A 1. b   3. f   5. c
   2. d   4. a   6. e

B 1. Sí.
  2. Sí.
  3. El padre de la niña era español.
  4. Sí.
  5. La madre rogaba por su niña.

C 1. c   4. a
  2. a   5. b
  3. c

D 1. Porque era criolla.
  2. Porque el padre pensaba en irse al Perú.
  3. Lloraba porque no quería irse lejos de su isla querida.
  4. La niña rogaba a la Virgen blanca y a Yocahu.
  5. La niña quería que no la dejaran marchar. (Quería quedarse en la isla.)
  6. El padre rogaba a los pies del altar cristiano.
  7. El padre quería irse, la niña no.
  8. El cielo.
  9. Un dios de los indios taínos.

E Answers will vary but may include:
  1. La niña hacía cosas de los españoles y de los indios.
  2. Rogaba a los dioses españoles y a los dioses indios.
  3. El padre veía los mismos reflejos liláceos de las tardes de Castilla.

441

Literatura 4

RESOURCES

- CD-ROM, Discs 1, 2, 3, 4, pages 442–447

National Standards

Cultures
Students experience, discuss, and analyze an expressive product of the culture: an excerpt from the novel of the Mexican Revolution, *Tierra*, by Gregorio López y Fuentes.

¡OJO! You can present this story to the entire class, or have students read it silently and do the **Después de leer** activities on their own.

TIERRA

TEACHING VOCABULARY

A. Have students open their books to page 442. Have them repeat the new vocabulary words after you.

B. Quickly go over **Práctica A** and **Práctica B** on page 443 orally to make sure that the students can recognize the vocabulary for receptive purposes.

442

TIERRA
de Gregorio López y Fuentes

Vocabulario

el portal   puerta principal
el tianguis   un mercado indio
el corneta   soldado que toca la corneta
el cabo   rango inferior al de sargento

voltear   dar la vuelta
alargarse   hacer más largo
la esperanza   *hope*

442 ∽ *cuatrocientos cuarenta y dos*

LITERATURA

⟡Práctica⟡

A **La hacienda** Completen.

1. En ese espacio grande los indios hacían el _____; compraban y vendían sus productos.
2. Cuando abrieron el _____ todos entraron al patio.
3. Cerca del patio estaba la _____ donde estaban los caballos y los coches.
4. Había seis soldados, un _____ y un sargento.
5. El sargento no tenía barba, pero sí tenía un gran _____.

B **¿Cuál es?** Expliquen.

1. ¿Cuáles son dos suboficiales militares?
2. ¿Cuál será la diferencia entre «el corneta» y «la corneta»?

Una hacienda, Cocoyoc, México

Literatura 4

⟡Práctica⟡

A Have students point to the objects in the illustration on page 442 as they answer each item in **Práctica A.**

B In **Práctica B,** Item 2, have students identify the two terms using the illustration on page 442.

ABOUT THE SPANISH LANGUAGE

The word **tianguis** comes from the Aztec **tianquiztli.** It is not a physical market, in the sense of a building or structure. In the story, the author says **un espacio... en él** *se hace* **el tianguis.** It is a place where the indigenous people gather on fixed days to buy and sell.

ANSWERS

Práctica

A 1. **tianguis**
 2. **portal**
 3. **cuadra**
 4. **cabo**
 5. **bigote**

B 1. **el cabo, el sargento**
 2. **«El corneta» es la persona que toca «la corneta».**

Literatura 4

DISCUSSING LITERATURE

INTRODUCCIÓN

You may go over the **Introducción** with the class or you may decide to omit it and just have them read the story.

Tierra

A. You may wish to have students take a few minutes to read each paragraph silently before going over it orally in class.

B. Since this reading is rather long, you may wish to go over only certain sections orally and just have students read the other parts silently.

C. Call on a more able student to give a synopsis of each paragraph. This helps less able students understand the selection.

Estatua de Emiliano Zapata, Chinameca, México

TIERRA (FRAGMENTO)
de Gregorio López y Fuentes

INTRODUCCIÓN Gregorio López y Fuentes (1895–1966) escribió la novela *Tierra* inspirada en la lucha de Emiliano Zapata por los indígenas del sur de México. Zapata fue traicionado y asesinado por tropas bajo el mando del Coronel Jesús María Guajardo. Guajardo le invitó a Zapata a cenar con él en la hacienda de Chinameca. Le dijo que quería unirse a su movimiento. El fragmento que sigue nos dice lo que pasó.

Emiliano Zapata

Tierra

La casa de la hacienda, en Chinameca, es enorme, con un portal inmenso. Tiene habitaciones para las visitas y una gran cuadra para coches y caballos. Frente a la casa, un espacio cuadrangular, tan grande, que en él se hace el tianguis. El rectángulo está encerrado por una muralla. A derecha e izquierda, la muralla tiene anchas puertas. En Chinameca esperaba Guajardo al general Zapata. Dentro de la casa estaban los soldados, situados en los mejores y más ocultos lugares. La persona que llegara no vería más que seis hombres armados en cada una de las puertas de la muralla. Allí también había un corneta.

El general Zapata tardaba en llegar. Pronto llegó un emisario. No se le permitió entrar. Pocos momentos después comenzó a llegar la escolta del general. También a estos hombres se les negó entrar al patio. Los soldados tenían órdenes de no dejarlos pasar porque tenían que hacer los honores al jefe. El general entraría por la puerta derecha. Los seis soldados estaban formados impecablemente, en actitud de firmes.

Apareció el jefe. Se le conocía por la bravura de su caballo, por sus grandes bigotes y por algo que siempre se nota en los acompañantes de un jefe. Cuando estaban a veinte metros de la puerta el corneta comenzó a tocar «marcha de honor». En cuanto sonó la corneta el cabo ordenó con voz enérgica:
—Presenten... ¡armas!

El caballo se adelantó, todo nervioso, todo electrizado con el toque de la corneta. Los soldados seguían presentando armas. El general había avanzado cinco metros y estaba dentro del patio. Entonces, los seis hombres que presentaban armas hicieron un pequeño movimiento,... y se escuchó una descarga.

LITERATURA

443

El general Zapata, violentamente, intentó voltear el caballo, quizás con la idea de salir de allí. Pero él se quedó a la mitad del movimiento. Se cayó al suelo. Pero el animal salió y se escapó. El cabo se acercó al general. Con la carabina le dio el tiro de gracia. Pusieron el cadáver en una mula. Los pies por un lado y los brazos por el otro lado. Tomaron el camino a Cuautla. Al trotar de la mula, las piernas hacían un movimiento como el de andar, como si Zapata seguía corriendo por el Estado de Morelos. Los brazos parecían alargarse, quizás queriendo tocar la tierra para sus muchachos, por la que tanto luchó, tan cerca y al mismo tiempo tan distante.

En Cuautla fue exhibido el cadáver y en voz baja comenzó la leyenda:

No es el general.

¡No va a ser! Está así, deformado, por haber venido como vino. La sangre se le fue a la cabeza.

No, compadre, el general tenía una seña muy particular, allí en la cara, y éste no la tiene.

¡Claro! Allí mismo le entró el tiro de gracia.

¡Quién sabe!

Y el «quién sabe» lleno de esperanzas, era como un lamento. Pero otros decían, muy contentos: —¡Vaya, por fin cayó este bandido!

Hacienda de San Juan Bautista, Taxco, México

HISTORY CONNECTION

Un héroe mexicano Emiliano Zapata was one of the giants of the Mexican Revolution of the first two decades of this century. He was born in 1883 in San Miguel Anenencuilco and died in Chinameca in 1919. He was a fighter for agrarian reform. He wanted to wrest the land from wealthy landowners and distribute it to the peasants.

FINE ART CONNECTION

Emiliano Zapata You may wish to show the Fine Art Transparencies entitled **"Campamento Zapatista"** (F-9) and **"Emiliano Zapata"** (F-12) from the Transparency Binder for **¡Buen viaje! Level 3.** You may also want students to do the activities accompanying these transparencies.

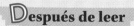

Después de leer

Note Students should read the entire selection before doing the **Después de leer** activities.

Después de leer

A **Estudio de palabras**   Pareen.

1. el espacio		**a.** lament
2. encerrado		**b.** discharge, gunshot
3. oculto		**c.** companion
4. armado		**d.** space
5. el emisario		**e.** enclosed
6. impecablemente		**f.** occult, hidden
7. en actitud de firmes		**g.** deformed
8. el acompañante		**h.** armed
9. avanzar		**i.** to trot
10. la descarga		**j.** to advance
11. trotar		**k.** emissary, representative
12. deformado		**l.** impeccably, perfectly
13. el lamento		**m.** escort
14. la escolta		**n.** at attention

B **¿Sí o no?**   Si no es verdad, hagan la corrección.

1. La casa de la hacienda en Chinameca es pequeña.
2. El portal de la casa es grande.
3. El tianguis se hace en un espacio enfrente de la casa.
4. El espacio donde se hace el tianguis es triangular.
5. Guajardo era general.
6. La casa donde Guajardo esperaba estaba en Chinameca.

C **La palabra, por favor.**   Escojan.

1. Alrededor del espacio donde hacían el tianguis había _____.
   a. una cuadra   **b.** una muralla   **c.** un portal

2. La muralla tiene dos _____, una a la derecha y la otra a la izquierda.
   a. puertas   **b.** habitaciones   **c.** cornetas

3. Los soldados dentro de la casa estaban en lugares muy _____.
   a. anchos   **b.** firmes   **c.** ocultos

4. Antes de llegar el general, llegó un _____.
   a. cabo   **b.** emisario   **c.** soldado

5. En la cara del general se le veía unos grandes _____.
   a. ojos   **b.** bigotes   **c.** tiros

ANSWERS

Después de leer

A 1. d   8. c
2. e   9. j
3. f   10. b
4. h   11. i
5. k   12. g
6. l   13. a
7. n   14. m

B 1. La casa de la hacienda en Chinameca es enorme.
2. Sí.
3. Sí.
4. El espacio donde se hace el tianguis es cuadrangular.
5. Guajardo era coronel.
6. Sí.

C 1. b
2. a
3. c
4. b
5. b

445

D Comprensión Completen.

1. Al llegar a la casa, una persona podría ver solamente a _____ soldados.
2. Junto con los soldados había otro que tocaba la _____.
3. Primero llegó el emisario del general y después llegaron los hombres de su _____.
4. Pero ni al emisario ni a la escolta les permitieron _____.
5. El general iba a entrar por la puerta de la _____.

E Discusión Reaccionen.

1. En tus propias palabras explica las dos oraciones que comienzan con: «Al trotar de la mula... » y terminan con «... tan cerca y al mismo tiempo tan distante».
2. ¿Cómo reaccionó la gente en Cuautla al ver el cadáver?

F Interpretación ¿Qué crees que representan los comentarios de la gente de Cuautla?

Las tropas de Emiliano Zapata

ANSWERS

D 1. **seis**
   2. **corneta**
   3. **escolta**
   4. **entrar**
   5. **derecha**

E Answers will vary.

F Answers will vary.

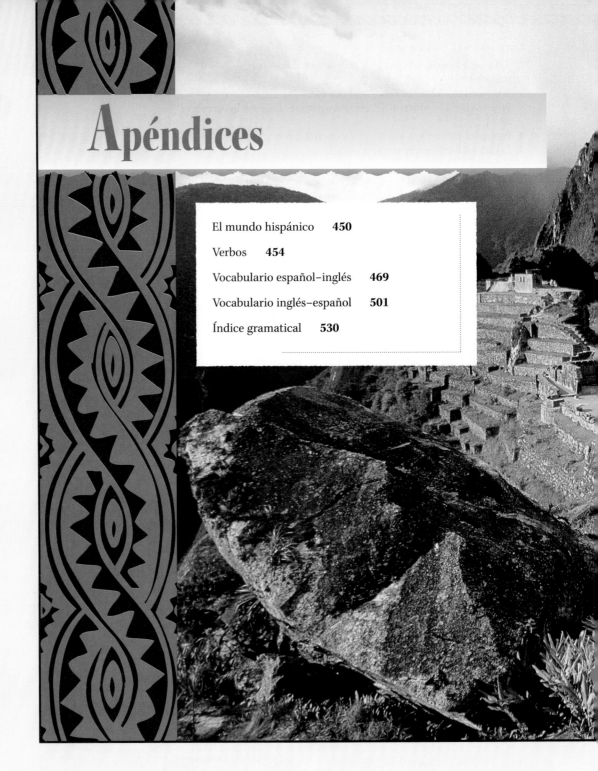

Apéndices

447

El mundo hispánico

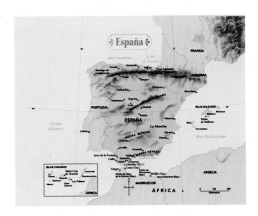

PAÍS	CAPITAL
Argentina	Buenos Aires
Belice	Belmopan
Bolivia	Sucre
Chile	Santiago
Colombia	Santafé de Bogotá
Costa Rica	San José
Cuba	La Habana
Ecuador	Quito
El Salvador	San Salvador
España	Madrid
Guatemala	Guatemala
Honduras	Tegucigalpa
México	México
Nicaragua	Managua
Panamá	Panamá
Paraguay	Asunción
Perú	Lima
Puerto Rico	San Juan
República Dominicana	Santo Domingo
Uruguay	Montivideo
Venezuela	Caracas

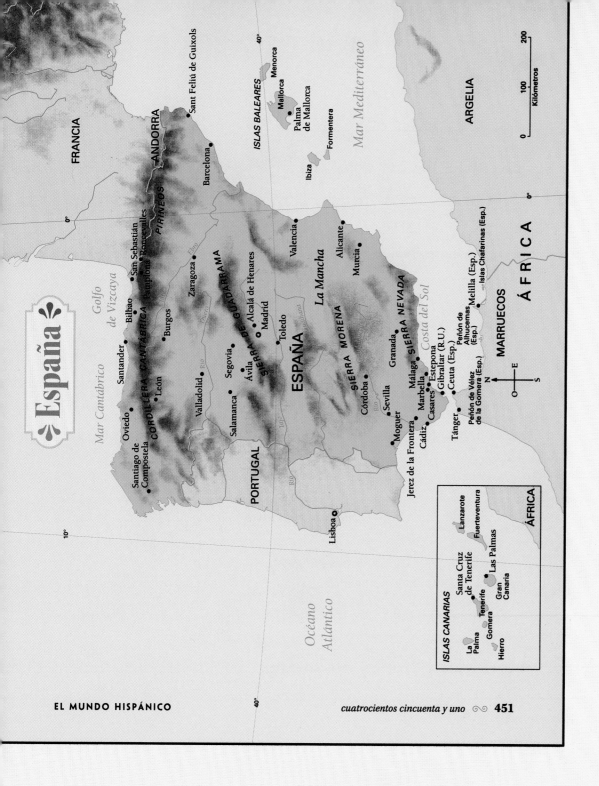

España

FRANCIA

Mar Cantábrico

Golfo de Vizcaya

ANDORRA

PIRINEOS

Santiago de Compostela

Oviedo

Santander

Bilbao

San Sebastián

Pamplona

Roncesvalles

CORDILLERA CANTÁBRICA

León

Burgos

Zaragoza

Río Ebro

Valladolid

Salamanca

Segovia

Ávila

SIERRA DE GUADARRAMA

Alcalá de Henares

Madrid

Río Tajo

Toledo

ESPAÑA

PORTUGAL

Río

Lisboa

La Mancha

SIERRA MORENA

Córdoba

Sevilla

Moguer

Jerez de la Frontera

Cádiz

Marbella

Casares

Estepona

Gibraltar (R.U.)

Ceuta (Esp.)

Tánger

Málaga

SIERRA NEVADA

Granada

Costa del Sol

Valencia

Alicante

Murcia

Mar Mediterráneo

ISLAS BALEARES

Menorca

Mallorca

Palma de Mallorca

Ibiza

Formentera

Sant Feliú de Guixols

Barcelona

ARGELIA

ÁFRICA

MARRUECOS

Peñón de Vélez de la Gomera (Esp.)

Peñón de Alhucemas (Esp.)

Melilla (Esp.)

Islas Chafarinas (Esp.)

Océano Atlántico

ISLAS CANARIAS

La Palma

Santa Cruz de Tenerife

Gomera

Tenerife

Hierro

Lanzarote

Fuerteventura

Las Palmas

Gran Canaria

ÁFRICA

N

O

E

S

0 100 200

Kilómetros

40°

10°

0°

40°

❧ La América del Sur ❧

Mar Caribe

Océano Atlántico

Océano Pacífico

Maracaibo
Cartagena
Caracas
VENEZUELA
GUYANA
Medellín
Georgetown
SURINAM
Tolima
Santafé de Bogotá
Paramaribo
Cayena
Cali
COLOMBIA
GUAYANA FRANCESA

Islas Galápagos (Ecuador)

Otavalo
Quito
Volcán Cotopaxi
ECUADOR
Guayaquil
Cuenca
Iquitos

Río Orinoco

Río Amazonas

BRASIL

PERÚ
Lima
MACHU PICCHU
Cuzco
Pisac
Brasilia
Miraflores
BOLIVIA
Ica
La Paz
TIWANAKU
Sucre

São Paulo
Río de Janeiro
PARAGUAY
Salta
Asunción

Vicuña
Córdoba
URUGUAY
Viña del Mar
Mendoza
Valparaíso
Rosario
Montevideo
Santiago
Buenos Aires
CHILE
ARGENTINA

Lago Villarrica
Pucón
Mar del Plata

Puerto Montt
Bariloche
Chiloé

CORDILLERA DE LOS ANDES

ATACAMA DESERT

PATAGONIA

Islas Malvinas (R.U.)

| 0 | 500 | 1000 |
Kilómetros

N
O · E
S

PARQUE NACIONAL TORRES DEL PAINE
Punta Arenas

452 ∾ *cuatrocientos cincuenta y dos*

EL MUNDO HISPÁNICO

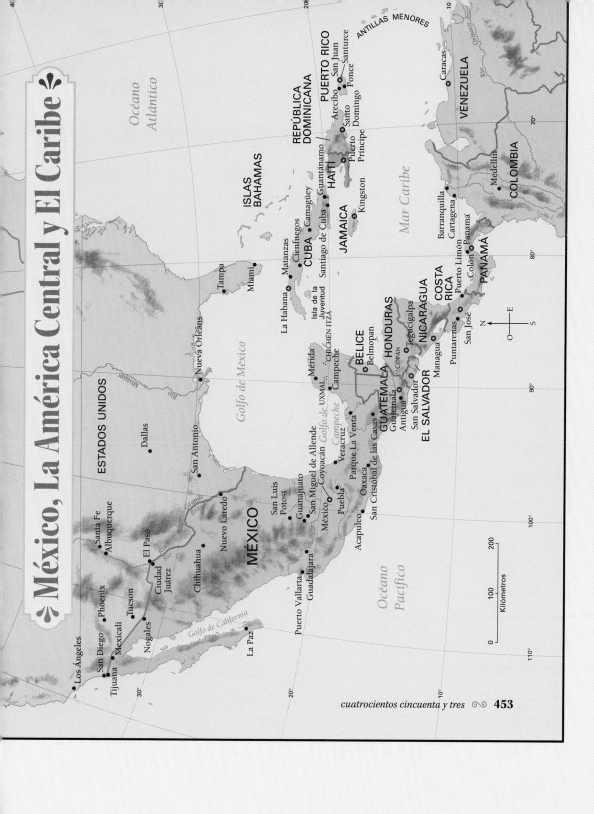

México, La América Central y El Caribe

Océano Atlántico

ESTADOS UNIDOS

Los Angeles
San Diego
Tijuana
Mexicali
Nogales
Phoenix
Tucson
Santa Fe
Albuquerque
El Paso
Ciudad Juárez
Chihuahua
Nuevo Laredo
San Antonio
Dallas
Nueva Orléans

Río Grande / Río Bravo

Golfo de California
La Paz
Puerto Vallarta
Guadalajara

MÉXICO

San Luis Potosí
Guanajuato
San Miguel de Allende
México
Coyoacán
Puebla
Acapulco
Oaxaca
San Cristóbal de las Casas
Mérida
Veracruz
Parque La Venta
Campeche

UXMAL
CHICHÉN ITZÁ

Golfo de México

Tampa
Miami

ISLAS BAHAMAS

La Habana
Matanzas
Cienfuegos
Isla de la Juventud

CUBA
Camagüey
Santiago de Cuba

JAMAICA
Kingston

Mar Caribe

REPÚBLICA DOMINICANA
HAITÍ
Puerto Príncipe
Santo Domingo
Guantánamo

PUERTO RICO
Arecibo
San Juan
Santurce
Ponce

ANTILLAS MENORES

VENEZUELA
Caracas
Medellín
COLOMBIA
Barranquilla
Cartagena

Golfo de Campeche

BELICE
Belmopan

GUATEMALA
Guatemala
Antigua
COPÁN
San Salvador
EL SALVADOR

HONDURAS
Tegucigalpa

NICARAGUA
Managua

COSTA RICA
Puntarenas
Puerto Limón
San José

PANAMÁ
Colón
Panamá

Océano Pacífico

N
O   E
S

0   100   200
Kilómetros

cuatrocientos cincuenta y tres ❧ **453**

Verbos

453

Verbos regulares

INFINITIVO	hablar *to speak*	comer *to eat*	vivir *to live*
PRESENTE PROGRESIVO	estar hablando	estar comiendo	estar viviendo
PRESENTE	yo hablo tú hablas él, ella, Ud. habla nosotros(as) hablamos *vosotros(as) habláis* ellos, ellas, Uds. hablan	yo como tú comes él, ella, Ud. come nosotros(as) comemos *vosotros(as) coméis* ellos, ellas, Uds. comen	yo vivo tú vives él, ella, Ud. vive nosotros(as) vivimos *vosotros(as) vivís* ellos, ellas, Uds. viven
PRETÉRITO	yo hablé tú hablaste él, ella, Ud. habló nosotros(as) hablamos *vosotros(as) hablasteis* ellos, ellas, Uds. hablaron	yo comí tú comiste él, ella, Ud. comió nosotros(as) comimos *vosotros(as) comisteis* ellos, ellas, Uds. comieron	yo viví tú viviste él, ella, Ud. vivió nosotros(as) vivimos *vosotros(as) vivisteis* ellos, ellas, Uds. vivieron
IMPERFECTO	yo hablaba tú hablabas él, ella, Ud. hablaba nosotros(as) hablábamos *vosotros(as) hablabais* ellos, ellas, Uds. hablaban	yo comía tú comías él, ella, Ud. comía nosotros(as) comíamos *vosotros(as) comíais* ellos, ellas, Uds. comían	yo vivía tú vivías él, ella, Ud. vivía nosotros(as) vivíamos *vosotros(as) vivíais* ellos, ellas, Uds. vivían
FUTURO	yo hablaré tú hablarás él, ella, Ud. hablará nosotros(as) hablaremos *vosotros(as) hablaréis* ellos, ellas, Uds. hablarán	yo comeré tú comerás él, ella, Ud. comerá nosotros(as) comeremos *vosotros(as) comeréis* ellos, ellas, Uds. comerán	yo viviré tú vivirás él, ella, Ud. vivirá nosotros(as) viviremos *vosotros(as) viviréis* ellos, ellas, Uds. vivirán
POTENCIAL	yo hablaría tú hablarías él, ella, Ud. hablaría nosotros(as) hablaríamos *vosotros(as) hablaríais* ellos, ellas, Uds. hablarían	yo comería tú comerías él, ella, Ud. comería nosotros(as) comeríamos *vosotros(as) comeríais* ellos, ellas, Uds. comerían	yo viviría tú vivirías él, ella, Ud. viviría nosotros(as) viviríamos *vosotros(as) viviríais* ellos, ellas, Uds. vivirían
PRESENTE PERFECTO	yo he hablado tú has hablado él, ella, Ud. ha hablado nosotros(as) hemos hablado *vosotros(as) habéis hablado* ellos, ellas, Uds. han hablado	yo he comido tú has comido él, ella, Ud. ha comido nosotros(as) hemos comido *vosotros(as) habéis comido* ellos, ellas, Uds. han comido	yo he vivido tú has vivido él, ella, Ud. ha vivido nosotros(as) hemos vivido *vosotros(as) habéis vivido* ellos, ellas, Uds. han vivido
SUBJUNTIVO PRESENTE	yo hable tú hables él, ella, Ud. hable nosotros(as) hablemos *vosotros(as) habléis* ellos, ellas, Uds. hablen	yo coma tú comas él, ella, Ud. coma nosotros(as) comamos *vosotros(as) comáis* ellos, ellas, Uds. coman	yo viva tú vivas él, ella, Ud. viva nosotros(as) vivamos *vosotros(as) viváis* ellos, ellas, Uds. vivan
IMPERATIVO FORMAL	hable (Ud.) hablen (Uds.)	coma (Ud.) coman (Uds.)	viva (Ud.) vivan (Uds.)
IMPERATIVO FAMILIAR	habla (tú)	come (tú)	vive (tú)

[1] Verbos con gerundio irregular: *caer: cayendo, construir: construyendo, contribuir: contribuyendo, distribuir: distribuyendo*

[2] Verbos con participio pasado irregular: *abrir: abierto, cubrir: cubierto, devolver: devuelto, escribir: escrito, freír: frito, morir: muerto, ver: visto*

Verbos con cambio radical

INFINITIVO	preferir³ (e>ie) *to prefer*	volver⁴ (o>ue) *to return*	pedir⁵ (e>i) *to ask for*
PRESENTE PROGRESIVO	estar prefiriendo	estar volviendo	estar pidiendo
PRESENTE	yo prefiero tú prefieres él, ella, Ud. prefiere nosotros(as) preferimos *vosotros(as) preferís* ellos, ellas, Uds. prefieren	yo vuelvo tú vuelves él, ella, Ud. vuelve nosotros(as) volvemos *vosotros(as) volvéis* ellos, ellas, Uds. vuelven	yo pido tú pides él, ella, Ud. pide nosotros(as) pedimos *vosotros(as) pedís* ellos, ellas, Uds. piden
PRETÉRITO	yo preferí tú preferiste él, ella, Ud. prefirió nosotros(as) preferimos *vosotros(as) preferisteis* ellos, ellas, Uds. prefirieron	yo volví tú volviste él, ella, Ud. volvió nosotros(as) volvimos *vosotros(as) volvisteis* ellos, ellas, Uds. volvieron	yo pedí tú pediste él, ella, Ud. pidió nosotros(as) pedimos *vosotros(as) pedisteis* ellos, ellas, Uds. pidieron
IMPERFECTO	yo prefería tú preferías él, ella, Ud. prefería nosotros(as) preferíamos *vosotros(as) preferíais* ellos, ellas, Uds. preferían	yo volvía tú volvías él, ella, Ud. volvía nosotros(as) volvíamos *vosotros(as) volvíais* ellos, ellas, Uds. volvían	yo pedía tú pedías él, ella, Ud. pedía nosotros(as) pedíamos *vosotros(as) pedíais* ellos, ellas, Uds. pedían
FUTURO	yo preferiré tú preferirás él, ella, Ud. preferirá nosotros(as) preferiremos *vosotros(as) preferiréis* ellos, ellas, Uds. preferirán	yo volveré tú volverás él, ella, Ud. volverá nosotros(as) volveremos *vosotros(as) volveréis* ellos, ellas, Uds. volverán	yo pediré tú pedirás él, ella, Ud. pedirá nosotros(as) pediremos *vosotros(as) pediréis* ellos, ellas, Uds. pedirán
POTENCIAL	yo preferiría tú preferirías él, ella, Ud. preferiría nosotros(as) preferiríamos *vosotros(as) preferiríais* ellos, ellas, Uds. preferirían	yo volvería tú volverías él, ella, Ud. volvería nosotros(as) volveríamos *vosotros(as) volveríais* ellos, ellas, Uds. volverían	yo pediría tú pedirías él, ella, Ud. pediría nosotros(as) pediríamos *vosotros(as) pediríais* ellos, ellas, Uds. pedirían
PRESENTE PERFECTO	yo he preferido tú has preferido él, ella, Ud. ha preferido nosotros(as) hemos preferido *vosotros(as) habéis preferido* ellos, ellas, Uds. han preferido	yo he vuelto tú has vuelto él, ella, Ud. ha vuelto nosotros(as) hemos vuelto *vosotros(as) habéis vuelto* ellos, ellas, Uds. han vuelto	yo he pedido tú has pedido él, ella, Ud. ha pedido nosotros(as) hemos pedido *vosotros(as) habéis pedido* ellos, ellas, Uds. han pedido
SUBJUNTIVO PRESENTE	yo prefiriera tú prefirieras él, ella, Ud. prefiriera nosotros(as) prefiriéramos *vosotros(as) prefirierais* ellos, ellas, Uds. prefirieran	yo volviera tú volvieras él, ella, Ud. volviera nosotros(as) volviéramos *vosotros(as) volvierais* ellos, ellas, Uds. volvieran	yo pidiera tú pidieras él, ella, Ud. pidiera nosotros(as) pidiéramos *vosotros(as) pidierais* ellos, ellas, Uds. pidieran
IMPERATIVO FORMAL	prefiera (Ud.) prefieran (Uds.)	vuelva (Ud.) vuelvan (Uds.)	pida (Ud.) pidan (Uds.)
IMPERATIVO FAMILIAR	prefiere (tú)	vuelve (tú)	pide (tú)

³ **Verbos similares:** *sugerir: sugiriendo*

⁴ **Verbos similares:** *morir: muriendo, jugar*

⁵ **Verbos similares:** *freír: friendo, pedir: pidiendo, repetir: repitiendo, seguir: siguiendo, sentir: sintiendo, servir: sirviendo*

Verbos irregulares

INFINITIVO	andar *to walk*	conocer *to know*	dar *to give*
PRESENTE PROGRESIVO	estar andando	estar conociendo	estar dando
PRESENTE	yo ando tú andas él, ella, Ud. anda nosotros(as) andamos *vosotros(as) andáis* ellos, ellas, Uds. andan	yo conozco tú conoces él, ella, Ud. conoce nosotros(as) conocemos *vosotros(as) conocéis* ellos, ellas, Uds. conocen	yo doy tú das él, ella, Ud. da nosotros(as) damos *vosotros(as) dais* ellos, ellas, Uds. dan
PRETÉRITO	yo anduve tú anduviste él, ella, Ud. anduvo nosotros(as) anduvimos *vosotros(as) anduvisteis* ellos, ellas, Uds. anduvieron	yo conocí tú conociste él, ella, Ud. conoció nosotros(as) conocimos *vosotros(as) conocisteis* ellos, ellas, Uds. conocieron	yo di tú diste él, ella, Ud. dio nosotros(as) dimos *vosotros(as) disteis* ellos, ellas, Uds. dieron
IMPERFECTO	yo andaba tú andabas él, ella, Ud. andaba nosotros(as) andábamos *vosotros(as) andabais* ellos, ellas, Uds. andaban	yo conocía tú conocías él, ella, Ud. conocía nosotros(as) conocíamos *vosotros(as) conocíais* ellos, ellas, Uds. conocían	yo daba tú dabas él, ella, Ud. daba nosotros(as) dábamos *vosotros(as) dabais* ellos, ellas, Uds. daban
FUTURO	yo andaré tú andarás él, ella, Ud. andará nosotros(as) andaremos *vosotros(as) andaréis* ellos, ellas, Uds. andarán	yo conoceré tú conocerás él, ella, Ud. conocerá nosotros(as) conoceremos *vosotros(as) conoceréis* ellos, ellas, Uds. conocerán	yo daré tú darás él, ella, Ud. dará nosotros(as) daremos *vosotros(as) daréis* ellos, ellas, Uds. darán
POTENCIAL	yo andaría tú andarías él, ella, Ud. andaría nosotros(as) andaríamos *vosotros(as) andaríais* ellos, ellas, Uds. andarían	yo conocería tú conocerías él, ella, Ud. conocería nosotros(as) conoceríamos *vosotros(as) conoceríais* ellos, ellas, Uds. conocerían	yo daría tú darías él, ella, Ud. daría nosotros(as) daríamos *vosotros(as) daríais* ellos, ellas, Uds. darían
PRESENTE PERFECTO	yo he andado tú has andado él, ella, Ud. ha andado nosotros(as) hemos andado *vosotros(as) habéis andado* ellos, ellas, Uds. han andado	yo he conocido tú has conocido él, ella, Ud. ha conocido nosotros(as) hemos conocido *vosotros(as) habéis conocido* ellos, ellas, Uds. han conocido	yo he dado tú has dado él, ella, Ud. ha dado nosotros(as) hemos dado *vosotros(as) habéis dado* ellos, ellas, Uds. han dado
SUBJUNTIVO PRESENTE	yo ande tú andes él, ella, Ud. ande nosotros(as) andemos *vosotros(as) andéis* ellos, ellas, Uds. anden	yo conozca tú conozcas él, ella, Ud. conozca nosotros(as) conozcamos *vosotros(as) conozcáis* ellos, ellas, Uds. conozcan	yo dé tú des él, ella, Ud. dé nosotros(as) demos *vosotros(as) deis* ellos, ellas, Uds. den
IMPERATIVO FORMAL	ande (Ud.) anden (Uds.)	conozca (Ud.) conozcan (Uds.)	dé (Ud.) den (Uds.)
IMPERATIVO FAMILIAR	anda (tú)	conoce (tú)	da (tú)

Verbos irregulares

INFINITIVO	decir *to say, to tell*	empezar *to begin*	estar *to be*
PRESENTE PROGRESIVO	estar diciendo	estar empezando	
PRESENTE	yo digo tú dices él, ella, Ud. dice nosotros(as) decimos *vosotros(as) decís* ellos, ellas, Uds. dicen	yo empiezo tú empiezas él, ella, Ud. empieza nosotros(as) empezamos *vosotros(as) empezáis* ellos, ellas, Uds. empiezan	yo estoy tú estás él, ella, Ud. está nosotros(as) estamos *vosotros(as) estáis* ellos, ellas, Uds. están
PRETÉRITO	yo dije tú dijiste él, ella, Ud. dijo nosotros(as) dijimos *vosotros(as) dijisteis* ellos, ellas, Uds. dijeron	yo empecé tú empezaste él, ella, Ud. empezó nosotros(as) empezamos *vosotros(as) empezasteis* ellos, ellas, Uds. empezaron	yo estuve tú estuviste él, ella, Ud. estuvo nosotros(as) estuvimos *vosotros(as) estuvisteis* ellos, ellas, Uds. estuvieron
IMPERFECTO	yo decía tú decías él, ella, Ud. decía nosotros(as) decíamos *vosotros(as) decíais* ellos, ellas, Uds. decían	yo empezaba tú empezabas él, ella, Ud. empezaba nosotros(as) empezábamos *vosotros(as) empezabais* ellos, ellas, Uds. empezaban	yo estaba tú estabas él, ella, Ud. estaba nosotros(as) estábamos *vosotros(as) estabais* ellos, ellas, Uds. estaban
FUTURO	yo diré tú dirás él, ella, Ud. dirá nosotros(as) diremos *vosotros(as) diréis* ellos, ellas, Uds. dirán	yo empezaré tú empezarás él, ella, Ud. empezará nosotros(as) empezaremos *vosotros(as) empezaréis* ellos, ellas, Uds. empezarán	yo estaré tú estarás él, ella, Ud. estará nosotros(as) estaremos *vosotros(as) estaréis* ellos, ellas, Uds. estarán
POTENCIAL	yo diría tú dirías él, ella, Ud. diría nosotros(as) diríamos *vosotros(as) diríais* ellos, ellas, Uds. dirían	yo empezaría tú empezarías él, ella, Ud. empezaría nosotros(as) empezaríamos *vosotros(as) empezaríais* ellos, ellas, Uds. empezarían	yo estaría tú estarías él, ella, Ud. estaría nosotros(as) estaríamos *vosotros(as) estaríais* ellos, ellas, Uds. estarían
PRESENTE PERFECTO	yo he dicho tú has dicho él, ella, Ud. ha dicho nosotros(as) hemos dicho *vosotros(as) habéis dicho* ellos, ellas, Uds. han dicho	yo he empezado tú has empezado él, ella, Ud. ha empezado nosotros(as) hemos empezado *vosotros(as) habéis empezado* ellos, ellas, Uds. han empezado	yo he estado tú has estado él, ella, Ud. ha estado nosotros(as) hemos estado *vosotros(as) habéis estado* ellos, ellas, Uds. han estado
SUBJUNTIVO PRESENTE	yo diga tú digas él, ella, Ud. diga nosotros(as) digamos *vosotros(as) digáis* ellos, ellas, Uds. digan	yo empiece tú empieces él, ella, Ud. empiece nosotros(as) empecemos *vosotros(as) empecéis* ellos, ellas, Uds. empiecen	yo esté tú estés él, ella, Ud. esté nosotros(as) estemos *vosotros(as) estéis* ellos, ellas, Uds. estén
IMPERATIVO FORMAL	diga (Ud.) digan (Uds.)	empiece (Ud.) empiecen (Uds.)	esté (Ud.) estén (Uds.)
IMPERATIVO FAMILIAR	di (tú)	empieza (tú)	está (tú)

457

Verbos irregulares

INFINITIVO	hacer *to do*	ir *to go*	leer *to read*
PRESENTE PROGRESIVO	estar haciendo	estar yendo	estar leyendo
PRESENTE	yo hago tú haces él, ella, Ud. hace nosotros(as) hacemos *vosotros(as) hacéis* ellos, ellas, Uds. hacen	yo voy tú vas él, ella, Ud. va nosotros(as) vamos *vosotros(as) vais* ellos, ellas, Uds. van	yo leo tú lees él, ella, Ud. lee nosotros(as) leemos *vosotros(as) leéis* ellos, ellas, Uds. leen
PRETÉRITO	yo hice tú hiciste él, ella, Ud. hizo nosotros(as) hicimos *vosotros(as) hicisteis* ellos, ellas, Uds. hicieron	yo fui tú fuiste él, ella, Ud. fue nosotros(as) fuimos *vosotros(as) fuisteis* ellos, ellas, Uds. fueron	yo leí tú leíste él, ella, Ud. leyó nosotros(as) leímos *vosotros(as) leísteis* ellos, ellas, Uds. leyeron
IMPERFECTO	yo hacía tú hacías él, ella, Ud. hacía nosotros(as) hacíamos *vosotros(as) hacíais* ellos, ellas, Uds. hacían	yo iba tú ibas él, ella, Ud. iba nosotros(as) íbamos *vosotros(as) ibais* ellos, ellas, Uds. iban	yo leía tú leías él, ella, Ud. leía nosotros(as) leíamos *vosotros(as) leíais* ellos, ellas, Uds. leían
FUTURO	yo haré tú harás él, ella, Ud. hará nosotros(as) haremos *vosotros(as) haréis* ellos, ellas, Uds. harán	yo iré tú irás él, ella, Ud. irá nosotros(as) iremos *vosotros(as) iréis* ellos, ellas, Uds. irán	yo leeré tú leerás él, ella, Ud. leerá nosotros(as) leeremos *vosotros(as) leeréis* ellos, ellas, Uds. leerán
POTENCIAL	yo haría tú harías él, ella, Ud. haría nosotros(as) haríamos *vosotros(as) haríais* ellos, ellas, Uds. harían	yo iría tú irías él, ella, Ud. iría nosotros(as) iríamos *vosotros(as) iríais* ellos, ellas, Uds. irían	yo leería tú leerías él, ella, Ud. leería nosotros(as) leeríamos *vosotros(as) leeríais* ellos, ellas, Uds. leerían
PRESENTE PERFECTO	yo he hecho tú has hecho él, ella, Ud. ha hecho nosotros(as) hemos hecho *vosotros(as) habéis hecho* ellos, ellas, Uds. han hecho	yo he ido tú has ido él, ella, Ud. ha ido nosotros(as) hemos ido *vosotros(as) habéis ido* ellos, ellas, Uds. han ido	yo he leído tú has leído él, ella, Ud. ha leído nosotros(as) hemos leído *vosotros(as) habéis leído* ellos, ellas, Uds. han leído
SUBJUNTIVO PRESENTE	yo haga tú hagas él, ella, Ud. haga nosotros(as) hagamos *vosotros(as) hagáis* ellos, ellas, Uds. hagan	yo vaya tú vayas él, ella, Ud. vaya nosotros(as) vayamos *vosotros(as) vayáis* ellos, ellas, Uds. vayan	yo lea tú leas él, ella, Ud. lea nosotros(as) leamos *vosotros(as) leáis* ellos, ellas, Uds. lean
IMPERATIVO FORMAL	haga (Ud.) hagan (Uds.)	vaya (Ud.) vayan (Uds.)	lea (Ud.) lean (Uds.)
IMPERATIVO FAMILIAR	haz (tú)	ve (tú)	lee (tú)

Verbos irregulares

INFINITIVO	oír *to hear*	poder *to be able*	poner *to put*
PRESENTE PROGRESIVO	estar oyendo		estar poniendo
PRESENTE	yo oigo tú oyes él, ella, Ud. oye nosotros(as) oímos *vosotros(as) oís* ellos, ellas, Uds. oyen	yo puedo tú puedes él, ella, Ud. puede nosotros(as) podemos *vosotros(as) podéis* ellos, ellas, Uds. pueden	yo pongo tú pones él, ella, Ud. pone nosotros(as) ponemos *vosotros(as) ponéis* ellos, ellas, Uds. ponen
PRETÉRITO	yo oí tú oíste él, ella, Ud. oyó nosotros(as) oímos *vosotros(as) oísteis* ellos, ellas, Uds. oyeron	yo pude tú pudiste él, ella, Ud. pudo nosotros(as) pudimos *vosotros(as) pudisteis* ellos, ellas, Uds. pudieron	yo puse tú pusiste él, ella, Ud. puso nosotros(as) pusimos *vosotros(as) pusisteis* ellos, ellas, Uds. pusieron
IMPERFECTO	yo oía tú oías él, ella, Ud. oía nosotros(as) oíamos *vosotros(as) oíais* ellos, ellas, Uds. oían	yo podía tú podías él, ella, Ud. podía nosotros(as) podíamos *vosotros(as) podíais* ellos, ellas, Uds. podían	yo ponía tú ponías él, ella, Ud. ponía nosotros(as) poníamos *vosotros(as) poníais* ellos, ellas, Uds. ponían
FUTURO	yo oiré tú oirás él, ella, Ud. oirá nosotros(as) oiremos *vosotros(as) oiréis* ellos, ellas, Uds. oirán	yo podré tú podrás él, ella, Ud. podrá nosotros(as) podremos *vosotros(as) podréis* ellos, ellas, Uds. podrán	yo pondré tú pondrás él, ella, Ud. pondrá nosotros(as) pondremos *vosotros(as) pondréis* ellos, ellas, Uds. pondrán
POTENCIAL	yo oiría tú oirías él, ella, Ud. oiría nosotros(as) oiríamos *vosotros(as) oiríais* ellos, ellas, Uds. oirían	yo podría tú podrías él, ella, Ud. podría nosotros(as) podríamos *vosotros(as) podríais* ellos, ellas, Uds. podrían	yo pondría tú pondrías él, ella, Ud. pondría nosotros(as) pondríamos *vosotros(as) pondríais* ellos, ellas, Uds. pondrían
PRESENTE PERFECTO	yo he oído tú has oído él, ella, Ud. ha oído nosotros(as) hemos oído *vosotros(as) habéis oído* ellos, ellas, Uds. han oído	yo he podido tú has podido él, ella, Ud. ha podido nosotros(as) hemos podido *vosotros(as) habéis podido* ellos, ellas, Uds. han podido	yo he puesto tú has puesto él, ella, Ud. ha puesto nosotros(as) hemos puesto *vosotros(as) habéis puesto* ellos, ellas, Uds. han puesto
SUBJUNTIVO PRESENTE	yo oiga tú oigas él, ella, Ud. oiga nosotros(as) oigamos *vosotros(as) oigáis* ellos, ellas, Uds. oigan	yo pueda tú puedas él, ella, Ud. pueda nosotros(as) podamos *vosotros(as) podáis* ellos, ellas, Uds. puedan	yo ponga tú pongas él, ella, Ud. ponga nosotros(as) pongamos *vosotros(as) pongáis* ellos, ellas, Uds. pongan
IMPERATIVO FORMAL	oiga (Ud.) oigan (Uds.)	pueda (Ud.) puedan (Uds.)	ponga (Ud.) pongan (Uds.)
IMPERATIVO FAMILIAR	oye (tú)	puede (tú)	pon (tú)

459

Verbos irregulares

INFINITIVO	querer *to want*	saber *to know*	salir *to leave*
PRESENTE PROGRESIVO	estar queriendo	estar sabiendo	estar saliendo
PRESENTE	yo quiero tú quieres él, ella, Ud. quiere nosotros(as) queremos *vosotros(as) queréis* ellos, ellas, Uds. quieren	yo sé tú sabes él, ella, Ud. sabe nosotros(as) sabemos *vosotros(as) sabéis* ellos, ellas, Uds. saben	yo salgo tú sales él, ella, Ud. sale nosotros(as) salimos *vosotros(as) salís* ellos, ellas, Uds. salen
PRETÉRITO	yo quise tú quisiste él, ella, Ud. quiso nosotros(as) quisimos *vosotros(as) quisisteis* ellos, ellas, Uds. quisieron	yo supe tú supiste él, ella, Ud. supo nosotros(as) supimos *vosotros(as) supisteis* ellos, ellas, Uds. supieron	yo salí tú saliste él, ella, Ud. salió nosotros(as) salimos *vosotros(as) salisteis* ellos, ellas, Uds. salieron
IMPERFECTO	yo quería tú querías él, ella, Ud. quería nosotros(as) queríamos *vosotros(as) queríais* ellos, ellas, Uds. querían	yo sabía tú sabías él, ella, Ud. sabía nosotros(as) sabíamos *vosotros(as) sabíais* ellos, ellas, Uds. sabían	yo salía tú salías él, ella, Ud. salía nosotros(as) salíamos *vosotros(as) salíais* ellos, ellas, Uds. salían
FUTURO	yo querré tú querrás él, ella, Ud. querrá nosotros(as) querremos *vosotros(as) querréis* ellos, ellas, Uds. querrán	yo sabré tú sabrás él, ella, Ud. sabrá nosotros(as) sabremos *vosotros(as) sabréis* ellos, ellas, Uds. sabrán	yo saldré tú saldrás él, ella, Ud. saldrá nosotros(as) saldremos *vosotros(as) saldréis* ellos, ellas, Uds. saldrán
POTENCIAL	yo querría tú querrías él, ella, Ud. querría nosotros(as) querríamos *vosotros(as) querríais* ellos, ellas, Uds. querrían	yo sabría tú sabrías él, ella, Ud. sabría nosotros(as) sabríamos *vosotros(as) sabríais* ellos, ellas, Uds. sabrían	yo saldría tú saldrías él, ella, Ud. saldría nosotros(as) saldríamos *vosotros(as) saldríais* ellos, ellas, Uds. saldrían
PRESENTE PERFECTO	yo he querido tú has querido él, ella, Ud. ha querido nosotros(as) hemos querido *vosotros(as) habéis querido* ellos, ellas, Uds. han querido	yo he sabido tú has sabido él, ella, Ud. ha sabido nosotros(as) hemos sabido *vosotros(as) habéis sabido* ellos, ellas, Uds. han sabido	yo he salido tú has salido él, ella, Ud. ha salido nosotros(as) hemos salido *vosotros(as) habéis salido* ellos, ellas, Uds. han salido
SUBJUNTIVO PRESENTE	yo quiera tú quieras él, ella, Ud. quiera nosotros(as) queramos *vosotros(as) queráis* ellos, ellas, Uds. quieran	yo sepa tú sepas él, ella, Ud. sepa nosotros(as) sepamos *vosotros(as) sepáis* ellos, ellas, Uds. sepan	yo salga tú salgas él, ella, Ud. salga nosotros(as) salgamos *vosotros(as) salgáis* ellos, ellas, Uds. salgan
IMPERATIVO FORMAL	quiera (Ud.) quieran (Uds.)	sepa (Ud.) sepan (Uds.)	salga (Ud.) salgan (Uds.)
IMPERATIVO FAMILIAR	quiere (tú)	sabe (tú)	sal (tú)

Verbos irregulares

INFINITIVO	ser *to be*	tener *to have*	traer *to bring*
PRESENTE PROGRESIVO	estar siendo	estar teniendo	estar trayendo
PRESENTE	yo soy tú eres él, ella, Ud. es nosotros(as) somos *vosotros(as) sois* ellos, ellas, Uds. son	yo tengo tú tienes él, ella, Ud. tiene nosotros(as) tenemos *vosotros(as) tenéis* ellos, ellas, Uds. tienen	yo traigo tú traes él, ella, Ud. trae nosotros(as) traemos *vosotros(as) traéis* ellos, ellas, Uds. traen
PRETÉRITO	yo fui tú fuiste él, ella, Ud. fue nosotros(as) fuimos *vosotros(as) fuisteis* ellos, ellas, Uds. fueron	yo tuve tú tuviste él, ella, Ud. tuvo nosotros(as) tuvimos *vosotros(as) tuvisteis* ellos, ellas, Uds. tuvieron	yo traje tú trajiste él, ella, Ud. trajo nosotros(as) trajimos *vosotros(as) trajisteis* ellos, ellas, Uds. trajeron
IMPERFECTO	yo era tú eras él, ella, Ud. era nosotros(as) éramos *vosotros(as) erais* ellos, ellas, Uds. eran	yo tenía tú tenías él, ella, Ud. tenía nosotros(as) teníamos *vosotros(as) teníais* ellos, ellas, Uds. tenían	yo traía tú traías él, ella, Ud. traía nosotros(as) traíamos *vosotros(as) traíais* ellos, ellas, Uds. traían
FUTURO	yo seré tú serás él, ella, Ud. será nosotros(as) seremos *vosotros(as) seréis* ellos, ellas, Uds. serán	yo tendré tú tendrás él, ella, Ud. tendrá nosotros(as) tendremos *vosotros(as) tendréis* ellos, ellas, Uds. tendrán	yo traeré tú traerás él, ella, Ud. traerá nosotros(as) traeremos *vosotros(as) traeréis* ellos, ellas, Uds. traerán
POTENCIAL	yo sería tú serías él, ella, Ud. sería nosotros(as) seríamos *vosotros(as) seríais* ellos, ellas, Uds. serían	yo tendría tú tendrías él, ella, Ud. tendría nosotros(as) tendríamos *vosotros(as) tendríais* ellos, ellas, Uds. tendrían	yo traería tú traerías él, ella, Ud. traería nosotros(as) traeríamos *vosotros(as) traeríais* ellos, ellas, Uds. traerían
PRESENTE PERFECTO	yo he sido tú has sido él, ella, Ud. ha sido nosotros(as) hemos sido *vosotros(as) habéis sido* ellos, ellas, Uds. han sido	yo he tenido tú has tenido él, ella, Ud. ha tenido nosotros(as) hemos tenido *vosotros(as) habéis tenido* ellos, ellas, Uds. han tenido	yo he traído tú has traído él, ella, Ud. ha traído nosotros(as) hemos traído *vosotros(as) habéis traído* ellos, ellas, Uds. han traído
SUBJUNTIVO PRESENTE	yo sea tú seas él, ella, Ud. sea nosotros(as) seamos *vosotros(as) seáis* ellos, ellas, Uds. sean	yo tenga tú tengas él, ella, Ud. tenga nosotros(as) tengamos *vosotros(as) tengáis* ellos, ellas, Uds. tengan	yo traiga tú traigas él, ella, Ud. traiga nosotros(as) traigamos *vosotros(as) traigáis* ellos, ellas, Uds. traigan
IMPERATIVO FORMAL	sea (Ud.) sean (Uds.)	tenga (Ud.) tengan (Uds.)	traiga (Ud.) traigan (Uds.)
IMPERATIVO FAMILIAR	sé (tú)	ten (tú)	trae (tú)

Verbos irregulares

INFINITIVO	venir *to come*	ver *to see*	
PRESENTE PROGRESIVO	estar viniendo	estar viendo	
PRESENTE	yo vengo tú vienes él, ella, Ud. viene nosotros(as) venimos *vosotros(as) venís* ellos, ellas, Uds. vienen	yo veo tú ves él, ella, Ud. ve nosotros(as) vemos *vosotros(as) veis* ellos, ellas, Uds. ven	
PRETÉRITO	yo vine tú viniste él, ella, Ud. vino nosotros(as) vinimos *vosotros(as) vinisteis* ellos, ellas, Uds. vinieron	yo vi tú viste él, ella, Ud. vio nosotros(as) vimos *vosotros(as) visteis* ellos, ellas, Uds. vieron	
IMPERFECTO	yo venía tú venías él, ella, Ud. venía nosotros(as) veníamos *vosotros(as) veníais* ellos, ellas, Uds. venían	yo veía tú veías él, ella, Ud. veía nosotros(as) veíamos *vosotros(as) veíais* ellos, ellas, Uds. veían	
FUTURO	yo vendré tú vendrás él, ella, Ud. vendrá nosotros(as) vendremos *vosotros(as) vendréis* ellos, ellas, Uds. vendrán	yo veré tú verás él, ella, Ud. verá nosotros(as) veremos *vosotros(as) veréis* ellos, ellas, Uds. verán	
POTENCIAL	yo vendría tú vendrías él, ella, Ud. vendría nosotros(as) vendríamos *vosotros(as) vendríais* ellos, ellas, Uds. vendrían	yo vería tú verías él, ella, Ud. vería nosotros(as) veríamos *vosotros(as) veríais* ellos, ellas, Uds. verían	
PRESENTE PERFECTO	yo he venido tú has venido él, ella, Ud. ha venido nosotros(as) hemos venido *vosotros(as) habéis venido* ellos, ellas, Uds. han venido	yo he visto tú has visto él, ella, Ud. ha visto nosotros(as) hemos visto *vosotros(as) habéis visto* ellos, ellas, Uds. han visto	
SUBJUNTIVO PRESENTE	yo venga tú vengas él, ella, Ud. venga nosotros(as) vengamos *vosotros(as) vengáis* ellos, ellas, Uds. vengan	yo vea tú veas él, ella, Ud. vea nosotros(as) veamos *vosotros(as) veáis* ellos, ellas, Uds. vean	
IMPERATIVO FORMAL	venga (Ud.) vengan (Uds.)	vea (Ud.) vean (Uds.)	
IMPERATIVO FAMILIAR	ven (tú)	ve (tú)	

Verbos reflexivos

INFINITIVO	**lavarse** *to wash oneself*		
PRESENTE PROGRESIVO	estar lavándose		
PRESENTE	yo me lavo tú te lavas él, ella, Ud. se lava nosotros(as) nos lavamos *vosotros(as) os laváis* ellos, ellas, Uds. se lavan		
PRETÉRITO	yo me lavé tú te lavaste él, ella, Ud. se lavó nosotros(as) nos lavamos *vosotros(as) os lavasteis* ellos, ellas, Uds. se lavaron		
IMPERFECTO	yo me lavaba tú te lavabas él, ella, Ud. se lavaba nosotros(as) nos lavábamos *vosotros(as) os lavabais* ellos, ellas, Uds. se lavaban		
FUTURO	yo me lavaré tú te lavarás él, ella, Ud. se lavará nosotros(as) nos lavaremos *vosotros(as) os lavaréis* ellos, ellas, Uds. se lavarán		
POTENCIAL	yo me lavaría tú te lavarías él, ella, Ud. se lavaría nosotros(as) nos lavaríamos *vosotros(as) os lavaríais* ellos, ellas, Uds. se lavarían		
PRESENTE PERFECTO	yo me he lavado tú te has lavado él, ella, Ud. se ha lavado nosotros(as) nos hemos lavado *vosotros(as) os habéis lavado* ellos, ellas, Uds. se han lavado		
SUBJUNTIVO PRESENTE	yo me lave tú te laves él, ella, Ud. se lave nosotros(as) nos lavemos *vosotros(as) os lavéis* ellos, ellas, Uds. se laven		
IMPERATIVO FORMAL	lávese (Ud.) lávense (Uds.)		
IMPERATIVO FAMILIAR	lávate (tú)		

Verbos reflexivos con cambio radical

INFINITIVO	acostarse (o>ue) *to go to bed*	despertarse (e>ie) *to wake up*	dormirse (o>ue, u) *to fall asleep*
PRESENTE PROGRESIVO	estar acostándose	estar despertándose	estar durmiéndose
PRESENTE	yo me acuesto tú te acuestas él, ella, Ud. se acuesta nosotros(as) nos acostamos *vosotros(as) os acostáis* ellos, ellas, Uds. se acuestan	yo me despierto tú te despiertas él, ella, Ud. se despierta nosotros(as) nos despertamos *vosotros(as) os despertáis* ellos, ellas, Uds. se despiertan	yo me duermo tú te duermes él, ella, Ud. se duerme nosotros(as) nos dormimos *vosotros(as) os dormís* ellos, ellas, Uds. se duermen
PRETÉRITO	yo me acosté tú te acostaste él, ella, Ud. se acostó nosotros(as) nos acostamos *vosotros(as) os acostasteis* ellos, ellas, Uds. se acostaron	yo me desperté tú te despertaste él, ella, Ud. se despertó nosotros(as) nos despertamos *vosotros(as) os despertasteis* ellos, ellas, Uds. se despertaron	yo me dormí tú te dormiste él, ella, Ud. se durmió nosotros(as) nos dormimos *vosotros(as) os dormisteis* ellos, ellas, Uds. se durmieron
IMPERFECTO	yo me acostaba tú te acostabas él, ella, Ud. se acostaba nosotros(as) nos acostábamos *vosotros(as) os acostabais* ellos, ellas, Uds. se acostaban	yo me despertaba tú te despertabas él, ella, Ud. se despertaba nosotros(as) nos despertábamos *vosotros(as) os despertabais* ellos, ellas, Uds. se despertaban	yo me dormía tú te dormías él, ella, Ud. se dormía nosotros(as) nos dormíamos *vosotros(as) os dormíais* ellos, ellas, Uds. se dormían
FUTURO	yo me acostaré tú te acostarás él, ella, Ud. se acostará nosotros(as) nos acostaremos *vosotros(as) os acostaréis* ellos, ellas, Uds. se acostarán	yo me despertaré tú te despertarás él, ella, Ud. se despertará nosotros(as) nos despertaremos *vosotros(as) os despertaréis* ellos, ellas, Uds. se despertarán	yo me dormiré tú te dormirás él, ella, Ud. se dormirá nosotros(as) nos dormiremos *vosotros(as) os dormiréis* ellos, ellas, Uds. se dormirán
POTENCIAL	yo me acostaría tú te acostarías él, ella, Ud. se acostaría nosotros(as) nos acostaríamos *vosotros(as) os acostaríais* ellos, ellas, Uds. se acostarían	yo me despertaría tú te despertarías él, ella, Ud. se despertaría nosotros(as) nos despertaríamos *vosotros(as) os despertaríais* ellos, ellas, Uds. se despertarían	yo me dormiría tú te dormirías él, ella, Ud. se dormiría nosotros(as) nos dormiríamos *vosotros(as) os dormiríais* ellos, ellas, Uds. se dormirían
PRESENTE PERFECTO	yo me he acostado tú te has acostado él, ella, Ud. se ha acostado nosotros(as) nos hemos acostado *vosotros(as) os habéis acostado* ellos, ellas, Uds. se han acostado	yo me he despertado tú te has despertado él, ella, Ud. se ha despertado nosotros(as) nos hemos despertado *vosotros(as) os habéis despertado* ellos, ellas, Uds. se han despertado	yo me he dormido tú te has dormido él, ella, Ud. se ha dormido nosotros(as) nos hemos dormido *vosotros(as) os habéis dormido* ellos, ellas, Uds. se han dormido
SUBJUNTIVO PRESENTE	yo me acueste tú te acuestes él, ella, Ud. se acueste nosotros(as) nos acostemos *vosotros(as) os acostéis* ellos, ellas, Uds. se acuesten	yo me despierte tú te despiertes él, ella, Ud. se despierte nosotros(as) nos despertemos *vosotros(as) os despertéis* ellos, ellas, Uds. se despierten	yo me duerma tú te duermas él, ella, Ud. se duerma nosotros(as) nos durmamos *vosotros(as) os durmáis* ellos, ellas, Uds. se duerman
IMPERATIVO FORMAL	acuéstese (Ud.) acuéstense (Uds.)	despiértese (Ud.) despiértense (Uds.)	duérmase (Ud.) duérmanse (Uds.)
IMPERATIVO FAMILIAR	acuéstate (tú)	despiértate (tú)	duérmete (tú)

Verbos reflexivos con cambio radical

INFINITIVO	divertirse (e>ie, i) *to enjoy oneself*	sentarse (e>ie) *to sit down*	vestirse (e>i, i) *to dress oneself*
PRESENTE PROGRESIVO	estar divirtiéndose	estar sentándose	estar vistiéndose
PRESENTE	yo me divierto tú te diviertes él, ella, Ud. se divierte nosotros(as) nos divertimos *vosotros(as) os divertís* ellos, ellas, Uds. se divierten	yo me siento tú te sientas él, ella, Ud. se sienta nosotros(as) nos sentamos *vosotros(as) os sentáis* ellos, ellas, Uds. se sientan	yo me visto tú te vistes él, ella, Ud. se viste nosotros(as) nos vestimos *vosotros(as) os vestís* ellos, ellas, Uds. se visten
PRETÉRITO	yo me divertí tú te divertiste él, ella, Ud. se divirtió nosotros(as) nos divertimos *vosotros(as) os divertisteis* ellos, ellas, Uds. se divirtieron	yo me senté tú te sentaste él, ella, Ud. se sentó nosotros(as) nos sentamos *vosotros(as) os sentasteis* ellos, ellas, Uds. se sentaron	yo me vestí tú te vestiste él, ella, Ud. se vistió nosotros(as) nos vestimos *vosotros(as) os vestistéis* ellos, ellas, Uds. se vistieron
IMPERFECTO	yo me divertía tú te divertías él, ella, Ud. se divertía nosotros(as) nos divertíamos *vosotros(as) os divertíais* ellos, ellas, Uds. se divertían	yo me sentaba tú te sentabas él, ella, Ud. se sentaba nosotros(as) nos sentábamos *vosotros(as) os sentabais* ellos, ellas, Uds. se sentaban	yo me vestía tú te vestías él, ella, Ud. se vestía nosotros(as) nos vestíamos *vosotros(as) os vestíais* ellos, ellas, Uds. se vestían
FUTURO	yo me divertiré tú te divertirás él, ella, Ud. se divertirá nosotros(as) nos divertiremos *vosotros(as) os divertiréis* ellos, ellas, Uds. se divertirán	yo me sentaré tú te sentarás él, ella, Ud. se sentará nosotros(as) nos sentaremos *vosotros(as) os sentaréis* ellos, ellas, Uds. se sentarán	yo me vestiré tú te vestirás él, ella, Ud. se vestirá nosotros(as) nos vestiremos *vosotros(as) os vestiréis* ellos, ellas, Uds. se vestirán
POTENCIAL	yo me divertiría tú te divertirías él, ella, Ud. se divertiría nosotros(as) nos divertiríamos *vosotros(as) os divertiríais* ellos, ellas, Uds. se divertirían	yo me sentaría tú te sentarías él, ella, Ud. se sentaría nosotros(as) nos sentaríamos *vosotros(as) os sentaríais* ellos, ellas, Uds. se sentarían	yo me vestiría tú te vestirías él, ella, Ud. se vestiría nosotros(as) nos vestiríamos *vosotros(as) os vestiríais* ellos, ellas, Uds. se vestirían
PRESENTE PERFECTO	yo me he divertido tú te has divertido él, ella, Ud. se ha divertido nosotros(as) nos hemos divertido *vosotros(as) os habéis divertido* ellos, ellas, Uds. se han divertido	yo me he sentado tú te has sentado él, ella, Ud. se ha sentado nosotros(as) nos hemos sentado *vosotros(as) os habéis sentado* ellos, ellas, Uds. se han sentado	yo me he vestido tú te has vestido él, ella, Ud. se ha vestido nosotros(as) nos hemos vestido *vosotros(as) os habéis vestido* ellos, ellas, Uds. se han vestido
SUBJUNTIVO PRESENTE	yo me divierta tú te diviertas él, ella, Ud. se divierta nosotros(as) nos divirtamos *vosotros(as) os divirtáis* ellos, ellas, Uds. se diviertan	yo me siente tú te sientes él, ella, Ud. se siente nosotros(as) nos sentemos *vosotros(as) os sentéis* ellos, ellas, Uds. se sienten	yo me vista tú te vistas él, ella, Ud. se vista nosotros(as) nos vistamos *vosotros(as) os vistáis* ellos, ellas, Uds. se vistan
IMPERATIVO FORMAL	diviértase (Ud.) diviértanse (Uds.)	siéntese (Ud.) siéntense (Uds.)	vístase (Ud.) vístanse (Uds.)
IMPERATIVO FAMILIAR	diviértete (tú)	siéntate (tú)	vístete (tú)

VERBOS

Verbos con cambio ortográfico

INFINITIVO	car → qu (before e) **buscar** *to look for*	gar → gu (before e) **llegar** *to arrive*	zar → c (before e) **empezar** *to begin*
PRESENTE PROGRESIVO	estar buscando	estar llegando	estar empezando
PRESENTE	yo busco tú buscas el, ella, Ud. busca nosotros(as) buscamos *vosotros(as) buscáis* ellos, ellas, Uds. buscan	yo llego tú llegas el, ella, Ud. llega nosotros(as) llegamos *vosotros(as) llegáis* ellos, ellas, Uds. llegan	yo empiezo tú empiezas el, ella, Ud. empieza nosotros(as) empezamos *vosotros(as) empezáis* ellos, ellas, Uds. empiezan
PRETÉRITO	yo busqué tú buscaste el, ella, Ud. buscó nosotros(as) buscamos *vosotros(as) buscasteis* ellos, ellas, Uds. buscaron	yo llegué tú llegaste el, ella, Ud. llegó nosotros(as) llegamos *vosotros(as) llegasteis* ellos, ellas, Uds. llegaron	yo empecé tú empezaste el, ella, Ud. empezó nosotros(as) empezamos *vosotros(as) empezasteis* ellos, ellas, Uds. empezaron
IMPERFECTO	yo buscaba tú buscabas el, ella, Ud. buscaba nosotros(as) buscábamos *vosotros(as) buscabais* ellos, ellas, Uds. buscaban	yo llegaba tú llegabas el, ella, Ud. llegaba nosotros(as) llegábamos *vosotros(as) llegabais* ellos, ellas, Uds. llegaban	yo empezaba tú empezabas el, ella, Ud. llegaba nosotros(as) llegábamos *vosotros(as) llegabais* ellos, ellas, Uds. llegaban
FUTURO	yo buscaré tú buscarás el, ella, Ud. buscará nosotros(as) buscaremos *vosotros(as) buscaréis* ellos, ellas, Uds. buscarán	yo llegaré tú llegarás el, ella, Ud. llegará nosotros(as) llegaremos *vosotros(as) llegaréis* ellos, ellas, Uds. llegarán	yo empezaré tú empezarás el, ella, Ud. empezará nosotros(as) empezaremos *vosotros(as) empezaréis* ellos, ellas, Uds. empezarán
POTENCIAL	yo buscaría tú buscarías el, ella, Ud. buscaría nosotros(as) buscaríamos *vosotros(as) buscaríais* ellos, ellas, Uds. buscarían	yo llegaría tú llegarías el, ella, Ud. llegaría nosotros(as) llegaríamos *vosotros(as) llegaríais* ellos, ellas, Uds. llegarían	yo empezaría tú empezarías el, ella, Ud. empezaría nosotros(as) empezaríamos *vosotros(as) empezaríais* ellos, ellas, Uds. empezarían
PRESENTE PERFECTO	yo he buscado tú has buscado el, ella, Ud. ha buscado nosotros(as) hemos buscado *vosotros(as) habéis buscado* ellos, ellas, Uds. han buscado	yo he llegado tú has llegado el, ella, Ud. ha llegado nosotros(as) hemos llegado *vosotros(as) habéis llegado* ellos, ellas, Uds. han llegado	yo he empezado tú has empezado el, ella, Ud. ha empezado nosotros(as) hemos empezado *vosotros(as) habéis empezado* ellos, ellas, Uds. han empezado
SUBJUNTIVO PRESENTE	yo busque tú busques el, ella, Ud. busque nosotros(as) busquemos *vosotros(as) busquéis* ellos, ellas, Uds. busquen	yo llegue tú llegues el, ella, Ud. llegue nosotros(as) lleguemos *vosotros(as) lleguéis* ellos, ellas, Uds. lleguen	yo empiece tú empieces el, ella, Ud. empiece nosotros(as) empecemos *vosotros(as) empecéis* ellos, ellas, Uds. empiecen
IMPERATIVO FORMAL	busque (Ud.) busquen (Uds.)	llegue (Ud.) lleguen (Uds.)	empiece (Ud.) empiecen (Uds.)
IMPERATIVO FAMILIAR	busca (tú)	llega (tú)	empieza (tú)

Vocabulario

Vocabulario español–inglés

The **Vocabulario español–inglés** contains all productive and receptive vocabulary from the text. The reference numbers following each productive entry indicate the chapter and vocabulary section in which the word is introduced. For example, **3.2** means that the word was taught in **Capítulo 3, Palabras 2**. **BV** refers to the preliminary **Bienvenidos** lessons in Level 1. Words without a chapter reference indicate receptive vocabulary (not taught in the **Palabras** sections). Words taught in Level 1 appear in regular type and those taught in Level 2 are in bold type. Note that **Capítulos 1** and **2** of Level 2 repeat **Capítulos 13** and **14** of Level 1 (e.g., 13.1; **1.1**).

A

a at; to
  a bordo de aboard, on board, **7.1**
  a eso de at about (time), 4.1
  a fines de at the end of
  a la española Spanish-style
  a lo menos
  a menudo often, **3.2**
  a pie on foot, 4.1
  a plazos in installments
  a propósito by the way
  a solas alone
  a tiempo on time, 11.1
  a veces sometimes, 7.1
  a ver let's see
abandonar el cuarto to check out, **6.1**
abarrotes: la tienda de abarrotes grocery store, **4.2**
la **abeja** bee, **8.1**
el/la **abogado(a)** lawyer, **14.1**
  abordar to get on, board
el **abrigo** overcoat, **4.1**
  abril April, BV
  abrir to open, 8.2
  abrocharse to fasten, **7.1**
  abrocharse el cinturón de seguridad to fasten one's seatbelt, **7.1**
la **abuela** grandmother, 6.1

el **abuelo** grandfather, 6.1
los **abuelos** grandparents, 6.1
  abundante plentiful
  aburrido(a) boring, 2.1
  aburrir to bore
el **abuso** abuse
  acabar de to have just (done something), **8.1**
la **academia** academy, school
  acariciar to caress
el **acceso** access
el **accidente** accident, **8.1**
la **acción** action
el **aceite** oil, 14.2; **2.2**
  aceptar to accept
la **acera** sidewalk, **9.1**
  acerca de about, concerning
  acercarse (a) to approach
  acertar (ie) to guess right
  acomodar to accommodate
el **acompañamiento** accompaniment
  acompañar to accompany
  aconsejar to advise
  acostarse (ue) to go to bed, 12.1
el **acrílico** acrylic
la **actividad** activity
  activo(a) active
el **actor** actor, 10.2
la **actriz** actress, 10.2
la **actuación** behavior
  actualmente at the present time

la **acuarela** watercolor
  acuático(a): el esquí acuático water-skiing, 9.1
  acuerdo: de acuerdo OK, all right; in agreement
  acuñar to coin, mint
  adaptar to adapt
  adecuado(a) adequate
  adelante ahead
  adelantar to overtake, pass (car), **11.2**
  además moreover; besides
  además de in addition to
la **adicción** addiction
  adiós good-bye, BV
  adivinar to guess
  admirar to admire
  admitir to admit, **8.2**
la **adolescencia** adolescence
el/la **adolescente** adolescent, teenager
  ¿adónde? where?, 1.1
la **adoración** adoration
  adorar to adore
  adornar to adorn
el **adorno** ornament
la **aduana** customs, 11.2
  advertir to warn
  aérea: la línea aérea airline
  aeróbico(a) aerobic
el **aerodeslizador** hydrofoil
el **aeropuerto** airport, 11.1
  afeitarse to shave, 12.1

la crema de afeitar shaving cream, 12.1
aficionado(a) a fond of, 10.1
el/la aficionado(a) fan (sports)
africano(a) African
afroamericano(a) African American
afortunado(a) fortunate
las afueras outskirts, 9.1
la agencia agency
    la agencia de empleos employment agency
el/la agente agent, 11.1
    el/la agente de aduana customs agent, 11.2
    el/la agente de policía police officer
agosto August, BV
agradable pleasant
agregar to add, 10.2
agrícola agricultural
el/la agricultor(a) farmer, 9.2
el agua (f.) water, 9.1
    el agua corriente running water
    el agua mineral mineral water, 12.2
    esquiar en el agua to water-ski, 9.1
el aguacate avocado, 10.2
el águila (f.) eagle
el agujero hole
ahora now, 4.2
ahorrar to save
el aire air, 11.1
    al aire libre outdoor (adj.)
el aire acondicionado air conditioning, 6.2
el ajedrez chess, 5.1
el ají chili pepper
el ajo garlic, 14.2; 2.2
el ajuar de novia trousseau
ajustar to adjust
al to the
    al aire libre outdoor (adj.)
    al bordo de alongside, on the banks of (river)
    al contrario on the contrary
    al lado de beside, 5.2
    al máximo at the most
    al principio at the beginning
alarmarse to be alarmed
el/la albañil bricklayer, 14.1

la alberca swimming pool, 9.1
el albergue para jóvenes (juvenil) youth hostel, 12.2
el álbum album
la alcachofa artichoke, 14.2; 2.2
el alcalde mayor, 14.1
la alcaldesa female mayor
la alcaldía city hall, 14.1
alcanzar to reach, attain
el alcohol alcohol
el alcoholismo alcoholism
alegrarse de to be glad about, 13.1
alegre happy
la alegría happiness
el alemán German (language), 2.2
la alergia allergy, 8.2
el álgebra algebra, 2.2
algo something, 5.2
    ¿Algo más? Anything else?, 5.2
el algodón cotton, 12.1
alguien someone
algunos(as) some, 4.1
el alimento food, 14.2; 2.2
allá there
allí there
almacenar to store
la almeja clam, 14.2; 2.2
la almohada pillow, 6.2
el almuerzo lunch, 5.2
    tomar el almuerzo to have, eat lunch
alojarse to stay, lodge
la alpargata sandal
alquilar to rent, 5.2
alrededor de around, 6.2
los alrededores outskirts
alternar to alternate
el altiplano high plateau, 7.2
la altitud altitude, 7.2
altivo arrogant, haughty
alto(a) tall, 1.1; high, 4.2
    en voz alta aloud
    la nota alta high grade, 4.2
la altura height; altitude, 7.2
el/la alumno(a) student, 1.1
amar to love
amarillo(a) yellow, 3.2
amazónico(a) Amazonian
ambicioso(a) hardworking, 1.1
el ambiente environment; atmosphere

la ambulancia ambulance, 8.1
ambulante itinerant
la América Central Central America
la América del Norte North America
la América del Sur South America
americano(a) American, 1.1
el/la amigo(a) friend, 1.1
el amor love
el análisis analysis
analítico(a) analytical
analizar to analyze
anaranjado(a) orange, 3.2
el/la anarquista anarchist
ancho(a) wide, 4.1
anciano(a) old, 6.1
el/la anciano(a) old person
andaluz(a) Andalusian
andante: el caballero andante knight errant
andar to walk, to go to, 13; 1
el andén railway platform, 13.1; 1.1
andino(a) Andean
la anécdota anecdote
angosto(a) narrow, 9.1
el anillo ring, 4.1
el animal animal
    el animal doméstico farm animal, 9.2
el aniversario anniversary
anoche last night, 9.2
el anorak parka, 9.2
la Antártida Antarctic
anteayer the day before yesterday
antenupcial prenuptial
los anteojos de sol sunglasses, 9.1
antes de before, 5.1
el antibiótico antibiotic, 8.2
anticipación: de anticipación ahead of time
anticuado(a) antiquated
la antigüedad antiquity
antiguo(a) old, ancient, 5.1
anunciar to announce
el anuncio announcement; 7.1; advertisement, 14.2
    dar anuncios to make announcements, 7.1
añadir to add, 10.2

el **año** year, BV

  cumplir... años to be . . . years old

  el año pasado last year, **9.2**

  este año this year, **9.2**

  tener... años to be . . . years old, 6.1

el **Año Nuevo** New Year, **13.2**

  ¡Próspero Año Nuevo! Happy New Year!, **13.2**

apagar to turn off, **3.1**

el **aparato** appliance, device, **3.2**

el **aparcamiento** parking lot

aparcar to park, **11.2**

aparecer to appear

la **apariencia** appearance

el **apartamento** apartment, 6.2

  la casa de apartamentos apartment house, 6.2

apasionado(a) passionate

el **apellido** last name

la **apendicitis** appendicitis

la **apertura** opening

  la apertura de clases beginning of the school year

aplaudir to applaud, 10.2

el **aplauso** applause, 10.2

  dar aplausos to applaud, **10.2**

  recibir aplausos to receive applause, 10.2

aplicar to apply

el **apóstol** apostle

aprender to learn, 5.1

apropiado(a) appropriate

la **aptitud** aptitude

el **apunte: tomar apuntes** to take notes, 4.2

aquel, aquella that

  en aquel entonces at that time

aquí here

  Aquí tiene (tienes, tienen)... Here is (are) . . .

  por aquí right this way

el/la **árabe** Arab

aragonés(esa) from Aragon (Spain)

el **árbol** tree

  el árbol de Navidad Christmas tree, **13.2**

el **arco** arc

el **área** (*f.*) area

la **arena** sand, 9.1

el **arete** earring, **4.1**

argentino(a) Argentinian, 2.1

el **argumento** plot

árido(a) arid

la **aritmética** arithmetic, 2.2

el **arma** (*f.*) weapon

el **armario** closet, **6.2**

la **arqueología** archeology

arqueológico(a) archaeological

el/la **arqueólogo(a)** archaeologist

el/la **arquitecto(a)** architect, **14.1**

arrancar to pull out

arrogante arrogant

el **arroyo** stream, brook

el **arroz** rice, 5.2

arrugar to wrinkle

el **arsenal** arsenal

el **arte** (*f.*) art, 2.2

  las bellas artes fine arts

el **artefacto** artifact

el/la **artista** artist, 10.2

artístico(a) artistic

asado(a) roasted

asar to roast, **10.1**

la **ascendencia** background

  de ascendencia mexicana (peruana, etc.) of Mexican (Peruvian, etc.) extraction

ascender to rise

el **ascensor** elevator, 6.2

asegurar to assure

el **aseo** restroom, **7.1**

así so; thus

el **asiento** seat, 11.1

  el número del asiento seat number, 11.1

la **asignatura** subject, discipline, 2.1

el/la **asistente de vuelo** flight attendant, 11.2

asistir to attend

el **asno** donkey

el **aspa** sail (of a windmill)

el **aspecto** aspect

el/la **aspirante** candidate, **14.2**

la **aspirina** aspirin, 8.2

astuto(a) astute

asustarse to be frightened

atacar to attack

el **ataque** attack

la **atención: prestar atención** to pay attention, 4.2

atender (ie) to assist, wait on (customer), **4.1**

atento(a) polite, courteous

el **aterrizaje** landing, **7.2**

aterrizar to land, 11.2

el/la **atleta** athlete

atlético(a) athletic

la **atmósfera** atmosphere

atrapar to catch, 7.2

las **atracciones** amusement park rides, **5.2**

  el parque de atracciones amusement park, **5.2**

atractivo(a) attractive

atrás behind, in the rear

atravesar (ie) to cross

el **atún** tuna, 5.2

los **audífonos** earphones, **7.1**

aumentar to increase

el **aumento** increase

aun even

aún yet

aunque although

el **auricular** telephone receiver, **3.2**; headphone, **7.1**

austral former Argentine unit of currency

auténtico(a) authentic

el **autobús** bus, 10.1

  perder el autobús (la guagua, el camión) to miss the bus, 10.1

automáticamente automatically, **7.1**

el **automóvil** automobile

la **autopista** highway, **11.2**

el/la **autor(a)** author, 10.2

autorizado(a) authorized

el **autorretrato** self-portrait

la **autovía** highway, **11.2**

  los auxilios: los primeros auxilios first aid

el **avance** advance

el **ave** (*f.*) bird

la **avenida** avenue, **9.1**

la **aventura** adventure

la **avería** breakdown

  averiado(a) broken down

la **aviación** aviation

el **avión** airplane, 11.1

el **avión de reacción** jet, **7.2**

la **avioneta** small airplane, **7.2**

ayer yesterday, 9.2

  ayer por la mañana yesterday morning, 9.2

ayer por la tarde
yesterday afternoon, 9.2

la **ayuda** assistance, help
ayudar to help, 13.1; **1.1**

el **azafrán** saffron

el **azúcar** sugar, 10.1

azul blue, 3.2

azul oscuro dark blue

B

el **bache** pothole

el **bachillerato** bachelor's degree

la **bacteria** bacteria

la **bahía** bay

bailar to dance, 4.2

el **baile** dance

bajar to lower; to go down, 9.2; to get off, 13.2; **1.2**
bajar(se) del tren to get off the train, 13.2; **1.2**
bajar las maletas to take the luggage down, **6.1**

bajo: bajo cero below zero, 9.2

bajo(a) short, 1.1; low, 4.2
la planta baja ground floor, 6.2
la nota baja low grade, 4.2

el **balneario** beach resort, 9.1

el **balón** ball, 7.1
tirar el balón to throw (kick) the ball, 7.2

el **baloncesto** basketball, 7.2

la **banana** banana, **10.2**

bancario(a) banking

la **banca** banking

el **banco** bank, **12.2**

la **banda** music band

la **banda elástica** elastic band

la **bandeja** tray, **7.1**

el **bando** team

el **bañador** bathing suit 9.1
bañarse to take a bath, 12.1

la **bañera** bathtub, **6.2**

el **baño** bathroom, 6.2; bath
el cuarto de baño bathroom, 6.2
el traje de baño bathing suit, 9.1

barato(a) cheap, inexpensive, 3.2

la **barba** beard

el/la **barbero(a)** barber, **12.1**

la **barra** bar

la **barra de jabón** bar of soap, 12.2

el **barrio** neighborhood, **9.1**

basado(a) based (on)
basar to base
basarse to be based

la **báscula** scale, 11.1

la **base** base, 7.2; basis
básico(a) basic

el **básquetbol** basketball, 7.2
la cancha de básquetbol basketball court, 7.2

bastante enough, rather, quite, 1.1

el **bastón** ski pole, 9.2

la **batalla** battle

el **bate** bat, 7.2

el/la **bateador(a)** batter, 7.2
batear to hit (baseball), 7.2

la **batería** battery

el **batú** Taíno Indian game

el **baúl** trunk, **11.1**

el **bautizo** baptism

el/la **bebé** baby
beber to drink, 5.1

la **bebida** beverage, drink, **7.1**

la **beca** scholarship

el **béisbol** baseball, 7.2
el campo de béisbol baseball field, 7.2
el juego de béisbol baseball game, 7.2
el/la jugador(a) de béisbol baseball player, 7.2

el/la **beisbolista** baseball player

la **belleza** beauty
bello(a) beautiful, pretty, 1.1
las bellas artes fine arts

la **bendición** blessing

el **beneficio** benefit

la **berenjena** eggplant, 14.2; **2.2**

bíblico(a) biblical

la **bicicleta** bicycle
ir en bicicleta to go by bike, 12.2

bien fine, well, BV
muy bien very well, BV

los **bienes y servicios** goods and services

la **bienvenida: dar la bienvenida** to welcome, 11.2

el **bife** beef

el **biftec** steak, 14.2; **2.2**

bilingüe bilingual

el **billete** ticket, 11.1; bill (currency), **12.2**
el billete de ida y vuelta round-trip ticket, 13.1; **1.1**
el billete sencillo one-way ticket, 13.1; **1.1**

la **biografía** biography

la **biología** biology, 2.2
biológico(a) biological

el/la **biólogo(a)** biologist

el **bizcocho** cake, **13.1**
blanco(a) white, 3.2

el **blanqueador** bleach

el **bloc** notebook, writing pad, 3.1
bloquear to stop, block, 7.1

el **blue jean** jeans, 3.2

la **blusa** blouse, 3.2

la **boca** mouth, 8.2
boca abajo face down, **3.1**
boca arriba face up, **3.1**
la boca del metro subway entrance, 9.1

la **bocacalle** intersection, 11.2

el **bocadillo** sandwich, 5.1

la **bocina** horn, **11.1**
tocar la bocina to honk the horn

la **boda** wedding, **13.1**

la **bola** ball

la **boletería** ticket window, 9.2

el **boleto** ticket, 9.2

el **bolígrafo** ballpoint pen, 3.1

la **bolsa** bag, 5.2
la bolsa de plástico plastic bag, **4.2**

el **bolsillo** pocket, **4.1**
bonito(a) pretty, 1.1
bordear to border

el **borde** border, side, shoulder (road)

la **bota** boot, 9.2

el **bote** can, 5.2; boat, **5.2**

la **botella: la botella de agua mineral** bottle of mineral water, 12.2

el **botón** button (on a machine), **3.1**; (on clothing), **4.1**

el **botones** bellman, **6.1**

el **brazo** arm, 7.1; branch (of candelabra, menorah, etc.), **13.2**

breve brief

brillante bright
brillar to shine, **9.1**
el **bronce** bronze, **10.2**
bronceado(a) tan
bronceador(a): la loción bronceadora suntan lotion, **9.1**
bucear to dive; to swim underwater, **9.1**
el **buceo** diving, underwater swimming, **9.1**
buen good
  estar de buen humor to be in a good mood, **8.1**
  Hace buen tiempo. The weather is nice., **9.1**
la **buenaventura** fortune
bueno(a) good, **1.2**
  Buenas noches. Good evening., **BV**
  Buenas tardes. Good afternoon., **BV**
  Buenos días. Hello, Good morning., **BV**
  sacar una nota buena to get a good grade, **4.2**
  tener buena pinta to look good (food), **4.2**
la **bufanda** scarf, **4.1**
el **bufete del abogado** lawyer's office, **14.1**
el **bulevar** boulevard, **9.1**
el **bus** bus, **4.1**
  el bus escolar school bus, **4.1**
busca: en busca de in search of
buscar to look for, **3.1**
la **butaca** seat (theater), **10.1**
el **buzón** mailbox, **12.2**

C

el **caballero** knight; gentleman, man, **4.1**
  el caballero andante knight errant
  la tienda de ropa para caballeros men's clothing shop, **4.1**
el **caballete** easel
el **caballito** carousel horse, **5.2**
el **caballo** horse
  pasear a caballo to go horseback riding
el **cabello** hair, **12.1**

caber to fit, **7.1**
la **cabeza** head, **7.1**
la **cabina** cabin, **7.1**
  la cabina de mando (vuelo) cockpit, **7.1**
el **cacahuete (cacahuate)** peanut
la **cacerola** saucepan, **10.2**
cada each, every, **1.2**
la **cadena** chain (necklace), **4.1**
  la cadena de oro gold chain, **4.1**
caerse to fall, drop, **7.1**
el **café** coffee, **BV**; café, **5.1**
  el café al aire libre outdoor café
  el café con leche coffee with milk, **5.1**
  el café solo black coffee, **5.1**
la **cafetería** cafeteria
la **caja** cash register, **3.1**; box, **4.2**
el/la **cajero(a)** teller, **12.2**; cashier, **14.1**
el **cajero automático** automatic teller
los **calamares** squid, **10.2**
los **calcetines** socks, **3.2**
la **calculadora** calculator, **3.1**
calcular to calculate
el **cálculo** calculus, **2.2**
calentarse (ie) to heat
la **calidad** quality
la **calificación** qualification
la **calle** street, **6.2**
  la calle de sentido único one-way street, **11.2**
  la calle peatonal pedestrian street
la **callecita** narrow street, alley, **9.1**
el **calor: Hace calor.** It's hot., **9.1**
la **caloría** calorie
calzar to take, wear (shoe size), **3.2**
la **cama** bed, **8.1**
  guardar cama to stay in bed, **8.1**
  hacer la cama to make the bed, **6.2**
la **camarera** maid, **6.2**
el/la **camarero(a)** waiter, waitress, **5.1**
los **camarones** shrimp, **14.2**; **2.2**

cambiar to change; exchange, **12.2**
  cambiar de tren to change trains (transfer), **13.2**; **1.2**
  cambiar las toallas to change the towels, **6.2**
el **cambio** change, exchange, **12.2**
  la casa de cambio foreign exchange office, **12.2**
  el tipo (la tasa) de cambio exchange rate, **12.2**
el/la **cambista** money changer, **12.2**
el **camello** camel, **13.2**
la **camilla** stretcher, **8.1**
caminar to walk, **5.1**
  caminar por la senda to walk along the path, **5.2**
la **caminata: dar una caminata** to take a hike, **12.2**
el **camino** trail, path
el **camión** bus (Mexico), **10.1**, truck
la **camisa** shirt, **3.2**
  la camisa de mangas cortas short-sleeved shirt, **4.1**
  la camisa de mangas largas long-sleeved shirt, **4.1**
la **camiseta** T-shirt, undershirt, **3.2**
la **campaña** campaign
el/la **campeón(ona)** champion, **5.1**
el **campeonato** championship
el/la **campesino(a)** farmer, peasant **9.2**
el **campo** country; field, **9.2**
  el campo de béisbol baseball field, **7.2**
  el campo de fútbol soccer field, **7.1**
  la casa de campo country home
canadiense Canadian
el **canal** channel (TV)
la **canasta** basket, **7.2**
la **cancha** court, **7.2**
  la cancha cubierta enclosed court, **9.1**
  la cancha de básquetbol basketball court, **7.2**
  la cancha de tenis tennis

court, 9.1
la **canción** song
el/la **candidato(a)** candidate,
14.2
cansado(a) tired, 8.1
cantar to sing, 4.2
el **cante jondo** traditional
flamenco singing
la **cantidad** amount
el **canto** singing
el **cañón** canyon
el **capacho** cloth shopping
bag
la **capital** capital
el/la **capitán** captain
el **capítulo** chapter
el **capó** hood (automobile),
11.1
la **cara** face, 12.1
el **carácter** character
la **característica**
characteristic
el **carbohidrato** carbohydrate
cardinal: los puntos
cardinales cardinal
points
la **cardiología** cardiology
el/la **cardiólogo(a)** cardiologist
el **cardo** thistle
los **cargos** charges
el **Caribe** Caribbean
el mar Caribe
Caribbean Sea
el/la **caricaturista** caricaturist
la **carne** meat, 5.2
la carne de res beef,
14.2; **2.2**
la **carnicería** butcher shop,
meat market, **4.2**
caro(a) expensive, 3.2
la **carpeta** folder, 3.1
el/la **carpintero(a)** carpenter,
14.1
la **carrera** race, career
la **carretera** highway, **11.2**
el **carril** lane (of highway),
11.2
el **carrito** cart (shopping),
4.2; (airplane), **7.1**
empujar el carrito to
push the cart, **4.2**
el **carro** car, 4.1
el carro deportivo
sports car, **11.1**
en carro by car, 4.1

la **carta** letter, **12.2**
la carta de
recomendación
letter of
recommendation
la **casa** home, house, 6.2
la casa de
apartamentos
(departamentos)
apartment house, 6.2
la casa de campo
country home, **9.2**
la casa privada
(particular) private
house, 6.2
en casa at home
la **casa de cambio** foreign
exchange office, **12.2**
casado(a): estar
casado(a) to be married
casarse to get married,
13.1
el **casete** cassette, 4.2
casi almost, practically
el **caso** case, 7.1
castellano(a) Castillian
el **castigo** punishment
el **castillo** castle
el **catarro** cold (illness), 8.1
tener catarro to have a
cold, 8.1
el/la **cátcher** catcher, 7.2
la **catedral** cathedral
la **categoría** category
católico(a) Catholic
catorce fourteen, BV
la **causa** cause
causar to cause
la **cazuela** pot, 10.1
el **CD-ROM** CD-ROM, **3.1**
la **cebolla** onion, 10.1
la **celebración** celebration
celebrar to celebrate, **13.1**
célebre famous
la **célula** cell
celular: el teléfono
celular cell phone,
3.2
la **cena** dinner, 5.2
cenar to have dinner
el **centavo** penny
central central
el **centro** downtown, **5.1;**
center
cepillarse to brush one's

hair, 12.1
cepillarse los dientes to
brush one's teeth, 12.1
el **cepillo** brush, 12.2
el cepillo de dientes
toothbrush, 12.2
cerca de near, 6.2
cercano(a) nearby
el **cerdo** pig (pork), 14.2; **2.2**
el **cereal** cereal, 5.2; grain,
9.2
la **ceremonia** ceremony, 13
cero zero, BV
cerrar (ie) to close, 8.2
cerrar la herida to close
the wound, **8.2**
la **cesta** basket (jai alai)
el **cesto** basket, 7.2
la **chabola** shack
el **chaleco** vest
el **chaleco salvavidas** life
jacket, **7.1**
el **chalet** chalet
el **champú** shampoo, 12.2
¡Chao! Good-bye!, BV
la **chaqueta** jacket, 3.2
charlar to chat
la **chaucha** string beans
el **cheque de viajero** traveler's
check, **12.2**
la **chequera** checkbook
el/la **chico(a)** boy (girl)
chileno(a) Chilean
la **chimenea** chimney
la **china** orange (fruit)
el **chisme** piece of gossip
¡chist! shh!
el **choclo** corn
el **chocolate: de chocolate**
chocolate (adj.), 5.1
el **chófer** chauffeur
el **chorizo** pork and garlic
sausage, 10.1
la **chuleta** chop, 10.1
la chuleta de cerdo pork
chop, 10.1
el **churro** (type of) doughnut
el **ciclismo** cycling
el **cielo** sky, 9.1
la **ciencia-ficción** science
fiction
las **ciencias** science, 2.2
las ciencias naturales
natural sciences
las ciencias políticas

political science **las ciencias sociales** social sciences, 2.2

el/la **científico(a)** scientist

científico(a) scientific

cien(to) one hundred, 3.2

cierto: Es cierto que... It is certain that

cierto(a) certain

cinco five, BV

el **cine** movie theater, 10.1

cincuenta fifty, 2.2

la **cinta** ribbon

el **cinturón** belt, 4.1

el cinturón de seguridad seat belt, 7.1

circular to circulate, travel, drive

el **círculo** circle

el/la **cirujano(a)** surgeon, 8.2

el/la cirujano(a) ortopédico(a) orthopedic surgeon, 8.2

cítrico(a) citric

la **ciudad** city, 9.1

la **claridad** clarity

el **clarinete** clarinet

claro(a) clear

¡Claro! Certainly!, Of course!

¡Claro que no! Of course not!

la **clase** class (school), 2.1; class (ticket), 13.1; **1.1**; kind, type

la apertura de clases beginning of the school year

la sala de clase classroom, 4.1

el salón de clase classroom, 4.1

primera clase first-class, 13.1; **1.1**

segunda clase second-class, 13.1; **1.1**

clásico(a) classic

clasificar to classify

la **clave de área** area code, **3.2**

el **claxon** horn, **11.1**

el **clic** click

el/la **cliente** customer, 5.1; hotel guest, **6.1**

el **clima** climate

climático(a) climatic

la **clínica** clinic

el **club** club, 4.2

el Club de español Spanish Club, 4.2

cobrar to charge

cobrar el cheque to cash the check, **12.2**

la **Coca-Cola** Coca-Cola, 5.1

la **cocción** cooking

el **coche** car, 4.1; train car, 13.2; **1.2**

el coche deportivo sports car, **11.1**

en coche by car, 4.1

el **coche-cafetería** cafeteria (dining) car, 13.2; **1.2**

el **coche-cama** sleeping car, 13.2; **1.2**

el **coche-comedor** dining car, 13.2; **1.2**

el **coche deportivo** sports car, **11.1**

el **cocido** stew

la **cocina** kitchen, 6.2

cocinar to cook, **10.1**

el/la **cocinero(a)** cook, 14.1; **2.1**

el **coco** coconut, **10.2**

el **cóctel** cocktail party

el **codo** elbow, **8.1**

la **coincidencia** coincidence

cojo(a) lame

la **cola** line (queue), 10.1

hacer cola to line up, to stand in line, 10.1

la **colección** collection

coleccionar to collect, **5.1**

el/la **coleccionista** collector, **5.1**

la **colecta: hacer una colecta** to take up a collection

el **colector** collector

el **colegio** school, 1.1

el **colesterol** cholesterol

el **colgador** clothes hanger, **6.2**

colgar (ue) to hang, hang up

la **coliflor** cauliflower, **10.1**

el **colmado** grocery store, **4.2**

la **colocación** placement

colocar to put, place

colombiano(a) Colombian, 1.1

la **colonia** suburb, colony

el **color** color, 3.2

de color marrón brown, 3.2

de color colored

¿De qué color es? What color is it?, 3.2

el **colorido**

el/la **comandante** pilot, captain, 11.2

la **comedia** comedy

el **comedor** dining room, 6.2

comenzar (ie) to begin

comer to eat, 5.1

comercial: la zona comercial business district, **9.1**

el/la **comerciante** businessman(woman), **14.1**

el **comercio** business

el **comestible** food, 14.2; **2.2**

cómico(a) funny, 1.1

la **comida** food, meal, 5.2

la **comisión** commission

el **comité** committee

como like; as; since, 1.2

¿cómo? how?, what?, 1.1

¿Cómo está...? How is...?, 8.1

¡Cómo no! Of course!

la **comodidad** comfort

compacto(a): el disco compacto compact disk, CD, 4.2

el/la **compañero(a)** friend, 1.2

la **compañía** company

la **comparación** comparison

comparar to compare

el **compartimiento** compartment, 13.2; **1.2**

el compartimiento sobre la cabeza overhead compartment, **7.1**

el compartimiento superior overhead compartment, **7.1**

la **competencia** competition

la **competición** competition, contest

competir (i, i) to compete

completar to complete

completo(a) full (train), 13.2; **1.2**

a tiempo completo full-time *(adj.)*, **14.2**

componer to compose

comportarse to behave

la **composición** composition

la **compra** buying, **4.1**

comprar to buy, 3.1

las **compras** shopping;

purchases, **4.2**
hacer las compras to go shopping, **4.2**
ir de compras to go shopping, to shop, 5.2
comprender to understand, 5.1
comprometerse to get engaged
el **compromiso** engagement
la **computadora** computer, **3.1**
común common
la **comunicación** communication
comunicarse to communicate with each other, **3.1**
la **comunidad** community
con with
con cuidado carefully, cautiously, **11.1**
con frecuencia often, **3.2**
con mucha plata rich
¿con quién? with whom?
con retraso with a delay, 13.2; **1.2**
con una demora with a delay, late, 11.1
el **concierto** concert
conciliar to reconcile
el/la **conde(sa)** count(ess)
la **condición** condition
el **condimento** seasoning
el **condominio** condominium, **9.1**
conducir to drive, **11.1**
el/la **conductor(a)** driver, **11.1**
conectar to connect
la **conexión** connection
la **conferencia** lecture
confirmar to confirm
la **confitería** café, tearoom
Conforme. Agreed, Fine., 14.2; **2.2**
confrontar to confront
congelado(a): los productos congelados frozen food, 5.2
el **congelador** freezer, **10.1**
el **conjunto** set, collection
conocer to know, to be familiar with, **11.1**
el/la **conocido(a)** acquaintance
el **conocimiento** knowledge
la **conquista** conquest

el **conquistador** conquerer
conquistar to conquer
el/la **consejero(a) de orientación** guidance counselor
el **consejo** advice
consentir (ie, i) to allow, tolerate
conservar to save
considerar to consider
consiguiente: por consiguiente consequently
consistir (en) to consist of
construir to construct
la **consulta del médico** doctor's office, 8.2
consultar to consult, 13.1; **1.1**
el **consultorio** medical office, 8.2
el/la **consumidor(a)** consumer
el **consumo** consumption
consumir to consume
la **contabilidad** accounting
el/la **contable** accountant, **14.1**
el **contacto** touch
contagioso(a) contagious
la **contaminación** pollution
contaminado(a) polluted
contaminar to pollute
contemporáneo(a) contemporary
contener (ie) to contain
contento(a) happy, 8.1
la **contestación** answer, response
el **contestador automático** answering machine, **3.2**
contestar to answer, **3.2**
el **continente** continent
continuar to continue, 7.2
contra against, 7.1
contrario(a) opposite
lo contrario the opposite
contrastar to contrast
contribuir to contribute
el **control** inspection, 11.1
el control de pasaportes passport inspection, 11.1
el control de

seguridad security check, 11.1
el/la **controlador(a)** air traffic controller
controlar to control
convencer to convince
conveniente convenient
el **convento** convent
la **conversación** conversation
conversar to talk, speak
el **convertible** convertible, **11.1**
convertir (ie, i) to convert, transform
la **coordinación** coordination
la **copa: la Copa mundial** World Cup
la **copia** copy
copiar to copy
el/la **co-piloto** copilot, 11.2
el **corazón** heart
la **corbata** tie, 3.2
el **cordero** lamb, 14.2; **2.2**
la **cordillera** mountain range, **7.2**
el **cordoncillo** piping (embroidery)
la **coreografía** choreography
coreográfico(a) choreographic
la **córnea** cornea
el **coro** choir, chorus
el **correo** mail; post office, 12.2
el correo aéreo airmail, **12.2**
el correo electrónico e-mail, electronic mail, **3.1**
el correo ordinario regular mail, 12.2
correr to run, 7.2
la **correspondencia** correspondence
corriente: el agua corriente running water
cortar to cut, 8.1
cortarse el pelo to get one's hair cut
la **corte** court, **14.1**
el **corte de pelo** haircut, **12.1**
cortés courteous
la **cortesía** courtesy, BV
corto(a) short, 3.2
el pantalón corto shorts, 3.2
las mangas cortas (largas) short (long) sleeves, **4.1**

la **cosa** thing

la **cosecha** crop, harvest, **9.2**

cosechar to harvest, **9.2**

coser to sew

la **costa** coast

costar (ue) to cost, 3.1

costarricense Costa Rican

la **costilla** rib, **10.1**

el **costo**

la **costumbre** custom

la **costura** sewing

el **cráter** crater

la **creación** creation

crear to create

crecer to grow, increase

crédito: la tarjeta de crédito credit card, 14.1; **2.1**

el **crecimiento** growth

creer to believe, 8.2; to think so

la **crema: la crema de afeitar** shaving cream, 12.1

la **crema protectora** sunblock, 9.1

criar to raise, 9.2

criollo(a) Creole

cristiano(a) Christian

el **cruce** crossing, intersection, **11.2**

el **cruce de peatones** crosswalk, **9.1**

el **crucigrama** crossword puzzle, **5.1**

llenar un crucigrama to do a crossword puzzle, **5.1**

cruel cruel

cruzar to cross, **9.1**

el **cuaderno** notebook, 3.1

la **cuadra** (city) block, **11.2**

el **cuadro** painting, 10.2

cuadros: a cuadros check, plaid

¿cuál? which?, what?, BV

¿Cuál es la fecha de hoy? What is today's date?, BV

¿cuáles? which ones?, what?

cualquier any

cuando when, 4.2

¿cuándo? when?, 4.1

cuanto: en cuanto a in regard to

¿cuánto? how much?, 3.1

¿A cuánto está(n)... ? How much is (are) . . . ?, 5.2

¿Cuánto es? How much does it cost?, 3.1

¿Cuánto cuesta(n)... ? How much do(es) . . . cost?, 3.1

¿cuántos(as)? how many?, 2.1

¿Cuántos años tienes que cumplir? How old do you have to be?

cuarenta forty, 2.2

el **cuarto** room, bedroom 6.2; quarter, 2.2

el **cuarto de baño** bathroom, 6.2

el **cuarto de dormir** bedroom

el **cuarto doble** double room, **6.1**

el **cuarto sencillo** single room, **6.1**

menos cuarto a quarter to (the hour), 2.2

y cuarto a quarter past (the hour), 2.2

cuarto(a) fourth, 6.2

cuatro four, BV

cuatrocientos(as) four hundred, 3.2

cubano(a) Cuban

cubanoamericano(a) Cuban-American

cubrir to cover

la **cuchara** tablespoon, 14.1; **2.1**

la **cucharita** teaspoon, 14.1; **2.1**

el **cuchillo** knife, 14.1; **2.1**

el **cuello** neck, **4.1**

la **cuenca** basin

la **cuenta** bill, check, 5.1

la **cuenta corriente** checking account, **12.2**

la **cuenta de ahorros** savings account

el/la **cuentista** short-story writer

el **cuento** story

la **cuerda** string (instrument)

el **cuerpo** body, **8.1**

el **Cuerpo de Paz** Peace Corps

el **cuestionario** questionnaire

¡cuidado! careful!

con cuidado carefully

el **cuidado intensivo** intensive care

tener cuidado to be careful

cuidar to raise, look after, care for

cultivar to cultivate, to grow, **9.2**

el **cultivo** cultivation, growing, **9.2**

culto(a) cultured

cultural cultural

el **cumpleaños** birthday, 6.1

¡Feliz cumpleaños! Happy birthday!, **13.1**

cumplir: cumplir... años to be . . . years old, 6.1

el **cupé** coupe, **11.1**

la **cura** cure, treatment

el/la **curandero(a)** folk healer

curar to heal, get well

el **curso** course, class, 2.1

el **curso obligatorio** required course

el **curso opcional** elective course

D

la **dama** lady-in-waiting, woman

la dama de honor maid of honor, **13.1**

las **damas** checkers, **5.1**

la **danza** dance

dañar to hurt

daño: hacerse daño to hurt oneself, **8.1**

dar to give, 4.2

dar a to open onto, look out on

dar a entender to imply that

dar auxilio to help

dar énfasis to emphasize

dar la mano to shake hands

dar la vuelta to turn around

dar las doce to strike twelve, **13.2**

dar un examen to give a test, 4.2

dar un paseo to take a walk, **5.2**

dar una fiesta to give (throw) a party, 4.2

dar una representación to put on a performance, 10.2

datar to date

los **datos** data, information, 3.1

entrar los datos to enter, keyboard information, 3.1

de of, from, for, BV

de... a... from (time) to (time), 2.2

de joven as a young person

De nada. You're welcome., BV

de ninguna manera by no means, 1.1

¿De parte de quién? Who's calling?, 3.2

de vez en cuando sometimes

debajo (de) under, below, 7.1

deber must; should; to owe

la **década** decade

decidir to decide

décimo(a) tenth, 6.2

decir to say, 13

¡Diga! Hello! (answering the telephone–Spain), 14.2; **2.2**

declarar to declare

la **decoración** decoration

decorado(a) decorated

decorar to decorate

dedicarse to devote oneself, **14.1**

el **dedo** finger, 4.1

el **defecto** fault, flaw

defender to defend

la **definición** definition

definir to define

definitivamente once and for all

dejar to leave (something), 14.1; **2.1**; to let, allow

dejar un mensaje to leave a message, 3.2

del of the, from the

delante de in front of, 10.1

delantero(a) front (adj.)

delgado(a) thin

delicado(a) delicate

delicioso(a) delicious

demás other, rest

demasiado too (much)

la **demografía** demography

el/la **demógrafo(a)** demographer

la **demora: con una demora** with a delay, 11.1

demostrar (ue) to demonstrate

la **densidad** density

dentífrico(a): la pasta dentífrica toothpaste, 12.2

el/la **dentista** dentist

dentro de within

dentro de poco soon

el **departamento** apartment, 6.2; department, **14.2**

la **casa de departamentos** apartment house, 6.2

el **departamento de personal** personnel department, **14.2**

el **departamento de recursos humanos** human resources department, **14.2**

depender (ie) (de) to depend (on)

el/la **dependiente(a)** salesperson, 3.1

el **deporte** sport, 7.1

el **deporte de equipo** team sport

el **deporte individual** individual sport

deportivo(a) (related to) sports, 6.2

la **emisión deportiva** sports program (TV), 6.2

el **depósito** deposit

derecho(a) right, 7.1

a la derecha to the right, **5.2**

derecho straight (ahead), 11.2

seguir derecho to go straight, **11.2**

la **dermatología** dermatology

el/la **dermatólogo(a)** dermatologist

derrotar to defeat

desagradable unpleasant

desamparado(a): los niños desamparados homeless children

desaparecer to disappear

el **desarrollo** development

el **desastre** disaster

desastroso(a) disastrous

desayunarse to eat breakfast, 12.1

el **desayuno** breakfast, 5.2

tomar el desayuno to eat breakfast, 12.1

descansar to rest

el **descapotable** convertible, **11.1**

el/la **descendiente** descendant

descolgar (ue) to pick up (the telephone), 3.2

describir to describe

descubrir to discover

el **descuento** discount

desde since, from

desear to want, wish, 3.2

¿Qué desea Ud.? May I help you? (in a store), 3.2

el **deseo** desire

los **desechos** waste

desembarcar to disembark, 11.2

desembocar to lead, go (one street into another), 9.1; to empty

el **desenlace** conclusion

el **desierto** desert

despachar to sell, 8.2

despacio slowly

despegar to take off (airplane), 11.2

el **despegue** take-off (airplane), **7.2**

despertarse (ie) to wake up, 12.1

después (de) after, 5.1; later

el **destino** destination, 11.1

con destino a to

la **desventaja** disadvantage

el **detalle** detail

el **detergente** detergent, **4.2**

determinar to determine

detrás de behind, **5.2**

devolver (ue) to return (something), 7.2

el **día** day, BV

Buenos días. Good morning., BV

el Día de los Reyes Epiphany (January 6), **13.2**

hoy (en) día nowadays, these days

¿Qué día es (hoy)? What day is it (today)?, BV

la **diagnosis** diagnosis, 8.2

el **diálogo** dialogue
el **diamante** diamond
diario(a) daily
dibujar to draw
el **dibujo** drawing
diciembre December, BV
diecinueve nineteen, BV
dieciocho eighteen, BV
dieciséis sixteen, BV
diecisiete seventeen, BV
el **diente** tooth
  cepillarse los dientes to
    brush one's teeth, 12.1
  el cepillo de dientes
    toothbrush, 12.2
la **dieta** diet
diez ten
la **diferencia** difference
diferente different
difícil difficult, 2.1
la **dificultad** difficulty
¡Diga! Hello! (telephone),
  14.2; **2.2**
diminuto(a) tiny, minute
la **dinamita** dynamite
el **dinero** money, 14.1; **2.1**
  el dinero en efectivo cash,
    12.2
¡Dios mío! Gosh!
el/la **diplomado(a)** graduate
diplomático(a) diplomatic
la **dirección** direction; address
  en dirección a toward
las **direccionales** turn signals,
  11.1
directo(a) direct
el/la **director(a)** director,
  principal
dirigir to direct
la **disciplina** subject area
  (school), 2.2
el **disco** dial (of telephone), **3.2**
el **disco compacto** compact
  disk, CD, 14.2; **3.1**
discutir to discuss
el/la **diseñador(a)** designer
el **diseño** design
disfrutar to enjoy
disponible available
la **disputa** quarrel, argument
el **disquete** disk, diskette, 3.1
la **distancia** distance
distinto(a) different, distinct
distraer to distract
la **distribución** distribution

la **distribuidora** parking
  meter that dispenses
  tickets
distribuir to pass out,
  distribute, **7.1**
la **diversión** amusement
divertido(a) fun, amusing
divertirse (ie, i) to enjoy
  oneself, 12.2
dividir to divide
la **división** division
divorciarse to get divorced
doblado(a) dubbed, 10.1
doblar to turn, **11.2**
doble: el cuarto doble
  double room, **6.1**
dobles doubles, 9.1
doce twelve, BV
la **docena** dozen, **4.2**
el/la **doctor(a)** doctor
la **documentación**
  documentation
el **documento** document, **3.1**
el **dólar** dollar
doler (ue) to hurt, 8.2
  Me duele(n)... My . . .
    hurt(s) me, 8.2
el **dolor** pain, ache, 8.1
  el dolor de cabeza
    headache, 8.1
  el dolor de estómago
    stomachache, 8.1
  el dolor de garganta sore
    throat, 8.1
  Tengo dolor de... I have a
    pain in my . . . , 8.2
doméstico(a): los animales
  domésticos farm animals,
  9.2
  la economía doméstica
    home economics, 2.2
el **domingo** Sunday, BV
dominicano(a) Dominican,
  2.1
  la República Dominicana
    Dominican Republic
el **dominio** control, authority
el **dominó** dominos, **5.1**
don courteous way of
  addressing a man
donde where, 1.2
¿dónde? where?, 1.2
doña courteous way of
  addressing a woman
dorado(a) golden

dormido(a) asleep
el/la **dormilón(ona)** sleepy-head
dormir (ue, u) to sleep
  el saco de dormir sleeping
    bag, 12.2
dormirse (ue, u) to fall
  asleep, 12.1
el **dormitorio** bedroom, 6.2
dos two, BV
doscientos(as) two hundred,
  3.2
la **dosis** dose, 8.2
el/la **dramaturgo(a)** playwright
driblar to dribble, 7.2
la **droga** drug
la **drogadicción** drug addiction
la **ducha** shower, 12.1
  tomar una ducha to take
    a shower, 12.1
la **duda** doubt
dudar to doubt
duele(n): Me duele(n)
  mucho. It (They) hurt(s)
  me a lot., **8.2**
dudoso(a) doubtful
dulce sweet
  el pan dulce sweet roll, 5.1
la **duración** duration
durante during
durar to last, **13.2**
duro(a) hard, difficult, 2.1

E
la **ebullición** boiling
echar to throw
  echar la carta (en el
    buzón) to mail the letter,
    12.2
  echar (tomar) una siesta
    to take a nap
  echarle flores to pay
    someone a compliment
la **ecología** ecology
ecológico(a) ecological
la **economía** economics;
  economy
  la economía doméstica
    home economics, 2.2
económico(a) economical,
  12.2
la **ecuación** equation
ecuatoriano(a) Ecuadorean,
  2.1
la **edad** age
el **edificio** building, **9.1**

la **educación** education
  la educación física
    physical education, 2.2
educar to educate
efectivo: el dinero en
  efectivo cash
efectuar to carry out
ejemplo: por ejemplo for
  example
ejercicio: hacer los
  ejercicios to exercise
el **ejote** string beans
el the *(m. sing.),* 1.1
él he, 1.1
la **electricidad** electricity
el/la **electricista** electrician, **14.1**
eléctrico(a) electric
electrónico(a): el correo
  electrónico e-mail,
  electronic mail
la **elegancia** elegance
elegante elegant, **13.1**
el **elemento** element
la **elevación** elevation
elevado(a) elevated, high
el **elevador** elevator, **6.1**
elevar to elevate
eliminar to eliminate
ella she, 1.1
ellos(as) they, 2.1
el **elote** corn (Mex.)
el/la **embajador(a)** ambassador
embarcar to board, 11.2
embarque: la tarjeta de
  embarque boarding pass,
  11.1
  la puerta de embarque
    departure gate
la **emergencia** emergency, **7.1**
  la sala de emergencia
    emergency room, **8.1**
la **emisión** program (TV), 6.2;
  emission
  la emisión deportiva
    sports program, 6.2
emitir to emit
la **emoción** emotion
emocional emotional
empalmar to connect
empatado(a) tied (score), 7.1
  El tanto queda empatado.
    The score is tied., 7.1
empezar (ie) to begin, 7.1
el/la **empleado(a)** employee, clerk,
  3.1

emplear to employ
el **empleo** employment, job
  una solicitud de
  empleo a job
  application, **14.2**
la **empresa** business
el/la **empresario(a)** entrepreneur,
  businessperson
empujar to push, **4.2**
  empujar el carrito to push
    the cart, **4.2**
en in; on
  en aquel entonces at that
    time
  en caso de in case of
  en punto on the dot,
    sharp, 4.1
  en sí in itself
el/la **enamorado(a)** sweetheart,
  lover
encantador(a) charming
encantar to delight
encargarse to take charge
encender (ie) to light,
  13.2
encestar to put in (make) a
  basket, 7.2
la **enchilada** enchilada, BV
encima (de) above
  por encima de above, 9.1
encontrar (ue) to find
encontrarse (ue) to meet
la **encuesta** survey
endosar to endorse, **12.2**
el/la **enemigo(a)** enemy
la **energía** energy
enero January, BV
enfadado(a) angry
el **énfasis: dar énfasis** to
  emphasize
enfatizar to emphasize
la **enfermedad** illness
la **enfermería** nursing
el/la **enfermero(a)** nurse, **8.2**
enfermo(a) sick, 8.1
el/la **enfermo(a)** sick person, 8.1
enfrente de in front of
el **enganche** down payment
¡Enhorabuena!
  Congratulations!, **13.1**
el **enlace** union
enlatado(a) canned
enlazar to join, connect
enorme enormous
la **ensalada** salad, 5.1

enseguida right away,
  immediately, 5.1
enseñar to teach, 4.1; to
  show, **4.1**
entablar to start, begin
entero(a) entire, whole
enterrar (ie) to bury
el **entierro** burial
entonces then
  en aquel entonces at
    that time
la **entrada** inning, 7.2;
  admission ticket, 10.1;
  entrance, **5.2**
entrar to enter, 4.1
  entrar en escena to
    come (go) on stage,
    10.2
entre between, 7.1
entregar to deliver
el **entrenamiento** training
entretenido(a)
  entertaining
la **entrevista** interview, 14.2
el/la **entrevistador(a)**
  interviewer, **14.2**
entrevistar to interview
entusiasmado(a)
  enthusiastic
el/la **envejeciente** aging person
enviar to send
envuelto(a) wrapped
el **episodio** episode
la **época** period of time,
  epoch
el **equilibrio** equilibrium
el **equipaje** baggage, luggage,
  11.1
  el equipaje de mano
    carry-on luggage, 11.1
el **equipo** team, 7.1;
  equipment
  el deporte de equipo
    team sport, 7.2
el **equivalente** equivalent
erróneo(a) wrong,
  erroneous
la **escala** stopover, **7.2**
  hacer escala to stop
    over, make a stop,
    7.2
la **escalera** stairway, 6.2
  la escalera mecánica
    escalator, **9.1**
los **escalofríos** chills, 8.1

escamotear to secretly take
escapar to escape
el escaparate shop window, **4.1**
la escasez shortage
la escena stage
 entrar en escena to come (go) on stage, 10.2
el escenario scenery, set (theater), 10.2
escoger to choose, **5**
escolar (related to) school, 2.1
 el bus escolar school bus, 4.1
 el horario escolar school schedule
 la vida escolar school life
 los materiales escolares school supplies, 3.1
esconder to hide
escribir to write, 5.1
escuchar to listen (to), 4.2
el escudero squire, knight's attendant
la escuela school, 1.1
 la escuela intermedia middle school
 la escuela primaria elementary school
 la escuela secundaria high school, 1.1
 la escuela superior high school
el/la escultor(a) sculptor, 10.2
la escultura sculpture
esencial essential
ese(a) that
eso that (one)
 a eso de at about (time), 4.1
esos(as) those
el espacio space
el espagueti spaghetti
espantoso(a) frightful
la España Spain, 1.2
el español Spanish (language), 2.2
español(a) Spanish (adj.)
la espátula palette knife, spatula
la especia spice
especial special
la especialidad specialty, specialization
el/la especialista specialist, **14.1**

especializar to specialize
especialmente especially
el espectáculo show, 10.2
 ver un espectáculo to see a show, 10.2
el/la espectador(a) spectator, 7.1
el espejo mirror, 12.1
espera: la sala de espera waiting room, 13.1; **1.1**
esperar to wait (for), 11.1; to hope
espontáneo(a) spontaneous
la esposa wife, spouse, 6.1
el esposo husband, spouse, 6.1
el esquí skiing, 9.2; ski
 el esquí acuático water skiing, 9.1
el/la esquiador(a) skier, 9.2
esquiar to ski, 9.2
 esquiar en el agua to water-ski, 9.1
la esquina corner, **9.1**
establecerse to settle
el establecimiento establishment
la estación season, BV; station, 10.1
 la estación de esquí ski resort, 9.2
 la estación de ferrocarril train station, 13.1; **1.1**
 la estación del metro subway station, 10.1
 la estación de servicio service station, **11.1**
el estacionamiento parking
estacionar to park
la estadía stay
el estadio stadium, 7.1
la estadística statistic
el estado state
 los Estados Unidos United States
 el estado del banco bank statement
estadounidense from the United States
la estancia ranch (Argentina)
estar to be, 4.1
 ¿Está... ? Is . . . there?, **3.2**
 estar cansado(a) to be tired, **8.1**
 estar contento(a) (triste, etc.) to be happy (sad, etc.), **8.1**

estar de buen (mal) humor to be in a good (bad) mood, **8.1**
estar enfermo(a) to be sick
estar nervioso(a) (tranquilo[a]) to be nervous (calm), **8.1**
estar resfriado(a) to have a cold, 8.1
estatal pertaining to state (adj.)
la estatua statue, 10.2
este(a) this
el este east
estereofónico(a) stereo
el estilo style
estimado(a) esteemed
esto this (one)
el estómago stomach, 8.1
estornudar to sneeze, 8.1
estos(as) these
la estrategia strategy
estrecho(a) narrow, **4.1**
la estrella star
la estructura structure
el/la estudiante student
 el/la estudiante de intercambio exchange student
 la residencia para estudiantes student housing, dormitory, **3.2**
estudiantil (relating to) student
estudiar to study, 4.1
el estudio study, 14
la estufa stove, 10.1
estupendo(a) stupendous
eterno(a) eternal
étnico(a) ethnic
la Europa Europe
europeo(a) European
exactamente exactly
exacto(a) exact
exagerado(a) exaggerated
exagerar to exaggerate
el examen test, exam, 4.2
examinar to examine, 8.2
la excavación excavation
excavar to dig, excavate
exceder to exceed
excelente excellent
la excepción exception
exclamar to exclaim

exclusivamente exclusively
la **exhibición** exhibition
exigir to demand
la **existencia** existence
existir to exist
el **éxito** success
la **expedición** expedition
la **experiencia** experience
experimentar to experiment
el/la **experto(a)** expert, 9.2
explicar to explain, 4.2
el/la **explorador(a)** explorer
la **explosión** explosion
exportar to export
la **exposición (de arte)** (art)
  exhibition, 10.2
la **expresión** expression
  el modo de expresión
    means of expression
la **extensión** extension
extranjero(a) foreign
  el país extranjero foreign
    country, 11.2
el/la **extranjero(a)** foreigner
  en el extranjero abroad
extraordinario(a)
  extraordinary
extravagante strange
extremo(a) extreme

F

la **fábrica** factory, 9.1
fabricado(a) manufactured
fabuloso(a) fabulous
fácil easy, 2.1
facilitar to facilitate
el **facsímil** fax, 3.1
la **factura** bill, 6.1; invoice
  facturar el equipaje to check
    luggage, 11.1
la **Facultad** school (of a
  university)
la **faja** sash
la **falda** skirt, 3.2
falso(a) false
la **fama: tener fama de** to have
  the reputation of
la **familia** family, 6.1
familiar (related to the)
  family
famoso(a) famous, 1.2
fantástico(a) fantastic, 1.2
el/la **farmacéutico(a)** druggist,
  pharmacist, 8.2
la **farmacia** drugstore, 8.2

fascinar to fascinate
Favor de (+ *infinitive*)
  Please (+ *verb*), 11.1
favorito(a) favorite, 11
el **fax** fax, 3.1
  mandar (transmitir) un
    fax to send a fax, to fax,
    3.1
febrero February, BV
la **fecha** date, BV
  ¿Cuál es la fecha de hoy?
    What is today's date?, BV
la **felicidad** happiness
¡Felicitaciones!
  Congratulations!, 13.1
feliz happy
  ¡Feliz cumpleaños! Happy
    birthday!, 13.1
  ¡Feliz Hanuka! Happy
    Hanukah!, 13.2
  ¡Feliz Navidad! Merry
    Christmas!, 13.2
feo(a) ugly, 1.1
el **ferrocarril** railroad, 13.1, 11.1
  la estación de ferrocarril
    train station, 13.1, 1.1
festejar to fete
la **ficción** fiction
la **ficha** piece (game), 5.1;
  registration card, 6.1
ficticio(a) fictitious
la **fiebre** fever, 8.1
  tener fiebre to have a
    fever, 8.1
fiel faithful
la **fiesta** party, 13.1
  dar una fiesta to give
    (throw) a party, 4.2
la **Fiesta de las luces** The
  Festival of Lights, 13.2
la **figura** figure
figurativo(a) figurative
fijar to fix
fijo(a) fixed
la **fila** row (of seats); line
  (queue), 10.1
el **filete** fillet
el **film** film, 10.1
el **fin** end
  a fines de at the end of
  el fin de semana weekend,
    BV
el **final: al final (de)** at the end
  (of)
financiero(a) financial

las **finanzas** finances
la **finca** farm, 9.2
fino(a) fine
firmar to sign, 12.2
la **física** physics, 2.1
físico(a): la educación física
  physical education, 2.2
flaco(a) thin, 1.2
flamenco(a) flamenco
la **flauta** flute
flechar to become enamored
  of (to fall for)
la **flor** flower
el **folleto** pamphlet
el **fondo** fund
el/la **fontanero(a)** plumber,
  14.1
la **forma** shape
formar to make up, to form
el **formulario** form, 8.2
  llenar un formulario to
    fill out a form, 8.2
la **fortaleza** strength
la **fortificación** fortification
la **foto** photo
la **fotografía** photograph
el/la **fotógrafo(a)** photographer
la **fractura** fracture, 8.1
el **fragmento** fragment
el **francés** French, 2.2
franco(a) frank, candid,
  sincere
el **frasco** jar, 4.2
la **frase** phrase, sentence
la **frazada** blanket, 6.2
frecuentemente frequently
freír (i, i) to fry, 14.1; 2.1
los **frenos** brakes, 11.1
la **frente** forehead, 8.1
fresco(a) fresh, 4.2
el **frijol** bean, 5.2
  los frijoles negros black
    beans, 10.2
el **frío: Hace frío.** It's cold.,
  9.2
frito(a) fried, 5.1
  las papas fritas French
    fries, 5.1
el **frontón** wall (of a jai alai
  court)
la **fruta** fruit, 5.2
la **frutería** fruit store, 4.2
el **fuego** fire, 10.2
  a fuego lento on a low
    flame, heat

quitar (retirar) del fuego to take (something) off the heat, **10.2**
la **fuente** source
fuerte strong
la **fuerza** strength; force
fumar: la sección de (no) fumar (no) smoking area, 11.1
la señal de no fumar no smoking sign, **7.1**
la **función** performance, 10.2; function
el **funcionamiento** functioning
el/la **funcionario(a)** city hall employee, 14.1
la **fundación** foundation
fundado(a) founded, established
fundar to found, establish
la **furia** fury
furioso(a) furious
el **fútbol** soccer, 7.1
el campo de fútbol soccer field, 7.1
el **futbolín** table soccer, **5.1**
el **futuro** future

G

la **gabardina** raincoat, **4.1**
las **gafas de sol** sunglasses, 9.1
el **galán** beau, heartthrob
la **galaxia** galaxy
la **galería comercial** shopping mall
el **galón** gallon
gallardo(a) gallant, fine-looking
la **gallina** hen, **9.2**
las **gambas** shrimp, **10.2**
el **ganado** cattle, **9.2**
ganar to win, 7.1; to earn
ganar la vida to earn one's living
la **ganga** bargain
el **garaje** garage, 6.2
la **garantía** garantee
la **garganta** throat, 8.1
la **garita de peaje** toll booth, **11.2**
la **gasolina** gasoline, **11.1**

la **gasolinera** service station, **11.1**
gastar to spend
el/la **gato(a)** cat, 6.1
el/la **gemelo(a)** twin
general: en general generally
por lo general in general, usually
generalmente usually, generally
el **género** genre
generoso(a) generous, 1.2
la **gente** people
la **geografía** geography, 2.2
la **geometría** geometry, 2.2
geométrico(a) geometric
gerencial managerial
el/la **gerente** manager, **14.1**
el **gesto** gesture
el **gigante** giant
el **gimnasio** gymnasium
la **ginecología** gynecology
el/la **ginecólogo(a)** gynecologist
la **gira** tour, 12.2
el **globo** balloon, **5.2**
el **gobierno** government, 14.1
el gobierno estatal state government
el gobierno federal federal government
el gobierno municipal municipal government
el **gol: meter un gol** to score a goal, 7.1
el **golfo** gulf
el **golpe** coup (overthrow of a government)
golpear to hit, 9.2
la **goma** tire, **11.1**
la **goma de borrar** eraser, 3.1
gordo(a) fat, 1.2
la **gorra** cap, hat, 3.2
gozar to enjoy
Gracias. Thank you., BV
gracioso(a) funny, 1.1
el **grado** degree (temperature), 9.2; grade
graduarse to graduate
la **gramática** grammar
el **gramo** gram
gran, grande big, large, great
las Grandes Ligas Major Leagues
el **grano** grain
la **grasa** fat

grave serious, grave
el/la **griego(a)** Greek
la **gripe** flu, 8.1
gris gray, 3.2
el **grupo** group
la **guagua** bus (Puerto Rico, Cuba), 10.1
el **guante** glove, 7.2
guapo(a) handsome, 1.1
guardar to guard, 7.1; to keep, save, **3.1**
guardar cama to stay in bed, 8.1
el/la **guardia** police officer
guatemalteco(a) Guatemalan
la **guerra** war
la **guerrilla** band of guerrillas
el/la **guía** tour guide; guide
la **guía telefónica** telephone book, **3.2**
el **guisante** pea, 5.2
la **guitarra** guitar
gustar to like, to be pleasing
el **gusto** pleasure; taste
Mucho gusto. Nice to meet you.

H

haber to have (in compound tenses)
la **habichuela** bean, 5.2
las habichuelas negras black beans, **10.2**
la habichuela tierna string bean
la **habitación** bedroom, room, **6.1**
el/la **habitante** inhabitant
habla: los países de habla española Spanish-speaking countries
hablar to speak, talk, 3.1
hace: Hace... años ... years ago
Hace buen tiempo. The weather is nice., 9.1
Hace calor. It's hot., 9.1
Hace frío. It's cold., 9.2
Hace mal tiempo. The weather is bad., 9.1
Hace sol. It's sunny., 9.1
hacer to do, to make
hacer caso to pay attention

hacer cola to line up, 10.1
hacer la cama to make the bed, **6.2**
hacer la maleta to pack one's suitcase
hacer las compras to shop, **4.2**
hacer las tareas to do homework, **3.1**
hacer preguntas to ask questions, **14.2**
hacer un viaje to take a trip, **11.1**
hacer una llamada telefónica to make a telephone call, **3.2**
hacerse daño to hurt oneself, **8.1**
hacia toward
la **hacienda** ranch
hallar to find
la **hamburguesa** hamburger, 5.1
hambre: tener hambre to be hungry, 14.1; **2.1**
Hanuka Hanukah, **13.2**
¡Feliz Hanuka! Happy Hanukah!, **13.2**
armonioso(a) harmonious
hasta until, BV
¡Hasta luego! See you later!, BV
¡Hasta mañana! See you tomorrow!, BV
¡Hasta pronto! See you soon!, BV
hay there is, there are, BV
hay que one must
Hay sol. It's sunny., 9.1
No hay de qué. You're welcome., BV
hebreo(a) Hebrew, **13.2**
hecho(a) made
helado(a): el té helado iced tea, 5.1
el **helado** ice cream, 5.1
el helado de chocolate chocolate ice cream, 5.1
el helado de vainilla vanilla ice cream, 5.1
el **helicóptero** helicopter, **7.2**
el **hemisferio norte** northern hemisphere
el **hemisferio sur** southern hemisphere
la **herencia** inheritance

la **herida** wound, **8.1**
el/la **herido(a)** injured person
la **hermana** sister, 6.1
el **hermano** brother, 6.1
hermoso(a) beautiful, pretty, 1.1
el/la **héroe** hero
hervir (ie) to boil, 10.1
el **hidrofoil** hydrofoil
la **higiene** hygiene
higiénico(a): el papel higiénico toilet paper, 12.2
la **hija** daughter, 6.1
el **hijo** son, 6.1
los hijos children, 6.1
hinchado(a) swollen, 8.1
el **hipermercado** hypermarket, **4.2**
la **hipoteca** mortgage
hispano(a) Hispanic
hispanoamericano(a) Spanish-American
hispanohablante Spanish-speaking
el/la **hispanohablante** Spanish speaker
la **historia** history, 2.2; story
el/la **historiador(a)** historian
histórico(a) historical
la **historieta** little story
el **hobby** hobby, **5.1**
la **hoja: la hoja de papel** sheet of paper, 3.1
¡Hola! Hello!, BV
el **hombre** man
¡hombre! good heavens!, you bet!
el **hombro** shoulder, 8.1
honesto(a) honest, 1.2
el **honor** honor
la **hora** hour; time
¿A qué hora? At what time?, 2.2
la hora de salida departure hour
la hora de la cena dinner hour
el **horario** schedule, 13.1; **1.1**
el horario escolar school schedule
la **horchata** cold drink made from almonds, milk, and sugar
la **hornilla** stove burner, **10.1**

el **hornillo** portable stove, 10.1
el **horno** oven, 10.1
el **horno de microondas** microwave oven, **10.1**
horrible horrible
hospedarse to lodge, stay
el **hospital** hospital, **8.1**
la **Hostia** Host (relig.)
el **hostal** inexpensive hotel, 12.2
el **hotel** hotel, **6.1**
hoy today, BV
hoy (en) día nowadays, these days
el **huarache** sandal
el/la **huerto(a)** vegetable garden, orchard, **9.2**
el **hueso** bone, **8.2**
el/la **huésped** guest, **6.1**
el **huevo** egg, 5.2
humano(a): el ser humano human being
húmedo(a) humid
humilde humble
el **humor** mood, 8.1
estar de buen humor to be in a good mood, 8.1
estar de mal humor to be in a bad mood, 8.1
el **huso horario** time zone

I

el **icono** icon
ida: de ida y vuelta round-trip (ticket), 13.1; **1.1**
la **idea** idea
ideal ideal, 1.2
el/la **idealista** idealist
identificar to identify
idílico(a) idyllic
el **idioma** language
la **iglesia** church
igual equal, alike
igual que like, as
la **ilusión** illusion
ilustre distinguished
la **imagen** image
la **imaginación** imagination
imaginado(a) imagined, dreamed of
imaginar to imagine
imaginario(a) imaginary
impar: el número impar odd number
el **imperativo** imperative
el **impermeable** raincoat, 4.1

importante important
importar to be important
imposible impossible
impresionar to affect, influence
la **impresora** printer, **3.1**
inaugurar to inaugurate
el/la **inca** Inca
incluido(a): ¿Está incluido el servicio? Is the tip included?, 5.1
incluir to include, 5.1
increíble incredible
la **independencia** independence
el **indicador: el tablero indicador** scoreboard, 7.1
indicar to indicate, 11.1
indígena native, indigenous
el/la **indígena** native person
indio(a) Indian
indispensable indispensable
individual individual
  el deporte individual individual sport
el **individuo** individual
industrial: la zona industrial industrial area, **9.1**
la **inferencia** inference
la **influencia** influence
la **información** information
informar to inform, 13.2; **1.2**
la **informática** computer science, 2.2
el **informe** report
la **ingeniería** engineering
el/la **ingeniero(a)** engineer, **14.1**
el **inglés** English, 2.2
el **ingrediente** ingredient
ingresar to make a deposit (bank)
inhospital inhospitable
inhóspito(a) desolate, inhospitable
inmediatamente immediately
inmediato(a) immediate
inmenso(a) immense
la **innovación** innovation
inocente innocent
el **inodoro** toilet, **6.2**
insistir to insist
inspeccionar to inspect, 11.1

la **instalación** installation
instantáneo(a) instantaneous
el **instante** instant
la **instrucción** instruction
el **instrumento** instrument
  el instrumento musical musical instrument
íntegro(a) integral
inteligente intelligent, 2.1
el **intercambio** exchange
  el/la estudiante (alumno[a]) de intercambio exchange student
el **interés** interest
interesante interesting, 2.1
interesar to interest
intergaláctico(a) intergalactic
intermedio(a): la escuela intermedia middle school
internacional international
Internet Internet, 3.1
la **interpretación** interpretation
el/la **intérprete** interpreter
interrumpir to interrupt
la **interrupción** interruption
intervenir to intervene
íntimo(a) intimate, close
la **introducción** introduction
introducir to insert, 3.2
  introducir la tarjeta telefónica to insert the phone card, **3.2**
el **invento** invention
inverso(a) reverse
la **investigación** investigation
el/la **investigador(a)** researcher
el **invierno** winter, BV
la **invitación** invitation
el/la **invitado(a)** guest
invitar to invite, 6.1
la **inyección** injection, shot, 8.2
  poner una inyección to give a shot
ir to go, 4.1
  ir a + infinitive to be going to (do something)
  ir a pie to go on foot, to walk, 4.1
  ir de compras to go shopping, 5.2
  ir en bicicleta to go by bicycle, 12.2

ir en carro (coche) to go by car, 4.1
ir en tren to go by train
la **irrigación** irrigation
la **isla** island
italiano(a) Italian
izquierdo(a) left, 7.1
  a la izquierda to the left, **5.2**

J

el **jabón** soap, 12.2
  la barra (pastilla) de jabón bar of soap, 12.2
jamás never
el **jamón** ham, 5.1
el **jardín** garden, 6.2
el/la **jardinero(a)** outfielder, 7.2
la **jaula** cage, **5.2**
el/la **jefe(a)** boss
el **jet** jet
el **jonrón** home run, 7.2
joven young, 6.1
  de joven as a young person
el/la **joven** youth, young person, 10.1
la **joya** jewel, **4.1**
la **joyería** jewelry store, **4.1**
la **judía verde** green bean, 5.2
el **juego** game
  el juego de béisbol baseball game, 7.2
  el juego de tenis tennis game, 9.1
  el juego de video video game, **5.1**
  los Juegos Olímpicos Olympic Games
  la sala de juegos game arcade, **5.1**
el **jueves** Thursday, BV
el/la **juez** judge, **14.1**
el/la **jugador(a)** player, 7.1
  el/la jugador(a) de béisbol baseball player, 7.2
jugar (ue) to play, 7.1
  jugar (al) béisbol (fútbol, baloncesto, etc.) to play baseball (soccer, basketball, etc.), 7.1
el **jugo** juice
  el jugo de naranja orange juice, 12.1
el **juguete** toy

julio July, BV

la **jungla** jungle

junio June, BV

juntos(as) together

juvenil: el albergue juvenil youth hostel, 12.2

la **juventud** youth

K

el **kilo** kilogram, 5.2

el **kilómetro** kilometer

L

la the *(f. sing.)*, 1.1; it, her *(pron.)*

el **labio** lip, **8.1**

el **laboratorio** laboratory

el **lado** side

   al lado de beside, next to, **5.2**

el **lago** lake, **5.2**

   remar por el lago to go rowing on the lake, **5.2**

el **lamento** lament

la **lana** wool, **12.1**

la **langosta** lobster, 14.2; **2.2**

la **lanza** lance

el/la **lanzador(a)** pitcher, 7.2

   lanzar to throw, 7.1; to launch

el **lápiz** pencil, 3.1

   largo(a) long, 3.2

   de largo recorrido long-distance (trip)

   las them *(f. pl. pron.)*

la **lástima: ser una lástima** to be a pity (a shame)

   lastimarse to get hurt, **8.1**

la **lata** can, 5.2

   lateral side *(adj.)*, 13.2; **1.2**

el **latín** Latin, 2.2

   latino(a) Latin *(adj.)*

   Latinoamérica Latin America, 1.1

   latinoamericano(a) Latin American

el **lavabo** washbasin, **6.2**; restroom, **7.1**

el **lavado** laundry, **12.1**

la **lavandería** laundromat

   lavar: la máquina de lavar washing machine, **12.1**

   lavarse to wash oneself, 12.1

   lavarse los dientes to brush one's teeth, 12.1

le to him, to her; to you *(formal) (pron.)*

la **lección** lesson, 4.2

la **leche** milk

   el café con leche coffee with milk, 5.1

el **lechón** suckling pig

la **lechuga** lettuce, 5.2

la **lectura** reading

   leer to read, 5.1

la **legumbre** vegetable, 14; **2**

   lejos far, **12.2**

la **lengua** language, 2.2

el **lenguaje** language

la **lenteja** lentil

   lento(a) slow, 10.2

el **león** lion

   les to them; to you *(formal pl.) (pron.)*

el/la **lesionado(a)** injured person

la **letra** letter (of alphabet)

   levantar to lift, to raise

   levantarse to get up, 12.1; to rise up (against)

   levantarse el sol the sun rises

el/la **libertador(a)** liberator

la **libra** pound

   libre free, 5.1

   al aire libre outdoor *(adj.)*

el **libro** book, 3.1

la **licencia** driver's license, **11.1**

el **liceo** high school

el **lienzo** canvas (painting)

la **liga** league

   las Grandes Ligas Major Leagues

   ligero(a) light (cheerful)

la **lima** lime, **10.1**

   limeño(a) from Lima (Peru)

el **límite de velocidad** speed limit

el **limón** lemon, **10.1**

la **limonada** lemonade, BV

   limpiar to clean, 6.2

   limpiar el cuarto to clean the room, **6.2**

   limpiar en seco to dry clean, **12.1**

   limpio(a) clean

la **limusina** limousine

   lindo(a) pretty, 1.1

la **línea** line

   la línea aérea airline

   la línea ecuatorial equator

   la línea paralela parallel line

   la línea telefónica telephone line

el **lípido** lipide, fat

   líquido(a) liquid

   lírico(a) lyric

la **lista** list

   listo(a) ready; clever, **5.1**

la **litera** berth, 13.2; **1.2**

   literal literal

   literario(a) literary

la **literatura** literature, 2.1

el **litro** liter

la **llamada larga** long-distance call, **3.2**

la **llamada telefónica** telephone call, **3.2**

   hacer una llamada telefónica to make a (telephone) call, **3.2**

   poner la llamada to put the call through

   llamado(a) called

   llamar to call; to telephone, **3.2**

   llamarse to be named, to call oneself, 12.1

la **llanta** tire, **11.1**

   la llanta de recambio (repuesto) spare tire, **11.1**

la **llanura** plain, **7.2**

la **llave** key, **6.1**

la **llegada** arrival, arriving, 11.1

   llegar to arrive, 4.1

   llenar to fill, fill out

   llenar un crucigrama to do a crossword puzzle, **5.1**

   llenar el formulario to fill out the form, **8.2**

   lleno(a) full

   llevar to carry, 3.1; to wear, 3.2; to bring, 6.1; to bear; to have (subtitles, ingredients, etc.); to take, **8.1**

   llover (ue) to rain

   Llueve. It's raining., 9.1

la **lluvia** rain

   lo it; him *(m. sing.) (pron.)*

   lo que what, that which

   local local, 13.2; **1.2**

la **loción: la loción bronceadora** suntan lotion, **9.1**

loco(a) insane

el **lodo** mud

lógico(a) logical

los them (*m. pl.*) (*pron.*)

el **loto** lotto

las **luces** headlights, **11.1**

luchar to fight

luego later; then, BV

¡Hasta luego! See you later!, BV

el **lugar** place

tener lugar to take place, **8.1**

lujo: de lujo deluxe

lujoso(a) luxurious

la **luna** moon

la **luna de miel** honeymoon

lunares: con lunares with polka dots

el **lunes** Monday, BV

la **luz** light

la luz roja red light, **11.2**

M

la **madera** wood

la **madre** mother, **6.1**

madrileño(a) native of Madrid

la **madrina** godmother

el/la **maestro(a)** teacher; master

magnífico(a) magnificent

el **maíz** corn, **14.2; 2.2**

mal bad, **14.2; 2.2**

estar de mal humor to be in a bad mood, **8.1**

Hace mal tiempo. The weather's bad., **9.1**

la **maleta** suitcase, **11.1**

el/la **maletero(a)** trunk (of a car), **11.1;** porter, **13.1; 1.1**

malhumorado(a) bad-tempered

malo(a) bad, **2.1**

sacar una nota mala to get a bad grade, **4.2**

la **mamá** mom

el **mambo** mambo

mandar to send, **3.1;** to order

manejar to drive, **11.1**

la **manera** way, manner, **1.1**

de ninguna manera by no means, **1.1**

la **manga** sleeve, **4.1**

a mangas cortas (largas) short- (long-) sleeved, **4.1**

el **maní** peanut

la **mano** hand, **7.1**

dar la mano to shake hands

la **mano de obra** workforce

la **manta** blanket, **6.2**

el **mantel** tablecloth, **14.1; 2.1**

mantener to maintain

mantenerse en forma to keep in shape

la **mantequilla** butter, **10.2**

la **manzana** apple, **5.2**

el **manzano** apple tree, **9.2**

mañana tomorrow, BV

¡Hasta mañana! See you tomorrow!, BV

la **mañana** morning

de la mañana A.M. (time), **2.2**

por la mañana in the morning

el **mapa** map

el **maquillaje** makeup, **12.1**

poner el maquillaje to put one's makeup on, **12.1**

maquillarse to put one's makeup on, **12.1**

la **máquina** machine, device

la máquina de lavar washing machine, **12.1**

prender la máquina to turn (a device) on, **3.1**

el **mar** sea, **9.1**

el mar Caribe Caribbean Sea

maravilloso(a) marvelous

el **marcador** marker, **3.1**

marcar to dial, **3.2**

marcar el número to dial the number, **3.2**

marcar un tanto to score a point, **7.1**

marchar to march

el **marfil** ivory

el **marido** husband, **6.1**

el/la **marino(a)** sailor

los **mariscos** shellfish, **5.2**

marrón: de color marrón brown, **3.2**

el **martes** Tuesday, BV

marzo March, BV

más more, **2.2**

más tarde later

más o menos more or less

la **masa** mass

la **máscara de oxígeno** oxygen mask, **7.1**

matar to kill

las **matemáticas** mathematics, **2.1**

la **materia** matter, subject; material

la materia prima raw material

el **material** supply, **3.1;** material

los materiales escolares school supplies, **3.1**

el **matrimonio** marriage

máximo(a) maximum, **11.2**

la velocidad máxima speed limit, **11.2**

el/la **maya** Maya

mayo May, BV

la **mayonesa** mayonnaise, **4.2**

mayor greater, greatest; elderly, older

la mayor parte the greater part, the most

la **mayoría** majority

me me (*pron.*)

el/la **mecánico(a)** mechanic

la **medalla** medal

media average

y media half-past (time)

mediano(a) medium, **4.1**

la **medianoche** midnight

las **medias** stockings, pantihose

el **medicamento** medicine (drugs), **8.2**

la **medicina** medicine (discipline), **8.2;** medicine

el/la **médico(a)** doctor, **8.2**

la **medida** measurement

el **medio** medium, means

el medio de transporte means of transportation

medio(a) half, **5.2;** average

media hora half an hour

el **medio ambiente** environment

el **mediodía** noon

medir (i, i) to measure
la mejilla cheek, **8.1**
los mejillones mussels, **10.2**
mejor better
el/la mejor the best
melancólico(a) melancholic
el melocotón peach, **10.1**
la memoria memory
mencionar to mention
menor lesser, least
la menora menorah, **13.2**
menos less, fewer
a menos que unless
menos cuarto a quarter to (the hour)
el mensaje message, **3.2**
dejar un mensaje to leave a message, **3.2**
la mensualidad monthly installment
mentiroso(a) lying
el menú menu, 5.1
el mercadeo marketing
el mercado market, 5.2
la mercancía merchandise, **14.1**
el merengue merengue
la merienda snack, 4.2
tomar una merienda to have a snack, 4.2
la mermelada jam, marmalade
el mes month, BV
la mesa table, 5.1; plateau
la mesera waitress, 5.1
el mesero waiter, 5.1
la meseta plateau, **7.2**
la mesita tray table, **7.1**
el/la mestizo(a) mestizo
el metabolismo metabolism
el metal: instrumentos de metal brass (instruments in orchestra)
meter to put, place, 7.1; to put in, insert, **3.1**
meter un gol to score a goal, 7.1
el método method
la métrica metrics
el metro subway, 10.1; meter, **7.2**

mexicano(a) Mexican, 1.1
mexicanoamericano(a) Mexican American
la mezcla mixture
mi my
mí me
el microbio microbe
microscópico(a) microscopic
el microscopio microscope
el miedo fear
tener miedo to be afraid
el miembro member, 4.2
mientras while
el miércoles Wednesday, BV
la migración migration
mil (one) thousand, 3.2
el militar soldier
la milla mile
el millón million
el/la millonario(a) millionaire
el/la mimo(a) mime, **5.2**
la miniatura miniature
la miniaturización miniaturization
el ministerio ministry
el minuto minute
mirar to look at, watch, 3.1
mirarse to look at oneself, 12.1
¡Mira! Look!
el/la mirón(ona) spectator
la miseria poverty
mismo(a) same, 2.1; myself, yourself, him/her/itself, ourselves, yourselves, themselves
el misterio mystery
misterioso(a) mysterious
la mitad half
la mitología mythology
mixto(a) co-ed (school)
la mochila backpack, 3.1; knapsack, 12.2
la moción motion
la moda style
de moda in style
la modalidad mode, type

el/la modelo model
el módem modem
la moderación moderation
moderno(a) modern
el modo manner, way
el modo de expresión means of expression
el molino de viento windmill
el momento moment
el monasterio monastery
la moneda coin, currency, **3.2**
el monitor monitor, computer screen, **3.1**
el mono monkey, **5.2**
monocelular single-celled
el monstruo monster
la montaña mountain, 9.2
la montaña rusa roller coaster, **5.2**
montañoso(a) mountainous
montar (caballo) to mount, get on (horse)
el monumento monument
moreno(a) dark, brunette, 1.1
morir (ue, u) to die
el/la moro(a) Moor
morrón: el pimiento morrón sweet pepper
la mortalidad mortality
el mostrador counter, 11.1
mostrar (ue) to show
el motivo reason, motive; theme
el motor motor
mover (ue) to move
el movimiento movement
el/la mozo(a) porter (train station) 13.1; **1.1;** bellman (hotel), **6.1**
la muchacha girl, 1.1
el muchacho boy, 1.1
mucho(a) a lot; many, 2.1
Mucho gusto. Nice to meet you.
mudarse to move
los muebles furniture
la muerte death
la mujer wife, 6.1
el/la mulato(a) mulatto

la **muleta** crutch, **8.2**
la **multa** fine
multinacional multinational
la **multiplicación** multiplication
multiplicar to multiply
mundial worldwide, (related to the) world
    la **Copa mundial** World Cup
    la **Serie mundial** World Series
el **mundo** world
    todo el mundo everyone
la **muñeca** wrist, **4.1**
el **mural** mural, 10.2
el/la **muralista** muralist
la **muralla** wall
    muscular muscular
el **museo** museum, 10.2
la **música** music, 2.2
el/la **músico(a)** musician
muy very, BV
    muy bien very well, BV

N

nacer to be born, **13.1**
nacido(a) born
nacional national
la **nacionalidad** nationality, 1.2
    ¿de qué nacionalidad? what nationality?
nada nothing, 5.2
    De nada. You're welcome., BV
    Nada más. Nothing else., 5.2
    Por nada. You're welcome., BV
nadar to swim, 9.1
nadie no one
la **naranja** orange, 5.2
el **narcótico** narcotic
la **nariz** nose, **8.1**
la **narración** narration
narrar to narrate
la **natación** swimming, 9.1
natural: los recursos naturales natural resources, 2.1
    las ciencias naturales natural sciences
la **naturaleza** nature
la **navaja** razor, 12.1

navegar to navigate
    navegar por la red to surf the Net
la **Navidad** Christmas, **13.2**
    el árbol de Navidad Christmas tree, **13.2**
    ¡Feliz Navidad! Merry Christmas!, **13.2**
necesario(a) necessary
la **necesidad** necessity
necesitar to need, 3.1
negativo(a) negative
negro(a) black, 3.2
nervioso(a) nervous, 8.1
el **neumático** tire, **11.1**
nevar (ie) to snow, 9.2
la **nevera** refrigerator, **10.1**
la **nieta** granddaughter, 6.1
el **nieto** grandson, 6.1
la **nieve** snow, 9.2
ninguno(a) not any, none, no
    de ninguna manera by no means, 1.1
el/la **niño(a)** child
    los niños desamparados homeless children
el **nivel** level
    el nivel del mar sea level
no no, BV
    No hay de qué. You're welcome., BV
    no hay más remedio there's no other alternative
noble noble
la **noche** night, evening
    Buenas noches. Good night., BV
    esta noche tonight, 9.2
    de la noche P.M. (time), 2.2
    por la noche in the evening, at night
la **Nochebuena** Christmas Eve, **13.2**
la **Nochevieja** New Year's Eve, **13.2**
nombrar to mention
el **nombre** name
    ¿a nombre de quién? in whose name?, 14.2; **2.2**
la **noria** Ferris Wheel, **5.2**
normal regular (gas), **11.1**
el **noroeste** northwest
el **norte** north

norteamericano(a) North American
nos (to) us (pl. pron.)
nosotros(as) we, 2.2
la **nota** grade, 4.2
    la nota buena (alta) good (high) grade, 4.2
    la nota mala (baja) bad (low) grade, 4.2
    sacar una nota buena (mala) to get a good (bad) grade, 4.2
notable notable
notar to note
las **noticias** news, 6.2
novecientos(as) nine hundred, 3.2
la **novela** novel
el/la **novelista** novelist
noveno(a) ninth, 6.2
noventa ninety, 2.2
noviembre November, BV
la **novia** bride, **13.1**; fiancée, girlfriend
el **novio** groom, **13.1**; fiancé, boyfriend
los **novios** bride and groom, newlyweds, **13.1**
la **nube** cloud, 9.1
    Hay nubes. It's cloudy, 9.1
nublado(a) cloudy, 9.1
nuestro(a) our
nueve nine, BV
nuevo(a) new
    de nuevo again
el **número** number, 1.2; size (shoes), 3.2
    el número de teléfono telephone number, **3.2**
    el número del asiento seat number, 11.1
    el número del vuelo flight number, 11.1
    el número equivocado wrong number
numeroso(a) numerous
nunca never
nupcial nuptial, wedding
la **nutrición** nutrition

O

o or
    o sea in other words
el **objetivo** objective

el **objeto** object
la **obligación** obligation
obligatorio(a): el curso obligatorio required course
la **obra** work
la obra de arte work of art
la obra dramática play
la obra teatral play, 10.2
el/la **obrero(a)** worker, **9.1**
la **observación** observation
el/la **observador(a)** observer
observar to observe
el **obstáculo** obstacle
obtener to obtain
obvio(a) obvious
la **ocasión** occasion
occidental western
el **océano** ocean
ochenta eighty, 2.2
ocho eight, BV
ochocientos(as) eight hundred, 3.2
octavo(a) eighth, 6.2
octubre October, BV
ocupado(a) taken, 5.1; busy (phone); occupied, **7.1**
ocurrir to happen
el **oeste** west
oficial official
la **oficina** office, **9.1**
el **oficio** trade, **14.1**
ofrecer to offer, **14.2**
la **oftalmología** ophthalmology
el/la **oftalmólogo(a)** ophthalmologist
el **oído** ear, **4.1**
oír to hear
oír el tono to hear the dial tone, **3.2**
ojalá I hope, **14.1**
el **ojo** eye, 8.2
la **ola** wave, 9.1
el **óleo** oil
la **oliva: el aceite de oliva** olive oil
la **olla** pot, **10.1**
once eleven, BV
la **oncología** oncology
el/la **oncólogo(a)** oncologist
la **onza** ounce
opcional: el curso opcional elective course
la **ópera** opera
el/la **operador(a)** operator

operar to operate
la **opereta** operetta
opinar to think, to express an opinion, **10.2**
la **opinión** opinion
la **oportunidad** opportunity
oprimir to push
opuesto(a) opposite
oralmente orally
la **orden** order (restaurant), 5.1
el **ordenador** computer, **3.1**
la **oreja** ear, **4.1**
el **orfanato** orphanage
el **organillo** barrel organ
el **organismo** organism
organizar to organize
el **órgano** organ
oriental eastern
el **origen** origin
original: en versión original in its original (language) version, 10.1
la **orilla** bank (of a river, lake, etc.)
a orillas de on the shores of
el **oro** gold
de oro (made of) gold, **4.1**
la **orquesta** orchestra, **13.1**
la orquesta sinfónica symphonic orchestra
la **ortiga** nettle
la **ortopedia** orthopedics
oscuro(a) dark
la **ostra** oyster, **10.2**
otavaleño(a) of or from Otavalo, Ecuador
el **otoño** autumn, BV
otro(a) other, another
el **oxígeno** oxygen
¡oye! listen!

P

la **paciencia** patience
el/la **paciente** patient
el **padre** father, 6.1
el padre (religioso) father (relig.)
los padres parents, 6.1
el **padrino** godfather; best man, **13.1**
los padrinos godparents
pagar to pay, 3.1
pagar en la caja to pay at the cashier, **4.2**

pagar la factura to pay the bill, **6.1**
la **página** page
la página Web Web page
el **pago** payment
el pago mensual monthly payment
el **país** country, 11.2
el país extranjero foreign country
el **paisaje** landscape
la **paja** straw, **13.2**
el **pájaro** bird
el **paje** page (wedding)
la **palabra** word
el **palacio** palace
la **palma** palm tree
el **pan** bread, **4.2**
el pan dulce sweet roll, 5.1
el pan tostado toast, 5.2
la **panadería** bakery, **4.2**
panameño(a) Panamanian, 2.1
panamericano(a) Panamerican
el **panqueque** pancake
la **pantalla** screen (movies), 10.1; computer monitor, **3.1**
la pantalla de salidas y llegadas arrival and departure screen, 11.1
el **pantalón** pants, trousers, 3.2
el pantalón corto shorts, 3.2
el **pañuelo** handkerchief, **4.1**
la **papa** potato, 5.1
las papas fritas French fries, 5.1
el **papá** dad
la **papaya** papaya, **10.2**
el **papel** paper, 3.1; role, part, **5.1**
el papel higiénico toilet paper, 12.2
la hoja de papel sheet of paper, 3.1
la **papelería** stationery store, 3.1
el **paquete** package, 5.2
par: número par even number
el **par** pair, **4.1**
el par de tenis pair of tennis shoes, 3.2
para for
¿para cuándo? for when?, 14.2; **2.2**

VOCABULARIO ESPAÑOL-INGLÉS

el **parabrisas** windshield, **11.1**
la **parada** stop, 13.2; **1.2**
   la parada de bus bus stop, **9.1**
el **parador** inn
el **paraíso** paradise
parar to stop, to block, 7.1
parcial: a tiempo parcial part-time *(adj.)*, **14.2**
pardo(a) brown
parear to pair, match
parecer to look like; to seem, **8.1**
parecido(a) similar
la **pared** wall
la **pareja** couple
el/la **pariente** relative, 6.1
el **parque** park, **5.2**
   el parque de atracciones amusement park, **5.2**
el **parquímetro** parking meter, **11.2**
el **párrafo** paragraph
la **parrilla** grill, **10.1**
la **parte** part, **8.1**
   ¿De parte de quién? Who's calling?, **3.2**
   la mayor parte the greatest part, the most
   la parte superior upper part
   por todas partes everywhere
particular private, 6.2
   la casa particular private house, 6.2
particularmente especially
la **partida** departure
el **partido** game, match, 7.1
el **pasado** the past
pasado(a) past; last
   el (año) pasado last (year)
el/la **pasajero(a)** passenger, 11.1
el **pasaporte** passport, 11.1
pasar to pass, 7.2; to spend; to happen
   Lo están pasando muy bien. They're having a good time., 12.2
   pasar por to go through, 11.1
   pasar el tiempo to spend time, **5.1**
   ¿Qué te pasa? What's the matter (with you)?, 8.1

el **pasatiempo** hobby, **5.1**
el **pase** pass (permission)
   pasear a caballo to go horseback riding
el **pasillo** aisle, 13.2; **1.2**
el **paso** step
la **pasta dentrífica** toothpaste, 12.2
el **pastel** pastry, **4.2**; cake, **13.1**
la **pastelería** bakery, **4.2**
la **pastilla** pill, 8.2
   la pastilla de jabón bar of soap, 12.2
la **patata** potato, **10.1**
el **patinaje lineal** roller blading
el **patrón** pattern
   pavimentado(a) paved
el **pavimento** pavement
el **payaso** clown, **5.2**
el **peaje** toll, **11.2**
   la garita de peaje tollbooth, **11.2**
el **peatón** pedestrian, **9.1**
el **pecho** chest, **8.1**
el **pedacito** little piece, **10.2**
el **pedazo** piece
la **pediatría** pediatrics
el/la **pediatra** pediatrician
pedir (i, i) to ask for, 14.1; **2.1**
   pedir la cuenta to ask for the bill, **6.1**
   pedir prestado to borrow
el **peinado** hairdo
peinarse to comb one's hair, 12.1
el **peine** comb, 12.1
pelar to peel, **10.2**
la **película** film, movie, 6.2
   ver una película to see a film, 10.1
el **peligro** danger
   peligroso(a) dangerous
el **pelo** hair, 12.1
la **pelota** ball (tennis, baseball, etc.), 7.2
   la pelota vasca jai alai
el/la **pelotari** jai alai player
la **peluca** wig
la **peluquería** hair salon, **12.1**
el/la **peluquero(a)** hair stylist, **12.1**
el **pendiente** earring, **4.1**
la **península** peninsula
el **pensamiento** thought
   pensar (ie) to think

la **pensión** boarding house, 12.2
   peor worse, worst
   el/la peor the worst
el **pepino** cucumber, **10.1**
   pequeño(a) small, 2.1
la **pera** pear, **9.2**
el **peral** pear tree, **9.2**
la **percha** clothes hanger, **6.2**
la **percusión** percussion
   perder (ie) to lose, 7.1; to miss, 10.2
   perder el autobús (la guagua, el camión) to miss the bus, 10.2
   perdón excuse me
el/la **peregrino(a)** pilgrim
   perezoso(a) lazy, 1.1
   perfeccionar to perfect
el **período** period
el **periódico** newspaper, 6.2
el **permiso de conducir** driver's license, **11.1**
   permitir to permit, 11.1
   pero but
el **perrito** puppy
el **perro** dog, 6.1
la **persona** person, 1.2
el **personaje** character
la **personalidad** personality
el **personal** personnel, 14.2
   el departamento de personal personnel department, 14.2
   personalmente personally
   pertenecer to belong
   peruano(a) Peruvian
la **pesa** weight
   pesado(a) heavy
   pesar to weigh, **12.2**
la **pescadería** fish market, **4.2**
el **pescado** fish (food), 5.2
la **peseta** Spanish unit of currency
el **peso** peso (monetary unit of several Latin American countries), BV; weight
la **petición** petition
el **petróleo** petroleum, oil
   petrolero(a) oil
el **piano** piano
la **picadura** sting, **8.1**
   picar to sting, **8.1**; to dice, **10.2**
el/la **pícher** pitcher, 7.2

el **pico** peak, **7.2**
   y pico just after (time)
el **pie** foot, 7.1; down payment
   a pie on foot, 4.1
   al pie de at the foot of
   de pie standing
la **piedra** stone
la **pierna** leg, 7.1
la **pieza** room
la **píldora** pill, 8.2
el/la **piloto** pilot, 11.2
la **pimienta** pepper, 14.1; **2.1**
el **pimiento** bell pepper, **10.2**
el **pimiento morrón** sweet
   pepper
   pinchado(a) flat
el **pincel** brush, paintbrush
la **pinta** pint
   pinta: tener buena pinta
     to look good (food), **4.2**
   pintar to paint, **14.1**
el/la **pintor(a)** painter
   pintoresco(a) picturesque,
     9.1
la **pintura** painting
la **piragua** ice with syrup over
   it, **5.2**
los **pirineos** Pyrenees
la **pirueta** pirouette, maneuver
la **piscina** swimming pool, 9.1
el **piso** floor, 6.2, apartment
la **pista** (ski) slope, 9.2; runway,
   7.2
la **pizarra** chalkboard, 4.2
el **pizarrón** chalkboard, 4.2
la **pizca** pinch
la **pizza** pizza, BV
la **placa** license plate
la **plaga** plague, menace
la **plancha de vela** sailboard,
   9.1
   practicar la plancha de
     vela to go windsurfing,
     9.1
   planchar to iron, **12.1**
   planear to plan
el **plano** plan, map, **9.1**
la **planta** floor, 6.2; plant
   la planta baja ground
     floor, 6.2
   plástico(a) plastic, **4.2**
   la bolsa de plástico
     plastic bag, **4.2**
la **plata** money (income)
el **plátano** banana, plantain, 5.2

el **platillo** base, 7.2; saucer, 14.1;
   2.1
el **plato** plate, dish, 14.1; **2.1**
la **playa** beach, 9.1
   playera: la toalla playera
     beach towel, 9.1
la **plaza** seat, 13.2; **1.2**; town
   square, **9.1**
   plazo: a corto (largo) plazo
     short- (long-)term
   pleno: en pleno + *noun* in
     the middle of *(noun)*
el/la **plomero(a)** plumber, **14.1**
   plomo: con plomo leaded
     (gasoline), **11.1**
   sin plomo unleaded, **11.1**
la **pluma** pen, 3.1
la **población** population, people
   pobre poor
el/la **pobre** the poor boy (girl)
el/la **pobretón(ona)** poor man
   (woman)
   poco(a) little, few, 2.1
   un poco (de) a little
   poder (ue) to be able, 7.1
el **poema** poem
la **poesía** poetry
el/la **poeta** poet
el/la **policía** police officer
   policíaco(a): novela
     policíaca detective fiction,
     mystery
   político(a) political
el **pollo** chicken, 5.2
el **poncho** poncho, shawl, wrap
   poner to put, 11.1
   poner en un yeso to put a
     cast on, **8.2**
   poner la mesa to set the
     table, 14.1; **2.1**
   ponerse to put on, 12.1
   ponerse el maquillaje to
     put on makeup, 12.1
   ponerse la ropa to dress
     oneself, to put on clothes,
     12.1
   popular popular, 2.1
la **popularidad** popularity
   por for
   por aquí over here
   por ciento percent
   por ejemplo for example
   por eso therefore, for this
     reason, that's why
   por favor please, BV

   por fin finally
   por hora per hour
   por la noche in the
     evening
   por lo general in general
   Por nada. You're welcome.,
     BV
   ¿por qué? why?
   por tierra overland
el **porche** porch
el **pordiosero** beggar
el **poroto** string bean
   porque because
   portátil portable
el/la **porteño(a)** inhabitant of
   Buenos Aires
la **portería** goal line, 7.1
el/la **portero(a)** goalkeeper, goalie,
   7.1
   poseer to possess
la **posibilidad** possibility
   posible possible
la **posición** position
la **postal** postcard, **12.2**
el **postre** dessert, 5.1
el/la **practicante** nurse
   practitioner
   practicar to practice
   practicar el surfing (la
     plancha de vela, etc.) to
     go surfing (windsurfing,
     etc.), 9.1
el **precio** price
   precioso(a) precious,
     beautiful
   preciso(a) precise
   precolombino(a) pre-
     Columbian
la **predicción** prediction
   predominar to predominate
el **predominio** predominance
   preferir (ie, i) to prefer
el **prefijo de país** country code,
   3.2
la **pregunta** question
   preguntar to ask (a
     question)
el **premio: el Premio Nóbel**
   Nobel Prize
   prender to turn on, **3.1**
   prender la máquina to
     turn (a device) on,
     3.1
la **preparación** preparation
   preparar to prepare

la **presencia** presence
la **presentación** presentation
presentar to show (movie); to present
presente present *(adj.)*
el/la **presidente** president
la **presión** pressure, **11.1**
    la **presión arterial** blood pressure, **8.2**
prestado: pedir prestado to borrow
el **préstamo** loan
prestar: prestar atención to pay attention, 4.2
el **prestigio** prestige
prevalecer to prevail
primario(a): la escuela primaria elementary school
la **primavera** spring, BV
primero(a) first, BV
    en primera (clase) first-class, 13.1; **1.1**
    los primeros auxilios first aid
el/la **primo(a)** cousin, 6.1
primordial fundamental
la **princesa** princess
principal main, principal
principalmente mainly
el/la **principiante** beginner, 9.2
prisa: a toda prisa as fast as possible
privado(a) private
    la casa privada private house, 6.2
probable probable
probarse (ue) to try on, **4.1**
el **problema** problem
procesar to process
la **procesión** procession
el **proceso** process
proclamar to proclaim
pródigo prodigal
la **producción** production
producido(a) produced
producir to produce
el **producto** product, 5.2
    los productos congelados frozen food, 5.2
la **profesión** profession, 14.1
el/la **profesor(a)** teacher, professor, 2.1
profundo(a) deep
el **programa** program

el/la **programador(a) de informática** computer programmer, 14.1
el **progreso** progress
prohibido(a) forbidden, 11.2
la **promesa** promise
la **promiscuidad** promiscuity
la **promoción** promotion
promover (ue) to promote
el **pronombre** pronoun
el **pronóstico** forecast
pronto: ¡Hasta pronto! See you soon!, BV
la **propaganda** publicity, advertising
la **propina** tip, 14.1; **2.1**
propio(a) (one's) own
la **prosa** prose
próspero(a): ¡Próspero Año Nuevo! Happy New Year, **13.2**
el/la **protagonista** protagonist
la **protección** protection
protector(a): la crema protectora sunblock, 9.1
la **proteína** protein
protestar to protest
el **protoplasma** protoplasm
el/la **proveedor(a)** provider
proveer to provide
la **provisión** provision
próximo(a) next,13.2; **1.2**
    en la próxima parada at the next stop, 13.2; **1.2**
proyectar to project, 10.1
el **proyecto** project
la **psiquiatría** psychiatry
el/la **psiquiatra** psychiatrist
publicar to publish
el **público** audience, 10.2
el **pueblo** town, 9.2
    los pueblos jóvenes shantytowns (Peru)
el **puerco** pork
la **puerta** gate, 11.1; door, **6.1**
    la puerta de salida departure gate, 11.1
puertorriqueño(a) Puerto Rican
pues well
el **puesto** market stall, **4.2**; position, **14.2**
la **pulgada** inch
pulsar: pulsar el botón to push the button, 3.1

la **pulsera** bracelet, **4.1**
el **pulso: tomar el pulso** to take one's pulse, **8.2**
puntual punctual
el **punto** stitch, 8.1; dot, point
    en punto on the dot, sharp, 4.1
    los puntos cardinales cardinal points
    poner puntos to give (someone) stitches
el **puré de papas** mashed potatoes
puro(a) pure

Q

qué what; how, BV
    ¡Qué absurdo! How absurd!
    ¡Qué enfermo(a) estoy! I'm so sick!
    ¿Qué tal? How are you?, BV
    ¿Qué te pasa? What's the matter (with you)?, 8.2
quechua Quechuan
quedar to remain, 7.1
    quedar: No me queda(n) bien. It (They) doesn't (don't) look good on (fit) me., **4.1**
los **quehaceres** chores
querer (ie) to want, wish; to love
el **queso** cheese, 5.1
el **quetzal** quetzal (Guatemalan money)
    ¿quién? who?, 1.1
    ¿De parte de quién? Who is calling?, **3.2**
    ¿quiénes? who? *(pl.)*, 2.1
la **química** chemistry, 2.2
químico(a) chemical
quince fifteen, BV
la **quinceañera** fifteen-year-old (girl)
quinientos(as) five hundred, 3.2
quinto(a) fifth, 6.2
el **quiosco** newsstand, 13.1; **1.1**
el **quirófano** operating room
Quisiera... I would like . . . , 14.2; **2.2**
quitar to take off, remove, **10.2**
quizás perhaps, 14.2

R

el **radiador** radiator, **11.1**
la **radiografía** X-ray, **8.2**
la **raíz** root
  rallar to grate, **10.2**
la **rama** branch
la **ranura** disk drive, **3.1**; slot, **3.2**
  rápidamente quickly
  rápido quickly
la **raqueta** racket (sports), 9.1
  raro(a) rare
el **rascacielos** skyscraper, **9.1**
el **rato** while
el **ratón** mouse (computer), **3.1**
la **raya** part (in hair), **12.1**
  rayas: a rayas striped
los **rayos equis** X-rays
la **razón** reason
  razonable reasonable
la **reacción** reaction
  real royal
  realista realistic
el/la **realista** realist
  realmente really
la **rebanada** slice, **4.2**
  rebanar to slice, **10.2**
  rebotar to rebound
la **recámara** bedroom, **6.2**
la **recepción** front desk (hotel), **6.1**; admissions (hospital), **8.2**; reception (party)
el/la **recepcionista** hotel clerk, **6.1**
el/la **receptor(a)** catcher, 7.2
la **receta** prescription, 8.2; recipe, **10.2**
  recetar to prescribe, 8.2
  recibir to receive, 5.1
el **reciclaje** recycling
  recién recently
  reciente recent
  recitar to recite
  reclamar to claim (luggage), 11.2
el **reclamo de equipaje** baggage claim, 11.2
  reclutar to recruit
  recoger to pick up
    recoger el equipaje to claim one's luggage, 11.2
la **recomendación** recommendation
  recomendar (ie) to recommend
  reconocer to recognize

  recordar (ue) to remember
  recorrer to travel through
el **recorrido** trip, distance traveled
    de largo recorrido long-distance
el **recreo** recreation
el **rectángulo** rectangle
el **recuerdo** memory, recollection
la **recuperación: la sala de recuperación** recovery room
el **recurso: los recursos naturales** natural resources
    el departamento de recursos humanos human resources department, **14.2**
la **red** net, 9.1
    navegar por la red to surf the Net
  reducido(a) reduced (price)
  reducir to set (bone), **8.2**
  reemplazar to replace
  referir (ie, i) to refer
  reflejar to reflect
el **reflejo** reflection
  reflexionar to reflect
la **reforestación** reforestation
el **refresco** drink, beverage, 5.1
el **refrigerador** refrigerator, **10.1**
el **refugio** refuge
  regalar to give
el **regalo** gift, 6.1
la **región** region
  regional regional
el **regionalismo** regionalism
  registrar to register
la **regla** rule
  regresar to return
el **regreso** return
    el viaje de regreso return trip, trip back
  regular regular, average, 2.2
la **reina** queen
  reír to laugh
la **relación** relation
  relacionado(a) related
  relativamente relatively
  religioso(a) religious
  rellenar to fill
el **reloj** watch, **4.1**; clock, **13.2**

  remar to row, 5.2
el **remedio** solution
  renombrado(a) well-known
  rentar to rent
  renunciar to renounce, give up
  reparar to repair
  repentinamente suddenly
  repetir (i, i) to repeat; to take seconds (meal)
el **reportaje** report
la **representación** performance (theater), 10.2
    dar una representación to put on a performance, 10.2
el/la **representante** representative
  representar to represent
  representativo(a) representative
la **república** republic
la **República Dominicana** Dominican Republic
  requerir (ie, i) to require, **14.1**
el **requisito** requirement
la **reservación** reservation, **6.1**
  reservado(a) reserved, 13.2; **1.2**
  reservar to reserve, 14.2; **2.2**
  resfriado(a): estar resfriado(a) to have a cold, **8.1**
la **residencia: la residencia para estudiantes** student housing, dormitory, **3.2**
el/la **residente** resident
  resolver (ue) to solve
el **respaldo** back (of seat), **7.1**
la **respiración** breathing
  respirar to breathe
  responder to respond
la **responsabilidad** responsibility
  responsabilizarse to make oneself responsible
la **respuesta** answer
  restar to subtract
el **restaurante** restaurant, 14.1; **2.1**
  restaurar to restore
el **resto** rest, remainder
los **restos** remains
el **resultado** result
la **retina** retina

el **retintín** jingle
retirar del fuego to remove
from the heat (stove), **10.1**
el **retrato** portrait
el **retraso: con retraso** with a
delay, late, 13.2; **1.2**
la **reunión** gathering
reunirse to get together
revisar to inspect, 11.1; to
check
revisar el boleto to check
the ticket, 11.1
revisar el aceite to check
the oil (car), **11.1**
el/la **revisor(a)** (train) conductor,
13.2; **1.2**
la **revista** magazine, 6.2
la **revolución** revolution
revolver (ue) to turn around;
to stir, **10.1**
el **rey** king
los **Reyes Magos** Three Wise
Men, **13.2**
el Día de los Reyes
Epiphany (January 6), **13.2**
rico(a) rich; delicious, 14.2; **2.2**
el/la **rico(a)** rich person
riguroso(a) rigorous
el **río** river, **7.2**
el **ritmo** rhythm
el **rito** ritual
el **rival** rival
la **roca** rock
rodar (ue) to roll
la **rodilla** knee, 7.1
rogar (ue) to beg, to plead
rojo(a) red, 3.2
el **rol** role
el **rollo de papel higiénico** roll
of toilet paper, 12.2
el/la **romano(a)** Roman
romántico(a) romantic
romperse to break, **8.1**
la **ropa** clothing, 3.2
la ropa interior
underwear, **4.1**
**la ropa para caballeros
(señoras)** men's
(women's) clothing, **4.1**
la ropa sucia dirty
laundry, **12.1**
la tienda de ropa clothing
store, 3.2
la **rosa** rose
rosado(a) pink, 3.2

el **rótulo** sign, **11.2**
rubio(a) blond(e), 1.1
las **ruedas: la silla de ruedas**
wheelchair, **8.2**
la **ruina** ruin
el **rumor** rumor
la **ruta** route
la **rutina** routine, 12.1
rutinario(a) routine (adj.)

S

el **sábado** Saturday, BV
la **sábana** sheet, **6.2**
el/la **sabelotodo** know-it-all
saber to know (how), 11.2
sabio(a) wise
sabroso(a) delicious
sacar to get, 4.2; to take out,
3.1
sacar un billete to buy a
ticket
**sacar una nota buena
(mala)** to get a good
(bad) grade, 4.2
el **sacerdote** priest
el **saco** jacket, **4.1**
el saco de dormir sleeping
bag, 12.2
el **sacrificio** sacrifice
sacrificar to sacrifice
la **sal** salt, 14.1; **2.1**
la **sala** room; living room, 6.2
la sala de clase classroom,
4.1
la sala de consulta
doctor's office, **14**
la sala de emergencia
emergency room, **8.1**
la sala de espera waiting
room, 13.1; **1.1**
la sala de juegos game
arcade, **5.1**
la sala de recuperación
recovery room
la sala de salida departure
area, 11.1
la sala de urgencias
emergency room
el **salario** salary
la **salchicha** sausage, **10.1**
el **saldo** balance (bank)
la **salida** departure, leaving,
11.1; exit, **11.2**
la hora de salida
departure hour, 13.1; **1.1**

**la pantalla de llegadas y
salidas** arrival and
departure screen, 11.1
la sala de salida departure
area, 11.1
la salida de emergencia
emergency exit, **7.1**
salir to leave, 10.1; to go out;
to turn out
salir a tiempo to leave on
time, 11.1
salir bien (en un examen)
to do well (on an exam),
10.1
salir tarde to leave late,
11.1
el **salón** hall, **13.1**; room
el salón de clase
classroom, 4.1
saltar to jump
la **salud** health
saludar to greet
el **saludo** greeting, BV
salvaje wild
salvar to save
salvo(a) safe
la **sandalia** sandal, **4.1**
la **sandía** watermelon, **10.2**
el **sándwich** sandwich, BV
la **sangre** blood
sano(a) healthy
el **santo** saint
el/la **sartén** frying pan, **10.1**
satisfacer to satisfy
satisfecho(a) satisfied, **14.1**
el **saxofono** saxophone
sazonar to season
el **secador** hair dryer, **12.1**
secar to dry, 12.2
la **sección de (no) fumar** (no)
smoking section, 11.1
seco(a) dry
el/la **secretario(a)** secretary, **14.1**
el **secreto** secret
secundario(a) secondary
la escuela secundaria
high school, 1.1
sed: tener sed to be thirsty,
14.1; **2.1**
el **sedán** sedan, **11.1**
la **sede** seat (of government)
seguir (i, i) to follow, 14; **2**; to
continue, **11.2**
Sigue derecho. Go straight.
según according to

segundo(a) second, 6.2
  el segundo tiempo second half (soccer), 7.1
  en segunda (clase) second-class, 13.1; **1.1**
la **seguridad** security, **7.1**
  el control de seguridad security (airport), 11.1
el **seguro** insurance
  seguro(a): estar seguro(a) to be sure
  seis six, BV
  seiscientos(as) six hundred, 3.2
la **selección** selection
  seleccionar to select
el **sello** stamp, **5.1**
la **selva** jungle
el **semáforo** traffic light, **9.1**
la **semana** week, BV
  el fin de semana weekend, BV
  el fin de semana pasado last weekend
  la semana pasada last week, 9.2
  sembrar to sow, plant, **9.2**
el **semestre** semester
el/la **senador(a)** senator
  sencillo(a) easy, simple
  el billete sencillo one-way ticket, 13.1; **1.1**
  el cuarto sencillo single room, **6.1**
la **senda** path, **5.2**
  caminar por la senda to walk along the path, **5.2**
  sentarse (ie) to sit down, 12.1
el **sentido** meaning, significance; direction, **11.2**
  el sentido contrario opposite way, **11.2**
  en cada sentido in either direction, **11.2**
  una calle de sentido único one-way street, **11.2**
  sentir (ie, i) to be sorry
  sentirse (ie, i) bien (mal) to feel well (ill), **8.1**
la **señal de no fumar** no smoking sign, **7.1**
la **señal de tránsito** traffic sign
el **señor** sir, Mr., gentleman, BV

la **señora** Ms., Mrs., madam, BV
la **señorita** Miss, Ms., BV
  separado(a) separated
  septiembre September, BV
  séptimo(a) seventh, 6.2
  ser to be
  ser una lástima to be a pity
el **ser: el ser humano** human being
  el ser viviente living creature, being
la **serie** series, 7
  la Serie mundial World Series
  serio(a) serious, 1.1
  en serio seriously
el **servicio** service, tip, 5.1
  ¿Está incluido el servicio? Is the tip included?, 5.1
el **servicio de primeros auxilios** first aid service, paramedics, **8.1**
la **servilleta** napkin, 14.1; **2.1**
  servir (i, i) to serve, 14.1; **2.1**
  ¿En qué puedo servirle? How may I help you?, **4.1**
  sesenta sixty, 2.2
la **sesión** show (movies), 10.1
  setecientos(as) seven hundred, 3.2
  setenta seventy, 2.2
el **sexo** sex
  sexto(a) sixth, 6.2
el **show** show
  si if
  sí yes
el **SIDA** AIDS
la **siembra** sowing
  siempre always, 7.1
  de siempre y para siempre eternally, forever
la **sierra** sierra, mountain range
  siete seven, BV
el **siglo** century
el **significado** meaning
  significante meaningful
  significar to mean
  significativo(a) significant
  siguiente following
la **silla** chair
la **silla de ruedas** wheelchair, **8.2**
el **sillón** armchair, **6.2**

  similar similar
  simpático(a) nice, 1.2
  simple simple
  sin without
  sin escala nonstop
  sincero(a) sincere, 1.2
  singles singles, 9.1
el **síntoma** symptom, 8.2
el **sirope** syrup
el/la **sirviente** servant
el **sistema** system
  el sistema métrico metric system
el **sitio** place
la **situación** situation
  situar to situate
  sobre on top of; over; on, about
  sobre todo especially
el **sobre** envelope, **12.2**
  sobresaltar to jump up
  sobrevolar to fly over, **7.2**
la **sobrina** niece, 6.1
el **sobrino** nephew, 6.1
  social: las ciencias sociales social sciences
la **sociedad** society
la **sociología** sociology
  socorrer to help
el/la **socorrista** paramedic, **8.1**
el **socorro** help
el **sofá** sofa, **6.2**
el **sol** Peruvian coin; sun, 9.1
  Hace (Hay) sol. It's sunny., 9.1
  tomar el sol to sunbathe, 9.1
  solamente only
el/la **soldado** soldier
  soler (ue) to be accustomed to, tend to
la **solicitud de empleo** job application, **14.2**
  solitario(a) solitary, lone
  sólo only
  solo(a) alone
  a solas alone
  el café solo black coffee, 5.1
  soltero(a) single, bachelor
la **solución** solution
el **sombrero** hat
  sonar (ue) to ring, 3.2
el **sonido** sound
la **sonrisita** little smile
la **sopa** soup, 5.1

el **sorbete** sherbet, sorbet

el/la **sordo(a)** deaf person

sorprender to surprise

sostener to support

su his, her, their, your

subir to go up, **6.2**; to board, to get on; to take up

subir al tren to get on, to board the train, 13.1; **1.1**

subterráneo(a) underground

el **subtítulo** subtitle, 10.1

con subtítulos with subtitles, 10.1

el **suburbio** suburb

suceder to happen

suceso: el buen suceso great event

sucio(a) dirty

la ropa sucia dirty laundry, **12.1**

la **sucursal** branch (office)

sudamericano(a) South American

el **sudoeste** southwest

el **suegro** father-in-law

el **suelo** ground

el **suelto** small change, **12.2**

el **sueño** dream

la **suerte** luck

¡Buena suerte! Good luck!

el **suéter** sweater, **4.1**

suficiente enough

sufrir to suffer

la **sugerencia** suggestion

sugerir (ie, i) to suggest

la **Suiza** Switzerland

sumar to add

súper super (gas), **11.1**

la **superficie** surface

superior: la escuela superior high school

el **supermercado** supermarket, **5.2**

la **superstición** superstition

supuesto: por supuesto of course

el **sur** south

sureste southeast

el **surf de nieve** snowboarding

el **surfing** surfing, 9.1

practicar el surfing to surf, 9.1

el **suroeste** southwest

el **surtido** assortment

sus their, your *(pl.)*, 6.1

suspirar to sigh

la **sustancia: la sustancia controlada** controlled substance

la **sutura** stitch

T

el **T-shirt** T-shirt, 3.2

la **tabla: la tabla hawaiana** surfboard, 9.1

el **tablero** board, 7.1; gameboard, **5.1**

el **tablero de llegadas** arrival board, 13.1; **1.1**

el **tablero de salidas** departure board, 13.1; **1.1**

el **tablero indicador** scoreboard, 7.1

la **tableta** pill, 8.2

el **taco** taco, BV

el **tacón** heel, **4.1**

taíno(a) Taino

la **tajada** slice, **4.2**

tal: ¿Qué tal? How are you?, BV

el **talento** talent, **14.1**

la **talla** size, 3.2

el **talón** luggage claim ticket, 11.1

el **talonario** check book

el **tamal** tamale, BV

el **tamaño** size, 3.2

también also

tampoco either

tan so

tan... como as . . . as, **8.2**

el **tango** tango

el **tanque** gas tank, **11.1**

llenar el tanque de gasolina to fill the tank with gas, **11.1**

el **tanto** point, 7.1

marcar un tanto to score a point

tanto(a) so much

tanto(a)... como as much . . . as

tantos(as)... como as many . . . as, **8.2**

tapar to cover, **10.2**

la **taquilla** box office, 10.1

tardar to take time

tarda el viaje the trip takes (+ time)

tarde late

la **tarde** afternoon

Buenas tardes. Good afternoon., BV

esta tarde this afternoon, 9.2

por la tarde in the afternoon

la **tarea** task

hacer las tareas to do one's homework, **3.1**

la **tarifa** fare, rate

la **tarjeta** card, 11.1; registration card (hotel), 6.1

la tarjeta de crédito credit card, 14.1; **2.1**

la tarjeta de embarque boarding pass, 11.1

la tarjeta de identidad estudiantil student I.D. card

la tarjeta postal postcard, **12.2**

la tarjeta telefónica telephone card, 3.2

la **tasa** rate

la tasa de cambio exchange rate, **12.2**

la tasa de desempleo unemployment rate

el **taxi** taxi, 11.1

la **taza** cup, 14.1; **2.1**

te you *(fam. pron.)*

el **té** tea, 5.1

el té helado iced tea, 5.1

teatral theatrical, 10.2

el **teatro** theater, 10.2

salir del teatro to leave the theater, 10.2

la **tecla** key (on keyboard), **3.2**

el **teclado** keyboard, 3.1; telephone keypad, **3.2**

el/la **técnico(a)** technician, 8.2

la **tecnología** technology

la **telecomunicación** telecommunication, 3.1

telefonear to telephone

telefónico(a) (related to the) telephone

la línea telefónica telephone line

la llamada telefónica telephone call, 3.2

el **teléfono** telephone

el teléfono celular cellular telephone, 3.2

el **teléfono de botones**
push-button telephone,
3.2
el **teléfono público** public
(pay) telephone, **3.2**
hablar por teléfono to
talk on the phone
el **telesilla** chairlift, 9.2
el **telesquí** ski lift, 9.2
la **televisión** television, 6.2
el **televisor** television set, **6.2**
el **telón** curtain (stage), 10.2
el **tema** theme, subject
temer to fear
la **temperatura** temperature, 9.2
templado(a) temperate
temprano early, 12.1
el **tenedor** fork, 14.1; **2.1**
tener (ie) to have, 6.1
tener un accidente to
have an accident, **8.1**
tener... años to be . . .
years old, 6.1
tener buena pinta to look
good, **4.2**
tener cuidado to be careful
tener hambre to be
hungry, 14.1; **2.1**
tener lugar to take place,
occur, **8.1**
tener miedo to be afraid
tener que to have to
tener sed to be thirsty,
14.1; **2.1**
el **tenis** tennis, 9.1
los **tenis** tennis shoes, 3.2
el par de tenis pair of
tennis shoes, 3.2
el/la **tenista** tennis player
la **tensión arterial** blood
pressure, **8.2**
tercer(o)(a) third, 6.2
la **terminal: la terminal de
pasajeros** passenger
terminal, **7.2**
terminar to end, finish, 3.1
el **término** term
la **ternera** veal, 14.2; **2.2**
la **terraza** terrace (sidewalk
café)
terrible terrible
el **terror** terror, fear
el **tétano** tetanus
la **tía** aunt, 6.1
el **ticket** ticket, 9.2

el **tiempo** time; weather, 9.1;
half (game)
a tiempo on time, 11.1
**a tiempo completo
(parcial)** full- (part-)
time *(adj.)*, **14.2**
el **segundo tiempo** second
half (game), 7.1
pasar el tiempo to spend,
pass time, **5.1**
la **tienda** store, 3.2
la tienda de abarrotes
grocery store, **4.2**
**la tienda de
departamentos**
department store
la tienda de ropa clothing
store, 3.2
**la tienda de ropa para
caballeros** men's
clothing store, **4.1**
**la tienda de ropa para
señoras** women's
clothing store, **4.1**
la tienda de ultramarinos
grocery store, **4.2**
la tienda de videos video
store
tierno(a) tender
la **tierra** land
por tierra by land,
overland
el **tigre** tiger
las **tijeras** scissors, 12.1
el **tilde** accent
tímido(a) timid, shy, 1.2
la **tintorería** dry cleaner, 12.1
el/la **tintorero(a)** dry cleaner, **12.1**
el **tío** uncle, 6.1
los **tíos** aunt and uncle, 6.1
el **tiovivo** merry-go-round, 5.2
típicamente typically
típico(a) typical
el **tipo** type
el **tipo de cambio** exchange
rate, **12.2**
el **tique** ticket, 9.1
tirar to kick, 7.1; to throw
tirar el balón to kick
(throw) the ball, 7.2
el **título universitario**
university degree, 14.1
la **toalla** towel, 6.2
la toalla playera beach
towel, 9.1

el **tobillo** ankle, **8.1**
tocar to touch; to play
(music)
tocar la bocina to honk
the horn
todavía yet, still
todo: todo el mundo
everyone
todos(as) everybody, 2.2;
everything, all
por todas partes
everywhere
tomar to take, 4.1
tomar agua (leche, café)
to drink water (milk,
coffee)
tomar apuntes to take
notes, 4.2
tomar el bus (escolar) to
take the (school) bus, 4.1
tomar el desayuno to eat
breakfast, 12.1
tomar el pulso to take
one's pulse, **8.2**
tomar el sol to sunbathe,
9.1
tomar fotos to take photos
**tomar la tensión (presión)
arterial** to take one's
blood pressure, **8.2**
tomar un jugo to drink
some juice
tomar una radiografía to
take X-rays
tomar un refresco to have
(drink) a beverage
tomar un vuelo to take a
flight, 11.1
tomar una ducha to take
a shower, 12.1
tomar una merienda to
have a snack, 4.2
el **tomate** tomato
el **tomo** volume
la **tonelada** ton
el **tono** dial tone, **3.2**; hue
tonto(a) foolish
torcerse (ue) to twist, **8.1**
el **torniquete** turnstile, **9.1**
la **toronja** grapefruit, **10.1**
torpe stupid
la **torre: la torre de control**
control tower, **7.2**
la **torta** cake, **13.1**
la **tortilla** tortilla, 5.1

la **tos: tener tos** to have a
cough, 8.1
toser to cough, 8.1
la **tostada** toast
tostadito(a) sunburned,
tanned
tostado(a): el pan tostado
toast, 5.2
tostar to toast
el **tostón** fried plantain slice
totalmente totally,
completely
tóxico(a) toxic
el/la **trabajador(a)** worker
trabajar to work, 3.2
trabajar a tiempo
completo to work full
time, **14.2**
trabajar a tiempo parcial
to work part time, **14.2**
el **trabajo** work; job, **14.2**
el trabajo a tiempo
completo (parcial) full-
time (part-time) job, **14.2**
la **tradición** tradition
tradicional traditional
traer to bring, 14.1; **2.1**
el **tráfico** traffic
la **tragedia** tragedy
el **traje** suit, 3.2
el traje de baño bathing
suit, 9.1
el traje de gala evening
gown, dress
el **tramo** stretch
tranquilo(a) peaceful; calm;
quiet
transbordar to transfer, 13.2;
1.2
transformar to transform
transmitir to send, to
transmit, **3.1**
el **transporte** transportation
tras after
trasladar to transfer, move
el **tratamiento** treatment
tratar to treat; to try
el **trayecto** stretch (of road)
trece thirteen, BV
treinta thirty, BV
treinta y uno thirty-one,
2.2
el **tren** train, 13.2; **1.2**
el tren directo nonstop
train, 13.2; **1.2**

el tren local local train,
13.2; **1.2**
la **trenza** braid
tres three, BV
trescientos(as) three
hundred, 3.2
la **tribu** tribe
el **tribunal** court, **14.1**
el **trigo** wheat, **9.2**
la **tripulación** crew, 11.2
triste sad, 8.1
triunfante triumphant
el **trocito** piece, **10.2**
el **trombón** trombone
la **trompeta** trumpet
tropical tropical
tu your *(sing. fam.)*
tú you *(sing. fam.)*
el **tubo de escape** exhaust pipe
el **tubo de pasta dentífrica**
tube of toothpaste,
12.2
la **turbulencia** turbulence, 7.2
el/la **turista** tourist, 10.2

U

u or (used instead of **o** before
words beginning with **o** or
ho)
Ud., usted you *(sing. form.)*
3.2
Uds., ustedes you *(pl. form.)*,
2.2
último(a) last
ultramarinos: la tienda de
ultramarinos grocery
store, **4.2**
un(a) a, an, 1.1
la **una** one o'clock, 2.2
único(a) only; unique
la **unidad: la unidad de**
cuidado intensivo
intensive care unit
el **uniforme** uniform
la **universidad** university
universitario(a) (related to)
university
uno one, BV
unos(as) some
urbano(a) urban
urgencias: la sala de
urgencias emergency
room
la **urología** urology
el/la **urólogo(a)** urologist

usado(a) used
usar to wear (size), 3.2; to use
utilizar to use
las **uvas** grapes, 10.1

V

la **vaca** cow, **9.2**
la **vacación** vacation, **6.2**
el/la **vago(a)** loafer, idler
el **vagón** train car, 13.1; **1.1**
la **vainilla: de vainilla** vanilla
(adj.), 5.1
la **vainita** string bean
¡vale! OK!
valer to be worth
valeroso(a) brave
valiente brave
el **valle** valley, 7.2
el **valor** value, worth
el valor real true value
vamos a let's go
la **variación** variation
variado(a) varied
variar to vary, change
la **variedad** variety
vario(a) various
el **varón** male
vasco(a) Basque
la pelota vasca jai alai
el **vaso** (drinking) glass, 12.1
el **váter** toilet, 6.2
el/la **vecino(a)** neighbor
el **vegetal** vegetable, 5.2
el/la **vegetariano(a)** vegetarian
veinte twenty, BV
veinticinco twenty-five,
BV
veinticuatro twenty-four,
BV
veintidós twenty-two, BV
veintinueve twenty-nine,
BV
veintiocho twenty-eight,
BV
veintiséis twenty-six, BV
veintisiete twenty-seven,
BV
veintitrés twenty-three, BV
veintiuno twenty-one, BV
la **vela** candle, 13.1
la **velocidad** speed, 11.2
la velocidad máxima
speed limit, 11.2
vencer to conquer
el **vendaje** bandage, 8.2

poner un vendaje to put a bandage on, **8.2**

el/la **vendedor(a)** salesperson, **11.1**

vender to sell, 5.2

el **veneno** poison

venenoso(a) poisonous

venezolano(a) Venezuelan

venir to come, 11.1

el viernes (sábado, etc.) que viene next Friday (Saturday, etc.)

la **venta** sale, **14.1**

la **ventaja** advantage

la **ventanilla** ticket window, 9.2; window (airplane), **7.1**; teller's window, **12.2**

ver to see; to watch, 5.1

el **verano** summer, BV

el **verbo** verb

la **verdad** truth

¡verdad! that's right (true)!

verdadero(a) true, real

verde green, 3.2

la judía verde green bean, 5.2

la **verdulería** greengrocer store, **4.2**

la **verdura** vegetable

verificar to check, 13.1; **1.1**

la **versión: en versión original** in (its) original version, 10.1

el **verso** verse

vertical vertical

vestido(a) dressed

el **vestido** dress, **4.1**

los vestidos clothes *(pl.)*

vestirse (i, i) to get dressed

el/la **veterinario(a)** veterinarian

la **vez** time

a veces at times, sometimes, 7.1

de vez en cuando now and then

en vez de instead of

una vez más one more time, again

la **vía** track, 13.1; **1.1**

viajar to travel

viajar en avión to travel by air, 11.1

el **viaje** trip

el viaje de novios honeymoon

el viaje de regreso return trip

hacer un viaje to take a trip, 11.1

el/la **viajero(a)** traveler

viceversa vice versa

víctima victim, **8.1**

victorioso(a) victorious

la **vida** life

la vida escolar school life

el **video** video

viejo(a) old, 6.1

el/la **viejo(a)** old person

el **viento** wind

el **viernes** Friday, BV

villa: villa miseria shantytown (Arg.)

el **vinagre** vinegar

la **viola** viola

el **violín** violin

visible visible

visitar to visit

la **Víspera de Año Nuevo** New Year's Eve, **13.2**

la **vista** view

vital vital

la **vitamina** vitamin

la **vitrina** shop window, **4.1**

la **vivienda** housing

viviente: el ser viviente living creature, being

vivir to live, 5.2

vivo(a) living, alive

la **vocal** vowel

volar (ue) to fly, **7.2**

el **voleibol** volleyball

el/la **voluntario(a)** volunteer

volver (ue) to return, 7.1

volver a casa to return home, 10.2

la **voz** voice

en voz alta aloud

el **vuelo** flight, 11.1

el número del vuelo flight number, 11.1

el vuelo directo direct flight, **7.2**

el vuelo nacional domestic flight

tomar un vuelo to take a flight, 11.1

la **vuelta: dar la vuelta** to turn around

Y

y and, BV

y cuarto a quarter past (the hour)

y media half past (the hour)

y pico just after (the hour)

ya now; already

la **yarda** yard

el **yeso** cast, **8.2**

yo I, 1.1

el **yogur** yogurt

Z

la **zanahoria** carrot, 5.2

la **zapatería** shoe store, **4.1**

el **zapato** shoe, 3.2

la **zona** zone, area, neighborhood

la zona comercial business zone, **9.1**

la zona industrial industrial area, **9.1**

la zona residencial residential area, **9.1**

el **zumo de naranja** orange juice

Vocabulario inglés–español

The **Vocabulario inglés–español** contains all productive and receptive vocabulary from the text. The reference numbers following each productive entry indicate the chapter and vocabulary section in which the word is introduced. For example, **3.2** means that the word was taught in **Capítulo 3, Palabras 2. BV** refers to the preliminary **Bienvenidos** lessons in Level 1. Words without a chapter reference indicate receptive vocabulary (not taught in the **Palabras** sections). Words taught in Level 1 appear in regular type and those taught in Level 2 are in bold type. Note that **Capítulos 1** and **2** of Level 2 repeat **Capítulos 13** and **14** of Level 1 (e.g., 13.1; **1.1**).

A

a, an un(a), 1.1
aboard, on board a bordo de
about sobre; acerca de;
  (time) a eso de, **4.1**
above encima; por encima de,
  9.1
abroad en el extranjero
abstract abstracto(a)
abuse el abuso
academic académico(a)
academy la academia
accent el tilde
to **accept** aceptar
access el acceso
accident el accidente, **8.1**
to **accommodate** acomodar
accompaniment el
  acompañamiento
to **accompany** acompañar
according to según
account (bank) la cuenta
  checking account la
    cuenta corriente,
    12.2
  savings account la cuenta
    de ahorros
accountant el/la contable,
  14.1
ache el dolor, 8.1
to **ache: My . . . ache(s).** Me
  duele(n)... , **8.2**
acrylic el acrílico
action la acción

active activo(a)
activity la actividad
actor el actor, 10.2
actress la actriz, 10.2
to **adapt** adaptar
to **add** sumar; agregar, añadir,
  10.2
addition: in addition to
  además de
addiction la adicción
address la dirección
adequate adecuado(a)
to **adjust** ajustar
to **admire** admirar
admission ticket la entrada,
  10.1
to **admit** admitir, **8.2**
adolescence la adolescencia
adolescent el/la adolescente
adorable adorable
adoration la adoración
to **adore** adorar
to **adorn** adornar
advance el avance
advantage la ventaja
adventure la aventura
advertisement el anuncio,
  14.2
advertising la propaganda
advice el consejo
to **advise** aconsejar
aerobic aeróbico(a)
to **affect** impresionar
African africano(a)

African American
  afroamericano(a)
after después (de), 5.1; tras
afternoon la tarde
  Good afternoon. Buenas
    tardes., BV
  in the afternoon por la
    tarde
  this afternoon esta tarde,
    9.2
again de nuevo
against contra, 7.1
age la edad
  **How old do you have to
    be?** ¿Cuántos años
    tienes que cumplir?
agency la agencia
  employment agency la
    agencia de empleos
agent el/la agente, 11.1
  customs agent el/la
    agente de aduana, 11.2
aging person el/la
  envejeciente
Agreed, Fine. Conforme.
  14.2; **2.2**
agricultural agrícola
ahead adelante
AIDS el SIDA
air el aire, **11.1**
air conditioning el aire
  acondicionado, **6.2**
air traffic controller el/la
  controlador(a), **7.2**

airline la línea aérea
airmail el correo aéreo, **12.2**
airplane el avión, 11.1
  small airplane la avioneta, **7.2**
airport el aeropuerto, 11.1
aisle el pasillo, 13.2; **1.2**
album el álbum
alcohol el alcohol
alcoholism el alcoholismo
algebra el álgebra, 2.2
alive vivo(a)
all todos(as)
allergy la alergia, 8.2
to allow consentir (ie, i); dejar
almost casi
alone solo(a); a solas
aloud en voz alta
already ya
also también
to alternate alternar
although aunque
altitude la altitud, la altura, **7.2**
always siempre, 7.1
ambassador el/la embajador(a)
ambulance la ambulancia, **8.1**
American americano(a), 1.1
amount la cantidad
amusement la diversión
amusement park el parque de atracciones, **5.2**
  amusement park ride la atracción, **5.2**
amusing divertido(a)
analysis el análisis
analytical analítico(a)
to analyze analizar
ancient antiguo(a), **5.1**
and y, BV
Andalusian andaluz(a)
Andean andino(a)
anecdote la anécdota
angry enfadado(a)
animal el animal
  farm animal el animal doméstico, **9.2**
ankle el tobillo, **8.1**
anniversary el aniversario
to announce anunciar
announcement el anuncio, **7.1**
another otro(a)

to answer contestar, **3.2**
answer la respuesta
answering machine el contestador automático, **3.2**
Antarctic la Antártida
antibiotic el antibiótico, 8.2
antiquated anticuado(a)
antiquity la antigüedad
any cualquier
apartment el apartamento, el departamento, 6.2; el piso
  apartment house la casa de apartamentos (departamentos), 6.2
apostle el apóstol
to appear aparecer
appearance la apariencia
appendicitis la apendicitis
to applaud aplaudir, 10.2
applause el aplauso, 10.2
  to receive applause recibir aplausos, 10.2
apple la manzana, 5.2
apple tree el manzano, **9.2**
application (job) la solicitud (de empleo)
to apply (for a job) solicitar trabajo
to approach acercarse (de)
appropriate apropiado(a)
April abril, BV
aptitude la aptitud
Arab el/la árabe
archaeological arqueológico(a)
archaeologist el/la arqueólogo(a)
archeology la arqueología
architect el/la arquitecto(a), **14.1**
area el área (f.); la zona
area code la clave de área, **3.2**
Argentinian argentino(a), 2.1
argument la disputa
arid árido(a)
arithmetic la aritmética, 2.2
arm el brazo, 7.1
armchair el sillón, **6.2**
around alrededor de, 6.2
arrival la llegada, 11.1
  arrival and departure screen la pantalla de llegadas y salidas, 11.1

to arrive llegar, 4.1
arrogant altivo(a), arrogante
art el arte (f.), 2.2
  fine arts las bellas artes
artichoke la alcachofa, 14.2; **2.2**
artifact el artefacto
artist el/la artista, 10.2
artistic artístico(a)
as como, 1.2
  as . . . as tan... como, **8.2**
  as many . . . as tantos(as)... como, **8.2**
  as much . . . as tanto(a) . . . como
to ask (a question) preguntar; (questions) hacer preguntas, **14.2**
to ask for pedir (i, i), 14.1; **2.1**
  to ask for the bill pedir la cuenta, **6.1**
  to ask questions hacer preguntas, **14.2**
asleep dormido(a)
aspect el aspecto
aspirin la aspirina, 8.2
to assist atender (ie), **4.1**
assortment el surtido
to assure asegurar
astute astuto(a)
at a
  at that time en aquel entonces
athlete el/la atleta
athletic atlético(a)
atmosphere el ambiente; la atmósfera
to attack atacar
attack el ataque
to attend asistir
  attention: to pay attention prestar atención, 4.2
attractive atractivo(a)
audience el público, 10.2
August agosto, BV
aunt la tía, 6.1
  aunt and uncle los tíos, 6.1
authentic auténtico(a)
author el/la autor(a), 10.2
automatic teller el cajero automático
automatically automáticamente

automobile el automóvil
autumn el otoño, BV
available disponible
avenue la avenida, **9.1**
average medio(a); regular, 2.2
aviation la aviación
avocado el aguacate, **10.2**

B

baby el/la bebé
bachelor's degree el
  bachillerato
back (of seat) el respaldo, **7.1**
background la ascendencia
backpack la mochila, 3.1
bacteria la bacteria
bad malo(a), 2.1; mal, 14.2;
  2.2
  to be in a good (bad)
    mood estar de buen
    (mal) humor, **8.1**
bad-tempered
  malhumorado(a)
bag la bolsa, 5.2
  cloth shopping bag el
    capacho
  plastic bag la bolsa de
    plástico, **4.2**
baggage el equipaje,
  11.1
  baggage claim el reclamo
    de equipaje, 11.2
  carry-on baggage el
    equipaje de mano
bakery la panadería, la
  pastelería, **4.2**
balance (bank) el saldo
ball (soccer, basketball) el
  balón 7.1; (baseball,
  tennis) la pelota , 7.2
balloon el globo, **5.2**
ballpoint pen el bolígrafo,
  3.1
banana el plátano, 5.2; la
  banana, **10.2**
band (music) la banda
bandage el vendaje, **8.2**
  to put a bandage on
    poner un vendaje, **8.2**
bank (of a river) la orilla
bank el banco, **12.2**
  bank statement el estado
    del banco
banking bancario(a)
baptism el bautizo

bar: bar of soap la barra
  de jabón, la pastilla de
  jabón, 12.2
barber el barbero, **12.1**
bargain la ganga
to base basar
base la base, 7.2
baseball el béisbol, 7.2
  baseball field el
    campo de béisbol, 7.2
  baseball game el juego
    de béisbol, 7.2
  baseball player el/la
    beisbolista; el/la
    jugador(a) de béisbol,
    7.2
based (on) basado(a)
basic básico(a)
basket (basketball) el
  canasto, la canasta, el
  cesto, 7.2; (jai alai) la
  cesta
basketball el baloncesto,
  el básquetbol, 7.2
  basketball court la
    cancha de
    básquetbol, 7.2
  to put in (make) a
    basket encestar, 7.2
Basque vasco(a)
bat el bate, 7.2
bath el baño
  to take a bath bañarse,
    12.1
bathing suit el bañador,
  el traje de baño, 9.1
bathroom el baño, el
  cuarto de baño, 6.2
bathtub la bañera, 6.2
batter el/la bateador(a),
  7.2
battery la batería
battle la batalla
bay la bahía
to be ser, 1.1; estar, 4.1
  to be afraid tener
    miedo
  to be in a good (bad)
    mood estar de buen
    (mal) humor
  to be happy (sad)
    estar contento(a)
    (triste)
  to be hungry tener
    hambre, 14.1; **2.1**

to be married estar
  casado(a)
to be sick estar enfermo(a)
to be thirsty tener sed,
  14.1; **2.1**
to be tired estar
  cansado(a)
to be . . . years old tener
  . . . años, 6.1
to be able poder (ue), 7.1
to be accustomed to, tend to
  soler (ue)
to be alarmed alarmarse
to be based basarse
to be born nacer, 13.1
to be called llamarse, 12.1
to be familiar with conocer,
  11.1
to be frightened asustarse
to be glad about alegrarse de,
  13.1
to be going to (do something)
  ir a + infinitive
to be important importar
to be named llamarse, 12.1
to be sorry sentir (i, i)
to be worth valer
  beach la playa, 9.1
  beach resort el balneario,
    9.1
  beach towel la toalla
    playera, 9.1
  bean el frijol, la habichuela,
    5.2
    black bean la habichuela
      negra, el frijol negro,
      10.2
    string (green) bean la
      habichuela tierna
to bear llevar
  beard la barba
  beau, heartthrob el galán
  beautiful bello(a),
    hermoso(a), 1.1; precioso(a)
  beauty la belleza
  because porque
to become enamored of (to fall
    for) flechar
  bed la cama, 8.1
    to go to bed acostarse (ue),
      12.1
    to make the bed hacer la
      cama, **6.2**
    to stay in bed guardar
      cama, 8.1

bedroom el cuarto de dormir; el cuarto, el dormitorio, la recámara, 6.2; la habitación, **6.1**

bee la abeja, **8.1**

beef la carne de res, 14.2; **2.2**

before antes de, 5.1

to **beg** rogar (ue)

to **begin** comenzar (ie); empezar (ie), 7.1

beginner el/la principiante, 9.2

beginning: at the beginning al principio

beginning of the school year la apertura de clases

to **behave** comportarse

behavior la actuación

behind atrás; detrás de, **5.2**

to **believe** creer, 8.2

bell pepper el pimiento, **10.2**

bellman el botones, **6.1**

to **belong** pertenecer

below debajo (de), 7

below zero bajo cero, 9.2

belt el cinturón, **4.1**

seat belt el cinturón de seguridad, **7.1**

benefit el beneficio

berth la litera, 13.2; **1.2**

beside al lado de, **5.2**

besides además

best man el padrino, **13.1**

better, best mejor

between entre, 7.1

beverage el refresco, 5.1; la bebida, **7.1**

biblical bíblico(a)

to **bicycle** ir en bicicleta, 12.2

bicycle la bicicleta

big gran, grande

bilingual bilingüe

bill la factura, **6.1**; **(money)** el billete, **12.2**; **(check)** la cuenta, 5.1

biography la biografía

biological biológico(a)

biologist el/la biólogo(a)

biology la biología, 2.2

bird el ave (f.); el pájaro

birthday el cumpleaños, 6.1

black negro(a), 3.2

blanket la frazada, la manta, **6.2**

bleach el blanqueador

blessing la bendición

block (city) la cuadra, **11.2**

to **block** bloquear, parar, 7.1

blond(e) rubio(a), 1.1

blood la sangre

blood pressure la presión arterial, la tensión arterial, **8.2**

blouse la blusa, 3.2

blue azul, 3.2

dark blue azul oscuro

blue jeans el blue jean, 3.2

to **board** embarcar, 11.2; subir, 13.1; **1.1**; abordar

to board the train subir al tren, 13.1; **1.1**

board el tablero, 7.1

arrival board el tablero de llegadas, 13.1; **1.1**

departure board el tablero de salidas, 13.1; **1.1**

scoreboard el tablero indicador, 7.1

boarding house la pensión, 12.2

boarding pass la tarjeta de embarque, 11.1

boat el bote, **5.2**

body el cuerpo, **8.1**

to **boil** hervir (ie, i), **10.1**

boiling la ebullición

bone el hueso, **8.2**

to set the bone reducir el hueso, **8.2**

book el libro, 3.1

boot la bota, 9.2

to **border** bordear

border el borde

to **bore** aburrir

boring aburrido(a), 2.1

born nacido(a)

to **borrow** pedir prestado

boss el/la jefe(a)

bottle la botella, **4.2**

bottle of mineral water la botella de agua mineral, 12.2

boulevard el bulevar, **9.1**

box office la taquilla, 10.1

boy el muchacho, 1.1; el chico

boyfriend el novio

bracelet la pulsera, **4.1**

braid la trenza

to **brake** poner los frenos

brakes los frenos, **11.1**

branch (office) la sucursal; la filial

branch (of menora) el brazo, **13.2**

branch (tree) la rama

brass (instruments in orchestra) instrumentos de metal

brave valeroso(a); valiente

bread el pan, **4.2**

to **break** romperse, **8.1**

breakdown la avería

breakfast el desayuno, 5.2

to **breathe** respirar

breathing la respiración

bricklayer el/la albañil, **14.1**

bride la novia, **13.1**

brief breve

bright brillante

to **bring** llevar, 6.1; traer, 14.1; **2.1**

broken down averiado(a)

bronze el bronce, 10.2

brook el arroyo

brother el hermano, 6.1

brown de color marrón, 3.2; pardo(a)

brunette moreno(a), 1.1

brush el cepillo, 12.2; **(paint)** el pincel

to **brush one's hair** cepillarse, 12.1

to **brush one's teeth** cepillarse los dientes, lavarse los dientes, 12.1

building el edificio, **9.1**

burner (stove) la hornilla, **10.1**

burial el entierro

to **bury** enterrar (ie)

bus el bus, 4.1; el autobús, 10.1; **(Mexico)** el camión, 10.1; **(Puerto Rico, Cuba)** la guagua, 10.1

school bus el bus escolar, 4.1

bus stop la parada de bus, **9.1**

business el comercio; la empresa, **14.1**

business district la zona comercial, **9.1**

businessman(woman) el/la comerciante, **14.1**; el/la empresario(a)

busy (phone) ocupado

but pero

butcher shop la carnicería, **4.2**

butter la mantequilla, **10.2**

button el botón, **3.1**

to **buy** comprar, 3.1

buying la compra, **14.1**

by no means de ninguna manera, 1.1

by the way a propósito

C

cabin la cabina, **7.1**

café el café, 5.1; la confitería

  outdoor café el café al aire libre

cafeteria la cafetería

cage la jaula, **5.2**

cake el bizcocho, la torta, el pastel, **13.1**

to **calculate** calcular

calculator la calculadora, 3.1

calculus el cálculo, 2.2

to **call oneself, be named,** llamarse, 12.1

to **call; to telephone** llamar, **3.2**

  Who is calling? ¿De parte de quién?, **3.2**

call la llamada (telefónica), **3.2**

  long distance call la llamada larga, **3.2**

called llamado(a)

calm tranquilo(a)

calorie la caloría

camel el camello, **13.2**

campaign la campaña

can el bote, la lata, 5.2

Canadian canadiense

candid franco(a)

candidate el/la aspirante, el/la candidato(a), **14.2**

candle la vela, **13.1**

canned enlatado(a)

canvas (painting) el lienzo

canyon el cañón

cap la gorra, 3.2

capital la capital

captain (airplane) el/la comandante, 11.2

car el carro, el coche, 4.1

by car en carro, 4.1

dining car el coche-comedor, el coche-cafetería, 13.2; **1.1**

sleeping car el coche-cama, 13.2; **1.1**

sports car el carro deportivo, **11.1**

train car el coche, 13.2; **1.1**

carbohydrate el carbohidrato

card la tarjeta, 11.1

  credit card la tarjeta de crédito, 14.1; **2.1**

  registration card (hotel) la tarjeta, la ficha, **6.1**

  student I.D. card la tarjeta de identidad estudiantil

  telephone card la tarjeta telefónica, **3.2**

cardinal points los punto cardinales

cardiologist el/la cardiólogo(a)

cardiology la cardiología

care: intensive care el cuidado intensivo

career la carrera

careful! ¡cuidado!

  to be careful tener cuidado

carefully con cuidado

to **caress** acariciar

Caribbean el Caribe

  Caribbean Sea el mar Caribe

caricaturist el/la caricaturista

carousel horse el caballito, **5.2**

carpenter el/la carpintero(a), **14.1**

carrot la zanahoria, 5.2

to **carry** llevar, 3.1

to **carry out** efectuar

cart el carrito, 4.2

case el caso, **7.1**

cash el dinero en efectivo, **12.2**

cash register la caja, 3.1

to **cash the check** cobrar el cheque, **12.2**

cashier el/la cajero(a), **14.1**

cassette el casete, 4.2

cast el yeso, **8.2**

Castillian castellano(a)

castle el castillo

cat el/la gato(a), 6.1

to **catch** atrapar, 7.2

catcher el/la cátcher, el/la receptor(a), 7.2

category la categoría

cathedral la catedral

Catholic católico(a)

cattle el ganado, **9.2**

cauliflower la coliflor, **10.1**

to **cause** causar

cause la causa

CD-ROM el CD-ROM, **3.1**

to **celebrate** celebrar, **13.1**

celebration la celebración

cell phone el teléfono celular, **3.2**

cellular celular

center el centro

central central

Central America la América Central

century el siglo

cereal el cereal, 5.2

ceremony la ceremonia

certain cierto(a)

Certainly!, Of course! ¡Claro!

chain (necklace) la cadena, **4.1**

  gold chain la cadena de oro, **4.1**

chair la silla

  armchair el sillón, **6.2**

chairlift el telesilla, 9.2

chalkboard la pizarra, el pizarrón, 4.2

champion el/la campeón(ona), **5.1**

championship el campeonato

change el cambio, **12.2**

to **change** variar; cambiar, **12.2**

  to change the towels cambiar las toallas, **6.2**

  to change trains (transfer) transbordar, 13.2; **1.2**

channel (TV) el canal

chapter el capítulo

character el carácter; el personaje

characteristic la característica

to **charge** cobrar

charges los cargos

charming encantador(a)

to **chat** charlar
chauffeur el chófer
cheap barato(a), 3.2
check (plaid) a cuadros
to **check luggage** facturar el equipaje, 11.1
to **check out** abandonar el cuarto, 6.1
to **check the oil** revisar el aceite, 11.2
to **check the ticket** revisar el boleto, 11.1
checkbook la chequera; el talonario
checkers las damas, 5.1
checking account la cuenta corriente, 12.2
cheek la mejilla, 8.1
cheese el queso, 5.1
chemical químico(a)
chemistry la química, 2.2
chess el ajedrez, 5.1
chest el pecho, 8.1
chicken el pollo, 5.2
child el/la niño(a)
children los hijos, 6.1
Chilean chileno(a)
chili pepper el ají
chills los escalofríos, 8.1
chimney la chimenea
chocolate (adj.) de chocolate, 5.1
choir el coro
cholesterol el colesterol
to **choose** escoger
chop la chuleta, 10.1
chores los quehaceres
chorus el coro
Christian cristiano(a)
Christmas la Navidad, 13.2
 Christmas Eve la Nochebuena, 13.2
 Christmas tree el árbol de Navidad, 13.2
 Merry Christmas! ¡Feliz Navidad!, 13.2
church la iglesia
circle el círculo
to **circulate** circular
citric cítrico(a)
city hall la alcaldía, 14.1
 city hall employee el/la funcionario(a), 14.1
city la ciudad, 9.1
to **claim (luggage)** reclamar, 11.2

to **claim one's luggage** recoger el equipaje, 11.2
clam la almeja, 14.2; 2.2
clarinet el clarinete
clarity la claridad
class la clase, el curso, 2.1
 first-class primera clase, 13.1; 1.1
 second-class segunda clase, 13.1; 1.1
classic clásico(a)
to **classify** clasificar
classroom la sala de clase, el salón de clase, 4.1
clean limpio(a)
to **clean** limpiar, 6.2
 to clean the room limpiar el cuarto, 6.2
clear claro(a)
clerk el/la dependiente(a); el/la empleado(a), 3.1
clever listo(a), 5.1
click el clic
climate el clima
clinic la clínica
close cercano(a)
to **close** cerrar (ie)
 to close the wound cerrar la herida, 8.2
closet el armario, 6.2
clothes (pl.) la ropa, los vestidos
 to put on (one's) clothes ponerse la ropa, 12.1; vestirse (i, i)
 clothes hanger el colgador, la percha, 6.2
clothing la ropa, 3.2
 clothing store la tienda de ropa, 3.2
 men's clothing store la tienda de ropa para caballeros, 4.1
 women's clothing store la tienda de ropa para señoras, 4.1
cloud la nube, 9.1
cloudy nublado(a), 9.1
 It's cloudy. Hay nubes., 9.1
clove (of garlic) el diente (de ajo)
clown el payaso, 5.2
club el club, 4.2
 Spanish Club el Club de español, 4.2

co-ed (school) mixto(a)
coast la costa
coat el abrigo, 4.1
Coca-Cola la Coca-Cola, 5.1
cockpit la cabina de mando (vuelo), 7.1
coconut el coco, 10.2
code: country code el prefijo de país, 3.2
 area code la clave de área, 3.2
coffee el café, BV
 black coffee el café solo, 5.1
 coffee with milk el café con leche, 5.1
coin, currency la moneda, 3.2
coincidence la coincidencia
cold (illness) el catarro, 8.1
 It's cold. Hace frío., 9.2
 to have a cold tener catarro, estar resfriado(a), 8.1
to **collect** coleccionar, 5.1
collection el conjunto; la colección; la colecta
collector el/la coleccionista, 5.1
Colombian colombiano(a), 1.1
colonial colonial
colony la colonia
color el color, 3.2
 What color is it? ¿De qué color es?, 3.2
colored de color
comb el peine, 12.1
to **comb one's hair** peinarse, 12.1
to **come** venir, 11.1
 to come (go) on stage entrar en escena, 10.2
comedy la comedia
comfort la comodidad
commission la comisión
committee el comité
common común
to **communicate with each other** comunicarse, 3.1
communication la comunicación
community la comunidad
compact disk, CD el disco compacto, 4.2
company la compañía

to **compare** comparar
comparison la comparación
compartment el
  compartimiento, 13.2; **1.2**
  overhead compartment el
   compartimiento superior,
   el compartimiento sobre
   la cabeza, 7.1
to **compete** competir (i, i)
competition la competencia;
  la competición
to **complete** completar
completely totalmente
compliment: to pay
  someone a compliment
  echarle flores
to **compose** componer
composition la composición
computer el ordenador, la
  computadora, **3.1**
computer programmer el/la
  programador(a) de
  informática, **14.1**
computer science la
  informática, 2.2
concert el concierto, 2.1
conclusion el desenlace
condition la condición
condominium el
  condominio, **9.1**
conductor (train) el/la
  revisor(a), 13.2; **1.2**
to **confirm** confirmar
to **confront** confrontar
Congratulations!
  ¡Enhorabuena!,
  ¡Felicitaciones!, **13.1**
to **connect** conectar; enlazar
connection la conexión
to **conquer** conquistar; vencer
conqueror el conquistador
conquest la conquista
consequently por
  consiguiente
to **consider** considerar
to **consist of** consistir (en)
to **construct** construir
to **consult** consultar, 13.1;
  1.1
to **consume** consumir
consumer el/la
  consumidor(a)
consumption el consumo
contagious contagioso(a)
to **contain** contener (ie)

contemporary
  contemporáneo(a)
contest la competición
continent el continente
to **continue** continuar, 7.2;
  seguir (i, i), **11.2**
contrary: on the contrary al
  contrario
to **contrast** contrastar
to **control** controlar
  control tower la torre de
   control, **7.2**
convenient conveniente
convent el convento
conversation la conversación
to **convert** convertir (ie, i)
convertible el convertible, el
  descapotable, **11.1**
to **convince** convencer
to **cook** cocinar, **10.1**
  cook el/la cocinero(a), 14.1;
   2.1
  cooking la cocción
coordination la
  coordinación
copilot el/la co-piloto, 11.2
to **copy** copiar
  copy la copia
corn (Mex.) el elote; el
  choclo; el maíz, 14.2; **2.2**
cornea la córnea
corner la esquina, **9.1**
correspondence la
  correspondencia
corridor el pasillo, 13.2; **1.2**
to **cost** costar (ue), 3.1
  How much do(es) it
   (they) cost? ¿Cuánto
   cuesta(n)?
Costa Rican costarricense
cotton el algodón, **12.1**
cough la tos, 8.1
  to have a cough tener tos,
   8.1
to **cough** toser, 8.1
counter el mostrador,
  11.1
country el país, 11.2; el
  campo, **9.2**
  foreign country el país
   extranjero
coup (overthrow of a
  government) el golpe
coupe el cupé, **11.1**
couple la pareja

course el curso, 2.1
  elective course el curso
   opcional
  required course el curso
   obligatorio
court la corte, el tribunal,
  14.1
court la cancha, 7.2
  basketball court la cancha
   de básquetbol, 7.2
  enclosed court la cancha
   cubierta, 9.1
  outdoor court la cancha al
   aire libre, 9.1
  tennis court la cancha de
   tenis, 9.1
courteous atento(a); cortés
courtesy la cortesía, BV
cousin el/la primo(a), 6.1
to **cover** cubrir; tapar, **10.2**
cow la vaca, **9.2**
to **create** crear
credit card la tarjeta de
  crédito, 14.1; **2.1**
Creole criollo(a)
crew la tripulación, 11.2
crop la cosecha, **9.2**
to **cross** atravesar (ie); cruzar, **9.1**
crossing el cruce, **11.2**
crosswalk el cruce de
  peatones, 9.1
crossword puzzle el
  crucigrama, **5.1**
  to do a crossword puzzle
   llenar un crucigrama,
   5.1
crutch la muleta, **8.2**
Cuban cubano(a)
Cuban American
  cubanoamericano(a)
cucumber el pepino, **10.1**
to **cultivate** cultivar, **9.2**
cultivation el cultivo
cultural cultural
cultured culto(a)
cup la taza, 14.1; **2.1**
cure la cura
curtain (stage) el telón, 10.2
custom la costumbre
customer el/la cliente, 5.1
customs la aduana, 11.2
  customs agent el/la agente
   de aduana, 11.2
to **cut** cortar, **8.1**
cycling el ciclismo

D

dad el papá
daily diario(a)
to dance bailar, 4.2
dance el baile
dance la danza
danger el peligro
dangerous peligroso(a)
dark oscuro(a)
dark-haired moreno(a), 1.1
data los datos, 3.1
to date datar
date la fecha, BV
   What is today's date?
     ¿Cuál es la fecha de hoy?,
     BV
daughter la hija, 6.1
day el día, BV
   What day is it (today)?
     ¿Qué día es (hoy)?,
     BV
death la muerte
decade la década
December diciembre,
   BV
to decide decidir
to declare declarar
to decorate decorar
decorated decorado(a)
decoration la
   decoración
to dedicate dedicar, 14.1
deep profundo(a)
to defeat derrotar
to defend defender
to define definir
definition la definición
degree (temperature) el
   grado, 9.2
delay: with a delay con una
   demora, 11.1; con retraso,
   13.2; 1.2
delicate delicado(a)
delicious rico(a), 14.2; 2.2;
   delicioso(a), sabroso(a)
to delight encantar
to deliver entregar
deluxe de lujo
to demand exigir
demography la demografía
to demonstrate demostrar (ue)
density la densidad
dentist el/la dentista
department el
   departamento, 14.2

department of human
   resources el
   departamento de
   recursos humanos, 14.2
department store la
   tienda de departamentos
personnel department el
   departamento de
   personal, 14.2
departure la salida, 11.1; la
   partida
departure area la sala de
   salida, 11.1
departure gate la puerta
   de salida, 11.1; la puerta
   de embarque
departure hour la hora de
   salida, 13.1; 1.1
to depend (on) depender (ie)
   (de)
deposit el depósito
   to make a deposit
     ingresar
dermatologist el/la
   dermatólogo(a)
dermatology la dermatología
descendant el/la
   descendiente
to describe describir
desert el desierto
design el diseño
designer el/la diseñador(a)
dessert el postre, 5.1
destination el destino, 11.1
detail el detalle
detective policíaco(a)
detergent el detergente, 4.2
to determine determinar
development el desarrollo
device el aparato, 3.1
to devote oneself to dedicarse,
   14.1
diagnosis la diagnosis, 8.2
dial (of telephone) el disco,
   3.2
to dial marcar (el número), 3.2
dial tone el tono, 3.2
dialogue el diálogo
diamond el diamante
to dice picar, 10.2
to die morir (ue, u)
diet la dieta
difference la diferencia
different diferente
difficult difícil, duro(a), 2.1

difficulty la dificultad
to dig excavar
to dine, have dinner cenar
dining car el coche-
   comedor, el coche-
   cafetería, 13.2; 1.2
dining room el comedor,
   6.2
dinner la cena, 5.2
diplomatic diplomático(a)
direct directo(a)
to direct dirigir
direction la dirección; el
   sentido, 11.2
   in each direction en cada
     sentido, 11.2
   in the opposite direction
     en el sentido contrario,
     11.2
director el/la director(a)
dirty sucio(a), 11.1
   dirty laundry la ropa
     sucia, 12.1
disadvantage la desventaja
to disappear desaparecer
disaster el desastre
disastrous desastroso(a)
discount el descuento
to discover descubrir
to discuss discutir
to disembark desembarcar,
   11.2
dish el plato, 14.1; 2.1
disk, diskette el disquete,
   3.1
   disk drive la ranura, 3.1
distance la distancia
distinct distinto(a)
distinguished ilustre
to distract distraer
to distribute distribuir, 7.1
distribution la distribución
to dive bucear, 9.1
to divide dividir
   diving el buceo, 9.1
division la división
divorce: to get divorced
   divorciarse
to do hacer
   to do homework hacer las
     tareas, 3.1
   to do well (on an exam)
     salir bien (en un examen)
doctor el/la doctor(a); el/la
   médico(a), 8.2

doctor's office la consulta (el consultorio) del médico, 8.2; la sala de consulta
document el documento, 3.1
documentation la documentación
dog el perro, 6.1
dollar el dólar, 11
Dominican dominicano(a), 2.1
Dominican Republic la República Dominicana
dominos el dominó, 5.1
donkey el asno
door la puerta, 6.1
dose la dosis, 8.2
dot el punto
  on the dot, sharp en punto, 4.1
doubles dobles, 9.1
to **doubt** dudar
doubt la duda
doubtful dudoso(a)
down payment el enganche
downtown el centro; en el centro (de la ciudad)
dozen la docena, 4.2
to **draw** dibujar
drawing el dibujo
dream el sueño
dress el vestido, 4.1
to **dress oneself, to put on clothes** ponerse la ropa, 12.1
  to get dressed vestirse (i, i)
dressed (in) vestido(a) (de)
to **dribble** driblar, 7.2
to **drink** beber, 5.1
  to drink a beverage tomar un refresco
  to drink water (milk, coffee) tomar agua (leche, café)
drink el refresco, 5.1; la bebida, 7.1
to **drive** conducir, manejar
driver el/la conductor(a), 11.1
driver's license la licencia, el permiso de conducir, 11.1
drug la droga
drug addiction la drogadicción

druggist el/la farmacéutico(a), 8.2
drugstore la farmacia, 8.2
to **dry** secar, 12.2
dry seco(a)
to **dry clean** limpiar en seco, 12.1
dry cleaner el/la tintorero(a), 12.1
dry cleaners la tintorería, 12.1
dubbed doblado(a), 10.1
during durante

E
e-mail, electronic mail el correo electrónico, 3.1
each cada, 1.2
  in each direction en cada sentido, 11.2
eagle el águila (f.)
ear la oreja, 4.1; el oído, 8.1
early temprano, 12.1
to **earn** ganar
  to earn one's living ganar la vida
earphones los audífonos, los auriculares, 7.1
earring el arete, el pendiente, 4.1
easel el caballete
east el este
eastern oriental
easy fácil, 2.1; sencillo(a)
to **eat** comer, 5.1
  to eat breakfast desayunarse, tomar el desayuno, 12.1
  to eat dinner cenar
ecological ecológico(a)
ecology la ecología
economical económico(a), 12.2
economics la economía
  home economics la economía doméstica, 2.2
economy la economía
Ecuadorean ecuatoriano(a), 2.1
to **educate** educar
education la educación
  physical education la educación física, 2.2
egg el huevo, 5.2

eggplant la berenjena, 14.2; 2.2
eight ocho, BV
eight hundred ochocientos(as), 3.2
eighteen dieciocho, BV
eighth octavo(a), 6.2
eighty ochenta, 2.2
either tampoco
elbow el codo, 8.1
elective course el curso opcional
electric eléctrico(a)
electrician el/la electricista, 14.1
electricity la electricidad
electronic electrónico(a)
  electronic mail el correo electrónico, 3.1
elegance la elegancia
elegant elegante, 13.1
element el elemento
elementary school la escuela primaria
to **elevate** elevar
elevated elevado(a)
elevation la elevación
elevator el ascensor, 6.2; el elevador, 6.1
eleven once, BV
to **eliminate** eliminar
emergency la emergencia, 7.1
  emergency exit la salida de emergencia, 7.1
  emergency room la sala de emergencia, la sala de urgencias, 8.1
emission la emisión
to **emit** emitir
emotion la emoción
emotional emocional
to **emphasize** dar énfasis; enfatizar
to **employ** emplear
employee el/la dependiente(a), el/la empleado(a), 3.1
enchilada la enchilada, BV
end el fin
  at the end (of) al final (de); a fines de
to **end** terminar, 3.1
to **endorse** endosar, 12.2
enemy el/la enemigo(a)

energy la energía
engagement el compromiso
engine el motor
engineer el/la ingeniero(a), **14.1**
engineering la ingeniería
English el inglés, 2.2
to **enjoy** disfrutar; gozar
to **enjoy oneself** divertirse (ie, i), 12.2
enormous enorme
enough bastante, 1.1; suficiente
to **enter** entrar, 4.1
entertaining entretenido(a)
enthusiastic entusiasmado(a)
entire entero(a)
entrance la entrada, **5.2**
entrepreneur el/la empresario(a)
envelope el sobre, **12.2**
environment el ambiente; el medio ambiente
episode el episodio
epoch la época
equal igual; par
equation la ecuación
equator la línea ecuatorial
equilibrium el equilibrio
equipment el equipo
equivalent el equivalente
eraser la goma de borrar, 3.1
erroneous erróneo(a)
escalator la escalera mecánica, **9.1**
to **escape** escapar
especially especialmente; particularmente; sobre todo
essential esencial
to **establish** establecer, fundar
establishment el establecimiento
eternal eterno(a)
eternally de siempre y para siempre
ethnic étnico(a)
Europe la Europa
European europeo(a)
even aun
evening la noche
  in the evening por la noche
evening gown el traje de gala

event: great event el buen suceso
every cada, 1.2
everybody todos(as), 2.2
everyone todo el mundo
everything todos(as)
everywhere por todas partes
exact exacto(a)
exactly exactamente
to **exaggerate** exagerar
exaggerated exagerado(a)
exam el examen, 4.2
to **examine** examinar, 8.2
example: for example por ejemplo
to **excavate** excavar
excavation la excavación
to **exceed** exceder
excellent excelente
exception la excepción
to **exchange** cambiar, **12.2**
exchange: exchange rate el tipo (la tasa) de cambio, **12.2**
  exchange student el/la estudiante de intercambio
to **exclaim** exclamar
exclusively exclusivamente
excuse me perdón
to **exercise** hacer los ejercicios
exhaust pipe el tubo de escape
exhibition (art) la exposición (de arte), 10.2; la exhibición
to **exist** existir
existence la existencia
exit la salida, **11.2**
expedition la expedición
expensive caro(a), 3.2
experience la experiencia, **12**
to **experiment** experimentar
expert el/la experto(a), 9.2
to **explain** explicar, 4.2
explorer el/la explorador(a)
explosion la explosión
to **export** exportar
to **express an opinion** opinar, **10.2**
expression la expresión
  means of expression el modo de expresión
expressway la autopista, **11.2**

extension la extensión
extraction: of Mexican (Peruvian, etc.) extraction de ascendencia mexicana (peruana, etc.)
extraordinary extraordinario(a)
extreme extremo(a)
eye el ojo, 8.2

fabulous fabuloso(a)
face la cara, 12.1
face down boca abajo, **3.1**
face up boca arriba, **3.1**
to **facilitate** facilitar
factory la fábrica, 9.1
  factory worker el/la obrero(a), **9.1**
faithful fiel
to **fall** caerse
to **fall asleep** dormirse, 12.1
false falso(a)
fame la fama
family la familia, 6.1
  family (related to the) familiar
famous famoso(a), 1.2; célebre
fan (sports) el/la aficionado(a)
fantastic fantástico(a), 1.2
far lejos, 12.2
fare la tarifa
farm la finca, 9.2
  farm animals los animales domésticos, 9.2
farmer el/la agricultor(a)
to **fascinate** fascinar
fast: as fast as possible a toda prisa
to **fasten** abrocharse, **7.1**
fat gordo(a), 1.2
fat la grasa
father el padre, 6.1
father-in-law el suegro
fault el defecto
favorite favorito(a), **11**
fax el facsímil, el fax, **3.1**
fear el miedo; el terror
to **fear** temer
February febrero, BV
to **feel** sentirse (ie), 8.1
Ferris Wheel la noria, **5.2**
to **fete** festejar

fever la fiebre, 8.1
   to have a fever tener fiebre, 8.1
few poco(a), 2.1
fewer menos
fiancé(e) el/la novio(a)
fiction la ficción
fictitious ficticio(a)
field el campo, 9.2
   baseball field el campo de béisbol, 7.2
   soccer field el campo de fútbol, 7.1
fifteen quince, BV
fifteen-year-old (girl) la quinceañera
fifth quinto(a), 6.2
fifty cincuenta, 2.2
to fight luchar
figurative figurativo(a)
figure la figura
to fill rellenar
to fill out llenar, 5.1
   to fill out the form llenar el formulario, 8.2
fillet el filete
film la película, 6.2; el film, 10.1
   to see a film ver una película, 10.1
finally por fin
finances las finanzas
financial financiero(a)
to find encontrar (ue); hallar
fine bien, BV
fine la multa
finger el dedo, 4.1
to finish terminar, 3.1
fire el fuego, 10.2
first primero(a), BV
   first aid service el servicio de primeros auxilios, 8.1
   first-class en primera (clase), 13.1; 1.1
fish (food) el pescado, 5.2
fish market la pescadería, 4.2
to fit caber, 7.1
   It (They) do(es)n't fit me. No me queda(n) bien., 4.1
five cinco, BV
five hundred quinientos(as), 3.2
to fix fijar
   fixed fijo(a)

flamenco flamenco(a)
   traditional flamenco singing el cante jondo
flat (tire) pinchado(a)
flaw el defecto
flight el vuelo, 11.1
   direct flight el vuelo directo
   domestic flight el vuelo nacional
   flight number el número del vuelo, 11.1
   to take a flight tomar un vuelo, 11.1
flight attendant el/la asistente de vuelo, 11.2
floor el piso, la planta, 6.2
   ground floor la planta baja, 6.2
flower la flor
flu la gripe, 8.1
flute la flauta
to fly volar (ue), 7.2
to fly over sobrevolar, 7.2
folder la carpeta, 3.1
folk healer el/la curandero(a)
to follow seguir (i, i), 14; 2
following siguiente
fond of aficionado(a) a, 10.1
food la comida, 5.2; el alimento, el comestible, 14.2; 2.2
foolish tonto(a)
foot el pie, 7.1
   on foot a pie, 4.1
for de, BV; para; por
   for example por ejemplo
   for when? ¿para cuándo?, 14.2; 2.2
forbidden prohibido(a), 11.2
forecast el pronóstico
forehead la frente, 8.1
foreign extranjero(a)
   foreign country el país extranjero, 11.2
   foreign exchange office la casa de cambio, 12.2
foreigner el/la extranjero(a)
forever de siempre y para siempre
fork el tenedor, 14.1; 2.1
form el formulario, 8.2
to form formar
fortification la fortificación
fortunate afortunado(a)

fortune la buenaventura
forty cuarenta, 2.2
to found fundar
foundation la fundación
four cuatro, BV
four hundred cuatrocientos(as), 3.2
fourteen catorce, BV
fourth cuarto(a), 6.2
fracture la fractura, 8.1
fragment el fragmento
frank franco(a)
free libre, 5.1
freezer el congelador, 10.1
French el francés, 2.2
French fries las papas fritas, 5.1
frequently frecuentemente, con frecuencia, 3.2
fresh fresco(a), 4.2
Friday el viernes, BV
fried frito(a), 5.1
friend el/la amigo(a), 1.1; el/la compañero(a), 1.2
frightful espantoso(a)
from de, BV; desde
   from (time) to (time) de... a... , 2.2
front delantero(a)
   in front of delante de, 10.1
frozen congelado(a), 4.2
   frozen food los productos congelados, 5.2
fruit la fruta, 5.2
fruit store la frutería, 4.2
to fry freír (i, i), 14.1; 2.1
frying pan el/la sartén, 10.1
full lleno(a)
   full (train) completo(a), 13.2; 1.2
   full-time job un trabajo a tiempo completo, 14.2
fun divertido(a)
function la función, 10.2
functioning el funcionamiento
fund el fondo
fundamental primordial
funny cómico(a), gracioso(a), 1.1
furious furioso(a)
furniture los muebles
fury la furia
future el futuro

G

galaxy la galaxia
gallant gallardo(a)
gallon el galón
game arcade la sala de juegos, **5.1**
game el juego; (match) el partido, 7.1; (of dominos, etc.) la partida
  baseball game el juego de béisbol, 7.2
  Olympic Games los Juegos Olímpicos
  tennis game el juego de tenis, 9.1
  video game el juego de video, **5.1**
game board el tablero, **5.1**
game piece la ficha, **5.1**
garage el garaje, 6.2
garantee la garantía
garden el jardín, 6.2
garlic el ajo, 14.2; **2.2**
gas station la gasolinera, **11.1**
gas tank el tanque, **11.1**
gasoline la gasolina, **11.1**
  regular (super) gasoline normal (súper), **11.2**
  (un)leaded con (sin) plomo, **11.1**
gate la puerta, 11.1
gathering la reunión
generally en general; generalmente
  in general, usually por lo general
generous generoso(a), 1.2
genre el género
gentleman el caballero, **4.1**
geography la geografía, 2.2
geometric geométrico(a)
geometry la geometría, 2.2
German (language) el alemán, 2.2
gesture el gesto
to get sacar, 4.2
  to get a good (bad) grade sacar una nota buena (mala), 4.2
  to get, buy a ticket sacar un billete
to get engaged comprometerse
to get off bajar, 13.2; **1.2**

to get off the train bajar(se) del tren, 13.2; **1.2**
to get on subir, 13.2; **1.1**; abordar
  to get on the train subir al tren, 13.1; **1.1**
to get together reunirse
to get up levantarse, 12.1
giant el gigante
gift el regalo, 6.1
girl la muchacha, 1.1; la chica
girlfriend la novia
to give dar, 4.2
  to give back devolver
  to give (throw) a party dar una fiesta, 4.2
  to give (someone) a present regalar
  to give (someone) a shot (an injection) poner una inyección
  to give a test dar un examen, 4.2
to give up renunciar
  glass (drinking) el vaso, 12.1
  glove el guante, 7.2
to go ir, 4.1
  let's go vamos a
  to go back volver, 7.1
  to go back home volver a casa, 10.2
  to go by bicycle ir en bicicleta, 12.2
  to go by car ir en carro (coche), 4.1
  to go by train ir en tren
  to go on a trip viajar, 11.1
  to go on foot ir a pie, 4.1
  to go shopping ir de compras, 5.2
  to go through pasar por, 11.1
to go down bajar, 9.2
to go surfing (windsurfing, etc.) practicar el surfing (la plancha de vela, etc.), 9.1
to go swimming nadar, 9.1
to go to bed acostarse (ue), 12.1
to go up subir, 6.2
  goal line la portería, 7.1
  goalkeeper, goalie el/la portero(a), 7.1
  godfather el padrino, **13.1**
  godmother la madrina

godparents los padrinos
gold el oro
  gold chain una cadena de oro, **4.1**
golden dorado(a)
good buen; bueno(a), 1.2
  Good afternoon. Buenas tardes., BV
  Good evening. Buenas noches., BV
  Good heavens!, You bet! ¡hombre!
  Good morning. Hello. Buenos días., BV
  to be in a good mood estar de buen humor, 8.1
good-bye adiós, ¡Chao!, BV
goods and services los bienes y servicios
Gosh! ¡Dios mío!
gossip item el chisme
government el gobierno, **14.1**
  federal government el gobierno federal
  municipal government el gobierno municipal, **14.1**
  state government el gobierno estatal
grade el grado; la nota, 4.2
  high grade la nota alta, 4.2
  low grade la nota baja, 4.2
  to get a good (bad) grade sacar una nota buena (mala), 4.2
graduate el/la diplomado(a)
to graduate graduarse
grain el cereal, **9.2**
grain el grano
gram el gramo
grammar la gramática
granddaughter la nieta, 6.1
grandfather el abuelo, 6.1
grandmother la abuela, 6.1
grandparents los abuelos, 6.1
grandson el nieto, 6.1
grapes las uvas, 10.1
grapefruit la toronja, 10.1
to grate rallar, 10.2
grave (serious) grave
gray gris, 3.2
great gran, grande
greater, greatest mayor
  greater part, the most la mayor parte
Greek el/la griego(a)

green verde, 3.2
green bean la judía verde, 5.2
greengrocer store la verdulería, **4.2**
to **greet** saludar
greeting el saludo, BV
grill la parrilla, **10.1**
grocery store el colmado, la tienda de abarrotes, la tienda de ultramarinos, **4.2**
groom el novio, **13.1**
ground el suelo
group el grupo
to **grow** cultivar, **9.2**
growth el crecimiento
to **guard** guardar, 7.1
Guatemalan guatemalteco(a)
guerrilla band la guerrilla
to **guess** adivinar
to **guess right** acertar (ie)
guest el/la invitado(a); el/la huésped, **6.1**
guidance counselor el/la consejero(a) de orientación
guide el/la guía
guitar la guitarra
gulf el golfo
gymnasium el gimnasio
gynecologist el/la ginecólogo(a)
gynecology la ginecología

H

hair el pelo, 12.1; el cabello, **12.1**
hair dryer el secador, **12.1**
hair salon la peluquería, **12.1**
hair stylist el/la peluquero(a), **12.1**
haircut el corte de pelo, **12.1**
hairdo el peinado
half la mitad
half medio(a), 5.2
  half an hour media hora
  half-past (time) y media
  half (game) el tiempo
  second half (game) el segundo tiempo, 7.1
hall el salón, **13.1**
ham el jamón, 5.1
hamburger la hamburguesa, 5.1

hand la mano, 7.1
  to hand out distribuir, **7.1**
  to shake hands dar la mano
handkerchief el pañuelo, **4.1**
handsome guapo(a), 1.1
to **hang, hang up** colgar (ue)
Hanukah Hanuka, **13.2**
  Happy Hanukah! ¡Feliz Hanuka!, **13.2**
to **happen** ocurrir, suceder; pasar
happiness la alegría; la felicidad
happy contento(a), 8.1; alegre
  Happy birthday! ¡Feliz cumpleaños!, **13.1**
hard duro(a), 2.1
hardworking ambicioso(a), 1.1
harmonious armonioso(a)
to **harvest** cosechar, **9.2**
harvest la cosecha, **9.2**
hat el sombrero; la gorra, 3.2
to **have** tener (ie), 6.1
  to have (subtitles, ingredients, etc.) llevar
  to have a cold tener catarro, estar resfriado(a), 8.1
  to have a cough tener tos, 8.1
  to have a headache tener dolor de cabeza, 8.1
  to have a snack tomar una merienda, 4.2
  to have a sore throat tener dolor de garganta, 8.1
  to have to tener que
to **have just (done something)** acabar de, **8.1**
he él, 1.1
head la cabeza, 7.1
headache el dolor de cabeza, 8.1
health la salud
healthy sano(a)
to **hear** oír
  to hear the dial tone oír el tono, **3.2**
heart el corazón
heat: on low heat a fuego lento
heavy pesado(a)

heel el tacón, **4.1**
height la altura, **7.2**
helicopter el helicóptero, **7.2**
Hello! ¡Hola!, BV
  Hello! (answering the telephone–Spain) ¡Diga!, 14.2; **2.2**
to **help** ayudar, 13.1; **1.1**; dar auxilio; socorrer
help el socorro, la ayuda
hemisphere: northern hemisphere el hemisferio norte
  southern hemisphere el hemisferio sur
hen la gallina, **9.2**
her (f. sing.) (pron.) la
her su
here aquí
  Here is (are)... Aquí tiene (tienes, tienen)...
hero el/la héroe
to **hide** esconder
high alto(a), 4.2; elevado
high school el liceo; la escuela secundaria, 1.1; la escuela superior
highway la carretera, **11**; la autovía, la autopista, **11.2**
hike: to take a hike dar una caminata, 12.2
him (m. sing.) (pron.) lo
  to him, to her; to you (formal) (pron.) le
his su
Hispanic hispano(a)
historian el/la historiador(a)
historical histórico(a)
history la historia, 2.2
to **hit** golpear, 9.2
to **hit (baseball)** batear, 7.2
hobby el pasatiempo, el hobby, **5.1**
hole el agujero
home la casa, 6.2
  at home en casa
  country home la casa de campo, **9.2**
  home economics la economía doméstica, 2.2
home run el jonrón, 7.2
homeplate el platillo, 7.2
honest honesto(a), 1.2
honeymoon la luna de miel

to **honk the horn** tocar la bocina

honor el honor

    maid of honor la dama de honor, **13.1**

hood (automobile) el capó, **11.1**

to **hope** esperar

    I hope ojalá, **14.1**

horn el claxon, la bocina, **11.1**

horrible horrible

horse el caballo

horseback: to go horseback riding pasear a caballo

hospital el hospital, **8.1**

hot: It's hot. Hace calor., 9.1

hotel el hotel, **6.1**

    inexpensive hotel el hostal, 12.2

hour la hora

    departure hour la hora de salida

house la casa, 6.2

    apartment house la casa de apartamentos (departamentos), 6.2

    private house la casa privada (particular), 6.2

housing la vivienda

how? qué, BV; ¿cómo?, 1.1

    How absurd! ¡Qué absurdo!

    How are you? ¿Qué tal?, BV

    How is . . . ? ¿Cómo está . . . ?, 8.1

    How may I help you? ¿En qué puedo servirle?, **4.1**

    How much do(es) . . . cost? ¿Cuánto cuesta(n)... ?, 3.1

    How much is (are) . . . ? ¿A cuánto está(n) . . . ?, 5.2

how many? ¿cuántos(as)?, 2.1

how much? ¿cuánto?, 3.1

human being el ser humano

humble humilde

humid húmedo(a)

hungry: to be hungry tener hambre, 14.1; **2.1**

to **hurt** doler (ue), 8.2

    My . . . hurt(s) me Me duele(n) . . ., 8.2

to **hurt oneself** hacerse daño, lastimarse, 8.1

husband el marido, el esposo, 6.1

hydrofoil el aerodeslizador; el hidrofoil

hygiene la higiene

hypermarket el hipermercado, **4.2**

I

I yo, 1.1

ice cream el helado, 5.1

    chocolate ice cream el helado de chocolate, 5.1

    vanilla ice cream el helado de vainilla, 5.1

icon el icono

idea la idea

ideal ideal, 1.2

idealist el/la idealista

to **identify** identificar

if si

illness la enfermedad

illusion la ilusión

image la imagen

imaginary imaginario(a)

imagination la imaginación

to **imagine** imaginar

    imagined, dreamed of imaginado(a)

immediate inmediato(a)

immediately enseguida, 5.1; inmediatamente

immense inmenso(a)

imperative el imperativo

to **imply that** dar a entender

important importante

impossible imposible

in en

    in case of en caso de, **7.1**

    in general por lo general

    in itself en sí

    in regard to en cuanto a

to **inaugurate** inaugurar

Inca el/la inca

inch la pulgada

to **include** incluir, 5.1

to **increase** aumentar

incredible increíble

independence la independencia

Indian indio(a)

to **indicate** indicar, 11.1

indigenous indígena

indispensable indispensable

individual el individuo

individual: individual sport el deporte individual

industrial industrial

inexpensive barato(a), 3.2

to **influence** impresionar

influence la influencia

to **inform** informar, 13.2; **1.2**

information la información; los datos, **3.1**

ingredient el ingrediente

inhabitant el/la habitante

inheritance la herencia

inhospitable inhospital

injection la inyección, 8.2

    to give (someone) an injection poner una inyección

inn el parador; el albergue

inning la entrada, 7.2

innocent inocente

innovation la innovación

insane loco(a)

to **insert** meter, **3.1**; introducir, **3.2**

to **inspect** inspeccionar, 11.1

inspection el control, 11.1

installation la instalación

installments: in installments a plazos

instant el instante

instantaneous instantáneo(a)

instead of en vez de

instruction la instrucción

instrument el instrumento

insurance el seguro

integral íntegro(a)

intelligent inteligente, 2.1

interest el interés

to **interest** interesar

interesting interesante, 2.1

international internacional

Internet Internet, **3.1**

interpretation la interpretación

interpreter el/la intérprete

to **interrupt** interrumpir

interruption la interrupción

intersection el cruce, la bocacalle, **11.2**

to **intervene** intervenir

to **interview** entrevistar

interview la entrevista, **14.2**

interviewer el/la entrevistador(a), **14.2**
introduction la introducción
invention el invento
investigation la investigación
invitation la invitación
to **invite** invitar, 6.1
invoice la factura, **6.1**
to **iron** planchar, **12.1**
irrigation la irrigación
island la isla
it la, lo
Italian italiano(a)
itinerant ambulante
ivory el marfil

J

jacket la chaqueta, 3.2; el saco, **4.1**
jai alai la pelota vasca
jai alai player el/la pelotari
jam la mermelada
January enero, BV
jar el frasco, **4.2**
jeans el blue jean, **3.2**
jet el avión de reacción, el jet, **7.2**
jewel la joya, **4.1**
jewelry store la joyería, **4.1**
Jewish hebreo(a), **13.2**
job el trabajo
   job application la solicitud de empleo, **14.2**
   full- (part-) time job el trabajo a tiemp completo (parcial), **14.2**
to **join** enlazar
judge el/la juez, **14.1**
juice el jugo
   orange juice el jugo de naranja, 12.1
July julio, BV
to **jump** saltar
June junio, BV
jungle la jungla; la selva
just: just after (time) y pico
   to have just (done something) acabar de (+ infinitive), **8.1**

K

to **keep** guardar, **3.1**
to **keep in shape** mantenerse en forma

key la tecla, **3.2**; la llave, **6.1**
keyboard el teclado, **3.1**
to **keyboard** entrar los datos, **3.1**
to **kick** tirar, 7.1
   to kick (throw) the ball tirar el balón, 7.2
to **kill** matar
kilogram el kilo, 5.2
kilometer el kilómetro
kind la clase
king el rey
   The Three Kings (Wise Men) Los Reyes Magos, **13.2**
kitchen la cocina, 6.2
knapsack la mochila, 12.2
knee la rodilla, 7.1
knife el cuchillo, 14.1; **2.1**
knight el caballero
   knight errant el caballero andante
to **know** conocer, 11.1
to **know (how)** saber, 11.2
knowledge el conocimiento

L

laboratory el laboratorio
lady-in-waiting la dama
lake el lago, **5.2**
lamb el cordero, 14.2; **2.2**
lame cojo(a)
lament el lamento
lance la lanza
to **land** aterrizar, 11.2
land la tierra
   by land, overland por tierra
landing el aterrizaje, **7.2**
landscape el paisaje
lane (of highway) el carril, **11.2**
language la lengua, 2.2; el lenguaje; el idioma
large gran, grande
to **last** durar, **13.2**
last pasado(a); último(a)
   last (year) el (año) pasado
late tarde; con una demora, 11.1; con retraso, 13.2; **1.2**
later luego, BV; después; más tarde
   See you later! ¡Hasta luego! , BV

Latin el latín, 2.2
Latin *(adj.)* latino(a)
Latin America Latinoamérica, 1.1
Latin American latinoamericano(a)
to **laugh** reír
to **launch** lanzar
laundromat la lavandería
laundry el lavado, 12.1
   dirty laundry la ropa sucia, **12.1**
lavatory el aseo, el lavabo, **7.1**
lawyer el/la abogado(a), **14.1**
lawyer's office el bufete del abogado, **14.1**
lazy perezoso(a), 1.1
to **lead, go (one street into another)** desembocar, **9.1**
leaded (gasoline) con plomo, **11.1**
league la liga
   Major Leagues las Grandes Ligas
to **learn** aprender, 5.1
to **leave (something)** dejar, 14.1; **2.1**
   to leave a tip dejar una propina, 14.1; **2.1**
to **leave** salir, 10.1
   to leave late salir tarde, 11.1
   to leave on time salir a tiempo, 11.1
   to leave the theater salir del teatro, 10.2
lecture la conferencia
left izquierdo(a), 7.1
   to the left a la izquierda, **5.2**
leg la pierna, 7.1
lemon el limón, **10.1**
lemonade la limonada, BV
lentil la lenteja
less menos
lesser, least menor
lesson la lección, 4.2
to **let** dejar
   letter (of alphabet) la letra
letter la carta, **12.2**
   letter of recommendation la carta de recomendación
lettuce la lechuga, 5.2
level el nivel

liberator el/la libertador(a)
license plate la placa
life jacket el chaleco
  salvavidas, **7.1**
life la vida
  school life la vida escolar
to **lift** levantar
light (cheerful) ligero(a)
to **light** encender (ie), **13.2**
light la luz, **11.1**
  red light la luz roja,
  11.2
like como, 1.2
to **like, to be pleasing** gustar
lime la lima, **10.1**
limousine la limusina
line (queue) la cola, 10.1; la
  fila, **5.2**
  to stand (wait) in line
  hacer cola, **10.1**
line la línea
  parallel line la línea
  paralela
  telephone line la línea
  telefónica
to **line up** hacer cola, 10.1
lion el león
lip el labio, **8.1**
liquid líquido(a)
list la lista
to **listen (to)** escuchar, 4.2
  Listen! ¡Oye!
liter el litro
literal literal
literary literario(a)
literature la literatura, 2.1
little poco(a), 2.1
  a little un poco (de)
to **live** vivir, 5.2
  living: to earn one's living
  ganar la vida
  living room la sala, 6.2
loan el préstamo
lobster la langosta, 14.2; **2.2**
local local, 13.2; **1.2**
to **lodge** alojarse; hospedarse
logical lógico(a)
long largo(a), 3.2
to **look at** mirar, 3.1
  Look! ¡Mira!
  to look at oneself mirarse,
  12.1
to **look for** buscar, 3.1
to **look good (food)** tener
  buena pinta, **4.2**

to **look like** parecer, **8.1**
to **lose** perder (ie), 7.1
lotto el loto
love el amor
to **love** querer; amar; encantar
low bajo(a), 4.2
to **lower** bajar, 9.2
luck la suerte
  Good luck! ¡Buena suerte!
luggage el equipaje, 11.1
  carry-on luggage el
  equipaje de mano, 11.1
  to check luggage facturar
  el equipaje, 11.1
  to claim luggage reclamar
lunch el almuerzo, 5.2
  to have, eat lunch tomar
  el almuerzo
luxurious lujoso(a)
lying mentiroso(a)
lyric lírico(a)

M
made hecho(a)
magazine la revista, 6.2
magnificent magnífico(a)
maid la camarera, **6.2**
maid of honor la dama de
  honor, **13.1**
mail el correo, **12.2**
  air mail el correo aéreo,
  12.2
  e-mail el correo
  electrónico, **3.1**
  regular mail el correo
  ordinario, **12.2**
to **mail the letter** echar la carta
  (en el buzón), **12.2**
mailbox el buzón, **12.2**
main principal
mainly principalmente
to **maintain** mantener
majority la mayoría
to **make** hacer
  to make a telephone call
  hacer una llamada
  telefónica, **3.2**
  to make the bed hacer la
  cama, 6.2
to **make up** formar
makeup el maquillaje, 12.1
  to put one's makeup on
  maquillarse, poner el
  maquillaje, 12.1
male el varón

man el hombre; el caballero,
  4.1
manager el/la gerente, **14.1**
manner el modo; la manera,
  1.1
manufactured fabricado(a)
many; a lot muchos(as), 2.1
map el mapa; el plano, **9.1**
March marzo, BV
to **march** marchar
marker el marcador, 3.1
market el mercado, 5.2
  meat market la carnicería,
  4.2
marketing el mercadeo
marmalade la mermelada
marriage el matrimonio
  to get married casarse,
  13.1
marvelous maravilloso(a)
mass la masa
master el/la maestro(a)
to **match** parear
material el material
  raw material la material
  prima
mathematics las
  matemáticas, 2.1
matter la materia
maximum máximo(a),
  11.2
May mayo, BV
Maya el/la maya
mayonnaise la mayonesa
mayor el alcalde, **14.1**; la
  alcaldesa
me *(pron.)* me
  to me a mí
meal la comida, 5.2
  to prepare the meal
  preparar la comida
to **mean** significar
meaning el significado; el
  sentido
meaningful significante
means el medio
  means of expression el
  modo de expresión
  means of transportation
  el medio de transporte
to **measure** medir (i, i)
measurement la medida
meat la carne, 5.2
mechanic el/la mecánico
medal la medalla

medical office el consultorio, 8.2

medicine (discipline) la medicina, 8.2

medicine (drugs) el medicamento, 8.2

medium mediano(a), **4.1**

medium el medio

to **meet** encontrarse (ue)

melancholic melancólico(a)

member el miembro, 4.2

memory la memoria; el recuerdo

men: men's clothing store la tienda de ropa para caballeros, **4.1**

menace la plaga

menorah la menora, **13.2**

to **mention** mencionar

menu el menú, 5.1

merchandise la mercancía, **14.1**

merengue el merengue

merry-go-round el tiovivo, **5.2**

message el mensaje, **3.2**

mestizo el/la mestizo(a)

metabolism el metabolismo

meter el metro

method el método

metrics la métrica

metro entrance la boca del metro, **9.1**

Mexican mexicano(a), 1.1

Mexican-American mexicanoamericano(a)

microbe el microbio

microscope el microscopio

microscopic microscópico(a)

microwave oven el horno de microondas, **10.1**

middle: in the middle of (noun) en pleno + *noun*

middle school la escuela intermedia

midnight la medianoche

migration la migración

mile la milla

milk la leche

million el millón

millionaire el/la millonario(a)

mime el/la mimo, **5.2**

miniature la miniatura

miniaturization la miniaturización

ministry el ministerio

to **mint** acuñar

minute diminuto(a)

minute el minuto

mirror el espejo, 12.1

to **miss** perder (ie), 10.2

    to miss the bus perder el autobús (la guagua, el camión), 10.1

Miss, Ms. la señorita, BV

mixture la mezcla

mode la modalidad

model el/la modelo

modem el módem

moderation la moderación

modern moderno(a)

mom la mamá

moment el momento

monastery el monasterio

Monday el lunes, BV

money el dinero, 14.1; **2.1**

    money (income) la plata

money changer el/la cambista, **12.2**

monitor el monitor, **3.1**

monkey el mono, **5.2**

monster el monstruo

month el mes, BV

monthly installment la mensualidad

monument el monumento

mood el humor, 8.1

    to be in a bad (good) mood estar de mal (buen) humor, 8.1

moon la luna

Moor el/la moro(a)

more más, 2.2

    more or less más o menos

moreover además

morning la mañana

    A.M. (time) de la mañana

    in the morning por la mañana

mortality la mortalidad

mortgage la hipoteca

mother la madre, 6.1

motion la moción

motive el motivo

motor el motor

to **mount, get on (horse)** montar (caballo)

mountain la montaña, 9.2

mountain range la sierra; la cordillera, **7.2**

mountainous montañoso(a)

mouse el ratón, **3.1**

mouth la boca, 8.2

to **move** mover (ue), mudarse

movement el movimiento

movie la película, 6.2

movie theater el cine, 10.1

Ms., Mrs., madam la señora, BV

much; a lot mucho(a), 2.1

mud el lodo

mulatto el/la mulato(a)

multinational multinacional

multiplication la multiplicación

to **multiply** multiplicar

mural el mural, 10.2

muralist el/la muralista

muscular muscular

museum el museo, 10.2

music la música, 2.2

    musical instrument el instrumento musical

musician el/la músico(a)

mussels los mejillones, **10.2**

must deber

mute mudo(a)

my mi

mysterious misterioso(a)

mystery el misterio

mythology la mitología

N

name el nombre

    in whose name? ¿a nombre de quién?, 14.2; **2.2**

    last name el apellido

nap: to take a nap echar (tomar) una siesta

napkin la servilleta, 14.1; **2.1**

narcotic el narcótico

to **narrate** narrar

narration la narración

narrow estrecho(a), **4.1**; angosto(a), **9.1**

    narrow street la callecita, **9.1**

national nacional

nationality la nacionalidad, 1.2

    what nationality? ¿de qué nacionalidad?

native indígena
native person el/la
  indígena
natural resources los
  recursos naturales, 2.1
natural sciences las ciencias
  naturales
nature la naturaleza
navegable navegable
to navigate navegar
near cerca de, 6.2
nearby cercano(a)
necessary necesario(a)
necessity la necesidad
neck el cuello, 4.1
to need necesitar, 3.1
negative negativo(a)
neighbor el/la vecino(a)
neighborhood el barrio, 9.1;
  la zona
nephew el sobrino, 6.1
nervous nervioso(a), 8.1
Net la red, 9.1
nettle la ortiga
never jamás; nunca
new nuevo(a)
newlyweds los novios, 13.1
New Year el Año Nuevo, 13.2
  Happy New Year!
    ¡Próspero Año Nuevo!,
    13.2
  New Year's Eve la
    Nochevieja, la Víspera de
    Año Nuevo, 13.2
news las noticias, 6.2
newspaper el periódico, 6.2
newsstand el quiosco,
  13.1; 1.1
next próximo(a),13.2; 1.2
  at the next stop en la
    próxima parada, 13.2; 1.2
nice simpático(a), 1.2
niece la sobrina, 6.1
night la noche
  Good night. Buenas
    noches., BV
  in the evening, at night
    por la noche
  last night anoche, 9.2
  P.M. (time) de la noche
nine nueve, BV
nine hundred
  novecientos(as), 3.2
nineteen diecinueve, BV
ninety noventa, 2.2

ninth noveno(a), 6.2
no no, BV
no one nadie
no smoking sign la señal de
  no fumar, 7.1
Nobel Prize el Premio Nóbel
noble noble
none, not any ninguno(a)
  by no means de ninguna
    manera, 1.1
nonstop sin escala
noon el mediodía
north el norte
North America la América
  del Norte
North American
  norteamericano(a)
northwest el noroeste
nose la nariz, 8.1
notable notable
to note notar
notebook el cuaderno, 3.1
notes: to take notes tomar
  apuntes, 4.2
nothing nada, 5.2
  Nothing else. Nada más.,
    5.2
novel la novela
novelist el/la novelista
November noviembre, BV
now ahora, 4.2; ya
  now and then de vez en
    cuando
nowadays, these days hoy
  (en) día
number el número, 1.2
  flight number el número
    del vuelo, 11.1
  local number el número
    local
  seat number el número
    del asiento, 11.1
  telephone number el
    número de teléfono
  wrong number el número
    equivocado
numerous numeroso(a)
nuptial, wedding nupcial
nurse el/la enfermero(a), 8.2;
  el/la practicante
nutrition la nutrición

O

object el objeto
objective el objetivo

obligation la obligación
observation la observación
to observe observar
observer el/la observador(a)
obstacle el obstáculo
to obtain obtener
obvious obvio(a)
occasion la ocasión
occupied, taken ocupado(a),
  5.1
ocean el océano
October octubre, BV
odd: odd number el número
  impar
of de, BV
  Of course! ¡Cómo no!; por
    supuesto
  of the, from the del
to offer ofrecer, 14.2
office la oficina, 9.1
official oficial
often con frecuencia, a
  menudo, 3.2
oil el aceite, 14.2; 2.2; el óleo
oil petrolero(a)
OK, all right; in agreement
  de acuerdo; ¡vale!
old viejo(a), anciano(a), 6.1;
  antiguo(a), 5.1
old person el/la anciano(a);
  el/la viejo(a)
olive oil el aceite de oliva
on en; sobre
  on foot a pie, 4.1
  on the dot, sharp en
    punto, 4.1
once and for all
  definitivamente
oncologist el/la oncólogo(a)
oncology la oncología
one uno, BV
  one o'clock la una
  one-way street la calle de
    sentido único, 11.2
  one-way ticket el billete
    sencillo, 13.1; 1.1
  one hundred cien(to),
    3.2
onion la cebolla, 10.1
only único(a); sólo; solamente
to open abrir, 8.2
opening la apertura
opera la ópera
to operate operar
operating room el quirófano

operator el/la operador(a)
operetta la opereta
ophthalmologist el/la
    oftalmólogo(a)
ophthalmology la
    oftalmología
opinion la opinión
opportunity la oportunidad
opposite opuesto(a);
    contrario(a)
    the opposite lo contrario
    the opposite direction el
        sentido contrario, 11.2
or o; u (used instead of o
    before words beginning
    with o or ho)
orally oralmente
orange (fruit) la china; la
    naranja, 5.2
orange anaranjado(a), 3.2
    orange juice el jugo de
        naranja, 12.1; el zumo de
        naranja
orchard el/la huerto(a), 9.2
orchestra la orquesta, 13.1
    symphonic orchestra la
        orquesta sinfónica
order (restaurant) la orden,
    5.1
to order mandar; (restaurant)
    pedir (i, i)
organ el órgano
organism el organismo
to organize organizar
origin el origen
ornament el adorno
orthopedic surgeon el/la
    cirujano(a) ortopédico(a),
    8.2
orthopedics la ortopedia
other otro(a)
ounce la onza
our nuestro(a)
outdoor (adj.) al aire libre
    outdoor café (market,
        etc.) el café (mercado,
        etc.) al aire libre
outfielder el/la jardinero(a),
    7.2
outskirts los alrededores; las
    afueras, 9.1
oven el horno, 10.1
over sobre
overcoat el abrigo, 4.1
overland por tierra

to overtake adelantar, 11.2
to owe deber
    own: one's own propio(a)
    oxygen el oxígeno
        oxygen mask la máscara
            de oxígeno, 7.1
    oyster la ostra, 10.2

P

to pack one's suitcase hacer la
    maleta
    package el paquete, 5.2
    page la página
    pain el dolor, 8.1
        I have a pain in my . . .
            Tengo dolor de..., 8.2
to paint pintar, 14.1
    paintbrush el pincel
    painter el/la pintor(a)
    painting el cuadro, 10.2; la
        pintura
    pair el par, 4.1
        pair of tennis shoes el par
            de tenis, 3.2
    palace el palacio
    palette knife la espátula
    palm tree la palma
    pamphlet el folleto
    Panamanian panameño(a),
        2.1
    Panamerican
        panamericano(a)
    pancake el panqueque
    pants el pantalón, 3.2
    papaya la papaya, 10.2
    paper el papel, 3.1
        sheet of paper la hoja de
            papel, 3.1
        toilet paper el papel
            higiénico, 12.2
    paradise el paraíso
    paramedics el servicio de
        primeros auxilios, los
        socorristas, 8.1
    paragraph el párrafo
    parents los padres, 6.1
to park aparcar, estacionar
    park el parque, 5.2
    parka el anorak, 9.2
    parking el estacionamiento
    parking lot el
        aparcamiento
    parking meter el
        parquímetro
    part (in hair) la raya

part la parte
    the greatest part, the
        most la mayor parte
    upper part la parte
        superior, 7
party la fiesta, 13.1
    to give (throw) a party dar
        una fiesta, 4.2
pass (permission) el pase
to pass pasar, 7.2; (car)
    adelantar, 11.2
passenger el/la pasajero(a),
    11.1
passionate apasionado(a)
passport el pasaporte, 11.1
    passport inspection el
        control de pasaportes,
        11.1
past pasado(a)
pastry el pastel, 4.2
path el camino; la senda, 5.2
    to walk along the path
        caminar por la senda,
        5.2
patience la paciencia
patient el/la paciente
pattern el patrón
paved pavimentado(a)
pavement el pavimento
to pay pagar, 3.1
    to pay at the cashier
        pagar en la caja, 4.2
    to pay attention hacer
        caso; prestar atención, 4.2
    to pay the bill pagar la
        factura, 6.1
payment el pago
    monthly payment el pago
        mensual
pea el guisante, 5.2
Peace Corps el Cuerpo de Paz
peaceful tranquilo(a)
peak el pico, 7.2
peanut el cacahuete
    (cacahuate); el maní
pear la pera, 9.2
pear tree el peral, 9.2
pedestrian el peatón, 9.1
    pedestrian street la calle
        peatonal, 9.1
pediatrician el/la pediatra
pediatrics la pediatría
to peel pelar, 10.2
    pen la pluma, 3.1
    pencil el lápiz, 3.1

peninsula la península
penny el centavo
people la gente
pepper la pimienta, 14.1; **2.1**
   bell pepper el pimiento,
   10.2
percent por ciento
percussion la percusión
to perfect perfeccionar
performance la función,
   (theater) la
   representación, 10.2
perhaps quizás, **14.2**
period el período
period of time la época
to permit permitir, 11.1
person la persona, 1.2
personality la personalidad
personally personalmente
personnel department el
   departamento de personal,
   14.2
Peruvian peruano(a)
petition la petición
petroleum el petróleo
pharmacist el/la
   farmacéutico(a), 8.2
phone el teléfono
   cell phone el teléfono
   celular, **3.2**
   pay phone el teléfono
   público, **3.2**
   phone book la guía
   telefónica, **3.2**
   phone call la llamada
   telefónica, **3.2**
   push-button phone el
   teléfono de botones, **3.2**
photo la foto
photograph la fotografía
photographer el/la
   fotógrafo(a)
phrase la frase
physics la física, 2.2
piano el piano
to pick up recoger
to pick up (the telephone)
   descolgar (ue), **3.2**
picturesque pintoresco(a),
   9.1
piece el pedazo, **10**; el trocito,
   10.2
   little piece el pedacito,
   10.2
pig (pork) el cerdo, 14.2; **2.2**

pilgrim el/la peregrino(a)
pill la pastilla, la píldora, la
   tableta, 8.2
pillow la almohada, **6.2**
pilot el/la piloto, 11.2
pinch la pizca
pink rosado(a), 3.2
pint la pinta
piping (embroidery) el
   cordoncillo
pirouette la pirueta
pitcher el/la lanzador(a),
   el/la pícher, 7.2
pity la lástima
pizza la pizza, BV
to place colocar; meter, 7.1
place el lugar; el sitio
placement la colocación
plague la plaga
plaid a cuadros
plain la llanura, **7.2**
plan el plano, **9.1**
to plan planear
plant la planta
to plant sembrar, **9.2**
plantain el plátano, 5.2
   fried plantain slice el
   tostón
plastic plástico(a), **4.2**
plate el plato, 14.1; **2.1**
plateau la mesa; la meseta,
   7.2
   high plateau el altiplano,
   7.2
to play (music) tocar
to play jugar (ue), 7.1
   to play baseball (soccer,
   basketball, etc.) jugar
   (al) béisbol (fútbol,
   baloncesto, etc.), 7.1
play la obra teatral, 10.2; la
   obra dramática
player el/la jugador(a), 7.1
playwright el/la
   dramaturgo(a)
to plead rogar (ue)
pleasant agradable
please por favor, BV; favor de,
   11.2
pleasure el gusto
plentiful abundante
plot el argumento
plumber el/la fontanero(a),
   el/la plomero(a), 14.1
pocket el bolsillo, 4.1

poem el poema
poet el poeta
poetry la poesía
point el tanto, 7.1; el punto
poisonous venenoso(a)
police officer el/la guardia;
   el/la agente de policía; el/la
   policía
polite atento(a)
political político(a)
   political science las
   ciencias políticas
polka dots: with polka dots
   con lunares
to pollute contaminar
polluted contaminado(a)
pollution la contaminación
poncho el poncho
poor pobre
   poor boy (girl) el/la pobre
   poor man (woman) el/la
   pobretón(ona)
popular popular, 2.1
popularity la popularidad
population, people la
   población
porch el porche
pork el puerco
portable portátil
porter el/la maletero(a), el/la
   mozo(a), 13.1; **1.1**
portrait el retrato
position la posición; el
   puesto, **14.2**
to possess poseer
possibility la posibilidad
possible posible
post office el correo, **12.2**
postcard la postal, la tarjeta
   postal, **12.2**
pot la cazuela, la olla, **10.1**
potato la papa, 5.1; la patata
   mashed potatoes el puré
   de papas
pothole el bache
pound la libra
practically casi
to practice practicar
pre-Columbian
   precolombino(a)
precious precioso(a)
precise preciso(a)
prediction la predicción
predominance el predominio
to predominate predominar

to **prefer** preferir (ie, i)
prenuptial antenupcial
preparation la preparación
to **prepare** preparar
to **prescribe** recetar, 8.2
prescription la receta, 8.2
presence la presencia
to **present** presentar
present (adj.) presente
  at the present time
    actualmente
presentation la presentación
president el/la presidente
pressure la presión, **11.1**
prestige el prestigio
pretty bello(a), bonito(a),
  hermoso(a), lindo(a),
  1.1
to **prevail** prevalecer
price el precio
to **prick** picar, **8.1**
priest el sacerdote
princess la princesa
principal el/la director(a)
principal principal
printer la impresora, **3.1**
private particular, 6.2;
  privado(a)
  private house la casa
    particular, la casa
    privada, 6.2
probable probable
problem el problema
process el proceso
to **process** procesar
procession la procesión
to **proclaim** proclamar
produced producido(a)
product el producto, 5.2
production la producción
profession la profesión,
  14.1
professor el/la profesor(a),
  2.1
program (TV) la emisión,
  6.2; el programa
  sports program la emisión
    deportiva, 6.2
progress el progreso
project el proyecto
to **project** proyectar, 10.1
promiscuity la promiscuidad
promise la promesa
to **promote** promover (ue)
promotion la promoción

pronoun el pronombre
prose la prosa
prosperous próspero(a)
protagonist el/la
  protagonista
protection la protección
protein la proteína
to **protest** protestar
protoplasm el protoplasma
to **provide** proveer
provider el/la proveedor(a)
provision la provisión
psychiatrist el/la psiquiatra
psychiatry la psiquiatría
public público(a)
publicity la propaganda
to **publish** publicar
Puerto Rican
  puertorriqueño(a)
to **pull out** arrancar
pulse el pulso, **8.2**
punctual puntual
punishment el castigo
puppy el perrito
pure puro(a)
to **push** oprimir; pulsar, **3.1**;
  empujar, **4.2**
to **put** poner, 11.1; colocar
  to put a cast on poner en
    un yeso, **8.2**
to **put in** meter, **3.1**
to **put on** ponerse, 12.1
  to put on a performance
    dar una representación,
    10.2
  to put on makeup ponerse
    el maquillaje, 12.1
Pyrenees los pirineos

Q

qualification la calificación
quality la calidad
quarrel la disputa
quarter el cuarto, 2.2
  quarter after (the hour) y
    cuarto
  quarter to (the hour)
    menos cuarto
queen la reina
question la pregunta
questionnaire el
  cuestionario
quickly rápidamente; rápido
quiet tranquilo(a)
quite bastante, 1.1

R

race la carrera
racket (sports) la raqueta,
  9.1
radiator el radiador, **11.1**
railroad el ferrocarril,
  14.1
railway platform el andén,
  13.1; **1.1**
rain la lluvia
to **rain** llover (ue)
  It's raining. Llueve., 9.1
raincoat el impermeable, la
  gabardina, **4.1**
to **raise** criar, **9.2**
ranch la hacienda;
  (Argentina) la estancia
rare raro(a)
rate la tarifa; la tasa
  exchange rate el tipo de
    cambio, la tasa de
    cambio, **12.2**
  unemployment rate la
    tasa de desempleo
rather bastante, 1.1
razor la navaja, 12.1
reaction la reacción
to **read** leer, 5.1
reading la lectura
ready listo(a)
realist el/la realista
realistic realista
really realmente
reason el motivo; la razón
reasonable razonable
to **rebound** rebotar
to **receive** recibir, 5.1
recent reciente
recently recién
reception la recepción,
  6.1
receptionist el/la
  recepcionista, **6.1**
recipe la receta
to **recite** recitar
to **recognize** reconocer
recollection el recuerdo
to **recommend** recomendar (ie)
recommendation la
  recomendación
to **reconcile** conciliar
recreation el recreo
to **recruit** reclutar
rectangle el rectángulo
recycling el reciclaje

red rojo(a), 3.2
to reduce (dislocated bone) reducir, 8.2
reduced (price) reducido(a)
to refer referir (ie, i)
to reflect reflejar; reflexionar
reflection; reflex el reflejo
reforestation la reforestación
refrigerator el refrigerador, la nevera, 10.1
refuge el refugio
region la región
regional regional
regionalism el regionalismo
to register registrar
registration card la ficha, 6.1
regular (gasoline) normal, 11.1
related relacionado(a)
relation la relación
relative el/la pariente, 6.1
relatively relativamente
religious religioso(a)
to remain quedar, 7.1
remainder el resto
remains los restos
to remember recordar (ue)
to renounce renunciar
to rent alquilar, 5.2; rentar
to repair reparar
to repeat; to take seconds (meal) repetir (i, i)
to replace reemplazar
report el informe; el reportaje
to represent representar
representative el/la representante
representative representativo(a)
republic la república
to require requerir (ie, i)
requirement el requisito
researcher el/la investigador(a)
reservation la reservación, 6.1
to reserve reservar, 14.2; 2.2
reserved reservado(a), 13.2; 1.2
residence la residencia
resident el/la residente
resort la estación, 10.1
to respond responder

responsibility la responsabilidad
to make oneself responsible responsabilizarse
rest demás; el resto
to rest descansar
restaurant el restaurante, 14.1; 2.1
to restore restaurar
result el resultado
retina la retina
to return regresar; volver (ue), 7.1
to return home volver a casa, 10.2
to return (something) devolver (ue), 7.2
return el regreso
return trip, trip back el viaje de regreso
reverse inverso(a)
revolution la revolución
rhythm el ritmo
rib la costilla, 10.1
ribbon la cinta
rice el arroz, 5.2
rich rico(a), 14.2; 2.2; con mucha plata
rich person el/la rico(a)
ride la atracción, 5.2
right derecho(a), 7.1
to the right a la derecha, 5.2
right: that's right (true)! ¡verdad!
right away enseguida, 5.1
rigorous riguroso(a)
ring el anillo, 4.1
to ring sonar (ue), 3.2
to rise ascender
ritual el rito
rival el rival
river el río, 7.2
to roast asar, 10.1
roasted asado(a)
rock la roca
role el rol; el papel
roll of toilet paper el rollo de papel higiénico, 12.2
to roll rodar (ue)
roller blading el patinaje lineal
roller coaster la montaña rusa, 5.2

Roman el/la romano(a)
romantic romántico(a)
room el cuarto, la sala, 6.2; la pieza
double room el cuarto doble, 6.1
recovery room la sala de recuperación
single room el cuarto sencillo, 6.1
waiting room la sala de espera, 13.1; 1.1
root la raíz
rose la rosa
round-trip (ticket) de ida y vuelta, 13.1; 1.1
route la ruta
routine (adj.) la rutina, 12.1
routine rutinario(a)
row (of seats) la fila, 10.1
to row remar, 5.2
royal real
ruin la ruina
rule la regla
rumor el rumor
to run correr, 7.2
runway la pista
rural rural

S

sacrifice el sacrificio
to sacrifice sacrificar
sad triste, 8.1
safe salvo(a)
saffron el azafrán
sail (of a windmill) el aspa
sailboard la plancha de vela, 9.1
sailor el/la marino(a)
saint el santo
salad la ensalada, 5.1
salary el salario
sale la venta, 14.1
salesperson el/la dependiente(a), 4.1; el/la vendedor(a), 11.1
salt la sal, 14.1; 2.1
same mismo(a), 2.1
sand la arena, 9.1
sandal el huarache; la alpargata; la sandalia, 4.1
sandwich el sándwich, BV; el bocadillo, 5.1
sash la faja
satisfied satisfecho(a), 14.1

to **satisfy** satisfacer
Saturday el sábado, BV
saucepan la cacerola, **10.2**
saucer el platillo, 14.1; **2.1**
sausage (pork and garlic) el chorizo, la salchicha, **10.1**
to **save** ahorrar; conservar; salvar; guardar, **3.1**
savings account la cuenta de ahorros
saxophone el saxofono
to **say** decir
scales la báscula, 11.1
scarf la bufanda, **4.1**
scene la escena
scenery, set (theater) el escenario, 10.2
schedule el horario, 13.1; **1.1**
school schedule el horario escolar
scholarship la beca
school (of a university) la Facultad
school (related to) escolar, 2.1
school bus el bus escolar, 4.1
school life la vida escolar
school schedule el horario escolar
school supplies los materiales escolares, 3.1
school el colegio, la escuela, 1.1; la academia
elementary school la escuela primaria
high school la escuela secundaria, 1.1; la escuela superior
middle school la escuela intermedia
science las ciencias, 2.2
science fiction la ciencia-ficción
scientific científico(a)
scientist el/la científico(a)
scissors las tijeras, **12.1**
to **score a goal** meter un gol, 7.1
to **score a point** marcar un tanto, 7.1
scoreboard el tablero indicador, 7.1
screen la pantalla, 10.1

arrival and departure screen la pantalla de salidas y llegadas, 11.1
sculptor el/la escultor(a), 10.2
sculpture la escultura
sea el mar, 9.1
sea level el nivel del mar
search: in search of en busca de
season la estación, BV
to **season** sazonar
seasoning el condimento
seat el asiento, 11.1; la plaza, 13.2; **1.2**
seat (of government) la sede
seat (theater) la butaca, 10.1
seat number el número del asiento, 11.1
seat belt el cinturón de seguridad, **7.1**
second segundo(a), 6.2
second-class en segunda (clase), 13.1; **1.1**
second half (soccer) el segundo tiempo, 7.1
secondary secundario(a)
secret el secreto
secretary el/la secretario(a), **14.1**
to **secretly take** escamotear
security la seguridad, **7.1**
security check el control de seguridad, 11.1
sedan el sedán, **11.1**
see: See you later! ¡Hasta luego!, BV
See you soon! ¡Hasta pronto!, BV
See you tomorrow! ¡Hasta mañana!, BV
to **see** ver, 5.1
to see a show ver un espectáculo, 10.2
to **seem** parecer, **8.1**
to **select** seleccionar
selection la selección
self-portrait el autorretrato
to **sell** vender, 5.2; despachar, 8.2
semester el semestre
senator el/la senador(a)
to **send** enviar; mandar, transmitir, **3.1**

sentence la frase
separated separado(a)
September septiembre, BV
series la serie
World Series la Serie mundial
serious serio(a), 1.1; grave
servant el/la sirviente
to **serve** servir (i, i), 14.1; **2.1**
How may I help you? ¿En qué puedo servirle?, **4.1**
service el servicio, 5.1
service station la estación de servicio, la gasolinera, **11.1**
set el conjunto
to **set the bone** reducir el hueso, **8.2**
to **set the table** poner la mesa, 14.1; **2.1**
seven siete, BV
seven hundred setecientos(as), 3.2
seventeen diecisiete, BV
seventh séptimo(a), 6.2
seventy setenta, 2.2
to **sew** coser
sewing la costura
sex el sexo
shack la chabola
to **shake hands** dar la mano
shampoo el champú, 12.2
shantytown la villa miseria (Arg.); el pueblo jóven (Peru)
shape la forma
shawl el poncho
to **shave** afeitarse, 12.1
shaving cream la crema de afeitar, 12.1
she ella, 1.1
sheet la sábana, **6.2**
sheet of paper la hoja de papel, 3.1
shellfish los mariscos, 5.2
sherbet, sorbet el sorbete
shh! ¡chist!
to **shine** brillar, 9.1
shirt la camisa, 3.2
long-sleeved shirt la camisa de mangas largas, **4.1**
short-sleeved shirt la camisa de mangas cortas, **4.1**

shoe el zapato, 3.2
shoe store la zapatería, **4.1**
to **shop** ir de compras, 5.2; hacer las compras, **4.2**
shop window el escaparate, la vitrina, **4.1**
shopping: to go shopping hacer las compras, **4.2**; ir de compras, **5.2**
shopping mall la galería comercial
short bajo(a), 1.1; corto(a), 3.2
short- (long-) term a corto (largo) plazo
shortage la escasez
shorts el pantalón corto, 3.2
shot: to give (someone) a shot poner una inyección
should deber
shoulder el hombro, **8.1**
to **show (movie)** presentar; mostrar
show (movies) la sesión, 10.1
show el espectáculo, 10.2; el show
shower la ducha, 12.1
to take a shower tomar una ducha, 12.1
shrimp los camarones, 14.2; **2.2**; las gambas, **10.2**
shy tímido(a), 1.2
sick enfermo(a), 8.1
sick person el/la enfermo(a), 8.1
side *(adj.)* lateral, 13.2; **1.2**
side el borde; el lado, **12**
sidewalk la acera, **9.1**
to **sigh** suspirar
sign el rótulo, **11.2**
traffic sign la señal de tránsito
to **sign** firmar, **12.2**
significance el sentido, **11.2**
significant significativo(a)
similar parecido(a); similar
simple sencillo(a); simple
since como, 1.2; desde
sincere franco(a); sincero(a), 1.2
to **sing** cantar, 4.2
singing el canto
single soltero(a)
singles singles, 9.1
sir, Mr., gentleman el señor, BV

sister la hermana, 6.1
to **sit down** sentarse (ie), 12.1
to **situate** situar
situation la situación
six seis, BV
six hundred seiscientos(as), 3.2
sixteen dieciséis, BV
sixth sexto(a), 6.2
sixty sesenta, 2.2
size (shoes) número, 3.2
size el tamaño, la talla, 3.2
What size (shoe) do you wear (take)? ¿Qué número calza Ud.?, **3.2**
What size (clothing) do you wear (take)? ¿Qué tamaño (talla) usa Ud.?, **3.2**
ski el esquí
to **ski** esquiar, 9.2
ski lift el telesquí, 9.2
ski pole el bastón, 9.2
ski resort la estación de esquí, 9.2
ski slope la pista, 9.2
skier el/la esquiador(a), 9.2
skiing el esquí, 9.2
skirt la falda, 3.2
sky el cielo, 9.1
skyscraper el rascacielos, **9.1**
to **sleep** dormir (ue, u)
to fall asleep dormirse (ue, u), 12.1
sleeping bag el saco de dormir, 12.2
sleeve la manga, **4.1**
long- (short-) sleeved a mangas largas (cortas), **4.1**
slice la rebanada, la tajada, **4.2**
to **slice** rebanar, **10.2**
slot la ranura, **3.1**
slow lento(a), **10.2**
slowly despacio
small pequeño(a), 2.1
smile: little smile la sonrisita
smoking: (no) smoking area la sección de (no) fumar, 11.1
snack la merienda, 4.2
to have a snack tomar una merienda, 4.2
to **sneeze** estornudar, 8.1

snow la nieve, 9.2
to **snow** nevar (ie), 9.2
snowboarding el surf de nieve
so así
so, so much tan, tanto(a)
soap el jabón, 12.2
bar of soap la barra (pastilla) de jabón, 12.2
soccer el fútbol, 7.1
soccer field el campo de fútbol, 7.1
social sciences las ciencias sociales, 2.2
society la sociedad
sociology la sociología
socks los calcetines, 3.2
sofa el sofá, **6.2**
soldier el militar; el/la soldado
solitary, lone solitario(a)
solution el remedio; la solución
to **solve** resolver (ue)
some algunos(as), 4.1; unos(as)
someone alguien
something algo, 5.2
sometimes de vez en cuando; a veces, 7.1
son el hijo, 6.1
song la canción
soon dentro de poco
sore throat el dolor de garganta, 8.1
sorry: to be sorry sentir (ie, i)
sound el sonido
soup la sopa, 5.1
source la fuente
South America la América del Sur
South American sudamericano(a)
south el sur
southeast el sureste
southwest el sudoeste; el suroeste
to **sow** sembrar, **9.2**
sowing la siembra
space el espacio
spaghetti el espagueti
Spain la España, 1.2
Spanish *(adj.)* español(a)
Spanish (language) el español, 2.2

Spanish speaker el/la hispanohablante

Spanish-American hispanoamericano(a)

Spanish-speaking hispanohablante

Spanish-speaking countries los países de habla española

Spanish-style a la española

spare tire la llanta de recambia (repuesto), **11.1**

to **speak** hablar, 3.1; conversar

special especial

specialist el/la especialista, **14.1**

to **specialize** especializar

specialty la especialidad

spectator el/la espectador(a), 7.1; el/la mirón(ona)

speed la velocidad, **11.2**

speed limit el límite de velocidad

to **spend** pasar; gastar

to spend time pasar el tiempo, **5.1**

spice la especia

spontaneous espontáneo(a)

sport el deporte, 7.1

individual sport el deporte individual

(related to) sports deportivo(a), 6.2

sports program (TV) la emisión deportiva, 6.2

team sport el deporte de equipo

spring la primavera, BV

squid los calamares, 10.2

squire, knight's attendant el escudero

stadium el estadio, 7.1

stage: to come (go) on stage entrar en escena, 10.2

stairway la escalera, 6.2

stall el puesto, **4.2**

stamp el sello, la estampilla **5.1**

to **stand on line** hacer cola

standing de pie

star la estrella

to **start** entablar

state el estado

station la estación, 10.1

subway station la estación del metro, **10.1**

train station la estación de ferrocarril, 13.1; **1.1**

stationery store la papelería, 3.1

statistic la estadística

statue la estatua, 10.2

to **stay** alojarse

to stay in bed guardar cama, 8.1

stay la estadía

steak el biftec, 14.2; **2.2**

step el paso

stereo estereofónico(a)

still todavía

sting la picadura, **8.1**

to **stir** revolver (ue), **10.1**

stitch el punto, la sutura, **8.1**

stomach el estómago, 8.1

stomachache el dolor de estómago, 8.1

stone la piedra

to **stop** bloquear, parar, 7.1

stop la parada, 13.2; **1.2**

stopover la escala, 7.2

to **store** almacenar

store la tienda, 3.2

story el cuento; la historia

little story la historieta

stove la estufa, 10.1

stove burner la hornilla, **10.1**

straight derecho, **11.2**

to go straight seguir derecho, **11.2**

strange extravagante

strategy la estrategia

straw la paja, **13.2**

stream el arroyo

street la calle, 6.2

one-way street la calle de sentido único, **11.2**

pedestrian street la calle peatonal

strength la fortaleza

stretch (of road) el trayecto; el tramo

stretcher la camilla, **8.1**

to **strike twelve** dar las doce, **13.2**

string (instrument) la cuerda

string bean la judía verde; el poroto; la vainita; el ejote; la chaucha

striped a rayas

strong fuerte

structure la estructura

student (relating to) estudiantil

student el/la alumno(a), 1.1; el/la estudiante

student housing la residencia para estudiantes, **3.2**

study el estudio

to **study** estudiar, 4.1

stupendous estupendo(a)

stupid torpe

style el estilo; la moda

in style de moda

subject la asignatura, 2.1; la materia; el tema

subject area (school) la disciplina, 2.2

substance: controlled substance la sustancia controlada

subterranean subterráneo(a)

subtitle el subtítulo, 10.1

with subtitles con subtítulos, 10.1

to **subtract** restar

suburb el suburbio; la colonia

subway el metro, 10.1

subway station la estación de metro, 10.1

success el éxito

suckling pig el lechón; el cochinillo

suddenly repentinamente

to **suffer** sufrir

sugar el azúcar, **10.1**

to **suggest** sugerir (ie, i)

suggestion la sugerencia

suit el traje, 3.2

suitcase la maleta, 11.1

summer el verano, BV

sunny: It's sunny. Hace (Hay) sol., 9.1

to **sunbathe** tomar el sol, 9.1

sunblock la crema protectora, 9.1

sunburned, tanned tostadito(a)

Sunday el domingo, BV

sunglasses las gafas de sol, los anteojos de sol, 9.1
suntan lotion la loción bronceadora, 9.1
supermarket el supermercado, 5.2
  supermarket cart el carrito, **4.2**
superstition la superstición
to **support** sostener
sure seguro(a)
to **surf** practicar el surfing (la tabla hawaiana), 9.1
  to surf the Net navegar por la red
surface la superficie
surfboard la tabla hawaiana, 9.1
surfing el surfing, 9.1
surgeon el/la cirujano(a), **8.2**
to **surprise** sorprender
survey la encuesta
sweater el suéter, **4.1**
sweet dulce
  sweet roll el pan dulce, 5.1
sweetheart, lover el/la enamorado(a)
to **swim** nadar, 9.1
to **swim underwater** bucear, 9.1
swimming la natación, 9.1
swimming pool la alberca, la piscina, 9.1
swollen hinchado(a), **8.1**
symptom el síntoma, 8.2
syrup el sirope
system el sistema
  metric system el sistema métrico

T-shirt la camiseta, el T-shirt, 3.2
table la mesa, 5.1
table soccer el futbolín, **5.1**
tablecloth el mantel, 14.1; **2.1**
tablespoon la cuchara, 14.1; **2.1**
taco el taco, BV
to **take** tomar, 4.1
  to take notes tomar apuntes, 4.2

to take out sacar, **3.1**
to take one's blood pressure tomar la tensión (presión) arterial, **8.2**
to take one's pulse tomar el pulso, **8.2**
to take photos tomar fotos
to take place tener lugar, **8.1**
to take the luggage down bajar las maletas, **6.1**
to take the (school) bus tomar el bus (escolar), 4.1
to **take charge** encargarse
  takeoff (of an airplane) el despegue, **7.2**
to **take off** quitar, **10.2**
  to take off (airplane) despegar, **11.2**
  to take off the fire retirar del fuego, **10.1**
to **take time** tardar
talent el talento
to **talk** hablar, 3.1; conversar
tall alto(a), 1.1
tamale el tamal, BV
tan bronceado(a)
tank el tanque, **11.1**
task la tarea
taxi el taxi, 11.1
tea el té, 5.1
  iced tea el té helado, 5.1
to **teach** enseñar, 4.1
teacher el/la maestro(a); el/la **profesor(a)**, 2.1
team el bando; el equipo, 7.1
  team sport el deporte de equipo, 7.2
tearoom la confitería
teaspoon la cucharita, 14.1; **2.1**
technician el/la técnico(a), **8.2**
technology la tecnología
teenager el/la adolescente
telecommunication la telecomunicación
to **telephone** telefonear
  to talk on the phone hablar por teléfono
telephone el teléfono
  cell phone el teléfono celular, **3.2**

public (pay) telephone el teléfono público, **3.2**
push-button telephone el teléfono de botones, **3.2**
(related to the) telephone telefónico(a)
telephone book la guía telefónica, **3.2**
telephone call la llamada telefónica, **3.2**
telephone keypad el teclado, **3.2**
telephone line la línea telefónica
telephone receiver el auricular, **3.2**
television la televisión, 6.2
television set el televisor, **6.2**
teller el/la cajero(a), **12.2**
  teller's window la ventanilla, **12.2**
temperate templado(a)
temperature la temperatura, 9.2
ten diez
tender tierno(a)
tennis el tenis, 9.1
  pair of tennis shoes el par de tenis, 3.2
tennis player el/la tenista
tennis shoes los tenis, 3.2
tenth décimo(a), 6.2
term el término
terminal el terminal
  passenger terminal el terminal de pasajeros, **7.2**
terrace (sidewalk café) la terraza
terrible terrible
terror el terror
test el examen, 4.2
tetanus el tétano
Thank you. Gracias., BV
that (one) eso
that aquel, aquella; ese(a)
the la, el, 1.1
theater el teatro, 10.2
theatrical teatral, 10.2
their su, sus, 6.1
them las, los
  to them; to you *(formal pl.) (pron.)* les
theme el motivo; el tema
then luego, BV; entonces

there allí, allá
there is, there are hay, BV
therefore, for this reason, that's why por eso
these estos(as)
they ellos(as), 2.1
thin delgado(a); flaco(a), 1.2
thing la cosa
to think pensar (ie); opinar, **10.2**
third tercer(o)(a), 6.2
thirsty: to be thirsty tener sed, 14.1; **2.1**
thirteen trece, BV
thirty treinta, BV
thirty-one treinta y uno, 2.2
this (one) esto
this este(a)
thistle el cardo
those aquellos(as), esos(as)
thought el pensamiento
thousand mil, 3.2
three tres, BV
three hundred trescientos(as), 3.2
Three Wise Men los Reyes Magos, **13.2**
throat la garganta, 8.1
to throw echar; lanzar, 7.1; tirar
to throw (kick) the ball tirar el balón, 7.2
Thursday el jueves, BV
thus así
ticket el boleto, el ticket, 9.2; el billete, 11.1; el tique, **9.1**
luggage claim ticket el talón, 11.1
one-way ticket el billete sencillo, 13.1; **1.1**
round-trip ticket el billete de ida y vuelta, 13.1; **1.1**
ticket window la boletería, la ventanilla, 9.2
tie la corbata, 3.2
tied (score) empatado(a), 7.1
The score is tied. El tanto queda empatado., 7.1
tiger el tigre
time la hora; el tiempo, **9.1**
At what time? ¿A qué hora?
on time a tiempo, 11.1
What time is it? ¿Qué hora es?
time la vez

at times, sometimes a veces, 7.1
one more time, again una vez más
at that time en aquel entonces
time zone el huso horario
timid tímido(a), 1.2
tiny diminuto(a)
tip el servicio, 5.1; la propina, 14.1; **2.1**
Is the tip included? ¿Está incluido el servicio?, 5.1
tire el neumático, la goma, la llanta, **11.1**
flat tire la llanta pinchada
spare tire la llanta de recambio (repuesto), **11.1**
tired cansado(a), 8.1
to a
to the al
toast la tostada; el pan tostado, 5.2
to toast tostar
today hoy, BV
together juntos(as)
toilet el inodoro, el váter, **6.2**
toilet paper el papel higiénico, 12.2
to tolerate consentir (ie, i)
toll el peaje, **11.2**
toll booth la garita de peaje, **11.2**
tomato el tomate
tomorrow mañana, BV
ton la tonelada
tonight esta noche, 9.2
too much demasiado
tooth el diente
toothbrush el cepillo de dientes, 12.2
toothpaste la pasta dentífrica, 12.2
tortilla la tortilla, 5.1
totally totalmente
touch el contacto
to touch tocar
tour la gira, 12.2
tour guide el/la guía
tourist el/la turista, 10.2
toward en dirección a; hacia
towel la toalla, **6.2**
beach towel la toalla playera, 9.1
tower la torre

control tower la torre de control, **7.2**
town el pueblo, **9.2**
town square la plaza, **9.1**
toxic tóxico(a)
toy el juguete
track la vía, 13.1; **1.1**
trade el oficio, 14.1
tradition la tradición
traditional tradicional
traffic el tráfico
traffic light el semáforo, **9.1**
traffic sign la señal de tránsito
tragedy la tragedia
trail el camino
train el tren, 13.2; **1.2**
local train el tren local, 13.2; **1.2**
nonstop train el tren directo, 13.2; **1.2**
train car el coche, el vagón, 13.1; **1.1**
cafeteria (dining) car el coche-cafetería, el coche-comedor, 13.2; **1.2**
sleeping car el coche-cama, 13.2; **1.2**
train conductor el/la revisor(a), 13.2; **1.2**
train station la estación de ferrocarril, 13.1; **1.1**
training el entrenamiento
to transfer transbordar, 13.2; **1.2**; trasladar
to transform convertir (ie, i); transformar
to transmit transmitir, **3.1**
transportation el transporte
to travel circular; recorrer; viajar
to travel by air viajar en avión, 11.1
traveler el/la viajero(a)
traveler's check el cheque de viajero, 12.2
tray la bandeja, **7.1**
tray table la mesita, **7.1**
treat tratar
treatment el tratamiento; la cura
tree el árbol
triangle el triángulo
tribe la tribu
trip el viaje

return trip el viaje de regreso
to take a trip hacer un viaje, 11.1
trip, distance traveled el recorrido
triumphant triunfante
trombone el trombón
trousers el pantalón, 3.2
trousseau el ajuar de novia
true verdadero(a)
trumpet la trompeta
trunk (of a car) el/la maletero(a), 11.1; la maletera, 13.1; **1.1** el baúl, **11.1**
to **try** tratar
to **try on** probarse (ue), **4.1**
tube of toothpaste el tubo de pasta dentífrica, 12.2
Tuesday el martes, BV
tuna el atún, 5.2
turbulence la turbulencia, **7.2**
to **turn** doblar, **11.2**
to **turn around** revolver (ue), **10.1**
to **turn off** apagar (gu), **3.1**
to **turn on** prender, **3.1**
turning signal la direccional, **11.1**
turnstile el torniquete, **9.1**
twelve doce, BV
twenty veinte, BV
twenty-eight veintiocho, BV
twenty-five veinticinco, BV
twenty-four veinticuatro, BV
twenty-nine veintinueve, BV
twenty-one veintiuno, BV
twenty-seven veintisiete, BV
twenty-six veintiséis, BV
twenty-three veintitrés, BV
twenty-two veintidós, BV
twin el/la gemelo(a)
twist torcer (ue), **8.1**
two dos, BV
two hundred doscientos(as), 3.2
type el tipo; la modalidad
typical típico(a)

U

ugly feo(a), 1.1
uncle el tío, 6.1

under debajo (de)
undershirt la camiseta, 3.2
to **understand** comprender, 5.1
underwater swimming el buceo, 9.1
underwear la ropa interior, **4.1**
uniform el uniforme
union el enlace
unique único(a)
unit la unidad
United States los Estados Unidos
from the United States estadounidense
university la universidad
related to university universitario(a)
university degree el título universitario, **14.1**
unleaded sin plomo, **11.1**
unless a menos que
unpleasant desagradable
until hasta, BV
urban urbano(a)
urologist el/la urólogo(a)
urology la urología
us (to) *(pl. pron.)* nos
to **use** utilizar
used usado(a)
usually generalmente

V

vacation la vacación, **6.2**
valley el valle, **7.2**
value el valor
vanilla *(adj.)* de vainilla, 5.1
variation la variación
varied variado(a)
variety la variedad
various varios(as)
to **vary** variar
veal la ternera, 14.2; **2.2**
vegetable el vegetal, 5.2; la legumbre, 14; **2**
vegetable garden el/la huerto(a), **9.2**
vegetarian el/la vegetariano(a)
Venezuelan venezolano(a)
verse el verso
version: in its original (language) version en versión original, 10.1

very muy, BV
vest el chaleco
veterinarian el/la veterinario(a)
vice versa viceversa
victim la víctima, **8.1**
victorious victorioso(a)
video el video
video store la tienda de videos
view la vista
vinegar el vinagre
violin el violín, 2.1
to **visit** visitar
vitamin la vitamina
voice la voz
volleyball el voleibol
volume el tomo
volunteer el/la voluntario(a)
vowel la vocal

W

to **wait (for)** esperar, 11.1
waiter, waitress el/la camarero(a), el/la mesero(a), 5.1
waiting room la sala de espera, 13.1; **1.1**
to **wake up** despertarse (ie), 12.1
to **walk** ir a pie, 4.1; andar; caminar, 9.1
to take a walk dar un paseo, **5.2**
wall la muralla; la pared
to **want** desear, 3.2; querer (ie)
I would like . . . Quisiera... , 14.2; **2.2**
war la guerra
to **warn** advertir (ie,i)
to **wash oneself** lavarse, 12.1
washbasin el lavabo, **6.2**
washing machine la máquina de lavar
waste los desechos
watch el reloj, **4.1**
to **watch** mirar, 3.1
water el agua *(f.)*, 9.1
mineral water el agua mineral, 12.2
running water el agua corriente
to **water-ski** esquiar en el agua, 9.1
water-skiing el esquí acuático, 9.1

watercolor la acuarela
watermelon la sandía, **10.2**
wave la ola, 9.1
way el modo; la manera, 1.1
we nosotros(as), 2.2
weapon el arma (*f.*)
to wear llevar, 3.2
to wear (size) usar, 3.2; **(shoe size)** calzar, 3.2
weather el tiempo, 9.1
   It's cold. Hace frío., 9.2
   It's hot. Hace calor., 9.1
   It's sunny. Hace sol., 9.1
   The weather is bad. Hace mal tiempo., 9.1
   The weather is nice. Hace buen tiempo., 9.1
Web page la página Web
wedding la boda, **13.1**
Wednesday el miércoles, BV
week la semana, BV
   last week la semana pasada, 9.2
weekend el fin de semana, BV
   last weekend el fin de semana pasado
to weigh pesar
weight la pesa; el peso
welcome dar la bienvenida, 11.2
   You're welcome. De nada., Por nada., No hay de qué., BV
well bien, BV; pues
   very well muy bien, BV
well-known renombrado(a)
west el oeste
western occidental
what? ¿qué?, BV
   What's the matter (with you)? ¿Qué te pasa?, 8.2
what, that which lo que
wheat el trigo, **9.2**
wheelchair la silla de ruedas, **8.2**
when cuando, 4.2
when? ¿cuándo?, 4.1
where donde, 1.2
where? ¿adónde?, 1.1; ¿dónde?, 1.2
which?, what? ¿cuál?, BV
while el rato; mientras
white blanco(a), 3.2

who? ¿quién?, 1.1; *(pl.)* ¿quiénes?, 2.1
   Who is calling? ¿De parte de quién?, **3.2**
whole entero(a)
why? ¿por qué?
wide ancho(a)
wife la mujer, la esposa, 6.1
wig la peluca
wild salvaje
to win ganar, 7.1
wind el viento
windmill el molino de viento
window (post office, etc.) la ventanilla; **(shop)** el escaparate, la vitrina, **4.1**
windshield el parabrisas, **11.1**
winter el invierno, BV
wise sabio(a)
   The Three Wise Men Los Reyes Magos, **13.2**
to wish desear, 3.2
with con
within dentro de
without sin
woman la dama
wood la madera
wool la lana, **12.1**
word la palabra
work el trabajo
to work trabajar, 3.2
   to work full time trabajar a tiempo completo, **14.2**
   to work part time trabajar a tiempo parcial, **14.2**
work la obra
   work of art la obra de arte
worker el/la trabajador(a); el/la obrero(a), **9.1**
workforce la mano de obra
world el mundo
World Cup la Copa mundial
World Series la Serie mundial
worldwide, (related to the) world mundial
worse, worst peor, el/la peor
wound la herida, **8.1**
wounded person el/la herido(a)
wrapped envuelto(a)
to wrinkle arrugar
wrist la muñeca, **4.1**
to write escribir, 5.1

writing pad el bloc, 3.1
wrong erróneo(a)

X

X-ray la radiografía, los rayos equis, **8.2**

Y

yard la yarda
year el año, BV
   to be . . . years old tener... años, 6.1; cumplir... años
   last year el año pasado, 9.2
   this year este año, 9.2
yellow amarillo(a), 3.2
yes sí
yesterday ayer, 9.2
   day before yesterday anteayer
   yesterday afternoon ayer por la tarde, 9.2
   yesterday morning ayer por la mañana , 9.2
yet aún; todavía
yogurt el yogur
you *(sing. fam.)* tú; *(sing. form.)* Ud., usted, 3.2; *(pl. form.)* Uds., ustedes, 2.2
You're welcome. De nada., No hay de qué., BV
young joven, 6.1
   as a young person de joven
your *(sing. fam.)* tu; *(form.)* su, sus, 6.1
youth la juventud
youth hostel el albergue juvenil, el albergue para jóvenes (juvenil), 12.2
youth, young person el/la joven, 10.1

Z

zero cero, BV
zone la zona
   commerical zone la zona comercial, **9.1**
   industrial zone la zona industrial, **9.1**
   residential zone la zona residencial, **9.1**
zoo el parque zoológico, **5.2**

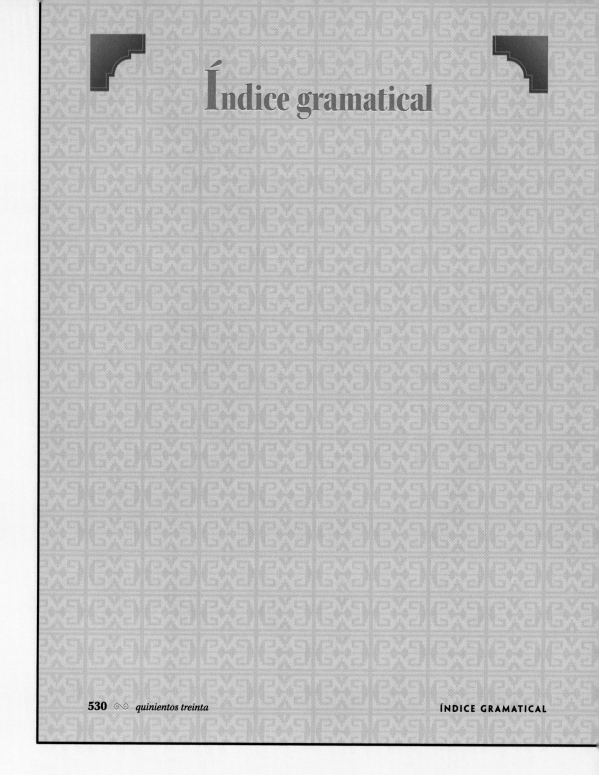

Índice gramatical

533

Credits

Photography

Abshier, Andrew: 184BL, 184BR. Allison, Glen/Tony Stone Images: 200TR. Antman, M./The Image Works: 248, 406. Arakaki, Roberto/International Stock: 246L, 307T. Artists Rights Society (ARS), New York/SPADEM, Paris: 346. Aubry, Daniel/Odyssey: 273. Augustin, Byron/DDB Stock: 319B. Bachmann, Bill/Tony Stone Images: 140B. Baker, Jeff/FPG: 126. Balaguer, Alejandro/Tony Stone Images: 292L. Bognar, Tibor/The Stock Market: 331. Booher, Andrea/Tony Stone Images: 263C. Bryant, D. Donne/DDB Stock: 249T, 268, 318, 443. Burckhalter, David: 217. Burgess, Michele/The Stock Market: 211, 234B. Byers, Bruce/FPG: 240. Bzdak, Zbigniew/The Image Works: 250C. Carr, Melanie/The Viesti Collection: 69B. Carrasco, Demetrio/Tony Stone Images: R51. Carton, J.C./Bruce Coleman, Inc.: R40. Cassidy, Anthony/Tony Stone Images: 433. Castro, Haroldo/FPG: 265B, 267. Chaplow, Michelle: R07, R20R, R52L, R52R, 2TR, 3, 6, 23BR, 24, 39B, 46R, 49, 60C, 61BR, 61CR, 63L, 63TR, 69TR, 72, 73BR, 75T, 79L, 79R, 89, 102, 133, 138, 143T, 145, 154B, 169B, 170R, 189R, 221T, 228T, 229, 231, 238L, 247B, 249B, 260, 276C, 283T, 285, 294T, 301, 307B, 308, 310, 311, 316, 320R, 321C, 330B, 350, 352, 354, 356T, 360, 373B, 379, 384, 415, 432B, 435. Cody, Dennie/FPG: 287. Cohen, Stuart/Comstock: R31, 254, 259T, 359BL. Coleman, Bruce/Bruce Coleman, Inc.: 198R, 320L. Collins, C.J./Photo Researchers: 234T. Contreras Chacel, Jorge/International Stock: 53B. Corbis-Bettman: 444 center, 447. Courau, J.P./DDB: 207. Cover/The Image Works: 144T, 373TL, 373TR, 386T. Crandall, Rob/The Image Works: 134C. Daemmrich, Bob: R44BL, R44BR, R44TC, R44TL, R44TR, R46, R49L, 152CL, 421. Dawes, Sonda/The Image Works: 220L. Delgado, Luis: R03, R15B, 1, 2, 4B, 4T, 8B, 8T, 10, 16, 18BL, 18T, 23Ba, 23Bb, 23C, 23CR, 23TR, 29, 32, 33T, 36BL, 36BR, 46T, 47T. Donadoni, Danilo/Bruce Coleman, Inc.: 299. Doyle, David: 56, 60TL, 256, 290, 295B, 295T. During, Richard/Tony Stone Images: 161. Edmonson, Paul/Tony Stone Images: 107B. Edwards, Gregory/International Stock: 147. Egan, Shaun/Tony Stone Images: 202R. Ehlers, Chad/International Stock: 129. Elmer, Carlos/FPG International: R26. Englebert, Victor: 179, 220R, 293BR, 353, 390L. Englebert, Victor/Photo Researchers: 235. Faris, R./Westlight: 261B. Fenton, Cheryl: R58, 28B. Freeman, M./Bruce Coleman Inc.: 21. Fischer, Curt: R01, R56L, R56R, 23TL, 30, 34, 44B, 46C, 48, 227, 236. Fisher, Ken/Tony Stone Images: R15T. FoodPix: 289B. Franklin, Stuart/Magnum Photos: 263B. Frazier, David R.: R25, R47, 132, 184T, 194B, 286, 361, 407T, 419. Frerck, Robert/Odyssey: R12, R14B, R21, R22, R23R, R39, 20BL, 55, 58T, 67, 85, 101B, 105, 106B, 106T, 107TR, 123, 141T, 146, 165, 195, 198L, 199, 200BR, 200L, 203B, 221B, 243, 253L, 253R, 261T, 262B, 264B, 266L, 271, 277T, 296, 309R, 312, 313, 317, 319T, 321BR, 323T, 327, 342TL, 355C, 355T, 357, 359TL, 365, 367, 370, 377, 381, 388L, 399T, 401L, 408, 413, 414L, 417, 418, 422, 445. Frerck, Robert/The Stock Market: 101T, 103, 252B. Frerck, Robert/Tony Stone Images: 77B, 185B, 448. Frerck, Robert/Woodfin Camp & Assoc.: R05, R13, R17. Fried, Robert: 9R, 14T, 19B, 19T, 20CR, 20TL, 47B, 100T, 154T, 186B, 210, 247C, 250L, 251L, 252T, 262T, 293L, 337, 386B, 440B. Fried, Robert/DDB Stock: 264T. Fried, Robert/Stock Boston: 20CL. Fuller, Tim: R6, R19, R20L, R34, R38, R43, R50, R54TL, 35BL, 35BR, 35T, 44T, 56, 58B, 62, 65BL, 68, 80B, 91, 92B, 94, 104B, 122, 125R, 139B, 142B, 142T, 152BR, 152T, 153, 155, 157L, 157R, 159, 162L, 162R, 164, 166, 180R, 181, 183, 185TL, 185TR, 188B, 188T, 189L, 192, 196, 197, 208T, 209, 224, 228B, 233, 238R, 259B, 266R, 280, 283B, 289C, 300, 303, 306, 315T, 323B, 340L, 340R, 341B, 341T, 344T, 348T, 369, 373CR, 378, 380, 382, 385B, 385T, 388R, 392L, 392R, 396, 397, 398, 404, 407B, 410, 411B, 411TL, 411TR, 414R, 418, 423, 424. Gainer, Gordon R./The Stock Market: 246R. Goldberg, Beryl: 130B, 130T, 345L. Graham, Ken/Tony Stone Images: xiv. Grant, Spencer/FPG: 276B. Greenberg, Jeff/David R. Frazier Photolibrary: 437. Greenberg, Jeff/Photo Edit: 322B. Grehan, Farrell/FPG: 329. Griffin, John/The Image Works: 375. Harris, Paul/Tony Stone Images: 137. Heaton, Dallas & John/Westlight: 114. Heilman, Grant Photography: 251R. Hollenbeck, Cliff: R37, 194T. Ikeda, Miwako/International Stock: 9L. In Focus Int'l/Image Bank: R54CR. Inman, Nick: 170L, 288, 312T, 315C, 321TR, 347, 425. Johnston, Greg/International Stock: R48, 139T. Jongen, Antoinette/FPG International: 117, 345R. Kahl, M.P./Bruce Coleman, Inc.: 107TL. Karp, Ken: R04T, R11T, R14T, R30, 9T, 11L, 15T, 39T, 41T, 42. Kittle, Kit/The Viesti Collection: 359R. Komer, Daniel/DDB Stock: 187. Lansner, Erica/Tony Stone Images: 141B. Leah, David/Allsport: R27. Little, Blake/SYGMA: 144B. Mangino, Larry/The Image Works: 180L. Manske, Thaine/The Stock Market: R08. Marco/ASK Images/The Viesti Collection: 322T. Martson, Sven/The Image Works: 395. Maruka/International Stock: 328. Mays, Buddy/International Stock: R53B. McGee, E. Alan/FPG: 277B. Menzel, Peter: R09. Mitchell, Robert & Linda: 444T. Miyazaki, Yoichiro/FPG: 13. Moffett, Mark/Minden Pictures: 440C. Morgan Cain & Associates: R06. Morgan, Francis: 104T, 305, 321BL, 321CL, 321TC, 321TL. Murphy-Larronde, Suzanne/FPG International: R11M. Murphy-Larronde, Suzanne L./DDB Stock: 77T, 441. National Gallery of Art, Washington: 284, 391R. National Palace, Mexico City: 45. North Wind Picture Archives: 440T. O'Roarke, Randy/The Stock Market: 376. Oldershaw, Dominic: 86B, 86T, 342TR, 343, 368, 374, 399B, 402L, 402R, 403B. Pape, Maria/FPG: 276T. Pcholkin, Vladimir/FPG: 297, 387. Peace Corps: 412B. Peacock, Barbara/FPG: 436T. Pefley, Chuck/Tony Stone Images: 436B. PhotoDisc: 336. Pokempner, Marc/Tony Stone Images: 435. Preston, Louisa: R35. Raga, José Fuste/The Stock Market: 432T. Raurich, Miguel/Tony Stone Images: 291. Reiff, Robert/FPG: 265T. Resnick, Lorne/Tony Stone Images: 304. Ries, Stan/International Stock: 274. Rivadamar, Daniel/Odyssey: 247T, 358L, 363. Rosendo, Luis/FPG: R53T, 190, 309L. Rumack, Gary: 371. Sauer, Jennifer: R48R, 70, 403T. Scala/Art Resource, NY: 100, 391L. Schafer, Kevin/Tony Stone Images: R16, 200CR. Schermeister, Phil: 115. Sharp, Chris/Photo Researchers: 263T. Shumway, Gail/FPG: 151. Sipa Press: 328T. Smestad, Mark: 72, 135, 225, 289T, 330T, 348B, 383. Smetzer, Don/Tony Stone Images: 92T. Smith, Jeff/FOTOSMITH: R42, 54, 80TR, 84, 87L, 124, 125R, 150, 178, 216, 218, 219, 222, 232, 244, 272, 275BR, 275L, 275TR, 279B, 279C, 279TL, 279TR, 338, 339, 366. Smith, Phillip & Karen/Tony Stone Images: 204. Spence,

Illustration

Vista credits

Maps